HARVARD SEMITIC SERIES

VOLUME XXI

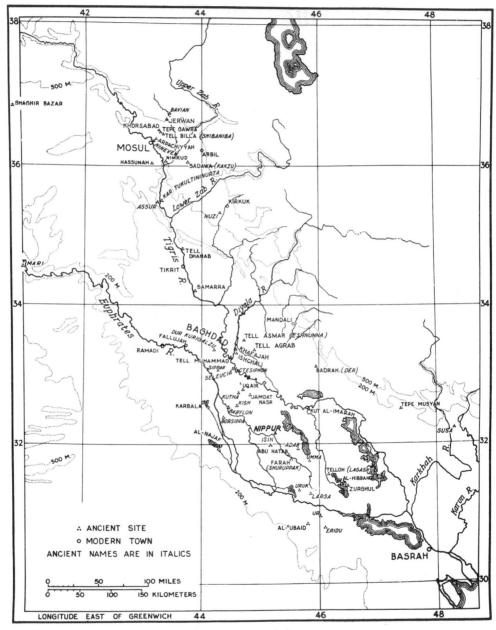

38   42   44   46   48   38

Upper Zab R.

500 M.

∴ SHAGHIR BAZAR

∴ BAVIAN
∴ JERWAN
KHORSABAD ∴ TEPE GAWRA
∴ ARPACHIYYAH ∴ TELL BILLA (*SHIBANIBA*)
MOSUL ∘ NINEVEH
HASSUNAH ∴ NIMRUD
    ∘ ARBIL

36   SADAWA (*KAKZU*)   36

∴ KAR TUKULTININURTA
ASSUR   *Lower Zab R.*
    ∘ KIRKUK
    NUZI

∴ *MARI*
    Tigris R.
    TELL DHAHAB
    200 M.
    TIKRIT
Euphrates R.
    SAMARRA

34   *Diyala R.*   34

    ∘ MANDALI
BAGHDAD ∘
DUR KURIGALZU
FALLUJAH ∘   TELL ASMAR (*ESHNUNNA*)
RAMADI ∘   TELL AGRAB
    KHAFAJAH
TELL MUHAMMAD ∴ ISHCHALI
SIPPAR   BADRAH (*DER*)
SELEUCIA CTESIPHON   500 M.
    200 M.
    UQAIR   TEPE MUSYAN
KUTHA JAMDAT NASR
KARBALA ∘ *KISH*   KUT AL-IMARAH
BABYLON
BORSIPPA   *SUSA*
AL-NAJAF ∘ **NIPPUR**   *Karkhah R.*

32   *ISIN*   32

500 M.
ABU HATAB *ADAB*
    UMMA
FARAH (*SHURUPPAK*)
    TELLOH (*LAGASH*)
    AL-HIBBAH
    ZURGHUL
    URUK
    200 M. *LARSA*
    UR
    AL-UBAID ∴ *ERIDU*

∴ ANCIENT SITE
∘ MODERN TOWN
ANCIENT NAMES ARE IN ITALICS
    BASRAH

    30

0   50   100 MILES
0   50   100   150 KILOMETERS

LONGITUDE EAST OF GREENWICH   44   46   48

Assyria and Babylonia

Toward the Image of Tammuz
and
Other Essays on Mesopotamian
History and Culture

Thorkild Jacobsen

Edited by William L. Moran

Harvard University Press
Cambridge, Massachusetts
1970

© Copyright 1970 by the President and Fellows of Harvard College
Distributed in Great Britain by Oxford University Press, London
Library of Congress Catalog Card Number 76-95925
SBN 674-89810-9
Printed in the United States of America

Foreword

The writings of Thorkild Jacobsen, which span a period of more than forty years, have ranged over a broad field of inquiry. They are the work of an archaeologist, a linguist, a textual and literary critic, an historian of religious thought as well as of social, legal, and political institutions. As the translator of Sumerian poetry he has also been much more than the learned philologist, as is evident from the astonishment of the critic David Grene in finding poetry of such skill and sensitivity in so very ancient times. The contribution of this extensive and many-sided scholarship to our understanding of ancient Mesopotamian civilization has been distinguished and often fundamental.

Yet the work of any scholar, however versatile, usually reveals areas of major interest and the underlying unity of his research. For Jacobsen it will be noted that he has concentrated largely on the earlier phases of Mesopotamian civilization. The explanation of this emphasis is perhaps his dominant concern with the basic forms of the culture, the matrix of geographical conditions, institutions, and conceptual patterns which, though subject to modification in the course of historical development, shaped the beginnings of this culture and continued to define it as Mesopotamian. Thus, characteristically, in religion he studies "formative tendencies" and "central concerns," the relation between pantheon and regional economy, the primary analogies in which religious experience articulated itself and the fundamental values which were sought and found expression in a cult. Similarly, he investigates the "early political development" in which kingship and its specifically Mesopotamian ideology gradually emerged, or introducing new methods he traces the irrigation system, which fixed the lines of human settlement, and the connection of the

shifts of this system with the ever-recurring problem of soil salinization and of the latter with the fall of dynasty and empire. In this
respect, therefore, Jacobsen's work appears as a sustained effort of
synthesis and definition of the essential structures and conditions
that gave Mesopotamian culture its specific character and determined
so much of its history.

What he believes this task of synthesis involves is seen from a
further concern—and this is most characteristic—with the problem of
whether it is really possible to understand Mesopotamian thought,
especially its mythological literature, which is its most typical form
of expression. By understanding he means an intellectual and emotional response that is faithful to the original and approaches that of
the ancients themselves. Such appreciation demands first that the
past be understood in its own terms and categories. Here alone the
difficulties are formidable, and no one is more aware of them than
Jacobsen; he could not stress more emphatically how remote and
alien the Mesopotamian world is to our own, nor reject more
vigorously facile comparisons that would make the Sumerians appear
to be pretty much like ourselves. But he also sees that to achieve this
inner resonance with the past much more is required than exact and
painstaking philology, however basic it may be. Ultimately, he argues,
it demands that one renounce his own world and, in complete
sympathy, enter another. He is accordingly openly diffident of the
chances of success, including his own, but if anyone has succeeded,
he has, and most notably in his essay "Toward the Image of
Tammuz." In many ways this is the most characteristic of Jacobsen's
writings, and it seemed therefore the most appropriate title for· this
volume.

The essays in this volume attempt to be representative of all aspects
of Jacobsen's work, but they stress his studies in history and religion,
many of which are not easily accessible. It is in these studies that he
has made his most important contribution to our knowledge of
Mesopotamian culture and the origins of our Western civilization.

William L. Moran

September 1969

Acknowledgments

The editor wishes to acknowledge his gratitude to the scholars, institutions, and publishers for permission to reprint: to the University of Chicago Press for "The Investiture and Anointing of Adapa in Heaven" (Chapter 4), "The Myth of Inanna and Bilulu" (Chapter 5), "Toward the Image of Tammuz" (Chapter 6), "Sumerian Mythology: A Review Article" (Chapter 7), "Primitive Democracy in Ancient Mesopotamia" (Chapter 9), "About the Sumerian Verb" (Chapter 15), "*Ittallak niāti*" (Chapter 16), and "The Akkadian Ablative Accusative" (Chapter 17); to the Oriental Institute of the University of Chicago for the map of Mesopotamia and the selections of *Most Ancient Verse*; to Doubleday and Company, Inc. for "Formative Tendencies in Sumerian Religion" (Chapter 1); to the *Encyclopaedia Britannica* for "Mesopotamian Gods and Pantheons" (Chapter 2); to the American Philosophical Society for "Ancient Mesopotamian Religion: The Central Concerns" (Chapter 3); to W. de Gruyter (Berlin) for "Early Political Development in Mesopotamia" (Chapter 8); to the American Schools of Oriental Research for "The Reign of Ibbī-Suen" (Chapter 10); to the American Oriental Society for "The Assumed Conflict Between the Sumerians and Semites in Early Mesopotamian History" (Chapter 11); to the Pontifical Biblical Institute (Rome) for "An Ancient Mesopotamian Trial for Homicide" (Chapter 12); to E. Munksgaard (Copenhagen) for "On the Textile Industry at Ur under Ibbī-Sîn" (Chapter 13); to the British School of Archaeology in Iraq for "The Waters of Ur" (Chapter 14); to Professors Samuel N. Kramer and John A. Wilson, who collaborated, respectively, on "The Myth of Inanna and Bilulu" and *Most Ancient Verse* (the part on Egyptian poetry), and who expressed their pleasure at the republication of their colleague's contribution.

The general index was prepared by Mary K. Brown and Diane Taylor; the lexical index, by Israel Abusch, John Durham, and Stephen Lieberman, whose cooperation also considerably lightened the editorial labors.

Contents

Toward the Image of Tammuz

The Kishkanu of White Magic

This dark kishkanu tree, grown forth in Eridu
    in a holy place,
Was to behold as clear (blue) lapis lazuli
    stretching out above the Deep.

Full of bounty are Enki's haunts in Eridu,
In his seat is the place of the portals
    to the nether world,
On a couch in the bedroom is Nammu,
From his holy dwelling the shadows fall
    as from a forest—inside no man may go with him,
Inside are the sun-god and Ama-ushumgal-anna,
    between the mouths of the two rivers.

The gods Kahegal, Igihegal, and Kanabdu of Eridu
Have dug out that kishkanu, have laid into it
    the spell of the Deep.

An incantation, part of a magic ritual of healing in which the kishkanu was used, and for which it was consecrated by this recounting of its holy origin. Enki was the god of the sweet waters and son of Nammu, goddess of pools. His sacred city was Eridu in southern Babylonia, built on a lake or a freshwater lagoon. The two rivers mentioned are the Tigris and the Euphrates. The gods named in the last stanza were minor deities in Enki's service. From Nineveh, Ashurbanipal's library, about 600 B.C., but the poem was composed much earlier and probably goes back at least to about 1700 B.C.

1. Formative Tendencies
in Sumerian Religion

1. RELIGION AS RESPONSE

Basic to all religion, formal or otherwise, is a unique experience which, with a term coined by Rudolph Otto, is usually called the "numinous" experience. Otto has analyzed it as the experience of a *mysterium tremendum et fascinans*, a confrontation with the "Wholly Other," outside normal experience and indescribable in terms of normal experience; terrifying, ranging from sheer demonic dread through awe to sublime majesty; and fascinating, with irresistible attraction demanding unconditional allegiance. It is the human response to this experience in thought (mythology and theology) and action (cult) which constitutes religion, and it is with the manifold forms which the response takes that the study of religion properly concerns itself. The aim of such study must be, beyond all, to understand and to interpret the varied religious forms as reponse, as ultimately meaningful in relation to the underlying numinous experience only.[1]

To the student of Sumerian religion such understanding is not readily come by. Remoteness in time and great differences of culture separate him, and the forms of religious response meaningful to him, from those of the ancients; imperfect knowledge of the language closes his ear to overtones; different habits of thought and differences

NOTE: First published in *The Bible and the Ancient Near East: Essays in Honor of William Foxwell Albright*, ed. G. Ernest Wright (New York, 1961), pp. 267–278 = Anchor Books edition (Garden City, 1965), pp. 353–368. Copyright © 1961 by The Biblical Colloquium. Reprinted by permission of Doubleday & Company, Inc.

in values tend to leave him uncomprehending or mistaken. He must wonder at every step whether his interpretation is leaving the ancient forms dry, empty of content, or whether he is unconsciously filling them with his own new wine only to shatter them. But no way is open to him in his dilemma other than to persevere in attempts to understand with continued attention to inner consistency in his results.

The following pages are part of such a preliminary attempt. They seek to point up the two major psychological tendencies which seem to us to structure the Sumerian response: namely, (1) an early spontaneous reliance upon features and values of the situations in which man experienced the numinous for guidance to its nature and approachability, and (2) a later similarly spontaneous reliance upon social forms and attitudes taken from the developing human society as vehicles for further understanding and approach.

Inasmuch as we are dealing in these pages with viewpoints for materials generally familar and readily adduced by the reader, documentation has been held at a minimum.[2]

2. ATTRIBUTION OF FORM

It is characteristic for Sumerian religion, especially in its older phases, that the human reaction to the experience of the numinous remained singularly bound by the situation in which the numinous was encountered, and by some central phenomenon or group of phenomena in it particularly. The numinous appears to be immediately and unreflectingly apprehended as a power in, underlying, and willing the phenomenon, as a power within it for it to come into being, to unfold in this its particular and distinctive form. In consequence the phenomenon largely circumscribes the power, for the numinous will and direction appear as fulfilled in the phenomenon and do not significantly transgress it.

This boundness to a phenomenon one might describe with a grammatical metaphor as intransitivity; it is found typically in such figures of the Mesopotamian pantheon as Nissaba, the goddess of the reeds; Sumukan, god of the wildlife in the desert; Nintu, goddess of birth; Ninkasi, goddess of beer; and many others. These deities are little more than active principles underlying certain specific forms, numinous powers for certain things to be, reeds, animals, births, beer; they act not, they suffer not, they appear, are, and vanish only.

It may be confidently assumed that such intransitivity is a general and an old feature, for an unmistakable intransitive core is traceable in all figures of the Sumerian pantheon. In figures where transcendence is met with, involving concerns beyond the being of some phenomenon, active intervention in human affairs—these aspects of the god are always connected with, and expressed under, inherently late anthropomorphic forms borrowed from human society and its human dignitaries.

The boundness of the numinous will as a will to a phenomenon makes it natural to attribute to it as its external form the form for which it strives, in which it fulfills its aspirations. We find that the earliest expressions of the nature of the gods, their names, and their earliest external forms are like those of the phenomena in which they were seen to reveal themselves. Utu is the numinous power that comes into being as the sun, the sun-god, and the visible form which that power takes is the flaming sun disk; the language allows no distinction between the two. Nanna is the power in the moon and the moon itself, the form that power wills and takes. An is heaven and the god of heaven. Ezinu is the power in the grain and the grain itself in all its forms. The single seed corn dropped by the farmer in the furrow is Ezinu dropped. The green stalks coming up are also Ezinu "standing in the furrow like an attractive young girl."

These early forms of the gods, the forms of the phenomena in which they reveal themselves, survive to the latest times as divine emblems: the sun disk of Utu, the moon sickle of Nanna/Enzu, the gate symbol of the goddess of the storehouse, Inannak, the lion-headed bird of the god of the thunderstorm, Ningirsuk/Ninurta, and many others. That the emblems are but variant forms of the gods to whom they belong may be seen clearly from the fact that when these gods follow the armies into battle, or when they are present at oath ceremonies, they go in their emblem form.

The anthropomorphic forms of the gods, which eventually came to rule supreme, were imposed relatively late and supplanted the older forms slowly and only with difficulty. To the latest time, the divine will to other, nonhuman form is alive under the human exterior and threatens it: rays pierce through the human body of the sun-god; ears of corn grow out through the human shoulders of the grain goddess; serpent heads look at the beholder each side of Ningishzida's human head in reminder of the true nature of the power within.

At times the long struggle to bring the gods closer to man and to human understanding under the human form resulted in open hostility toward the older forbidding shape. An example may be seen in the case of the god of the thundercloud, whose early shape, after becoming his emblem, ended up as his enemy. The numinous power in the thundershowers, which in the early spring clothe the bare desert with green and transform it into pastureland overnight, was named from the phenomenon Imdugud, "shower." It took external form from the floating cloud as an enormous bird with outstretched wings; its head, to account for the lionlike roar of the thunder, that of a lion. In this form Lugalbanda met the god in the Lugalbanda epic. The earliest evidence of tendencies to humanize the bird shape dates from the Second Early Dynastic period. On seal cylinders of this period the bird shape is shown with the legs and lower parts of a human body draped in a kilt. Completely humanized, the god appears in the cult statue from Tell Asmar, where the bird shape occurs only as an embled carved on the base of the statue. The advent of the human form seems to have been accompanied by a tendency to designate the god under his new form by some epithet other than the old name Imdugud, so closely associated was the latter with the earlier shape. In Girsu the god was known as Ningirsuk "the lord of Girsu"; in Nippur as Ninurta, and in Eshnunnak as Aba-ú, "Old Man Pasture." The victory for the human shape was not easily won. In Girsu, as late as Enannatum I, a macehead dedicated to Ningirsuk still shows the ruler adoring him under his bird shape; and later still, when Gudea sees the god in a dream in partially human shape, he still retains the outspread wings of the Imdugud shape. After the time of Gudea, as the human form comes to reign more and more supreme, a growing hostility toward the older form begins to show itself. In the Nippur versions of *Lugal-e*, Imdugud is included in the list of Ninurta's conquered enemies. In Akkadian mythology, as the evil Zû-bird, it becomes his archfoe. On Assyrian reliefs, finally, Ninurta, still with the wings of his original bird shape, is shown fighting and routing the thunderstorm, his own former self, the lion bird.[3] The hostility toward the older nonhuman form which here changed it into an enemy is, it may be added, probably part of a general and growing tendency, as anthropomorphism became more and more established. A very similar instance is found in Mummu and Apsû, both old forms of the god Enkik/Ea, who in Enuma-elish, the creation epic, are depicted as enemies of the god, captured and slain by him.

3. SITUATIONAL VALUES: GOOD AND EVIL

As the immediate apprehension of numinous power as power and will to a given phenomenon became determining for the inner and outer form under which the power was envisaged, so under this immediate apprehension were human values inherent in the phenomenon unhesitatingly accepted as incentives or deterrents to the ever present human urge to seek security and salvation by establishing ties of allegiance to the numinous power.

A clear case is that of the "evil god" (*dingir hul*). The term *dingir* "god" was used generally by the Sumerians to designate any numinous power known to them, but specifically it applied to the protective genius of an individual and his family, a "personal god." The situation of numinous experience which underlies this latter concept is reasonably clear from the use of the term "to acquire a god" (*dingir tuku*), used to denote unbelievable and conspicuous good fortune. The "uncanny" feeling of some outside supernatural agency at work which may accompany extraordinary luck or success is well known. In Sumerian religion the power whose presence was felt in such experiences was given form from the situation and was envisaged as a benevolent father or mother figure concerned with the individual in question and bent on furthering his fortunes. Inviting spontaneous allegiance as "good," the personal god was made the object of a permanent cult in the house of his or her protégée.

But a very similar numinous experience may accompany instances of spectacular misfortune, which may equally be felt as uncanny. The numinous power recognized in such cases was also a "god" (*dingir*), but the very different situation in which this power was encountered determined it as evil, bent on destruction, and the human response was one of avoidance and defense through incantations and other magical means. No allegiance was invited or offered, no cult developed. The "evil god" took its place among the innumerable other destructive numinous powers, demons, and evil spirits who are inimical to man and for whom it is characteristic and very particularly terrifying that they are altogether inhuman, have nothing in common with us, are purely a dread unreachable wholly other:

> Neither males are they, nor females,
> They are winds ever sweeping along,
> They have not wives, engender not children,
> Know not how to show mercy,
> Hear not prayer and supplication.

As indicated by their various names, these demons are forms given to the numinous power experienced in sudden illness and pain, or other situations of uniformly terrifying nature. They are the supernatural wills and power which come into being in evil things.

4. SITUATIONAL VALUES: OUR DAILY BREAD

The tendency for the human response to take color as negative or positive from the human values inherent in the situation in which the numinous power was encountered could not but act to single out for special attention certain situations and certain powers which were recognized as good and approachable. Human allegiance and the establishment of regular cult naturally centered on those numinous powers which from the situations in which they revealed themselves were recognizable as approachable and friendly toward man. To some such process of natural selection we may ascribe the marked uniformity with which the major deities of the older Mesopotamian pantheon prove, on closer inspection, to be powers in phenomena or activities of primary economic importance to their worshipers. On the more primitive economic levels, with their terrible uncertainties and ever present threat of famine and slow, horrible death from hunger, the all-important security sought by man is economic security: "Give us today our daily bread." The powers confronting him in the sources of his food supply, in numinous experience on the hunt, with his cattle, in his fields, commanded an allegiance born of values in the situation, forced by the anguish of his deepest anxieties, and irresistibly invited by the element of fascination in the numinous.

That the major deities of the Sumerian pantheon are powers in phenomena and activities of primary economic importance also means, of course, that they differ in character from region to region, as natural conditions give prominence now to one, now to another type of economy. From the marsh-lands of the hunter and fisherman in the south, over the grasslands in the center, to the farms in the north and east, each had its own pantheon determined by its particular economy.

Beginning with the south and the chief deities of the ancient cities of the marshlands we find ourselves in the world of the hunter and fisherman. In Eridug resides Enkik, the "Ibex of the Deep" (*Dara-abzuk*), the numinous inner will to form in the Deep, visualized as a gigantic hart or ibex, the antlers of which showed above the water as reeds. As a will to the ibex form this power, the "ibex-fashioner" (*Dara-dím*), provided the hunter with his game, as a will to reeds the "Lord Reedbundle" (*En-uru*) it provided him his reed hut for protection. As numinous will in the Deep to the form of the reed bundle and imbued with the cleansing power of water, Enkik is also the power behind all purification magic.

If Enkik may be seen as the power behind the game of the marshes, his daughter Nanshe in Nina is the numinous will that produces the teeming schools of fish moving under the surface and gives the fisherman his livelihood. Fish are everywhere around her; a scepter fish is the scepter in her hand; sandal fish are the sandals on her feet. South of Nina, in Kinirsha, finally, is the home of Dumuzid-abzuk, the "quickener of the child (in mother's womb)" of the Deep. Under the form of a goddess we meet here the mysterious numinous power that brings new life into being, lets life multiply and thrive in the marshlands.

Through the marshlands along the Euphrates from Kiabrig over Ur up to Uruk runs the country of the ox herdsman, and here the numinous powers behind the bovine form are supreme. In Kiabrig resides the bull-god Nin- EZEN × LA and his consort Nin-é-ì-garak, "The Lady of the Creamery." In Ur we find Nanna, the moon-god, envisaged by the herdsman as a frisky young bull with gleaming horns grazing in the heavenly pastures. In Uruk lastly are Nin-sún, "Lady Wild Cow," and her bull-god husband, Lugalbanda.

In Uruk the cow country borders upon the sheep country, the broad grassy steppe in the center of southern Babylonia which the ancients called the *edin*. Here cult cities of the gods of the shepherds, Dumuzid, the "quickener of the young one (in mother's womb)" and his young wife Inannak, personification of the storehouse in which the produce of the flocks was kept, ring the *edin* around: Uruk, Bad-tibira, Umma, Zabalam. From these cities, when lambing time is over and Dumuzid, the numinous power which miraculously gave life to the lambs and filled their mothers' udders with milk, has ceased to be, there issued each year the sorrowful processions to lament in the desert the dead god, killed by invaders from the mountains, the land of death, as happened so often to the human young shepherds in the *edin*. Two other important cult centers on the borders of the *edin* should also be mentioned. In the north lies IM^ki, the city of Ishkur, god of thunder and rain who yearly makes the desert green with grass for the flocks to feed on. In the south lies Larsa, the city of the sun-god Utu and his son Sumukan, god of goats and of all four-legged wild creatures of the plain, providing herdsman and hunter alike with their means of existence.

North and east of the *edin*, finally, lie the plowlands with cities dedicated to the cereal and chthonic deities which dominate the pantheon of the tiller of the soil. In Shuruppak we find Sud, goddess of the ear of corn, daughter of Ninshebargunu, the "mottled barley," and bride of Enlil, the numinous power in the wind which pollenizes the grain. Further north is Nippur with Enlil and his wife Ninlil, who is identical with the grain goddess Sud. Here also is Enlil's divine store, Dukug, "the pure mound" in which grain, wool, and milk were kept in the morning of time before men were given a share in them. Nippur is also the home of Enlil's son Ninurta, god of the thunder-showers and god of the plow. Under the name of Pabilsag he is worshiped as husband of the city goddess of nearby Isin, and as Nin-girsuk he is the chief god of Girsu in the fertile regions southeast of the *edin*. Further north, in Kutha, resides Nergal, the death- and life-giving will in the soil, a power to receive and hold the dead, the dark will of the grave, but also a power to life and growth from which the roots of grain, plants, and trees draw strength, a will to fertility and plenty. In Babylon we find Marduk, also an agricultural deity, originally the powers in the spade (*mar*), the chief tool of the irrigator and orchardman. In the northeast, finally, resides Ninazu, like Nergal a chthonic god combining death- and life-giving powers. His city, Eshnunnak, is the capital of the fertile lands of the Diyala region.

5. ACTS OF ALLEGIANCE

With numinous power apprehended directly as will in specific phenomena, and with attention tending to focus on those powers which informed and willed phenomena of crucial economical importance, it is but natural that the early response in action to the numinous experience should direct itself to assisting these favorable powers in their will to be and to assuring their presence in the community. Two means were available to these ends, the cult drama and the temple. In the cult drama[4] man takes on the identity of a numinous power and, thus identified, activates it by letting its will to be in its appropriate form realize itself externally in the cult act. The cult act makes it present, and once present it will manifest itself everywhere. The most important of the Sumerian cult dramas were: (1) the *hieros gamos* in which the king took the identity of the god Dumu-zid, the "quickener of the little ones (in mother's womb)" and through a ritual act of coitus ensured magically that the power of fertility, which was the god, became present to pervade all nature and ensure plenty in the new year; (2) the battle drama at new year in Babylon, where the king in symbolic action fought and won as embodiment of Marduk the battle against chaos which established the ordered cosmos for the new year as it had done primevally; and (3) lastly—slightly differently oriented—the dramatic lament for the dead god Dumuzi which, in its vivid expression of grief and longing, served to strengthen the community's ties with the lost power of engendering new life and to give it such succor against oblivion and total extinction as mention of its name and maintaining it in living memory could provide.

As man in the cult drama endeavored to bring into being and give reality to the numinous powers of his allegiance, so he sought by creation of the visual tangible form of the power, the divine image, and by providing the power with a dwelling among the houses of the community, a temple, to keep the power present and with him always. The purpose of the temple as a dwelling for the god is clear from the fact that Sumerian had no special word for temple. The structure was but a house (*é*) among other houses, differing only by having a god rather than a human magnate as owner. Further confirmation is offered by its plan, which, as one follows it back in time, proves to be the simple plan of a dwelling house.

6. ANTHROPOMORPHISM: NEW SOCIOPOLITICAL PATTERNS

The strong urge to tender allegiance and therein to achieve security and salvation, which characterizes the human response to the numinous experience, contains in it a temptation to remodel the image of the numinous ever closer to the heart's desire, to see it more and more under human forms, to soften estrangement in its stark otherness by seeing it under familiar images taken from human society and human interrelations, so as to broaden the basis for community and contact.

In ancient Mesopotamia this tendency early led to the development of a finely spun, closely interwoven, and complete pattern. This guided the human response to the numinous into channels parallel to those developed for relations of dependence in human society. Thus in a progressively more differentiated, stratified, and complex society, the image of the numinous powers, individually and as a functioning group, was subtly molded into the likeness of an early landed aristocracy. In blunt fact the gods came to be part of society, the ruling caste exercising all basic economic and political functions of the country.

Central in this new view stands the temple, the god's mighty house, the center of a great estate with extensive holdings of land. At its head, as owner and administrator, is the great god himself, and with him his divine consort and children, who may themselves own similar estates. The house is run by the god's wife, who directs a staff of divine servants. These in turn guide and lend their divine efficacy to a corps of human servants, the priests. There are chamberlains, who make the divine bed, see to the bathing and anointing of the god, keep his rooms clean and swept. There are cooks who prepare his daily meals, carvers and cupbearers, who serve at table, singers and musicians, who entertain the god and his guests, and also singers of elegies who soothe his darker moods. In the administration of his estates and in looking after his far-flung interests, the god has the aid of a divine vizier, a *sukkal*, who announces visitors and states their business, and who also goes on errands for his lord. Divine and human stablemen care for the god's donkey teams and keep his war chariot in good order. Overseers of fields, canals, forests, and fisheries look after the running of the estate according to the god's orders, all assisted by human personnel guided in ordinary matters by their knowledge of the job, in all exceptional matters by direct orders from the god given in omens and extispicy. As a great and influential personage, the god participates in the political councils of his peers, the divine assemblies, in which all major decisions affecting the country are taken, laws passed, and political offices assigned. Here the god may have been chosen "king" (*lugal*) to lead the country in war through his human representative, or "lord" (*en*) to guide as administrator the internal affairs of the country. He may also hold traditional office by virtue of his special talents and abilities. Thus, for example, Utu, the sun-god, is judge; Enkik, god of the subsoil waters, through his organizing abilities, rises to a position comparable to that of a secretary of the interior, planning and directing the whole of the economic life of the country. In these offices (*me*) of the god, held traditionally or by appointment, we find in slightly reinterpreted form most of the old relation between numinous power and features of the situation in which that power was experienced. But the earlier immediate apprehension of the numinous as direction and will in and to the phenomenon in which it was seen revealed is now yielding to a more reflected mode: the numinous has receded from the visible phenomenon, is no longer one with it as mind with body but appears as a power in charge of it, administering, owning it. Thus countless individual phenomena and processes of nature and human life, both once alive with numinous will and power, have become works, the outcome of conscious, organized, dutifully carried out tasks of numerous divine functionaries, tasks which in their planned inter-related totality structure world order and maintain the universe as a cosmos.

7. RELATION TO EARLIER VIEWS

The form of a divine aristocracy on earth, dividing the cosmic tasks between its members, living the life of human landed gentry on big estates, can obviously have been neither as cleanly set off from earlier very different forms, nor as barren and empty of real religious content as it must appear on brief modern restatement. It is easy to sense that the old immediate apprehension of the numinous as awesome inner will in a phenomenon of the universe still lives under the anthropomorphic image of the human lords and rulers. What at first seems metaphor will on occasion spring to sudden life as the true reality, a terrifying nonhuman form taking the place of the familiar human image. In Gudea's dream the man who reaches from heaven to earth does not have arms, but instead the outstretched black wings of the thundercloud, while his body below becomes a raging flood wave. And even where the older form does not break the human image, that form still pulses under it as a deeper truth, endowing the metaphors and similes applied with almost uncanny life and making it capable of carrying rather more numinous content than we are at first likely to allow it to. Gudea's humanizing terms "master" and "lord" convey in his prayer to Ningirsuk his profound awe before a *mysterium tremendum*, the wholly other terrifying power in the flood wave sweeping down from the mountains:

O my master Ningirsuk, lord, fiercely eroding (flood-) water,
good lord, (seminal) water emitted by the great mountain (Enlil),
hero without challenger,
Ningirsuk, I am to build you your house,
but I have nothing to go by.
Warrior, you have called for the things that are proper,
But, son of Enlil, lord Ningirsuk,
I cannot know what that means.
Your heart, rising as (rise the waves in) mid-ocean,
Crashing down as (does the falling) *ushu* tree,
Roaring like the water pouring out (through a breach in a dike),
Destroying cities like the flood wave,
Rushing at the enemy country like a storm,
O my master, your heart, an outpouring (from a breached dike) not
    to be stemmed,

Warrior, your heart, remote (and unapproachable) like the far-off
   heavens,
How can I know it?

8. THE TEMPLE AS CENTRAL SYMBOL

Particularly powerful and concrete in the new anthropomorphic
view was the symbol of the temple, the god's house. Towering over
the flat roofs of the surrounding town, it gave the townsmen visible
assurance that the god was present among them. The vast expanses
of temple fields and orchards were unspoken testimony that his ties
were the strong ties of a landowner to his land, and the numerous
ways in which man served him as house servant and worker in the
fields gave man status: needed by the god, belonging to him as a
servant belongs to his master, bound to absolute obedience in
unquestioning loyalty, unprotected against arbitrary moods and
unjust punishment, but always belonging, never under any circumstances to be abandoned.

In this strong human tie between master and servant, transferred to
man's relation with the numinous powers which ruled the universe,
lay Mesopotamian religion's warrant of human salvation; its answer
to the human need for security. It was a limited security that it
offered. Sonship man had only to his personal god, who was usually
a minor power able at most to intercede for him with other greater
gods, not to save him on its own. It was, furthermore, security in
life only. Outside the kingdom of the gods was a foreign power in the
eastern mountains. Death's kingdom raided the land of the living and
carried its people away to eternal servitude in regions where the gods
of the living were powerless.

And even in life, security was not so absolute as might have been
thought. The power of even the strongest gods could not prevail
against the combined will of the divine assembly; and the assembly,
swayed by inscrutable motives, might order death and destruction
of its own. At such times the gods flee their city, flutter like terrified
doves before the terrible enemy who enters their sanctuaries con-
temptuously with shod feet. The city is sacked and plundered, its
people killed or carried off into captivity. In the ruins around the
destroyed temple the survivors face the utter collapse of their world,

the terrible reality of being abandoned by their gods. Only one means is still at hand—the lament.

The lament is rightly central to Sumerian ritual and to Sumerian religious poetry, for it alone plumbs the depths of utmost despair without giving in to it. In magical emphasis the emotional ties to god and temple are strengthened, the god and goddess are implored, are called back into existence, the turbulent dark despairing mind of the god is soothed by music of harps and drums that it may once more regain strength to act, strength to rebuild what is lost:

My Lady, your city cries for you as for its mother,
Ur seeks you as were it a child lost in the streets.
Your house reaches forth its hand for you, as does one who has lost
    something,
Your bricks in the good house, as were they mortals, say: Where is
    she?

9. CONCLUSIONS

We have sought in the preceding pages to point up two successive attitudes to the numinous in Sumerian religion. An older attitude which attempted to understand the numinous power directly from the situation in which it revealed itself as a power willing that situation or some specific phenomenon central to it. The numinous power was seen as intransitive, its relation to man lay essentially in a community of interest when the numinous will and man both desired the phenomenon informed by the power to manifest itself. The younger attitude, gaining ground slowly but eventually emerging victorious, was born of a growing conviction that the numinous power was primarily to be understood in human terms, even in terms of known social and political power. The numinous was given form as master and ruler; man became a concern to it in so far as he was a needed and useful servant. Therein man found a limited security.

After Sumerian times, a span of the development not of direct concern here, the application of the human social and political forms of the ruler to the numinous drew into the form of the divine a growing emphasis on the ruler's duty to dispense justice. Also the old political forms of a primitive democracy applied to the gods tended to lose meaning and to yield subtly to monocratic attitudes, which mostly took henotheistic forms.

To the end, however, the polarity of human and nonhuman essence in the numinous continued to give Mesopotamian religious expression its peculiar vibrant tension, and both modes of viewing the numinous contributed to it valid and profound insights.

2. *Mesopotamian Gods and Pantheons*

THE GROWTH AND DEVELOPMENT
OF RELIGIOUS THOUGHT

The basic characteristic of ancient Mesopotamian religion was a tendency to a pluralistic view of the numinous (i.e., the mysterious element in the holy and the feelings of awe or fear it elicits): many different numina (or divine powers) were seen in many different phenomena, each such numen being the life force and will of its particular phenomenon, nameable from the phenomenon and wearing the external form of the phenomenon. As an example of the last, representations from the Protoliterate period show that the numinous power in the rain cloud, Imdugud, was given form as an enormous lion-headed black bird, floating on outstretched wings and roaring its thunder cry.

With the numina that constituted the will of phenomena vital to human survival, especially those phenomena that were essential to the economy—as flocks and herds, grain, the earth, etc.—man felt a sense of solidarity that found its expression in endeavors to ensure the "presence" of the numen by such means as cult images, temples, service, and the ritual drama. The earliest Mesopotamian religion appears to have been one of solidarity with nature and its powers, upon which man depended.

This early tendency to give situationally determined, nonhuman form to the numinous, however, probably at no time excluded attribution also of human form. Thus the Erech vase, which dates to Protoliterate time, shows the sacred marriage between two deities in

NOTE: First published as "Religion," in the article "Babylonia and Assyria," *Encyclopaedia Britannica* (1963), II, 972–978.

human form, and so do numerous representations on seals from this period. The fact that human agents could embody the gods and take on their identity in the ritual drama also indicates that the human form as such must have been considered possible and appropriate for divinity.

Nonetheless, attribution of human form to the divine did not come to dominate religious thought until Early Dynastic times. From the latter half of that period onward it is the form under which gods and goddesses ordinarily are represented. The older nonhuman forms, with their close ties to natural phenomena, tended to recede into the background as divine emblems (*shu-nir*) associated with the anthropomorphic god—the sun disk next to the human figure of the sun-god Utu, the lion-headed bird accompanying Ningirsu/Ninurta, the ibex accompanying Enki, and the dog associated with Nininsina. At times animosity against the now unpopular older form even seems to have made of it an enemy vanquished by the human-shaped god; in later mythology, for example, the lion-headed bird develops into the chief opponent of the god Ningirsu/Ninurta, whose older form it is. Parallel to this process of divorcement of the older nonhuman form from the human form of the god there seems to go a similar general tendency to divorce phenomenon from god and to see it as a distinct, not divine, entity. The god comes to own or control the phenomenon, becomes a power behind it rather than in it and of it.

The victory of the human form was not easy or rapid and for long periods not complete. Enannatum I at the end of the Early Dynastic period still was depicted in attitude of worship before Ningirsu's old form of lion-headed bird. As late as Old Babylonian times the goddess Nininsina was still imagined with the head of a dog, and over and over again nonhuman features vie with human ones in monumental representations: rays flare from the body of the sun-god, serpent heads peep out from the shoulders of Ningishzida next to his human head, grain sprouts from the body of the grain-goddess.

The approach to understanding of the numinous that led during the Early Dynastic period to attribution of external human form to divinity paralleled a similar new understanding of activity and function of the numinous in a human pattern, that of the "ruler." The growth and the progressive differentiation of society during Proto-literate times, and the accompanying development of governmental forms, had created a type of human ruler vastly more powerful than the early chiefs and village headmen, and hence the object of feelings of distance, reverence, dependence, and awe. This evolving concept of the ruler made possible a new metaphor for understanding and expressing central elements in the numinous, its awesomeness and majesty. The term *en*, "lord," with implications of "manager who causes to thrive," is attested from the early part of the Protoliterate; its application to a god is first known from the late Protoliterate in the divine name En-lil, "Lord Wind." It soon came to be an integral part of many such names (Enlil, Enki, Enamash, Engara, Enduku, etc.). The term *lugal*, "king," especially leader in war, first occurs in the middle of the Early Dynastic period. It too was used as title for deities and forms part of divine names such as Lugalbanda, Lugalgirra, Lugalkisaa, Lugalmarada, etc.

The gods became a divine landed aristocracy with great manors (the temples), managed by a vast retinue of divine and human servants; as rulers of cities they became responsible for the social and political as well as the economic welfare of the community. At the end of the Early Dynastic period, at the word of Enlil, Ningirsu of Girsu agreed with Shara of Umma on their mutual boundary line, and later on, when Umma violated the line, Ningirsu declared war. The politically active gods were organized in a "primitive democracy" in which the highest authority was a general assembly meeting at Nippur under the presidium of An and Enlil to elect "lords" and "kings" from among the member gods, and to decide on the rise and downfall of dynasties and cities. The gods who were powers in nature had become powers in history: the numinous power in the phenomenon of birth, the "Lady Birthgiver," Nintu, became an officeholder endowed with the office (*garza*) of furthering birthgiving, an office conferred upon her by Enki; Dumuzi, the mysterious power in the ewe of begetting and of giving milk, became a divine shepherd whose office was to manage and look after cattle pens and sheepfolds, and so forth.

The classical image of the god as ruler, responsible for defense against external enemies and for prosperity and order internally, sharpened in the late phase. The national character of Marduk and Ashur as supreme gods identified them closely with external national interests; through signs and omens they actively guided the policies of their countries, so that religion and politics became more inextricably linked than ever before. In the struggle of the Sargonids to subdue Babylon, cult and ritual were in the center of the fray; Sennacherib even appears to have tried to transplant the New Year festival of Babylon bodily to Assyria, with Ashur as the chief figure rather than Marduk, and groups of fragmentary Assyrian texts testify to the use of astoundingly virulent religious political propaganda.

In internal affairs, divine concern with social order, questions of morality and ethics were prominent, dominating the image of the gods. The concept of the god as ruler—now given its special color from the everyday experience of absolute monarchy—tended to produce a piety bordering at times on subservience and anxious avoidance of even the semblance of independent initiative: "Take not to heart matters of strength and power, seek Nabu and Marduk and let them kill your foes" is the advice Nabopolassar hands on to later rulers. In the private prayers that have survived the penitent crawls before the god in veritable orgies of self-abasement, pleading for mercy for sins he is not aware he has committed.

The utter dependence of man on the gods in all matters raises the question of the righteous sufferer. By Old Babylonian times it became general belief that all men had personal gods who watched over them and that—in contrast to what had been thought earlier—the personal god was easily capable of withstanding all demons and evil forces. Sickness or other ills meant therefore that the protective deity had turned away from his ward in anger or disgust, leaving him a prey to evil, and that the ward must have committed a ritual or moral sin to alienate his god. With time the emphasis shifted more and more to the latter type of sin, and elaborate rituals with penitential psalms were used to regain the good graces of the angered god or goddess. Out of this literature grew attempts to deal with the paradox of the righteous sinner, the pious and upright man who was yet allowed to suffer. The solution found was a humble realization of the limitation of human insight and human judgment; man lacks the larger perspective of the eternal gods.

The full realization of distance between human and divine that flowed from the ruler metaphor, as well as the living sense of a mighty power of nature still inherent in the god, is shown in Gudea's prayer to Ningirsu:

O my master Ningirsu, lord who sends the awesome waters,
Potent lord, engendered by the Great Mountain,
Warrior whom none can challenge,
Ningirsu, I am to build you your house, but have no sign!
Warrior, you have called for what is fitting,
But, son of Enlil lord Ningirsu,
I cannot know what that means!
Your heart, which lifts like the swell in mid-ocean,
Comes crashing down like great ebony trees,
Which roars like the waters of the breech in a dike,
Destroys cities like a flood,
Which rushes at the enemy country like a storm,
O my master, your heart, the onrushing waters of a breach in a dike,
      not to be restrained,
Warrior, your heart, remote like the Heavens,
How can I know it?

It affected deeply man's place in the scheme of things. Ruled by the gods, working on their estates as servant or field hand, he became the serf of the god, who might be harshly treated but could not be abandoned. As lord of the manor (the temple) the god was tied to his lands and people; hence the greatest crisis life could know was destruction of the temple, the threat of breaking forever the bond between god and man. Around this direst of all calamities center the most important, most fervent, and perhaps most profound expressions of Sumerian religious feeling, the public laments, designed to strengthen and repair the bonds that had become severed, to calm the god and induce him to undertake the task of reconstruction.

The last phase of ancient Mesopotamian religion may be counted as beginning in the Old Babylonian period and lasting to the end of Babylonian and Assyrian civilization. It is marked by the rise of two national gods, Marduk and Ashur, to positions of supreme power in the world of the gods, and reflects the eventual crystallization of Mesopotamia into the two rival national states, each under an absolute monarch. The old pantheon and religious framework generally remained relatively unchanged, but the emphasis had subtly shifted; power and decision were now centered in Marduk or in Ashur, the other gods acting as their agents or as intercessors with

them. The strong feeling of unified central power found its expression
in henotheistic tendencies; the various gods were seen as in essence
one with aspects of a supreme god. We are told that Enlil is Marduk
(as god) of lordship and counsel, Nabu is Marduk (as god) of accounting, Sin is Marduk (as god) illuminating the night, Shamash is Marduk
(as god) of justice, Adad is Marduk (as god) of rain, etc. Similarly
the other gods may be identified with parts of the body of Ninurta:
his eyes are Enlil and Ninlil, the iris of his eyes Sin, his lips Anu and
Antum, and so on. There is a recognizable drive to see the forces
that govern the cosmos as basically one and unified.

SUMERIAN PANTHEON

The Sumerian pantheon was exceedingly numerous—it seems to
have contained some 3,000 to 4,000 deities—hence only a few of the
more prominent gods can be considered here. This article concentrates
on such as ranked as chief deity of a city and lists them in regional
arrangement according to the location of their cult city.

1. Southeastern Marshes

The marshes and lakes that in ancient times separated the inhabited
areas of Sumer from the Persian Gulf seem to have begun southeast
of a line from Eridu (Abu Shahrain) in the desert west of Ur up to
Nina (Surghul) in the southern part of the Lagash region. The deities
worshiped in the cities located there all appear to represent powers
vital to men who derived their livelihood from the marshes; they are
powers in the waters and the reeds, in the birds and fishes, and they
are seen in shapes drawn from the familiar forms of animal and
vegetal life in the marshes. They belong to a single family, that of
Enki in Eridu, and Enki himself was the figure among them who gave
rise to stories and myths about how he organized the country and its
economy, how he outwitted the goddess of the gravelly desert lands
in the west, always with creative results. The deities of this group of
cities, the early pantheon of the marshlanders, are:

1. Enki (Ea), the city-god of Eridu, situated in antiquity on a
lake or lagoon. He was god of the fresh water of rivers, lakes, and
marshes, was known for great wisdom, and the power of water to

cleanse made him god of ablution and lustration magic. His earliest name and form seems to have been Abzu, "the Watery Deep," later seen as an opponent vanquished by him. His name Enki, "Lord of the Earth," probably has reference to the fertilizing power of the irrigation waters. As creator god his name was Nudimmud; as god of ablution magic he was usually called En-uru, "Lord Reed Bundle," after the reed bundles out of which was constructed the reed hut in which the rites were performed. In historical times he was generally envisaged in human form, but an earlier nonhuman form of the god survives in his emblem, the ibex, which often is depicted under his feet. Other emblems, also seemingly older nonhuman forms of the god, were a goat the body of which tapers into that of a fish, and a ram-headed curved stick. The Akkadians identified Enki with their god Ea, and in later times a variety of gods of special crafts were identified with him.

As father of Enki the texts mention the god of the wind, Enlil of Nippur; his mother was Enlil's housekeeper, Nammu. As Enki's father, perhaps to be understood as his grandfather, occurs sometimes also the god of the sky, An. Enki's spouse was Damgalnunna, "The Great Spouse of the Prince," whom the Akkadians called Damkina. The Janus-faced god Sha (Akkadian Usmu) served as his vizier.

Of the more noteworthy myths dealing with Enki may be mentioned the Tilmun myth, which tells how he engendered a great variety of deities, among them Uttu, the spider, goddess of weaving; the "Myth of Enki and Ninmah," which tells about the creation of man and of how human freaks came into the world through a contest between these two creator gods; and "Enki Organizes Sumer," which tells how Enki blessed the major cities of Sumer, arranged for the rivers, marsh, and sea, and instituted agriculture and husbandry and other important features of the economic life of the country.

2. Asalluhe (Marduk), city-god of Ku'ar, in the general vicinity of Eridu. Asalluhe was active with Enki in rituals of lustration magic and was considered his son. His name, "Man-Drenching Asal," suggests that he was originally a god of thundershowers and corresponded in the marshman's pantheon to Ishkur in the herder's and Ninurta in the farmer's. His epithet *lu-he*, "man-drenching," also is applied to Ishkur. In the incantations he is regularly the one who first

observes and calls Enki's attention to existing evils, perhaps in his role of thundercloud surveying the world from on high. He was later identified with Marduk of Babylon.

3. Dumuzi-abzu, city-goddess of Kinirsha in the southeastern part of the Lagash region. Dumuzi-abzu was the power for fertility and new life in the marshes. Her name means "the Quickener [of] the Young [in mother's womb] of the Deep," and she corresponds in the marshman's pantheon to Dumuzi in the herder's. She was considered a goddess in the Lagash region, but in the region around Eridu she was viewed as male—possibly due to influence from Dumuzi of the herder's pantheon—and as son of Enki.

4. Nanshe (or perhaps better Nazi), city-goddess of Nina (Surghul) in the southeastern part of the Lagash region. Goddess of fish and fishing, Nanshe was envisaged as dressed altogether in fish. Among her accomplishments was skill in interpreting dreams, and an important hymn to Nanshe and many references in other texts stress her concern for equity and social justice. Her father was Enki, her husband, Nindara, called the "tax-gatherer" of the sea.

5. Ninmar, city-goddess of Guabba, situated on the shore of a lake or lagoon in the southeastern part of the Lagash region. She seems to have been a bird-goddess, and her emblem, a bird, probably represents her original nonhuman form. She was the daughter of Nanshe and thus granddaughter of Enki.

2. SOUTHERN ORCHARDS

In the south, the region along the lower course of the ancient Euphrates from Erech past Ur, three different early economies and their gods came together. Cities of the marshlander's family of gods descended from Enki can be followed from Eridu and Ku'ar in this region over toward Nina in the east; cities of the herdsman's family of gods descended from Nanna in Ur show connection northward to cities in the central grasslands; and lastly there is a group of cities that have city-gods belonging to still a third family of gods descended from Ninazu. The gods of this group all have pronounced chthonian character as powers of the nether world, and several of them appear closely connected with trees and vegetation. Since the region in which their cities lie is one of the chief centers of date cultivation in the country, and seems to have been equally so in antiquity, it is perhaps not unlikely that they represent the pantheon of the early fruit growers and their settlements along the riverbanks, dependent on the powers for growth in the earth. To this group of deities belonged probably originally also Inanna in Erech as goddess of the storehouse of dates and her bridegroom, Dumuzi-Amaushumgalana, the power for growth and new life in the date palm, both of whom were later absorbed in large measure into the pantheon of the herders. Inanna seems to have been the figure that gave rise to the major myths in the fruit growers' pantheon, such as the myth of Inanna and Shukallituda, which tells of the origins of shade-tree gardening, and the myth of Inanna's descent to the nether world, which seems to be a mythopoeic elaboration of the partly subterranean character of the storehouse. The gods of this group of cities are:

1. Ninazu, the city-god of Enegir, located on the lower ancient Euphrates between Larsa and Ur. Another city of his was Eshnunna (Tell Asmar) in the Diyala region. Ninazu was an underworld deity whose precise nature is not clear; the name seems to mean "Water Knower." He counted in Enegir as son of the queen of the nether world, Ereshkigal; a variant tradition made him a son of Enlil and Ninlil. His spouse, Ningirda, was a daughter of Enki.

2. Ningishzida, city-god of Gishbanda in the vicinity of Ur. Ningishzida was likewise a power of the nether world, where he held the office of "throne-bearer." Originally he seems to have been a tree-god, for his name appears to mean "Lord Productive Tree," specifically perhaps god of the winding tree roots, as he was originally envisaged in serpent shape. When he is pictured in human form, two serpent heads grow from his shoulders in addition to the human one, and he rides on a dragon. He was a son of Ninazu and Ningirda and was married to Ninazimua, "Lady Productively Grown Branch."

3. Damu, city-god of Girsu on the Euphrates in the general vicinity of Ur. Damu, son of Ningishzida and Ninazimua, was a vegetation god, especially, it seems, god of the sap that rises in trees and plants in the spring. His name means "the Child," and his cult—which seems to have been preponderantly a woman's cult—centered in rites of lamentation and search for the god, who had lain under the bark of his nurse, the cedar tree, and had disappeared. The search ended in the finding of the god, who reappeared out of the river. A

particularly interesting feature of the Damu cult is that it recognized as incarnations of the disappearing and sleeping god all the dead kings of the third dynasty of Ur and the early kings of the following dynasty of Isin. The cult of Damu influenced and in time blended with the very similar cult of Dumuzi the shepherd, at home farther north among the shepherds of the central grasslands.

3. HERDING REGIONS

In the south around the lower ancient Euphrates was a group of cities—Ur, Gaesh, Kiabrig, Larsa, and Kullab—the chief gods of which seem to have been herdsmen's gods belonging to the family of Nanna. Farther north, in the center of Sumer between the Iturungal and the ancient Euphrates, lay grasslands ringed around by the ancient cities of Erech, Bad-tibira, Umma, Zabalam, and Bitkarkara, which likewise have city-gods connected with herding and belonging to the family of Nanna. The gods of these cities, however, especially Inanna and her young husband, Dumuzi the shepherd, seem to be shepherds' rather than cowherds' gods. Lastly may be noted the two cities of Adab on the northern edge of the grasslands and Kesh, probably to be identified with Ishan Abu Salabikh, north of Nippur on the edge of the gravelly western desert, both cities of Ninhursaga, whose connections were with asses (onagers) and ass herding.

These groups of city-gods form, as it were, a herdsman's pantheon, a family of gods headed by Nanna of Ur—cowherds' gods in the south, shepherds' in the central grasslands. More loosely connected is the separate family of Ninhursaga to the north of them, the ass herders' gods. Characteristic for this pantheon of the herdsmen is a prominence of astral deities: Nanna, the moon; Utu, the sun; Inanna, the morning and evening star; and seemingly An, the sky. Deities of this group have forms derived from the world familiar and particularly meaningful to the herdsman: the animal of the herd or flock, the herdsman himself.

Southern Cowherds' Gods. 1. Nanna (Sin), city-god of Ur and of the neighboring Gaesh and god of the moon. His name Nanna may have designated him particularly as the full moon; another of his names, Ensun, "Lord Wild Bull," as the half-moon; a third, Ashimbabbar, as the new light. His original form, the moon, was sometimes visualized as a boat, sometimes as the horned crown of divinity, but most characteristically it was seen with the herdsman's eye as the horns of a great bull leading the herd of stars. In human form the god became a cowherd driving his herd over the sky, and in this form the Sumerian hymns most often present him. Nanna counted as son of Enlil and Ninlil; his spouse was Ningal.

2. Ninhar, city-god of Kiabrig in the region of Ur, probably toward the south. Ninhar was god of the thunder and rainstorms that make the desert green with pasturage in the spring and was envisaged under the shape of a mighty roaring bull. He was son of Nanna and Ningal and married to Ninigara, the "Lady of Butter and Cream," goddess of the dairy.

3. Utu (Shamash), city-god of Zararim (Akkadian Larsa) in the south and of Sippar in Akkad. In both cities his temple was called Ebabbar. Utu was god of the sun and of justice and equity. His name means "sun," and his original form, the sun disk, seen through the eyes of the cowherd became the round head of a bison. This form survived as the god's emblem, "the Bison's Head, the emblem of Utu," mentioned by Gudea, and in the two crossed bison-headed figures often shown under his chair. When he is depicted in human shape his solar character usually is indicated by rays issuing from his body; often he holds in his hand another of his emblems, a saw. Utu was son of Nanna and Ningal and married to Shenirda. Their son was Shakan, god of goats and goat herding and of the gazelles and wild four-legged creatures of the steppe generally. As viziers of Utu occur the personified justice, Niggina, and equity, Nigsisa. The Akkadians identified their solar deity Shamash with Utu and their goddess Aia with Shenirda.

4. Ninsun, city-goddess of Kullab, an ancient city generally assumed to have merged into Erech but perhaps more likely identical with Larsa or with a part of it. Ninsun seems to be the divine power behind, and the embodiment of, all those qualities the herdsman hoped for in his cows—she is the "good cow," a "mother of good offspring that loves the offspring." As her name Ninsun, "Lady Wild Cow," indicates, she was originally imaged in cow shape, but in human shape she could also give birth to human offspring. Thus Gudea, whose personal goddess she was, is said to have been borne by Ninsun, "the good cow in its [form as] woman." In the cowherd's pantheon

the good cow that loves the offspring became the type of the mother. The "wild bull" Dumuzi of the cowherds, as distinct from Dumuzi the shepherd of the shepherds, was her son whom she lamented— often very movingly—in the yearly ritual of lament for his death. As type of the mother, Ninhursaga in the pantheon of the ass herder and, in lesser degree, Ninlil in the pantheon of the farmer are counterparts to her. Her husband was Lugalbanda.

5. An (Anu), worshiped in Erech but not counted as city-god. An was god of the sky and father of all the gods. His name means "sky," and he seems originally to have been envisaged under the form of a great bull, a form later disassociated from the god as a separate mythological entity, the "bull of heaven," which he owned. The bovine imagery suggests that he belonged originally to the herdsman's, specifically the cowherd's pantheon, likely enough in view of the general predilection in that pantheon for celestial powers. As father of the gods An presides in divine assemblies and grants the highest offices, kingship and lordship. He is himself, more than any other god perhaps, the embodiment of majesty and supreme authority.

Central Grasslands Shepherds' Gods. 1. Inanna (Ishtar), city-goddess of Erech and Zabalam (Bzeikh), also of Hursagkalamma (Uhaimir) in Akkad. Inanna appears originally to have been a personification of the powers in the storehouse for dates and to have belonged to the pantheon of the orchardman. She lives in Eanna, "the House of the Date Clusters," her name means "the Lady of the Date Clusters," her young husband is Dumuzi-Amaushumgalana, the power in the single great bud of the date palm, and their wedding takes place in the "storehouse." The reed bundles and rolled-up screen of the gate of the storehouse served as her emblem and original nonhuman form. As goddess of the storehouse more generally—the storehouse for wool, meat, and dairy products—she seems to have been received early into the pantheon of the herdsman, where she appears as bride both of Dumuzi the shepherd and of "the wild bull" Dumuzi, and as daughter of the head of the herdsman's pantheon, Nanna. From this came probably her astral aspect as goddess of the evening and morning star, which led in post-Sumerian times to a reinterpretation of her name as "Queen of the Sky." As a personification of the storehouse awaiting union with the year's produce she early became typed —although the gods Shara and Lulal (Latarak) counted as her sons—as a young marriageable girl and bride rather than as wife and mother. Since the union of storehouse and produce is not a lasting one (stores are used up), her husband dies young soon after marriage. To her typing as a young marriageable girl she probably owes her role as incarnation of the rage of battle, for in early Sumer, as still among the Bedouins, it appears to have been the accepted function of young unmarried girls to encourage and egg on the young warriors in battle with praise and taunts. To her typing as unmarried girl she may possibly owe also her role of harlot and protectress of harlots. In the process of recasting the pantheon in human aristocratic pattern she became the type of the independent, willful, and spoiled young noblewoman.

Of noteworthy myths about Inanna may be mentioned "Inanna and Shukallituda," which tells how the orchardman Shukallituda invented shade-tree gardening, found Inanna asleep in the shade under one of his trees and lay with her, and how she tried to find him afterward, sending various plagues upon the country but to no avail. The end of the story is not preserved. "The Descent of Inanna" tells how she attempted to take over rule of the nether world from her sister Ereshkigal, was changed into a cut of meat and held prisoner in the nether world, but was eventually revived through the agency of Enki and released on condition that she furnish a substitute to take her place. On her return, finding that her husband Dumuzi did not appear sorrowful enough at her disappearance, she delivered him up in a fit of jealous rage to substitute for her in the nether world. The myth "Inanna and the Powers of Office" tells how Inanna journeyed to Eridu, was granted a medley of offices and powers by Enki after a banquet in her honour when he was mellowed by wine, and left next morning to take them safely to Erech. She succeeded, although Enki seven times stopped the boat and tried to get the powers back. The myth was probably a *hieros logos* of a yearly ritual journey of the image of Inanna by boat to Eridu for purification and re-appointment to divine office. "Inanna and Ebeh" tells of Inanna's conquest of the mountain range Ebeh, the present Jabal Hamrin.

2. Dumuzi (Tammuz), city-god of Bad-tibira (Madinah) is god of fertility and the producer of new life. His name means "the Quickener of the Young [in Mother's Womb]" and he occurs in various forms: as Dumuzi-Abzu, "Dumuzi of the Watery Deep," in the marsh-

man's pantheon; as Dumuzi-Amaushumgalana, "Dumuzi, the One Great Source [lit. 'mother'] of the Date Clusters," a deification of the heart of palm, the single great bud of the date palm, in the orchard-man's pantheon, where Damu is a related figure; as "the Wild Bull" (*am*) Dumuzi, son of Ninsun, in the cowherd's; and as Dumuzi "the shepherd" (*sibad*), son of Duttur, goddess of the ewe, in the shepherd's pantheon. It is in the latter form (as the divine power to produce lambs and milk in the ewes in springtime) that he is city-god of Bad-tibira.

The cult of Dumuzi centers around two poles, the marriage of the god to Inanna, and the lamenting of his early death. The marriage was ritually consummated in a cult drama, a *hieros gamos*, in which the king took on the identity of the god, a priestess that of the goddess. It expressed different things in the various Dumuzi cults. In Erech the marriage of Inanna as goddess of the storehouse to Dumuzi-Amaushumgalana was essentially a harvest festival. It celebrated the relief of the community in knowing itself safely provisioned for a new year under the ritual image of the young girl finding security in marriage. In the marriage of Inanna to "the wild bull Dumuzi" of the cowherds in Nippur the rite was essentially a fertility rite of spring, the king's potency in the consummation of it being coincident with the shooting up of the flax, the grain, and the verdure of the steppe.

The end of spring and of new life in nature, of the milking and lambing season, heralded the death of Dumuzi, the power who had produced it. His death was variously conceived. In the herdsmen's rites it was usually brought about by an attack on the young herdsman in the desert by raiders from the nether world. In the rites he was mourned by his bereaved mother, his sister, and his young widow in laments that often reach great heights of beauty and compassion.

3. Shara, city-god of Umma and son of Inanna. The precise character of this god remains obscure.

4. Ishkur (Adad), city-god of Bitkarkara, a city mentioned between Zabalam and Adab and perhaps to be identified with the modern site of Tell Jidr. Ishkur was god of the rain and thunderstorms of spring, so vital to the herdsman because the pasturage in the desert depends on them. As Ninhar, whom he greatly resembles, Ishkur was imagined in the shape of a great bull and was son of Nanna.

When he is depicted in human shape he often holds his symbol, the lightning fork. As god of rain and thunder he corresponds in the herdsman's pantheon to Asalluhe in the marshman's and has the epithet *lu-he*, "man-drenching," in common with him. In the farmer's pantheon his counterpart is Ninurta. Ishkur's wife was the goddess Shala. He was identified by the Akkadians with their god of thunderstorms, Adad.

Gods of the Northern Ass Herders. Ninhursaga (Belitili), city-goddess of Adab and of Kesh, is the goddess of the stony, rocky ground, the *hursag*, as it is found in the mountains to the east and as it comes out in the vast gravelly and stony desert to the west, contrasting so sharply with the alluvial soil of Sumer proper. Particularly she is the power in the foothills and in the desert to produce wildlife, and especially the wild onagers of the western desert are her offspring. Her name Ninhursaga denotes her as the "Lady of the Stony Ground." Other names for her are Dingirmah, the "Exalted Deity"; Ninmah, the "Exalted Lady"; Aruru, the "Dropper" (i.e., who lets fall in birth); and Nintu, "Lady Birthgiver." As the sorrowing mother animal she appears in a lament for her son, a young colt, but as goddess of birth she is not only the goddess of animal birth but "the mother of all children." In curses on evil-doing future rulers she may be asked to stop all birthgiving in the land. Her husband is the god Shulpae. Of their children the sons Mululil and Ashshirgi and the daughter Egime may be mentioned. Mululil appears to have been a dying god, comparable with Dumuzi and Damu, whose death was lamented in yearly rites.

4. Farming Regions

The ancient cities situated north of the central grasslands and up into Akkad, and to the east in the northern parts of the Lagash region, have city-gods, most of whom show connections with cereals or agricultural implements or otherwise indicate that they belong to the world of the farmer with its characteristic values and forms. They belong to a single divine family, that of Enlil in Nippur, and may be assumed to have constituted the farmer's pantheon. Their most distinctive features seem to be a pronounced fierceness and warlikeness in the male gods, who tend to the type of the warrior, and a stress on chthonian aspects. The figure that occupied the myth-making fantasy most centrally in the farmer's pantheon was Enlil. Late in the myth-making period, on the verge of that of the epic, interest seems to have shifted to Enlil's son Ninurta. The gods of this group are:

1. Enlil, city-god of Nippur, god of the wind. His name Enlil designates him directly as "Lord Wind," but with time the form in which he manifested himself came to be viewed more particularly as the breath issuing from his mouth, his "word" or "command." The wind, in the eyes of the Mesopotamian farmer, is not only the raging, destructive storm but also, and as significantly, the moist reviving wind of the spring that brings the rains and makes desert and fields green. At harvest time when the grain is winnowed Enlil, the wind, cleans it. The grain is Ninlil or Sud, his wife, "the Princess of the Copper [winnowing] Pan," the daughter of the goddess of the varicolored barley. In the divine assembly Enlil is enthroned on Duku, "the Pure Mound," apparently the mythological prototype of the storage pile covered with mats and with earth to hold them down. There are indications that Enlil had to go away to the nether world, that he sleeps "the treacherous sleep," and is reawakened by Inanna. Details of this side of his nature—presumably the disappearance of the pleasant winds of spring and early summer is involved—are, however, not clear.

Enlil was son of An and presided with him in the divine assembly, which met in the court Ubshuukkinna in Ekur in Nippur. As "king of all lands," he granted with An kingship and lordship. Enlil's word, the wind, was the executive agent of the divine assembly, carrying out its decisions. When the gods had decided on the overthrow of a city it was Enlil's word that blew as a storm against it, enveloped and overwhelmed it—his word "which as stormcloud lies massively grounded on the earth, its interior inscrutable, his word which up above makes the heavens tremble, which down below makes the earth quake, his word with which the gods destroy." This divine word is the image under which the destroying, conquering enemy hordes were seen; or rather, it represented the inner truth of what was happening, the deeper reality for which the enemy horde of actuality was incidental.

Myths about Enlil include the "Myth of the Creation of the

Pickax," which tells how Enlil created this basic agricultural tool and used it to break the hard crust of the earth in Uzumua in Nippur, letting the first men grow forth from the earth like plants there; the "Myth of Enlil and Ninlil," which tells how Enlil raped Ninlil when he first met her and was banished to the nether world, how Ninlil followed him, how under various disguises he united with her again and how she conceived, besides Ninna, the moon-god, the chthonian deities Meslamtaea and Ninazu and still a third god whose name is only imperfectly preserved in the text.

2. Ninlil, city-goddess of Tummal near Nippur, where she was known as Egitummal, and of Shuruppak, where she was known as Sud. Ninlil is "the varicolored ear [of barley]," goddess of the grain (particularly, perhaps, of the seed corn), and counts as the daughter of Haia, god of the stores, and Ninshebargunu, "Lady varicolored Barley," the goddess of the ripening barley, a form of the goddess Nissaba. The goddess Ezinu of the green barley issued from the seed corn seems to have been Ninlil's daughter.

3. Nissaba, city-goddess of Eresh on the ancient Euphrates not far upstream from Erech, was goddess of the grasses generally, including the reeds and the cereals. As goddess of the reeds and provider of the reed stylus of the scribe she became the patroness of writing and the scribal arts, particularly of accounting.

4. Ninurta, city-god of Girsu (Telloh) in the Lagash region, where he was known by his name Ningirsu, "Lord of Girsu." Ninurta was the farmer's version of the god of the thunder and rainstorms of the spring. Since it is the early rains that melt the snow in the mountains and swell the rivers, he was also the power in the floods of spring; and since it is the rains and the general humidity in the air in spring that makes the ground soft enough to be broken by the plow, he is also god of the plow and of plowing, much as his father, Enlil, is god of the older implement, the pickax. Ninurta's earliest name was Imdugud, which means "Rain-Cloud," and his earliest form was that of the thundercloud, envisaged as an enormous black bird floating on outstretched wings, roaring its thunder cry from a lion's head. With the growing tendency toward anthropomorphism the old form and name were gradually disassociated from the god as merely his emblem; enmity toward the older, inacceptable shape eventually made it evil, an ancient enemy of the god, a develop-

ment culminating in the Akkadian myth about it as Anzu. The preferred names for the new human form of the god tended to be colorless epithets like Ningirsu, "Lord of Girsu," in Girsu.

Ninurta was the son of Enlil and Ninlil and was married to Bau, in Nippur called Ninnibru, "Queen of Nippur." A major festival of his, the *gudsisu* festival, marked in Nippur the beginning of the plowing season.

Myths about Ninurta are first of all the epic *Lugal-e*, which depicts the god as the type of the king as young leader of raids and wars. It tells of his battle with the rival king of the plants and the stones, the monster Asakku, in the mountains; his victory; his construction of a rocky ridge, the *hursag*, to regulate the irrigation supplies of Sumer; and of how he gave this ridge to his mother, Ninlil, when she paid him a visit after his victory (hence her name Ninhursaga, "Queen of the Hursag"). Lastly it recounts his judgments on the stones after his victory, judgments in which he assigned to them their various characteristics and uses. A second myth about Ninurta tells of his return to Nippur after victory in battle. An Akkadian myth deals with his victory over Anzu—his own earlier form of Imdugud, which now takes the place of Asakku as his opponent—and regains from it the tablets of destiny which it had stolen from Enlil.

5. Bau, city-goddess of Uruku in the Lagash region, and, under the name Nininsina, "The Queen of Isin," city-goddess of Isin, south of Nippur. Bau seems originally to have been goddess of the dog and her name, Bau, to have constituted an imitation of the dog's bark, as English "bowwow." As Nininsina she is till late envisaged with a dog's head, and the dog is her emblem. She became—probably because the licking of sores by dogs was supposed to have curative value—a goddess of healing. Her father was An, her husband Pabilsag, another name for Ninurta/Ningirsu. The Akkadians called her Gula or Ninkarrak as well as Bau.

6. Meslamtaea (Nergal), city-god of Cuthah in Akkad. His temple in Cuthah was called Emeslam or Meslam, "Luxuriant Mesu Tree," and the god's name Meslamtaea, "He Who Issues From Meslam," indicates perhaps origin as a tree-god, which would agree with his general chthonian character. He was son of Enlil and Ninlil and appears in hymns as a warrior and so like Ninurta as to be almost indistinguishable. One difference, however, is that the weapons of

Meslamtaea seem frequently to be turned against his own people and their herds, whom he kills as the divine power in the great plagues that so often sweep ancient countries. Another name of Meslamtaea, Nergal, designates him as ruler of the nether world and as spouse of its queen, Ereshkigal. This may not have been original with the god, since other gods are mentioned as Ereshkigal's spouse in the older tradition, and since an Akkadian myth explicitly tells how he came to occupy that exalted position, the "Myth of Nergal and Ereshkigal."

AKKADIAN PANTHEON

The gods worshiped by the Akkadians when they infiltrated Akkad are very largely unknown, but some idea of what the Akkadian pantheon was like can be gained from divine names occurring as part of Akkadian personal names of the period of the dynasty of Agade and just before. They show the presence of a not very clearly defined major god Il and of the astral triad Sin, god of the moon; Shamash, deity of the sun, seemingly a goddess; and Ashtar, later Ishtar, goddess of the morning and evening star. The deities of this triad were identified with the Sumerian deities Nanna, Utu, and Inanna respectively and merged into them.

A relatively large number of goddesses devoted to raids and battle are present: Anuna, "Skirmish," and Anunitum, "She of the Skirmish"; Inin, "Skirmishing"; Irnina, "Victory." Here belong perhaps also Shilabat, "She is a Lioness," and Shiduri, "She is My Fortress." All these figures tended in time to blend into that of Ishtar.

Lastly there was a group of deities of the thunder and rainstorms of the spring, similar to the Sumerian Ishkur and Ninurta. Most of these, it is perhaps worth noting, became city-gods: Dagan, seemingly a god of storm and rain, is the city-god of Tuttul on the Euphrates. Zababa in Kish seems to have belonged to this type also. Aba in Agade is known mainly as warrior and god of war. Tishpak, who replaced Ninazu as city-god of Eshnunna, was perhaps originally a rain-god; his name may mean "the Down-pouring One." To the gods of rain and thunder belongs also Adad.

Of frequent occurrence is Ea, probably a river-god, who was identified with Sumerian Enki. The gods Malik, "the Counsellor," the chthonian god and goddess Erra and Allatum, and the goddesses Mama and Ishhara may at least be mentioned.

Generally speaking, the early Akkadian pantheon with its prominent astral triad of moon, sun, and morning and evening star, and with its gods of the rain and thundershowers that bring out grass and pasture in the spring, seems fairly close to the Sumerian herdsman's pantheon and constituted itself very probably the indigenous pantheon of pasturing nomadic tribesmen.

ASSYRO-BABYLONIAN PANTHEON

To the end of Mesopotamian civilization the long lists of gods of the Sumerians continued to be copied and hymns to ancient Sumerian gods in the Sumerian language continued to be sung in the temples; none of the old gods was deliberately discarded. Yet, as in the second millennium, when the two national states of Babylonia and Assyria arose, decided changes in emphasis and attention took place. Two young autocrats, Marduk of Babylon and Ashshur (Ashur) of Assyria, came to occupy the foreground and the older gods receded, still prominent and worshiped but seen less and less as primary sources of power. The major figures besides Marduk and Ashur were in later time Marduk's son Nabu of Borsippa, god of the scribal art and secretary in the assembly of the gods, and the older gods An, Enlil, Ea (Enki), Sin (Nanna), Shamash (Utu), Adad (Ishkur), Ishtar (Inanna), Ninurta—especially in Assyria—and Nergal. Of these Marduk and Ashur may be discussed in more detail.

1. *Marduk.* Marduk, the city-god of Babylon, would seem to have been in origin a Sumerian god and go back to times when Akkad and Babylon were both still Sumerian, for both Marduk's own name and the names of his temple Esangila and its ziggurat Etemenanki are Sumerian. His original character was probably—like that of Asalluhe with whom he was identified and with whom he shows intimate relation—that of a god of thunder and rainstorms, and he seems, like Asalluhe and other gods of thunder and rainstorms, to have been imagined under the outer form of a bull, the bellow of which was heard in the thunder. His weapons, with which he gained victory over the forces of primeval chaos, were the bow and arrow, probably representing the lightning shot by the god of

thunder, and his symbol is an arrowhead or head of a spear. In the course of time, by a process of syncretism, Marduk came to absorb a number of other, originally independent gods such as, for example, the god of spells, Tutu; the god of irrigation, Enbilulu; the grain-gods Ezinu and Gil; and many others. As a result Marduk presents a highly complex and opaque figure. In later time the god is usually depicted in human shape and accompanied by a dragon known as the *mushhushshu*. Marduk was the son of Ea and Damkina (Enki and Damgalnunna) and was married to the goddess Sarpanitum. Around the figure of Marduk centers the Babylonian creation story, a myth that in its kernel (the battle between the god of the thunderstorm and the god of the sea) does not really fit in a Mesopotamian natural setting and seems to have been borrowed from Western myths.

The most important festival for Marduk, the New Year festival in the spring, was in its essence a reenactment and reaffirmation of his original achievement of reducing the universe to order. The first days of the month of Nisan were given over to preparations and purification of the temples for the festival. On the fourth the whole of the creation myth was recited before the god. On the fifth, when Marduk's son Nabu arrived from Borsippa, the festival proper began with a cermony of reinvestiture of the king. The high priest took the royal insignia away from the king, smote him on the cheek, and made him kneel before Marduk to say a prayer in which he assured the god that he had done no wrong but had ruled properly. The high priest then assured him of the god's favor, restored to him the insignia of office, and struck his cheek a second time. If the blow brought tears to the king's eyes it was a sign that the god was friendly; if not, that he was angry. On the eighth Marduk took his seat amidst the assembled gods in the chamber of destinies, Duku, for the deciding of destinies, probably a reenactment of the divine assembly in which Marduk was made king. On the tenth followed a great procession and journey by boat out of town to the *akitu* temple, the king leading Marduk. This seems to reflect the march to battle with Tiamat, as related in the myth. On the eleventh the assembled gods again paid homage to Marduk in the chamber of destinies, presumably a reenactment of the celebration of Marduk's victory, his feats of organization, and his election as "lord" by the gods. On the twelfth day the festival ended and the gods returned to their temples.

2. *Ashur*. Ashur, the city-god of Ashur and national god of Assyria, is in origin and essence a most elusive figure. Possibly he was in the beginning merely a *numen loci* of the city that shares his name. In later times, from Shamshi-Adad I onward, there appear to have been strong tendencies to identify him with the Sumerian Enlil, and not only titles of Enlil but deities associated with him and cult places of his in Nippur are duplicated in Ashur in Assyria. Still later, under Sargon II, there were tendencies to identify Ashur with Anshar, the father of An in the creation myth. Under Sennacherib abundant materials testify to deliberate and thorough attempts to transfer to Ashur the primeval achievements of Marduk as told in the myth, as well as the whole ritual of the New Year festival of Babylon— attempts that clearly have their background in the political struggle with Babylonia. In view of this it may be asked whether also the earlier tendency to identify Ashur with Enlil may not have had mainly political motivation and to have implied a political program of domination over Sumer and Akkad rather than any actual affinity of nature and function between the two gods. As a consequence, the image of Ashur seems to lack all real distinctiveness and contains little that is not implied in his position as the city-god of a vigorous and warlike city that became the capital of an empire. He grants rule over Assyria, supports Assyrian arms against enemies, and even receives detailed written reports from the Assyrian kings about their campaigns. He appears a mere personification of the interests of Assyria as a political entity, with little character of his own.

THE INDIVIDUAL AND THE POWERS

During the classical period Mesopotamian religion underwent a process of structuring along the lines of political organization; all of the cosmos became a great state in which the gods held the supreme offices and wielded the supreme authority. In seeking to understand the viewpoint and position of the individual worshiper it is well to keep this in mind. The individual had direct and personal relations mainly to his own personal god, the power who took a personal interest in him and his fortunes, whom he worshiped in a daily private cult, to whom he brought his immediate personal problems, and whom he occasionally badgered if he did not think he was properly taken care of. The major gods were more like high officials in the state, whom one might see on official occasions—*in casu* at the great festivals—but with whom an ordinary citizen had few personal dealings. This does not mean, however, that the relationship to them and dependency on them was any less real and important. As the government is responsible for the smooth running of a nation's economy, for defense and for internal peace, law and order, so the gods were the responsible powers for order in nature, for peace and prosperity in social life. Direct contact with the higher gods the individual would seek mainly when he felt himself harmed, much as a citizen in such cases will turn to the government and the courts for protection. Such contacts were sought by the individual in cases of illness, attacks on him by the lawless demons of disease, when help from the higher gods was needed to restrain the demons and to pacify and reconcile the personal god who had turned from the man in anger, exposing him to attack.

Not only in illness but in every situation of anxiety and uncertainty the individual was likely to seek divine guidance through omens, that he might know the will of the gods. And such guidance was sought assiduously, even by the greatest rulers and kings, in all matters of import. The state was directly ruled in its major policies by divine instructions.

The religious framework thus affected and conditioned life in ancient Mesopotamian society intensely and on all levels. It may be assumed that, as in most societies, the majority of men in ancient Mesopotamia had normal aptitude for, and sensitivity to, religion and religious values. Occasional individuals lacking in such normal sensitivity, who could see in religion only meaningless restrictions on their personal inclinations, will of course have been found, perhaps especially among the slaves and brutalized poor. To balance them the civilization seems to have had an unusually large number of highly sensitive minds, religiously creative poets, thinkers, and priests. Mesopotamian religious literature at its best is the literature of a people highly gifted in religion, capable of profound religious insights and of finding profound and moving expression for them.

3. Ancient Mesopotamian Religion:
The Central Concerns

The best way to begin a paper entitled "Ancient Mesopotamian Religion: The Central Concerns" is perhaps to say what the words "religion" and "central concerns" were meant to convey.

By "religion"—and so also by "ancient Mesopotamian religion"—we would wish to understand the human response to a unique type of experience, the one William James called religious experience and Rudolph Otto "numinous" experience. Otto has analyzed it as a confrontation with power not of this world, a wholly other, outside of normal experience and indescribable in its terms; terrifying, ranging from sheer demonic dread through awe to sublime majesty; and fascinating with irresistible attraction, inviting unconditional allegiance: mysterium tremendum et fascinans.[1]

While this experience seems to be essentially one, the human response to it is demonstrably manifold and—since it is human—contingent, and dependent on many factors. As a particularly powerful such factor must be counted the urge in man to seek security and salvation in his allegiance with the power. The urge arises out of the inherent uncertainties of the human condition and is so dominant in man that under it his immediate understanding of the power, and of allegiance to it, comes in very considerable measure to reflect his own self, his deepest needs, his most profound fears. It is these most profound fears, conditioning and shaping the religious response, lending it different emphases from age to age, that we would attempt to trace for ancient Mesopotamia.[2]

NOTE: First published in *PAPS* 107/6 (1963) 473–484.

In thus dealing with ancient man in his most profoundly contingent and insecure aspect we must needs present a side of him that is not at all that of the self-assured resolute man of action, builder of cities and maker of history, that we know so well from the monuments. Rather, we must try to make our own the lines in "The Waste Land" that say:

> And I will show you something different from either
> Your shadow at morning, striding behind you,
> Or your shadow at evening, rising to meet you;
> I will show you fear in a handful of dust.

THE FOURTH MILLENNIUM:[3] FAMINE

Fear in a handful of dust.—The fear at the very roots of existence that long ago, down through the fourth millennium, gave to the religious response in Mesopotamia its major direction would seem to have been a simple one: fear of starvation.

Early Mesopotamian economy was unquestionably a remarkable achievement, able for the first time to provide sufficient food so that large numbers of humans could congregate in cities. But it was also a precarious and uncertain economy, for it was based on artificial irrigation, the most touchy and tricky basis imaginable, nervously reacting to vagaries of nature and man alike.[4] Disasters, famine, slow or quick death must have been always with those early men.[5] And the character of their religion as we know it bears this out. The powers to whom they turned were powers in and behind their primary economies on which life depended: fishing, herding, agriculture, as even the briefest look at the character of the chief gods of their cities will show. Aim and purpose of their cults were to insure the presence of these essential powers for fertility, produce, and food. Houses—temples—were built for them so that they might dwell with men as members of the human community; rituals, such as the one shown on the Uruk Vase and on numerous roll-seals, celebrated the sacred marriage between the power for fertility and crops, Dumuzid, and the power in the community stores, the goddess Inannak, thus binding the power for fertility to the community in the strong bonds of marriage. We may surmise that other rites, lamenting the absence or the death of the power for fertility, endeavored to bring him back through the magic of human longing and desire. In brief: man felt solidaric with the powers in nature for fertility and produce and food, on which he depended so utterly, and, feeling solidaric, he did his utmost to help and enhance them, to insure that they would realize themselves, appear tangibly before his eyes in their own desirable mode of being.[6]

If we wish to gain an impression of what such a religion was like we must turn to survivals of the cult shown on the Uruk Vase, to the continuing worship of the god of fertility and new life, Dumuzid, under one of his varying aspects.[7] We have chosen as an example a section of a lament for the god under the name and aspect of Damu;[8] the god is far away in the nether world and the dry season with its growing threat of death drags on from day to day:[9]

For him of the faraways...the wailing for (fear) that he may not come,[10]
For my child of the faraways...the wailing for (fear) that he may not come,
For my Damu of the faraways...for my anointed[11] one of the faraways...,
From the pure cedar[12] where I, the mother, gave birth...,
From Eannak high and low..., the wailing for (fear) that he may not come,
The wailing from the lord's house...for (fear) that he may not come,
The wailing from the lord's town...for (fear) that he may not come,
That wailing is surely wailing for the flax—the flax-plot may not give it birth,
That wailing is surely for the grain—the furrow may not give it birth,[13]
That wailing is surely wailing for the great river—it may not give birth to its waters,
That wailing is surely for the field—it may not give birth to the mottled barley,
That wailing is surely for the marsh—it may not give birth to carp and trout,
That wailing is surely for the reed-thicket—the old reeds may not give birth to (new) reeds,

That wailing is surely for the woods—they may not give birth to
  stag and deer,
That wailing is surely for the orchards—they may not give birth to
  honey and wine,
That wailing is surely for the garden-beds—they may not give birth
  to lettuce and cress,
That wailing is surely for the palace—it may not give birth to long
  life.

In her distress the mother of the god goes out into the desert to
seek her child, and in another hymn we follow her as she is calling
and calling for him there. But he is captive in the realms of death and
cannot answer her cry:[14]

> I am not one who can answer my mother, who cries for
>   me in the desert,
> Who makes the cry for me echo in the desert,
> She will not be answered!
> I am not the grass—may not come up for her (again)
> I am not the waters—may not rise for her (again)
> I am not the grass, sprouting in the desert,
> I am not the new grass, coming up in the desert.

Eventually the god's sister finds him in the nether world and tries
to comfort him and promises to stay with him:[15]

> Who is your sister?—I am your sister,
> Who is your mother?—I am your mother.
> The day that dawns for you will also dawn for me,
> The day you see—I shall also see.

When eventually the god is allowed to sail back to life and the living
from the realms of death the aura of death is still upon him, so that a
cry of warning sounds before him:[16]

> O (city of) Ur! At my loud cry
> Lock your house, lock your house, city lock your house!
> O temple of Ur! Lock your house, city lock your house,
> Your priestess-bride must not go out of (her house) the Giparu,
> City lock your house!

THE THIRD MILLENNIUM:[17] AND THE SWORD

With the coming of the third millennium B.C. a new fear took its place at the center of existence together with the fear of starvation—the fear of war and its ravages.

As the settled areas of the country grew and joined, the protection that had been afforded by relative isolation was no longer there and fear of enemy attack, death, or slavery became a part of life ever present in the depth of consciousness. The intensity of the danger and of the fear it engendered can be gauged by the great city-walls that arose around the towns in this period and the staggering amount of labor that must have gone into them. For a shield against danger men looked to the now vitally important institutions of collective security, the great leagues and their officers, and particularly to the new institution of kingship as it took form and grew under the pressures of these years.[18] The king, awesome and majestic in his power over men, was alike the defender against outside foes and the righter of wrongs among his people.[19] The new concept—opening up, as it did, a possibility of approach to the elements of majesty in the divine—was early applied to the gods[20] and it profoundly influenced the religious outlook. The gods, seen as kings and rulers, were no longer powers in nature only, they became powers in human affairs—in history. As great lords they defended their cities against attack, and through decrees of social reform and covenants with their servant the human king that he would not deliver up the orphan and the widow to the powerful man,[21] they maintained justice and righteousness.[22] Meeting as needed in assembly at Nippur the gods deliberated on human affairs and shaped history.[23] Against the decisions of this assembly no single god could prevail and so—for all the relative security the rule of one's own city-god could provide—basically fear could not be stilled.

We have the lament of the goddess of Ur, Ningal, when the divine assembly had decreed that Ur should be destroyed:[24]

Dread of the storm's floodlike destruction weighed on me
And of a sudden on my couch at night,
Upon my couch at night no dreams were granted me,
And of a sudden on my couch oblivion,
Upon my couch oblivion, was not granted.

Because (this) bitter weeping had been destined for my land
And I could not, even if I scoured the earth—a cow seeking her calf—
    Have brought my people back,
Because (this) bitter sorrow had been destined for my city,
Even if I, birdlike, had stretched my wings
And, like a bird, flown to my city,
Yet my city would have been destroyed on its foundation,
Yet Ur would have perished where it lay.
Because that day of storm had raised its hand
And even had I screamed out loud and cried
"Turn back, O day of storm, (turn) to (thy) desert"
The breast of that storm would not have been lifted from me.

The imagery in the laments of the times show how real, how often and how matter-of-factly experienced, such disasters were:[25]

(Dead) men, no potsherds,
Covered the approaches.
The walls were gaping,
The high gates, the roads,
Were piled with dead.
In the wide streets, where feasting crowds would gather,
Scattered they lay.
In all the streets and roadways bodies lay
In open fields that used to fill with dancers
They lay in heaps
. . . .
The country's blood now filled its holes like metal in a mould
Bodies dissolved—like fat left in the sun.

THE SECOND MILLENNIUM:[26] GUILT

In our sources for religion in the fourth and third millennia B.C. just considered the individual seems almost totally immersed in his community as part of which he suffers and rejoices. But with the beginning second millennium the personal fortunes of the individual worshiper, his fears of personal misfortune, anxieties in illness and suffering, begin to be voiced; and the fear that may torture individual existence takes its place with the earlier central, conditioning fears, adding a personal dimension to the relation with the divine.

The new development has its beginnings in the concept of the "personal god,"[27] originally a personification of a man's "luck" and ability to effective thinking and acting, but very early identified with some known figure of the pantheon, usually a minor deity, who took a specially paternal interest in this particular man and his fortunes. In texts from the beginning of the second millennium, such as the Sumerian composition "Man and his God" treated by Dr. Kramer,[28] the emphasis is still very largely on the basic element of individual effectiveness. The man complains that what he knows does not come out right, what he says quite truthfully turns out to be false, he does things in all innocence and finds that he has been duped into committing wrong.[29] His god—his powers of clear and fast thinking—is not there to suggest an answer when friends deceive or impute falsehood to him, or when evildoers abuse him,[30] his god has abandoned him and lost interest in him.[31] He realizes that the blame lies with himself—pleading, however, that no man is perfect[32] —and asks to be shown his faults, his transgressions, that he may confess them before his god and be forgiven.[33] And the god is moved by his contrition and takes him back into favor. There is here the beginnings of a searching of the heart: the insight gained in the preceding millennium that the divine stands for, and upholds, a moral law is now bearing fruit in a realization of individual human responsibility, but also of innate human inability to live up to that responsibility. In his plight—estranged from his personal god—the penitent may have to seek intercession by higher deities. In an Old Babylonian lamentation to the goddess Ishtar the condition of the penitent sinner is described:[34]

> Ishtar, who but you can clear a path for him?
> Hear his entreaties!
> He has turned to you and seeks you,
> Your servant who has sinned, have mercy on him!
> He has bowed down and loudly implored you,
> For the wrongs he committed he shouts a psalm of penance,
> In full he counts up the benefactions of Ishtar,
> What he remembers—and what he had forgotten . . . . .
> He has sinned, all his conduct he lays open,
> The weariness with which he wearied himself he recounts:
> "I have done wrong!—The wrongs I committed

Ishtar has made good for me, I weep ardently!
I had no qualms, Ishtar ......"

and so on.

As the second millennium further explored the question of man's acceptability before his god the problem of the righteous sufferer led on to realization of man's finiteness and the altogether finite character of his insights and his moral judgments:[35]

What seems good to one's self, is a crime before the god,
What to one's heart seems bad, is good before one's god.
Who may comprehend the minds of gods in heaven's depth
The thoughts of (those) divine deep waters, who could
　　　fathom them?
How could mankind, beclouded, comprehend the ways of gods?

In this realization that all human values are finite—and that yet man is held responsible to absolutes beyond him—Mesopotamian religious thought reaches perhaps its finest insights.[36]

THE FIRST MILLENNIUM

We have considered, thus, three millennia and seen how the human prayer slowly grew from "give us this day our daily bread" to "preserve us from evil" and—lastly—"forgive us our trespasses." There is left the first millennium b.c. in which Mesopotamian civilization drew toward a close without producing any major new religious directions. The new beginnings were elsewhere, in Israel and in Greece, who jointly were to become the fountainheads of Western civilization. Yet in the case of Israel the new beginnings were not in all respects new; Israel came into being in a millennium when the concept of a moral universe had been achieved and when men could enter into a covenant of social justice with God as acting in History and under this covenant live collectively and individually in moral responsibility. And one need only leaf through the books of the Old Testament to see—and see in detail—how major themes and modes of approach directly continue Mesopotamian themes and approaches, but with a new freshness and with a deeper profundity. Israel is heir—and a worthy heir—to preceding millennia.

Deadly Diseases

The shivers and chills (of death) that fritter the sum of things, spawn
    of the god of Heaven, spawned on an evil spirit,
The death warrants, beloved sons of the storm-god born of the
    queen of the nether world,
Who were torn out of Heaven and hurled from the Earth as castoffs
    Are creatures of Hell, all.

Up above they roar, down below they cheep,
They are the bitter venom of the gods,
They are the great storms let loose from Heaven,
They are the owl (of ill omen) that hoots in the town,
Spawn spawned by the god of Heaven, sons born by Earth are they.

Over high roofs, over broad roofs like a flood wave they surge,
From house to house they climb over,
Doors do not hold them, locks do not restrain them,
Through the doors they glide like snakes,
Through the hinge boxes they blow like wind.

From the man's embrace they lead off the wife,
From the man's knee they make the child get up,
And the youth they fetch out of the house of his in-laws;
They are the numbness, the daze
    that treads on the heels of man.

*From an incantation against diseases describing the death-dealing demons who
were thought to be the cause of most bodily ills. They are seen as evil wind
demons, children of the god of Heaven, Anu, and of the storm-god Enlil. From
Nineveh, Ashurbanipal's library, about 600 B.C.*

4. The Investiture and Anointing of Adapa in Heaven

In working over the Adapa-myth for the *Chicago Dictionary* I happened to come across the interesting note by Pater Burrows in *Orientalia*, XXX, 24, in which he discusses the experiences of Adapa in heaven. In working with the text my interest had been caught by exactly the same section of the myth as Pater Burrows discusses, but I had come to quite a different opinion as to the meaning of it.

Pater Burrows thinks that the anointing and investiture of Adapa means that Anu wishes to take this wise son of Ea, whose magic powers had been able to subdue even the south wind, into his own service. The food of immortality was to prevent his return to earth. Ea foresaw this and by a lying description of the food insured Adapa's refusal, and so brought about his return to earth equipped with the heavenly powers. The closing lines of the narrative are a common incantation against sickness fortified by the preceding history of the Ea-given wisdom and the Anu-given authority of the founder of the ritual.

As will be seen at once, the basic point upon which this ingenious theory rests is really the interpretation of the anointing and the investiture of Adapa. Was the clothing of our hero an investiture to the old Babylonian and was the fact that he was anointed an anointment in the ritual sense of the world? I will not deny the possibility that these actions under certain conditions may have had

NOTE: First published in *AJSL* 46 (1930) 201–203.

the above-mentioned significance in the Babylonian culture; but I doubt very much that this would be the interpretation most likely to occur to the ordinary Babylonian reader.

In all oriental countries hospitality is considered a principal virtue; and very early it developed a set scheme of formalities, all of them based upon very real needs of a weary guest coming from afar. To this set scheme in the reception of a guest belonged washing, and in the hot Babylonian climate anointing, the presenting of a new garment to the guest, and as the last item, food and drink. A few examples may suffice to show the prevalance of these customs in Babylonia. When Gilgamesh, weary from his long journey, came to Ut-napishtim he was taken to the place of washing, where he was thoroughly washed and had the dirt from the journey removed from his body; thereafter he was presented with a new garment which—as one could expect in such a place—was not an ordinary garment but possessed magic qualities; this, however, does not weaken the impression that Ut-napishtim only followed the established rules for receiving a guest. A still more elaborate description of how a guest was treated we find in the same epic, where we hear of how Engidu was received by the shepherds when the courtesan led him out of the wilderness. First food was placed before him and plenty of wine to quench his thirst; then he was anointed with oil, and at last he put on a garment. From the historical literature I might mention Ashurbanipal's treatment of the Babylonian ambassadors whom he caused to sit down at a splendid banquet and clothed with linen clothes and various-colored garments. Plenty of similar evidence could be adduced also from the related cultures; I need only remind the reader of the role which the garment plays as a gift to guests of honor in the Arabic civilization, but this may be enough for the present.

It would seem, then, that what Anu does to Adapa is only to comply with the laws of good taste in receiving his guest.

Now we can turn to the meaning of the story itself. The wise Adapa, the son of Ea, breaks with his spell the wing of the south wind, and by so doing brings down upon himself the punishment of Anu, the king of the gods. To rescue Adapa his father, Ea, thinks out a cunning scheme by which he gets the two doorkeepers of Anu to soothe his wrath toward Adapa. The scheme works out and Anu is appeased; astonished he looks at Adapa: why has Ea shown the heart of heaven to an impure* human? I.e., why has Ea given such magic power as the one Adapa has displayed in his encounter with the south wind to an "impure" human? Such powers had apparently hitherto been confined to the gods. Anu does not know what to do to this new mixture of divine powers and human nature; but at last he decides to treat him as a guest, i.e., as a being of equal rights to the host, in this case as a god. Accordingly he complies with the laws of hospitality and brings him food, drink, a garment, and oil for anointing. While the last two items are of little importance the food is food of life and the drink water of life. It is most natural to assume that food of immortality was what the gods generally ate and drank in parallel to the ambrosia of the Greeks and the apples of Ydun in the old Northern mythology.

The cunning Ea, however, had foreseen that Anu, when appeased, would treat Adapa as a guest and give him of the foods of the gods; but he did not wish that Adapa, who is here apparently the first man or at least the symbol of man, should eat of the food and live eternally; so he had taken measures to prevent Adapa from eating by his lying description of the food and drink which Anu would offer him.

The old explanation of the myth as an action which should explain why man is not immortal—even if he once upon a time was very near to obtaining this desired immortality—it seems to me still holds good. The fact that the myth—as Pater Burrows has rightly seen—is imbedded in an incantation does not weaken this point. Although we often find that the myths used to strengthen the power of incantations were made to order, it is not infrequent that the magician took an old myth which originally was not intended for such purpose and used it in an incantation. A clear example of such a procedure is found in the Ea and Atrahasis story, which is used to strengthen an incantation to relieve women in childbirth; also the Erra epic might be quoted in this place, though its magic power to keep away pestilence from the house in which it is found is apparently not essential to the meaning nor to the form of the epic itself.

---

* I.e., not possessing the "purity," the "holiness," "mana" of the gods.

In our case the incantation priest may have chosen this legend because in the story of Adapa's magic power (great enough to break the wing of the south wind) and the wisdom of his father (great enough to rescue Adapa from Anu's wrath) he found a description of the founder of his science sufficiently impressive to gain the upper hand over the demons of disease.

5. The Myth of Inanna and Bilulu

The new Sumerian myth here published is inscribed on a somewhat damaged four-column tablet, which forms part of the Nippur collection of the Museum of the Ancient Orient in Istanbul. The tablet carries the museum number Ist. 4486. Professor Samuel N. Kramer, arrested by the rather unusual contents of this text, copied it in Istanbul some years ago and subjected it to a preliminary study through which he established its character as a Dumuzi text and clarified the main lines of the story it tells. However, on hearing later that I was engaged in a general study of the Sumerian Dumuzi materials he not only made the text available to me but suggested with characteristic generosity a joint publication to which he would contribute primarily the autograph copy of the text, I the transliteration and translation.

It is this joint undertaking which is here presented. In preparing my part of it I have had the benefit of Professor Kramer's initial clarification of the story and of his reading and criticism of the finished manuscript. In addition Professor Benno Landsberger has discussed the text with me in detail, and I am indebted to him for numerous valuable references and illuminating suggestions. Whenever possible the contributions of these two scholars have been specifically indicated. It is perhaps unnecessary to add that what is here presented aims at no more than a first and tentative beginning at interpreting this most interesting but highly difficult text.[3]

I. FORM AND AFFINITIES

The Sumerian literary genre to which the composition contained in Ist. 4486 belongs seems to be indicated in a note at the end of the

NOTE: First published in *JNES* 12 (1953) 160–187 (with cuneiform copy and an appendix of S. N. Kramer, which are omitted here).

text which reads: ù-líl-lá ᵈInanna-kam, "It is an ù-líl-lá (pertaining to the cult) of Inanna." This genre is new and Ist. 4486 seems so far the only composition which can be assigned to it with certainty. As far as one can judge from a single example the ù-líl-lá would seem to occupy a middle position between the lamentation and the praise-hymn, partaking in the nature of both. Since the situation which Ist. 4486 celebrates, Inanna's revenge for Dumuzi, may be considered an instance of a typical situation: "The avenger's return," and since that is a situation which—because of its emotional ambivalence—is likely to have given rise to a distinctive type of song blending jubilation at the avenger's victory with sorrow and lament for the loss avenged, it seems possible that the peculiar emotional and stylistic range of Ist. 4486, from lament to heroic narrative to paean of victory, may prove a central characteristic of the ù-líl-lá generally. Certainty can, of course, not be reached until more examples of the genre come to hand.[4]

Except by its range Ist. 4486 does not stand notably apart stylistically. It employs, even in its narrative section, a strikingly vivid, semi-dramatic style characterized by abrupt transitions to and from direct speech and by frequent and sudden changes of characters and scene of action. These are, however, not distinctive characteristics. Narrative in that style—which undoubtedly owes its peculiarities to a background in ritual of a more or less dramatic nature—is found also in laments of the balag and ershemma types, particularly in the Dumuzi texts of these genres.

In wording Ist. 4486 shows itself terse to the point of sparseness. Adjectives and descriptive relative clauses are almost completely absent. This terseness together with the heroic values which underlie the tale give an archaic cast to the composition and suggest high age for it.

In structure the composition appears to be exceptionally intricate and it is rather unfortunate that the large lacunas make a complete structural reconstruction difficult. The better preserved sections suggest an arrangement of stanzas, which can be distichs or tristichs, into what we have termed "megastrophes." The megastrophes, which form couplets and perhaps triplets, grow regularly in length from one couplet or triplet to the next as the composition moves toward its climax. With the last couplet they again decrease.[5]

Leaving the problems of form and literary classification to one side and turning to questions of literary and mythological affinities of the text, we may assign it with a fair amount of probability to the Bad-tibira branch of the Dumuzi tradition.[6] To that branch of the tradition point the place names, with it the divine epithets occurring in the story are compatible, and one of the main motifs, the death of Dumuzi in a raid on his fold, is attested in Badtibira mythology.[7] It may therefore be assumed that the text was originally composed for use at the yearly rites of lamentation for Dumuzi in that city.

II. STORY

The beginning of the story as we have it is badly damaged. Since the remains of lines 1–6 parallel closely the text of the dirge in ll. 179–83, we may assume, however, that the composition began with a lament for Dumuzi.[8] When the text becomes better preserved (i. 28 ff.) the scene is—if our interpretation is correct—Bad-tibira. Inanna, whom we may imagine as recently married and still living in her parental home,[9] longs for her young husband, Dumuzi, whose duties keep him in the desert with the flocks. In her loneliness she yearns for him in tears, calls upon his name with many endearing epithets, and finally, it seems, goes before her mother, Ningal, asking to be sent on an errand to the fold. When the request is granted Inanna, with expert skill, sets about preparing for the journey.

At this point a new sizable lacuna interrupts the story. We would conclude from the events that follow that the missing passage told of a raid upon Dumuzi's fold by a certain Bilulu and her son Girgire, a raid in which Dumuzi met his death. When the text resumes a servant[10] is telling Inanna that he has found his master lying with head beaten in and has seen his sheep driven off through the desert, strangers walking beside them.

It is a noteworthy psychological point that Inanna's first reaction is one neither of personal loss and grief nor of revenge, but of love and pride in her slain husband, a desire to tell him of his value. And thus a paean is born, simple, full of tenderness, lauding the shepherd who steadfastly guarded his sheep:

You who lie at rest, shepherd who lie at rest, you stood guard
    over them!

Dumuzi, who lie at rest, you stood guard over them!
Ama-ushumgal-anna, who lie at rest, you stood guard over
  them!
Rising with the sun you stood guard over my sheep!
Lying down by night (only) you stood guard over my sheep!

Meanwhile in Edin-líl-lá, the house of Bilulu,[11] Girgire, as befits a good householder, is busy with practical tasks: he fills pens and folds with the cattle taken on his raids, he stores his grain. Those he has slain he lets lie scattered in the fields. A third member of the household, sìr-ru of Edin-líl-lá, sits before him keeping him company and conversing with him.

Very soon, however, Inanna's thoughts turn to revenge and her heart urges her to kill Bilulu that Dumuzi may rest more easy.[12] She takes the road to Edin-líl-lá, enters the alehouse where, it would seem, Bilulu and her people have gathered after the work with the harvest is ended, steps up on a bench and lays a terrible curse upon Bilulu:

> Begone!—I have killed you, verily so is it; and with you
>   I destroy (also) your name!

Bilulu is to become a water skin such as the traveler in the desert uses, and she and Girgire will be *genii* of the desert. 'sìr-ru of Edin-líl-lá, "no one's child and no one's friend," is to stand in the desert to keep count (?) of offerings of flour. Whenever water is libated and flour strewn from the water skin for "the lad wandering in the desert" (presumably the spirit of the slain Dumuzi) the *genii* of the desert must call out so that he may be present at his offering; thus will Bilulu serve to gladden his heart. Inanna's curse takes effect immediately and all becomes as she has said.

At this point the text is again broken by a lacuna. When it resumes at the beginning of col. iv the connection with what has gone before is unfortunately obscure: a bird, which is perhaps the partridge(?),[13] takes counsel with itself about Dumuzi and his mother, Duttur.[14] The remainder of the text deals with the setting up of a lament for Dumuzi by his sister Geshtin-anna and Inanna. That lament, built around the reiterated cry "the wail for you" and accompanied by praise of Inanna as the avenger of Dumuzi, is given twice, first as sung by Geshtin-anna and then as repeated by the narrator. On this note the text ends.

III. MYTHOLOGICAL INTERPRETATION

To understand a myth on its most basic level one must attempt to clarify as far as possible what the various figures with which it deals represent. In the present case this holds true especially of Dumuzi and of his adversaries Bilulu and Girgire. We may consider Dumuzi first.

Dumuzi represents, we would suggest, the life-giving powers in the milk. When the short milking season in the spring comes to an end, and with it the fresh milk, it means that Dumuzi has died. This death of the god was given form by the mythopoeic imagination in various ways. In the mythological tradition of Bad-tibira—and with distinctive variations also in that of Uruk—it is seen as caused by an attack upon his sheepfold, as a consequence of which he perishes.[15]

The identification of Dumuzi with the powers in milk here proposed[16] is based, of course, primarily on the form under which the god was characteristically envisaged, that of the shepherd, on the general emphasis laid on his role as provider of milk and milk products, on the fact that his "mother," i.e., his source of origin, was the ewe,[17] and on the direct testimony offered by his name dAma-ga,[18] which means "Mother Milk." The identification has, however, also the support of other evidence. In one of the myths about Dumuzi, which may be called "The myth of Dumuzi's dream,"[19] we are told how Dumuzi dreamt an ominous dream presaging his death, how he was later attacked by highwaymen, how he fled, and how he was finally overtaken in his sheepfold and died. The death of the god, both as it occurs in the dream and later on in reality, is stated by the myth in terms of the overturning of churn and drinking vessel: "When the fifth (highwayman) entered the fold and the pen the churn was lying (on its side), no milk flowed, the drinking vessel was lying (on its side), Dumuzi lived no more, the fold had been thrown to the winds."[20] The coincidence of Dumuzi with the milk could hardly find more pregnant expression. That same coincidence underlies a line in the section dealing with Dumuzi's flight. The god

there says that he "dances on the pure knees, the knees of Inanna." [21]
Since Dumuzi is pictured in the myth as a full-grown young man,
the statement at first seems more than puzzling. It becomes meaningful, however, in the light of Dumuzi's coincidence with the milk as a
reference to the primitive method of churning butter by jogging
a skin with milk on the knees, a method still practiced by bedouin
women. [22] Lastly we may mention that the name Dumuzi itself seems
to point to the milk and its life-giving powers, for it would appear to
mean "He who quickens the young ones." [23]

Turning from Dumuzi to his adversaries we are faced with the
difficulty that a deity Bilulu, envisaged as a wise old woman, does not
seem to occur elsewhere in Sumero-Akkadian mythology. This
difficulty is, however, more apparent than real, for it is well known
that the sex of Sumerian deities was not always rigidly fixed; the
same divine power might be envisaged at different times and places
under a male or under a female aspect. And as a male deity, as En-
bilulu, "Lord Bilulu," a Bilulu is abundantly attested. We know this
deity as a form of the weather-god Ishkur/Adad, as a form of Marduk
of Babylon, and, of course, as a separate god in his own right. [24]
The character of En-bilulu is clear from the quite precise analysis of
his nature given in *Enuma elish* in the section which deals with
Marduk's various names and forms. [25] The En-bilulu passage begins
with a—highly ungrammatical—translation of his name as "the
lord who makes plenteous" and goes on to describe him generally as
a god of pasture and drinking places, who opens the deep and distrib-
utes the waters. Then follows a closer analysis which distinguishes
three sides of his being: he is (1) ^{d}En-bilulu ^{d}E-pa$_5$-dun, the "opener
of dike and ditch," god of irrigation and ploughing, he is (2) ^{d}En-
bilulu ^{d}Gú-gal, the "supervisor of canals," [26] granter of large harvests,
prosperity, lambs, and grain; and finally he is (3) ^{d}En-bilulu ^{d}Hé-gál,
"abundance," god of the rains, who makes grass and plants plentiful.
From this it is not difficult to recognize the essence of his being: he is
god of the fructifying waters, whether they rise in the rivers and
canals to be led out over the fields or whether they fall from heaven as
rain, making grass and plants sprout in the desert. He is thus a god
almost exactly parallel in nature to Ninurta/Ningirsu, who likewise
is god both of the yearly floods and (especially clearly in his older form
Im-dugud, the thundercloud) [27] of rain and thunder.

Considering, then, in the light of this evidence, the Bilulu who occurs in Ist. 4486, we may look for indications of her nature first to the known form, the water skin, into which Inanna changed her. The connection with water is here clear. In terms of a natural phenomenon which a mythopoeic imagination might have connected with the water skin, one would venture the opinion that the dark, rounded, billowy skin, full of water, suggests rather plausibly the rain cloud, which could well be imagined as a huge water skin floating in the skies. The rain cloud, more specifically the thundercloud, may therefore have been Bilulu's original form from which she was changed by Inanna. Her connection with the winds—she lives in the "house of the winds"[28]—and the stress on the fact that she is "her own mistress" point in this direction, for the independence of the thunder cloud, which will frequently appear to move against the wind, seems to have been observed by the Sumerians and to have intrigued them.[29] That Bilulu should be the thundercloud and thus correspond to the aspect of En-bilulu which is connected with rain, and in which he is a form of Ishkur/Adad, god of rain and thunder, gains decisively in probability when we consider her together with her son Girgire. For Girgire (gir-gir-e[d]) means "the flash of lightning."[30] And the "mother" who gives birth to the flash of lightning is the thundercloud. With Girgire's character as the lightning agrees the statement about him that "his (victims) struck down with the mace he (left) scattered in the fields," for that is how the bodies of those struck by lightning are afterwards found. The emphasis on his husbandry, a point not directly demanded by the requirements of the story, is likewise understandable if he is the lightning. For the set pattern for Sumerian gods of thunder and lightning makes them at the same time gods of the yearly flood, of ploughing, and of agriculture generally. Ninurta/Ningirsu is the outstanding example.

It would have been gratifying if also the third member of Bilulu's household, sìr-ru Edin-líl-lá could have been identified. So far, however, even his name cannot be read with certainty. One might expect, because of the constant epithet "of Edin-líl-lá"[31] some connection with the wind, and possibly that the name designated him as some kind of domestic functionary.

With the suggested identifications of Dumuzi as the power in the milk and of Bilulu and Girgire as powers of the thunderstorm, the background of the myth begins to emerge in its main lines. In the Mesopotamian spring thundershowers and short but violent downpours clothe almost overnight the desert with grass and greenery; large pools of rainwater are to be found everywhere and remain in hollows and low-lying places for a considerable length of time. Then the black tents of the shepherds, who seek grazing for their flocks, begin to dot the desert; it is the lambing season and consequently the milking season. But the milking season is short, as it draws to a close thundershowers become infrequent and finally cease; the desert vegetation disappears, the water holes dry up, and the traveler in the desert must carry a water skin on his journey, for the drinking places are gone.

It is this sequence of events with its interplay of forces in nature that our myth unfolds in direct knowledge of what takes place. When the milking season ends and Dumuzi, the power in milk, is no more, his death can be laid to the thunderstorm, to Bilulu and Girgire. That they should figure as enemies and killers of Dumuzi is understandable enough, for as is well known milk tends to curdle and sour in a thunderstorm. On a different level the bitter and deep antagonism between shepherd and farmer, which is ever present in ancient cultures, would, of course, make the assumption of enmity between Dumuzi and the agricultural deities of rain and thunder both natural and readily acceptable.

Soon after Dumuzi's death the thunderstorms cease. They in their turn have been killed in revenge for Dumuzi. Through Inanna's curse the bounteous waters that poured from the thundercloud have become the trickle from the traveler's water skin. And in this new and lowly form Bilulu now pays homage to Dumuzi, whom she killed, whenever libations are poured to him by the traveler in the desert.

IV. POSSIBILITIES OF APPRECIATION

Attempts at mythological interpretation of a myth ought rightly to go hand in hand with an attempt to interpret it in human and psychological terms. However, in the present case that may perhaps be dispensed with since the simplicity of the feelings expressed—

longing, love, sorrow, and revenge—makes it easy for us to understand them directly even over the distance of four thousand years. In fact the human truth and appeal of the myth lies largely in that very simplicity.

The real difficulty in understanding myths, and, symptomatically, in appreciating them as works of literature, lies neither on the level of mythological interpretation nor on that of sympathetic psychological insight, but rather in our failing to fuse the two levels of reading. Our natural inclination is to puzzle out mythological connections, not to experience them directly as a form of truth; and we read about the powers the myth presents to us as if they were purely human, which they are not. In fact the more one reads myths the more one feels the sting in Rilke's reproach:[32]

> Ich will immer warnen und wehren: Bleibt fern.
> Die Dinge singen hör' ich so gern.
> Ihr rührt sie an: sie sind starr und stumm.
> Ihr bringt mir alle die Dinge um.

For our modern inability to understand myth is very largely our inability to "commune" with matter and the powers that inform it. Matter and its powers are no longer of us, can no longer touch our human selves in awe or pity, or even in a feeling of wonder. The best we can do with such knowledge as that Dumuzi is the life-giving power in milk is to push it aside as irrelevant information, disturbing to our enjoyment while we read the myth.

But such choosily anthropocentric reading must of necessity shatter any myth. And it would be ironic to call it understanding. Its insufficiency is demonstrated rather well in the myth with which we are here dealing. No reader, even he who can accept without serious loss of enjoyment that Bilulu is the thundercloud, can fail to be brought up sharply by the anticlimax of her becoming a water skin. Not only is that like suddenly feeling sand between one's teeth, but the myth lets us chew on it for a long time. For to the myth *that* is climax which to us is anticlimax and the myth emphasizes it as such.

There is, then, truly no other way toward understanding myths either as myths or as literature than the laborious one of trying to recapture the lost unity of the human soul with the universe as matter and phenomenon, that direct communication out of which Rilke speaks. For the myth lives and breathes—also as a work of art—in that unity. Its characters are true to the extent that they give pregnant expression to the nonhuman no less than the human "psyche," to the character and will in things, to their ways. In the world of the myth there is one common level of dignity and the powers in things are not stripped, by being of things, of claim on our emotional response. Rather, these powers in things and phenomena have their own dignity on a par with, often even higher than, that of man. It is only in the effort to recapture that world that one may in glimpses begin to see the shattered myth come together again and regain unity as a work of literature.[33] If one could wholly recreate within oneself a believable world in which the homely water skin saved thirsting men's life out of the bounty of its inherent nature, and where that water skin, itself in its innermost being divine, was doing penance to other divine powers that it had wronged, then one could perhaps recapture some of the old meaning of the episode of Inanna's curse. Perhaps it had in it feelings of sudden illumination, of pity, and of wonder, rather as if, on the human level, one should learn unexpectedly who the blind slave grinding away at the mill in Gaza once was.

The degree to which we in our world of today can recreate and recapture the conditions of the original intellectual and emotional response to Sumerian myths across the millennia that separate us from them must thus always be problematical. And our attempts at understanding will again and again subtly fail. If ever we should get to the point where we have elucidated every word and difficult construction, and ferreted out every intricate reference, we should still be faced with the greater difficulty of renouncing our own world and becoming momentarily to the old book of clay like Kierkegaard's reader:

> ...that sympathetic person who accepts the book and gives to it a good place, that sympathetic person who, by accepting it, does for it through himself and through his acceptance, what the treasury did for the widow's mites: hallows the gift, gives it significance, and transforms it into much.[34]

Transliteration[35]

[edin-na ᵈDumu-zi-mu i-lu za-ra i-lu za-ra]
  [i-lu] ⌜balag⌝(?) ⌜mu-un⌝-da-⌜di⌝-d[i][36]
[É-a-r]a-⌜li⌝ ⌜mu-un⌝-
⌜Bàd⌝-tibiraᵏⁱ ⌜mu⌝-un-
5 Du₆(!?)-šuba-a [m]u-un-
  ki(!?)-nam-siba-da ⌜mu-un-da⌝-⌜di⌝(!?)-⌜di⌝(!?)
  ki(!?)-nam-siba-da ⌜mu-un-da⌝-⌜di⌝(!?)-⌜di⌝(!?)
      amaš ᵈDumu-zi-da-ka . . . .][37]
siba lú [. . . . .]
[. . . . .]
10 [. . . . .] ᵈ⌜Dumu⌝(!?)-[zi]
[. . . . .] . . . [. . . . .]
[. . . . .]
[. . . . .]
[. . . . .]-⌜mu⌝(!?)-un
15 [. . . . .] . . .
[. . . . .] ⌜ka⌝-zal-m[u]
[. . . . .] ⌜gar⌝-ra
[. . . . .] . . . UG
[. . . . .] . . . KA(!?)
20 [. . . . .] . . . .[. . . .]
[. . . . .] . . .[. . . . .]
[. . . . .]
[. . . . .] . . . .[. . . . .] . . . .
[. . . . .] . . .
25 [.] . . . . .[. . .] . .-la mu-⌜da⌝(?) . . . . ⌜-ba⌝-e
      i-⌜si-iš⌝ [. . .] . . mu(?) . . . .
[. . .] . . . . .[. . . . .] . . . .[. . . . .]
[. . . . .] . . ka-zal-la-ke₄ . . . .[. . . . .]
[. . .] . . . . . ne . . . ⌜ad⌝-e-eš . . .-. . .-gi₄[38]
30 [ᵈDumu-z]i ka-kù igi sa₆-sa₆[39]
      i-si-iš-bi mu-un-kúš-ù[40]
[k]a-kù
[g]uruš(?) ⌜nitalam⌝ ⌜ù⌝(?)-m[u]-⌜un⌝ ⌜zú⌝(?)-lum
[. . . . . .] ⌜ᵈ⌝Dumu-zi-dè mu-un-kúš-ù[41]
35   [i-si-iš-bi] mu-un-kúš-ù
⌜kù⌝ ⌜ᵈ⌝⌜Inanna⌝-ke₄ . . . .[. . . . .]
⌜SANGA GAR⌝ nam-SAL-. . .-⌜ne⌝ . . . ⌜GAR⌝ ⌜nam⌝-[. . . . .]
in-nin lú-gar-ra[42] . . . . gar-[ra . . . .]
⌜ki⌝-sikil ᵈInanna lú-gar-ra

Translation[85]

In the desert, my Dumuzi, I sing with her the wail,
    the wail for you, the wail for you;
In the temple Arali I sing with her;
In Bad-tibira I sing with her;
5   In Dushuba I sing with her;
In the shepherding country I sing with her,
    in the sheepfold of Dumuzi....................

....

(Some twenty to twenty-one lines of the text are missing at
this point. From a few broken words that remain one would
conclude that they described—after the introductory motif
of lament had come to a close—the young Inanna longing
in her mother's house to be reunited with her husband,
Dumuzi, who is in the desert with the flocks. When the
text resumes she is in tears:)

    ....she broods on it:
30   "O Dumuzi of the fair(-spoken) mouth, of the ever kind eyes!"
    in tears she sobs forth,
"O you of the fair(-spoken) mouth, of the ever kind eyes!
Lad, husband, provider, (sweet as the) date,
    O Dumuzi!" she sobs forth,
35   in tears she sobs forth.
A a Holy Inanna ....
    b ....
    a The lady ....
    b The maiden Inanna ....

40 ⌜ama₅⌝(?)⁴³ ⌜ama⌝ u-gù-na-ka mu-un-DU-DU
   e(?) ⌜a⌝-ra-zu ⁴⁴ du₉-du₉ mu-un-na-su₈-ug
   a .[. . . . .]. ama-mu ⌜da⌝ . . . . -dib⁴⁵
             amaš-šè ga ⁴⁶-m[a]-e-⌜da⌝-du
   ama-mu Ga-ša(!?)-an-gal-e da-[. . . . . .]

45 aia-mu ma-ra-bu₇ ⁴⁷ du₉-na ga(?) ⁴⁸-da- . . .-dib
   ᵈSú.en ma-ra-bu₇ du₉-na ga ⁴⁸(?)-da(?)- . . .-dib
   dumu ama u-gù-ni kin-gi₄-a-ge₁₈ ⌜ama₅⌝(?)-ta im(?)-ma-ta-è(?)
   ama Ga-ša-an-gal-e kin-gi₄-a-ge₁₈
   nin-mu gal mu-un-zu gal in-ga-an-tù-mu

50 kù ᵈInanna-ke₄ gal mu-un-zu
   kaš u₄-dal u₄-sù(?)-du(?) dùr-ru-na-bi-a

col. ii   (gap of ca. 18 lines)

70 [. . . . .] . . . .[. . . . .]
   [. . . . .]⌜amaš⌝-⌜ta⌝(?)[. . . . .]
   [. . . . .] . . . .[. . . . .]
   si[g₄(?) É]-⌜d⌝Be-li-li-šè⁴⁹ . .[. . . . .]
   ki-bi-a siba sag-a ra[. . . .]
75 ⌜d⌝Dumu-zi sag-a ra
   ᵈAma-ušum.gal-an-na sag-a ra
   udu lugal-mà ᵈDumu-zi-[d]a-ke₄ edin-na[. . .] . .
   ᵈInanna lú siba nu-me-a
   udu lugal-mà zà-ba mu-un-gi₄-gi₄
80 ⌜nin⌝-e nitalam-ni-ir sìr mu-un-ši-íb-ù-tu
             ⌜sìr⌝ mu-un-ši-ib-dím-e
   [kù ᵈInan]na-ke₄ ᵈDumu-zi-ra
   [mu-l]u ná ⁵⁰ su₈-ba mu-lu ⌜ná⌝ en-nu-un-ba me-⌜gub⌝¹⁵¹

40 a In the chamber of her mother who bore her was pacing (to and
fro),

b While in prayer and supplication respectfully they stood in
attention on her.

B a "O my mother . . . .
to the fold with your permission I would go!

b "O my mother Ningal . . . . to the fold with
your permission I would go!"

45 a My father has shone forth for me, in lordly fashion . . . .

b Sin (the Moon) has shone forth for me, in lordly fashion. . . . "

a Like a child sent on an errand by its mother from. . . . she went out,

b Like one sent on an errand by Mother Ningal from the chamber
she went out.

[C(?)] a Full knowledgeable My-lady was, and also she was full apt,

50 b Full knowledgeable holy Inanna was, and also she was full apt:

a (Lager) beer laid up in remote days, in long (past) days
. . . .

> (At this point some eighteen lines are missing. It may be
> assumed that they told of Inanna's preparations for the
> journey to the fold and—with a temporary change of scene—
> of an attack on Dumuzi's fold by Bilulu and Girgire in which
> Dumuzi was killed. When the text resumes Inanna would
> seem to be nearing, or to have arrived at, the fold. A
> messenger, perhaps the partridge mentioned later in the
> composition, is bringing her the terrible news:)

70 . . . .
. . . .

A a " . . . .[I went(?)]

b To the brick-built house of Belili [I went(?)]

a There the shepherd, head beaten in,. . .[lay on the ground(?)]

75 b Dumuzi, head beaten in . . . .[lay on the ground (?)]

a Ama-ushumgal-anna, head beaten in,. . . . .[lay on the ground(?)]

b The sheep of my master, of Dumuzi, [I saw] in the desert,

a O Inanna, a man who was not the shepherd

b Was returning beside my master's sheep!"

80 B a (My) lady gave birth to a song to her young husband,
fashioned a song to him,

b Holy Inanna gave birth to a song to Dumuzi, fashioned a song to
him:

a "O you who lie at rest, shepherd who lie at rest, you stood guard
over them,

ᵈDumu-zi mu-lu ná en-

85 ᵈAma-ušum.gal-an-na mu-
ᵈUtu-da⁵² gub-ba si₈⁵³-mà en-
ge₆-da⁵² ná-ná si₈-mà en-nu-un-ba me-gub⁵⁴
u₄-bi-a um-ma⁵⁵ ᵈBi-lu-lu
bur-šu-ma nin ní-te-na-ka

90 dumu-ni Gír-gír-e lú dili-àm⁵⁶
ul₄-ul₄-e àm-túm⁵⁷ lú ì-zu-àm⁵³
gu₄ dab₅-ba-ni⁵⁹ tùr-amaš-e àm-si
gur₇-du₆-ra-ni gú àm-gur-gur⁶⁰
ul₄-ul₄-la rìg⁶¹-tag-ga-na ság mu-un-ne-du₁₁

95 dumu-ni⁶² ku-li-na sìʀ-ru Edin-líl-lá
igi-ni-šè ì-tuš inim mu-un-da-ab-bi
u₄-bi-a nin-e šà-ga-ni a-na àm-túm. .⁶³
kù ᵈInanna-ke₄ šà-ga-ni a-na àm-⌐túm⌐(!?)
ù-mu-un⁶⁴ ᵈBi-lu-lu ug₅-g[e-dè]

100   šà-ga-ni à[m-túm]
col. iii nitalam ki-ág-gá-ni ᵈDumu-zi ᵈAma-[ušum.]g[al]-an-na-ra]
ki-ná du₁₀-du₁₀-ge-dè⁶⁵ šà-ga(!?)-ni nam-[túm]⁶⁶
nin-mu ᵈBi-lu-lu Edin-líl-lá ba-an [. . .   ]
dumu-ni Gír-gír-e líl-lá-a-⌐bi⌐ bí-i[n(?)-. . .   ]

105 dumu-na ku-li-na sìʀ-ru ⌐Edin⌐-líl-⌐lá⌐[   ]
kù ᵈInanna-ke₄⁶⁷ éš(!?) -dam-ma⁶⁸ ba-ni-in-tu[   ]
ki(!?)-tuš-a ⌐ba⌐-e-gub nam mu-ni-ib-tar-re
gen-na ba-ug₅-ge-en na-nam-ma-àm
            mu-zu ga-ba-da-ku₆-lam-e

110 kuš a-edin-lá⁶⁹ a šeₓ níg-edin-na hé-me-en
dumu-ni Gír-gír-re ⌐e⌐-ne-bi-da
ᵈudug edin-na ᵈlamma edin-na hé-em-ma-da-me-eš-àm
dumu-na ku-li-na sìʀ-ru e[din]-líl-lá
edin-na ha-mu-ni-íb-du zì hu-mu-ni-íb-šID-e⁷⁰

115 guruš edin-⌐na⌐ du⁷¹ a ub-ta-an-bal-bal zì ub-ta-an-dub-dub
ᵈudug edin-na ᵈlamma edin-na
⌐. . šeₓ(?)⁷²-a⌐ hu-mu-ni-⌐ib-bi⌐ dub(?)⁷³-a hu-mu-ni-ib-bi
ki-⌐sa⌐-ha-⌐a⌐-na⁷³ [edin-n]a hu-mu-un-gál
um-ma ᵈBi-lu-lu ⌐šà⌐(?)-⌐ga⌐(?)-⌐ni⌐ hu-mu-húl-le

       b Dumuzi, who lie at rest, you stood guard over them,

85 c Ama-ushumgal-anna, who lie at rest, you stood guard over them,

       a Rising with the sun you stood guard over my sheep,

       b Lying down by night (only), you stood guard over my sheep!"

A a That day the son of the old woman Bilulu,

       b Matriarch and her own mistress,

90 a Girgire, the good householder,

       b He being fit to govern and a knowledgeable man,

       a Was filling pen and fold with his captured cattle,

       b And was stacking his stacks and piles (of grain).

       c His (victims) struck down with the mace he (left) scattered in the
          fields,

95 a sìr-ru of Edin-líl-lá, no(one's) child and no(one's) friend,

       b Sat before him, with him he held converse.

B a That day what was in (My-)lady's heart?

       b What was in holy Inanna's heart?

       a To kill the provider Bilulu,

100   (that) was in her heart!

       b To make good the resting place for her beloved young husband,
          for Dumuzi, for Ama-ushumgal-anna, (that) was in her heart!

       a To (?) Bilulu in Edin-líl-lá My-lady went(?)

       b Her son Girgire like the wind there did........

105 c sìr-ru of Edin-líl-la, no(one's) child and no(one's) friend, did.....

       a Holy Inanna entered the alehouse,

       b Stepped unto a seat, determined fate:

A a "Begone! I have killed you, so is it verily,

A a "Begone! I have killed you, so is it verily,

          and with you I destroy (also) your name:

110 b May you become the water skin for cold water that (men carry)
          in the desert!"

       a "(Yea: and) may her son Girgire and she

       b Become the utukku and the lamma (the *numina*) of the desert,

       a May sìr-ru of Edin-líl-lá, no(one's) child and no(one's) friend,

       b Stand in the desert and keep count of flour.

115 a When for the lad wandering in the desert water is libated and
          flour strewn from the (water skin)

       b Let the utukku of the desert and the lamma of the desert

       c Call out: 'A libation!', call out: 'A strewing!'

       a and (thereby) cause him to be present in the place from which he
          vanished, in the desert,

       b Let the old woman Bilulu gladden his heart!"

120 ì-bí-še ᵈUtu u₄-ne ⌜ur₅⌝ hé-en-na-n[am] [74]
    kuš a-⌜edin⌝-lá [a še_x níg-edin-na ì-me]
    ⌜dumu⌝-ni [Gír-g]ír-re ⌜e-ne-bi⌝-[da]
    [ᵈ]⌜udug⌝ edin-na ᵈlamma edin-na im(!?)-ma-an-da-an-me-
        eš-⌜àm⌝
    [dumu-n]a ku-li-na SÌR-ru Edin-líl-lá

125 [edin-n]a mu-ni-íb-DU zì(!?) mu-ni-ib-ŠID-e
    [guruš edin]-⌜na⌝ du a ub-ta-⌜an-bal-bal zì ub⌝-ta-
    ᵈudug edin-na [ᵈ]lamma edin-na   ]
    ⌜ .. še_x(?)-a⌝(?) mu-ni-ib-bi ⌜dub⌝[-a mu-ni-ib-bi   ]
    ki-⌜sa⌝-ha-a-na edin-na [mu-un-gál   ]

130 um-ma ᵈBi-lu-lu ⌜šà⌝-⌜ga⌝-[ni mu-húl-e   ]
    ᵈInanna-ke₄ ⌜guruš⌝(?) ki-e šu m[u-.....................]
    ᵈDumu-zi ⌜ki⌝(?)[-e šu mu-....................]
    šu-dù-a-[ni [75].................................]
    .....[...]
                    (gap of some eleven lines)

col. iv ..[...]-še ...   [...] mu-na-⌜ÍL⌝(?) [76]
    [.]..[...]...-ba-še buru₅-⌜habruda⌝mušen-e [77] nam ⌜ÍL⌝(?) [76]
    ki SIG₇-ALAM ᵈDumu-zi-da-⌜še⌝ buru₅-⌜habruda⌝mušen-e ......
    tumušen-ge₁₈ ab-làl-ba [78] ní-bi-a ad-e-eš ba-ni-íb-gi₄
150 buru₅-⌜habruda⌝mušen-e Á-BÙR-ba [78] ad-e-eš ba-ni-ib-gi₄
    lugal-mu ama-ni ᵈDur_x-t[ur]-ra-àm ì-húl-le [79]
    ᵈDumu-zi-dè ama-ni [79]
    in-nin-mu ù-tu-da Ku₆-aki
    ki-sikil amar-sig₇-ga men-bi
155 u₆-ti₄ níg-me-gar sag-gi₆-ga
    e-ne du₁₁-du₁₁ i-lu akkil ⌜du⌝₁₁(?)-du₁₁
    nam-šita_x du₁₁-du₁₁ lugal-la[............]
    ᵈGeštin-an-na-ke₄ ⌜nin⌝(?)[............]
    ⌜A⌝AN⌜SÙ⌝(?) KE₄(?)[..............]..
160 ki-sikil u₆-ti₄..[.................]...
    ᵈGeštin-an-na-ke₄...[......] mi-ni-......
    nu-gig-e šu[......-n]e-ne ⌜šu⌝-a mi-ni-⌜TUR⌝(?)

120 B a And immediately, on that day and (under that) sun, it truly
        became so.
      b She became the water skin for cold water that (men carry) in the
        desert,
      a And while her son Girgire and she
      b Became the utukku and the lamma of the desert
      a sìR-RU of Edin-líl-lá, no(one's) child and no(one's) friend,
125   b stood in the desert and kept count of flour.
      a When for the lad wandering in the desert water is libated and flour
        strewn from the (water skin)
      b The utukku of the desert and the lamma of the desert
      c Call out: 'A libation!', call out: 'A strewing!'
      a And (thereby) cause him to be present in the place from which he
        vanished, in the desert
130   b And the old woman Bilulu gladdens his heart.
[C(?)] a Inanna [put out her] hand to the lad on the ground,
       b [Put out her hand] to Dumuzi on the ground,
       a his (death-)bound hands..............................
         ....

         (Some eleven lines or more are missing here. They may have
         told how Inanna carried out her second purpose: to make
         good the resting place for Dumuzi. When the text resumes
         the partridge(?) is taking counsel with itself. Its role here and
         its words are not clear.)
         ....

       a To the......of its......the partridge(?) did...............
       b To the birthplace(?) of Dumuzi the partridge(?) did...........
       a Like a dove in its nest it took counsel with itself,
150   b the partridge(?) in its shelter took counsel:
       a "Only his mother Duttur can gladden my master
       b Only his mother Duttur can gladden Dumuzi!"
    B a My-lady, born in Kuar,
      b The maiden who is the crown of (all)......,
155   a The admiration and acclaim of the black-headed (people),
      b The (fore-)dancer who voices the wail and the cry,
      a Spokesman of prayer to the king,
      b Geshtin-anna, to (My-)lady did...................
      a ....
160...b The maiden the admiration..............
      a Geshtin-anna to Inanna did...........................
      b The sacred one, (Inanna)..................in (her) hand.....

......-ni [........]-ba(?) teš-bi ba-ra-gá-⌐gá⌐(?)

[...] ka ni ...[......] ba(?) an-ta(?)-gi$_4$-gi$_4$

165 [i-l]u za-ra i-lu za-ra [.......] ⌐ṭu⌐[80]-mu-ri-ib-⌐du⌐$_{11}$

[...] šeš-e mà i-lu za-ra

[......].........i-lu za-ra[81]
[..........].. i-lu za-ra[81]
[.........].. i-lu za-ra[81]
170 [......]... ..[..]... i-lu[81]
[ki nam]-siba-da ...[...]... ⌐ṭu⌐-mu-ri-i[b-...]
[in-ni]n mu-ut-na-ni ⌐ne⌐-⌐nam⌐ ⌐íb⌐-d⌐a-di⌐[82]
[kù Ga-š]a-an-an-na su$_8$-ba ^{d}[Dumu-zi ne]-⌐nam⌐ [i]b-
[ki-n]ú zé(!?)-zé-ba [in-nin]-⌐ra⌐(?)

175 [šu-ga]r-gi$_4$-a Ga-ša-an-an-na-ra(?)[83] š[u-a ba-n]a-an-si
[i-lu za]-ra i-lu za-ra i-lu ṭu-m[u-ri-i]b-du$_{11}$

[i]-lu za-ra i-lu za-ra
[ki]-⌐sìG⌐$_7$-⌐ALAM⌐ i-lu za-ra[84]
edin-na ^{d}Dumu-zi i-lu za-ra[84]

180 É-a-ra-li(!?)-a i-lu za-ra[84]
⌐Du$_6$⌐-⌐šuba⌐-⌐ra⌐ [i-lu] ⌐za⌐-ra[84]
⌐Bàd⌐-tibira⌐ki⌐-a i-[lu za-ra][84]
ki nam-siba-da i-lu za-ra ⌐i⌐(?)-lu ṭ[u-mu-ri-ib-du$_{11}$]
^{d}Dumu-zi ne-nam ⌐íb⌐(?)-da-di-e šu-[gar gi$_4$-a]

185 ^{d}Bi-lu-lu ug$_5$[-ge]
^{d}Inanna ⌐íb-da⌐-d[i]
ù-líl-lá ^{d}Inanna-kam

a ....together..........

a ....together..........

b ....was countering (in song:)

165 A a "I will sing with you (Inanna) the wail (for Dumuzi): 'The wail for you, the wail for you!'"

b In the temple(?) I will sing with you (Inanna): 'O (my)....brother! the wail for you!'

a In.....................I will sing: 'The wail for you!'

b In....................I will sing: 'The wail for you!'

a In....................I will sing: 'The wail for you!'

170 b In..............I will sing: 'The wail for you!'

c In the shepherding country I will sing with you (Inanna): 'The wail for you!'"

a How (truly) the lady proved the equal of her betrothed,

b How (truly) holy Inanna proved the equal of the shepherd Dumuzi,

a To make good his resting place, unto the lady—

175 b To avenge (him), unto Inanna was (granted and) given into her hand!

B a "I will sing with you (Geshtin-anna) the wail (for Dumuzi), 'The wail for you, the wail for you!'

b "I will sing with you (Geshtin-anna) 'The wail for you, the wail for you!'

a In the place of bringing forth(?) 'The wail for you'

b In the desert, 'O my Dumuzi the wail for you!'

180 a In the temple Arali 'The wail for you!'

b In Dushuba 'The wail for you'

a In Bad-tibira 'The wail for you!'

b In the shepherding country 'The wail for you!', the wail (for Dumuzi) I will sing with you (Geshtin-anna)!"

a How (truly) she proved the equal of Dumuzi, avenged (him);

185 b (By) killing Bilulu

c Inanna proved equal to him!

An ù-líl-lá (song) for Inanna

The Bride Sings

Going to the lad, my young husband
To my young husband, to whom I cling as the apple to the bough,
O lad, my young husband, whom I so love,
To whom I, Inanna, cleave as the date to the date leaf,
Whom I, the maiden Inanna, so love;
My young husband, to whom I cling as the grape to the stalk,
Ama-ushumgal-anna, whom I so love.

Part of a procession hymn used in connection with the ritual of the sacred marriage between Inanna and Ama-ushumgal-anna. Findspot unknown.

6. Toward the Image of Tammuz

I. UNITIES AND INDIVIDUAL CACHET

One of the goals we set for ourselves when we began these lectures*
was to find the way back to the specific religious experiences that
underlie the figure of Tammuz or Dumuzi, the "Quickener of the
Child," the divine power to new life, of the ancient Mesopotamians.

"We must try," we said, "to identify the concrete loci in the external world in which a feeling of being in the presence of divine power
of that particular kind, suggestive of that particular symbolization,
may naturally have arisen. For it is only there that we may hope to
find common ground in reality with the myth." And we continued:
"Once we have identified the loci in the external world in which the
particular experience that is symbolized and given form in the god
came to the ancients, we can try, out of our own human experience,
to recapture in sympathetic understanding such value and truth as
that symbolization may possess as an expression of the 'unchanging
human heart.'"

Analyzing thus the figure of Tammuz in terms of the places and
phenomena in which the power for new life that was the god was
encountered by the ancient Mesopotamians we were able to distinguish four different aspects: (1) a power in the sap that rises in
trees and plants, Damu; (2) a power in the date palm and its fruits,

* The above inquiry constituted the last in a series of lectures on the cult of Tammuz
given as the Haskell Lectures at Oberlin College. The original lecture form has been
retained, but some sections, especially in the latter part, have been rewritten for clarity
of statement. The quotations from the ancient sources are all directly from the original
Sumerian texts, published and unpublished. The texts date in general from around
2000 B.C. In many cases they are here translated for the first time. We hope on another
occasion to present them in detailed philological treatment.
NOTE: First published in *History of Religions* 1 (1961) 189–213.

Dumuzi Ama-ushumgal-anna; (3) a power in grain and beer, Dumuzi of the Grain; and (4) a power in milk, Dumuzi the Shepherd. From the relevant texts we traced in detail how each of these different aspects was symbolized, what particular myths were told, what specific forms the human response to each of them took. It remains for us in this last lecture to gather our various impressions into a single comprehensive picture of the god and to see how far it may be possible to understand the experience of him as ethical and religious experience. We shall consider first the general picture gained of the god in its underlying unities, and proceed from there to the varying emphases possible, the aspects of their individual cachet.

II. THE GOD: UNITIES

UNITIES OF THE LOCI

The approach to the god, if it hopes to be successful, must, as we have suggested, be made through the loci, the phenomena in the external world in which he was thought to be present: the sap in the trees, the date palm and its dates, the grain, and the milk.

All of these phenomena have one thing in common: they are foods or connect with foods. Under varying forms and in varying ways they reveal an indwelling same basic power to life: manifesting new life in nature, its fertility and abundance, they embody life, are means of preserving and sustaining it. The milk is a basis for the pastoral economy of Mesopotamia; the grain, both as bread and as beer, is a chief source of nourishment and cheer; the date was from time immemorial an indispensable part of the diet of the poor, that which beyond anything else kept them alive. Only Damu, the power in the sap of trees and plants, stands a little apart insofar as he is not the power in any specific, important food but rather a power for reviving vegetation generally, making it possible for food as such to be grown. He was—as we have seen—absorbed into the figure of Tammuz at a relatively late date.

INTRANSITIVENESS

If we seek to pass from contemplation of the phenomena in which the god is present—the various foods—to contemplation of the god himself, we become conscious first of a singular circumscribedness. The power that is the god is not only immanent in the phenomenon; it is curiously bound, curiously circumscribed by it.

It is not so much that Tammuz as the power in milk dies when the churn and cup run dry and they lie empty, or that Tammuz as the power in grain dies when the grain is crushed between the mill-stones, floats dead with the malt in the mash tun; that one expects. It is rather that the power Tammuz in its total expression, whether alive or dead, has a character that may be expressed as wholly "intransitive." It does not, either in action or as will and direction, ever transcend the phenomenon in which it dwells.

If we would try to describe any of the four aspects of Tammuz mentioned in terms of his activity we should soon find that he does not act on anything or anybody in any true sense of the word. What seems to be activity dissolves itself into the simple contrast of "being" and "not being," of living and dying. The yearly cycle of the power in the milk is a "being there" in the spring—in the cult rite of the sacred wedding this "being there" is even passively expressed as a reception, a being acquired of the god as husband—and a "not being there," a loss when the milking season is over; a flight, a death, an empty place where the god once was. And this "being" or "not being" of the god is closely bound up with, is altogether coincident with, that of the phenomenon in which he inheres. Very similarly, if we attempt to describe the god in terms of basic will and direction, we find that this will is so bound to, and limited by, the phenomenon that it can be said at best to be a will for the phenomenon to be, a power for willing it into existence.

To the ancient worshiper this circumscribed nature of the will and power that was Tammuz, its innocent self-centeredness, as it were, must have discouraged all attempts to seek help from it generally. In the personal crises of a man's life, in sickness and despair, he had to look to other gods. Nor were the great public crises, victory and defeat, conquest or the utter destruction of one's city and country, the concern and responsibility of Tammuz. Accordingly, the very few prayers to him that we possess are in fact only requests that he will more copiously express his own being. In a text from Nippur, to which we have referred, Inanna asks her young husband for a variety of kinds of milk, which he freely grants her. An inscription by

Hammurabi's contemporary, Rimsin, tells of the building of a temple for Tammuz in Ur and expresses the wish that "therefore may his master Tammuz rejoice in him and make oxen and sheep numerous in pen and fold." We can think of only one exception to the rule. An Assyrian incantation for ridding a man of the ghost of a member of his family has the ingenious idea to appeal to Tammuz to take the troublesome ghost along with him when he sets out on his journey to the nether world.

The circumscribed nature of the will and power in Tammuz, its self-contained character, is seen most clearly, perhaps, if we compare other Mesopotamian gods such as Enlil, god of the storm, Enki, god of the sweet waters, Ninurta, god of the thunder cloud. These gods similarly are powers in specific phenomena. But they transcend their phenomena, have interests, activities, concerns outside and beyond them. They are rulers of cities and countries, they lend help in war, or they destroy in anger their own cities. Man can turn to them for aid in sickness and in health; they make moral demands upon him and enforce them. Correspondingly their mythology is replete with will and action, with deeds done, things created and achieved. They could, were we to describe them in a metaphor similar to the one we used for Tammuz, only be termed "transitive active" powers.

The fact that the power in Tammuz in the various aspects of the god has this pronounced intransitive, self-contained character removes it curiously from the moral sphere. It is not to be feared, or lauded, or blamed, for what it does; it does nothing, it interferes not in human life. Nor may help and support be expected from it in any general sense; it is not a deity into whose hands man would lay his fortunes, his hopes, his fears. It has no responsibilities. It is a good power—yes, but not in the sense of morally good. It is good by what it is, because dates, milk, grain, and so on are good things.

This aspect of the power in Tammuz as being rather than doing, as having no responsibilities, innocently self-centered, yet pleasing and attractive, is very finely expressed in its symbolization as a young boy, a youth, a symbol shared by all the aspects of Tammuz. In the youth, attractive for what he is, not for anything he has done or may do, unformed by responsibilities, still part of nature, immediate as a young animal, the element of sheer being, of intransitiveness, in Tammuz finds its right human form.

BELOVEDNESS

But the characteristic intransitiveness in Tammuz, the fact that he is singularly limited to, and circumscribed by, the phenomena in which he is immanent, the fact that he does not interfere actively in human life and in social activity does not mean that he is without influence. As Aristotle's first cause, God, moves without being moved because he is the object of desire and thought, because he is loved, so Tammuz, intransitive and self-contained, in sheer "being" and "not being" exerts an influence as strong as any he could have exerted through action, because he is loved. It is this love for him that is the mainspring of his cult and perhaps of his divinity: man wants nothing from him except what the lover wants from the beloved, that he be, so that the heart, enticed and taken captive, may dote on him and worship. We may thus add to the symbolization of Tammuz as a young boy the essential qualification "beloved," which renders his significance. He is a beloved lad. And we may proceed to a consideration of this love for the god, its nature and its ground, insofar as it is possible for us to divine it from the phenomena in which the god inheres.

The love for Tammuz as it appears in the texts is both a fascination with the god and an attainment to trust and security in inward dependence on him as sheer being. It is, furthermore, a love capable of inspiring both service and sacrifice. It finds expression as the love of the wife for her husband, of the mother for her son, and of the sister for her brother. In the aspect of Tammuz as Ama-ushumgal-anna the first of these expressions dominates, in Dumuzi the Shepherd and in Dumuzi of the Grain all three are present, and in Damu only the last two, mother- and sister-love, are found. Essentially, however, we seem to be dealing with very much the same basic emotion, and it is not always—especially in the laments—that we can say of a statement that its emotional content definitely marks it as that of a wife, or a mother, or a sister. It is therefore often difficult to determine who is speaking in a lament when it is not definitely stated. We may recall the elegies in "The Most Bitter Cry" in which Dumuzi is lamented alternately as the husband and the son of Inanna, or the dialogue in the nether world between Damu and his sister in which her tenderness for him takes the form: "O my brother...who is your sister?—I am your sister. Who is your mother?—I am your mother."

GROUND OF ENTICEMENT

In discussing the elements in this emotion we may consider first that of enticement: the immediate and unreflected yielding in irresistible attraction, in which the heart, enticed and taken captive, makes no demands but wishes only to dote fondly on the beloved object.

As an example of this element of inner captivation, of desire only to dote on the beloved object, the lament in "The Most Bitter Cry" may serve. The feeling is, of course, emphasized by that of the loss of Tammuz and blends with pity for him:

> "Woe for her husband!   Woe for her son!
> Woe for her house!   Woe for her town!
> For her captive husband,   her captive son,
> For her dead husband,   her dead son,
> For her husband lost for Uruk in captivity,
> Lost for Uruk and Kullab in death;
> Who no more bathes himself in Eridu,
> Who no more rubs himself with soap in Enun,
> As whose (loving) mother no guardian deity serves;
> Who no more sweetens the work for the maidens of his
>   town,
> Who no more tussles with the lads of his town,
> Who wields his sword no more among the guardsmen of
>   his town,
> The peer, who is shown honor no more!"

What is here remembered, what is here longed for, is the undemanding pleasure in the sheer being of the beloved Dumuzi, the grace of his body and his movements, the youthful charm of his talk and his play.

Another example of this feeling of inner captivation is the mother's lament in "The Lad in the Desert," in which she recalls her thoughts as she was traveling to join Dumuzi, and in which every one of those thoughts is colored by the one pleasure of being with him and near him: the approach to his camp, the recognition of their own people, and finally the hearing of his voice:

> "Servants, bring my mother in, bring her in, my mother is
>   coming,
> Bring in my younger sister with her, she will weave
>   cloth, my mother is coming!"

There is here again no demand for Dumuzi to do anything—only for him to be. Yet, whereas the feeling in the first passage quoted was completely self-contained, there is in this second passage an added element of reciprocity, of being also loved by him, which comes out in the words the mother imagines Dumuzi will say as she fondly contemplates their impending meeting.

The element of reciprocity, of loving and hope or certainty of being loved, informs the epithets "fair-spoken" and "of the ever-kind eyes" which Inanna uses of Dumuzi in the Bilulu story. They express the approachability, the promise of tender reception, in the god, and they underlie the expression "sweet" used by Inanna in "my sweet husband, my sweet son" in "The Most Bitter Cry." Both the contemplative and more sensuous pleasure in the beauty of the god and the promise of tenderness and affection in the kindness of his voice go together in two lines of a hymn which praises Damu as he returns from the river:

> "His voice is full of deliciousness,
> His limbs are covered with deliciousness."

In these last examples, in the terms "sweet" and "kind"—perhaps more precisely "pleasing"—and especially in the term "deliciousness," we come, we believe, rather close to the ground of the love for Tammuz in the basic experience of the god as a power in the phenomenon of food. The experience of the delicious, the rapture of the sweet, appears superficially not unlike the experience of, and the rapture of, the more significant and profound fascination and captivation that is love.

Why this should be we are unable to say, and we must content ourselves with pointing to the universal use of metaphors from the realm of eating and tasting for love, ranging from sexual "appetite" and "hunger" to the lover's desire to "eat" his beloved, and to his use of terms like sweet, delicious, honey. Conversely there is the extraordinary linguistic fact that it is possible to love and adore ice cream—at least if the speaker is a young girl, in which case ice cream may even be divine.

It is, of course, not our intention to say through these random examples of idioms that the psychological structure of the experiences of tastiness, of love, and of adoration are actually alike; merely that the strength of a feeling of attraction in one of these areas may be suggested metaphorically by the use of words belonging properly to the others. But that is all we need to make it probable that the response to a religious experience, a felt confrontation with a numinous power to life in and behind food, should become colored by, and seek its expression—its metaphor, as it were—in the feeling of love; in its fascination and rapture, in its deliciousness and sweetness.

In the tastiness of food—the sweetness of the date, of the fresh milk, and of malt and beer—we would thus see the ground of the element of love as attraction and enticement in the response to Tammuz. It was that feature of the situation, the locus in which the god was thought to be experienced, which gave to the experience of him this characteristic form.

Ground of "Bliss"

But the element of fascination in which the heart is enticed and captivated is not the only element in the love for Tammuz. Especially in the aspect of Tammuz as Dumuzi Ama-ushumgal-anna, but also in Dumuzi the Shepherd, we find the further element of deep inner trust and dependency on the god, a feeling which is—or at least comes close to—that of salvation, of fulfillment and security. We have met this element in the attitude toward the god in our earlier discussion of the texts dealing with the sacred marriage. Perhaps its most profound statement, and the one most in consonance with its symbolic expression, the marriage rite, occurs in Inanna's words:

> "Let them join(?) his hand in my hand,
> Let them join(?) his heart to my heart,
> Sweet is it to sleep hand in hand with him,
> And equally good the loveliness of joining heart to heart."

We described the emotional experience here rendered as one of attainment to right true end, to full inner and outer security. We could—perhaps even more precisely—have quoted of Inanna and of the community at large, which she represents, Patmore's lines: "The whole of life is womanhood to thee / Momently wedded with enormous bliss." For "bliss" renders the central feeling as well as any one word can do.

The statement by Inanna which we quoted gives the feeling of bliss and security in its deepest reaches, in its full emotional amplitude. Closest to it in emphasis on the security of belonging are perhaps the lines in the procession hymn from Nippur in which Inanna says:

"Going to the lad, my young husband,
  To my young husband, to whom I cling like the apple to the bough,
  O lad, my young husband, whom I so love,
  To whom I, Inanna, cleave like the date to the palm leaf,
  Whom I, the maiden Inanna, so love,
  My young husband, to whom I cling like the grape to the stalk,
  Ama-ushumgal-anna, whom I so love."

In most of the other expressions of the feeling that we have it tends to shrink imperceptibly from bliss, full inner and outer security, toward the more narrow compass of material security. This narrower emphasis appears in Inanna's lament in "The Lad in the Desert":

"O my husband, provider of plentiful food, provider of
        plentiful drink,
  My husband who is bound like the river Tigris,
  Who is captive like the river Euphrates."

And it comes out in the texts dealing with Dumuzi's and Dumuzi Ama-ushumgal-anna's wooing, where the qualifications of the suitor as provider play such a prominent, even decisive, role. It is stressed by Inanna in "The New Linens":

"I want to! It is the man of my heart, the man of my
        heart, the man my heart did speak of:
  He who wields the hoe, heaps up piles of grain,
  Who brings the grain to the barn,
  The farmer of many, many grain piles,
  The shepherd of the storehouse full of wool!"

And it forms the accepted basis for the rejection of Dumuzi the Shepherd in "The Shepherd and the Farmer" and is therefore the explicit point at which Dumuzi defends himself: what he has to offer as provider is as plentiful and as good as anything with which his rival, the farmer, can tempt.

This shrinking of the feeling of security in love away from the full amplitude of the soul, however much it must appear to us as a withdrawal and impoverishment of the experience, cannot be considered a deflection; rather we must see it as a withdrawal in the direction of the center, of the origins of the feeling; for the meaning of the rite of the sacred marriage as a harvest rite is clear and therewith the center of the feeling of bliss is given as that of material security induced by the plentiful supply of food:

> "Ama-ushumgal-anna has reached out for food and drink,
> The palace is in festive mood, the king is joyous,
> To make the people spend the day amidst plenty
> Has Ama-ushumgal-anna come in joy,
> Long may he remain on the pure throne."

Thus we are led by following the element of security in the feeling of love for the god to another aspect of the situation, of the locus, in which he was thought to be encountered: the nourishing, the life-sustaining qualities in food. And here again this experience of the locus, of the phenomenon in which the god inheres, seems to have served to color and to shape the experience of the god, in this case as one of bliss.

III. THE GOD: CACHET

It seems possible to continue the analysis of the god in terms of formative influences from his loci in the external world a good deal further. For the variety of loci in which the power that is Tammuz was encountered may be assumed to have found its reflection in the variety of aspects of the god which we distinguished and to correspond to essential differences of emphasis in the experience of encounter with the divine. Such differences are in fact traceable and give the experiences their cachet.

Ama-ushumgal-anna: Security

We may begin by considering Ama-ushumgal-anna, the power in and behind the date palm. As we pointed out in previous lectures, an outstanding characteristic of his cult and mythology is its joyous and light character. The side in the cult which in the other aspects of Tammuz turns toward death and sorrow is here wholly absent. And the reason is not difficult to see. The phenomenon in which the god inheres, the date, does not take the worshiper through the experience of absence and separation. The date—eminently storable and enduring—is life to have and to hold, life for the present but no less for the future. It is therefore understandable that the cult of Ama-ushumgal-anna should be centered in the rite of the sacred marriage and that the emotional response of bliss, love in security, should be more pronounced and attain to further emotional depth in his cult than in that of any of the other Tammuz aspects.

While the feature of the provider forms an element in the love of the god in all of the aspects, it does not, and could not, in the other aspects attain to supremacy, could not reach inward and down to the roots of existence, could not attain to the significance of filling the whole of the soul and its aspirations as it does in the inner and outer security, the bliss, of the Ama-ushumgal-anna experience. It is only there one can use Patmore's words quoted above to describe the experience of the community.

Dumuzi the Shepherd: Brevity and Loss

In contrast to the enduring date the milk is an inconstant, a seasonal food; only in slight degree is it storable. Therefore the sweetness of the encounter with the power in the milk, Dumuzi the Shepherd, when all life's powers revive in the spring, is made more poignant and intense by the bitter knowledge that it is short. This gives to the Dumuzi cult its ambivalence, its counterpoint of joy and sorrow; not only wedding, but also—and shortly—death and grief.

In Dumuzi the element of enticement and captivation of the heart comes out most clearly. Our most pregnant examples of this element in the love for Tammuz came from the texts about the shepherd, and characteristically from the laments for him, where the vision of experienced joy was sharpened by the recent loss. And it is perhaps no accident that the feeling of bliss that we meet in the texts about Dumuzi the Shepherd, especially in the idyllic stories of his suit and marriage, goes no deeper than to the idyllic. It is not allowed to ripen into security and salvation, to touch the root of being, for there is not in it the assurance of constancy. Certainly determined and not accidental is the greater violence of the emotion which occasionally comes to the fore. In the Bilulu story the reaction to Dumuzi's death is one of protest, of demand for retribution, for revenge. In the "Lad in the Desert" the inner protest at the loss turns against the slain Dumuzi himself—

"Woe, the bowels of your mother, Woe, the heart of your mother,
    heart of her you have completely destroyed!
  O lad, your mother wanders (restless, seeking) after you, cannot
    for the thought of you lie down to sleep,
Ninsun wanders (restless, seeking) after you, cannot for (the thought
    of) you lie down to sleep"—

and in Inanna's Descent the resentment at the briefness of Dumuzi's stay with the living flares out in white anger. The briefness becomes inconstancy, love turns to hate, Inanna—and the community, for which she stands—kills Dumuzi in a fury of jealousy. The story of "The Guilty Servant Girl," if we are right in assigning it to this tradition, follows the jealousy and the revenge to its bitter aftermath: its failure to heal the soul and make up for the loss of Dumuzi and his love, for being rejected and left by him:

> What did she confess to her in tears and lamentations?
> The mistress's heart is fain to break with groans,
> The heart of Inanna,—What might it be?
> The mistress's heart is fain to break with groans,
> What might it be? What might it not be?
> About him who looked with favor upon her by day,
> About him who passed the night with her.

Naturally given with the experience of the milk, with the tragic briefness of the encounter with Dumuzi the Shepherd, are the figures of the mother and sister. In the bliss which was the experience of Ama-ushumgal-anna mother and sister had no place. For bliss is fulfillment, and it is the wife who finds the fulfillment of life in her husband's arms. The mother's love for her son, the sister's for her brother, though it may fill their life to the exclusion of everything else, can never fulfill it.

But in the loss, in the bereavement, the strength of their attachment and the depth and intensity of their grief may stand beside—nay, may in some respects transcend—that of the widow, especially of the young widow, because of the more varied and intricate ways they were bound to the dead in memories of life together.

In the Dumuzi texts, in the experience of loss, the figure of the mother embodies therefore perhaps the highest intensity of grief. The wife and the sister still have a life before them or, more rightly, have the vitality and resilience of youth even under the hardest blow. But the mother is old and she loses all she had left to live for. She is—as in "The Lad in the Desert"—"her you have completely destroyed." And there is in all the Tammuz literature no picture of more complete and utter grief than the one in the reed-flute lament of the mother who goes slowly and alone up to her son's body, shudders, looks at his face, and has only this to say: "You look different." In the vast emptiness and silence of total inner destruction there can be heard only and always the precise articulation of some irrelevant, trivial, loving observation:

"A reed pipe, (the instrument) of dirges!—My heart plays a
    reed pipe, (the instrument) of dirges, for him in the desert,
I, the mistress of Eanna, who lay waste the mountains,
(And) I, Ninsun, mother of the lord,
(And) I, Geshtinanna, daughter-in-law of Heaven,

My heart plays a reed pipe, (the instrument) of dirges, for
    him in the desert,
Plays where the lad dwelt,
Plays where Dumuzi dwelt,
In Arali, on the Shepherd's Hill;

"My heart plays a reed pipe, (the instrument) of dirges, for
    him in the desert,
Where the lad dwelt, he who is captive,
Where Dumuzi dwelt, he who is bound,

Where the ewe surrendered the lamb,
—My heart plays a reed pipe, (the instrument) of dirges, for
    him in the desert,
Where the goat surrendered the kid.

"Treacherous are you, numen of that place,
  Where, though he said to me: 'May my mother join me!'
  —My heart plays a reed pipe, (the instrument) of dirges,
    for him in the desert,
  He may not move toward me his prostrate hands,
  He may not move toward me his prostrate feet."
   She neared the desert, neared the desert,
   —The mother in the desert, O what loss she has suffered!—
   She reached the desert where the lad dwelt,
   Reached the desert where Dumuzi dwelt,
   —The mother in the desert, O what loss has she suffered!—
   She looks at her slain (young) bull,
   Looks at his face,
   —The mother in the desert, O what loss has she suffered!—
   How she shudders...

.   .   .   .

   —The mother in the desert, O what loss has she suffered!—
  "It is you!" she says to him,
  "You look different!" she says to him.
  O what loss has she suffered,
  In woe for the house, in grief for her chamber....

While the death of Dumuzi in the figure of the mother is end and total destruction, it is in the figure of the sister a cruel but not a crushing blow. Her youth and vitality make her react with hope against all hope, or with compassion and pity; feelings which, however deep they may go, leave the center of the soul still intact. Her youth and her compassion are manifest in a touching passage in a Badtibira lament in which she comes rushing in to her mother to offer her own jewels as a ransom to buy her brother free. In her lament in "The Lad in the Desert" her compassion and pity for Dumuzi grow out of the youthfulness which she and Dumuzi share. It is an understanding of aspirations and hopes cut short before they could be fulfilled, and it is a girl's understanding of a boy, fastening on fulfillment in marriage and children rather than on action and masculine achievement:

> "Before the young wife was yet in his arms,
> And my mother might raise a (grand-)child on (her) knees;
> When (his) father- and mother-in-law had (just) thought of him
> And he had acquired them as father- and mother-in-law,
> When he was accepted among fellows as a friend, when he
>   was merely a young soldier,
> (Then) did (the powers) pass sentence upon him,
> On the noble young lord,
> And his god let the sentence befall him!"

How essentially timeless in its mood is this lament we may perhaps illustrate by quoting a few lines of a modern lament by a young woman: Gene Derwood's "Elegy on Gordon Barber, Lamentably Drowned in His Eighteenth Year":

> "Then did you dream of mother or hopes hatched
>   When the cold cramp held you from nape to foot
>   And time dissolved, promise dissolved, in Death?
>   Did you cry 'cruel' to all the hands that stretched
>   Not near, but played afar, when you sank down
>   Your sponge of lungs hurt to the quick
>   Till you had left the quick to join the dead,
>   Whom, now, your mother mourns grief-sick
>   You were too young to drown.
>
> "Never will you take bride to happy bed,
>   Who lay awash in water, yet no laving
>   Needed, so pure so young for sudden leaving."

There is here the same tender compassion, the same sense of unfulfillment, the same partial identification, the girl understanding the urge to fulfillment in marriage more immediately and more primarily than fulfillment in action.

DUMUZI OF THE GRAIN: GUILT

When we pass from consideration of Dumuzi the Shepherd to Dumuzi of the grain and malt we pass to an emotionally ambivalent situation. For it is peculiar to the grain that its death and sufferings as it is cut and ground are undergone at the hands of the very same human community that laments it. In none of the other encounters with Tammuz does man meet him in guilt, but he does so very distinctly here.

The rite of the lament is a necessary and an only possible human countermeasure against the loss incurred by death. In the lament, through the intensification to the highest point of the emotional ties with the departed, his unity with the community is emotionally asserted in the face of the powers that separate, and the separation is overcome—insofar as possible—through the vividness of the recall and the nearness and presence of the departed in the spirit and the heart of the mourners. And at the same time this emphasizing of emotional ties is a pacification and an act of love toward the departed, which he appreciates, as is made clear directly in "Dumuzi's Dream" where he himself calls for a lament for himself, or indirectly in "Inanna's Descent" where Dumuzi's lack of visible signs of sorrow infuriates Inanna.

In the cult of Dumuzi of the Grain, where man himself has caused the god's death and suffering, such lament, such assertion of unity with the god, was obviously especially needed—and also especially full of hidden guilt. We believe one may trace to this particular feature in the encounter with Dumuzi of the Grain the rather extreme limits of pity to which these materials go. Man's guilt seems to come out in the covert form of the god's self-pity which is nowhere more pronounced than in Dumuzi's description of his body floating on the river, his plaintive cry that his body hurts, and his unabashed crying:

> "O my sister, who must also be a mother for me,
> O Ama-Usan, who must also be a mother for me,
> Tears like a child I weep,
> Sobs like a child I sob to you."

Similarly the community—in the persons of the mother and sister —goes to extremes in its desire for reunion with Dumuzi in a search for him that takes it into the realms of the dead to try to comfort him. In all of this there is perhaps a shade of the too much: too much grief, too much effort to make good what cannot be made good. One is tempted, though very possibly unjustly, to see here the unbalancing effect of the feeling of guilt.

Damu: Anxiety

In the cult of Damu the character of the experience of the god seems determined by the point in time of Damu's return, which falls at the end of the long and exhausting dry season. At this point in the year the community, tired and worn down, feels distinctly the shadow of death upon it and a deep inner anxiety whether that shadow will prevail. This anxiety and the release from it are felt behind the mythological framework of the Damu texts. The descent of Damu's sister to join him in the dry world below and her anxiety lest she be left there reflect the spiritual experience of exhaustion of the community and give it expression. They have thus a psychological justification different from the corresponding descent in the Dumuzi of the Grain texts. The somewhat spooky mood of Damu's return may likewise be due to the sense of the direct presence of death in the state of exhaustion as the dry season drags on. An explicit statement of the anxiety is given in the lament in the story of the cedar nurse in which it is feared that the flax plot may not produce flax, the furrow not grain, the river not its flood, and so forth. The same text also voices the relief in its triumphant hymn to Damu when he appears out of the river.

IV. VALUES

We have tried to understand the human response to the power for new life called Tammuz by tracing it to the loci in the external world, various major foods, in which the power was thought to be encountered. In so doing we saw how closely it was bound up with its loci, how circumscribed it was by the phenomena in which it inhered. We called that the intransitive character of the god. We saw further that, like Aristotle's first cause which moves without being moved because it is the object of love, Tammuz, in spite of his intransitiveness, was a force in human life through being loved. And we traced the character of that love, suggesting that it was conditioned in its form by the loci and situations, the foods, in which the god was encountered: that the sensation of deliciousness gave the experience of the divine in food its form of love as fascination and enticement of the heart, and that the nourishing qualities added the form of love as security and bliss. We looked further for the cachet of the various experiences and found the feeling of bliss dominant with Ama-ushumgal-anna of the storable dates; that of intensity and briefness, counterpointing of joy and sorrow, wedding and death, as characteristic of Dumuzi the Shepherd, power in the seasonal milk. A certain excess of emotion in the reponse to Dumuzi of the Grain we tentatively put down to the effect of covert feelings of guilt; characteristic feelings of anxiety and release in the reponse to Damu we saw as given with the psychological situation of tiredness and tension at the end of the dry season.

From this analysis in terms of loci—the god an intransitive power bound up with the phenomena, foods, in which he was thought to manifest himself, the reponse to him closely conditioned by the response to the phenomena in their deliciousness and nourishing qualities, but expanding variously the underlying cravings for food into feelings of desire and love for the power for and in the foods, love in security and in insecurity, in guilt, and in tension and relief— we may move to seek further precision of outline by asking about the limits set by the particular situational conditioning of numinous experience. What is its range of more general values, ethical and religious? Does the love for Tammuz in its human symbolization carry with it ethical and moral values? How fully does the particular numinous experience that takes form as Tammuz allow the numinous to come to awareness in all of its essential elements?

In trying to find answers to these questions we may begin by considering the rather special background and setting in society of the Tammuz cult.

"THERE SAT WOMEN"

The wording of Ezekiel's brief reference to the cult of Tammuz (Ezek. 8:14), "There sat women weeping for Tammuz," is very clearly not accidental. The cult was primarily, perhaps exclusively, a woman's cult. We can see this from the whole structure of its ritual and mythology. The great events celebrated are the great events in a woman's life: the wedding, which, as we have noted, must be seen through the eyes of the bride; and death, which is the death of husband, son, brother. And as the participation of the community of worshipers in the wedding was expressed through the figure of the bride, so it finds expression in the laments through the figures of the mother, the sister, and the widow. Male representatives such as a sorrowing father or brother are absent and find no place.

In our consideration of values we must thus be prepared to find them conditioned by the specific psychological horizon of the ancient Mesopotamian woman, a world apart, a world with its own characteristic perspective, not to be identified simply with the man's world we know about from other ancient sources.

Ethical Values

As one turns to the materials asking for ethical content it becomes readily clear that Tammuz is not prophet and not teacher, neither by word nor by example. The values embodied in the god are such as flow from his role as object of love, youth, and charm, and they blend with qualities of defenselessness and suffering, which invite feelings of pity and compassion allied to those of love. These are, it will be seen, values that are at best ethically neutral, and "ethically neutral" seems about as far as one can venture about the god as the texts depict him. Though Tammuz is a male god, proper manly virtues such as one finds exemplified and celebrated in, for instance, the early epical texts—courage, resourcefulness, steadfastness—are in him almost conspicuously lacking. When he is attacked, or merely fears that he may be attacked, he takes to his heels with no thought of offering resistance. There is, correspondingly, no hesistation about depicting him in the grip of abject terror as in "Inanna's Descent," where he turns green with fear. The response confidently expected is ready and loving pity only. On any and all occasions he will weep in complete and abandoned self-pity, turning freely for help and comfort to the women around him, his mother and sister. Even to male relations his approach is basically the same. His appeal to the sun-god Utu for help to escape his pursuers in "Dumuzi's Dream" is the appeal of an irresistible darling, a pet who must be saved because he is a pet:

> "I am he who brings wedding gifts to Uruk,
>> I kiss the pure lips,
>> Dance on the pure knees, the knees of Inanna."

In all relationships he seems instinctively to take it for granted that he be only and always receiving. When he embarks to return from the realm of the dead, for instance, he has no thought for his sister who had followed him there to give him of her love and comfort and is apparently ready to leave her to her fate. Only because the boatman listens to her anxious plea and speaks up for her is she taken along back to life.

Other similar examples of the absence of seemingly basic and obvious virtues in Tammuz could be cited, virtues so basic that their absence cannot be mere accident; there was clearly no felt need for them. Tammuz was not loved for responsibility and maturity, rather, if anything, for their absence.

From the god, who seems almost as ethically neutral as food itself, we may turn, then, to the figures around him—mother, sister, and bride—to see whether the ethical content lacking in the god is perhaps to be found in them, whether their love for him has qualities to make it relevant within the fundamental ethical contrast of selfish and unselfish, is the real love Solovyev speaks of when he says, "The meaning and worth of love as a feeling consists in this, that it effectively constrains us, in all our nature, to acknowledge for *another* the unconditioned central significance, of which in virtue of our egoism, we are conscious only in our own selves."

Reluctantly—as one contemplates once more these appealing figures and considers the specific expression which their emotions find—one concludes that such is not the nature of their love. Their love is innocently selfish, innocently possessive, the loving self asks little from the beloved beyond his mere presence—at most, in the bride, material security: "the man of my heart, the man my heart did speak of, he who wields the hoe, heaps up piles of grain," and it is deeply infatuated, measures the beloved against no general scale of values, not even, as we have just seen, the simple one of the ancient epic. But also the loving self gives little; it is not conscious of the beloved as a person in his own right, in the separateness of his individuality; it has no real concern for his needs as such, as his, only for the occasion they afford of being prime among them, of being necessary to him. Very subtly this can be felt even in the urge that drives mother and sister to seek the god and to be with him, if necessary, among the dead. As expressed the urge appears fundamentally as a need in them, a necessity for their own selves; it is on their own need they act rather than to alleviate needs in another, in the god. He, the beloved, exists for the loving self only in a single one of his aspects, as satisfaction of needs in that self for being with, caring for, and being necessary to; as object, not also as subject.

In none of the situations in the Tammuz cult, therefore, is the love for the god ever conscious of, or yielding to, interests or desires in the beloved that could contrast, or even conflict, with those of the lover, whether mother, sister, or bride. The god has no content of his own, empties to mere projection of emotional needs in those who love him, no more, no else.

And as the love for Tammuz thus subsumes him under its own needs and sees only what satisfies needs in the loving self, so will that love abruptly cease to be love the moment suspicion of more than the projected content, independent will, or interests in him arises, as in the anger with the god for having died and so withdrawn himself, or in the cruelty of the jealousy that erupts in Inanna in "Inanna's Descent."

In the love we meet in the Tammuz cult the self is thus all-pervasive. It is love as infatuation, blind to any ethical or moral imperfections in the beloved; it is innocently unreflected, possessive love, never tempered in consideration for other than the self; it is in fact all self since it is incapable of letting the beloved come to awareness as another individuality.

But without the consciousness of another individuality there can be no awareness of the contrast of selfish and unselfish, no ethical choice, no ethical content. The figures around Tammuz are as is he ethically neutral.

These consistent findings of ethical neutrality in all the major figures of the cult are arresting enough to call for explanation. Why should this be so? Almost certainly because of the character of the love for the god as we have just seen it, a love for which the beloved does not exist as another individuality but merely as satisfaction of needs.

That being so, the beloved, the god, must be viewed for what he is, a figment, nothing in his own right, a mere projection of desires; his shortcomings a simple reflection of needs in a loving self, needs for being with, for comforting, and for being necessary to.

That being so, the lover—mother, sister, or bride—achieves no real personal relationship. In her love, since there is only self, not self and another individuality, there can be no ethical awareness of selfishness and unselfishness, no adjustment, no coming to terms, only a straight, one-sided drive to possess—as in the drive to possess things, where there is likewise no other individuality.

In a drive to possess things, in the physiological craving for foods and their nourishing deliciousness, we tended to see in our analysis in terms of loci the origins of the feeling which, variously expanded, took form in the cult as desire and love for the power for and in foods, love for Tammuz. In this same original drive for things, foods, we may now see the constraining factor which held love for the god to its one-sided, possessive, ethically neutral character and prevented it from rising to higher forms. The original physiological need could without loss of essential identity be satisfactorily symbolized by one-sided, possessive need-love as in the cult the personified numinous power for and in food, the god, took the place of food itself. It could not without becoming entirely transformed have been symbolized by real love, determined in its essence by the recognition of another individuality as centrally significant.

Religious Values

From consideration of the ethical values of the cult of Tammuz we may turn to a consideration of its religious values and ask in what measure and with what limitations the response to Tammuz is aware of and expresses a numinous mysterium tremendum et fascinans.

For such consideration the image of the god, ethically so neutral, must, very differently seen, once again move into the center of the inquiry, for it is the cult's primary and basic symbolization of the numinous: Dumu-zi, the "Quickener of the Child (in the womb)," power to new life in all of nature, to yields and foods sustaining life; young and beloved, son, brother, and bridegroom, closely held and suddenly lost, mourned in death, transformed, object of love, of pity and of horror, calling, beckoning, from out of the grave.

As one goes over the imprint this image has left in the texts one cannot very well doubt that numinous character is present and real. One cannot avoid noting also, however, that of the three elements in the numinous that of fascinans appears to dominate the image so exclusively as to allow those of mysterium tremendum only limited expression if at all, and that the special reponse in the Tammuz cult to the element of fascinans is one of such close intimacy of feeling that any sense of distance or reverence is ipso facto precluded. There is adoring, but no clarity from the feeling itself that it is directed toward a divinity.

"Mysterium tremendum." Seeking the possible expression of a sense of mysterium tremendum in the god, we may consider first, perhaps, the texts concerned with the living god, the Quickener of the Child. Here faint overtones of awe and wonder at the miracle of conception are possibly present in such description of the ritual of the sacred marriage between god and goddess as: "That the life of all lands be received in charge...do they at year's end, the day of the rite, set up a bed for Mylady" and, describing the actual sexual congress in that rite and its magic effect throughout nature, "With the exalted rising of the king's loins rose at the same time the flax, rose at the same time the barley, did the desert fill as with delicious gardens." But if in these passages overtones of awe and wonder at the miracle of new life are really present and have not merely been read into the language used by us, they are likely to have been fleeting and not widely shared. A related text reasserts the general climate of easy intimacy and familiarity when it sees as the purpose of setting up the bed for the rite that the god "be fondled." And it is without question significant that the characteristic words for numinous awe, *ní* and *melam*, so common in other religious texts, are almost entirely lacking from the Tammuz materials.

Far more real and clear than in the living god is the element of mysterium tremendum in the image of the dead god where it is present in its crude form of horror at the wholly other of the ghost. The shudder is still to be felt when the dead Tammuz, speaking from the grave, warns his mother not to follow him:

"The looks of that food is bad, how could you eat that food?
The looks of that water is bad, how could you drink that water?
The food I have eaten since yesterday, my mother, you must not eat,
The water I myself have drunk, my mother must not drink!"

The food and water he is speaking of are the decaying food and water left with him in the grave as an offering when he was buried the day before. Horror clings to him even when he returns to the living; a cry warning people not to look is sounded from the boat that brings him up from the dead:

> "O (city of) Ur! At my loud cry
> Lock your house, lock your house, city lock your house!
> O temple of Ur! Lock your house, city lock your house!
> Your *entu*-priestess must not go out of (her house) the Giparu,
> City lock your house!"

It is to be noted, however, that the note of dread of the ghostly Tammuz exists, as it were, only for outside observers. The mother's and sister's love for him renders them immune to any dread of him, and dread must have been overcome in the human mourners through emotional identification with them.

The attitude of mother and sister as they search for the dead god is throughout one of pure maternal instinct, as if they were searching for a small child who had become lost. They have but one thought: he is not there. The sister calls that she has food and drink for him. When she at last joins him in the nether world she senses only that she is with him and can mother and take care of him:

> "Who is your sister?—I am your sister!
> Who is your mother?—I am your mother!
> The day that dawns for you will also dawn for me,
> The day you see, I shall also see."

Nothing else comes to awareness. Thus in this single, all-pervasive maternal instinct to find Tammuz, to be with him and mother him, is not only any sense of his otherness as ghost not permitted to register; every awareness of him as a power, a deity, has likewise vanished. In fact, the very nature of the love for him insists on his helplessness; he is the more loved for his helplessness and weakness. Thus in an almost complete reversal of the normal roles of god and worshiper it is the god who is powerless. He clings to mother and sister. When on their search they turn away at the gate of the nether world he weeps:

> "Now it is truly death—my mother has turned away,
> My mother has turned away, my sister has turned away,
> My mother has turned away—there she turned away, a stranger,
> My mother has turned away!"

And when the sister comes to him:

> "O my sister, who must also be a mother for me,
> O Ama-usan, who must also be a mother for me,
> Tears like a child I weep,
> Sobs like a child I sob to you!'

There is no power in him and for others no hope:

> "I am not one who can answer my mother who cries for
>   me in the desert,
> Who makes the cry for me echo in the desert,
> She will not be answered!
> I am not the grass—may not come up for her (again),
> I am not the waters—may not rise for her (again),
> I am not the grass, sprouting in the desert,
> I am not the new grass, coming up in the desert!"

The lack of all hope in the god, the denial of any possibility of revival, the finality of death, is striking—not least because we know that the god did eventually return from the dead—and it is emphasized by the general fact that there is in the texts no looking forward to, and no hope of, such a revival. It is as if the return of the god were not properly a sequel to what has gone before, not a continuation beginning a new phase, not a victory and reassertion of life, not new hope. It is rather as if we were experiencing within a time sense different from ours, cyclical rather than linear, and not a movement from one cycle to another but a staying forever in the same one. The return of the god seems no new beginning; it is more we who are back again to the old beginning, to live over the cycle of life which has only one beginning, birth, and one end, death, both equally final and equally absolute.

"*Fascinans.*" While there is thus in the emotional response to the numinous experience of Tammuz relatively little room for expression of the element of mysterium tremendum, the reponse shows intense awareness of the element of fascinans. In fact, the intensity and particular mode of response to the fascinans, the very closeness and intimacy of the emotion it engendered, would seem to make it a main inhibiting factor. It has no sense of distance and so does not readily allow feelings which depend on a sense of distance, feelings of mystery and awe, of reverence, to rise to awareness and unfold. We have seen how language about the rite of the sacred marriage in which overtones of awe and wonder are at least conceivable has to compete with other merely familiarly intimate, in which the rite is for the "fondling" of the god. It is clear too that the intense emotions of maternal love which dominate the search demand for their fulfillment utter helplessness and dependence in their object to a point where reverence and any sense of power and divinity in the god must necessarily vanish.

In part, this closeness and intimacy in the response traces, of course, to the general closeness and intimacy of emotional experience in the woman's world, the home, which is the inner horizon of the cult. In part, however, it seems more than that, primary, already given with the easy and inviting character of the situations and phenomena in which the god was encountered. Tammuz is a will and power to new life in all of nature, a will that takes outward form in the new milk, the fresh dates, the grain, and that, presenting itself under these eminently attractive forms, invites closeness, caring for: the milk will be milked, the dates gathered, the grain prepared and lovingly handled; the encounter is one without any reserve and withdrawal. Correspondingly, its symbolization, the images under which the god is envisaged, are intimate and close, invite caressing care: the power to a new life in its promise, Tammuz the bridegroom, tenderly loved by the bride; the power in its fulfillment, Tammuz the child, tenderly adored by mother and sister.

Looking beyond the general character of closeness in the response to the fascinans in Tammuz for a distinctive essence in the love for the god, common to it in all of its aspects, we may recall what we found in the discussion of the figures of mother, sister, and bride: an enticing of the heart in emotion taking color half unconsciously from the phenomena, the foods, in which the power that was the god inhered, as "sweetness" and as "bliss," as security from want. In the presence of the god this love came to rest in quiet rapture, adoring, doting, letting the sensuous images of the god fill the soul which could never have enough of their sweetness and deliciousness:

> "His voice is full of deliciousness,
> His limbs are covered with deliciousness."

One is, with reservations, reminded of Rimbaud's "J'attend Dieu avec gourmandise."

A close and intimate feeling, then, is the response to the fascinans in Tammuz when not thwarted: a quiet, doting, sensuously contemplative love. Is it more? We have also seen, in the discussion of ethical content, that this emotion is in its essence one-sided and possessive; a most significant thing about it is its altogether extraordinary potential of emotional intensity, depth, and power. If thwarted in its possessive drive it becomes a total craving in the soul. And in the cult cycle it is thus thwarted. Having gathered momentum slowly in the happy love which comes to expression in the rite of the wedding, the sacred marriage, it is abruptly and cruelly damned, raised to the point of the unbearable, in the stunned moment of the death of the god. Thus the lament releases it. As it pours forth in full flow in the lament, the intimate closeness of its every image—son, brother, bridegroom—draws directly on depths of real, actual, and immediate emotional experience in the worshipers, encompassing the totality of the emotional relationships in which they stand. Veiled and hidden feeling, longing and sorrows of earlier years, well up in old intensity, all blending with the love for the god, transferring to him, urging toward him to follow him, to die with him:

"It it is demanded, O lad, I will go with you the road of no
      return. . . ."
She goes, she goes, to the breast of the nether world.
The daylight fades away, the daylight fades away, to the
      deepest nether world.

If one tries to imagine the effect of these laments in their original setting in the cult, sung far from human habitations in a lonely desert where the green grass of spring is now sere and withered, as night falls, their unrestrained, rushing flow of powerful, intensely personal emotion led on and on without ending by shrill wailing flutes and the deep vibrant tones of the harp, it is difficult not to become aware of how directly they must have invited abandonment to transports of love, grief, and religious exaltation, how very much, in fact, the mourning for Tammuz must have had in common with modern rites of ecstatic wailing in the regions where it once flourished, those which are now celebrated for Ali and Hussein.

V. ENDS

The inquiry into values in the cult of Tammuz and the narrow compass within which these values were seen to lie help greatly to pinpoint the essential concerns and ends of the cult. We saw, in the analysis in terms of loci, that the god was a numinous power and will for new life to be, for yields sustaining life, dates, new milk, grain, and vegetation generally; and that he was desired, loved with a love which took color from the desire for the deliciousness and nourishing qualities of the foods in which he manifested himself. We saw further, in considering the ethical values in the cult, that this love remained a one-sided, possessive emotion, a need-love; and we saw, in considering the religious values in the cult, that awareness of the elements of the numinous was very largely centered on the element of fascinans to which the possessive love was directed and to which it responded with extraordinary intensity of feeling.

From all of this it appears clear that the cult of Tammuz had in essence only one central value, the god himself in all his irresistible fascination; only one end, possessing him, having him present.

To this end the ritual of the cult, the major cult dramas of wedding and lament, is means. In the cult drama of the wedding the king takes on (as we know from direct statements in the texts) the identity of the god, becomes Tammuz, and thereby magically achieves the coming into being of the god as a power in all of nature. As the god he celebrates his wedding with his divine bride who is embodied in a priestess and who represents the community taking formal possession of him. In the cult drama of the death of the god and lament for him, celebrated at the end of spring, the loss of the god, the waning of the power for new life in nature, is counteracted by mourning and lament. Through the free expression of love for the dead god the close emotional ties with him are strengthened; through the magic power to bring back the dead, which inheres in all expression of intense human grief and longing, the return of the god is assured. Deliberately and intentionally the ancient community in this rite does as does the lover in the ballad "The Unquiet Grave":

> "I'll do as much for my truelove
> As any young man may;

> I'll sit and mourn all at her grave
> For a twelvemonth and a day."

> The twelvemonth and a day being up
> The dead began to speak:
> "Oh who sits weeping on my grave
> And will not let me sleep?"

The mourners for Tammuz will not let him sleep, in fact they cannot, cannot become resigned to the loss of him; for their very existence depends on the god, on bringing him back. They could never, as can the lover in the ballad, make themselves content:

> "'Tis down in yonder garden green,
>   Love, where we used to walk,
>   The finest flower that e'er was seen
>   Is withered to a stalk.

> "The stalk is withered dry, my love,
>   So will our hearts decay;
>   So make yourself content my love,
>   Till God calls you away."

The cult of Tammuz is thus of a piece, simple and direct throughout. At its center lies numinous experience undergone in specific situations, in the renewal of life and the abundance of the Mesopotamian spring. The human response to such experience, taking form from the situation in which it was undergone, is one of irresistible attraction, of possessive love. In cult rites of sacred marriage and of death and lament this possessive love finds its expression and finds its magic means to achieving its ends: presence of the god, possession of him.

The Wild Bull,

Who Has Lain Down

The wild bull, who has lain down, lives no more, the wild bull who
    has lain down, lives no more,
Dumuzi, the wild bull, who has lain down, lives no more, the wild
    bull, who has lain down, lives no more.

O you wild bull, how fast you sleep!
    How fast sleep ewe and lamb!
O you wild bull, how fast you sleep!
    How fast sleep goat and kid!

I will ask the hills and the valleys,
I will ask the hills of the Bison:
"Where is the young man, my husband?"
    I will say,
"He whom I no longer give to drink"
    I will say,
"And my lovely maids"
    I will say,
"And my lovely young men?"

"The Bison has taken thy husband away up into the mountains!"
"The Bison has taken thy young man away, up into the mountains!"

"Bison of the mountains, with the mottled eyes!
  Bison of the mountains, with the crushing teeth!
  Bison!—He sleeps sweetly, he sleeps sweetly,
  He whom I no longer serve food sleeps sweetly,
  He whom I no longer give to drink sleeps sweetly,
  My lovely maids sleep sweetly,
  My lovely young men sleep sweetly!"

"My young man who perished from me (at the hands of) your men,
  My young Ababa who perished from me (at the hands of) your men,
  Will never more calm me (with) his loving glance
  Will never more unfasten his lovely bright clasp (at night)

On his couch you made the jackals lie down,
In my husband's fold you made the raven dwell,
His reed pipe—the wind plays it,
My husband's songs—the north wind sings them."

The herders in the desert, far from the protection of the towns, were ever in danger from raiding bandits descending upon them from the mountains in the east. In the stories about the herder-god Dumuzi, his death is often laid to such a raid on his fold. There is, however, also a deeper level of meaning: in the mountains was, according to Sumerian beliefs, the realm of the dead: the powers of death itself reach out for him. In the present poem these powers are symbolized by the Bison—bisons roamed the foothills bordering the Mesopotamian plain in prehistoric and early historic times—and his followers.

Although Dumuzi appears in this poem as a shepherd, he is called—as son of the cow-goddess, Ninsun—"the wild bull," and once, perhaps as a caritative, "Ababa." Inanna, searching for him in the desert, has found him dead, "asleep," his fold raided, the servants he had with him and his flocks killed. In her anguish she asks for him of the hills only to be told that the Bison has led him, that is, his shade, captive into the mountains, that is, into the realm of the dead. Where Dumuzi's camp had been now roam undisturbed and unafraid the wild animals of the desert. Findspot unknown.

7. Sumerian Mythology:
A Review Article[1]

The study of ancient Mesopotamian civilization may be said to have reached the threshold of a new epoch. For only now does the vast and profoundly important early Sumerian literature begin to be accessible in a real sense. It is not that the task of publishing the thousands of fragments of clay tablets upon which this literature was inscribed has only now begun. Rather the major part, and in many respects the heavier end, of that task was accomplished in long years of valiant work by many devoted scholars. If any single name should be mentioned, it would perhaps be that of Edward Chiera, whose contribution—judged on the double standard of quality and quantity combined—is outstanding.[2] Chiera also accomplished the first and most difficult part of the task of distinguishing the various compositions involved and of assigning the relevant fragments to them so that now, when the style and subject matter of the major literary compositions are known, the placing of new fragments—even small ones—has become incomparably easier.[3]

With all this work done, however, the compositions remained fragmentary. For most of them the statement was true—and for many of them it still holds—that "the story seemed to make no connected sense; and what could be made out, seemed to lack intelligent motivation" (Dr. Kramer, with reference to the myth of Inanna and Enki).[4] Hence many more of the fragments lying unpublished in the museums of Istanbul and Philadelphia had to be made available, for each such fragment now promised unusual

NOTE: First published in *JNES* 5 (1946) 128–152.

returns: a few lines, unimportant in themselves, might furnish the link between large but separately unintelligible sections of a story and thus for the first time make that story understandable. It is greatly to Dr. Kramer's credit that he clearly realized the import of this situation and that he energetically bent his efforts toward publishing and placing more texts. In Istanbul he collated earlier publications and copied 170 hitherto unpublished fragments;[5] some 675 further fragments in the University Museum in Philadelphia are being prepared for publication by him. When these texts have been made available, Dr. Kramer will have lastingly inscribed his name in the annals of Sumerology, and Sumerology itself can enter upon a new era—an era of interpreting and evaluating Sumerian literature.

Dr. Kramer plans to publish the results of his researches in a series of seven volumes, of which the book here reviewed represents the first. Volumes II–VI will be devoted primarily to source material; they will give the text of the Sumerian compositions in transliteration accompanied by translation and notes. Hitherto unpublished documents utilized to establish the text will be added in autograph copy. Each volume will deal with one literary genre: epics, myths, hymns, lamentations, and wisdom texts. A concluding volume will endeavor to sketch the religious and spiritual concepts of the Sumerians as revealed in the previously published materials.

This plan seems excellently conceived. One might—considering the difficulties still attending the translation of Sumerian—have preferred that translations and notes should be published separately from transliterations and copies, but the point is not very important. The main thing is that the texts now unpublished or scattered in fragments in a variety of publications will be brought together in orderly, practical, and convenient fashion so that they will be readily available for study.

The first volume of the series is intended as introductory. It is meant, the author states, to give "a detailed description of our sources together with a brief outline of the more significant mythological concepts of the Sumerians as evident from their epics and myths" (p. ix). After the first chapter, which traces the decipherment of cuneiform and the history of Sumerology (pp. 1–25), follows a discussion of "The Scope and Significance of Sumerian Mythology" (pp.

26–29). Then comes the actual substance of the book, which retells
the more important Sumerian myths under the headings "Myths of
Origins" (pp. 30–75), "Myths of Kur" (pp. 76–96), and "Miscellaneous Myths" (pp. 97–103). Interspersed among the stories are
sections endeavoring to reconstruct and interpret in more systematic
fashion the Sumerian cosmogonic concepts as a whole. The book is
profusely illustrated with exccllent photographs of ancient Mesopotamian seal impressions, tablets, and copies of tablets. The latter—
uniting in one place copies which Kramer had previously published
in various journals, and adding a few unpublished ones—constitute
a most welcome feature. Very useful also are the notes in which
Kramer lists the fragments utilized for reconstructing the text of each
myth treated. A number of misprints in figures and abbreviations
will, we understand, be corrected by the author elsewhere. The
completeness with which the material has been utilized and the various
fragments assigned to their proper places is admirable. We have noted
only one omission: the bilingual fragment *OECT*, VI, Pl. XVI,
K. 2168, contains on the obverse the beginning of the myth which
Dr. Kramer calls "The Creation of Man" and on the reverse a few
lines dealing with the creatures formed by Ninmah.

Although the introductory chapters of Dr. Kramer's book—
sketching the history of Sumerology in a somewhat personal perspective and outlining the older history of Mesopotamia strictly in
racial terms—contains much which would normally have invited
comment, all such points are necessarily overshadowed by the
immediate importance of the chief subject matter of the book. Has
the author been able—as he is himself firmly convinced that he has—to
"reconstruct and translate in a scientific and trustworthy manner
the extant Sumerian literary compositions" (p. xi)? This issue is
crucial and must take the central place in any review. We shall
therefore proceed directly to a discussion of the statement of Sumerian
mythological concepts given by Dr. Kramer, considering first the
translations upon which that statement is based, then both specific
and general questions of interpretation.

It is perhaps hardly necessary to mention that two different translators will occasionally arrive at somewhat different results; for all
translating involves a choice between possibilities and allows the
personal factor a certain amount of play. A reviewer thus has the

advantage of being able to state alternatives whenever they seem to him to merit attention.

I. TRANSLATIONS

In trying to form an opinion about translations such as those offered in Dr. Kramer's book, one will consider—but will not attach undue importance to—instances of mere inexactitude. Lack of precision is unfortunate but rarely really serious even if, as here, instances of it occur in disproportionate numbers. A few examples chosen at random will show what we have in mind:

Ab-sín is "furrow" (see Landsberger, *ana ittišu*, p. 158) and not "crops" (p. 54 and *passim*). When the god Enki had put the plow in order, he did not roar at the crops (p. 61) but "opened the mouth of the furrow," that is, "opened up a furrow" (on the use of the locative construction here, cf. Poebel, *AOF*, 9 [1933/34], 254–255).

The correct rendering of the city name mentioned on page 100 is Aktab, not Shittab (see Poebel, *JOAS*, 57 [1937], 359 ff.).

Bára, borrowed by Akkadian as *parakku*, means "throne dais" (see Schott, *ZA*,n.F., 6 [1931], 19 ff.; Landsberger, *ibid.*, 7 [1933], 292 ff.), not "shrine" (p. 59 *passim*).

Ge-gun₄-na is not "grove" (p. 60) but a special kind of dwelling, or room in a dwelling, serving approximately as audience hall and dining hall combined (for the former use see especially the Eshtar hymn, *RA*, 22 [1925], 170–171, rev. 5–8).

Ḫi-ʟɪ-gùr-ru, said of a young woman, is not "bountiful" (p. 54) but "(physically) attractive." The meanings of ḫi-ʟɪ shade off from that of "sex appeal" (cf. Thureau-Dangin in *RA*, 11 [1914], 153).

Kù-gál[6] is not "knower" (pp. 51 and 61) but "inspector of canals." It was borrowed by Akkadian as *gugallu* and meant originally "one who stocks (ponds and rivers) with fish," ku₆-gál. (Cf. Thureau-Dangin, *RA*, 33 [1936], 111, and Meissner, *MAOG*, 13, No. 2, pp. 8–9. Meissner's meaning 2 belongs closely with 3 and here may belong also *gugallu* as an epithet of Adad. See also Gudea, Cyl. B xiv.26.)

Má and má-gur₈, the terms by which Nanna's vessel is designated do not mean "gufa" (pp. 41 and 48) but "boat" and "barge." One cannot travel upstream in a gufa; Nanna travels from Ur to Nippur in the story dealt with on pages 47–49.

Maškim is not "ambusher" (p. 35) but—rather differently—the legally empowered agent of a court or of a high judicial or executive official (see, e.g., Landsberger, *ZA*,n.F., 4 [1929], 276). The best English rendering (suggested to me by Dr. A. Heidel) would appear to be "deputy."

The canal of primeval Nippur is said to have been "sparkling" (mul; the Akkadian translation has *muttanbiṭum*), not merely "pure" (p. 43), and Karusar was not "its quay where the boats stand" (p. 43) but "its quay where the boats moor" for ús means "to lie up against" and is—like its Akkadian counterpart *emēdu*—the usual term for "to moor." The Akkadian translation of the story renders the whole phrase as *maklûtum*, "harbor quay."

The author not infrequently omits—without informing the reader —lines or parts of lines in connected translation. Thus on page 51, after the sentence "Emesh bent the knees before Enten," the phrase "making supplication to him" has been omitted. On page 54, after the description of Ashnan, "Grain," as "a maid kindly and bountiful is she," the line "lifting (her) head in trusting fashion from her field" has been omitted. On page 68, after "Falsely has he uttered the name of his power, the name of the Abzu," the line "guilefully has he sent thee as messenger to me" is missing. On page 98, after "Ziusudra opened *a window* of the huge boat," a line voicing his thoughts in so doing: "I shall let the light of the hero Utu (i.e., of the sun) enter into the interior of the huge boat," has fallen out. On page 102, after the line "The farmer more than I, the farmer more than I, the farmer what has he more than I?" two further lines, virtually repeating the previous sentence, but mentioning the farmer Enkimdu by name and epithet, have been omitted. While nothing much is lost by the last-mentioned omission one rather regrets that Dr. Kramer begins translating the myth of Enki and Ninhursaga with its fifth and not with its first line (p. 55) since the omitted section is important for the setting of the story:

When you were dividing the virgin earth (with your fellow gods),
        you!
The land of Tilmun was a region pure,

When you were dividing the pure earth (with your fellow gods), you!
The land of Tilmun was a region pure.[7]

The reference is to the beginning of time when the world and its
various cities and city-states were apportioned among the appropriate
gods, and Enki and Ninhursaga received Tilmun as their share. The
two deities are here in the opening lines of the myth addressed directly
in the second person; then the storyteller lapses into ordinary
narrative style.[8]

Lack of precision in renderings and translations and unadvertised
omission of phrases or whole lines, such as have been exemplified
above, undoubtedly constitute blemishes but hardly more.

Often the translation chosen is critical to our understanding of a
story, and the alteration of a single word in the translation will bring
that part of the story into a more intelligible context. We shall consider here only three such cases.

1. Recounting the myth which he has renamed "The Fears and
Exploits of Ninurta," Dr. Kramer writes:

> Hearing of her son's great and heroic deeds, his mother, Ninmah—
> also known as Ninhursag and Nintu, and more originally perhaps as
> Ki, the mother earth—is taken with love for him; she becomes so restless
> that she is unable to sleep in her bedchamber [p. 81].

The Sumerian word arḫuš, which underlies Dr. Kramer's paraphrase "is taken with love for him," corresponds to Akkadian *rêmu*
(root *r-ḥ-m*), "pity," "compassion," but not to *râmu* (root *r-ʾ-m*),
"love," which is ki-ág(a) in Sumerian. That *rêmu* and *râmu*, treated
as one in Delitzsch's *Handwörterbuch*, are distinct in both form and
meaning was shown long since by Barth (*ZA* 22 [1909], 1–5).

The mother's pity and compassion for her son, who is far from
home, alone in a foreign country, cannot take on the overtones of a
love affair without serious detriment to our understanding of the
myth.

2. In the myth of Enlil and Ninlil, Enlil is outlawed by the assembly
of the gods in Nippur for having raped young Ninlil. Banished by
the gods of the world above, Enlil can turn only to the one other
great realm of the Mesopotamian universe, that of the nether world,
and so—headed for those dark regions—he leaves Nippur.[9] In
Dr. Kramer's rendering (pp. 43–47) all reference to the arrest of

Enlil and to the verdict banishing him has been omitted. Enlil's journey to the underworld, accordingly, appears devoid of motivation.

When Enlil leaves Nippur, Ninlil, who is pregnant with his child, decides to follow. On her way she comes first to the city gate; she tells the gatekeeper that she is his queen and that she carries his king Enlil's child under her heart. The gatekeeper, who is actually Enlil himself in disguise, answers her—according to Dr. Kramer's translation (p. 45)—as follows:

The "water" of my king, let it go toward heaven, let it go toward earth,
Let my "water," like the "water" of my king, go toward earth.

Thereupon Enlil, in his guise of gatekeeper, unites with Ninlil, engendering the deity Ninazu.[10]

It is not clear to us how Dr. Kramer arrived at the above translation and what meaning he would assign to such a speech in this context. To us it appears to obscure the story. In the Sumerian the lines in question read:

a lugal-mu an-šè ḫé-du a-mu ki-šè ḫé-du
a-mu a lugal-mu-ge$_{18}$ ki-šè ḫé-im-ma-du

Let my precious scion of the king go to heaven, let *my* scion go to the earth,
Let *my* scion in place of my precious scion of the king go to the earth.[11]

This gives very good sense. When Enlil was banished, Ninlil faced a deep inner conflict. She was his, the mother of his child; she could not do otherwise than follow him wherever he might go. But, in so doing, she would take with her to live forever in the gloom of the underworld her unborn child, Sîn. In this her royal child and its fate centers all she most dearly values, all she lives for. She must therefore necessarily fall an easy pray when the gatekeeper—playing on her deepest fears in professed anxiety for the future fate of Sîn—holds out to her the possibility of saving him for the world of light: she willingly unites with the gatekeeper to conceive another—not royal—child, who may take Sîn's place in the underworld.

All this is essential for understanding the tale and is necessarily lost if the passages here discussed are omitted or inexactly rendered. Lost, too, is the further point that in due time Enlil's word—as must a god's word—comes true: Sîn, the bright moon-god, belongs to the world above while Ninazu belongs to the world below. Lost, finally, are the possible overtones: the constant fight of light and darkness in the waxing and waning moon as parallel to the fight of light and darkness over him before he was yet born.

3. As a last example may serve Dr. Kramer's rendering of the beginning of the myth of the pickax (pp. 51-53). Dr. Kramer is not altogether satisfied with his version, fears that it may seem "sodden, stilted, and obscure" (p. 51), but defends it on the ground that "the background and situation which these words and phrases imply and assume, still elude us; and it is this background and situation, part and parcel of the Sumerian mythological and religious pattern and well known to the Sumerian poet and his 'reader,' which are so vital to a full understanding of the text" (p. 52). The translation reads:

The lord, that which is appropriate verily he caused to appear,
The lord whose decisions are unalterable,
Enlil, who brings up the seed of the land from the earth,
Took care to move away heaven from earth,
Took care to move away earth from heaven.
In order to make grow the creature which came forth,
In the "bond of heaven and earth" (Nippur) he stretched out the. . . .

He brought the pickax into existence, the "day" came forth,
He *introduced labor*, decreed the fate,
Upon the pickax and basket he directs the "power."
Enlil make his pickax exalted,
His pickax of gold, whose head is of lapis lazuli,
The pickax of his house, of. . . .silver and gold,
His pickax whose. . . .is of lapis lazuli,
Whose *tooth* is a one-horned ox ascending a large wall.

The lord called up the pickax, decrees its fate,
He set the *kindu*, the holy crown, upon his head,
The head of man he placed in the mold,
Before Enlil *he* (man?) *covers* his land,
Upon his black-headed people he looked steadfastly.
The Anunnaki who stood about him,
He placed *it* (the pickax?) as a gift in their hands,

They soothe Enlil with prayer,
They give the pickax to the black-headed people to hold.

Checking through this translation to see what causes the impression
of which Dr. Kramer speaks, one's attention is drawn to the last of
the three sections. Here, after the second line, Dr. Kramer has followed
a version which omits a line of the original. This omitted line and the
lines following it read in Sumerian:

> uzu-è ^{giš}al-a-[ni mi-n]i-in-dù
> sag nam-lú-ulú ù-šub-ba mi-ni-gál
> ^{d}En-líl-šè kalam-ma-ni ki mu-un-ši-in-dar⟨-re⟩
> sag-gi$_6$-ga-ni-šè igi-zi nam-mi-in-bar [12]

(And) drove his pickax into the uzu-è.
In the hole (which he thus made) was the vanguard of mankind,
(And) while (the people of) his land were breaking up through the
   ground (like plants) toward Enlil
He eyed his black-headed ones in steadfast fashion.

The uzu-è, literally the "flesh producer," into which Enlil drove his
newly fashioned pickax, is called Uzu-mú-a, the "(place where) flesh
sprouted forth," in one of the variants of our text, and as such we
know it well.[13] It is a frequently mentioned sacred spot in Nippur,
and our text shows with all desirable clarity the reason for its sacred
character: here in primeval times the earth produced mankind; for
the first men grew up from the earth like plants according to a
tradition vouched for also in the introductory lines of the myth of
Enki and E-engurra:

> a-ri-a nam-ba-tar-ra-ba
> mu ḫé-gál ana ù-tu-da
> ukù-e ú-šim-ge$_{18}$ ki in-dar-a-ba

When destinies had been determined for (all) engendered things,
When in the year (known as) "Abundance, born in heaven,...."
The people had broken through the ground like grass (lit.: plants
   and herbs).[14]

   The meaning of Enlil's action thus becomes clear: with his pickax
he breaks the hard top crust of the earth which has thus far prevented
the first men, developed below, from sprouting forth, just as such

a crust will often prevent germinating plants from breaking through. At Enlil's blow man becomes visible in the ù-šub, i.e., in the hole left by the clod which Enlil's blow has broken loose;[15] and, as man after man shoots forth from the earth, Enlil contemplates his new creatures with approval.

Once this passage has been clarified, the structure of the story as a whole begins to stand out. After Enlil had separated heaven and earth, he bound up the wound occasioned to earth when the "bond of heaven and earth" which had united her with heaven was severed:

> uzu-è sag mú-mú-dè
> dur-an-ki-ka búru nam-mi-in-lá

(And) bound up for her (i.e., for earth) the gash[16] in the "bond of
    heaven and earth"
So that the "flesh producer" might grow the vanguard (of mankind).

The place of this wound, and of the severed bond, was in Nippur, the sacred area Dur-an-ki, for Dur-an-ki means "the bond of heaven and earth." In Dur-an-ki was located Uzu-mú-a, which, after the wound had been closed, grew the first men.

We may thus offer the following translation which, though we consider the main lines certain, is still open to much improvement in detail:

The lord did verily[17] produce the normal order,
The lord whose decisions cannot be altered,
Enlil, did verily speed to remove heaven from earth
So that the seed (from which grew) the nation could sprout (up) from
    the field;

Did verily speed to bring the earth out from (under) heaven (as a)
    separate (entity)
(And) bound up for her (i.e., for earth) the gash in the "bond of
    heaven and earth"
So that the "flesh producer" could grow the vanguard (of mankind).

He caused the pickax to be, (when) daylight was shining forth,
He organized the tasks, the pickman's way of life,
(And) stretching out (his) arm straight toward the pickax and the
    basket

Enlil sang the praises of his pickax.
His pickax was of gold, its head(?) of lapis lazuli,
His (well) trussed[18] pickax was of gold and *mesu* silver,
His pickax was...........
Its point was valiant, a lone bastion projecting from a great wall.[19]
The lord ...ed the pickax, giving it its qualities
..............., the pure crown he placed upon (his) head
(And) drove his pickax into the "flesh producer."
In the hole (which he thus made) was the vanguard of mankind
(And) while (the people of) his land were breaking through the
    ground toward Enlil
He eyed his black-headed ones in steadfast fashion.
The Anunnaki (gods) stepped up to him,
Laid their hands upon their noses (in greeting),
Soothing Enlil's heart with prayers,
Black-headed (people) they were requesting(?) of him.

Having thus considered specimens of the translations offered in the book under review, we turn next to questions of interpretation, to deal first with certain specific interpretational concepts presented in it.

II. SPECIFIC INTERPRETATIONAL CONCEPTS

A. The Creation of the Universe

Dr. Kramer bases his statement of Sumerian cosmogonic concepts on a passage in the introduction to the tale of "Gilgamesh, Enkidu, and the Nether World," which he translates (p. 37):

> After heaven had been moved away from earth,
> After earth had been separated from heaven,
> After the name of man had been fixed;
>
> After An had carried off heaven,
> After Enlil had carried off earth,...

This translation is substantially correct, as is the subsequent interpretation:

> Heaven and earth, originally united, were separated and moved away from each other, and thereupon the creation of man was or-

dained. An, the heaven-god, then carried off heaven, while Enlil, the air-god, carried off earth [p. 38].

Having established these facts, Dr. Kramer proceeds to ask three major questions: (1) Were heaven and earth conceived as created, and if so, by whom? (2) What was the shape of heaven and earth as conceived by the Sumerians? (3) Who separated heaven from earth? We shall consider his answers one by one.

1. *Before heaven and earth.* Dr. Kramer finds the answer to his first question in the text *TRS* 10, an early version of the great catalogue of divine names known as An *Anum*, which lists the divine name ᵈAma-ù-tu-an-ki, "The mother who gave birth to heaven and earth," as an epithet of the goddess Nammu. He writes:

> In a tablet which gives a list of the Sumerian gods, the goddess Nammu, written with the ideogram for "sea," is described as "the mother, who gave birth to heaven and earth." Heaven and earth were therefore conceived by the Sumerians as the created products of the primeval sea [p. 39].

By giving this, and only this, answer to his first question, Dr. Kramer creates the impression that Sumerian cosmogonic concepts were all smoothly integrated—that the Sumerians had a single answer to questions concerning ultimate beginnings. Such, however, was not the case. The very same text from which Dr. Kramer derives his evidence on Nammu contains two other, different traditions concerning world origins, one of which—since it is placed at the very beginning of the text—may even be surmised to have been considered the most important of the three. These two traditions, the "Genealogy of Anu" and the "Genealogy of Enlil," are both well deserving of attention.

The "Genealogy of Anu" carries the parentage of heaven deified back through An-šár-gal, "The greater horizon"—apparently the horizon where the greater heaven and the greater earth were thought to meet—to a divine entity En-uru-ulla, "The lord of the primeval city." Since this deity is known from other sources to be located in the nether world, we may assume that "the primeval city" is the city of the dead, the "great dwelling." Death, it would appear, was and ruled before life and all that is came into being—that is, all life originated in (or emanated from) death, lifelessness. The other tradition, the one which in *TRS* 10 is placed at the beginning, but which in later versions of the list appears as the genealogy of Enlil, traces cosmic origins back through fifteen divine pairs. Among these are the powers manifest in earth viewed in their male and female aspects as ᵈEn-ki, "The earth lord," and ᵈNin-ki, "The earth lady," and the powers manifest in heaven represented by ᵈEn-an-na and ᵈNin-an-na, "The sky lord" and "The sky lady." At the beginning of the genealogy, before everything else, stands the active principle of the world itself, its modus operandi,[20] personified as ᵈEn-me-šár-ra, "Lord (en) modus operandi (me) of the universe (šarr-a(k))" and ᵈNin-me-šár-ra, "Lady modus operandi of the universe." And from them issued life: "Lord days of life" and "Lady days of life." These highly interesting speculations concerning world origins cannot well be ignored in a statement of Sumerian cosmogonic concepts.

Returning to Dr. Kramer's treatment of the speculations centering in the goddess Nammu, it must be pointed out that the sign with which her name is written does not—as Dr. Kramer avers—mean "sea." "Sea" is a-abba(k) in Sumerian; the sign with which Nammu's name is written denotes—if read engur—primarily the body of sweet water which the Mesopotamians believed lay below the earth, feeding rivers and wells but best observable in the watery deep of the marshes. Nammu is therefore the "watery deep" of the Mesopotamian marshes extending below the surface of the earth as the water-bearing strata. She is not the sea.[21]

The point just made is not unimportant, for it places the ideas with which we are here concerned in a particular group of Meso-potamian cosmogonic speculations. That group envisages the origin of the world along lines suggested by the manner of formation of alluvial Mesopotamia itself: through continual deposits of silt in the riverain marshes. Nammu, the deep which deposits the silt, is to this day "giving birth" to earth in Mesopotamia. By identifying Nammu with the sea, Dr. Kramer must necessarily lose sight of the basic meaning of the speculations of which he treats. Accordingly, later on (p. 75), he is at a loss to explain why the particular combination Nammu-Ninmah-Enki should be involved in the creation of man. The answer is not difficult. In the text to which Dr. Kramer has reference man was made—as one would make a clay figurine—from "the clay above the *apsû*." This clay typifies the silt which the watery deep of the marshes (Nammu) deposits on the shore (Ninmah), and correspondingly Ninmah (Kramer rightly identifies her with Ki, "The firm ground") is in the myth to "stand above" Nammu to receive the child—the silt—when Nammu gives birth to it. The deposited clay owes its plasticity, its ability to receive form, to its content of water. This explains the presence of Enki, who represents the sweet waters and who himself issued from Nammu. Just as the deep which deposits the clay, the firm ground which receives it, and the water which gives it plasticity are all involved in the making of a clay figurine, so were these forces involved in the making of man, a process which the myth sees as entirely analogous.

2. *The shape of heaven and earth.* The second of Dr. Kramer's three questions has reference to the shape of heaven and earth: "What was the shape of heaven and earth as conceived by the Sumerians?" He finds the answer in two lines from the myth of Lahar and Ashnan on which he comments as follows (p. 39):

> The myth "Cattle and Grain"...., which describes the birth in heaven of the spirits of cattle and grain, who were then sent down to earth to bring prosperity to mankind, begins with the following two lines:
>
>> After on the mountain of heaven and earth,
>> An had caused the Anunnaki (his followers) to be born,....
>
> It is not unreasonable to assume, therefore, that heaven and earth united were conceived as a mountain whose base was the bottom of the earth and whose peak was the top of the heaven.

What Dr. Kramer here proposes is a Sumerian *Weltberg*. His argument rests, as will be seen, on a tacit assumption that the genitive in the Sumerian phrase ḫur-sag an-ki-bi-da-ke$_4$, "on the mountain of heaven and earth," can represent, and can represent only, an appositive genitive with identifying force: "the mountain of (= which is) heaven and earth." Such an assumption, however, is not admissible a priori. In the first place, the proposition that Sumerian possessed the appositive genitive is open to the gravest doubts. Nobody has yet demonstrated—or, as far as we know, even suggested—that this was the case. Second, one would hesistate—even if it could be shown that Sumerian possessed such a genitive—to interpret the particular genitive in ḫur-sag an-ki-bi-da-ke$_4$ as other than a normal "possessive" genitive (range of meaning approximately: in the sphere of), for the "possessive" genitive fits the context perfectly. The Sumerian word ḫursag usually has reference to the range of mountains bordering the Mesopotamian plain on the east. As seen on the eastern horizon, its shining peaks towering from earth up into heaven, the ḫursag appears indeed to belong equally to both of these cosmic entities, and the epithet here applied to it, "of both heaven and earth," is therefore as forceful as it is apt.

The interpretation of the phrase here given was seen and clearly set forth already by Chiera in *SRT*, page 27, note 2. Chiera also noted (ibid., p. 29, n. 3) that the scene of events as indicated in the introductory lines of the myth (the ḫursag on the eastern horizon) is in full agreement with the later statement that Lahar and Ashnan came into being in Du$_6$-kù, "the holy mound," for Du$_6$-kù was located by the Sumerians in the mountains on the eastern horizon where the sun rises.[22] Indeed, it was probably the luxuriant vegetation, the wondrously fresh green pastures of the foothills, contrasting so markedly with the barren Mesopotamian plain, that led the Sumerians to seek the origin and home of Lahar, the power manifesting itself in the thriving flocks, in the faraway green hills.

We must thus conclude that there is in these lines no evidence for a Sumerian *Weltberg*.

3. *The separation of heaven and earth.* Dr. Kramer's answer to his third question is correct. It was Enlil who separated heaven and earth.

B. THE ORGANIZATION OF THE UNIVERSE

On pages 41–75 Dr. Kramer deals with the organization of the universe, dividing the subject into the organization of heaven and the organization of earth; the latter, which subsumes the creation of man, we shall treat separately.

The section on the organization of heaven occupies only one of the thirty-four pages and is based largely on scattered phrases culled from a variety of literary texts. Important relevant myths are the "Myth of the Elevation of Inanna" (*RA*, 11 [1914], 144–145; cf. also *RA*, 12 [1915], 74–75), especially lines 24 ff., and the "Eclipse Myth'

(*CT*, XVI, 19). Both of these sources are ignored as, indeed, are most of the very large and very important Sumerian mythological materials which happen to have come down to us in late copies only. The reasons for the omission of this material, seemingly deliberate, are not clearly stated anywhere in the book.

Since we are discussing the organization of heaven, we would call attention to a passage on page 74:

> *Enlil*, the air-god, now found himself living in utter darkness, with the sky, which may have been conceived by the Sumerians as made of pitch-dark lapiz lazuli, forming the ceiling and walls of his house, and the surface of the earth, its floor. He therefore begot the moon-god *Nanna* to brighten the darkness of his house.

For the sake of clarity it should be said that this passage is not, to our knowledge, a paraphrase of any extant Sumerian myth. The conception of the universe as a dark house, and of the moon-god as a lamp begot to light it, is rather the author's own vivid synthesis, a suggestion as to what the Sumerians *may* have thought.

The organization of the earth Dr. Kramer presents by retelling nine different Sumerian myths. Some of these, such as "Enlil and Ninlil" and "Enki and Ninhursaga," are concerned primarily with origins (the former also with status: chthonic or celestial), while others, such as "The Myth of the Pickax," "Lahar and Ashnan," and "Emesh and Enten," deal with both origin and relative value. Only "Enki and Shumer" and in a sense "Inanna and Enki" deal primarily with organization—the latter in so far as it seeks to explain the scope of Inanna's powers. The myth of "Enki and Eridu," giving the building history of Enki's temple, stands somewhat apart. So, too, does "The Journey of Nanna," which seems concerned primarily with the prosperity of Ur.

We have commented on sections of two of these myths above ("Enlil and Ninlil" and "The Myth of the Pickax") and—since considerations of space prohibit detailed discussion—here add only a few remarks on the others.

The statement on page 53 ("Lahar and Ashnan"), "But the Anunnaki were unable to make effective use of the products of these deities; it was to remedy this situation that man was created," seems to rest on the lines translated: "The Anunnaki of the Dulkug eat, but remain unsated; in their pure sheepfolds milk,..., and good things, the Anunnaki of the Dulkug drink, but remain unsated" (p. 73). These lines, however, merely express the fact that the Anunnaki so liked the good products of Ashnan and Lahar (primarily bread and milk) that they never tired of eating and drinking them. This is the sense in which negated forms of *šebû*—to which si corresponds in the meaning "to satiate"—are used elsewhere in Mesopotamian literature (see, e.g., Delitzsch, *HW*, pp. 636–37). We should accordingly translate "insatiably" and not "but remained unsated." The meaning of the third section of the passage of Lahar and Ashnan translated on pages 72–73 and—much more serious—the greater part of the myth of Enki and Ninhursaga are fatally obscured through the erroneous interpretation of Uttu as "goddess of plants" instead of as goddess of "weaving" and/or "washing" clothes. The latter interpretation— and the only one which fits the myths—has been conclusively established by Scheil (see, e.g., Langdon, *Le Poème sumérien...*, pp. 152 ff., where the relevant syllabary passages are quoted). In the myth of Enki and Shumer the latter (as the principality centering around Nippur) stands on a line with the principality of Ur (not in the relation of country and capital) and with that of Meluhha. The blessing on Shumer, mentioning its "matrix" which gives birth to kings and *enu*'s, has been largely misunderstood in the translation on page 59.[23]

C. THE CREATION OF MAN

The tradition according to which man sprouted, as though he were a plant, from the soil of Uzumua has been discussed above.[24] The tradition which Dr. Kramer treats (pp. 68–72) assumes that man was formed from clay much as a figurine is made. Unfortunately, the section dealing with the actual birth of "the clay above the *apsû*" and the fashioning of man from it is lost in a lacuna of the text. The following sections deal not with man as such but rather with certain freak types of human existence (e.g., the eunuch, the barren woman) and unfortunate general forms of human life such as that of the old man suffering under the debilities of extreme age (typified in Enki's creature U_4-mu-ul, "My day is ancient"). The origin of these forms of human existence is traced to a mischievous contest between Enki and Ninmah when these gods were in their cups. One was to make freaks, the other was to cope with the freak, find a way to integrate it with the world order, a way in which it might gain a living. The meaning of this part of the myth seems to have escaped Dr. Kramer.

D. MYTHS OF KUR

A special section of Dr. Kramer's book, pages 76–96, is devoted to myths about a monster called Kur. He writes:

> *Kur* thus cosmically conceived is the empty space between the earth's crust and the primeval sea. Moreover, it is not improbable that the monstrous creature that lived at the bottom of the "great below" immediately over the primeval waters is also called Kur; if so, this monster Kur would correspond to a certain extent to the Babylonian Tiamat. In three of our "Myths of Kur," it is one or the other of these cosmic aspects of the world *kur* which is involved [p. 76].

Since the monster Kur is a new concept in Sumerian mythology— except for occasional references to it in earlier writings of Dr. Kramer —it will be worthwhile to consider briefly the material adduced for it.

1. *First myth of Kur.* The first "myth" quoted under the heading "The Destruction of Kur: The Slaying of the Dragon" (p. 76) appears—we can think of no other way of describing it—to have been derived by means of a series of conjectures from a misunderstood passage in the introduction to the tale of "Gilgamesh, Enkidu, and the Nether World." We may illustrate by quoting Dr. Kramer's own outline of the story, printing in italics the words which connect one such conjecture with the next:

> After heaven and earth had been separated, An, the heaven-god, carried off the heaven, while Enlil, the air-god, carried off the earth. It was then that the foul deed was committed. The goddess Ereshkigal was carried off violently into the nether world, *perhaps* by Kur itself. Thereupon Enki, the water-god, whose Sumerian origin is uncertain, but who toward the end of the third millennium B.C. gradually became one of the most important deities of the Sumerian pantheon, set out in a boat, *in all probability* to attack Kur and avenge the abduction of the goddess Ereshkigal. Kur fought back savagely with all kinds of stones, large and small. Moreover it attacked Enki's boat, front and rear, with the primeval waters which it *no doubt* controlled. Here our brief prologue passage ends, since the author of "Gilgamesh, Enkidu,

and the Nether World" is not interested in the dragon story primarily but is anxious to proceed with the Gilgamesh tale. And so we are left in the dark as to the outcome of the battle. *There is little doubt,* however, that Enki was victorious. Indeed it is *not at all unlikely* that the myth was evolved in large part for the purpose of explaining why, in historical times, Enki, like the Greek Poseidon, was conceived as a sea-god; why he is described as "lord of the abyss"; and why his temple in Eridu was designated as the "sea-house" [p. 79].

Since the whole story is built around the assumption that Ereshkigal in the beginning of time was abducted violently to the nether world, we may begin our comments with the three lines on which that assumption rests. They read:

> u_4 An-né an ba-an-túm-a-ba
> ^{d}En-líl-le ki ba-an-túm-a-ba
> ^{d}Ereš-ki-gal-la-ra (var. om. -ra) kur-ra sag-rig$_5$-ga-šè
>   im-ma-ab-rig$_5$-ga-a-ba

These lines are translated by Dr. Kramer on page 37 as follows:

> After An had carried off heaven,
> After Enlil had carried off earth,
> After Ereshkigal had been carried off into Kur as its prize.

In his comments on the text on page 38 he explains that "the goddess Ereshkigal, the counterpart of the Greek Persephone, whom we know as queen of the nether world, but who originally was probably a sky-goddess, was carried off into the nether world, perhaps by Kur." Actually, however, the verb phrase sag-rig$_5$-ga-šè....rig$_5$ does not mean, as Dr. Kramer translates it, "to carry off as a prize," but literally "to present as a presented present." It is a somewhat over-loaded variant of the phrase sag-šè....rig$_5$, "to present as a present," used typically of (1) votive offerings (including persons: votaries) presented to a deity and (2) the dowry given to a woman at her marriage. Ereshkigal, whom Dr. Kramer assumes to be the subject of the passive form of the verb, is actually the dative object, as shown by the dative suffix -ra which follows her name in the text given on Plate VIII. We must accordingly translate quite differently:

After An had carried off heaven,
After Enlil had carried off the earth,

(And) after it (the earth) had been presented as dowry to Ereshkigal
   in the nether world (var.: to Ereshkigal and the nether world).

For the concept that the earth (ki) belongs to Ereshkigal we might
perhaps be justified in quoting her Akkadian epithet *šarrat erṣetim*,
"Queen of the earth." It seems quite likely that "the earth" (ki)
should have been considered somehow to be associated with or to
have belonged originally to the "great(er) earth" (ki-gal), Dr.
Kramer's "great below," of which Ereshkigal's name (ereš-ki-gal-la)
indicates her to be ruler.

There is thus in the lines quoted no support whatever for the
assumption that a "foul deed" (p. 79), an abduction of Ereshkigal,
was ever committed. Nor is there any evidence for the related suggestion that Ereshkigal "originally was probably a sky-goddess"
(p. 38). Nor can Enki's boat ride, referred to in the following lines,
now be plausibly explained as an expedition undertaken to avenge
that abduction. For the time being we must content ourselves with
the fact that we do not yet know the myth to which it has reference.[25]
In passing, it may be noted that Enki's name is perfectly good Sumerian and means "The lord of the earth" (more originally, perhaps,
"Lord Earth"). It happens to be one of the first Sumerian divine
names attested, occurring already on tablets from Jemdet Nasr.[26] The
name also appears, immediately following that of Enlil, at the head of
our oldest Sumerian lists of gods, those from Fara.[27] The suggestion
that Enki's "Sumerian origin is uncertain" seems therefore particularly unfortunate. So also is the characterization of Enki as a sea-god
and the comparison with the utterly different Greek Poseidon. Enki
was primarily god of the sweet waters, of wells and canals, and of the
apsû. His connections with the salt water, the sea (a-abba (k)), are at
best peripheral, the sea playing a very small role in the life of the
Sumerians, a very large one in that of the Greeks.[28]

   2. *Second myth of Kur.* The second myth quoted under the heading
"The Destruction of Kur: The Slaying of the Dragon" is the well-
known lugal-e u₄ me-lám-bi nir-gál. Dr. Kramer retells the first
part of this myth—the only part here relevant—as follows:

   After a hymnal introduction the story begins with an address to
   Ninurta by Sharur, his personified weapon. For some reason not stated
   in the text as yet available, Sharur has set its mind against Kur. In

its speech, therefore, which is full of phrases extolling the heroic qualities and deeds of Ninurta, it urges Ninurta to attack and destroy Kur. Ninurta sets out to do as bidden. At first, however, he seems to have met more than his match and he "flees like a bird." Once again, however, Sharur addresses him with reassuring and encouraging words. Ninurta now attacks Kur fiercely with all the weapons at his command, and Kur is completely destroyed [p. 80].

This interpretation differs most strikingly from those given by earlier scholars who have worked on the myth in that it treats the word kur, "the mountains," "the enemy land," as if it were a proper name, the name of Ninurta's antagonist. This antagonist, Kur, is supposed to have been a "large serpent which lived in the bottom of the 'great below' where the latter came in contact with the primeval waters" (p. 78).

The texts concerned—as far as known to the reviewer—contain no evidence whatsoever that might support these assumptions. On the contrary, the Akkadian translation of lugal-e u_4 me-lám-bi nir-gál with unfailing consistency treats the word kur as a geographical term, translating it by *šadê*, "the mountains." Never once does the translator take this word over untranslated as is his custom with proper names. Thus the line from which Dr. Kramer concludes that "Sharur has set its mind against Kur" reads:

u_4-bi-a en-na (var. om.) ^{giš}tukul-a-ni kur-ra geštu mi-ni-i[n-gál]
i-nu-šú šá be-lí kak-ka-šú ina šadi-i uz-na-a-šú ba-[šá-a] [29]

In those days was the attention (lit.: the ear) of the weapon of the
    lord (directed) toward the mountains.

This means that Sharur, Ninurta's weapon personified, elsewhere called his "general," kept an eye on the mountains, that unruly region on the borders of the Mesopotamian plain whence danger of attack ever threatened. The phrase geštu....gál, which must be restored in our line, means "to direct one's attention toward," literally "(one's) ears being (toward)." It does not have the connotation "to set one's mind against." Kur is here, as elsewhere, translated by *šadê*, "the mountains," quite differently from the way in which the real name of Ninurta's opponent, Asag (Á-sàg), is treated. This name is not translated but is correctly taken over into Akkadian as *Asakku*. Asag, who is not mentioned by Dr. Kramer at all, is the enemy against whom Sharur warns. He has been begotten on Ki, the Earth, by the god of heaven, Anu, has been chosen king by the plants, and his warriors, various stones, raid the cities. Sharur calls upon Ninurta to protect the country against Asag and Ninurta defeats him. That Asag, and not a nonexistent being Kur, is Ninurta's antagonist has never been doubted by earlier translators. It is, besides, clearly stated in other literary texts.[30] Since there is thus no evidence for the existence of a personage Kur in Sumerian mythology, we need not discuss the question of his supposed outward form. As for Asag, we can offer no opinion; the myth seems to treat of him in human terms but gives no definite clue to his shape. Nor need we deal in detail with the meaning of the section which describes the conditions remedied by Ninurta after he had vanquished Asag. We shall state only that we believe Asag, "The Crippler,"[31] to typify the frigid cold of winter, Ninurta the forces of spring. Their battle, which takes place over the mountains, can be heard in the roar of the thunderstorms which herald the Mesopotamian spring. Before Asag was vanquished, the subterranean waters used to go up into the far mountains, where they froze, but Ninurta built the ḫursag, the near ranges, to prevent the waters from so doing and led them into the Tigris. This seems to have reference to that melting of the snows on the high mountains in spring which causes the yearly flood. Altogether the myth of Ninurta and Asag appears to be a nature myth telling of the yearly battle of spring and winter.

3. *Third and fourth myths of Kur.* Two more myths are listed as myths of Kur: "Inanna and Ebih" and "The Descent of Inanna." Since the word kur as used in these myths is not claimed by Dr. Kramer to refer to a personal being, monstrous or otherwise, we need not discuss these two myths in detail. We may therefore conclude our comments on the chapter "Myths of Kur" with the statement that—as far as we can see—evidence for the existence of such a being is still lacking.[32]

It remains to consider Dr. Kramer's interpretation of his material in the wider and more significant sense of the word: his evaluation of the Sumerian myths as a literary and as an intellectual achievement. Dr. Kramer is the first to undertake such an evaluation. He has endeavored to bring system and order into his materials, to understand—as he sees them—their underlying pattern of thought. The reviewer notices that the resultant synthesis differs not inconsiderably from the one to which his own research has led him and which he has recently had opportunity to clarify to himself in a few lectures soon to be published. Such difference, however—at the present stage of our knowledge—is not seriously disturbing. We are as yet in the earliest and most tentative stages of penetrating the inner structural coherence of these Sumerian materials, of clarifying the cultural system in which they are imbedded and from which alone they derive their intellectual and emotional meaning. The task is exceedingly difficult and most delicate. But each individual approach will contribute, will explore new possibilities. Differences of interpretation at this stage are therefore to be expected and even welcomed. For it is precisely in attention to and discussion of differences that we may hope to progress toward a truer insight.

It seems useful therefore to express clearly those divergencies of interpretation which seem to be of greatest significance in our various attempts to achieve a consistent picture.

III. GENERAL INTERPRETATIONAL APPROACH

Good interpretation undoubtedly has its mainspring in sincere love of that which is to be interpreted. But such love, if it is to lead to understanding, must be in a very special sense unselfish, neither closing its eyes in blind admiration nor impetuously trying to make over what it loves to suit its own desires. It must be the tempered passion of one who loves wisely.

These maxims, trite but true, are not always, it would seem, strictly observed in the book under discussion. Thus many of the aesthetic value judgments scattered through its pages seem overly enthusiastic and may thereby defeat their purpose, setting the reader aginst the Sumerian tale rather than leading him on to appreciation.

The myth of Enlil and Ninlil as given in the book tells how Ninlil's mother deliberately makes her daughter expose herself so that she may be raped by Enlil, how Enlil abandons her as soon as he has raped her, how she follows him and is seduced three times in succession by men whom she meets on the road—all of them, as it turns out, Enlil in disguise. The story is presented to the reader as "this delightful myth" (p. 43).

The story of Inanna and Enki tells how Enki while drunk presented to Inanna a great many powers, how Inanna made off with these powers in her boat, and how Enki, when he became sober, tried to stop the boat and take back his gift. The tale is introduced to the reader as "this magnificent myth with its particularly charming story" (p. 64).

Little is gained by such appreciation *quand même*.

As for the first story, Dr. Kramer was in a difficult position, since the motivations and meaning of the events in the story seem to have largely escaped him. Thus the story becomes merely brutal, losing the strange undertone of inevitability which it has when the psychology of its characters and the moral norms governing their actions are understood. Even so, however, an adjective like "wild" or even "brutal" would have done better to prepare the reader than does the incongruous "delightful."

As for the second story, Dr. Kramer understood the essentials of the tale correctly, but "magnificent" is out of tune. Here it might have been stressed that this story is one in a much lighter vein. The conflict is not serious, for, since Inanna is Enki's favorite daughter, he cannot lose much to her. Whatever he gives her stays—so to speak—in the family. Thus the listener is free to enjoy the unwonted spectacle of Enki, the most clever and crafty of all the gods, caught in a dilemma of his own making, a dilemma of which his quick-witted daughter is not slow to take advantage. It may be added that the prize for which they play is nothing as ponderous as "the basis of the culture pattern of Sumerian civilization" (p. 66), but merely a motley of powers and activities with which the many-sided Inanna was thought to have connection.

As overenthusiasm is unfavorable to understanding, so also is too harsh censure. In the myth of Enki and Ninhursaga the latter gives birth to various deities, each to heal a part of Enki's aching body. In each case the name of the healing deity is compounded with the Sumerian word for the relevant part of the body. This draws the following salvo:

Moreover, the superficiality and barren artificiality of the concepts implied in this closing passage of our myth, although not apparent from the English translation, are brought out quite clearly by the

> Sumerian original. For the fact is that the actual relationship between each of the "healing" deities and the sickness which it is supposed to cure, is verbal and nominal only;....[p. 59].

It would undoubtedly have helped the reader more toward appreciating the ancient tale if—instead of chiding the Sumerians for not being more modern in their thinking—the author had explained why they thought as they did. The conviction that a name somehow partakes of the reality of that which it denotes is a prominent feature of Sumerian, as of most other, mythopoeic thought. It has its basis in the fact that this form of thought does not recognize different levels of reality.

By closing one's heart against such ways of thought, one bars one's self from deeper understanding of the ancient mind and of ancient poetry. Thus Dr. Kramer—averse to mere "verbal" and "nominal" relationships—must fail to appreciate the rather fine piece of narration which the beginning of this self-same myth constitutes. The narrator of the myth—since a name partakes of the reality of what it means— refers to the deity Ninhursaga under her several names according as the essence of these names is manifest in or foreshadows Ninhursaga's role in the stream of events narrated. She is Nin-sikil-la, "The pure (i.e., virgin) lady," before Enki unites with her. In the section telling of Enki's advances to her she is Nin-tu ama kalamma, "The lady who gives birth, the mother of the land," the name bringing into focus the possibility latent in her, a possibility which begins to be realized with the event here related. When Ninhursaga finally accepts Enki, she is Dam-gal-nun-na, "The great spouse of the prince (i.e., of Enki)." And when—as the fertile soil—she conceives and gives birth to vegetation, she is Nin-ḫur-sag-gá, "The lady of the mountain," for on the lush green mountain slopes in the east the earth manifests its powers to produce the luxuriant vegetation of spring as it does nowhere else.

The student of ancient mythology dares not cling to his own criteria for what constitutes logical thinking so pertinaciously that these criteria become barriers preventing him from entering sympatheticaly into other, earlier modes of thought. So too must he ever be on guard against reading into the ancient words his own concepts, born, formed, and determined in a world of scientific outlook and experimental technique.

To a modern, scientifically trained mind the concept "fire" can mean: "oxidation, the oxygen of the atmosphere combining with the substance burnt." But something entirely different filled the mind of an ancient Mesopotamian when he consigned images of his enemies to the fire and addressed it as follows: "Scorching God Fire, warlike son of Heaven, thou, the fiercest of thy brethren, who like Moon and Sun decidest lawsuits, judge thou my case, hand down the verdict. Burn, O God Fire, the man and woman who bewitched me."[33] Concepts are not necessarily identical because their referent is the same. The words "God Fire," "fire," "combustion," "oxidation" may all refer to one objective reality, yet each symbolizes a different concept entirely. Were we—in the above prayer—to progress gradually through such stages as "God Fire," "fire," and "combustion," to "oxidation," we would remove with each "translation" one step further from understanding what filled the ancient speaker, until with "oxidation" all bridges had been cast off. The concept "oxidation," the total mental reaction which this world symbolizes, could not possibly have been entertained by him.

For the Mesopotamians, as for us, things are what we make them, that is to say, what our concepts of them are. And one·cannot add to, or subtract from, or make substitutions for, a concept without emerging with a new and different concept.

We are stating these rather obvious facts in order to make clear why we are reluctant to follow Dr. Kramer in his efforts to express Sumerian mythology "rationally." These efforts amount exactly—it seems to us—to substituting concepts such as "combustion" and "oxidation" for concepts like "God Fire"—under the impression that one is still rendering Sumerian thought.

Dr. Kramer states his method on page 73. Speaking of Sumerian cosmogony, he rejoices that "when these concepts are analyzed; when the theological cloak and polytheistic trappings are removed ...., the Sumerian creation concepts indicate a keenly observing mentality....etc." He seems quite unaware that what he is here removing is not a "cloak," not "trappings," but the very categories constitutive of Sumerian thought, its whole conceptual apparatus. When that has been removed, there can be nothing left. Those and none other were the terms in which the Sumerians could and did think. Without them there is no Sumerian thought.

A few of the results of this method may be considered in more detail. We quote:

> Heaven and earth were conceived as *solid* elements. Between them, however, and *from them*, came the gaseous element *air*, whose main characteristic is that of expansion. Heaven and earth were thus separated by the expanding element *air* [p. 73; italics are Dr. Kramer's].

For the god Enlil (i.e., the storm viewed as, and reacted to as, a personal being with divine powers: "Lord Storm") has been substituted the modern scientific concept "the gaseous element *air*, whose main characteristic is that of expansion." With the term "air" instead of "storm," "wind," we are already on dangerous ground. There is, as far as we know, no term for "air at rest" in either Sumerian or Akkadian: all those we have denote "air in motion," i.e., they symbolize concepts limited approximately as are those suggested by our words "wind" and "storm," and only thus may they be rendered. Constitutive for the further term "gaseous element" is the notion that there are various substances which have the same form as air. This was realized in Europe as late as the eighteenth century; up to that time it had been supposed that air is one homogeneous substance. That the main characteristic of air is that of expansion (Dr. Kramer has in mind, as the context shows, its ability to exert outward pressure) may—at least in a modified form—seem true to the physicist, but we doubt very much whether this is the characterization the man in the street would give; and we cannot imagine how the Sumerians, without experiments, would hit upon the notion that heated air expands more than does a comparable volume of solids or fluids heated to the same temperature. With the terms "solid," "gaseous," "element," the constitutive notion of a tripartite scheme of possible forms under which matter can exist (as solids, liquids, or gases) has been introduced and imputed to the Sumerians—if we understand Dr. Kramer's text correctly, consciously so. It seems unnecessary to go on demonstrating how utterly divorced these notions are from the Sumerian concept of a "Lord Storm," the essentials of which they are supposed to render. In the first paragraph on page 74 the reader may find language implying that the Sumerians were aware of a relation between density and gravitational pull: "Air, being lighter and far less dense than either heaven or earth, succeeded in producing the *moon*." He may then check with pages 43–47 to see how far the concepts involved are truly the same. The immediately following lines of the paragraph read like the Nebular Hypothesis of Laplace seen through a glass darkly.

But this must suffice. We hope that we have expressed ourselves clearly so that if we end up on a positive note by suggesting that Enlil, "Lord Storm," may have been imagined to have separated heaven and earth in somewhat the manner in which strong wind may momentarily blow under and lift a tent cloth or a large heavy sheet lying on the ground, neither the reader nor Dr. Kramer will conclude that this is "the same thing" that he has been saying all along. Differences of two worlds and of four millennia may not be ignored.

We have come to the end of our review and may sum up. We have found in Dr. Kramer's book much which calls for unqualified praise, especially in matters relating to the establishing of the text of the Sumerian compositions, which is a task of prime importance.

We have also found points on which we tend to differ with the author, almost exclusively, we may stress, in matters relating to translation and interpretation.

The fact that such differences exist in no way lessens our appreciation of the other wholly excellent aspects of the author's work and our clear recognition of the urgency, value, and extreme importance of the larger project of which the book under review forms a part. The central task of that project—the establishing of the text of the Sumerian literary compositions, the finding, placing, copying, and publication of new fragments—can be satisfactorily accomplished even though the meaning of the text may not always be fully understood. And that task, we repeat, is without question the most urgent of all those which confront Sumerologists today. Here Dr. Kramer has demonstrated his industry and ability so convincingly that in our considered opinion no other scholar would be as competent as he to carry this important work to a speedy and satisfactory conclusion.[34]

8. Early Political Development in Mesopotamia[1]

> "If, then, Socrates, we find ourselves in many
> points unable to make our discourse of the
> generation of gods and the universe in every way
> wholly consistent and exact, you must not be
> surprised. Nay, we must be well content if we
> can provide an account not less likely than another's."[2]

I. INTRODUCTION

1. *Desirability of Inquiry.* In the outgoing third millennium B.C. the Dynasty of Akkade built the world's first empire. It stretched from the mountains of present-day Iran in the East across the fertile plains of Iraq and Syria to the shore of the Mediterranean in the West; and the Akkade rulers were able to maintain it over a period of some three generations, from the founder, Sargon, to Naram-Sîn.[3]

This achievement, crude and primitive though it may have been, is one of the great landmarks in universal history, for in man's everlasting struggle to enlarge the political unit, on the long road from tribe to village, town, and city; from city-state to nation, empire, and attempts such as the United Nations of our day, the step to empire marks for better or worse the beginning of a major phase in the development of human political forms.

NOTE: First published in *ZA* 52 (1957) 91–140.

This great general significance of the Akkade achievement makes it particularly desirable to understand and to evaluate it in its proper historical setting, and an inquiry into the development which led up to it administratively and militarily, that is, into the general early political development in Mesopotamia, is therefore a tempting undertaking.

But the mere fact that such an inquiry would be desirable is hardly enough, it must necessarily also appear feasible in terms of the information at our disposal. Before attempting it, therefore, it may be well to glance briefly at the available sources in order to clarify to ourselves the nature of the answers which they may be able to give and the degree of validity of the account they will sustain.

2. *Special Conditions of Mesopotamian History.* Ancient Mesopotamian history generally suffers under scarcity of sources to a point where its very character of history in the strict sense of the word may be drawn in question, for of history proper[4] one must demand not only that it provide a consistent and meaningful account of past political and cultural development, but also that this account meet certain stringent tests of credibility; it must, in Oakeshott's words be, "What the evidence obliges us to believe."[5] In the ancient Mesopotamian field, however, that principle is not easily applied. The general scarcity of sources and the fact that the sources themselves are very frequently only of limited relevance to the questions which are historically of central importance leaves the historian in a position in which his sources "oblige" him to believe hardly anything except on matters of small import. If he insisted on the principle he would end up, therefore, with a direct antithesis of history, a mere collection of unconnected trivia.

Thus, if the ancient Mesopotamian historian is to give any meaningful account of his materials at all he must of a necessity relax the stringent claim of "what the evidence obliges us to believe" and substitute for it a modest "what the evidence makes it reasonable for us to believe," for it is only by taking account of evidence which is suggestive, when the suggestion is in itself reasonable, rather than restricting himself to wholly compelling evidence, that he will be able to integrate his data in a consistent and meaningful presentation. In replacing "what the evidence obliges us to believe," with "what the evidence makes it reasonable for us to believe" the historian—at the peril of his right to so call himself—leaves, of course, except for details of his work, the realm of knowledge to enter that of reasonable conjecture. This may not be altogether palatable to him, but since the nature of his materials allows him no other choice the best he can do is to accept it as gracefully as possible and with full awareness of its consequences in terms of limited finality of the results possible to him.

3. *Limited Goals of Inquiry.* The sources for an inquiry into the political developments which led up to the Akkade empire have their full measure of the deficiencies just discussed. Original sources dating from before the Akkade period are few, meager, and mostly of limited relevance to basic problems. Later tradition and survivals of early political concepts are somewhat more numerous and generally more centrally relevant, but they present by reason of their special character problems of reference and general evaluation. All in all such sources will be suggestive far more often than they can be compelling and a meaningful account based on them can only be given within the latitude that, as we have suggested, ancient Mesopotamian history must allow. The best that can be attempted from them is an ordered, coherent, and meaningful account which, though openly conjectural, is consistent with the known data and in itself reasonable.[6] We must, in Plato's words "be well content if we can provide an account not less likely than another's"; in itself no small task.

In submitting our inquiry to the present volume in honor of Professor Arno Poebel we hope he will enjoy recognizing in the varied textual materials on which it is based so very much to the elucidation of which he has contributed fundamentally and in all aspects: grammatically, lexically, and historically. It is a pleasant duty here to acknowledge all we have learned from him, in class, in discussions, from his writings, and—most of all, perhaps—in being forced to ground thoroughly any point on which one might differ with him.

II. COUNTRY AND SETTLEMENT

1. *Country.* An inquiry into the pre-Sargonic political development in Mesopotamia may profitably begin with the conditioning factors given with the country and its early settlement.

The country which was to become the heartland of the Akkade empire extends from slightly north of the present Baghdad region southward to the Persian Gulf. It is a flat alluvial plain originally laid down by the rivers Tigris and Euphrates which traverse it. Rain is scarce and the country depends almost exclusively on artificial irrigation for its crops, which in antiquity were primarily barley and dates. Settled human occupation, accordingly, is closely tied to rivers and canals and only occurs along them, but, since conditions for irrigation tend to vary considerably along the course of a river, habitation rarely forms an unbroken strip along the banks but rather clusters in favorable spots mutually separated by long stretches on which the river runs through desert or swamp.

Of the two major watercourses, the Euphrates and the Tigris, the former is by far the easier one to tap and on it depends, therefore, most of the ancient settlements. Beginning at a point north of the latitude of modern Baghdad a number of major canals were drawn from the Euphrates and carried with the surface contours southeast toward the Tigris, which in this stretch flows parallel with, and not very far to the east of, the Euphrates. The excellent drainage into the Tigris or into swamps along its bank made for stable irrigation conditions and gave rise to a block of more or less contiguous settlements which constitute the ancient land of Uri, or Akkad as it was called later on.

Further to the south, approximately at Babylon, the Euphrates divided in antiquity into two major branches which watered the country of Sumer. The easternmost of these, the Iturungal, flowed in southeastern direction well north of Nippur to Adab, then south over Zabalam and Umma to Badtibira, where it veered west and, over Larsa, seems to have rejoined the main, western branch. The western branch itself, the ancient Euphrates, followed a course somewhat to the north and east of that of the present Hilla branch, passed through Nippur, curved down to Shuruppak, and flowed from there due south over Uruk to Ur and on through extensive marshlands to the Persian Gulf. Besides these two major Euphrates branches there was a third important watercourse, the Sirara, which took off from the Iturungal at Zabalam and, flowing first southeast, then south, watered the district of Girsu, Lagash, and Ninâ, continuing southward through marshes to the gulf. This canal seems at various times to have fed also from the Tigris, most likely through a cut running down from a point somewhere near modern Kut-el-Amara.[7]

2. *Settlement.* The earliest settlement, insofar as we can form an idea about it, seems to have consisted of small villages scattered throughout the country where conditions permitted. These villages appear to have been located by preference on river-fed small lakes or swamps, and fishing was an economic factor of importance. As agriculture developed the villages in the extreme South grew in size and the earliest cities—Eridu, Ur, Uruk, Girsu, probably Lagash and Ninâ, Umma, and others as well—came into being. The northern boundary of the first cities would seem to have been approximately at the latitude of Uruk; north of that line we must assume the original small villages only.

This picture, growing cities in the South, small villages in the middle and North of the country, seems to have persisted through the Ubaid, Uruk and early Protoliterate periods. With the second part of the Protoliterate period (Jemdet Nasr), however, there are signs of a change. Shuruppak, Nippur, Kish, and Eshnunna, if not actually founded at this time, grew to city size then and we must assume that the southern pattern of the larger city was extended—possibly due to some major advance in agriculture as, e.g., planned large-scale irrigation—to the northern part of Sumer and to Uri.[8] Before and after this expansion of concentrated population patterns northward there appear signs of local worsening of economic conditions in the South. Eridu was to all practical purposes abandoned after the Ubaid period, a similar fate overtook Ninâ and Lagash in the I and II Early Dynastic periods. Probably the reason was salting up of the soil due to long cultivation with imperfect draining techniques.[9] Whether a connection can be established between this and the rise of cities further northward is as yet uncertain.

The picture emerging for the late Protoliterate and the following Early Dynastic periods is thus one of cities with surrounding villages separated by stretches of open country in which nomadic tribes may be assumed to have roamed. These cities, with their surrounding villages, were limited essentially to points along two separate lines: that of the Euphrates with Nippur, Shuruppak, Uruk, Ur, and that of the Iturungal-Sirara with Adab, Zabalam, Umma, Badtibira, and the Girsu and Lagash region. Between the two lines, effectively separating them, lay open desert, the Edin of the Sumerians, and also between the individual settlements on either line lay vast stretches of desert and swamp. This geographically imposed separateness of the settlements is noteworthy, for it sets narrow limits for the developing political units and must have tended to act, once the immediate borders of the individual settlements had been reached, as a powerful restraining factor encouraging separatism and hampering attempts at further effective unification of the country as a whole. We may see it as a constant background force in Sumerian political history responsible for—compared to Egypt—the very late unification of the country and for the always tenuous character of that unification; whenever opportunity presented itself Sumer would always fall apart again into the old city-states.

III. EARLIEST POLITICAL PATTERN: PRIMITIVE DEMOCRACY

1. *Sources.* Our sources for the earliest political forms in Meso-potamia are the ancient myths, stories told about the gods and their exploits. These stories—as even a cursory inspection will show—are all laid in a society governed by a characteristic, simple political pattern, the one we have elsewhere termed "Primitive Democracy." [10] The political pattern of the myths, "Primitive Democracy," differs from a comparable pattern found in the stories about human or semi-human heroes, the epics and epical tales, by its greater primi-tivity, and it stands apart altogether from anything we know of the political organization of the country in historical times.

Since it is difficult to conceive that the original myth-makers could have depicted as setting for their stories a society quite outside their experience and unrelated to anything they or their listeners knew, and since furthermore the myths of a people usually constitute the oldest layer of its tradition, one must assume that a political setting such as occurs in these tales once existed in Mesopotamia and was later replaced by more developed political forms.

2. *Primitive Democracy.* In the political pattern depicted in the myths ultimate authority, sovereignty, resides in a general assembly of the citizens (unkin).[11] Proceedings in this assembly are directed

by a leader—in the myths usually the god of heaven, An—and its verdicts, approved by the assenting votes[12] (heam "let it be!") of the individual members, were made law (nam-tar-a) through being formally announced by a small group of seven known as "the seven law-making gods" (dingir-nam-tar-a(k) imin-anene).[13] Particular weight in the discussions carried, as might be expected, the opinions of the older, experienced members, the "seniors." In the divine assembly they numbered fifty (dingir-gal-gal(-ak) ninnu-(a)nene).[14]

The assembly was called when a crisis threatened the community and it served two major purposes: it pooled all available experience and inventiveness, and it served as an instrument of achieving agreement for concerted action. There are some indications that an oath to abide by the decisions was imposed on the members beforehand.[15]

The crisis which might occasion the calling of an assembly were many, but certain typical ones stand out. In cases of serious offenses by individuals the assembly acted as a court of law, imposing punishment of death or banishment[16] on the culprit. In cases of internal administrative crises—need for organization of large communal undertaking or for checking banditry and lawlessness—the problem before the assembly was that of choosing a suitable organizer, a "lord" (en) and persuading him to serve.[17] The "lord" was chosen for proven administrative abilities (he would normally be the head of a large estate) and charismatic powers, magical ability to make things thrive, was the core of his office.[18] A similar problem of finding a suitable leader confronted the assembly in crises brought on by the threat of attack from outside, but here the qualities looked for were slightly different. The war leader or "king" (lugal) was chosen for skill in warfare and physical endurance. He was therefore typically a young man—usually he still lived at home under parental authority —and of noble family; his father was generally a rich landowner on whose servants and retainers the son could draw for followers on his military ventures.[19]

Viewed as a whole the most characteristic element of the primitive democracy pattern is probably its provisional and ad hoc character. It is called upon to function in emergencies only and the assembly called is determined not only as to time but also often as to size by the special emergency and the geographical extent of the threat it represents.[20] The assembly deals only with the specific crisis for which it was called and correspondingly the officers which it may appoint, the "lord" and the "king," are appointed for a limited term only, a bala,[21] essentially the duration of the emergency with which they are to cope. When that emergency had passed we must assume that the larger unit temporarily imposed on the community vanished with it and left the ordering of society to the numerous minor over-lapping power structures which crisscross any society:[22] family, household, estate, village, town, and so forth. Many of these minor power structures were in the early Mesopotamian society themselves organized along primitive democratic lines with a general assembly as highest authority: family council etc.

3. *Extension of Pattern.* The many different levels on which the pattern of primitive democracy could be applied and its general temporary ad hoc character raises the question whether it was ever extended from regional application to the country of Sumer as a whole. We tend to believe that the answer should be in the affirmative.

The main support for such an assumption comes from a considera-tion of the quite unique position held by the city of Nippur and its chief god, Enlil, in Sumerian politics. From the very beginning of historical times Nippur and Enlil were recognized as an undisputed source of rule over Sumer as a whole, and kings of Sumer would derive their authority from recognition in Nippur rather than from their own city and its city-god. Such singular prestige would, of course, be very simply explained if we could assume that at one time rulers of Nippur had conquered the whole of Sumer and thus established a precedent linking the right to rule all of the country specifically with Nippur. However, nowhere in our traditions is there a trace of any such original dominium by Nippur. In fact the traditions point in quite another direction, to Nippur as an original all-Sumerian place of assembly for purposes of electing a common ruler. In this role—slightly obscured by later transfer of the scene of the myth to Babylon—Nippur appears in Enuma elish, which de-scribes three successive general assemblies held in Ubshu-ukkinnak, the place of assembly in the Enlil temple in Nippur, for the purpose of electing first a war leader, a "king," later an administrator, a "lord." The all-Sumerian scope of these assemblies is indicated not only by the active part which Ea/Enkik, god of Eridug in the extreme South, plays in them, but also by the universal character of the myth itself;

it deals with the origins and ordering of the world as a whole. A similar all-Sumerian scope is indicated also for assemblies told about in other myths.

Even more explicit than Enuma elish is the political theory of kingship prevalent in historical times and expressed, e.g., in the royal hymns of Ur III and Isin-Larsa date.[23] According to their doctrine the king of all Sumer was nominated for office by his city-god, or another deity close to him, in an assembly of the gods of the various Sumerian cities meeting together in Nippur under the presidium of An and Enlil. After being duly nominated the new king was then elected by the assenting individual votes of the members. As this assembly chose the king so it could also depose him; it was a vote of the gods in the Nippur assembly which brought an end to the rule of the Third Dynasty of Ur.[24]

If we look, then, for original political realities which can have given Nippur its prestige as source of kingship over all of Sumer, and which at the same time can have shaped the specific concepts which we encounter in the myths and the later political theory, it is difficult to avoid the conclusion that Nippur was originally the meeting place to which the citizens of the Sumerian cities assembled to elect common leaders, "lords" or "kings" as the case might be.

With such an assumption agrees well the only term we have for Sumer as a political unit, the term Kengir; for there is good evidence that this term was originally a term for Nippur itself,[25] and it is understandable that a political organization created in Nippur meetings should take its name from the meeting place. Another term of interest is the designation bara(g)-bara(g) Kengir-a(k) used for rulers of cities forming part of the Kengir organization and which contrasts with ensi(g) kur-kur-a(k) "the ensiks of all the sovereign countries." It seems likely that bara(g), "throne dais," refers to the seats in the Nippur assembly and that the meaning of the term thus is "all the throne daises of Nippur."[26] To have a convenient name for the assumed original organization of Sumer as a whole under the form of primitive democracy we may—since its temporary and loose character preclude terms like "state" or even "nation"—choose the relatively noncommittal term "Kengir League."

4. *Date of Maximal Extension.* As to the time when the assumed Kengir League may have flourished very little can be surmised. The

pattern of primitive democracy is of small help when it comes to dating, for it is so closely similar to the political patterns which one typically finds in small primitive communities, tribes and villages, almost everywhere that it is likely to go back to the earliest village settlements in Mesopotamia and even to nomadic tribes before them. An upper time limit for the Kengir League is, however, given with Nippur itself which, on archaeological evidence, would seem to date—at least as a major city—not further back than the second part of the Protoliterate period (Jemdet Nasr period).[27] Correspondingly the widespread occurrence of city walls in Early Dynastic II suggests a probable lower limit, for they suggest conditions such as appear to have prompted the development of the more advanced political pattern mirrored in the epics.[28] A tentative date to the intervening period of Early Dynastic I would accordingly seem in order.

With such a date agrees quite well what little other, specific evidence we have. Of the terms connected with the pattern of primitive democracy, that for "assembly" (unkin) occurs, as might be expected, already in our earliest documents, the tablets of early Protoliterate times for Warka.[29] As for the officers chosen by the assembly the sign for "lord" (en) likewise appears in the earliest texts,[30] but it is not clear whether it is used in its political sense or with some of the several other meanings of which it is capable. The first occurrence of the term for "king," lugal, is in tablets dating from Early Dynastic I found in Ur,[31] but it is quite possible, of course, that earlier instances may turn up. With the occurrence of the term for "king" goes that for the "palace" (é-gal), the center of his administration,[32] and the same group of tablets also contains an example of early military organization, a list of soldiers under sergeants (ugula) formed into a company (un-sìr-ra) under colonels (nu-bánda), one of which seems to be in supreme command.[33] Of particular interest are the probable mention of Kengir[34] and a group of puzzling jar sealings impressed with "collective" seals. Each of these seals is inscribed with the names of a group of major Sumerian cities. Since such collective seals imply collective responsibility for the goods sent under the seal we may see in them evidence of official deliveries to Ur by groups of cities, a feature most easily understandable in terms of a league of cities such as the Kengir League. An obvious parallel is the bala deliveries[35] of later times.[36]

IV. GERMS OF NEW DIRECTION

The picture of extremely casual political forms given in the myths, with its crisis-determined, ad hoc, assembly and offices conferred for the duration of emergencies, shows at one point tendencies toward greater permanence. A "lord" or "king" appointed by the assembly, having once tasted the heady wine of exceptional prestige and influence, would be understandably disinclined to relinquish that position after the emergency which had created it was over, and would look for ways of perpetuating it. He would tend to keep his household troops in training by raids across the borders, he would welcome opportunities to make his power felt internally—opportunities which would be only too readily presented to him by people seeking his help in righting private wrongs—thus taking upon himself the task of a "judge" in the Old Testament sense, and he would, last but not least, ruthlessly put down any possible rival to his position, the first and most basic rule for defending and maintaining power.[37]

The tendencies here mentioned are well exemplified in a group of myths centering around the god Ninurta which, since they show close affinities with the epics and epic tales in their general outlook, are probably to be considered the latest stratum of myths that we possess. The one which gives the most complete picture is the longest of them, Lugal-e. In this myth the young king, Ninurta, appears to hold, even in peacetime, a position of relative permanence. Owing his influence and standing in the community largely to the established position of his father[38] he is yet able to vie with the older, prominent members of the community in public esteem.[39] He maintains a body of warriors with which he goes on raids outside the borders, but his main function is that of an Old Testament "judge," a powerful individual to whom people in trouble turn for help to get their rights.[40] In the jealousy with which he guards this prerogative we have an instructive example of "power defense." When the plants assemble and choose a king, the Asakku, who also maintains a body of warriors, the stones, and also "judges" in the land, Ninurta immediately sets about crushing him.[41] In a pitched battle the Asakku is killed and Ninurta follows up his victory by "judging" the Asakku's followers, thus establishing his position of sole "judge" in the country.[42] Those who have opposed him vigorously are condemned to death or otherwise severely punished, those who seem likely to transfer their allegiance to him are placed in positions of influence.

The further development of these trends toward primacy and permanence in the officers of the assembly may be seen in full flower in the picture of Mesopotamian society given in the epics.

V. DEVELOPING POLITICAL FORMS: PRIMITIVE MONARCHY

1. *Sources.* Our second major group of sources for Mesopotamian political forms from before the historical periods are the epics and epic tales. They differ formally from the myths by centering around a human or semi-human hero, Enmerkar, Lugalbanda, Gilgamesh, etc. rather than around a god. More significant to us, however, is a difference in the general picture of political conditions which they paint. In the myths life was on the whole peaceful, with only an occasional serious threat of war; in the epics war is the rule, the cities are ringed with huge defensive walls, their rulers think of war and conquest only, danger of sudden attack is ever present. The risks involved in such attacks, furthermore, are real and serious. Large prosperous cities may be looted and burned and even completely destroyed[43]; if a city yields to the attacker it may see the canal system on which it depends readjusted to favor the city of the victor[44] and may have to send its inhabitants off year after year to do forced labor in the victor's fields or on his building projects to the detriment of its own economy.[45] How real and constant these dangers were can be gauged from the prevalence of city walls in the epics, for no community would have accepted the enormous burden of constructing such walls were the need for them not both patent and pressing.

2. *Ascendency and Perpetuation of Offices.* The change from the relatively peaceful conditions of the myths to the all-out warlike world of the epics goes a long way toward explaining adjustments in the political pattern which the epics show. We have already noted certain inherent tendencies in the officers of the primitive democracy pattern, the "lord" and the "king," to perpetuate their position and power beyond the duration of the emergency for which they had been elected. With conditions such as those depicted in the epics these tendencies must have obtained the backing of political necessity

itself. For what used to be a passing emergency, war, has now taken on the aspect of a permanent condition, and the officer who was to deal with it could not but become permanent with it. The "king" and the "lord" thus had a free field for making their offices enduring institutions.[46]

The details of this development, as it can be seen in the epics, may be stated as follows:

The ever present need for defense acted to speed the development of the ruler's household troops from a band of raiders to a regular standing army. For purposes of defense—and of control—further, the king would establish "households" of his, "palaces" (é-gal) in major cities under his sway,[47] fully staffed with servants militarily organized, and functioning as garrisons.

In the building, maintaining, and guarding of the new city walls a further permanent task fell to the king and his forces, as may be seen, e.g., from the close connection between Gilgamesh and the building of the city wall of Uruk in the Gilgamesh Epic and in other traditions,[48] and in the figure of the god ᵈLugal, a personification of the royal office. This god, as Gudea tells us, had the duty of seeing to the patrolling of the temple and the guarding of the city wall.[49]

The role of the ruler as "righter of wrongs" in peacetime, which we first met with in the Ninurta myth Lugal-e, is continued in the epics. Thus in the story of Gilgamesh and the Huluppu Tree, when Inanna has been dispossessed of a tree she had planted and complains to the sun-god she is referred to the ruler of her city, Gilgamesh, and the latter repossesses her of her tree by armed force.[50] The related tendencies in the kings and lords to strengthen their position by ruthlessly suppressing all rivals may be seen as a reason why in the various regions of Mesopotamia, as we find them in the epics, only one ruler, either a "king" or a "lord," is met with. With this regional unification of power in one hand goes a gradual merging of the various functions of the two offices, for all of them were needed for a community to thrive. The general warlike conditions would, in the case of the "lord," stress his powers of maintaining order and expand his police powers to full military scope. The "king," on the other hand, could not well disregard internal administrative and economic problems in his realm and would thus naturally come to assume also the "lord's" responsibilities for fertility and abundant crops. Thus magic and ritual responsibilities were added to his earlier military and judiciary functions to form the combination so characteristic of later Mesopotamian kingship.[51]

The tendencies toward protecting and securing the position they held also led the rulers to seek a more independent and more stable basis for their power than that of popular favor and election in the popular assembly; divine favor and election were stressed instead. This was, of course, a natural stress in the case of the "lord," whose central task of securing prosperity was so immediately and patently linked to divine favor,[52] but it was applied equally to the "king," to whom the gods had entrusted the defense of their cities and their estates, the temples:

"Uruk, the handiwork of the gods,
  Eannak, the temple descended from heaven,
  their various parts the great gods made;
  their great wall, resting on the ground like a cloudbank,
  their exalted dwellings, founded by An,
  are entrusted to thee, thou art their king and defender."[53]

In this gradual shift of emphasis from human to divine election the groundwork is laid for a complete transfer of the human popular assembly to the divine plane, such as we find it in later political theory, where the king of all Sumer is elected in an assembly of city-gods in Nippur, discussed earlier on.[54]

The permanence and the growing power of "king" and "lord" which we find in the epics could not but force the assembly very decidedly into the background as an instrument of high policy. The assembly now appears in such function only when it is a question of challenging a ruler by force, that is, as a political instrument of organizing and declaring rebellion. In that role we meet it in the tale of Gilgamesh and Agga and in that function it survived to Akkade times.[55]

As an important influence in this whole development must be counted, lastly, the example of a new successful pattern of rule by force which was set at the time: the kingship of Kish. Kish, a city in the North, succeeded, aided by its advantageous tactical position, in subjecting by force all the other major cities in the country. Striking swiftly downstream its riverborne armies could make fast their longboats under the walls of any city in the South long before warning of the attack could reach the victim.[56] Its new pattern—rule over large territories imposed by force—could not but establish a new ideal in the minds of ambitious region rulers, an ideal which competed successfully with the older one of the Kengir League with its rule imposed by mutual agreement.

3. *Evaluation. Vulnerability of Assembly. New Type of Power.* The change in ideals—or perhaps better, in realizable possibilities—of rule over large areas from rule by agreement to rule by force sums up the essence of the development shown in the epics. In seeking to evaluate it in larger perspective and to note the reasons why the assembly, the central feature of primitive democracy, was so easily forced out from the top level of government of larger areas, two points stand out. Direct democracy, and most particularly in its primitive forms, is a form suited to small areas and to communities with common interests and outlook. If it is applied to larger areas it tends to become overextended: inertia acts to keep people from undertaking the long and wearisome journey to a faraway assembly place, and in assemblies in which many different regional interests are at play against each other agreement is difficult to obtain. It is therefore not until "Representative Democracy" is developed that the general form of democracy can be successfully applied over large territories. The exceedingly primitive character of the Mesopotamian primitive democracy, which had not developed regular meetings such as are necessary for control of officers and maintaining long-range policies, and which was without such techniques of decision as majority vote, was clearly both a cumbersome and vulnerable institution and therefore easy to bypass.[57]

The second point of note is the emergence, or rather the radical and systematic extension, of a new type of power, that of the master of a house over his household. The "king" was a "great householder" (lú gal)[58] presiding over a "great house" (é gal), the palace. His forces consisted of his personal servants and retainers bound to him by exceptionally strong ties of dominance and obedience. As shown by the epic tale of the Death of Gilgamesh and, slightly later, by the royal tombs at Ur, some of the personal attendants of a king would follow him even in death.[59] The exceptional character of the relation shows also in the fact that the term "king" (lugal) is the only one available in Sumerian to express a master's complete control over his slave, an owner's over his house.

This tight power structure formed by the king and his household troops was, moreover, readily extendable in space, for the king could establish a new "great house" of his wherever he needed one. Thus gradually grew a system of royal households staffed by servants and retainers owing the king complete allegiance, as slaves their master, and standing apart from the citizenry of the town where they were stationed by their unfree status and their allegiance to the king only. They are the erín, or soldier-teams, which meet us through all of later history.[60] With such a pliable and powerful instrument at their disposal it is small wonder that the kings looked to force rather than to the difficultly achieved free agreement as the effective means of extending their domain.

4. *Dating.* As to the dating of the picture presented by the epics and epical tales a probable upper limit seems indicated by the archaeological evidence for widespread appearance of city walls in Mesopotamia in the period of Early Dynastic II.[61] At that time, therefore, general warlike conditions such as form the background for the epics would seem to have developed. To Early Dynastic II or the beginning of Early Dynastic III point further the date suggested by the traditions of the Sumerian King List for the heroes of the epics, Enmerkar, Lugalbanda, and Gilgamesh. More weight should be given, probably, to the independent evidence of the proper names occurring in the epics such as Agga, Gilgamesh, etc., which are current into the period of the Fara texts, i.e., early Early Dynastic III, and then disappear.[62] An approximate dating to Early Dynastic II and the beginning of Early Dynastic III will therefore probably not be much off.

VI. PALACE RECORDS FROM SHURUPPAK

The picture of the development of royal power and organization just given is confirmed in some measure by the records of a palace of early Early Dynastic III date found in Fara, the ancient Shuruppak. This palace was, as the records show, staffed with an abundance of personnel: chamberlains (uri), deputies (maškim), pages (sukkal), cupbearers (sagi), cooks (mu-haldim), musicians (lú-AD) and so on down to craftsmen of various kinds: smiths, basketryworkers, etc.

The number of persons within these ranks employed by the palace appears almost impossibly high; there were, for instance, no less than 144 cupbearers, 113 musicians and singers, 65 cooks, and so on.[63] When one compares the relatively modest-sized building which may be assumed to represent the palace itself[64] it is difficult to escape the impression that we are dealing, in these accounts, less with an actual mammoth household than with an organization essentially other in purpose—presumably military—which is merely structured along the lines of a household. That the palace did in fact serve a military purpose is indicated by the occurrence of accounting for repairs made by the craftsmen on war chariots coming and going from battle[65] and lists of troops under their officers "going to battle."[66]

As to the general political situation obtaining at the time of the archive we get only glimpses. Relations to the North are suggested by the fact that one of the war chariots repaired belonged to the chief mason (DÍM-gal) of Kish[67] and by the mention of a man from Sippar as belonging to the king.[68] Rather closer, however, are the ties with the South. "Visitors to the city" (uru(.šé) du) from almost all of the major cities of Sumer appear in the accounts as working for the palace and receiving rations. Responsible for them is not, as with the natives, a foreman, but a police constable (nimgir).[69] Of particular interest are two texts which deal with "people stationed elsewhere, Sumerians" (lú ba.durun Ke-en-gi), that is, presumably, troups of the Kengir League moved from Shuruppak to other points. These troups hail from Uruk, Adab, Nippur, Lagash, Shuruppak itself, and Umma, and since the order of the listing is the same in both texts Uruk, which heads the list, may well have been the leading city at the time.[70]

VII. THE STRUGGLE FOR PRIMACY

1. *Development by Beginning of Early Dynastic III.* The type of the "king" which we have seen develop in the epics was set in its essentials already in the late myths, when the temporary war leader sought permanence and, backed by his household troops, set himself up as supreme "righter of wrongs," jealously guarding against any similar rival powers arising within his sphere of influence. The drive toward

permanence led, aided by the prevailing warlike conditions, to a transfer of the basis of royal power from popular to divine election and, in the period we are now to consider, to a special royal mythology and to the establishing of dynasties. The correlated drive toward primacy in force led in its turn to perfection of the household troops with their special obedience into a standing army garrisoned in key cities, and to a basic policy of suppressing any rival power inside or outside the borders. This policy culminated in the kingdom of Kish, with its undisputed primacy of force in all of Sumer and Uri, an impressive object lesson in what the new royal power was able to do with force alone.

The limits of the achievement are, however, also apparent. What the early king strove for was primarily the prestige of superior force; effective rule, with its detailed administrative control, was still of the future. The superiority of force on which the king relied was, moreover, superiority by a small margin only. The tale of Gilgamesh and Agga shows that a single rebellious city might successfully challenge a king and his army—he must have been even more vulnerable to coalitions—and likewise that the king's garrisons in outlying cities and their commanders were not always to be trusted.[70a]

It is therefore not to be wondered at that with such a precarious hold over its dependencies the early kingdom of Kish failed to endure, and still less that it could not weld the country into anything like a national state. Toward the early middle of Early Dynastic III, when our first historical inscriptions begin, Sumer is again back to rival regional kingdoms and even smaller independent city-states under ensiks.[71]

2. *Regional Kingdoms.* The sources for the time from some generations before Urnanshek[72] and down to Eannatum[73] show a mosaic of such little kingdoms covering the southern part of Sumer. There is a kingdom in the Lagash region, another immediately to the west around Ur, a third on its northwestern border around Umma, and just north of the Umma kingdom lies a fourth one centered in Adab.[74] In the texts of the following times, of Eannatum and his successors, the mosaic of little kingdoms in the South is completed by the mention of a further small kingdom around Uruk,[75] and the Adab kingdom seems to have been replaced by one with its capital in Ki-dingir,[76] not far southward. In the northern part of the country,

the later Akkad, we get glimpses of more such kingdoms. There is one in Kish, one in Akshak very close to it, and one in Mari.[77]

Since our sources give a fairly complete picture of only one of these small regional kingdoms, that in the Lagash region, we may turn to it for information about how the development of the royal office had progressed.

The drive toward permanence and independence of the office, it may be noted first, appears to have made great strides. The ruler, whether king or ensik, is given his regional office by a deity. Ningirsuk handpicks the king of Lagash "out of 3,600 men," the goddess Nanshe likewise confers the responsibility of kingship over the Lagash region, and Inannak grants the highest office, that of king of Kish.[78] Correspondingly the king's responsibilities and duties under these offices, as stated in the texts, are almost exclusively to the gods rather than to men. The inscriptions tell of continuous building and rebuilding of temples; wars are fought at divine command to defend or to recapture divine property.[79] The choice of the king by the gods, and the favor in which they hold him, has been developed into a special royal mythology: the future king is engendered by a god, born and nursed with divine milk by goddesses.[80]

The drive toward perpetuation and institutionalization of the royal office witnessed to by the search for a divine basis for it also produced a development now clearly attested for the first time: the dynastic principle. In order to avoid the disruptive factional strife contingent on the choice of a new ruler when a king died, a successor, usually the ruler's son, sometimes his brother, was designated during the king's lifetime and was given a share in the royal duties. Thus Entemenak led the armies of Lagash against Umma during the lifetime of his father, Enannatum,[81] and similarly Lugal-kisalsi of Uruk joined his father, Lugal-kigennish-dudud, in presenting votive offerings to the gods.[82] How thoroughly the dynastic principle had become established is shown in Lagash, where the same royal family maintained itself over at least five generations.[83] Similar dynasties are found wherever we are able to check: in Umma, Ur, and Uruk.

The king's old role of "righter of wrongs" likewise shows a significant new facet. Urukagenak's famous reform texts, which date from the end of the period with which we are dealing, constitute our first evidence of the king's right at the beginning of his reign to issue a set of decrees—often abrogating existing traditional law—aiming at righting social wrongs. This traditional royal right to impose "rightings" (Sum. níĝ-si-sá, Akk. *mîšarum*) produced in time the imposing series of reform decrees known as the royal codes of Ur-Nammuk, Lipit-Eshtar, Hammurabi, and Ammizaduga.[84]

Turning to the military aspect of kingship the original role of the king as "defender" is much in evidence in the Lagash materials. Lagash was situated on the southeastern border of Sumer and was continually exposed to raiders from the mountain countries in the East, as well as to conquerors invading and crossing Sumer from the north and west. In addition it had on its hands a long-standing boundary conflict with its northwestern neighbor Umma. The rulers of Lagash were therefore on the whole glad if they could hold their own, often exchanging the title of "king" for the less pretentious one of ensik, and ready, even when comparatively strong, to renounce further territorial advance in treaties of nonaggression ("brotherhood"), as happened in the case of Entemenak.[85] Only once, and fleetingly, did a ruler of Lagash ever attempt a bid for the "king of Kish" title and the hegemony over all of the country which it implied.[86]

3. *Hegemony. Kings of Kish.* But that the Lagash kingship was thus restrained by circumstances from too ambitious ventures does not mean that the ferment of the drive for primacy in the kingship and the allure of the old example set by Kish had lost their power in this period; on the contrary, they appear to have dominated almost completely the central political stage and to be behind most of the moves in the heartland of Sumer along the Euphrates.

At some time not very much earlier than Ur-Nanshek of Lagash, Mesalim, a ruler whose capital is not known, succeeded in establishing hegemony over Sumer and took the title king of Kish.[87] A little later—perhaps during or just after Urnanshek's reign—the founder of the First Dynasty of Ur, Mesannepada, held the title.[88] It was not claimed, however, by his successors Aannepada, and Meskiagnunnak, even though both seem to have controlled the Euphrates up to Nippur,[89] so the power of Ur would appear to have met with successful opposition further north. This accords with the fact that Kish itself appears to have been an active and independent power in the earlier part of Eannatum's reign[90]—approximately the time of

Aannepada—and that, when its power seems to wane slightly a little later on, its place is taken by its northern neighbor Akshak.[91] Eannatum's records from the end of his reign mention a defensive victory against Mari,[92] which was situated on the Euphrates far off to the northwest. Since campaigns by Mari penetrating as far south into Sumer as to touch the Lagash area cannot have been numerous, it is rather probable that Eannatum's brush with the Mari forces is to be connected with a temporary hegemony of Mari over Sumer under Ilshu,[93] recorded in the Sumerian King List and confirmed by the finding of inscriptions of Ilshu and his daughter Nin-me-ta-bar-rí in Ur.[94] It may tentatively be placed at the end of Meskiagnunnak's reign.

The weakening of Kish referred to above was probably connected—as result or merely as a background—with a spectacular victory gained by one Enshakushannak "lord of Kengir" over Enbiq-Eshtar, king of Kish, of which we have records.[95] This victory, which should likely be placed either just before or just after the Mari interlude, resulted in Enbiq-Eshtar's captivity and in rich tribute being handed over by the city rulers of both Kish and Akshak. There is some reason to believe that Enshakushannak's capital was Uruk,[96] a city now apparently in the ascendency over Ur as the major power in the South. Uruk was ruled, at the time of Entemenak, the nephew and second successor of Eannatum, by Lugal-kigennesh-dudud, who, after concluding a brotherhood pact with the expanding Lagash kingdom, succeeded in establishing a personal union between Ur and Uruk—the famous "joining of the lordship and the kingship" which continued to be remembered in the royal titulary as late as Isin-Larsa times—and to gain eventually the title "king of Kish"[97] and complete hegemony in the country. The hegemony thus won remained in the latter's successor, Lugaltarsi. After Lugaltarsi, however, the title "king of Kish" disappears and Lugalzagesi, a ruler of Umma, who after Lugaltarsi was accepted as king by both Uruk and Ur, claims neither in his titles nor in his inscriptions rule over more than Sumer itself. The North seems to have reasserted its independence. That Lugalzagesi was not, however, without ambitions to regain the Kish title is shown by the fact that it was an effort on his part[98] to subdue the North which led to his fateful encounter with Sargon of Akkad and to his final defeat.

4. *Nature of the "Kingship of Kish."* To attempt to gauge, even in the most general way, what the various "kingships of Kish" here reviewed may have amounted to in terms of actual rule is, naturally, not an easy task. The possibility that on occasion such kingship may have been little more than the power to raid and to exact tribute unopposed cannot be ruled out, but in the majority of cases more positive contributions springing from the nature and ideals of the royal office as then developed can undoubtedly be assumed. The king's traditional role as supreme righter of wrongs would make his power available for enforcing settlements of disputes even among the most redoubtable contestants and thus for imposing something like a "king's peace." His close dependence on divine favor would correspondingly tend to find expression in a program of public building, temples, and in general support of the cult throughout his domain. Thus Mesalim is known to have intervened in the long and vicious boundary dispute between Lagash and Umma and to have imposed a settlement,[99] and inscriptions of his as well as later traditions testify to his rebuilding of temples and making votive offerings in various cities under him.[100] Such royal building activity may well have been a task of the king's garrison forces on the spot when they were not needed for war. Interesting is likewise the finding of an inscription of Ilshu's daughter in Ur. It suggests that even this far-distant conqueror was sufficiently concerned with the cult of Ur to dedicate his daughter as the human consort of its god Nanna, a custom amply attested for later rulers.[101]

The most complete picture of the aspirations of a ruler of all of Sumer is given, however, by Lugalzagesi toward the end of the period. Lugalzagesi tells us that: "When Enlil, king of all sovereign countries had given him (Lugalzagesi) the kingship over the nation (kalam), had directed upon him the eyes of the nation, made all sovereign countries wait upon him, and made (everybody) from where the sun rises to where the sun sets submit to him; then he (Lugalzagesi) drew (lit. directed) toward him (self as the supreme source of assistance) the feet of (everybody) from the Persian Gulf (along) the Tigris and the Euphrates to the Mediterranean; from where the sun rises to where the sun sets Enlil let him have no opponent. All sovereign countries lay (peacefully as cows) in pastures under him, the nation was (peacefully) watering (its fields) in joy under him, all the dependent rulers of Sumer (Kengir) and the ensiks of all independent countries bowed to him before the arbitral office (me-nam-nun(.na) (held by him) in Uruk.[102]

The king here described is, it will be seen, a ruler whose power and prestige are so great that he is influential not only inside his own borders, where his subjects look to him for help, but also outside the borders, where the independent, smaller countries are eager to accommodate his wishes. Since he cannot be challenged peace reigns everywhere and all other rulers, both inside and outside the nation, bow to his arbitration. It need hardly be pointed out, of course, that this picture is a highly idealized one, but then ideals are interesting for what they tell about major goals and envisaged means. The major goal here is quite obviously peace, a natural goal after centuries of incessant war between rival kinglets. The means envisaged are power, sufficiently great to rise above the rivalry and, by being unchallengeable, to end it. Made available to complainants both inside and outside the borders such power will be able to impose settlement of all disputes usually through the mere respect it inspires, but if necessary by use of force. In this goal and in the means envisaged for reaching it there is little essentially new. Not only are the main lines the same within our period from Mesalim to Lugalzagesi, but we still recognize in the picture of Lugalzagesi that of the young king of the later myths jealously suppressing rivals and making his power available as righter of wrongs. It is, however, extended from a purely regional to a national scale. Still absent are the safe foundations of power, a centralized and effectively controlled administrative system reaching from the king directly down into everyday local affairs and providing the necessary intensity of domination. That was left for Ur III to establish generations later.

VIII. CONCLUSION

1. *Summary of the Early Development.* We have tried to trace in these pages the early development of Mesopotamian political forms from a "Primitive Democracy" based on mutual agreement, designed to deal with crisis situations, and centering in a general assembly appointing temporary officers, to a "Primitive Monarchy" based essentially on force, striving for permanence, and centering in a king

who, through his superiority in armed might, holds out promise of internal and external peace, through his relations to the gods of a thriving economy. In concluding our sketch we should perhaps say a few words about the lines leading onward from these developments:

2. *Primitive Empire. Akkade.* The rulers of Akkade extended the pattern of primitive monarchy to cover an empire. Their huge standing army was used both for conquest and for garrisoning a network of army posts along the major highways of the empire.[103] Difficulties of control over their regional commanders soon developed, however, and beginning with Sargon himself the Akkade rulers had to face rebellion after rebellion at the heart of the empire, in Sumer itself. They achieved a precarious mastery of the situation through policies of destroying city walls in the internal parts of the empire,[104] thus leaving rebels no strongholds, by appointing only citizens of Akkade to higher administrative positions,[105] backing them with all-Akkadian garrison troops,[106] and by holding members of local ruling families as hostages in Akkade.[107] On the economic front—largely dominated by the concept of the king's charismatic powers—the king was raised under Naram-Sîn to the status of personal god of the capital,[108] but his relations with the gods seem to have deteriorated to a point where a widespread famine sent by them shook the empire to its foundations and opened the way for raiders from the mountains, the Gutians, who eventually took control.[109]

3. *Bureaucratic National State. Ur III.* When Utuhegal and the Third Dynasty of Ur ended the Gutian domination they renounced on the whole the larger goal of empire to solve instead the problem of continual internal rebellion which had vexed the Akkade kings. The top provincial civil administrators, the ensiks, became proper governors, entirely dependent on the king, and were moved at will from one post to another to minimize the danger inherent in too strong local ties.[110] Military affairs were out of their hands entirely and sorted under the king's garrison commandants, the šagubs, conflicts between the military and the civil administration being adjudicated by the courts.[111] A corps of royal messengers kept the king continually informed of all developments both inside and outside the borders, and regular diplomatic relations were maintained with the numerous minor principalities outside the realm.

4. *Dissolution into Regional Kingdoms. Isin-Larsa.* The fall of the

Third Dynasty of Ur, which must be given credit for having established a new concept of rule—the first bureaucratic national state—seems to have been due again to economic causes, the king's charismatic powers and favor with the gods proving unable to ward off a severe famine,[112] which loosened the hold of the central government. There followed a return to regional rule, the period of Isin and Larsa, ending in the ephemeral unification of the country under Hammurabi and Samsuiluna of Babylon.

5. *Catastrophe in South. Political Stagnation.* Under Samsuiluna and his successors the economic difficulties which had been growing in Sumer came to a head. A major and definitive catastrophe—probably a final salting up of the fields cultivated over millennia—practically depopulated the South and changed it into wasteland and marshes.[113] A long period of relative political stagnation descended upon Mesopotamia.

6. *The Assyrian Empire.* It is not until Neo-Assyrian times that important political developments again occur in Mesopotamia. The Neo-Assyrian empire, which—to judge by the name of its founder, Sargon, and from traditions about the Akkade rulers carefully preserved in Assyrian libraries—was in no small degree inspired by memories of the earlier Akkade empire, succeeded in developing a harsh, but not inflexible, effective policy of governing dependencies[114] and thus laid secure administrative foundations for central rule of the entire Near East from Mesopotamia to Egypt. It was these secure foundations, laid by the Assyrians, which made first the Persian, later Alexander's[115] empire possible and which are therefore a—perhaps the—major conditioning factor behind all of the following Hellenistic and Roman history and, insofar as empire conditions influenced the spread and organization of the early church, behind much of the medieval history as well.

9. Primitive Democracy
in Ancient Mesopotamia[1]

Words which embody the hopes, the fears, and the values of generations are likely to lose in clarity what they gain in depth. One such word is "democracy," which denoted a form of government and now stands for a way of life. It may not be amiss, therefore, first to make clear in what sense we intend to use the word before we plunge in medias res.

We shall use "democracy" in its classical rather than in its modern sense as denoting a form of government in which internal sovereignty resides in a large proportion of the governed, namely in all free adult male citizens without distinction of fortune or class. That sovereignty resides in these citizens implies that major decisions—such as the decision to undertake a war—are made with their consent, that these citizens constitute the supreme judicial authority in the state, and also that rulers and magistrates obtain their positions with, and ultimately derive their power from, that same consent.

By "primitive democracy," furthermore, we understand forms of government which, though they may be considered as falling within the definition of democracy just given, differ from the classical democracies by their more primitive character: the various functions of government are as yet little specialized, the power structure is loose, and the machinery for social coordination by means of power is as yet imperfectly developed.

We should perhaps add that the contrast with which we are primarily concerned is the one between "democracy" as defined

NOTE: First published in *JNES* 2 (1943) 159–172.

above, on the one hand, and "autocracy," used as a general term for forms which tend to concentrate the major political powers in the hands of a single individual, on the other. "Oligarchy," which so subtly merges into democracy and which so often functions in forms similar to it, can hardly, at the present stage of our knowledge of ancient Mesopotamia, be profitably distinguished.

AUTOCRATIC ORIENTATION IN HISTORICAL TIMES

The political development in early historical times seems to lie under the spell of one controlling idea: concentration of political power in as few hands as possible.

Within small areas, in town and township, this principle had been realized—or was being realized—to a very substantial degree during the first centuries of Mesopotamian history.[2] The country formed a mosaic of diminutive, self-sufficient, autonomous city-states, and in each such state one individual, the ruler, united in his hands the chief political powers: legislative, judiciary, and executive. Only he could promulgate and carry into effect new law;[3] he alone was personally responsible by contract with the city-god for upholding justice and righteousness;[4] as supreme commander of all armed forces, he led the state in battle;[5] and, as administrator of the main temple complex,[6] he controlled the most powerful single economic unit within the state.

But the momentum of the autocratic idea was still far from spent with the realization of this idea within small separate areas. It drove Mesopotamia forward relentlessly toward the more distant aim: centralization of power within one large area. Each ruler of a city-state was forever striving to subdue his neighbors, striving to become the one who would unite all of southern Mesopotamia into a single centralized state under a single ruling hand—his own. From before the dawn of history[7] through the soldier-kingdoms of Lugalzagesi and the early Sargonids to the highly organized bureaucratic state of the Third Dynasty of Ur, we watch these efforts toward ultimate centralization steadily grow in power, in intensity, and in efficiency.[8]

DEMOCRATIC INSTITUTIONS IN THE JUDICIARY IN POST-IMPERIAL TIMES[9]

To find in a world so singularly autocratic in outlook, propelled in its domestic and foreign policies by the one urge for concentration of power, institutions based on diametrically opposite concepts, is somewhat unexpected. Yet in the judiciary branch of government, as a heterogeneous, unassimilated block, appear, even in the latest period of Sumero-Akkadian civilization,[10] features of a distinct and democratic character.

Assyria. As a particularly striking example may serve the Assyrian merchant colonies in Asia Minor on the border of our cultural province.[11] Here in early post-Imperial times (Isin-Larsa period) the highest judicial authority was not vested in any one individual but resided in a general assembly of all colonists: "the colony, young and old,"[12] as it is called. This general assembly was called into session by a clerk at the bidding of a majority of its senior members. Characteristically the clerk was not permitted to act at the bidding of any single individual and was severely punished if he did so.[13]

The general assembly tried and decided lawsuits which arose in the colony, and even commissaries sent by the legal authorities of the mother-city Assur could not proceed, if they met with resistance on the part of a colonist, except by authority of this local assembly.[14]

Babylonia. Turning from the "republican"[15] Assyrian colonies to the Babylonia of Hammurabi as it is revealed some generations later in documents of the Old Babylonian kingdom, we are very naturally struck first of all by the degree to which royal power is there in evidence. Anybody can turn to the king with complaints; he looks into the matter and delegates the case to a suitable court for decision. At his service stands a corps of royal officials and "judges of the king," dealing out justice according to the "legal practice of the king."[16]

But it is worth noting that alongside of, and integrated with, this judiciary organization centered in the king stands another having its center in the Babylonian city. The city as such deals out justice according to its own local ideas of right and wrong.[17] Town mayor and town elders[18] settle minor local disputes; other cases—perhaps the more especially difficult or especially important ones—are brought before the town as a whole, the "assembly," for decision. Our sources furnish a vivid and interesting picture of the workings of this assembly; we shall comment, however, on two significant points only—its composition and its competence.

That the Old Babylonian assembly comprises, as already mentioned, the citizens of a given town or village is apparent from the use of "town" and "assembly" as alternatives in our documents. In the text *VS* VII, 149, for instance, after a report has been made "in the assembly of (the town) Dilbat," the ensuing actions are carried out "as Dilbat commanded." The assembly of Dilbat is thus equivalent to the town itself.[19] Similar evidence is given by the letter *TCL* XVII, 30. The writer of this letter needed a tribunal before which to compose a legal dispute; so he "assembled the town" (*a-lam ú-pa-ḫi-ir-ma*). His phrase—since the act *puḫḫurum*, "to assemble," produces a *puḫrum*, "assembly"—shows again that the town constitutes the assembly.[20]

In interpreting this evidence, there is naturally some danger of going too far. Though citizens[21] and therefore part of the *âlum*, "the town," women are not likely to have participated in the assembly.[22] Even the men may not always have put in an appearance in numbers which we should consider adequate representation of the citizenry. One inference, however, may be drawn from the fact that *puḫrum* can alternate with the highly comprehensive term *âlum*: participation in the *puḫrum* and in the judicial functions which it exercised did not constitute the prerogative of some small favored class or group; it must have been open to the citizenry at large. And this is borne out by a Babylonian proverb[23] which prudently, though with conspicuous lack of public spirit, warns:

Do not go to stand in the assembly;
Do not stray in the very place of strife.
It is precisely in strife that fate may overtake you;
Besides, you may be made a witness for them
So that they take you along to testify in a lawsuit not your own.

As will be readily seen, this proverb presupposes that anybody who happened along and has a mind to could "stand"—that is, participate—in[24] the *puḫrum*.

The competence of the Old Babylonian assembly is in general

that of a court of law.[25] A plaintiff may himself "notify the assembly" (*puḫrum lummudum*),[26] or the case may be delegated to the assembly by the king[27] or other high authority. The assembly investigates the case (inim-inimma igi-du$_8$),[28] hears testimony, and may send one of the parties and his witness to some temple to prove their testimony by oath.[29] Finally, it renders its decision (e or du$_{11}$ and *qabû*).[30]

The cases tried by the assembly were, as shown by the records which have come down to us, both civil cases and criminal cases.[31] The assembly had, as proved by one such record dealing with a case of murder,[32] power to pronounce sentence of death. Occasional infliction of punishment in the assembly may represent a survival from times when the people met in assembly as both judge and executioner at the same time. The Code of Hammurabi decrees in paragraph 202 that "if a man has smitten the cheek of a man who is his superior (or "his senior"?) he shall be given sixty lashes with an ox whip in the assembly." It is also worth noting that if a judge has committed fraud in the carrying out of his duties he shall make twelvefold restitution, and "in the assembly they shall make him get up from his judge's seat not to return (ever) to sit in judgment with judges."[33]

Of particular interest for the light it throws on the relation between these popular tribunals and the royal power is an Old Babylonian letter which shows that a man who had been arrested by a royal official for seditious utterances was placed before the assembly, where the charges were proved against him before he was committed to prison. Note also that the king, as already mentioned, may delegate cases to the assembly.[34]

As will be readily perceived, the judiciary organization here outlined is democratic in essence. Judicial powers are vested in the community as a whole, in an assembly open to all citizens. Such institutions are manifestly not of a piece with the period in which they are found—a period dominated by the very opposite principle: that of concentration of powers in the hands of one single individual. The question then arises whether these institutions represent new ideas which are just beginning to gain momentum or something old which has been retained from earlier times.

The first alternative seems not very plausible, since the entire drift of Mesopotamian political life and thought in the historical periods is wholeheartedly in the other direction. Throughout we find no signs of growing democratic ideas. The second alternative, therefore, seems the more likely: these judiciary institutions represent a last stronghold, a stubborn survival, of ideas rooted in earlier ages.

WIDER SCOPE OF ASSEMBLY IN OLDER TIMES

This inference is confirmed when we turn to the material which bears on earlier periods, for as we go back in time the competence and influence of the "assembly" appears to grow and to extend from judiciary functions to other, even more vital, aspects of government.

Tradition relating to times no farther back than those of the kings of Akkad already shows that the assembly deemed it within its authority to choose a king:[35]

> In the "Common of Enlil," a field
> belonging to Esabad, the temple of Gula,
> Kish assembled
> and Iphurkish, a man of Kish,
>
> . . . .
> they raised to kingship.

When we consult still older tradition, tradition concerning Uruk in the time of Gilgamesh, beyond the border line of history proper, we find the ruler scrupulously refraining from action in the matter of peace or war until he obtains the consent of the assembly, in which, therefore, internal sovereignty of the state would seem to be vested.

The tradition in question[36] relates that King Agga of Kish sent messengers to Uruk. Gilgamesh, lord of Uruk, is bent on resistance; but the decision apparently does not rest with him. He first approaches the senate, the elders of Uruk, to lay his proposal before them:

> Gilgamesh before the elders of his town
> spoke up. . . . .[37]

His address—urging reasons which are not yet entirely clear—ends in the plea:

Let us not bow to the palace of Kish; let us smite (it) with weapons![38]

The elders consider the proposal in their assembly:

> After an assembly had been established, the elders of his town
> gave answer unto Gilgamesh concerning it.[39]

This answer is in the affirmative, exactly repeating Gilgamesh's words
and ending in the same exhortation. It greatly pleases Gilgamesh:

(As for) Gilgamesh, lord of Kullab,

. . . .

at the word of the elders of his town his heart rejoiced, his liver was
    made bright.[40]

But he is not yet through; the men of the town must be heard on the
issue:

> Next Gilgamesh before the men of his town
> spoke up.....[41]

His plea here is a word-for-word repetition of the plea before the
elders, and the "men of his town," "after an assembly had been
established," answer it. With differently worded reasons they urge
the same course of action: "May you not bow to the palace of Kish;
let us[42] smite it with weapons." They add a declaration of confidence and faith, and Gilgamesh is again highly pleased:

On that day (as for) Gilgamesh, lord of Kullab,
at the word of the men of his town his heart rejoiced, his liver was
    made bright.[43]

Now the road is clear before him, and he immediately sets about
arming for the coming conflict.

    Here, then, we seem to have portrayed a state in which the ruler
must lay his proposals before the people, first the elders, then the
assembly of the townsmen, and obtain their consent, before he can act.
In other words, the assembly appears to be the ultimate political
authority.[44]

PROJECTIONS OF THE OLD ASSEMBLY INTO
THE WORLD OF THE GODS

    Since the traces of this older, democratic form of political organiza-
tion in Mesopotamia all point back to a time before the earliest

historical inscriptions, it would normally be impossible to gain closer insight into its details and workings simply because we lack sources for the time when it was flourishing. A peculiar circumstance, however, comes to our aid.

The Sumerians and Akkadians pictured their gods as human in form, governed by human emotions, and living in the same type of world as did men. In almost every particular the world of the gods is therefore a projection of terrestrial conditions. Since this process began relatively early, and since man is by nature conservative in religious matters, early features would, as a matter of course, be retained in the world of the gods after the terrestrial counterpart had disappeared. The gods, to mention only one example, were pictured as clad in a characteristic tufted (sheepskin?) garment long after that material was no longer in use among men. In similar fashion must we explain the fact that the gods are organized politically along democratic lines, essentially different from the autocratic terrestrial states which we find in Mesopotamia in the historical periods. Thus in the domain of the gods we have a reflection of older forms, of the terrestrial Mesopotamian state as it was in prehistoric times.

The assembly which we find in the world of the gods rested on a broad democratic basis; it was, according to the Adad myth in *CT* XV, 3, an "assembly of all the gods."[45] Nor was participation limited by sex: goddesses as well as gods played an active part in its deliberations.[46]

The assembly was usually held in a large court called Ubshuukkinna. As the gods arrived, they met friends and relatives who had similarly come from afar to participate in the assembly, and there was general embracing.[47] In the sheltered court the gods then sat down to a sumptuous meal; wine and strong drink soon put them in a happy and carefree mood, fears and worries vanished, and the meeting was ready to settle down to more serious affairs.

They set (their) tongues (in readiness) [and sat down] to the banquet;
They ate bread (and) drank(?) [wine].
The sweet drink dispelled their fears;
(So that) they sang for joy as they drank the strong drink.
Exceedingly carefree were they, their heart was exalted;
For Marduk, their champion, they decreed the destiny.[48]

The description is psychologically interesting. Here, as so often in Mesopotamian mythology, the important decisions originate when the gods are in their cups. In the toilsome earthbound life of the primitive Sumerians wine and beer were evidently necessary to lift the spirit out of the humdrum existence of everyday cares to original thought and perspective.[49]

The leadership of the assembly belonged by right, it would seem, to An, god of heaven and "father of the gods"; but with him or alone appears also Enlil, god of the storm. An or Enlil usually broached the matters to be considered; and we may assume—our evidence does not allow us to decide the point—that the discussion which followed would be largely in the hands of the so-called *ilū rabiūtum*, the "great gods" or, perhaps better, "the senior gods," whose number is said to have been fifty.[50] In this discussion it was the intrinsic merit of a proposal which gave it weight: wise counsel, testifying to "intelligence, profundity, and knowledge,"[51] is much admired; and ability to make the others listen to one's words is a prized gift.[52] Through such general discussion—"asking one another,"[53] as the Babylonians expressed it—the issues were clarified and the various gods had opportunity to voice their opinions for or against, at times espousing proposals which they later bitterly regretted. Such regrets befell Ishtar, who had supported the proposal to wipe out mankind with a flood, when she saw the results of the decision:

> Ishtar shrieks like a woman in birth pangs,
> The lovely voiced lady of the gods yells aloud:
> "The times before are indeed turned to earth,
> Because I myself in the gods' assembly
> Gave the ill counsel!
>
> How could I in the gods' assembly
> Give such ill counsel,
> To decree the fight
> For the destruction of my mankind?
> I alone gave birth to my mankind.
> Now they fill, like the spawn of fishes, the sea!"[54]

A group of seven powerful gods, "the seven gods who determine destinies"—that is, whose word is decisive—had, it would seem, the final say,[55] and when an agreement had at last been reached in this manner—voting is a technique of much later origin—it was announced by An and Enlil as "the verdict, the word of the assembly of the gods, the command of An and Enlil."[56] The executive duties, carrying into effect the decisions of the assembly, seem to have rested with Enlil.[57]

The functions of this divine assembly were in part those of a court of law. Here the crime of a man who destroys an inscription is taken up, and the deity to whom the inscription was dedicated speaks against him and "makes bad his case."[58] Here sentence was once passed on all humanity because the constant noise which they made was obnoxious to divine ears.[59] Another cause célèbre was against Enlil in his youth, when he was ostracized by "the fifty senior gods and the seven gods who determine destiny" for raping young Ninlil.[60]

But the functions of the divine assembly which go beyond those of a court of law are the ones that command our greatest attention: the assembly is the authority which grants kingship. Once, we are told, great danger threatened: Ti'āmat, the primeval waters, and her host of monsters planned war against the gods. The gods learned that

They are angry, they are plotting, they rest not night and day;
they have taken up the fight, they fume, they rage like lions;
they have established an assembly and are planning the combat.
Mother Hubur, who fashions all things,
has added (thereunto) irresistible weapons, has borne monster serpents
sharp of tooth, with unsparing fang;
she has filled their bodies with poison for blood.
Dragons grim she has clothed with terror,
has crowned them with glory and made them like gods,
so that he who looks upon them shall perish from terror,
so that their bodies shall rear up and their breasts not be turned
　　back.[61]

In this emergency young Marduk proved willing to champion the case of the gods, but he demanded absolute authority:

If I am to be your champion,
vanquish Ti'āmat, and keep you alive;
then establish an assembly and proclaim my lot supreme.

Seat yourselves together gladly in Ubshuukkinna,
and let me when I open my mouth (have power to) determine
    destiny even as you,
(so that) whatever I frame shall not be altered
(and) the command of my lips shall not return (void), shall not be
    changed.[62]

So the call to assembly went out, the gods gathered in Ubshuukkinna,
and there, to meet the exigencies of the situation, they gave Marduk
supreme authority:

Thou carriest weight among the senior gods,
thy status is unequaled, thy command is (like that of) Anu.
Marduk, thou carriest weight among the senior gods,
thy status is unequaled, thy command is (like that of) Anu.
From this day onward thy order(s) shall not be altered;
to exalt and to abase—this shall be thy power.
True shall be what(ever) thou dost utter, not shall thy word prove
    vain (ever);
none among the gods shall encroach upon thy rights.[63]

They acclaimed him king and invested him with the insignia of
royalty:

They rejoiced (and) did homage, (saying:) "Marduk is king!"
They bestowed upon him the scepter, the throne, and the *palû*;
They gave him an unrivaled weapon to smite the enemy, (saying:)
"Go and cut off the life of Ti'āmat
May the winds carry her blood to out-of-the-way places."[64]

Then, having armed himself, Marduk led the gods to battle with
Ti'āmat.[65]

    As the assembly is the authority which grants kingship, it can also
take it back. The Sumerians counted kingship as a *bala*, an office to
be held by each incumbent for a limited period.[66] Similarly kingship
would be given for a time to one city and its god; then it would be
transferred to another city and god. The period—to mention an
example—during which Inanna's two cities, Kish and Akkad, held
sway over Mesopotamia was "the term (*bala*) of Inanna."[67]

The authority which determines when such a royal *bala* is to end is the assembly, as may be seen most clearly in a group of texts dealing with the fall of Ur. Under its famous Third Dynasty, Ur had dominated all of southern Mesopotamia. Its rule ended tragically in a savage attack by invading Elamites which all but wiped out the city. Among the texts which deal with this catastrophe we may first quote one in which the god of Ur, Nanna, is complaining to his father, Enlil, about what has happened. His complaint, however, evokes only a cool response:

> Enlil [answere]d his son Sîn concerning it:
> "The deserted city, its heart, sobbing, wee[ps bitterly];
>   in it [thou passest] in sobs the day.
>   (But), Nanna, through thy own 'submission' [thou didst accept(?)]
>   the 'Let it be!'
>   By verdict, by the word [of] the assembly [of the] g[ods],
>   by command of An and Enlil [. . . .]
>   [was the] k[ing]ship of Ur [. . . . carried away].
>   Since olden days when the country was founded [. . . .]
>   [are] the terms of kingship [constantly changed];
>   (as for) its (i.e., Ur's) kingship, [its] term [has (now) been changed
>   for a different term]."⁶⁸

Though the text here quoted has suffered considerable damage, the view which it takes of the fall of Ur stands out, fortunately, quite clearly: it was the normal end of Ur's—and of Nanna's—term of kingship; and it was brought about in the proper fashion, by a decision of the assembly of the gods.

This same view, that Ur's fall was a normal end to its term of reign, decided upon beforehand by the gods, underlies also the lament *BE* XXXI, 3. It finds, however, its most vivid expression in the long *Lamentation over the Destruction of Ur*, composed only a few generations after the disaster.⁶⁹ There, toward the end of the fourth song, we are taken to the very assembly of the gods in which the decision was made and witness the passionate plea of Ningal, Nanna's consort, for mercy for the doomed city:⁷⁰

> Next unto the assembly, where the people were still (tarrying) on
>   the ground,

the Anunnaki gods being still seated after they had given the
    binding promise,[71]
did I verily drag (my) legs, did I verily stretch out (my) arms.
I verily poured out my tears before An;
verily I myself mourned before Enlil.
"May my city not be destroyed!" I said indeed to them;
"May Ur not be destroyed!" I said indeed to them;
"May its people not be killed!" I said indeed to them.
But An the while never bent toward that word;
Enlil with a "It is pleasing; let it be!" never soothed my heart.
The destruction of my city they verily gave in commission;
the destruction of Ur they verily gave in commission;
that its people be killed, as its fate they verily determined.

There can thus be do doubt that the assembly had power to revoke,
as it had power to grant, kingship.

CONCLUSIONS

Our material seems to preserve indications that prehistoric Mesopotamia was organized politically along democratic lines, not, as
was historic Mesopotamia, along autocratic. The indications which
we have, point to a form of government in which the normal run of
public affairs was handled by a council of elders but ultimate sovereignty resided in a general assembly comprising all members—or,
perhaps better, all adult free men—of the community. This assembly
settled conflicts arising in the community, decided on such major
issues as war and peace, and could, if need arose, especially in a
situation of war, grant supreme authority, kingship, to one of its
members for a limited period.

Such a form of government is, it may be added, in no way unique
but can be abundantly paralleled from elsewhere. We call attention
especially to the early European material, for which we may quote
two summaries by W. J. Shephard:[72]

Among all the primitive peoples of the West there seems to have
been some kind of popular assembly which shared with the tribal chief
or king and with a council of lesser chieftains the powers of social
control.

Again, still more striking:

> The significant political institutions of the primitive Teutonic tribes who overran Western Europe were a folkmoot, or meeting of all the adult males bearing arms; a council of elders; and in time of war a war leader or chieftain. All important questions, such as peace and war, were decided by the folkmoot. The council of elders prepared questions to be submitted to the folkmoot and decided minor matters. It was a rude form of democracy in which government was not differentiated nor law clearly distinguished from religious or social custom.

It need hardly be stressed that the existence of such close parallels in other societies lends strong support to the correctness of the reconstruction here proposed and promises valuable help in the interpretation of the fragmentary Mesopotamian data.

Love Song to King Shu-Suen

Youth of my heart, my beloved one,
 O that to sweeten still more
 your charms, which are sweetness,
 are honey—

Lad of my heart, my beloved one,
 O that to sweeten still more
 your charms, which are sweetness,
 are honey.

You, my own warrior, might march against me—
 I would flee before you, youth,
 into the bed.

O that you, my own warrior, might march against me—
 I would flee before you, lad,
 into the bed.

O that you might treat me, youth, with all sweetness,
 my sweet and darling one,
 with whom I would speak (words of) honey,
 on the quilt of the bed
 we would rejoice in your charm
 and all your sweetness.

O that you might treat me, lad, with all sweetness,
 my sweet and darling one,
 with whom I would speak (words of) honey—
 youth, I am in love with you.

Shu-Suen was the last king but one of the famous Third Dynasty of Ur. The love song to him, of which we here give the first stanzas, is placed in the mouth of his young and impatient bride. Who she was does not appear, but it is tempting to identify her with Shu-Suen's concubine Kubātum, who figures in another love song which has the form of a dialogue with the king. These two songs and two others that look as if they might be from the same hand stand, so far, alone in Sumerian literature; they were probably the work of a gifted woman at Shu-Suen's court, either Kubātum herself or a girl in her entourage. That her work appealed to Sumerian taste may be gathered from the fact that it was still copied by scribes in Nippur some three hundred years later. From Nippur, about 1700 B.C. or earlier.

10. The Reign of Ibbī-Suen

To the memory of O. E. Ravn,
Beloved Teacher and Friend

The reasons for the dire catastrophes that befell the city of Ur in the reign of Ibbī-Suen, the sudden collapse of its great empire and the later utter destruction of the city itself at the hands of barbarian invaders, were in no way doubtful to those who lived through the fateful years or to the generations that followed them: Nanna, the god of Ur, had lost favor with his father, Enlil, and with the divine assembly that governed all things. Therefore the kingship that Ur had held was taken away from it, and therefore the destruction of the city was decreed in the assembly of the gods.[1]

To the modern historian trying to read behind the sense of threatening divine will that speaks to him from the ancient documents, causes or, better, full circumstances are far less apparent. How an empire like that of the Third Dynasty of Ur—to judge by our sources the most efficiently organized structure of its kind before Assyrian times—could so quickly and so completely collapse without pressure from any enemy state or states of comparable magnitude is really quite puzzling.

Whether we shall ever see with full clarity what happened in those years only time can tell. These present lines—in spite of the title—will attempt no more than to adduce some of the documents that have a bearing on the collapse, and to point to events that may have been contributory factors. The full story, we are convinced, is still far beyond our grasp.

NOTE: First published in *JCS* 7 (1953) 36–47.

I

When Shū-Suen died in the ninth year of his reign he was succeeded—before year's end[2]—by Ibbī-Suen. The new king appears
to have been the son of his predecessor[3]; not, though, by the
energetic and active Abī-simtī,[4] but by a less well known wife,
Mama.[5] He married shortly after his accession to the throne a princess of royal blood, Geme-Enlilla(k),[6] and may thus have become
king while still an unmarried youth.[7]

There is no reason to believe that the accession of Ibbī-Suen meant
more than a change in the person of the ruler. The old and experienced grand vizier Ir-Nanna(k) continued in his key position[8]
and there were no spectacular changes of the other high officials of
the realm. On the eastern frontier the traditional policy of alternating
punitive expeditions and political marriages of princesses of the royal
house to important local rulers continued as before. The third year of
Ibbī-Suen is named after a punitive expedition against Simurrum in
the far northeast, the fifth after the marriage of princess Tukîn-ḫatta-
migrisha to the *ensi(g)* of Zabshali, whose country it had been necessary
to punish not so many years previously under Shū-Suen.[9] Substantial
taxes flowed in from the various parts of the empire[10]—apparently
quite smoothly—and literature flourished.[11]

Soon, however, serious trouble developed. Documents dated
with formulas of Ibbī-Suen are relatively frequent all over the empire
in the king's first two years. Then they begin to cease in one part
after the other, a clear indication that his authority was no longer
recognized there. In Eshnunna(k) the Ibbī-Suen datings stop with his
second year,[12] in Susa with his third,[13] in Lagash with his fifth,[14] in
Umma with his sixth,[15] and in Nippur, emblem of the kingship over
Sumer, with his seventh year.[16] Correspondingly we find that the
ensi(g)s of the realm default in their duty to deliver sacrificial animals
for the royal *eššešu* offerings for Nanna after the sixth year, and
there are indications of a general curtailment of offerings in the seventh
and following years.[17] From the date formula for the sixth year it is
clear that the inner security of the realm is seriously threatened, for
it has become necessary to repair the defenses of Nippur and Ur,
two key cities in the very heart of the empire.

What happened in these years is stated in general terms by the later omen literature, in which the unhappy events left clear-cut memories. The omens tell of the people acting on their own, overriding the authority of the king, of uprisings and rebellions, and of the breaking up of Ibbī-Suen's kingdom.[18]

But while it is thus fairly clear in a general sense what happened, the question of just how it happened is still difficult to answer. Some light seems to come, though, from an unfortunately fragmentary letter from Ishbī-Erra, the later ruler of Isin, to his king Ibbī-Suen, and from a few unpretentious account texts from Ur recently published by Legrain.

The Ishbī-Erra letter, written when he was still a servant of Ibbī-Suen, reports on a grain-buying expedition on which he was sent. The beginning of the letter reads:[19]

$^{Id20}I\text{-}bí\text{-}^{21d}Sú.en$ [lugal-mu-ra ù-na]^{22}-$^{\ulcorner}a^{\urcorner}$ ^{23}-$^{\ulcorner}du^{\urcorner}$ ^{24}
$^{II\check{s}\text{-}bi}$ ^{25}-Èr-ra ír-[zu na-ab-bi-a] ^{22}
kaskal Ì-si-in^{ki}-na ^{26} K[a-zal-lu^{ki}-šè] ^{22}
še sa$_{10}$-sa$_{10}$-dè $^{\ulcorner}á^{\urcorner}$(!?)-$^{\ulcorner}$šè$^{\urcorner}$(!?) $^{\ulcorner}mu^{\urcorner}$[-e-da-a]-$^{\ulcorner}ág^{\urcorner}$ ^{27}
5 KI-LAM 1(!) še(!): gur(!)-ta-àm ^{28} še sá-di ^{29}
20 gú kù-babbar ŠE-$^{\ulcorner}SA_{10}^{\urcorner}$-re ^{30}-dè ba-gar
inim Mar-tu lú ^{31}-kúr ^{32}-ra ^{33} šà ma-da ba(!?)-tu-ra
giš ì ^{34}-tuku-àm
144,000 ^{35} še: gur še dù-a-bi šà Ì-si-in^{ki}-na ^{36}
ba-an-tu-$^{\ulcorner}ur^{\urcorner}$ ^{37}
a-da-al-la-bi Mar-$^{\ulcorner}tu^{\urcorner}$ dù-dù-[a-bi] ^{38}
šà kalam-ma-šè ba-an ^{39}-t[u-ur ^{40}]
10 bàd-gal-gal didli-bi im-m[i-in-dab$_5$-dab$_5$] ^{41}
mu Mar-tu še-ba síg-ge ^{42} nu-mu[-e-da-sì-mu] ^{41}
u-gù-mu mu-ta-ni-ib ^{43}-[kal ba-bu$_7$-en] ^{41}
lugal-mu(!) 600 ^{giš}má-gur$_8$ a-ga-àm . . . ^{44}
etc.

To Ibbī-Suen, my king,[45] speak
what Ishbī-Erra, your servant, says:
I was charged with[46] an expedition
to Isin and Kazallu to buy grain.
Grain is (now) reaching the rate of one *gur* (for) each (shekel)
and the 20 talents of silver for buying grain have been spent.
Reports that hostile Martus had entered the plains[47]
having been received (lit. "heard")

> 144,000 *gur* grain (representing) the grain in its entirety
>> was brought into Isin.
> Now the Martus in their entirety have entered
>> the interior of the country
> taking one by one all the great fortresses.
> Because of the Martus I am not able to provide...........for
>> that grain,
> it has become too difficult for me, I shall winnow(?) it
> and may my king have 600 boats of 120 *gur* each caulked and..
>> etc.

After a broken passage Ishbī-Erra concludes his letter with the suggestion that he be charged with the defense of Isin and nearby Nippur.

The situation outlined in this letter is not a happy one. The nomadic Martu tribes have broken through the line of fortresses on the border, counted upon to keep them out, and are now pouring unchecked into the interior of Sumer, bent on killing and plundering. Ishbī-Erra, to safeguard the large supplies of grain he was sent to buy, has withdrawn into Isin and wishes to be put formally in charge of defending it and Nippur.

The Martu breakthrough reported in the letter helps us in dating it, for it can hardly be other than that sudden danger at the very heart of the empire that prompted the repairs of the city-walls of Nippur and Ur commemorated in the date formula for Ibbī-Suen's sixth year. Assuming that events mentioned in date formulas in this period belong to the year named from them[48] and that Ishbī-Erra's grain-buying expedition, which bought at the exceedingly favorable rate of two *gur* to a shekel, could only have taken place at harvest time, we may with a fair degree of probability assume that he wrote early in Ibbī-Suen's sixth year.

Ishbī-Erra's report of the Martus's movements makes it clear that after they had penetrated the border defenses their further progress into the center of the country was rapid and unchecked. We can therefore conclude that no major forces able to offer effective resistance were available in the interior, or, in other words, that Sumer was a victim of what is nowadays called a "Maginot-Line mentality": overly great reliance on a single line of outer defenses so that a breach will quickly develop into a debacle of catastrophic proportions.

That the Martu breakthrough was in fact a catastrophe, militarily, administratively, and—worst of all—economically, cannot be doubted. It would act to isolate the major cities of the country from each other and from the capital; the people, forced to seek protection behind city walls, had to abandon their fields to the invaders. Coming at the time that it did, just after the harvest, the fields could not be made ready for cultivation that year and a severe famine was accordingly to be expected.

For no other city were the dangers greater than for the capital Ur itself. The Ishbī-Erra letter shows that Ur was dependent for its grain on very substantial imports from the north. Not only was it now cut off, but it was cut off just before the supplies on which it had counted for the year could reach it.

The reply of Ibbī-Suen to Ishbī-Erra's letter, preserved in part on an unpublished tablet, A 7475, in the Oriental Institute, shows that he was well aware of his plight: Enlil has dealt in wrath with Sumer, its fields are no more. How could the commandant of *Bàd-igi-ḫursag-gá* have failed to meet the Martus?

How seriously Ur needed the grain which Ishbī-Erra was sent to buy is vividly suggested by the fact that Ibbī-Suen offers to pay double for it: Ishbī-Erra can remit it at the rate of one *gur* a shekel even though he bought it at two *gur* a shekel. In answer to the inquiries about transport and boats Ibbī-Suen refers Ishbī-Erra to help from northern *ensi(g)s*. Whether that would be practicable under the circumstances we have no means to judge. It does show, however, that the capital itself did not have the means for loading and safely convoying its much needed grain. At the end of the letter Ibbī-Suen grants Ishbī-Erra's wish to be charged with the defense of Isin and Nippur and so appoints him. As we know, he proved very effective in that task though eventually carrying it out in his own rather than in Ibbī-Suen's interests.

The economic threat to Ur, which is clear from the letters, was not a danger of a passing nature but the beginnings of a severe famine. As mentioned above, the *ensi(g)s* of the realm—whether by necessity or choice—ceased to send in their *bala* contributions to the royal *eššešu* offerings to Nanna with Ibbī-Suen's sixth year, and the plight of the city is clear from the general curtailments of the offerings. The full measure of the crisis becomes apparent in the seventh and eighth years. In those years, as we learn from the new account texts from Ur, one could buy for one shekel of silver no more than $2\frac{1}{2}$ sila of oil, or 5 sila of grain, or, if one was so disposed, $12\frac{1}{2}$ sila of fresh fish.[49] These are truly staggering prices such as are found nowhere else except in times of the most extreme famine and complete economic collapse.[50] The price of grain has climbed to the inconceivable rate of 60 times the normal.

If it is permissible to assume—as the evidence we have quoted seems to suggest—that a breakthrough of the Martu tribes in year five tended to isolate the capital both militarily and economically and thus to precipitate a famine which paralyzed its power of action almost completely, the political events of these years become more understandable. The major cities of the realm, thrown upon their own resources and looking in vain for the customary effective leadership from Ur, would almost necessarily drift toward independence, first in fact, eventually in name. Moreover, such elements of loyalty and habit as could have tended to slow the process must have been rendered largely ineffective by the very nature of events in Ur. In a community such as the Sumerian, which held its king personally responsible through his ritual acts, divine favor, and charismatic powers for fertility and prosperity,[51] the adverse effect on his prestige and authority of years of dire famine must indeed have been profound. The complete collapse of royal authority such as apparently took place cannot be considered an unlikely consequence.

II

That the crumbling of the empire and the final destruction of Ur itself were distinct happenings was argued by us in *AS* XI pp. 199–201 and later in *AJSL* 58 (1941), 219–221. This interpretation seems now to be generally accepted. The brief outline of the events of Ibbī-Suen's reign given in the last-mentioned place may be supplemented and corrected as follows:

(1) The "rebellion" against Ibbī-Suen was in all probability not one clear-cut event but rather a long-drawn-out process of disintegration beginning as early as the sixth year. Its beginning has been dealt with in the first part of the present paper. The argument for placing it in the tenth year offered in *AS* XI overrated our means of dis-

tinguishing date formulas from the time when the empire was still intact from those of the time when Ibbī-Suen was in fact only a petty ruler.[52]

(2) The process of disintegration and of the discarding of loyalties toward Ibbī-Suen appears to have been not only slow but uneven, many *ensi(g)*s, while probably long independent in fact, still professing a degree of formal loyalty. In the most interesting case, that of Isin, Ibbī-Suen's commandant, Ishbī-Erra, would appear to have considered himself formally independent and to have begun issuing his own date formulas not earlier than the twelfth year of Ibbī-Suen.

Assuming that Ibbī-Suen reigned twenty-four years—though twenty-five is also possible and perhaps preferable, see *AS* XI p. 123, note 331—the placeable date formulas of his reign, the date-list of Ishbī-Erra published by Taha Baqir in *Sumer* 4 112–113, and column ii of the date-list from Ur published in *UET* I as no. 292 may be correlated as follows on page 180:

We have restored three years at the beginning of the Ishbī-Erra date-list, assuming with Baqir that no more than two or three lines are missing and that the list, when complete, contained all of Ishbī-Erra's formulas.[53] Both assumptions seem to us to have a very high degree of probability. If they are correct the correlation shows that Ishbī-Erra began to issue his own date formulas in or around Ibbī-Suen's twelfth year.

One difficulty should be mentioned. The archive of a certain *Lugal-sag₆(-ga)* from Isin, discussed by Goetze in this journal p. 32, appears to cover the reigns of Ibbī-Suen and Ishbī-Erra in Isin fairly representatively; and the only Ibbī-Suen dates occurring are those of the first eight years of his reign. From this Goetze drew the natural conclusion that in Isin the Ishbī-Erra datings followed directly upon the last of the Ibbī-Suen dates present in the archive. The force of this argument depends, naturally, on the degree of certainty with which gaps, i.e., years not represented by dated documents in the archive, can be ruled out.

(3) The point in time at which Ishbī-Erra began effectively to push his claim to kingship over Sumer falls some time after he made himself independent. This may be deduced from a copy of an inscription of his, recently found at Nippur, in which he contents himself with the modest title of "king of his land" (*lugal kalam-ma-na*). A closer

UR

1 mu ᵈI-bí- ᵈSú.en lugal-àm
2 mu en ᵈInanna............
3 mu Si-mu-ru-umᵏⁱ..........
4 mu en-am-gal-an-na........
5 mu dumu-munus lugal.......
6 mu bàd gal Nibruᵏⁱ Uríᵏⁱ-ma..

7 mu-ús-sa bàd gal........
8 mu-ús-sa bàd .. mu-ús-sa-bi
9
10
11
12
13
14
15
16
17
18
19
20
21
22
23
24

gibil⌈egir⌉(?) (UET I 292 ii) ᵈI-bí-
ᵈSú.en in-sig
mu ᵍⁱˢšu-nir gal ᵈEn-líl..
mu bàd Ri-im-ᵈEn-líl.......
mu Nin-me-an-ki...........

ISIN

1' [mu Iš-bi-Èr-ra lugal-àm]
2' [............]
3' [............]
4' mu nin-dingir ᵈNin-líl[l].....
5' mu Uruᵏⁱ_Mar-tu...........
6' mu-ús-sa Uruᵏⁱ_Mar-tu.......
7' mu a-šà-gibil a-ta...........
8' mu nin-dingir ᵈIškur.........
9' mu bàd I-ti-il-pá-šu-nu.......
10' mu en GABA................
11' mu bàd Li-bur-ᵈIš-bi-Èr-ra...
12' mu-ús-sa bàd.............
13' mu ugnim Elam ù lú Su-a......
14' mu bàd Eš-tár-tá-ra-am-........
= 15' mu ᵍⁱˢšu-nir gal ᵈEn-líl......
= 16' mu bàd Ri-im-ᵈEn-líl......
= 17' mu Nin-me-an-ki......

Martu breakthrough. Ishbī-
  Erra correspondence.
Famine in Ur.

Ishbī-Erra independent.

Kazallu correspondence.

Invasion by Elam and Sua.
Ur falls, Ibbī-Suen captive.

Ur under Ishbī-Erra.

etc.

dating can be obtained from the fact that it was the threatened enforcement of the wider claim that gave rise to the Kazallu correspondence.[54] In this correspondence the *ensi(g)* of Kazallu reports, among other things, that Ishbī-Erra has built the wall of Isin called Itil-pāshunu, has undertaken successful military exploits, and has now sent ambassadors to him demanding allegiance. The mention of Itil-pāshunu, the building of which is recorded in Ishbī-Erra's date formula for his ninth year, places, on the correlation given above, the correspondence sometime after Ibbī-Suen's twentieth year, that is, in the last three years or so of his reign.

(4) The end of Ur came, as argued in *AJSL* (1941), 220–221, by a general attack on Sumer by Elam and the Sua people, who ravaged the city and led Ibbī-Suen away captive to Elam. It is to be noted that, as shown ibid., note 4, the Sua were a mountain tribe located in the vicinity of Susa. They can accordingly not very well be identified with either the Sutians[55] or with Subir / Subartu,[56] which occupied territory near or including that of the later Assyria.

As we may not identify the Sua people with Subir,[57] so we may not take the further step of identifying them with the Assyrians themselves and assume that the great Lamentation over the Destruction of Ur (*AS* XII) refers, not to the destruction under Ibbī-Suen, but to a later, somewhat hypothetical destruction at the hands of Ilushumma of Assur (thus Falkenstein, *ZA*, 49, 320–321). Rather, the mention of Elam and the Sua in the Lamentation over the Destruction of Ur as responsible for the destruction groups it firmly with the Ibbī-Suen Lament[58] in which they are also mentioned. And the correctness of historical tradition in the laments is vouched for by the date formula for Ishbī-Erra's thirteenth year, which shows this particular combination of enemies to have been present in Sumer at the time of Ibbī-Suen's final defeat.[59]

The attack on Sumer by Elam and the Sua through which Ur fell appears to have been an independent undertaking, not tied in with the inner Sumerian rivalry between Ishbī-Erra and Ibbī-Suen, which, incidentally, as far as we know, never led to open war between them. The suggestion offered by Falkenstein (*ZA*, 49, 74 and 77) that Ibbī-Suen and Elam were in coalition against Ishbī-Erra, and the related suggestion that Ibbī-Suen went to Elam, not as a captive but voluntarily because of pressure from Ishbī-Erra or because of differences with Elamitic troop contingents (*WO* 1 [1950] 385) both rest on Falkenstein's tentative attribution of the meaning "zur Seite stehen," "helfen" to the phrase *zà....tag* which occurs in Ibbī-Suen's letter to Puzur-Numushda of Kazallu (See *ZA*, 49, 62 and 63 line 36 of the letter, and comment ibid., 72). Such a meaning is, however, hardly compatible with the other passages for *zà...tag* quoted by Falkenstein or otherwise known to us. Doubts were raised already by Kramer, see apud Falkenstein, *ZA*, 49, 72 and *ANET* p. 481, note. 35.[60] The preserved formulas of Ibbī-Suen suggest a rather constant enmity with Elam, often flaring into open war.

(5) After the fall of Ur an Elamitic garrison was left on the site.[61] To this occupation we would assume the first line of col. ii in *UET* I 292 to refer: *gibil* ⌈*egir*⌉(!?) *ᵈI-bí-ᵈSú.en in-sìg* "a new one (i.e., year) after he smote Ibbī-Suen." The line is probably a note about a year rather than a proper year formula, for the locution *mu gibil egir* "new year after..." may be considered characteristic of everyday language and did not enter the language of the date formulas (which use *mu ús-sa*) until the latter half of the Dynasty of Babylon. Very soon, however, what was left of Ur acknowledged Ishbī-Erra's sovereignty and dated with Isin formulas from Ishbī-Erra's 15′ onward. This is shown by *UET* I 292, which represents the practice followed in Ur. The Elamitic garrison—left undisturbed for a while—was eventually made to surrender.[62]

APPENDIX

We assume that the lady Abī-simtī, who is mentioned frequently in the economic texts of the Ur III period, was the consort of Amar-Suena(k) and—after his death—of his brother and successor Shū-Suen. The earliest occurrence of Abī-simtī's name is, as far as we know, in a document from the sixth year of Amar-Suena(k) (Gen. *Tr.D.* 27). She is last mentioned in the second year of Ibbī-Suen (*UET* III 1504 viii 49).

During the reign of Amar-Suena(k), Abī-simtī is referred to chiefly in connection with religious rites, of which she seems to have been in charge and which were celebrated monthly on the *bubbulum* day (*u₄ ná-a*), the day when the moon is invisible. The sacrificial animals taken in charge by her for this purpose (*níg-dab₅ u₄-ná-a*)[63] are sometimes gifts from the king.[64] Whether she ever furnished the requisite animals herself is uncertain.[65] In the clear instances in which Abī-simtī furnishes animals (mu-tù A-bi-zi-im-ti)[66] through her "cattle feeder(?),"[67] the animals were put to other uses. The deliveries for the *bubbulum* day cluster—as one might expect—around the 26th of the month.[68]

In the last years of Amar-Suena(k), Abī-simtī begins to be mentioned also as GÌR official in transactions involving the paying out of sacrificial animals for offerings. The gods and cult places in question are Nin-ḫursaga(k) (Oppenheim, *Eames Coll.* O 8, dated to A.S. 8 vii), the gate of the Giparu, and Nana in Ur (ibid., E 6 dated A.S. 9 iii). In the following reign of Shū-Suen her activity as GÌR official predominates and the references to the *bubbulum* rites cease. She acts as GÌR for offerings to Allatum in the palace (Gen. *Tr.D.* 16 dated Š.S. 1) and for Inanna of Zabalam (Hackm. *T.D.* 31, dated Š.S. 3; Schneider *An. Or.* VII, p. 241 dated Š.S. 4).[69]

Of various other references to Abī-simtī one may quote: Nesb. *SRD* XV (*sá-dug₄* for A. dated A.S. 2), Gen. *Tr.D.* 27 (A.S. 6), Langdon *TAD* 28 (*u₄ A-bí-zi-im-ti ᵈSataran in-da-a* "when A. .... Sataran" Š.S. 2), Jean, *SA* XLII (*5 udu ŠE é-ḫatim igi-guru₆ é Á-bí-la-ša-šè A-bi-zi-im-ti šu bí-in-ús,* "5 grain-fed sheep of the 'kitchen' Abī-simtī commandeered(?) for the inspection of the house of Awīlasha" Š.S. 3), Schn. *DDU* 234 (hides of sheep and goats to A. *mu giš-kin-ti-šè,* "for the craftsmen"). Note also *ITT* 3802 rev. 5. According to *UET* III 1509 r. i, Š.S. 4 and ibid., 1757, date lost, she had her own weaver.

The texts mentioning Abī-simtī make it clear that her position in the reigns of Amar-Suena(k), Shū-Suen, and Ibbī-Suen was that of a queen. Her deliveries were effected through the "cattle feeder(?) of the queen." In A.S. 8 (Nesb. *SRD* XIX, Legr. *TRU* 126, and *Nik.* 488) *Bí-zu-a,* who is styled "sister of the queen" (*nin nin*[70]) in Gen. *T.D.* 5484, A.S. 5, is probably her sister since she is mentioned later as "balag singer" (*balag(?)-di(?)*) of Abī-simtī the queen (*UET* III 1504 viii, I.S. 2 and 1505 ix, I.S. 1). In the texts from Shū-Suen's reign she is designated as queen (*nin*) in Hackm. *T.D.* 31, dated to Š.S. 3 and in *UET* III 1509 r. 1 dated to Š.S. 4. She retained that title under Ibbī-Suen, when she was presumbly a dowager queen, see *UET* III 1505 and 1504 dating from I.S. 1 and 2 respectively.

While there can thus be no no reasonable doubt that Abī-simtī was a queen there is some question as to which king or kings were her consort. We assume, as mentioned above, that she was the consort first of Amar-Suena(k) and later of Shū-Suen. We base this on the text Chiera *SRT* 23, which seems to us to mention her as a consort of Shū-Suen's and on the occurrence of her name with the title queen already under Amar-Suena(k), which would suggest that she was at that time married to him.

A different opinion based on a different interpretation of *SRT* 23 is held by Falkenstein. He assumes that Abī-simtī was the consort of Shulgi(r) and the mother of Shū-Suen. His interpretation of *SRT* 23 is given in *WO* 2 (1947) 44, where he translates the beginning of the text, on which his argument is founded, as follows:

"Den 'Reinen' hat sie geboren, den 'Reinen' hat sie ge[boren],
  den 'Reinen' hat die Königin geboren,
  den 'Reinen' hat Abīsimtī gebo[ren],
  den 'Reinen' hat die Königin geboren.
  Meine (Herrin), die mit (ihren) Gliedern Gefallen erweckt, meine
     Abīsimtī,
  meine (Herrin), die mit (ihrem) *Haupt* in.........ist, meine Herrin
     Dabbatum,
  mein (Herr), der mit (seinem) Scheitel [in.....] .... dasteht,
     mein Šūsîn,
  mein (Herr), der mit (seinem) Wort [...................], mein
     Sohn Šulgirs."

Assuming that "der 'Reine'," said in ll. 1–4 to have been born by Abī-simtī, is Shū-Suen, whom l. 8 considers as the son of Shulgi(r), Falkenstein concludes that Abī-simtī must have been Shulgi(r)'s consort.

Our different interpretation takes as point of departure the fact that *SRT* 23 is said to be a *bala-bala-e*, i.e., a "dialogue,"[71] and that its text therefore must likely be distributed onto different speakers. We recognize a male speaker in ll. 1–6, which are in *Eme-KU*,[72] and a woman replying to him in ll. 7–22, which are in *Eme-sal*.[73] In the last lines of the text, finally, ll. 23–27, we have again *Eme-KU*.[74]

In the male speaker of ll. 1–6 we would see Shū-Suen himself, for the reply to these lines, ll. 23 ff., is addressed to him. Conversely, since the speech of ll. 1–6, according to l. 6, seems to be addressed to the lady Kubātum,[75] we assume that she is the one who answers. In the lady Kubātum we see with Falkenstein the *lukur* (SAL-ME) of Shū-Suen, Kubātum, who is mentioned on a necklace from Uruk (Falkenstein, *WO* 2 [1947] 46. A *lukur* was not allowed to have children and would therefore often provide her husband with a concubine for purposes of procreation.[76] We are inclined to see a reference to Kubātum's status as *lukur* in Shū-Suen's metaphor for her "my warpbeam on whom no warp may be placed," contrasting with his metaphor for Abī-simtī, who has just had a child, "my cloth beam of pleasing cloth." The concubine whom she had provided for Shū-Suen was perhaps the tapstress mentioned by her in l. 19[77] and recommended to Shū-Suen for her physical and other charms. We would accordingly read and translate the beginning of *SRT* 23 as follows:

> *kù-ga-àm in-tu-ud kù-ga-àm in-t[u-ud]*
> *nin-e kù-ga-am in-tu-ud*
> *A-bi-zi-im-ti kù-ga-am in-tu-ud*
> *nin-e kù-ga-àm in-tu-ud*
> *giš-gi-na túg nam-sa₆-ga-mu A-bi-zi-im-ti-mu*
> *giš-sa₁₁-du túg ⟨dun-⟩dun na-gál-[la-]mu nin-mu Ku-ba-tum*
> *suḫur-e.. .... ..-gub-ba-mu ù-mu-un ᵈŠu-ᵈSú.en-mu*
> *ka ma........ .. ...-mu ṭu-mu ᵈŠul-gi-ra-mu (etc.)*

(Shū-Suen:)
"As a pure one[78] she has given birth, as a pure one she has given birth,
As a pure one the queen has given birth,
As a pure one Abī-simtī has given birth,
As a pure one the queen has given birth.
(She who is) my cloth beam[79] of pleasing cloth, my Abī-simtī,
(know this) O my (poor) warpbeam[79] on whom no warp may be
    placed, my lady Kubātum!"

(Kubātum:)
"O my ...., my king Shū-Suen!
O my ...., my son of Shulgi(r)!
(etc.)"

In the remainder of the text Kubātum, after her introductory address to Shū-Suen in ll. 7–8, alludes to gifts of personal ornaments (a golden pin, a lapis-lazuli seal, and rings of gold and silver) which Shū-Suen has given her because she broke out in jubilation at the news of the birth,[80] and she pleads with Shū-Suen that he make his gifts to her (of personal ornaments) attractive[81] so that she will catch his eye. After blessing Shū-Suen[82] she enlarges, as mentioned above, upon the charms of her handmaiden and recommends her to Shū-Suen. Perhaps she was the concubine through whom Kubātum hoped vicariously to equal Abī-simti's feat and to provide (*šuršû*) for Shū-Suen the sons she could not herself bear. The text ends with praise of Shū-Suen in *Eme*-KU, spoken perhaps by a chorus of courtiers or singers.[83] The final attribution of the text to the goddess Baba means presumably that it had found a place in her cult. Possibly Kubātum had connections with that goddess.

11. The Assumed Conflict Between the Sumerians and Semites in Early Mesopotamian History

According to accepted views the early history of Mesopotomia is essentially the history of a racial conflict; its events represent stages in a deadly struggle between two inimical racial groups, Sumerians and Semites. In that struggle the Semites, who could draw on racial reserves in Syria and Arabia, came out victorious. After a long-drawn and bitter fight lasting through generations they defeated, under their gifted leader Sargon, the Sumerians, who were forced thenceforth farther and farther south. Except for a short-lived Sumerian comeback under the Third Dynasty of Ur, that victory made the Semites masters of Babylonia forever after.

How thoroughly this view dominates at present accounts of Mesopotamian history may be seen from headings in Breasted's *Ancient Times* of 1935;[1] they are:

The Lands and Races of Western Asia
Rise of Sumerian Civilization in the Age of the City-kingdoms and the Early Struggle of Sumerian and Semite
The First Semitic Triumph: the Age of Sargon
Union of Sumerians and Semites: the Revival of Ur and the Kings of Sumer and Akkad
The Second Semitic Triumph: the Age of Hammurapi and After

Every phase is here presented in terms of racial conflict, the fight for supremacy between Sumerians and Semites constitutes the main theme.

NOTE: First published in *JAOS* 59 (1939) 485–495.

Now it must always be the fate of historical theories, however widely accepted, to be tested and retested as new material widens the horizon of the historian; so inasmuch as a considerable amount of new material has come to light since the theory stated above was first formulated, it seems indeed timely to test whether older Mesopotamian history actually centers around a racial conflict. Such a test will naturally have to concentrate on the period now called "The First Semitic Triumph," the age of Sargon of Akkad; for here, where according to present opinion the two races after long preliminary struggles clash in a decisive battle, we should, if anywhere, find clear lines. The fundamental theme—Sumerian versus Semite—must stand out supreme.

Stripped of all incidentals, the events of this period may be summarized as follows: Lugalzagesi, ruler of Umma, a small Sumerian city-state in the South, began his spectacular career by attacking and practically destroying the neighboring city-state of Lagash, burning and plundering its temples.[2] Next, possibly through other similar victories, we find Lugalzagesi as king of the important center Uruk.[3] The complete defeat and destruction of the city Kish in northern Bablyonia should in all probability also be ascribed to him.[4] His position as undisputed master of the country was officially recognized by the Enlil temple in Nippur.[5] Lugalzagesi's downfall was wrought by a former cupbearer of the king of Kish, Sargon, who had founded a new city, Agade.[6] In a series of battles Sargon succeeded in defeating first Lugalzagesi and afterwards other important city rulers, such as the rulers of Ur, E-Ninmar, and Umma.[7] He thus took over the dominating position which Lugalzagesi had held, and was likewise recognized by Enlil in Nippur.[8]

The question which we have to decide is this: Does this series of events, notably the war between Lugalzagesi and Sargon, represent a long-brewing decisive clash between the two races which formed the population of Babylonia—Sumerians and Semites—or is it merely a fight between purely political units, two city-states vying with each other for power and influence? In trying to answer this question let us consider first the authority of the two leaders, Lugalzagesi and Sargon, as they themselves express it in their titles. That should give us an indication concerning the nature of the groups they were leading—whether racial or political.

We find that Lugalzagesi designates himself first as king of a city, Uruk, then, in a second title, as "king of the land."[9] He has no titles indicating leadership of a racial group such as "leader of the Sumerians." Similarly, Sargon designates himself first as a city king, king of Agade, king of Kish, and secondly also as "king of the land."[10] There is no title such as "leader of the Semites." The groups which our two dominant figures are leading are thus, according to their titles, purely political: first a city-state, then a political-geographical entity, the land.[11]

The absence of any racial grouping shown by these titles becomes still more noticeable when we turn to the inscriptions of Lugalzagesi which we possess. Among them is one that had once been carved on a statue of Lugalzagesi himself, which stood in the temple of the chief Sumerian deity, Enlil, in the thoroughly Sumerian city of Nippur.[12] That inscription is written in Semitic! Would the leader in a bitter racial fight, writing on a statue of his own in the temple of his own god in his own city, use the language of his hated racial enemies? Is it not more natural to assume that no racial conflict existed and that Akkadian accordingly was considered as good a medium for expressing one's thoughts as Sumerian?

To the same conclusion leads the evidence from the northern part of the country, the names of the rulers of Kish in the period with which we are dealing. We find here a Sumerian queen, Ku(g)-ᵈBaba,[13] who gives her son a Semitic name, *Puzur-ᵈSîn*. *Puzur-ᵈSîn* in turn gives his son a Sumerian name, Ur-ᵈZababa(k), and this Sumerian Ur-ᵈZababa(k) employs a Semitic vizier, *Šarrum-kîn*.[14] Such interchange of Sumerian and Semitic names within the same family[15] can only mean that racial differences were of little importance to the people and that Sumerian and Semitic names were considered of equal standing.

Turning now to the war itself between Lugalzagesi and Sargon we again find evidence which proves incompatible with the idea of a racial struggle. The pantheon of the Semites in Mesopotamia can be pieced together from Old Akkadian proper names without difficulty. Sîn, Shamash, Eshtar, Ea, and a few others were the gods whom the Semites worshiped. If Sargon fought his battles as leader of the Semitic race, these gods should therefore be the ones who led him and his Semites on to victory and supported his cause. Actually, however, not a single one of them seems to have taken any interest in his fight. More puzzling still, the deities who did help him and indeed all those who appear in closer relation with him were Sumerian. We find in his inscriptions Inanna, An, Enlil, and Sargon's personal god, ᵈA-MAL.[16] It was Enlil who "judged" Sargon's "case" and made him undisputed master of the country, it was to him that Sargon presented the captured Lugalzagesi as trophy, and it is as his chief representative on earth, as ensi-gal ᵈEn-líl, that Sargon appears in the inscriptions.[17]

Can we believe that the gods of the Semites would play no part whatever in this all-important struggle of their people against the Sumerians? Can we believe that the Sumerian gods should have actively supported their deadly enemies, the Semites, and helped them to defeat and subdue their own worshipers, the Sumerians? Is it not perfectly clear that what the sources show is not a racial grouping: Semites with Semitic gods against Sumerians with Sumerian gods, but a purely political fight: two city-states, Agade and Uruk, bidding for hegemony in Babylonia? It is those purely political entities, Agade, Uruk, Babylonia, which are reflected in the deities involved.[18]

We may now leave the strictly contemporaneous sources to consider the impression which our events left upon the immediately following generations. How did this fight go down in history and literature? Do we find Semitic compositions glorifying the triumph of their race amidst Sumerian works lamenting Sumerian defeat and cursing the hated enemies?

We are fortunate in that we possess a Sumerian literary composition which has for its subject the rise and downfall of Sargon and his dynasty.[19] Nothing could be more fitting to show how the Sumerians felt about those rulers, no theme would more naturally serve as a vehicle for the hate which the Sumerian author should harbor against the oppressors of his race and for the "Schadenfreude" which should fill him when that dynasty was overthrown.

Yet the text has no vestige of such feelings. On the contrary, we find sympathy where we should have animosity. The text begins with a historical exposé: "When the displeasure of Enlil like the Bull of Heaven had killed Kish, when like a great ox it had trampled.... Uruk in the dust, and then and there(?)[20] Enlil had given to Sargon,

king of Agade, lordship and kingship from the south to the north"
(1–6) and goes on to tell how Inanna, the goddess of Agade, strove to
make her city prosperous (7–24). She filled Agade with gold, silver,
and precious stones (25–27), to its people she gave wisdom, gladness,
and military prowess (29–37). All lands had peace and security (38 f.).
The king shone like the sun on the throne dais in Agade (40 f.). The
city wall of Agade towered like a mountain range up toward heaven
(42). Inanna threw open the city gate,²¹ comparable—from the
traffic flowing through it—to the Tigris where it flows into the sea,
and precious wares poured into Agade from all the world (43–50).
The dependent city rulers and administrators sent the tribute straight
in,²² monthly and yearly, and it grew in the palace of Agade like
rising waters²³ (50–54). Inanna, however, for unknown reasons²⁴
decided to abandon the city. Agade was attacked, and before a fort-
night had passed, the kingship had been given elsewhere (55 ff.).

There is clearly no racial feud in this text. Right from the beginning, where the rise of Agade is mentioned as the last link in the series
Kish-Uruk-Agade, i.e., as one of three city-states which gained
supremacy in Babylonia, it is clear that the author is describing a city-
state at the height of its power, not one race triumphing over another.
There can be no doubt that he is in full sympathy with Agade, with
the riches which came to it, with its wise, joyous, militant inhabitants,
and with the peace and security which then reigned. He is certainly
not describing the rise and downfall of a hereditary, hated racial
enemy.

Written when the Agade kings were no longer in power, as a treatment of the rise and fall of these Semitic conquerors by one of the
conquered Sumerians, the text which we have here quoted can be
counted on to give a true picture of Sumerian feelings. As we have
seen, it shows only friendly feelings. There is no animosity, not
even indications that the Agade kings were considered strangers,
their hegemony different from the previous hegemonies of Kish and
Uruk. And indeed, this total lack of hatred or even animosity is
shared by all other Sumerian texts known to us and is obviously
incompatible with the idea of a racial struggle. The struggle supposed
to form the keynote to Mesopotamian history would, if the accepted
view were true, be at once a racial and a civil war. Yet we can comb
the entire Sumero-Akkadian literature without finding a single

expression of animosity, no "evil Semite," no "wicked Sumerian."

Consider for a moment this absence of animosity, the Sumerian writer's wise and peaceful Agade, and compare then the outburst after a "racial war" of much smaller proportions, but one which at least was real, the war against the Gutian conquerors:[25]

> Gutium, a stinging viper of the mountains, an enemy of the gods, ... who filled Sumer with evil, took the wife from him who had a wife, the child from him who had a child, who established iniquity and wickedness in the land.

Here is all the hate and all the bitterness for which we looked in vain in the presumed racial conflict between Sumerians and Semites.

Reviewing the evidence, we can thus state that in this allegedly racial conflict the leaders represent themselves in their inscriptions as leaders of political units, not as leaders of racial groups. The Sumerian leader, Lugalzagesi, writes in Semitic in the Sumerian temple of the chief Sumerian god, Enlil, in the Sumerian city of Nippur. Sumerian and Semitic names are given indiscriminately within the same royal family. The Semitic gods stand by passively and take no part in the decisive struggle of their race. The Sumerian gods actively support their racial foes and lead the Semites on to victory over their own worshipers. No single trace of animosity between Sumerians and Semites can be found anywhere in the texts; on the contrary, Sumerian writers describe the rise of their supposed oppressors with sympathy as a golden age.

We must accordingly abandon the idea of a racial war. The Semitic population was very likely to a large extent formed through constant filtering in of single families from the desert. It is obvious that such single families, settling and adapting themselves to life in the city or on the farm, would very soon feel as citizens of the city-state to which they had happened to immigrate and where they had become established. They would not constitute a common group, united across existing political boundaries. Semites and Sumerians lived thus, according to all the texts teach us, peacefully side by side in Mesopotamia. The wars which shook that country and the aims for which its rulers fought had nothing to do with differences of race; the issues were purely political and were determined solely by social and economic forces.[26]

12. An Ancient Mesopotamian Trial for Homicide

INTRODUCTION

The picture we can form of the early legal development in Mesopotamia and of the processes operative in it is gradually becoming
clearer. From the oldest times, it would appear, justice was normally
dispensed by local assemblies of villagers and townsmen, who judged
according to a body of traditional unwritten common law with which
everybody was familiar. How far the law that these assemblies
administered was real law in the sense that it was backed by force
or the threat of force is rather questionable. In certain cases involving
capital punishment such backing may have been present since the
assembly probably executed its own verdict by mob violence; in
others it perhaps depended for enforcement of its judgment on some
powerful individual in the community who had agreed beforehand
to sponsor the weaker party, but in a great many cases it must have
relied mainly on the general social pressure of public opinion. In
large measure the early courts must therefore have had the character
of mere courts of arbitration and they retained—except possibly for
a brief period under the Third Dynasty of Ur—much of that character
down to the time of Hammurabi and his successors.[1]

Into the relatively static setup which we have described the political
development projected in the Early Dynastic period a powerful
instrument for legal change: the king. Kingship seems to have

NOTE: First published in *Studia Biblica et Orientalia* III, *Analecta Biblica et Orientalia* XII
(Rome, 1959) 130–150.

achieved a fair degree of permanence and institutionalization in Mesopotamia during that period and the king—besides his central function of war leader—appears to have had from the beginning also certain general responsibilities for the peace and contentment of the society which he served. Old traditions preserved in myths and epics show that the king's aid could be enlisted in cases of grave wrong to individuals, and with the passing of time the king proved willing to make his power available more and more extensively to underpin justice. By the time of the Dynasty of Agade royal judgments were safeguarded by severe monetary sanctions,[2] and the use of oaths by the name of the king in private contracts, which appears at the same time, can have had no other purpose than that of bringing royal punitive power to bear in the event of a breach. The same type of oath by the name of the king was used later, in the Isin-Larsa period, to shore up court decisions accepted by the parties, decisions which would otherwise have been without forcible sanctions. Also attested for the Isin-Larsa period is the characteristic function of the king as assigner of lawsuits brought to his attention to suitable courts for trial. This function almost certainly traces back to an earlier function as sponsor; the king's power made him the ideal person to induce courts to accept cases for which means of enforcing the decision would otherwise have been lacking.

By thus in various forms making his power and influence available as backing for decisions and commitments under the common law the king became a force contributing toward the gradual transformation of the nature of the common law from being essentially a body of ethical rules backed mainly by the pressure of public opinion to becoming more and more a body of legal rules in the true sense, backed by force and the threat of force.

The same vague original responsibilities of the king for peace and contentment among his subjects to which we traced his later activities in support of the common law were in all probability the source also of a different, not less interesting, royal function, that of modifying and changing the common law. At the beginning of a reign a new king would often promulgate a decree of "equity" (níg-si-sá, Akkadian *mîšarum*) which had for its aim the alleviation of social conditions felt to be unjust or unfair. Since such conditions were often hallowed by time and intimately connected with practices tolerated by the common law, an "equity" decree would frequently interfere with existing law, modifying or even abrogating it in the interest of the general welfare of the community. The earliest such decree known to us, the Reformtexts of Urukagina, appears as a contract concluded between the new king and the chief god of his city. However, since kingship in older times was an elective office it is reasonable to surmise that originally, in not a few cases, the content of such "equity" decrees would reflect closely wishes and demands set forth in the popular assembly which had chosen the king. Due in great part to recent discoveries we can now follow these decrees from Urukagina over Ur-Nammu, Lipit-Eshtar, to Hammurabi and beyond. They comprise what we traditionally call the Mesopotamian law codes, including the most famous of them all, the great Code of Hammurabi. But they are, of course, very far from being codes in the proper sense of the word, codifications of existing law; rather, they are the opposite: statements of desirable modifications and changes in the law meant to compete with and to supersede it with the help of royal authority. The degree to which in individual cases they were successful and were able to win out against the ingrained traditional concepts and formulations of the common law is at our present stage of knowledge very much an open question.[3]

While our sources for the royal "equity" decrees, the "codes," have increased significantly and gratifyingly in recent years, giving us better insight into what we must now see as a powerful influence at work on the common law from the outside, as it were; our sources for the common law itself, court records, contracts, and other legal documents, have shown no comparable spectacular and significant gains. This is in many respects to be regretted, for one would imagine that increased knowledge would show that also inside the common law forces for change and development were at work and that royal decrees were not the only source of new law. One would in this connection think first, perhaps, of the popular assemblies which served as courts and of the opportunities they must have offered for discussion and divergence of opinion among the laymen who constituted their membership. Here if anywhere, one would surmise, new popular concepts of right and wrong would have had a hearing and the opportunity of making themselves felt.

But though such discussions may be surmised our actual sources have hitherto been disappointingly silent on this point and the court records which have come down to us deal almost exclusively with the establishing of the facts of the case, never touching on points of law. It is therefore particularly fortunate that at least one example of a court record setting forth in some detail a discussion about a point of law should now have turned up, and it is further gratifying that the case involved should be one of homicide. For homicide is an offense very differently viewed at different stages of legal development and a trial for homicide will therefore tend to throw special light upon development and achievements.

TEXT AND TRANSLATION (4)

The tablet here published, 2N-T.54, was found in the course of the excavations of the scribal quarter by the Oriental Institute and the University Museum, Philadelphia, in the second season of the Joint Expedition's work in Nippur. It was lying on the floor of a room TB 10, in a private house which, to judge by the latest of the dated documents found in that stratum (II 1) should belong to the early years of Rim-Sîn of Larsa. The tablet was unfortunately not intact, the upper left hand corner had been broken off anciently, and it was therefore a great satisfaction to discover later that a duplicate existed and had been published years ago by Chiera (*PBS* VIII 173). This duplicate, which came from the earlier excavations at Nippur, is now in Philadelphia. Though relatively small it happens to preserve exactly the parts which are missing in the tablet found later and it is, to judge from the writing, of approximately the same age. Noteworthy is the fact that it gives a fuller version of the text in some places.

Further duplicates turned up in the course of the third season. These duplicates—3N-T.340, 3N-T.403, 3N-T.426, and 3N-T.273— are all relatively later copies dating from the time of Samusiluna and later. They differ from the earlier versions, which both represent single tablets containing only the homicide trial, by including a number of other records of trials before the Assembly of Nippur. The first of these concerns a dispute over office between one Pa-ha-

hu-um son of Lugal-a-ma-ᵣruᴵ(?) (plaintiff) and Ma-áš-kum son of
ᵈNanna-ma-an-sum (defendant). The second deals with the seizure
of a slave girl belonging to one Ku-gu-za-ni (plaintiff) by Lugal-me-
lám son of ᵈNanna a-ra-mu-gi (defendant). These cases follow the
homicide trial in the text. The purpose of this collection of trial
records, whether didactic or otherwise, is unfortunately not clear.
Nor can we at the moment link with any degree of certainty any
of the principals in the trials with occupants of the houses in which
the records of them were handed down.

Transliteration

[^{Id}Nanna-sig$_5$[1] dumu Lú-^{d}E]n[2]-zu
[^{I}Kù-^{d}En-líl-lá dumu Kù][2]-⌈^{d}⌉Nanna šu-i
[ù ^{d}En-líl-en-nam ara][2]d Ad-da-kal-la nu-giri$_{11}$(GIŠ.SAR)
[^{I}Lú-^{d}Inanna dumu][2] Lugal-uru$_4$-du$_{10}$ nu-èš
5 ⟨[3]in-gaz-eš⟩
⟨u$_4$ Lú-^{d}Inanna[3] [4]dumu Lugal-uru$_4$-du$_{10}$-ke$_4$[4]⟩
[ba-úš-a][2]-ta
[^{I}Nin-da[5]-da dumu][2]-⌈munus⌉ Lú-^{d}Nin-urta
[dam Lú][2]-⌈^{d}⌉Inanna⟨-ra!⟩[6]
10 [[7]^{I}Lú-^{d}Inanna[7] dam][2]-⌈a⌉-ni
[al-gaz-][2]za
⌈in⌉-na-an-⌈ne⌉-eš
[8]^{I}Nin-da-da ⌈dumu⌉-[munus]-⌈Lú⌉-[^{d}Nin]-urta[8]
ka nu[9]-un-ba[9] ⌈TÚG⌉[10] ba-an-dul
15 di-bi Ì-si-in^{ki}-šè[11]
igi lugal-la-šè ba-DU
^{I}Ur-^{d}Nin-urta lugal-e
di-bi pu-úh[12]-ru-um
Nibru^{ki}-ka dab$_5$-bi-da[13] bi-in-du$_{11}$
20 ^{I}Ur-gu(?)[14]-la dumu Lugal-ibila
[15]^I⌈Du-du⌉ mušen-dù[15]
^{I}A-li-ella(t)-ti MAŠ.EN.DÀ
^{I}Pu-zu dumu Lú-^{d}En-zu
^{I}E-lu-ti dumu [16]Ti⟨-iz⟩-qar[16]-^{d}É-a
25 ^{I}Šeš-kal-la bahar (DUG-QA-BUR)[17]
^{I}Lugal-kam nu-giri$_{11}$ (GIŠ.SAR)
^{I}Lugal-á-zi-da dumu [18] ^{d}En-zu-an-dúl[18]
^{I}Šeš-kal-la dumu [19]ša-ra-HAR[19]
igi-ne-ne bí[20]-in-gar-re-eš-...[21]
30 lú-lú-ù [22]in-gaz-eš-àm[22]
lú-ti-la nu-me-eš[23]
⌈nitah⌉ [3]-a[24]-bi ù munus-bi
igi ^{giš}gu-za Lú-^{d}Inanna dumu Lugal uru$_4$-du$_{10}$ nu-èš-šè[25]
ì-gaz-dè-eš [26]bí-in-e-eš[26]
35 ^{I}Šu-qa-li-lum ERÍN-GAL-GAL uku-uš [27] ^{d}Nin-urta[27]
^{I}U-bar-^{d}En-zu nu-giri$_{11}$ (GIŠ.SAR)
igi-ne-ne in-gar-re-eš-ma[28]
Nin-da[29]-da dumu-munus Lú-^{d}Nin-urta[30]
dam-a-ni hé-en-gaz

Translation

Nanna-sig son of Lu-Enzu
Ku-Enlilla son of Ku-Nanna the barber
and Enlil-ennam slave of Adda-kalla the orchardman
killed
5 Lu-Inanna son of Lugal-uru-du the nishakku.
After Lu-Inanna son of Lugal-uru-du
had been put to death
they told
Nin-dada, daughter of Lu-Ninurta,
10 wife of Lu-Inanna,
that Lu-Inanna, her husband,
was killed.
Nin-dada, daughter of Lu-Ninurta,
opened not her mouth, covered it up.
15 Their case was taken
to Isin before the king.
King Ur-Ninurta
ordered their case
to be accepted for trial in the Assembly of Nippur.
20 Ur-gula, son of Lugal-ibila,
Dudu, the birdcatcher,
Ali-ellati, the client,
Puzu, son of Lu-Enzu,
Eluti, son of Tizkar-Ea,
25 Shesh-kalla, the potter,
Lugalkam, the orchardman,
Lugal-a-zida, son of Enzu-andul,
and Shesh-kalla, son of Shara-HAR,
addressed (the assembly):
30 "As men who have killed men
they are not live men,
the males (all) three of them and that woman
before the chair of Lu-Inanna, son of Lugal-uru-du, the nishakku,
shall be killed" they said.
35 Shuqalilum, the ERÍN-GAL-GAL, sergeant of Ninurta, and
Ubar-Enzu, the orchardman,
addressed (the assembly) as follows:
"Nin-dada, daughter of Lu-Ninurta,
may have killed her husband;

40 munus-e a-na [31]bí-in[31]-ag-e
   al-gaz-e[32]-d[è] bí-in-eš[33]
   pu-uh[34]-ru-um Nibru^ki-ka
   [35]igi-bi bi-⌈íb⌉-gar-ma[35]
   [36]munus dam-a-ni nu-un-na-kal-la[36]
45 lú-kúr-⌈ra⌉-a[37]-ni hé-en-[38]-zu-àm
   ⌈dam⌉-a-ni hé[38]-en-gaz
   [dam-a-ni][39] ⌈al⌉-gaz-za
   [giš ha-ba-an-tu][39]ku-àm
   [a-na-aš-àm KA(?) u-gù-⌈na⌉[39] ⌈li⌉-bi-in-si
50 [e-na-àm dam-a][39]-ni in-gaz
   [[40]nam-tag-ga(?)-a-ni lú-i][39]n-gaz-eš-àm[40]
   [[41]a-ab-diri bí-in-][39] eš[41]
   [pu-úh-ru-um[39] Nibru^kika
   ⟨inim búr-e-da-bi⟩[42]
55 [^IdNanna-sig_5 dumu Lú][39]-dEn-[zu]
   [^IKù-dEn-líl-lá dumu Kù-dNan][39]na šu-i
   [[43]ù dEn-líl-en-nam arad Ad-da][39]-⌈kal⌉-la nu.$giri_{11}$ (GIŠ.SAR)
   ⟨ù ^INin-da-da dumu-munus Lú-d⌈Nin-urta⌉ dam Lú-d ⌈Inanna⌉-
   ke_4⟩[44]
   [[45]gaz-dè ba-an-sum-mu][39]-uš[46]
   [[39]di-dab_5-ba pu-úh[39]-ru-um Nibr]u^ki-ka

Critical apparatus: N.B. there are many errors in the textual notes of the original publication, which, without being noted, are here corrected. [1]3N-T.340: sa_6-ga. [2]Restored from *PBS* VIII 173. [3]Thus *PBS* VIII 173 and 3N-T.340; 2N-T.54: om. [4]Thus *PBS* VIII 173; 3N-T.340: + nu-èš-a; 2N-T.54: om. [5]3N-T.340: -ad-. [6]Thus probably *PBS* VIII 173; 3N-T.340: -ke_4; 2N-T.54: om. [7]3N-T.340: om. [8]3N-T.340: om. [9]3N-T.340: -ba-e. [10]3N-T.340: TÚG. [11]3N-T.340: -šè(?)-i(?)... [12]3N-T.340: -uh-. [13]3N-T.340: -dè. [14]3N-T.340: -gú-. [15]3N-T.340: om. [16]3N-T.340: ...-KA. [17]3N-T.403: + -ra. [18]3N-T.403: Lú-dSú.en-na. [19]3N-T.403: dHAR-a-bi. [20]3N-T.403: om. [21]Perhaps -ma over erasure(?) in 2N-T.54; 3N-T.403: -àm. [22]3N-T.403: lú al-gaz-a. [23]3N-T.403: -en. [24]3N-T.403: om. [25]3N-T.526: -a. [26]3N-T.426: [ba-a]n-sum-mu-uš. [27]3N-T.426:

40 but what can a woman do in (such a matter)
that she is to be killed?" they said.
In the Assembly of Nippur
it (i.e., the assembly) addressed them as follows:
"A woman who values not her husband
45 may give information to his enemy and thus
he (i.e., the enemy) may (be able to) kill her husband.
That her husband is killed
he (i.e., the enemy) may (then) let her hear
—why should he not thus make her keep silent about him?—
50 *She* (more than anyone else) killed her husband,
her guilt is greater than (theirs:) that they killed a man"
they said.
In the Assembly of Nippur,
the matter having been solved,
55 Nanna-sig, son of Lu-Enzu,
Ku-Enlilla, son of Ku-Nanna, the barber,
Enlil-ennam, slave of Adda-kalla, the orchardman,
and Nin-dada, daughter of Lu-Ninurta, wife of Lu-Inanna,
were delivered up to be killed.

60 Case accepted for trial in the Assembly of Nippur.

---

dNin-urta(?)-ke₄(?). ²⁸3N-T.426: -àm. ²⁹3N-T.426: -ad-. ³⁰3N-T.426:
+ dam Lú-dInanna-ke₄. ³¹3N-T.426: ì-. ³²3N-T.426: om. ³³3N-T.426:
+ NE-...-...-... ³⁴3N-T.426: -uh-. ³⁵3N-T 426: èn tar-re-eš-àm igi-
ne-ne in-[...]. ³⁶3N-T.426: mùnus-e dam-a-ni igi-ni nu-mu-un(?)-
[...]. ³⁷3N-T.426: -ka-. ³⁸3N-T.426: om.(?). ³⁹Thus *PBS* VIII 173.
⁴⁰3N-T.273: [nam]-ᵣtagᵢ-a-ni SI.A.ᵣAN¹(?)[...]; *PBS* VIII 173: -a
instead of -àm. ⁴¹3N-T.273: [ab]-SI.ᵣA¹. ⁴²Thus *PBS* VIII 173; 3N-T.
273: om. ⁴³Thus *PBS* VIII 173; 2N-T.54 and 3N-T.273: om. ⁴⁴Restored
on the basis of 3N-T.273: [ù] Nin-ad-da dumu-munus Lú-dNin-urta
[dam] Lú-dᵣInanna¹-ke₄; *PBS* VIII 173 and 2N-T.54: om. ⁴⁵Thus *PBS*
VIII 173; 3N-T.273: om. ⁴⁶Thus PBS VIII 173; 3N-T.273: al-gaz-e-de-eš.

COMMENTARY

1. *The Statement of the Facts.* The text, as is customary in Sumero-Akkadian court records, opens with a concise statement of the facts of the case reported on. It is a characteristic of such statements that they do not, as might perhaps have been expected, present the facts as they appeared at the beginning of the trial but rather as they were eventually proved and as they underlie the verdict. In the present case the factual statement notes that three named men killed a high-ranking priest, Lu-Inanna, and that his widow, on hearing of the killing, kept her knowledge secret. One may wonder whether the neat distinction between the guilt of the three men, who did the killing, and that of the woman, who covered it up, was present from the outset or only appeared in the course of the discussion about the applicability of the verdict as first proposed. There is no cogent reason, however, why it should not have been original.

The victim was, as mentioned, a high-ranking priest. His title nu-èš, Akkadian *nišakku*, seems to indicate a position at the top or near the top of the priestly hierarchy of a temple. The highest official in Nippur in Cassite times, the guenna(k), was in at least one case a *nišakku* of Enlil, and the later Assyrian and Babylonian kings not infrequently call themselves *nišakku* in their titulatory. The ritual function of the *nišakku* is less clear. Since an Enlil hymn[5] mentions him as "holding the golden (or: 'the pure') cup" and since he is often listed with the guda priest who had responsibilities connected generally with the divine meals it is possible that the *nišakku* was the god's cupbearer. The title *nišakku* is sufficiently frequent in the texts to show that not all its bearers can have had the exalted position of the *nišakku* of Enlil, and it is likely that many headed smaller, even quite unimportant temples or chapels. There are no indications that the *nišakku* whose murder is dealt with in the text under discussion was especially prominent.

Among the accused men two have patronymics and were accordingly freemen. Rather interesting questions are raised, however, by the status of the third who is identified as a privately owned slave. The most striking fact is perhaps that no special consequences seem to flow from his unfree condition. We are left to wonder whether he participated in the killing on an equal footing with the two freemen or merely as their hired helper; he is given trial exactly as they are, and no question seems to have arisen about any responsibility on the part of his owner for what he had done. The widow of the slain man, a free woman, is identified both by patronymic and by the name of her husband.

2. *Assignation of the Case.* After the introductory factual statements the text notes that the case was brought before the king, Ur-Ninurta, in Isin and that he assigned it for trial in the Assembly in Nippur. The briefness of the statement leaves unsaid a great deal that we should have wished to know. Who, for instance, initiated the proceedings? Since in ancient Mesopotamia, at least since the times of the Third Dynasty of Ur, the right to make a charge of murder before the authorities and thereby to start an official investigation seems to have been fairly general, proceedings may in this case have been initiated by almost anybody. In the slightly older document *TEO* 6167 (Umma, Ur III) which deals with such a charge, it is the widow of the man allegedly murdered who accuses a named person before the authorities. The authorities, seemingly a court, on hearing the accusation immediately proceed to investigate it. In *TEO* 6165 (Umma, Ur III) an accusation of murder is made to the governor (ensi) of the city by a man who appears to have merely heard that a murder had been committed. A deputy (maškim) is assigned to him to look into the matter further. In the present case, since the widow so pointedly refrained from taking any steps, the initiative may perhaps best be imagined to have come from friends and neighbors alive with suspicions.

"The case was taken to Isin before the king." The verbal prefix used, ba-, "off," "away," suggests that the case originated in Nippur. If so its eventual assignation to trial before a Nippur court is very natural. Whether the phrase may be taken to imply that the original charge was made before the king or—as seems more probable—that it was made to local authorities in Nippur who in their turn referred it to the king is uncertain. Uncertain is also the precise reason why the case was brought before the king. Had this been a civil case or one involving especially powerful defendants one might have quoted the superiority of the royal sanctions or the pressure the king could exert on a court to accept an unattractive case as a reason; with a trial for homicide, however, such considerations would hardly enter. Rather one may guess that the monopoly on violence of the state—as embodied in the person of the king—had by this time become sufficiently entrenched for a feeling to prevail that cases involving capital punishment ought to proceed with the king's knowledge and approval.[6]

The proceedings before the king, leading to his assignation of the case to the assembly in Nippur involved in all probability a thorough examination into the charges and their factual foundations. That such examination regularly preceded royal assignation of cases has been made plausible by Lautner[7] and may be assumed also for this case even though no special record of it is preserved.

The Assembly in Nippur, to which the case was assigned, can claim considerable interest. Its ancestry probably traces back to early politico-judicial assemblies of sufficient fame and importance in their days to have served as a pattern for the concept of the divine assembly meeting in Nippur in Ubshuukkinna. By the time here concerned, however, the assembly had undoubtedly lost all political functions and served only as a court. The professions listed in our document for the members who participated in the debate about the case—bird-catcher, client, potter, orchardman, etc.—underline its popular and lay character; it was clearly composed largely of the common people in Nippur.

3. *Proceedings in the Assembly.* Since our knowledge of court procedure in older Mesopotamia derives almost exclusively from records of civil trials the record of a trial for homicide can obviously claim special attention. We find it to be concerned with law to the complete exclusion of facts; it is the record of the formulation of a verdict only. Proceedings in the assembly open with a statement made by a group of nine named men identifying the accused as killers and ordering the death penalty for them; this proposed verdict is followed by a question about the applicability of the term "kill" in the case of one of the accused, the woman, and then comes a ruling on the question by the assembly. The initial statement stands— and is allowed to stand throughout—unsupported by any show of proof, and this complete absence of a detailed establishing of the facts of the case through testimony of witnesses, confession, oath, or otherwise is most striking. Even if one would assume, as we have done above, that a thorough establishing of the facts had already

taken place before the king, before the case reached the assembly for trial, the lack of even the briefest presentation of those earlier findings leads again to the conclusion that the assembly was expected to reach its verdict on the basis of its members' personal knowledge and convictions rather than on facts established in court. This is so unlike all we know about procedure in the civil trials, where fact-finding looms so large as to constitute the bulk of the average trial record, that the question cannot but arise whether we might not here—since this is a case of homicide—be dealing with a separate and altogether distinct, criminal procedural tradition. Since there is no abundance of evidence for the specific development in Mesopotamia we are, of course, to some extent thrown upon fairly general considerations.

Civil procedure seems to have been always and everywhere litigious in origin, a competition between plaintiff and defendant to be arbitrated, later decided, by the court on the merits. The original role of the court as mere arbitrator enjoins from the beginning careful attention to the facts on both sides.

Rather different appears the original situation underlying the tradition of criminal procedure. The early "crime" is an act endangering the whole community, and the community, aroused and scared, is apt to deal with it along lines of lynch justice. In the emotionally highly charged lynch situation the facts and the guilt of the accused are generally taken for granted (it is the conviction that they are true that has aroused the community to action). At the tense moment when the community faces the accused the salient point is therefore merely the crystallization of the guilt in a precise and poignant formula that will trigger the punitive mass action. This formula fulfills the function of the later "verdict."

If, accordingly, our Nippur trial stands in a specific "criminal" procedural tradition going back to an original situation of lynch justice its exclusive concentration on the verdict and its lack of interest in the facts of the case would become far easier to understand. The question is thus whether such a specific "criminal" tradition existed in Mesopotamia and what was its nature.

In seeking an answer one will turn naturally to the evidence of the Mesopotamian myths since they, in the picture of social conditions which they present, seem generally to have preserved memories of greater antiquity than any other of our sources. Here, therefore, if anywhere, can we hope for information about early ways of dealing with "crime." The myths contain three cases which are of special interest to us. The first, and most detailed one, occurs in the myth generally known as "The Guilty Slavegirl."[8] In this myth—which probably continues, or at least has close connection with, the Descent of Inanna—Inanna sends out her vizier, Nin-shubur, to announce publicly charges against one of her slavegirls. The slavegirl, whose name Ama-namtagga means "the guilty one," has violated taboos, she has "sat in the pure chair, slept in the pure bed, learned coitus, learned kissing." As shown by what follows in the myth we must interpret this as referring to adultery with Inanna's husband, Dumuzi.

At the summons people gather to the city. The condemned Ama-namtagga lies prostrate in the dust and Inanna steps forward, she "looked upon her, it was the look of death, the lady cried out against her, it was the cry of 'guilty!' She grasped her at her fore-lock and threw the girl Ama-namtagga at the foot of the city-wall: 'Let the shepherd kill her with his shepherd's crook, let the *kalû*-priest kill her with his *mezû* instrument, let the potter kill her with his churn, let the *kurgarû*-priest kill her with his dagger and mace!'"

As will be seen we are here very close to the lynch situation. The charge is one of public concern, a breach of taboos, rather than one of private wrong. Its publication serves as a call to assembly. In the assembly there is no doubt about, or investigation into, the alleged facts, it is sufficient that the accuser with a trigger statement, the cry of "guilty!" throws the accused to the mob, which finishes her off in a surge of mob violence. That the fixing of the accused with a "look of death" and the crying out against him or her with a "cry of 'guilty!'" was a traditional formal act may be seen from its recurrence in similar situations elsewhere, e.g., in the Descent of Inanna when Ereshkigal in the court of the nether world imposes penalty upon Inanna and changes her into a cut of meat, and when Inanna later in the story gives Dumuzi into the hands of the deputies of the nether world.

Slightly more developed is the procedure described in *Enuma elish* when Kingu is tried for incitement to rebellion before the assembly of the gods, again, since rebellion is directed against society as a whole, a trial for a crime. The trigger statement, the verdict of guilty, is here no longer pronounced by the accuser—in this case

Marduk—but is delivered by the assembly on the basis of its own personal knowledge of the facts in reply to questions put to it by Marduk. When the verdict has been rendered Kingu is taken before Ea and killed; presumably this means that he was killed in and by the assembly, conveniently near the spot where Ea sat, since Ea, after he had been killed, was to create man out of his blood. There is again no inquiry into the facts of the charge made, they are taken to be common knowledge; however, the assembly from being merely an instrument of execution has taken on a judicial function inasmuch as it here renders the verdict. The verdict itself has grown from a mere trigger statement—"guilty!"—to a fuller definition of the guilt.

Still a little further advanced appears the procedure in the trial of Enlil for rape described in the myth of Enlil and Ninlil.[9] Here Enlil, passing through Ki-ur, is seized by the assembly, which immediately and apparently out of their own previous knowledge pass judgment upon him: "Enlil the sex criminal shall leave town, Nunamir, the sex criminal, shall leave town." The rape which Enlil has committed makes him ritually unclean, an uzug. This word, which we have translated "sex criminal," has wider connotations and denotes generally ritual uncleanness connected with matters of sex. It is this aspect, with its inherent dangers to the community, that makes the offense a crime. The punishment imposed is in form that of banishment, but since it seems to imply that Enlil must take the road to the nether world and the realm of death the story may reflect a development from an earlier punishment by death to a later one by banishment, or vice versa. The verdict, no longer prompted by an accuser, is delivered by the assembly, which has come to state in succinct fashion the identity of the accused and of his guilt: "Enlil the sex criminal," and the penalty imposed, "shall leave town."

From the stage of development represented by the trial of Enlil to that found in the court record here under discussion there is very little change. No accuser appears, the verdict is rendered by the assembly on the basis of personal knowledge of the facts and it has two parts: one linking the accused with his guilt, the other prescribing the penalty. New is the opportunity for challenging the verdict on points of law, a feature not attested earlier. Establishing of the facts of the case in court appears to be still absent.

4. *The Proposed Verdict.* The opening statement, which forms the basis for the discussion in the assembly, is made, as mentioned, by a group of nine men. It is in the form of a verdict and has two parts: (1) a pronouncement, recognizable from its style as a common saw or formula, quite obviously traditional, which identifies the accused as criminals and sets forth the grounds why a death penalty could and should be inflicted, and (2) a specific order for the infliction of that penalty on the accused, defining the place of execution.

The complete statement reads: "As men who have killed men they are not live men. The males (all) three of them and that woman shall be killed before the chair of Lu-Inanna, son of Lugal-uru₄-du₁₀, the nishakku."

That the first part of this statement sets forth grounds why a death penalty could and should be inflicted may not be immediately evident. As it stands it seems to deny that the accused are alive, and since they were undoubtedly present for all to see that would appear to be both absurd and *contra plenam et manifestam evidentiam.* The absurdity disappears and the real meaning becomes apparent, however, the moment we interpret the statement as rooted in the Mesopotamian magico-religious outlook—familiar to us, e.g., from the Babylonian omen literature—and as seeking to penetrate below appearances to inner essence.

In that outlook the world constituted underneath the visible surface a continuous conflict between different and mutually hostile modes of being. And what thus went on below was not hidden to the thoughtful. If, for instance, a desert animal or a desert plant should be seen in a city, where it did not belong, that was a symptom— much as a symptom of a disease—that the alien mode of being of the desert was at work within that city intruding upon its own proper mode of being, that of a city, and, if not checked, would eventually fully realize itself, making the city into wasteland. In very similar fashion the appearance of killers, of death-dealing forces, within the society of the living, would be a symptom that another mode of being, that of death, was encroaching upon it and at work within it, and would eventually take over if not checked. It was accordingly imperative to nip the contagion in the bud, to remove those who by their acts had shown that they had in them the alien essence of death, not of life, were not therefore "live men," and by returning them to death, which they represented and to which they belonged, to recreate clear lines.

The formula: "As men who have killed men they are not live men" thus sets the killers apart as having no share in the society of the living, as aliens not belonging there, and by its emphasis that they are not "live men" it effectively removes at the same time any stigma that might have attached to the execution of the death penalty on them as constituting a taking of life.

The view of killing here found—a symptom of an inner disease threatening society in its very essence—is obviously closely akin to the concept of killing as a "pollution," which in Greek and Hebrew law was influential in the shaping of the concept of homicide as a public crime. This kinship stands out even more clearly when we turn to the second part of the statement.

The second part of the statement, ordering the death penalty and specifying that it is to be imposed in front of the chair of the slain nishakku-priest, constitutes one of the very few survivals of the concept of blood revenge to be found in older Mesopotamian sources: the third for personal revenge in the soul of the slain man is to be assuaged by the killing of his slayer before his chair, that is, symbolically, in his presence.

It is to be noted that the concept of revenge here present is a fairly developed one. It is not the early idea that a killing is essentially a loss to a family or clan which may be made up for by wealth paid in composition; rather, killing is an individual affair, creating a personal grievance in the dead man, and the danger and compulsion of this lies in the fact that his unrelieved demand represents a new and strong impulse in the realm of the dead to interfere with that of the living. It is thus entirely on a line with the concepts active in the transformation of homicide in Hebrew law from a tort, a wrong which could be compensated for, into a public crime and a sin which demanded expiation: "Ye shall take no satisfaction for the life of a murderer... So ye shall not pollute the land wherein you are; for blood it defileth the land...."

5. *The Request for Clarification.* The statement by the group of nine, actually a proposed verdict, is questioned by a smaller group of two with regard to its applicability to one of the accused, the widow: "Nin-dada, daughter of Lu-Ninurta, may have killed her

husband, but what can a woman do in (such matters) that she is to be killed?"

The question is clearly directed to the definition of the crime of "killing." As shown by the concession with which the question is prefaced, "Nin-dada...may have killed her husband," the questioners do not consider Nin-dada clearly innocent; it is admitted that "to kill" (gaz) covers a variety of acts, among them such of which Nin-dada was guilty. However, the question itself presupposes that among these acts certain ones were to be distinguished as alone deserving of capital punishment. Since it is felt that a woman ipso facto could not be capable of them we may assume that the questioners have in mind mainly direct participation in the physical act of killing. In modern terms they seem to exclude approximately what we should call the abettor, "one who is actually or constructively present at the commission of the deed and contributing to it by moral or physical force" (Webster), but to include the accessory, "one who accedes to or becomes involved in the guilt of an offence by some act either previous or subsequent as of instigating, aiding, or concealing" (Webster). Whereas Nin-dada, to judge from the introductory statement of the facts of the case, and perhaps from the response of the assembly to the question raised, was certainly an accessory, it is quite obviously unlikely that as a woman she could have participated directly in the physical act of killing.

6. *The Ruling by the Assembly.* The question raised was answered by the assembly—according to a later variant after mutual consultation—in an affirmative sense: "A woman who values not her husband may give information to his enemy, and thus he (i.e., the enemy) may (be able to) kill her husband. That her husband has been killed he (i.e., the enemy) may (then) let her hear—why should he not thus make her keep silent about him?—She (more than anyone else) killed her husband, her guilt is greater than (theirs:) that they killed a man."

This answer, it may be noted first of all, seems to be given in general rather than in specific terms, that is to say it answers how "a woman" can be guilty under the questioned term rather than how this particular woman was guilty and it considers correspondingly only "a" hypothetical slayer rather than the three actual ones who figure in the case involved. In this we may see an indication that the discussion is properly one of a point of law and seeks to lay down a rule of general applicability.

Among the culpable actions listed is first that of "giving information" to an enemy of the husband. We assume that the information in question is intelligence about the husband's movements and about opportunities for attack on him that will aid a prospective slayer. We would not exclude, however, the possibility that the reference may be more immediately to the preceding statement that the woman "values not her husband." On the former interpretation the woman would aid in the perpetration of the deed whereas, should the latter interpretation prove the correct one, she would be guilty rather of instigation of the killing, the implication of her letting her disaffection for the husband be known probably amounting to offering her favors as inducement for removing him. For such an interpretation, which reads rather more into the facts than seems necessary, might speak the likely general connection of the case with that of CH §153 discussed below.

More significant—possibly only because more readily provable—seems the further act mentioned, that of concealment. Not only is this the only one which is specifically laid to Nin-dada in the introductory statement of the facts of the case given at the beginning of the document, but it is—if our interpretation of what is here said is correct—known by the slayer to constitute clear and incontrovertible evidence of complicity and the culpable knowledge is deliberately furnished her to involve her inextricably. Our translation assumes that the sentence "why would he not cause her to keep silent about him" belongs closely together with the preceding clause which is subordinated to it by means of its final -àm, "and in this manner," and states the means of insuring her silence: "That her husband is killed he may let her hear." Through imparting to her knowledge of the deed the slayer places her in a position in which she is forced to conceal culpable knowledge and by thus implicating her lessens the chances of a betrayal on her part.

With the statement "She (more than anyone else) killed her husband" the assembly turns from general considerations to the case in hand in order to evaluate the degree of Nin-dada's culpability. It is found to be even greater than that of the actual killers, undoubtedly because of the element of disloyalty which it involves and the difficulty for any husband to protect himself against such betrayal. This makes it morally far more reprehensible than the mere killing of a man by his enemy.

7. *The Case and CH* §153. The discussion surrounding the role of Nin-dada is illuminating in many ways. It shows, in the moral strictures passed upon her by the assembly, that a considerable intensity of public feeling against her offense was present. Even the two questioners who doubt whether capital punishment is in order instinctively feel her to be in some sense guilty: she "may have killed her husband." Their trouble is that they see no legal remedy, since in their view the crime of homicide is restricted to physical acts and the law can thus not reach her. Their view, with its concrete restriction to the physical act of killing and precise, clear applicability, can safely be assumed to represent the older, commonly held concept of what constituted the crime of homicide. The pressure operating to extend the concept in this instance is clearly occasioned by the moral aspects of Nin-dada's actions: aversion against a wife who seeks her husband's death, the dangerous, underhand, and treasonable character of what such a wife can do, and a resultant exceptionally violent repugnance to the thought that she should be allowed to escape punishment. Out of this conflict between the traditional definition of homicide on the one hand and the desire to find Nin-dada guilty on the other, arises a new definition which extends homicide from covering at most the abettor to including, in the case of a wife involved in the murder of her husband, also the accessory. In the discussion about Nin-dada and in the final ruling by the assembly we thus see a new crime coming into being.

This interpretation of the Nin-dada discussion as the creation of a new crime finds some support from §153 in the Code of Hammurabi. That paragraph occurs in a section devoted to the family between a law defining the liability of a husband for debts contracted by his wife, and vice versa, and more significantly, one which deals with incest between father and daughter. It reads: "If the wife of a man on account of another male has her husband murdered they shall impale that woman."

The character of the Code of Hammurabi as a collection of changes, substitutions, and complementation to the common law we have had occasion to mention earlier when dealing with the *mišarum* tradition. The occurrence in it of this relatively isolated and rather special rule suggests, therefore, that we are dealing with a complement to existing law, a rule designed to meet a need not effectively covered earlier. The need is very much the same as that with which the Assembly in Nippur was faced centuries earlier in the Nin-dada case: punishment for a wife who has successfully plotted her husband's death.

The remedy found is, as will be seen, very different in the two cases. In Nippur the definition of homicide was extended so that it would cover, under these particular circumstances, also the accessory. In the Code of Hammurabi an entirely separate crime is defined with a characteristic formulation, "has her husband killed," and a distinctive penalty—impalement. This new crime is not a subcase of homicide but rather is grouped vaguely with other capital offenses within the family, such as incest.

While there can thus be no question of a direct connection between the remedy evolved in Nippur and that presented in the Code of Hammurabi the general similarity of the situation with which they are concerned suggest that in these centuries common opinion of right and wrong had moved ahead of the formulations of the common law to demand capital punishment for this particular offense, the wife plotting her husband's death, and that legal development experimented with various solutions.

8. *The Execution of the Verdict.* The verdict, challenged, but upheld by the ruling of the assembly, is not announced for a second time. After the statement of the ruling the text continues: "In the Assembly of Nippur, the matter having been solved, Nanna-sig, son of Lu-Enzu, Ku-Enlilla, son of Ku-Nanna, the barber, Enlil-ennam, slave of Addakalla, the orchard man, and Nin-dada, daughter of Lu-Ninurta, wife of Lu-Inanna, were delivered up to be killed." There follows a subscription: "A trial in the Assembly of Nippur."

In our oldest version of this part of the text, *PBS* VIII 173, the line listing Nin-dada is accidentally omitted, a circumstance which long seemed to us to demand an interpretation of the document on which she was found not guilty. However, as variants from the later texts clarified the reading and meaning of the ruling by the assembly, and as her name appeared properly included in the list of the condemned in 3N-T.273, that assumption could no longer be maintained and the character of the omission in *PBS* VIII 173 as merely a scribal slip imposed itself.

The phrasing of the statement which records the commitment of the condemned into the hands of their executioners gives no indication who these were. The term used, sum: "to deliver up," "to hand over," "to give," is used in records of civil trials of the awarding of a disputed object to the winning party by the court or—with the losing party as object—of the awarding of a right *in personam*. Here clearly the emphasis is on recording merely that the condemned passed out of the temporary state of being in the charge of and under the protection of the court.

As our document gives no indication of who executed the verdict of death, so do the codes known to us use only noncommittal expressions such as "he/she/they shall be killed" or "they shall kill them." Who "they" in the latter case are is not stated.

The evidence for the execution of a death penalty by mob violence presented by the story of the guilty slavegirl comes from a myth. Since myths frequently preserve customs of a far earlier period we can only assume that such execution was at one time prevalent in Mesopotamia, not that it necessarily survived to the time of the trial with which we have here been concerned. It is tempting to assume that the royal power, especially because of the indications of a particular concern of the king with capital cases mentioned above, may have taken over the executive function quite early in historical times, but no certainty is yet possible, not even, perhaps, an informed guess.

Bucolic

His sister of the sweet-voiced lyre,
Maid Geshtin-anna, sits in the fold,
She milks the ewe and gives to the lamb,
She milks the goat and gives to the kid,
In her right hand she carries the churn,
In her left the young woman has a lyre and a harp.

In the spring the shepherds took to the desert in search of grazing for their flocks. The description of Geshtin-anna, sister of the god of flocks and herds, Dumuzi, here given shows Sumerian pastoral life from its idyllic side. It is taken from a longer poem about Dumuzi. From Nippur, about 1700 B.C. or earlier.

13. On the Textile Industry at Ur under Ibbī–Sîn

One of the many outstanding discoveries made by the Joint Expedition of the British Museum and the University Museum of the University of Pennsylvania in the course of its long and successful work at Ur is an archive of the time of Ibbī-Sîn, the bulk of which the expedition recovered in 1924–1925 in the so-called "Registrar's Office," a room in the Cassite É-Dub-lá-mah complex.[1]

The texts of this archive were published by Legrain in 1947 among other Ur III texts found by the expedition in his "Ur Excavations Texts III. Business Documents of the Third Dynasty of Ur." On the basis of that publication and of information kindly supplied by Professor Legrain himself we have recently made an attempt to single out the texts of the archive with a view to forming some idea of its character.[2] Rather to our surprise we found that although most of the remains of the archive were recovered in the immediate vicinity of the main temple of Ur, the Nanna temple, and though many of its accounts are of offerings to Nanna, yet the archive as a whole does not appear to represent temple accounts but seems rather to be the records of an accounting unit engaged in keeping track of specifically royal economic interests, perhaps not even very closely linked with those of the temple. Whether this unit was in fact a part of the temple's bookkeeping branch but on special assignment, or whether, as seems perhaps more likely, it was responsible directly to the crown, cannot yet be decided with certainty.

NOTE: First published in *Studia Orientalia Ioanni Pedersen dedicata* (Copenhagen, 1953), 172–187.

Among the various royal interests watched over in the archive perhaps the most interesting and important is the textile industry which was carried on in and around Ur at that time. The accounts give us an unusually full picture and allow us to follow in reasonable detail all of the major steps in the processing of the crown's wool from the time it came in to Ur from the great yearly sheepshearings and until it ended up as finished cloth ready for distribution.

In the following we shall try to sketch this process in broad outline. In so doing we have no thought of giving an exhaustive treatment of the subject, or even of studying fully the documents to which we refer. Our aim is a far more timid and modest one: to draw attention to an important group of sources and by tentatively suggesting the lines of their inner coherence perhaps to encourage others to pursue in earnest the problems which they raise.

I. THE INCOMING WOOL

The most important of the texts dealing with raw wool are nos. 1505 and 1504,[3] accounts for the years Ibbī-Sîn 1 and 2 respectively.[4] Unfortunately the reverse sides of both texts are completely destroyed, so that the sections dealing with expenditures remain incomplete. Worse still, we miss the subscripts, which might have given us precise information about the identity of the economic and administrative unit here rendering account. To judge by the amounts of wool handled and the scope of its activities generally it must have been of considerable importance in the country's economy.[5] Until more precise information is available we may call it the "Wool Office," merely to have a convenient name.[6] The following brief outline of the structure of its accounts is based on no. 1505, but no. 1504 is quoted for interesting variants and for the parts in which it goes farther than 1505.

A. The Credits

The credit items listed may be divided into three subsections as follows:

1. The first subsection, present only in 1505, gives the amount of wool left over from the preceding year: "Wool...placed at the gate (ᶜkáᵓ-e gál-[la]) in the year Shu-Sîn 9." The phrase used suggests

that every year at year's end the stock was taken out in the open and laid out for inspection near the gate of the storehouse in order to facilitate the stocktaking.[7]

2. The second subsection deals with new supplies. From the subscript we learn that these are: "Wool which has come out of (the estate of) the palace" (síg é-gal-ta è-a) or, as 1504 has it "From the (estate of the) palace of Shu-Sîn" (é-gal ^{dr}šu^1-$^{[d]r}$EN^1:^{r}ZU^1-ta).[8] This means that the "Wool Office" derived almost its total working capital from holdings of the crown and, of course, that for accounting purposes it was a separate entity. The more specific formulation in no. 1504 is perhaps best explained if we assume that the estate of Shu-Sîn had not yet been divided between his heirs when the account was written, i.e., in the second year of his successor.

The first listings under the subsection are of wool paid in by the herdsmen. These are of three different kinds: the shepherds of the fat-tailed sheep (sipa udu kungal-la(!?)-ke$_4$-ne),[9] the shepherds of the uligi(r) sheep (sipa udu uli-gi-ra-ke$_4$-ne),[10] and the goatherds (sipa úz-da-ke$_4$-ne). Between them they provide the bulk of the new wool, and since the items of the subsection are all derived from the estate of the palace we may assume that they were the king's herders.

After the payments from the herdsmen follow amounts of wool from the "fat-tailed sheep of the highlands" (síg udu kungal igi-nim-ma), presumably sheep of the East-Tigridian grasslands,[11] and of sheep of Eshnunna(?) (síg udu Áš(!?)-nun^{rki1}-ka).[12] Both are paid in by a certain ^{r}I^1(!?)-tu-ra-^{r}a^1(!?), ^{r}ensi^1, in whom we should perhaps recognize the Ituria who was ensi of Eshnunna in these years.[13] Next come amounts from one Du$_{11}$-ga-zi-da, the herdsman (sahar), representing wool from the sheep of Girsu (síg udu Gír-su^{ki}) and then amounts from ^{r}In^1-ni-^{r}si^1(?) from Lugal-KA-TUK(?), and from ^{d}Šul-gi-mi-šar. All of these deliveries, in contrast to those from the herdsmen, are authorized by comptrollers (šakan).[14] They represent presumably the yield of sheep of the crown additional to the main herds and maintained separately as part of separate accounting units. Since one of the persons mentioned, Shulgi(r)-mīshar, appears later on in the accounts of the fullers as a recipient of finished cloth, it seems possible that all or part of the wool he furnished was for processing only and reverted to him and the economic unit he stood for as finished cloth.

The wool delivered is distinguished, not only by its source, but also according to whether the selection (igi-sag-gá)[15] of the wool was made at the sheepshearing (šà ka-si-ka)[16] or in Ur (šà Ur^{ki}-ma) and, of course, according to the kind and quality of the wool in question. The imperfect standardization of weights and the corresponding different significance of the figures of weight from different weighing places is adjusted account-technically by amounts called sag-bi, which indicate by how much a given figure is to be raised in order to make up for the fact that it was arrived at on the basis of a "long" rather than a "short" ton or—to be precise—talent (gú).[17]

3. The third subsection of the credit items lists first amounts of wool deriving from votive gifts such as "votive gifts by(?) the king from various.....-houses"[18] (a-ru-a lugal é-du$_6$-la didli-ta) and "votive gifts for Sîn"[19] (a-ru-a ^{d}Sú.en), and "separate votive gifts" (a-ru-a didli). After the votive gifts follow "wool (from cloth ends left) on the loom beam"(?) (síg nir-ra gál(??)-la)[20] and amounts from a variety of persons, groups of persons, and establishments: wool from the É-x(?) (*RÉC* 344 or *RÉC* 345),[21] flax fibers[22] from the flax growers, this latter constituting "working materials" (á-giš-gar-ra ki engar-gu-ke$_4$-ne-ta), wool, linen, and flax fiber from the overseers of weavers (ki ugula-uš-bar-ke$_4$-ne-ta), which represents their complete stock since it is specified as "incomings" (mu-tù) and "positive balances returned" (LÁ-NI su-ga), wool from the book-keeper in charge of the ".......copper" (dub-sar urudu-níg-sun-nu-da),[23] who for reasons unknown to us paid the positive balance on his account in wool rather than in silver (mu kù LÁ-NI-šè), wool from the "house of the surveyors of Shulgi(r) (é-nam-sag-sug$_5$ ^{d}Šul-gi-ra), which is known to have engaged also in the textile industry,"[24] and finally from the šabra of (the temple of) Shulgi(r).

It will be seen from this rapid summary of the credit entries that the real source of income of the Wool Office was the royal herds supplemented by a number of other, smaller herds also belonging to the crown. To this come votive gifts entering the wool office directly, and a number of entries that are perhaps best classed as "actives" since they appear to represent remnants, working materials, and stock on hand in the various establishments that sorted under the Wool Office and were supplied from it. They are of interest for what they tell of the activities of the Wool Office since in most cases the corresponding debit entries are lost. Of particular importance in this respect is, of course, the entry showing that the "overseers of the weavers" worked for the Wool Office and that any stock they had on hand was counted as an asset by it. Of interest is also the obvious relations of many of these establishments with the crown. Two are named from king Shulgi(r), and one, the É-X, we know from other texts of the archive to have supplied the sacrificial animals for the royal *eššešu* offerings, which was an obligation of the crown.

B. The Debits

The section dealing with expenditures is, as already mentioned, only preserved in its first parts. The extant items are largely concerned with payment of wool for cult purposes (níg-dab₅),[25] wool allotments (síg-ba), and as part of stipends (níg-ba). The first subsection lists such payments insofar as they were made "in the house," the following one apparently deals with similar payments "out of the house." In the sections now lost we must place expenditures of wool and flax fiber as working materials for the overseers of the weavers; that such entries existed is clear from the credit entries which we just discussed.

1. The first subsection deals, as we have stated, with domestic expenditures (zi-ga šà-é-a-ka). It begins with a deficit from the preceding year and moves on to a series of expenditures of a cultic nature: cult needs (níg-dab₅) of Nanna, wool allotments (síg-ba) for the minor gods of his entourage (síg-ba dingir ...., 1505; édingir-TUR-TUR-ne,[26] 1504), wool allotments for the *entu* of the gods Shullat and Hanish[27] (síg-ba nin-dingir [ᵈŠul-la-at] ù ᵈ[Ha-ni-iš], 1505; 1504 has síg-ba(?) ezen ᵈ˹Šul˺-l[a]-at ù ᵈHa-ni-iš, "wool allotments for the festival of Shullat and Hanish"), cult needs (níg-dab₅) of the old woman of É-ga-nu-hu-um (níg-dab₅ ši-ib-tum é-ga-nu-hu-˹um˺, 1505; 1504 has níg-dab₅ ši-ib-ta é-ga-nu-hu-ka),[28] and flax fibers for the jewelry(-depository) of Nanna (za-gaba ᵈNanna) and the jewelry(-depository) (za-gaba) of ᵈŠul-pa-è.[29]

After some rather difficult and damaged entries follow allotment and stipends to personnel. The listings are "wool allotments for the slaves and slavegirls" (síg-ba geme-arad-e-ne), "stipends for the slavegirls working as weavers, oil pressers, and millers" (níg-ba geme uš-bar geme ì-sur geme kín-kín-ne),[30] and "stipends for the slavegirls working as porters(?)" (níg-ba geme ukù-gùru-ne). The amounts of wool paid out for these purposes are very considerable. If we can assume that the standard yearly wool consumption of an individual, 10 mana, applies in these cases, the number of slaves employed by— or at least paid by—the Wool Office must have run close to 9,000.

After the allotments and stipends to the slaves come allotments and stipends to members of the royal family, first to Bí-zu-a, lamentation priestess of Abī-simtī, the queen (níg-ba Bí-zu-a balag(?)-di(?) A-bí-zi-im-ti nin), a lady who is mentioned under Amar-Sîna(k) as sister of the queen,[31] then to "the queens" (nin-e-ne). At this point 1505 breaks off. No. 1504 continues with further items, unfortunately not all of them clear, and gives the subscript defining the section as one of domestic expenditures (zi-ga šà é-a-ka).

The picture we obtain of the Wool Office from these entries is that of a large establishment with chapels for Nanna and various minor deities. While presumably primarily a storehouse for wool it contained also treasuries for the jewelry of various gods.[32] It employed a large personnel of slaves, and—as we already gathered from the credit entries—it has close connections with the royal house, members of which receive stipends on it.[33]

2. The second subsection of the debits presumably listed outside expenditures, but it breaks off before reaching the subscript. It begins with entries listing stipends for the "runners" (níg-ba lú kas₄-ke₄-ne), stipends of síg-gi wool for "the men stationed on the wall" (lú bàd-e-ne) "because their garments were woven from síg-gi wool" (mu túg-bi [s]íg(!?)-gi(!?) ba-tuku₅-tuku₅-a-šè), a stipend—clearly incidental in nature—for the neatherd (sipa gu₄) ⌈Su-ú⌉-[ú] "because his grain-fed ox was slaughtered" (mu gu₄-šE-a-ni ba-šum-šum-a-šè). After this comes a section of deliveries against sealed receipt (kišib) to various individuals mentioned by name, often for distribution as wool allotments or stipends to groups of people in their charge. With these entries also 1504 breaks off, and we are left uninformed as to how it may have continued. One point of interest in the named entries should be noted. The wool stipend to "the runners" and the entries in the kišib group Ur-ᵈŠul-gi-ra mu Lugal-kù-zu-šè "Ur-Shulgira(k) for Lugal-ku(g)-zu" have their exact counterparts in the fullers' accounts of finished cloth with which we

shall deal later; they are a valuable indication of the close inner unity of the textile accounts as a whole.

II. ACCOUNTS OF THE OVERSEERS OF WEAVERS

From the Wool Office the wool and flax fiber went out to be spun and woven into cloth, and the accounts furnish a quite detailed picture of this section of the industry and its organization. We meet in the texts a considerable number of "overseers of weavers" (ugula uš-bar), who live in the villages (šà uru-bar-ra)[34] and towns around Ur such as Ki-mu-ra, Ambar-mah, É-^{d}Nin-mar^{ki}, Ga-eš, É-^{d}Šara, Lagash^{ki}, ^{d}Nanna-ki-gal, etc. These overseers were organized in units under headmen (nu-bànda), and a list of four such units, each numbering from eleven to fifteen overseers of weavers, is given in no. 1449. Since the headman is mentioned when overseers of weavers deliver cloth to the fullers, it is clear that this organization served—in part at least—purposes of industrial control. In addition it may, of course, have had military uses.

Each overseer had charge of a not inconsiderable number of slave-girls (geme uš-bar), who did the spinning and weaving. He was provided, further, with the necessary raw materials and had to account both for these and for the time and output of the slavegirls in his charge. An instructive example of such an accounting furnishes text no. 1554. The overseer is a certain Du$_{11}$-ga-ni-zi, whose weaving establishment (é-uš-bar) was located in the village of É-^{d}Nin-mar^{ki} (cf. 1519), and who specialized in the manufacture of linen. He gives a balanced account for the twelve months of the year of Ibbī-Sîn 6.

1. The Credits

As credits Dugani-zi(d) lists flax fibers, naǧa, and labor. His first subsection deals with stock in the weaving establishment remaining from the preceding year (níg-gál-la é-uš-bar-ra mu...I.S. 5..), his second with new supplies—the subscript, which is now broken away, probably read "incomings" (mu-tù)—and the third consists of summaries. All of this constitutes the "credits" (sag-níg-ga-ra-kam).

The flax fibers listed are of three kinds: "heart of the flax" (gu šà-gu), the highly valued innermost fibers of the flax plant, "fibers for linen of third grade" (gu gada 3-kam ús), and the "ordinary fibers" (gu gen). The new supplies of flax fibers were obtained from the "storehouse" (é-kišib-ba-ta). It is not impossible that this "storehouse" is the one we have called the Wool Office, but more likely it was merely one of its subsidiaries, conveniently located for Dugani-zi(d), for from receipts by overseers of weavers for wool procured as "working materials" (á-giš-gar-ra-aš) we know that at least three storehouses served as supply points, that of É-^dNanna-ki-gar-ra, that of ^dNin-gal-e-gar-ra, and that of the "House of the Butler" (É-zabar-dab₅).[35]

The ingredient naǧa listed in second place in the account is an alkaline plant used, among other things, for the manufacture of soap. It seems likely that it may have served in the bleaching of the linen. Dugani-zi(d) obtained his new supplies from the scribe of Gá-nun (ki dub-sar Gá-nun-na-ta).

The labor entries, which come last, are computed on the basis of a unit representing the working capacity of one slavegirl in one month (geme iti 1-šè). The listings under new supplies are unfortunately damaged, but we can see that various classes of workers such as "(at the) head of the roll, old (hands)" (sag-dub libir) were distinguished. The source of the labor supply, if noted, is lost in the lacuna. From the totals given we see that Dugani-zi(d) had at his disposal labor amounting to 2,751 "slavegirls for one month" which, distributed over the twelve months for which the account runs, would indicate an average of up to 230 girls employed in the establishment.

2. The Debits

The debit section lists first the yearly output of linen, specifying for each kind of cloth the number of pieces and the amount of raw materials (flax fiber and naǧa) and the labor (working time and number of workers) consumed in its manufacture. Sometimes the weight of the linen and the weight loss incurred—presumably in the bleaching—are stated; in one case the labor item lists separately the spinners and the weavers.

The output was taken over, for the greater part, by the fullers (gada ki-lá-tag-ga mu-tù šu-ti-a aslag),[36] and the remainder was "brought into the storehouse and credited" (é-kišib-ba-ka ba-an-tu a-ka-a ba-a-gar). This accounting for the output is called "The (lit. 'its') cost in linen incomings" (á gada mu-tù-ra-bi).

The debit section then moves on to a summary of labor costs, which includes such items as wages for "head girls" (zilulu)[37] and girls who were "ill" (tu-ra), in both cases distinctions are made between "old hands" (libir) and "extras" (taḫ-ḫu). This represents "the (lit. 'its') cost in workdays (lit. 'days of sitting')" (á u_4 tuš-a-bi). After this girls who have died during the year (ba-úš) are accounted for and the debit items generally are summed as "The (lit. 'its') cost in incomings(!),[38] working days (workers, and sundry expenditures. Slavegirls for one month" (á tu-ra u_4 tuš-a ù zi-ga didli-bi geme iti-1-šè).

The last column of the account lists the stock of flax fiber, naǧa, and still available labor remaining in the weaving establishment (níg-gál-la é-uš-bar-ra), adds it to the expenditures (zi-ga ù níg-gál-la), and notes the balances.[39] Then follow subscript and date.

III. ACCOUNTS OF WEIGHED CLOTH

As shown by the account just discussed the major part of the output of the overseer of weavers passed from his hands into those of a fuller. This transfer is recorded not only in the accounts of the overseers of weavers (as a debit), and in the accounts of the fullers (as a credit), but a whole separate account type, the "accounts of weighed cloth," is devoted to it exclusively.

In its origin, as may be seen from variants of the characteristic formula for this account type, the account of weighed cloth was a straight record of the weighing, guaranteeing through the person who performed the weighing that the weights were true.[40] In time, however, the emphasis appears to have shifted so as to make of these accounts essentially a record of the transfer of the weighed goods from one party to another. The practical usefulness of such a type of document at the time with which we are dealing is, unfortunately, not altogether clear. The fact that the type allows great freedom to group several transactions together in a single document, even in cases where several headmen and comptrollers (šakan) are concerned, would tend to limit the choice to a warehouse such as, e.g., the one in

Kimura(k) in which the fullers kept the cloth they received as working materials. To such a warehouse these records—as records of incoming stock—would probably have been useful. They would, of course, also serve as a check on the individual accounts of the overseers of weavers and of the fullers.

The accounts of weighed cloth that we have are yearly, monthly(?), and dated to the day. Their form varies somewhat according to whether one or more transations are recorded. The accounts of single trans-actions, found only among the accounts dated to the day, list first the number, kinds, and weights of the cloth in question; state then that N_1 a fuller, has received it (šu ba-an-ti), that it is weighed cloth or linen, incomings, that it is from N_2, an overseer of weavers, and mentions finally the name of the headman (nu-bànda) of the overseer of weavers and the name of the comptrollers (šakan) who authorized the transaction. The date is by day of the month and year.

When more than one transaction is recorded the arrangement is slightly different. The body of the account consists then of the details of the cloth transferred, followed for each transfer by the statement: "N_1 (fuller) received from N_2 (foreman of weavers)." The subscript sums this up as "cloth weighed, incomings, from overseers of weavers fullers received" (túg ki-lá-tag-ga mu-tù ugula uš-bar-ra-ke$_4$-ne aslag-e-ne šu ba-an-ti-éš). Then follow the name or names of the headman (nu-bànda) of the overseers, and the name or names of the comptrollers (šakan). The date may be by day of the month and year, or by month and year, or by year only.

A special group within the accounts of this type form accounts which have the additional phrase Lugal-á-zi-da (dub-sar) i-dab$_5$ "L. (the scribe) took it in charge." These accounts always mention the place where the transaction took place, the others never do so. We may conclude from this that certain outlying weaving establish-ments—or the fullers they served—found it inconvenient to bring the cloth the long way to the warehouse themselves, and that the scribe Lugal-á-zida was charged with collecting and conveying such cloth. The outlying localities mentioned are Ga-eš, É-^{d}Ninmar^{ki}, ^{d}Nanna-ki-gal, Ambar-mah, and Lagash^{ki}. The distribution of place-names and names of comptrollers (šakan) in these texts show very close corre-spondence. It would follow that the comptroller normally was located near the weaving establishment which delivered the cloth, and we may surmise that the essence of his function was to authorize an expenditure rather than a receipt of goods.[41] In one case, apparently because no local comptroller was readily available, Lugal-á-zida served in that capacity himself.

The accounts of weighed cloth, while stating that the cloth has been received by a fuller, do not usually give any indication of the purpose of the transfer, or of what the fuller is to do to the cloth. An exception forms a small group of three documents (nos. 1598, 1663, and 1674) which seems to belong to the "weighed cloth" type of account. In these texts the characteristic clause reads: "Weighed cloth, incomings, from N_1 (an overseer of weavers) to prepare it (sa gi_4-gi_4-dè)[42] has N_2, a fuller, received" etc. This may well be the full form of the clause, the more so since the term "prepare" appears to be the characteristic overall designation for the fuller's contribution to the manufacturing process and recurs in the accounts recording the fullers' delivery of finished work: túg sa-gi_4-a, "prepared cloth." The rather general and inclusive meaning of the term does not, it is true, materially help us to grasp the precise nature of the fuller's work, except that its inclusiveness suggests that a variety of different activities may be contained in it. As chief among these we should probably see the bleaching and fulling of the cloth by scouring or treading it in an alkaline medium, the process now known as the "milling" of woolen goods. In this direction point a number of texts which record the receipt of naǧa, an alkaline plant, and oil by the fullers for "'walking' on the cloth" (túg-ga-DU-a-aš (nos. 948, 953, and 1135) or of naǧa by overseers of weavers and fullers gada-a-DU-a-aš "for 'walking' on linen" (1627).[43]

IV. ACCOUNTS OF THE FULLERS

We have suggested that the fuller kept his working materials in a local warehouse, taking home only the cloth on which he was working. This seems to agree with what we can gather from the one specimen of a fuller's monthly account that we possess, no. 1779. This text is a balanced account of credits and debits, rendered by the fuller Abba-kalla in Šu(!?)-na-mu-gi_4[ki] and covering the first month of the year Ibbī-Sîn 3.

1. The Credits

The first credit item listed by Abba-kalla is cloth representing positive balance transferred from the previous year's account (si-ì-tum níg-šID-ag). Then follows his stock in Kimura(k)[44] (níg-gál-la Ki-mu-ra-ka mu...I.S. 2), also as of the preceding year. After that he lists fresh supplies. There are two items, both apparently representing cloth transferred by overseers of weavers. The first is described as "weighed cloth, incomings, from Níg-ga-^{d}En-líl, overseer of weavers" (túg ki-lá-tag-ga mu-tù ki Níg-ga-^{d}En-líl ugula uš-bar-ta); the second, unfortunately damaged, seems to have mentioned a different overseer of weavers as source. All of these entries are then summarized according to the number of pieces and type of cloth, and form "the credits" (sag níg-šID-ag).

2. The Debits

As debit items figure two payments, one of cloth received by Ur-Shul-gira(k) (Ur-^{d}Šul-gi šu-ba-an-ti), and one of cloth received by An-ki-a (An-ki-a šu-ba-an-ti). These two items are summed as "expenditures" (zi-ga-àm). Next are listed cloth in storage in Ki-mura(k) at the time of accounting (Ki-mu-ra-ka gál(!?)-[la-àm]) and the expenditures are added to the stores as "expenditure and stores" (zi-ga ù níg-gál-la) and balances, i.e., the amounts by which the debits of the various types of cloth exceed (diri) or fall short (LÁ-NI) of the corresponding credits are noted.

The subscript reads: "Balanced account (níg-šID-ag) of Abba-kalla, the fuller (aslag). Comptroller (šakan) Lugal-á-zida, the scribe, in Šu(!?)-na-mu-gi$_4$^{ki} (šà Šu(!?)-na-mu-gi$_4$^{ki}). First month (iti 1-kam) year I.S. 3."

It will be noted that Abba-kalla, although located in Šu-na-mu-gi$_4$^{ki} keeps his stock of cloth in Kimura(k). That this is true also of the new supplies transferred from the overseers of weavers may be concluded from the fact that his debits after delivery of his finished work to Ur-Shulgira(k) and An-ki-a indicate that he has nothing on hand in his workshop in Šu-na-mu-gi$_4$^{ki}, for all his remaining stores are listed as in Kimura(k).

V. ACCOUNTS OF FINISHED CLOTH

The account of Abba-kalla throws some light on the disposal of the fuller's cloth once he finished with it. As the credit entries reflect a separate account type recording the transfer of cloth from the overseers of weavers *to* the fullers, so the debit entries reflect another separate account type recording the transfer of cloth *from* the fullers. This latter type has, as far as we can now see, two major forms, depending on the destination of the cloth.

The first of these forms—not too copiously documented—lists first the number and kinds of pieces of cloth furnished by each fuller, giving the name of the fuller. It then summarizes the various types of cloth and, after listing the total number of pieces, states "prepared cloth, incomings, (from) fullers, has been brought into the storehouse of Gá-nun-mah" (túg sa-gi$_4$-a mu-tù aslag-e-ne é-kišib-ba Gá-nun-mah-ka ba-an-tu). The name of the comptroller (šakan) and dating by month and year follow (1581).

The second type, rather well represented, lists, when more than one transaction is involved, the number of pieces of cloth furnished by each fuller and his name. It then sums up the pieces of cloth according to kind and continues: "prepared cloth, incomings, (from) fullers, Ur-Shulgira(k) received" (túg sa-gi$_4$-a mu-tù aslag-e-ne Ur-^{d}Šul-gi-ra šu-ba-an-ti). The name of the comptroller and date by month and year only follow. If only one transaction is involved the arrangement is: first number and kinds of the pieces of goods, the "prepared cloth, incomings (from) N$_1$, the fuller, Ur-Shulgira(k) received etc." The texts distinguish between cases in which Ur-Shulgira(k) acts for himself (or for the institution which he represents) and cases in which the delivery is destined for others. In the latter case the phrases: "for ^{d}Shul-gi-URU-mu" (mu ^{d}Šul-gi-URU-mu-šè) or "for Lugal-ku(g)-zu" (mu Lugal-kù-zu-šè) are inserted before the words "Ur-Shulgira(k) received."

The official Ur-Shulgira(k), who from these texts appears to be the normal delivery point for the output of the fullers, is known to us from other documents also as in charge of receipts and deliveries of cloth. Unfortunately his precise position is not as clear as could be wished, nor are its institutional affinities well defined. He may have had particularly close relations with the Gá-nun-mah—the other recipient of cloth from the fullers—since in one document he receives materials for strengthening that structure.

The cloth which he receives is distributed mainly for three purposes:

(1) As cloth allotments to groups of employees: the fullers themselves, the runners (lú-kas$_4$-e-ne), and the corporals (uku-uš-e-ne). Other such deliveries by him to slaves and slavegirls are made with cloth from the "storehouse" (é-kišib-ba).

(2) As deliveries to ^{d}Šul-gi-URU-mu. This personage, who is mentioned in the accounts of finished cloth, may perhaps be identified with the herdsman (sahar) of that name who occurs in the credit section of the wool accounts in connection with wool deliveries from ^{d}Šul-gi-mi-šar.

(3) As deliveries to Lugal-ku(g)-zu, likewise mentioned in the wool accounts, but in the debit section.

Since most of these deliveries—not only the last ones, to named persons, but also those to groups of employees—seem to have close parallels in the wool accounts, whether in the credit or debit entries, it seems likely that we have come full circle, the wool returning as finished cloth to the Wool Office, which originally provided it, to be disposed of according to its various needs.

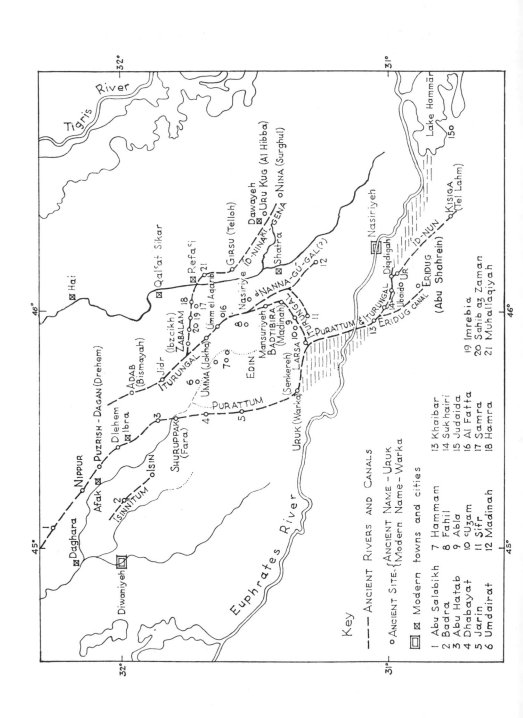

Key

— — ANCIENT RIVERS AND CANALS

o ANCIENT SITE- { ANCIENT NAME - URUK
⊠   { Modern Name - Warka

▣ Modern towns and cities

1 Abu Salabikh
2 Badra
3 Abu Hatab
4 Dhabayat
5 Jarin
6 Umdairat
7 Hammam
8 Fahil
9 Abla
10 ⁿUžam
11 Sifr
12 Madinah
13 Khaibar
14 Sukhairi
15 Judaida
16 Al Fatta
17 Samra
18 Hamra
19 Imrebia
20 Sahib az Zaman
21 Muhallaqiyah

14. The Waters of Ur

I. INTRODUCTION

The magnificent site plans which we owe—with so much else—to Sir Leonard Woolley's brilliant and painstaking work at Ur show on the northern and western edges of the mound two harbors, opening out upon the white unknown outside the plan and thus tacitly posing the question of how much we can ever know about the great canal system which once linked Ur and the other cities of Sumer in a net of intercommunication and—even more important—distributed to them the irrigation waters without which no city or other permanent human settlement could have existed.

The question is certainly legitimate, but not altogether an easy one; for it is well known that the major rivers of Iraq have substantially changed their courses since antiquity and also that in large sections of the country heavy deposits of new soil now securely hide all ancient river- and canal-beds deep under the present surface, out of reach of investigation. Special methods must therefore be brought to bear if the ancient system is eventually to be reconstructed and we should like to call attention here to one such method, that of Ceramic Surface Survey, which has already been applied with good results and moderately extensively.

The method of ceramic surface survey was first developed in 1937 in a survey of the Central Diyala region undertaken by the writer as part of the work of the Iraq Expedition of the Oriental Institute. The underlying assumption of the method is that in the semi-arid alluvial Mesopotamian plain, human settlement was possible only along rivers and canals. A systematic survey of all existing settlements (tells)

NOTE: First published in *Iraq* 22 (1960) 174–185, with Plate XXVIII.

in a region, dating the settlements by means of their surface pottery and plotting them on period maps, will therefore show that they are grouped in linear patterns representing the lines of the major water courses of the region in antiquity. Such maps, supplemented by information from inscriptional materials, will form a basic source for studies of ancient topography as well as of political and economic history.

Work with the method of ceramic surface survey was continued in a survey of Central Sumer carried out by Fuad Safar, Vaughn Crawford, and the writer in 1953–1954, in a survey of Akkad by Robert M. Adams and Vaughn Crawford in 1956–1957, on which the writer served as adviser, and lastly in a survey of the Diyala region as a whole, part of the program of the Diyala Basin Archaeological Project, undertaken by Fuad Safar, Robert M. Adams, Mohammed Ali Mustafa, and the writer in 1957–1958.[1]

In the case of the region of Ur, which forms the subject of the present paper, only marginal work if any is extant: a canal line, which may conceivably represent the boundary canal between Ur and Lagash, and a section of the Euphrates line between Uruk and Ur were noted on the Survey of Central Sumer, and important observations about an ancient canal in the Eridug plain have been made by Fuad Safar and Mohammed Ali Mustafa in connection with the excavations at Eridug. Scant as are these scattered observations on the ground, they may, however, provide just enough foothold to allow at least a preliminary attempt at sketching the major waterways of Ur in their dependence on the larger system of which they were part, even though such a sketch must of necessity lean more heavily on textual evidence, more lightly on evidence on the ground, than is altogether desirable. It must, needless to say, be open to correction even on major points once a systematic ceramic surface survey of the region can be undertaken.

II. PARENT SYSTEM: THE EUPHRATES TO URUK

1. Main Course

The primary source of water for the Ur region was at all times the Euphrates.[2] The course of this river in antiquity can now be fairly accurately plotted. The line of tells marking its course from Abu Ghubar north of Sippar over Sippar and down to Kish has been established by Adams and Crawford in their Akkad Survey. The course from Kish southeast into the line leading down to Abu Salabikh (Kesh?) and Nippur could not be investigated by them in similar detail, but must count as reasonably certain. From Abu Salabikh over Nippur, Drehem (*Puzriš-Dagan*), Dlehem, Abu Hatab (Kisurra), Fara (Shuruppak), Dharbayat, Jarin (Eresh??) to Warka (Uruk) the course was determined in the Survey of Central Sumer. Inscriptional evidence bear out the results.[3]

2. EFFLUENTS

Six major branches took off from the main Euphrates course between Abu Ghubar and Nippur in antiquity. They were:

(*a*) *The Zubi*. A line of tells marking the course of a major canal leaving the Euphrates from the left bank at Abu Ghubar was observed by Adams and Crawford. The line runs southeast over Deir, curves south at a point east of Jemdet Nasr, and eventually rejoins the main Euphrates course north of Abu Salabikh. It may on the basis of a topographical text published by Kraus plausibly be identified as the ancient Zubi canal.[4]

(*b*) *The Irninna*. A line of tells marking a canal leaving the Euphrates from the left bank at Sippar was observed by Adams and Crawford. The line runs southeast and south over Cutha, passes south of Jemdet Nasr, and joins the Zubi at a point east of that site. It may plausibly be identified with the ancient Irninna canal.[4]

(*c*) *The Araḫtum with the Apkallatum*. From the right bank of the Euphrates in the vicinity of Sippar branched the Araḫtum canal, flowing past *Luḫaiat* and a town . . . *bati* down through Babylon. Our knowledge of this branch is so far based on textual evidence alone since the Akkad Survey did not extend to the western bank of the Euphrates.[5]

South of Babylon the famous *Apkallatum* canal (Pallacottas) seems to have taken off from the Araḫtum and to have run southward, passing east of Aktab (ŠIT-TAB), then through Abiak, and continuing further south. This canal too is known only from inscriptional evidence.[6]

(d) The Me-^{d}En-líl-lá. The next important branch in order, the Me-Enlillak, left the Euphrates, likewise from the right bank, at Kish. Its course has been traced by Adams and Crawford from Kish down to Wannet-es-Saadun (Marad).[7]

(e) *The Iturungal with the* Íd-Nina^{ki}-g̃en-a and the ^{d}Nanna-gú-gal(?). At an as yet unidentified point, Ka-saḫar-ra, situated on the Euphrates a day's journey or so upstream from Nippur, the important effluent Iturungal took off, flowing first eastward, then southward. The line of its course was picked up in the Survey of Central Sumer at Bismayah (Adab), from where it continued southward over Jidr, past Bzeikh (Zabalam), over Jokha (Umma), Umm-el-Aqarib, Mansuriyah to Madinah (Bàd-tibira).[8] Here it veered west over Able and Senkereh (*Larsa*) to junction with the Euphrates again.[9]

Two effluents took off from the left bank of the Iturungal, the Íd-Nina^{ki}-g̃en-a, which over Bzeikh (Zabalam) flowed to Telloh (Girsu), Al Hibba (Uru-kù, Lagaš?), and Surghul (Nina),[10] and an anonymous branch which takes off from a point north of Mansuriyah, passes well to the east of Madinah (Bàd-tibira), and continues southeast down to a small mound also called Madinah. A branch takes off from the right bank and runs to Tell Sifr (Kutalla).

As to the possible identity of this anonymous branch it may be noted that it flows just about where one would reasonably expect the western border of the Lagash region toward Larsa and Ur to have been, and that inscriptional evidence gives some reason to believe that that boundary marched with a canal called ^{d}Nanna-gú-gal. Ur-Nammûk mentions in an inscription (*UET* I, 44(b) i. 9–12) that íd ^{d}Nanna-gú-gal íd-ki-sur-ra ⌜^{d}?⌝⌜Nin⌝(?)-⌜gír⌝(?)-⌜zu⌝ [m]u-ba-al, "he dug here the ^{d}Nanna-gú-gal, the boundary canal of Ningir-suk(?)," and a clay nail reported to come from Tello, probably picked up by a workman from a point on the canal in that general region, enlarges on this information (Ur-Nammûk Clay nail B, *SAK* p. 188 i): ^{1}^{d}Nanna ^{2}dumu-sag ^{d}En-líl-lá ^{3}lugal-a-ni ^{4}Ur-^{d}Nammu ^{5}nitah kala-ga ^{6}lugal Uri^{ki}-ma ^{7}lugal Ki-en-gi^{ki}-Uri-ke$_4$ ^{8}u$_4$ ⟨é⟩-^{d}En-líl-lá ^{9}in-dù-a ^{10}íd-da ^{11}^{d}Nanna-gú-gal mu-bi ^{12}íd-ki-sur-ra-kam ^{13}mu-ba-al ^{14}kun-bi a-ab-ba-ka ì-lá ^{15}di níg̃-gi-na ^{16}^{d}Utu-ta ^{17}bar bí-UD ^{18}KA bí-gi-in II ^{1}lú ^{2}^{d}Nanna-[da] ^{3}in-dab$_x$(URUDU)-kúr-[a] ^{4}lugal hé-[a] ^{5}ensi hé-[a] ^{6}lú áš-du$_{11}$-[ga] ^{7}^{d}Nanna-ge$_{18}$-[nam] ^{8}hé-[a] ^{9}ki-tuš ^{d}Nanna-[da] ^{10}hé-íb-gibil ^{11}uru-ni GI-KA-t[a] ^{12}hé-ta-dag-dag-ge [13]nam-ti-il [14]níg̃-gig-ga-ni [15]hé-na. "[1]For Nanna, [2]first-born son of Enlil, [3]his master, [4]did Ur-Nammûk, [5]the mighty male, [6]king of Ur, [7]king of Sumer and Akkad, [9-8]when he built the temple of Enlil, [13]here dig [10]the canal [11]the name of which is [d]Nanna-gú-gal [12]as boundary canal, [14]and connected its tail end with the sea. [15]Through a just judgment [16]by Utu [17]he cleared up the underlying facts [18]and confirmed the testimony (about the boundary). [II] [1]Whoever [3]shall engage in contention [2]with Nanna, [4]be he a king, [5]or be he a city ruler, [8]may he become [6-7]exactly as the man cursed by Nanna, [10]may he have to take up a new [9]abode with (each) Moon, [12]may he roam and roam [11]from his city and . . . . , [13]may health [15]be made (?) [14]a thing forbidden to him." Lastly it may be noted that a contract from Larsa mentions an orchard situated on the bank of the [d]Nanna-gú-gal and also a town called [d]Nanna-gú-gal, suggesting that [d]Nanna-gú-gal also touched on Larsa territory.[11] All of this would be consistent with an identification of the [d]Nanna-gú-gal with the anonymous branch of the Iturungal, though hardly, of course, conclusive.

(*f*) *The Isinnîtum.* From an unknown point on the right bank of the Euphrates north of Nippur branched off the Íd-SAL + SILA$_4$-SIG, Akkadian *Isinnîtum*, the Isin canal. The line of this canal was picked up by the Survey of Central Sumer at Seyyed Ridha southwest of Nippur and was followed southwest over Ishan Badra and Danghūz to Ishan Bahriyāt (Isin). That the canal fed from the Euphrates north of Nippur is indicated by the bilingual processional hymn to Nin-Insiannak (*KAR* 16), which describes how the goddess travels up this canal to the Euphrates and then floats down to Nippur (lines 27–40).

III. THE REGION OF UR: THE EUPHRATES BELOW URUK

1. Main Course

The Survey of Central Sumer was unable to pick up the line of the Euphrates course south of Warka until it reached Ishan Khaibar. Such interruption of a river- or canal-line by empty space without settlements usually indicates that the river or canal here passed through swamps or lakes anciently, and this may well have been the case with the Euphrates on this part of its course. A more detailed discussion will be found below in connection with the confluence of the Iturungal.

From Ishan Khaibar a well-defined line of tells marks a south-easterly course over Sukhairi West, Sukhairi East to Diqdiqah located one and a half miles northeast of the ziggurat at Ur. The tells forming the line are in order from northwest to southeast: (1) Ishan Khaibar. A medium-low mound with surface pottery of Cassite-Middle Babylonian period. (2) Mafshuq. A small mound with undistinctive surface pottery, possibly Cassite-Middle Babylonian in date. (3) Abu Thayeh. Small to medium tell with Cassite to Middle Babylonian surface pottery. (4) Sukhairi East. Medium to large mound with Cassite-Middle Babylonian surface pottery and some indications of destruction by fire. A cut made by robbers and a subsequent brief examination by the Department of Antiquities have exposed strata of Early Dynastic date. (5) Sukhairi West. Small mount with surface pottery of Cassite-Middle Babylonian date. (6) Diqdiqah. Small mound situated in direct continuation of the line of tells here discussed. It was not visited on the Survey of Central Sumer. A number of inscriptions of Ur III and Isin-Larsa date were picked up on the site and brought to Ur when work there was in progress.

After Diqdiqah the course of the Euphrates seems once more to be lost. The map shows no mounds. Most likely, therefore, we are again dealing with a stretch where the river anciently entered marshes or lakes and it seems quite possible that in antiquity the precursor of the present Lake Hammar, now some twenty miles further southeast, may have extended upward toward the vicinity of Diqdiqah.

2. CONFLUENCE WITH THE Iturungal

South and southeast of Warka, over toward Senkereh (*Larsa*), stretches, as we have mentioned above, empty space, and we have suggested that this space indicates ancient lakes or marshes through which the main course of the Euphrates here lay. To judge from a letter of Hammurabi's (*VAB* VI, no. 43. 27–28) which mentions [id]*Purattum ša iš-tu Larsa*[ki] *a-di Urí*[ki], "the Euphrates from Larsa to Ur," the course passed close by Senkereh, and since the course of the

Iturungal coming from the east could likewise be followed to Senkereh, the confluence of the two should likely be sought at or near that site. From Senkereh and south, along the edge of the empty space, a number of tells which we were unfortunately not able to investigate in the Survey of Central Sumer are shown on the map down to Ishan Khaibar. They could conceivably mark the joint course of the Euphrates and the Iturungal after their confluence, a course continued in the Ishan Khaibar line. Further investigation on the ground is much needed here.

Inscriptional evidence of interest for this stretch of the river is the description of the progress of the ceremonial barge of the god Nanna given in the myth of "The Journey of Nanna to Nippur"—clearly the hieros logos of an annual ritual journey of the image or emblem of the god by boat from Ur to Nippur and back. Proceeding up from Ur the boat is, when the text becomes available after a lacuna, moving along the banks of the Iturungal.[12] It passes in sequence Muru (IM^{ki}), Larsa, Uruk, and two cities the names of which are not preserved, one of them probably Shuruppak,[13] before it reaches Nippur. At each of these cities the chief goddess of the city comes out of her temple to hail the boat and wish it good speed.[14] Since the joint course of the Euphrates and the Iturungal south of Larsa, which Hammurabi calls the Euphrates, is here called the Iturungal, it seems probable that both names were in use, or one or the other may have been the preferred designation at different periods.

3. THE Eridug CANAL

In the course of the third season's work at Eridug in 1948–1949, Fuad Safar and Mohammed Ali Mustafa took occasion to investigate the surrounding plain. Fuad Safar reports on their findings in *Sumer* 6 (1950) p. 28 as follows: "At the same time several small mounds, situated in the flat depression of Eridu and not far away from the ruins of that city, were also sounded and carefully examined. The mounds were found to lie on the banks of the bed of a wide canal which, in ancient times, was undoubtedly connected with the River Euphrates. The recognition of this canal and the tracing of its course are now extremely difficult, as it has been filled with sand and soil drifted in from the surrounding plain. The course of the canal crosses the flat depression of Eridu from north-west to south-east and its nearest point to Eridu is about 3 kilometres from the south-west of that site. The mounds were not very high and carried surface pottery dating to not later than the second millennium B.C. A number of them, however, were covered with burials of a later period, though in a few there were burials of the Kassite period or even earlier, near the surface."

This wide canal which in the second—and presumably in the third—millennium B.C. traversed the plain of Eridug can hardly be other than the Íd-edin-Eriduga (NUN)^{ki}, "the canal of the Eridug plain," later called the *Susuka*, listed in Diri IV (II R 50, ii. 13); and it must have been on this canal that Inannak traveled back to Uruk with the many and varied divine offices which she had obtained from Enkik in Eridug as told in the myth of Inannak's Journey to Eridug, a myth which is almost certainly the hieros logos of a cult festival, an actual ritual journey of the divine barge Má-an-na from Uruk to Eridug and back with stops at the places indicated.[15]

The text of the myth recording the journey back from Eridug is unfortunately badly damaged, but it can be seen that Enkik tried to stop the boat at seven points of the journey, which are in order: (1) [. . .]. . .[ ] *HGT.* 25, i. 6, (2) HU [. . .]-kù-ga idem 41, (3) ⌜Du⌝$_6$-ul-ma idem ii.6', (4) Du$_6$-a-⌜šà⌝-ga idem ii.31' (5) [. . . . . .] idem, iii.11', (6) ID Iturungal (UD-NUN) . . . idem, iii.45, (7) Kar-babbar-ra idem, iv.63. These points must be located on the Eridug canal north and northeast of Eridug, each further upstream than the preceding one. With point (6) the boat must already have passed into the Euphrates, for the mention of Iturungal can only apply to the common bed of the canal with the Euphrates south of Larsa. The last point, (7), appears to be the quay on the Euphrates at Uruk itself.

In terms of the main Euphrates course it would thus seem that the river flowing southeast from Uruk first received the Iturungal entering from the left at Larsa and then, as it continued south, sent off the Eridug canal as a branch from its right bank.

4. THE DIQDIQAH FAN

As has been mentioned earlier the small mound of Diqdiqah yielded a number of inscriptions which were brought in to Ur when the excavations there were in progress. A striking fact about the Diqdiqah inscription is the frequency with which work on canals is mentioned and the number of different canals involved. We may list the following: (1) *UET*, I.45 (9 clay cones): digging of Íd-Urí^{ki}-ma, (2) *UET*, I.46 (5 clay cones): digging of Íd-En-erín-nun, (3) *UET*, I.42 (3 clay cones): digging of Íd-nun, and (4) *UET*, I.136 (several inscribed bricks. Provenience given as Diqdiqah?): digging of Íd^d-Nanna-šita₄ (ᴜ + ᴋɪᴅ).

Such coming together at a single point on a major river of three or four branch canals can in a pattern of gravity irrigation mean only one thing: a weir with the fan of branch canals which it serves. The distance to which a branch canal can carry water out into the surrounding country depends in gravity irrigation in large measure on the height obtainable at the point of takeoff where it feeds from the main river. It is therefore usual to raise the water level in the main river by means of a weir and to utilize the stretch of high water directly above the weir as takeoff point for branch canals flowing out from it fanwise. In addition to providing height the weir also serves to assure a supply of water to the branch canals more steady and less affected by fluctuations in water level in the main river than could otherwise have been obtained. Thus use of weirs was well known in antiquity. A characteristic example furnishes the Shad-hurwān-al-asfal on the Naharwān excavated by the Diyala Basin Archaeological Project and dating to Sassanian and early Islamic times. A far older example is the weir at Girsu, dating to shortly after the time of Gudea. The identification of this latter as a weir— it was interpreted as a Hypogeum by its excavator M. André Parrot in *RA* 29 (1932), 45–57—follows with certainty from its remarkable and detailed structural correspondence with the later Naharwān weir. Of inscriptional references to weirs Eannatum Boulder A, vii. 7–13 and Entemena Brick A, iii.10–iv.8 may be mentioned. It must appear highly probable, therefore, that part of Diqdiqah covers the remains of an ancient weir dating to the time of Ur-Nammûk or earlier, a weir serving to regulate the intake of a fan of three, four, or more branch canals watering the region around Ur. These branch canals, insofar as known to us, were:

(*a*) Íd-Urí^{ki}-ma. Mentioned in *UET*, I. 45: ^{1d}En-líl ²lugal kur-kur-ra ³lugal-a-ni ⁴Ur-^dNammu ⁵nitah kala-ga ⁶lugal Urí^{ki}-ma

[7]lugal Ki-en-gi[ki]-Uri-ke[4] [8]Íd-Urí[ki]-ma [9]íd-nindaba (PAD-[d]INANNA)-ka-ni [10]mu-na-ba-al, "[1]For Enlil, [2]king of all countries, [3]his master, [4]did Ur-Nammûk, [5]the mighty male, [6]king of Ur, [7]king of Sumer and Akkad, [10]here dig [8]the Íd-Urí[ki]-ma, ('The canal of Ur'), [9]his canal (productive) of food offerings." This canal, which seems to have been an irrigation canal serving the fields of the Enlil temple mentioned in *UET*, I. 46 (see below), may perhaps—because of its name, "The canal of Ur"—be assumed to have taken off from the right bank of the Euphrates since the city of Ur is to that side of the river.

(*b*) Íd-En-erín-nun. This canal, also serving fields of the Enlil temple, is mentioned in *UET*, I 46: [1d]En-líl [2]lugal kur-kur-ra [3]lugal-a-ni [4]Ur-[d]Nammu [5]lugal Urí[ki]-ma [6]lugal Ki-en-gi[ki]-Uri-ke[4] [7]é-a-ni [8]mu-na-du [9]Íd-En-erín-nun [10]íd-nindaba (PAD-[d]INANNA)-ka-ni [11]mu-na-ba-al, "[1]For Enlil, [2]king of all countries, [3]his master, [4]did Ur-Nammûk, [5]king of Ur, [6]king of Sumer and Akkad, [8]here build [7]his temple [11]and dug here for him [9]the Íd-En-erin-nun [10]his canal (productive) of food offerings." The Enlil temple here mentioned was most likely situated in Diqdiqah. The canal Íd-En-erín-nun may have watered fields of the temple on the left bank of the Euphrates.

(*c*) Íd-nun. This canal is mentioned in *UET*, I. 42: [1d]Nanna [2]lugal-a-ni-šè [3]Ur-[d]Nammu [4]nitah kala-ga [5]lugal Urí[ki]-ma [6]lugal Ki-en-gi[ki]-Uri-ke[4] [7]Íd-nun [8]íd-ki-ág-ni [9]mu-na-ba-al, "[1]For Nanna, [2]his master, [3]did Ur-Nammûk, [4]the mighty male, [5]king of Ur, [6]king of Sumer and Akkad, [9]here dig [7]the Íd-nun, [8]his beloved canal." The Íd-nun took off from the right bank of the Euphrates, for we know that it flowed directly past Ur itself. It is mentioned as Íd-nun-kù a-zal-le gal-gal-la... "pure Íd-nun, which makes great the.... waters...." in the praise of Ur in the Shulgir hymn (*SLTN* 79, l. 16) immediately before the mention of the city wall and it flowed, as shown by the location of the North and West harbors, along the west side of the city. One of these harbors—but so far not clear which—must have been the often-mentioned Kar-za-gìn, "the pure quay," of Nanna on which stood in late Ur III times a statue of Amar-[d]Enzunak.

From Ur the Íd-nun must have followed a course southeast along the gravelly ridge down to Tell Lahm, for we know from a brief entry in the Ur III text *UET* III, 1181: 3 sila ì-g̃iš má-a g̃ar-ra Kisiga[16] (EZEN × KÙ)-šè, "3 sila oil stowed on a boat for Kissik," that it was possible to ship from Ur down to Kissik. The identity of Kisiga/Kissik with Tell Lahm, further, seems to follow from a Nabonidus cylinder found at that site and published in photo by Fuad Safar in *Sumer* 5 (1949), pl. vii. 4. The end of col. 1 reads: —É-amaš-kù-ga bît ^{d}A-....-tim be-lit gi-me-er su-pur-ru bîtu el-li ša qí-ir-ba URU-EZEN[× KÙ]^{ki} ša i-na la-ba-ri i-ni-šu i-qu-pu i-ga-ru-šu etc. "...É-amaš-kù-ga, the temple of Anunîtum(?), mistress of all, the fold, the pure temple, which is in Kisiga, which had become weak from age, the walls of which buckled, ..." The Ishtar temple É-amaš-kù-ga in Kisiga here mentioned is also known from *SK* 199 rev. iii. 36, where the sign for the city is to be read as EZEN(!) × KÙ, and from *HGT* 157, i.14, where only the last part of the city name is preserved.

The Íd-nun is further mentioned in the Lament for Sumer which states: gú Íd-nun-na ^{d}Nanna-ka á dugud ba-ši-in-túm Maš-kán-é-danna ^{d}Nanna-ka tùr dugud-ge$_{18}$ ba-gul, "On the bank of Nanna's Íd-nun heavy hand (lit. 'arm') has been laid (lit. 'brought'), the Mashkan-edanna of Nanna has been destroyed like a .... cattle pen."[17] Where Mashkan-edanna ("The threshing floor of the double-mile house") is to be located is as yet uncertain. Nor can we know whether the localities Bára-an-na, É-[...], É-pu-úḫ-ru[um-ma], "the house of assembly," and Ki-abrig, mentioned in the following lines of the lament, are to be looked for in the region through which the Íd-nun flowed.

(*d*) Íd-^{d}Nanna-šita$_4$. This canal is mentioned on several bricks of Warad-Sîn assumed to come from Diqdiqah. They may have belonged to a sluice or similar construction at the head of the canal. The text reads: ^{1}^{d}Nanna ^{2}lugal-a-ni-ir ^{3}Warad-^{d}Sîn (EN-ZU) ^{4}ú-a Urí^{ki}-ma ^{5}É-babbar-da ní-tuk ^{6}lugal Zara^{ki}-ma ^{7}u$_4$ ^{d}Nanna ^{8}^{d}Nin-gal-bi ^{9}šà-ne mu-un-ne-ša$_4$-aš ^{10}ki-šu-íl-mà ^{11}mu-un-uš-en ^{12}Íd-^{d}Nanna-šita$_4$(U + KID) ^{13}mu-ba-al-la-a ^{14}ki-bi bí-in-gi$_4$-a, "^{1}For Nanna, ^{2}his master, ^{3}did (I) Warad-Sîn, ^{4}provider for Ur, ^{5}reverent toward Ebabbar, ^{6}king of Larsa $^{7-8}$until I had prevailed upon Nanna and Ningal ^{11}frequent (?) ^{10}the place where I pray. (My entreaty:) ^{13}that I (could) here dig ^{12}the Íd-^{d}Nanna-šita$_4$ ^{14}and restore it."

The canal is also mentioned in the list *OECT*, IV 162, ii. 10 as Íd-⟨d⟩Nanna-šita$_4$ but little further is known about it.

5. The "Sea"

Four clay cones with identical text: U.2520, 2701, 6019, and 7722 were found loose at Diqdiqah and were brought in to Ur, to judge by the excavation numbers at various times. The text of these cones, published in *UET* I as no. 50 reads: i. 1dNanna ^{2}dumu-saĝ ^{3d}En-líl-lá ^{4}lugal-a-ni ^{5}Ur-^{d}Nammu ^{6}nitaḫ kala-ga ^{7}lugal Urí^{ki}-ma ^{8}lugal Ki-en-gi^{ki}-Uri-ke$_4$ ^{9}lú é-^{d}Nanna ^{10}in-dù-a ii. 1níĝ-ul-lí-a-ke$_4$ pa mu-na-è ^{2}gaba a-ab-ba-ka ^{3}ki-sar-a nam-ga-eš$_8$ bí-silim^4 má-Má-gana šu-na mu-ni-gi$_4$, "i. 1For Nanna, ^{2}the first-born son ^{3}of Enlil, ^{4}his master, ^{5}did Ur-Nammûk, ^{6}the mighty male, ^{7}king of Ur, ^{8}king of Sumer and Akkad, $^{9-10}$did the man who built the temple of Nanna, ii. 1 have the primordial (state of) things (re)appear. ^{2}On the shore of the 'Sea' ^{3}in the registry place he saw the sea trade(rs) safely home^4 and returned the Magan ships to his (i.e., to Nanna's) hand."^{18} With this may be compared the Code of Ur-Nammûk ii, 30–37: ^{30}ki-[s]ar-ra ^{31}má-Má-gan^{ki}-na ^{32d}Nanna ^{33}á(?) ^{d}Nanna ^{34}lugal-⸢mà⸣-ta ^{35}ḫé-mi-gi$_4$ ^{36}Urí^{ki}-ma ^{37}ḫa-ba-UD, "^{30}In the registry place ^{31}the ships of Magan ^{32}of Nanna ^{33}by the might(?) of Nanna ^{34}my master ^{35}I verily detained ^{36}in Ur ^{37}I verily cleared them."

What Ur-Nammûk here tells us seems to be that he reestablished an earlier practice of detaining ships returning with cargoes from Egypt at a registry place on the shore of the sea until all accounting for and claims on merchandise and profits had been properly settled in orderly fashion in Ur, after which the ships were allowed to proceed to the harbor of the city to unload.

Since the cones from Diqdiqah can have come originally only from the walls and foundations of the place of registry on the shore of the "Sea," the establishing of which they commemorate, we must—if the provenience is to be trusted—look for the registry place and the "Sea" at Diqdiqah or in its immediate environs. This is perhaps not as unlikely a thought as it might at first seem. As we have mentioned earlier the line of tells marking the course of the Euphrates down toward Ur stops at Diqdiqah, leaving the kind of empty space usually associated with ancient marshes or lakes, and the ground between Diqdiqah and Lake Hammār some twenty miles further on is even now so low that it inundates in flood season. It seems, therefore, not at all impossible that in antiquity Lake Hammār, or a predecessor of it, may have sent an arm up toward Diqdiqah, and that it and the marshes to the south were considered by the ancients part of the Persian Gulf, with which they connected.

Girl under the Moon

Under Nanna's moon—a girl under Nanna's moon
    alone I lie,
Under Nanna's moon drifting over the pure mountains
    alone I lie,
Under the mountains of the cedars where sleeps Mullil
    alone I lie.

As it stands, the stanza comes from a formal lament by the grain-goddess about the destruction of her temple. That lament, however, clearly builds on a folk song, the plaint of a young girl longing for her lover. Findspot unknown.

15. *About the Sumerian Verb*

A Hair perhaps divides the False and True—
Yes; and a single Alif were the clue—
Could you but find it.

The Sumerian verb may be said[1] to consist generally of an invariant, the root, which carries the lexical meaning, and variables, affixes, which carry grammatical meanings and serve to modify the lexical meaning of the root according to a limited number of grammatical categories.

The variables, the affixes, consist in their turn of pronominal, nominal, and relater (i.e., casemark or "postpositional") components of various kinds joined together in partitive parataxis as for example -nda-, "with him," analyzable as -n.d (a).a-, "inside (.a) of forearm (.da.) of him (-n.)."

They relate as wholes to the root in predicate (nexal) relations specified by their relaters (casemarks) much as the members of a sentence relate to the verb governing them.

They stand as wholes to one another in conjunctive parataxis and thus constitute a series of modifiers of the root joined, as it were, by "and."

They follow one another in the form according to a fixed order of rank[2] much as the members of a sentence follow one another in syntactical order—only theirs is a morphological, fixed order, a frozen syntax as it were.

NOTE: First published in *Studies in Honor of Benno Landsberger, AS* XVI (Chicago, 1965), pp. 71–102.

They may be grouped into prefixes, such as precede the root in narrative forms of the verb, and suffixes, such as follow it. The prefixes can be further subdivided into (1) profixes, that is, affixes that must begin the form in which they occur, (2) prefixes in the narrower sense, that is, affixes that may begin the form but do not have to do so, and (3) infixes, that is, affixes that cannot begin the form.

PROFIXES (PR. 28)

The profixes must always begin the form in which they occur. Functionally they may be said to parallel modal sentence adverbs. They appear to convey will in the speaker to realize the event presented, but the kind of realization the speaker has in view can be either external realization in the outside world (injunctive use) or internal realization in the mind of the addressee (assertive use). The realization, further, may be expected to follow from the speaker's injunction or assertion simply, or it may be enjoined or asserted as outcome of other will. Besides this dimension of will to realization the profixes show another dimension, that of reality of the event. The reality can be affirmed, presumed, or negated. Diagrammatically the profixes may therefore be arranged according to the dimensions of will to realization and degree of reality.

	INJUNCTIVE		ASSERTIVE	
	Simple	Of outside will	Of outside will	Simple
Affirmative	Imperative $\sqrt{}$	Jussive $de/_{a, u}$	Contrapuntive $\check{s}i/_{a, u}$	Indicative #
Presumptive	Cohortative $ga/_{i, u}$	Optative $he/_{a, u}$	Presumptive volitive $ne/_a$	Presumptive negative $li/_a$
Negative	Frustrative nuš	Vetitive na	Nolitive bara	Negative nu

It may be noted that the dividing line between injunctive and assertive is not a sharp one; he- and na- may both be used also assertively to express mere potentiality, and bara- can be used also injunctively with prohibitive force.

The presumptive, which stands midway between affirmative and negative, seems to indicate a degree of uncertainty in the speaker. In the injunctives this uncertainty seems due to clearly felt dependence on other will: in the cohortative on the will of the addressee, in the optative on outside will or simply on fate. In the assertives the uncertainty is rather about the data asserted as not open to direct experience by the speaker: state of mind in the subject (na-) or negation of matters outside the speaker's here and now, in the b areas (li/ₐ).

In detail the profixes are the following.

AFFIRMATIVE

$\sqrt{}$-, the punctive root, mark of imperative, "do," as for example é-zu kala-ga-ab, "strengthen (kalag-a-b) your house" (Code of Lipiteshtar xiii 27). When the root moves to profix position from its normal place behind the infixes it gives the form imperative character as a demand for realization of the event it denotes. In profix position the root is incompatible with the prefix i/e- and with the stem suffixes -ed- and -e-. The form which it introduces is a virtual second person but has overt mark of subject only in the plural (-(en)zen). Only punctive roots can occur in profix position.

–de/ₐ,ᵤ, jussive, "be it that," as for example ukù g̃á mar-ma-an-zé-en ír-ra da-mar-re-en:*ni-ši li-hi-šá-nim-ma tak-rib-tú liš-ša-kin,* "People, hurry hither! Be it that I set up (da-a-mar-en) a lament" (*SBH,* p. 31, lines 18 f.); du₅-mu-u₈-ši-du, "O be it that you might march against me" (Kramer, *From the Tablets of Sumer* [Indian Hills, Colorado, 1956] Fig. 76, line 5). The element de- seems to enjoin— in semi-incantatory manner—the event itself to come into being, which explains the Akkadian preference for rendering it by a third neuter optative passive (for other examples see *GSG* §666). It varies in use with ga-, "let me," and he-, "may" (cf. *GSG* §§651 and 666), and is predominantly found in Emesal context.

–ši/ₐ,ᵤ, contrapuntive, "correspondingly," "he on his part," as for example, [umun íb-ba]-na an mu-un-da-ur-ur ᵈIškur súr-ra-na ki ši-in-ga-tuktuk, "the heavens tremble before the lord in his wrath, the earth on its part also shakes (ši-n.ga-tuktuk) at Ishkur in his raging" (IV R 28, No. 2:8 and 11). The profix ši- indicates that the speaker presents the occurrence denoted by the verb as a parallel, corresponding counterpart occurrence to something else.[3]

#, indicative. Absence of other profix, zero-profix, indicates indicative, statement of positive fact.

PRESUMPTIVE

ga/$_{i,u}$, cohortative, "let me/us," as for example ga-mu-ra-ab-dím: *lu-pu-ša-ku-um*, "let me make for thee (ga-mu-ra-b-dim)" (*MSL* IV 71, line 90). The element gives the form the character of a plea for assent to an activity; it is incompatible with the prefix i/e- and with the stem-suffixes -ed- and -e-. The element also is incompatible with durative root. The form introduced by ga- is a virtual first person but has overt mark of subject only in the plural (-(en)den). Its negative counterpart is na- of the vetitive.

he/$_{a,u}$, optative, "may," as for example hé-íb-dím-me:*li-pu-uš*, "may he make (he-b-dim-e)" (*MSL* IV 70, line 88). The profix he- indicates a favorable attitude in the speaker toward realization of the occurrence denoted by the verb. The realization which the speaker has in mind may be external realization, and his commitment may range from will to, or wish for, the occurrence (optative: "may he") to permission for it (permissive: "he may") or mere allowance for it as a possibility (potentialis: "he may"), which approaches use as an assertive. The realization of the occurrence which the speaker has in mind may, however, also be inner realization in the addressee, the acceptance of it as real by him. In the latter usage as a strong assertive he- is incompatible with the stem-suffixes -ed- and -e-; as example of it in this use may serve níĝ-erím níg-á-zi ka-ge (hé-mi-gi$_4$, "(words of) enmity and violence I verily barred (he-mi-gi) at the mouths (that wished to speak them)" (Code of Lipiteshtar xix 12–13). The negative counterpart of he- is bara-.

ne/$_a$, presumptive volitive, "(he) of his own," "(he) decided to," as for example geštug-ga-ni na-an-g[ub], "she took it into her head to set (na-a-n-gub) her heart upon (lit. 'her ear toward')" (Inanna's Descent, line 1). The profix ne$_6$/na- appears to indicate that the speaker projects himself by empathy into the subject and presents the act from inside as urged by will or wish or whim.[4]

li/a, presumptive negative, "not." The prefix li/a- takes the place of the negation nu- with verbal forms that show the area prefixes bi- and ba-, which indicate occurrences in area other than the speaker's here and now. It may be assumed to denote the degree of uncertainty connected with statements of matters out of view of speaker and hearer.

NEGATIVE

nuš, frustrative, "were it but that," used to express unrealizable wish, as for example nu-uš-ma-da-ǧál-la, "(my *pukku*) which I wish were here with me (nuš-ma-da-ǧal-a) (but which could not so be)."

na, vetitive, "may not," as for example ma-da-na suhuš-bi na-an-ge-né, "may he/she (a deity) not fix firmly (na-n-gen-e) into his land its supports (lit. 'its legs')" (Code of Lipiteshtar xx 46). The prefix na- indicates unfavorable attitude in the speaker toward the realization of the occurrence denoted by the verb and gives to the form the character of a plea for concurrence in a wish for non-realization or in allowing for the possibility of nonrealization. In the latter use it serves as a negative *potentialis*. As example may serve i-lu na-ám-er-ra, "the wailing that he may not come (na-m-er-a)" (*CT* XV, Pl. 26, line 1). The prefix na- is the negative counterpart of the cohortative ga-; cf. ga-àm-ma-sìg-ge-en-dè-en, "let us smite" (ga-a-m.ma-sig-e-enden), and the corresponding nam-ba-sìg-ge-en-dè-en, "let us not smite" (na-a-m.ba-sig-e-enden), in Gilgamesh and Agga, lines 8 and 14 (*AJA* 53 [1949] 7).

bara, nolitive, "must not." The prefix bara- indicates unfavorable attitude in the speaker toward realization of the occurrence denoted by the verb. If the speaker has external realization in view bara- indicates will to nonrealization, prohibition, and serves as a prohibitive. If the speaker has in view internal realization in the mind of the addressee bara-indicates will to the addressee not entertaining the notion and serves as assertion of nonfact; as such it is the negative counterpart of assertive he/a, u- and is, as the latter, incompatible with the stem-suffixes -ed- and -e-. As examples may serve ki-sur-ra ᵈNin-ǧír-zu-ka-ke₄ ba-ra-mu-bal-e, "(for vast eons) he (i.e., the

Ummean) must not cross hither (bara–mu–bal–e(d)) over the boundary of Ningirsu" (Stele of the Vultures, obv. xx 17–19); ud–ul–lí–a–ta
lugal–lugal–e–ne–er ba–ra–an–dím–ma ᵈUtu–lugal–g̃á gal–bi hu–mu–na–
dù, "what since days of yore a king among the kings verily had not
fashioned (bara–n–dim–a) I verily built in grand fashion for my
master Utu."

nu, negative, "not," as for example dumu nu–un–ši–in–tu–ud, "she
bore not unto him (nu–n.ši–n–tud) a son" (Code of Lipiteshtar xvii
11). The profix nu– serves to state negative fact and is the negative
counterpart of zero–profix, indicative, which serves to state positive
fact.

PREFIXES

The prefixes can begin a form but do not have to do so. They
would seem to denote various aspects of time and place under which
the lexical meaning of the root is to be viewed, so that functionally
they may be said to parallel adverbs of time and place. In form the
prefixes seem to be composites of pronominal (explicit or merely
understood), nominal, and relater elements joined in partitive parataxis.
As pronominal—or perhaps better pronominal-adverbial—elements
occur zero, n, l, m, and b; as nominal element occurs g; as relater or
casemark elements occur u, a, i/e, and zero. The reference of the
pronominal-adverbial elements appears to be—in order of their
occurrence in the form—to the subject (#), to preceding verbal
action (n) or phrase of time (m), to following verbal action (#), and
to various areas (m, b) and points (n, l).

The prefixes group into six successive ranks, three looking most
nearly to time and three to place.

Aspects of Time

The aspects of time relate to the degree of persistence of the action
in time or to its location in time relative to other actions referred to
by the speaker.

Aspects of Persistence (Pr. 27)

The persistence prefixes form a single rank and serve to indicate the
degree of persistence of the occurrence denoted by the verb, its effect,

in the subject. In form they may be analyzed as composed of an understood pronominal element referring to the subject and a relater or case element.[5]

u, mark of limited persistence. The prefix is so far attested in a few imperative forms only, for example ğál-lu, "open up without delay (ğal-u)" (Kramer, *SLTN*, No. 35 ii 11; Inanna's Descent, line 75, cf. line 76). The suggestion that it denotes limited persistence, that is, dominance of the occurrence and its effects over the subject for a limited span of time only, fits both the contexts in which the extant forms occur and the meaning pattern of the rank as a whole.

a, mark of persistence. The prefix a- presents the occurrence denoted by the verb as persisting in the subject, who is dominated and lastingly conditioned by it. Accordingly forms with a- denoting past action are regularly translated into Akkadian as permansives, not preterits, as for example in an-gub:*na-zu-uz* (*MSL* IV 111, line 20), ab-gub:*na-zu-uz* (ibid., p. 112, line 25, but ì-gub:*iz-zi-iz* in line 26); similarly, clauses with a- forms are preferentially rendered in Akkadian by participles—implying persistent tendency—and not by preterit subjunctive, for example ⁱˢkak ur₅ šà-ga an-da-ab-lá-àm:*u-ṣu mu-šak-kir lib-bi u ha-še-e*, "the arrow, nailer of lung and heart (i.e., the arrow, which—since that action persists in it and dominates it—nails lung to heart)" (*RA* 12 74–75, lines 1–2). In forms with a- denoting future action the characteristic aspect of inner conditioning and domination of the subject by a future act serves to express obligation or general inner urge to realization of the action, for example an-lá-e:*i-šaq-qal*, "he has to pay (the value difference in an exchange)" (*MSL* I, Tf. 4 iv 47), an-ta-bal-e-da, "who is minded to cross over" (Entemena Cone A vi 16). In imperative forms, finally, a- is the preferred choice of prefix. The preference is a natural one since the prefix presents the action as conditioning and compelling for the subject, for example zi-ga:*ti-bi*, "rise (zig-a)!" (*MSL* IV 76, col. i 1), more precisely "you are/have to rise!"

Note that the a- prefix is never explicitly rendered before second person singular ergative infix -e- but is left understood.

i/e, mark of transitory, nonconditioning aspect. The prefix i/e- presents the occurrence denoted by the verb as touching on the subject without inwardly conditioning him in any lasting manner. Forms with i/e- prefix denoting past action are therefore regularly translated by Akkadian preterits. Imperatives, since they imply some degree of inner conditioning of the subject, are not formed with i/e-. As example may serve tukum-bi lú-ù gud in-huĝ, "if a man hired (i-n-huĝ) an ox" (Code of Lipiteshtar xx 49–51).

Aspect of Conjunctivity (Pr. 26)

The prefixes of conjunctivity serve to link the action denoted by the verb to an action mentioned earlier.[6]

n-ga, mark of general conjunctivity, "also," for example niĝ-ĝá-e-i-zu-a-mu za-e in-ga-e-zu, "what I know you also know (i-n.ga-e-zu)" (*CT* XVII, Pl. 26, line 62).

m-ga, mark of specified contemporaneity, "at this (just specified) time," for example ud-5-ud-10-àm ba-zal-la-ba lugal-mu i-si-iš Ki-en-gi-ra-ke$_4$ sá(!) nam-ga-mu-ni-ib-du$_{11}$, "when five to ten days had passed, at this time (-m.ga) did the tears of Shumer happen (or 'see fit') to (na-) reach my king" (*PBS* X 2, No. 6, rev. i 16–20).

Aspect of Previousness (Pr. 25)

The prefix of previousness marks the occurrence denoted by the verb as previous and preconditioned to a subsequently stated occurrence.

u/a, i, mark of previousness, "when...(then)," for example lú é a-ba-sun ù-un-dù mu-sar-ra-bi ... ki-gub-ba-bi nu-ub-da-ab-kúr-re-a, "the man who, when the house has grown old and he has rebuilt it, does not change the place of its inscriptions..." (*UET* I, Pls. K and L, lines 26 ff.). The prefix occurs in the form a- before the prefix ba-, in the form i- before the prefix bi-. It is incompatible with the stem-suffixes -ed- and -e-. A form with this prefix is usually followed by a durative (pres./fut.) in -e.[7]

ASPECTS OF PLACE

The aspects of place relate the action of the verb to a point or an area.

Aspect of Propinquity I (Pr. 24)

The prefixes constituting the rank of Aspect of Propinquity I consist of a consonantal pronominal-adverbial element of place followed by zero mark of collative case, which denotes a relation of togetherness (see n. 13). Since it is unlikely that Sumerian had initial consonantal clusters we may assume that the pronominal-adverbial elements m and l—both sonors—were not true consonants but syllabic in nature and thus could begin a form as any other syllable (cf. n. 6).

m#, mark of propinquity to (zero mark for collative) the area of the speech situation (m). The prefix is neutral as to direction (accollative: "hither"; collative in narrower sense: "here"; decollative: "hence") of motion.[8] As example may serve an instance of the less frequent decollative use: ᵈInanna kur-šè i-im-du, "Inanna was walking hence (i-m-du) toward the nether world" (Inanna's Descent, line 25). The prefix m#- is incompatible with prefixes of Aspect of Propinquity II and seems to combine with no infixes other than -da-, -ta-, and -ši-.

l#, mark of propinquity to (zero mark for collative) a point relatively remote from the speaker (1). The point referred to by l#- is rarely specified; usually it is rather an ideal point, an implied goal or fulfillment point of the action as such. "Goal-aimed aspect" describes perhaps the function of the prefix best. As example may serve al-di-di-de-en nu-kúš-ù-dè-en ì-di-di-dè-en ù nu-ku-ku-me-en:*a-tal-lak* [*ul a*]*n-na-ah* ⌈*aˡ-dal-ma* [*ul a-ṣa-al*]*-lal*, "I walk and walk and do not tire, I prowl around and cannot sleep" (*STVC*, No. 3 iii 11 ff., and II R 8, No. 3:37–40). In the first of these forms, the one with l#, the walking is seen as purposeful, directed to a goal; in the second, without l#, it is aimless and without any goal.[9] The prefix l#- is incompatible with the Aspect of Propinquity II prefix and with all infixes.

Aspects of Regional Contact (Pr. 23)

The prefixes constituting the rank of regional contact prefixes or "generally" locating prefixes may be analyzed as consisting of a pronominal-adverbial element denoting a region (m, b) and a relater or casemark (u for tangentive, a for illative, i/e for allative). They serve to locate the occurrence denoted by the verb as in contact with a general region: internally adherent to border of it (u), included in it (a), and externally adherent to border of it (i/e). They are neutral with respect to achieving, maintaining, or ceasing from the position indicated, a neutrality that may in a measure be expressed as neutrality that may in a measure be expressed as neutrality as to direction (hither/hence); essential to the prefix is only insistence on the fact of regional contact, whether that contact is coming, extant, or past.

The regions to which the regionally locating prefixes refer are two: the area of the speech situation, denoted by the component m, and the area of the event related as other than that of the speech situation, the "area in question," denoted by the component b. Approximately, m may be translated as "here," b as "the place in question," "there." It may be noted further that while m and b primarily denote place they tend to carry also connotations of time: m, "here and now," b, "there and then." It may be noted also that, while the indication of place is primarily a general one of region, the line between general and specific indication, between area and entity indication, tends to blur in usage. Thus a degree of overlap in function between the general regional indication of the prefixes and the specific entity indication of the infixes is observable. It parallels the choice in English between general indication such as "thereon" in "he put his mark thereon" and specific entity indication such as "he put his mark there on it" for relation of position on near entity.[10]

mu, mark of location of the occurrence denoted by the verb on the inside border (. u) of the area of the speech situation (m.). This is typically the place of the two participants, speaker and addressee, so that depending upon which of them the speaker has in mind mu-locates approximately as Latin *hic* and *iste*. It adds to this implications of emotional involvement of the speaker, of his being personally engaged.[11] As example may serve mu-na-dù, "he built here for him (mu-na-(n-)du)." In functional overlap mu- can occur as specific indication of allative first person singular, for example saǧ-túm-ma mu-un-ǧar:*ma-gi-ir-tam iq-bi-a-am* but saǧ-túm-ma i-ni-in-ǧar:*ma-gi-ir-tam aq-bi-šum* (*MSL* IV 72), lines 173–176).

ma, mark of location of the occurrence denoted by the verb inside the area of the speech situation. The original meaning of the prefix is retained only in the sequence -m-ma-, which indicates appearance into view, "out here (before me)." As examples may serve é-níǧ-gur₁₁-ra-na kišib bí-kúr ǧiš im-ma-ta-ǧar, "he broke (lit. 'replaced') the seal on his storehouse, laid out here from it (i-m-ma-ta-(n-) ǧar) lumber" (Gudea Cyl. A vii 13–14); nam-erím-bi-ta im-ma-ra-gur-ra, "(because) he came back here (i.e., to the place of judgment) from the oath about it" (Falkenstein, *Gerichtsurkunden*, No. 205 [*ITT* III, No. 5286] line 23). The sequence –m-ma- often carries connotations of time: "here and now," for example ud na-an-ga-ma mušen-e gùd-bi-šè gušudi (KA× BULUG̃) un-gi₄ amar-bi gùd-bi-ta inim ba-ni-ib-gi₄ i-bi-šè mušen-e gùd-bi-šè gušudi (KA× BULUG̃) un-gi₄ amar-bi gùd-bi-ta inim nu-um-ma-ni-ib-gi₄, "any day when the bird had hailed its nest its young one answered it from its nest, now when the bird had hailed its nest its young one did not answer it from its nest" (Lugalbanda Epic, lines 75 ff.), where "any day" and "now" correspond with the prefixes ba- and -m-ma- respectively.

In functional overlap ma- occurs as specific indication of dative first person singular "for me," and this seems to be the only use of ma- when it occurs initially in the form, for example, ma-an-sum, "he gave me (ma-n-sum)" (*RTC*, No. 295). In functional overlap ma- occurs also in the sequence –m-ma- and serves then as specific indication of near dative third person neuter "for it (here)," for example gù àm-ma-dé-e, "it said to it as follows (durative)" (Dispute of Plow and Hoe, line 20 and passim).

ba, mark of location of the occurrence denoted by the verb inside relevant area, not that of the speech situation, for example ba-g̃en: *it-ta-lak*, "he went away," that is, into some area not here (*MSL* IV 90, line 90), 1 ma-na kù-luh-ha igi-nu-du₈-a šám-šám-dè Ur-é-muš tám-kàr É-muš-ke₄ ba-túm šà-bi-ta 1 igi-nu-du₈-kù-14-gín-kam mu-ku₄ Ur-ki nu-giri₆-ke₄ ba-túm 1 sag̃-nitah-kù-⅓-ša-ma-na-kam mu-ku₄ Lugal-da siba-udu-siki-ka-ke₄ ba-túm 1 igi-nu-du₈-kù-14-gín-kam mu-ku₄ An-a-mu nu-giri₆-ke₄ ba-túm, "1 mana refined silver to buy orchard workers (lit. 'blind ones') did Ur-Emush, merchant of Emush, take away (ba-(n)-tum). Out of it 1 orchard worker (to a value) of 14 shekel he brought in here (mu-(n-)kur). Urki, the orchard man, took him away (ba-(n-)tum). 1 male slave (to a value) of 20 shekel he brought in here (mu-(n-)kur); Lugalda, the shepherd of the wool sheep, took him away (ba-(n-)tum). 1 orchard worker (to a value) of 14 shekel he brought in here (mu-(n-)kur); Anamu, the orchard man, took him away (ba-(n-)tum)" (Nikolski I, No. 293). As will be noted, the taking of the silver away "into relevant area," that is, to the appropriate markets, is expressed by ba- prefix. The return with the persons bought to the speaker's area is expressed by mu- prefix. The taking of the bought persons away "into relevant area," that is, to their respective places of work, is again expressed by ba-. A very similar example is ud é-gal-e ba-ab-túm-ma-ta igi nu-ni-du$_8$-a ud [igi ì-í]b-du$_8$-a m[u-túm-mu-a] šeš Ur-^{d}[Ba-ba$_6$] nam-erím-[àm], "that he had not seen him (a deserter) since the government (lit. 'the palace') took him away (ba-prefix) and that when he sees him he will bring him in here (mu-prefix) did the brother of Ur-Baba swear" (Falkenstein, *Gerichtsurkunden*, No. 190: 46–49 [*ITT* III, No. 6545 iii 8–13]).

In functional overlap ba- occurs as specific indication of more remote dative third person neuter, for example šu-na ba-an-sum-ma, "which he had given into his hand" (*BE* VI 2, No. 42), ki-sur-ra ^{d}Mes-lam-ta-è-a A-bí-ak^{ki}-e inim ba-an-gi-in Ur-^{d}Nammu lugal-e, "Urnammu the king confirmed the boundary of Meslamtaea for (the city) Abiak" (Kraus in *ZA* 51 [1955] 46 ff., A ii 20–23; cf. B rev. iv 29–32); contrast dative third person personal a-šà ^{d}Nu-muš-da Ak$_x$-tab^{ki}-kam ^{d}Nu-muš-da-ra inim in-na-gi-in Ur-^{d}Nammu lugal-e, "Urnammu the king confirmed the territory of Numushda of Aktab for Numushda" (ibid., A i 13–16).

The prefix ba- often carries connotations of time, "there/then" denoting a degree of distance in time (see example given under ma-).

mi, mark of location of the occurrence denoted by the verb outside, on the outer border of, the area of the speech situation, "right over there." As example may serve na$_4$ kisal-mah-a mi-rú-a-né, "unto his stele which he erected over there (mi-(n-)ru-a) in the main court" (Gudea Cyl. A xiii 8 f.). The scribe apparently begins his enumeration of the steles with the one nearest to him; the following ones are described with prefix bi-. Another example is ^{d}Ama-ušum.gal-an-na kalam-ma mi-né-a-ra dingir-ud-te ša-mu-sa$_6$(!?)-ge kur-re ba-íl kur ša-mu-u$_8$-da-húl-la-àm, "in Amaushumgalanna coming forth right over there (mi-n(i)-e-a) in the country, it (i.e., the country) on its part takes pleasure in him (as) the god who makes daylight approach; he rises over the mountains yonder (ba-íl) while the mountains rejoice in him, they on their part" (*CT* XXXVI, Pl. 33, lines 15–16; cf. the parallel lines 13–14). The prefix mi- is used with the country, ba- with the far-off mountains.

In functional overlap the prefix mi- serves in the sequence -m-mi- as specific indication of near third person neuter allative and causative.

It often carries connotations of nearness also in time. As example may serve ì-mi-du$_{11}$, "he said (in answer) to it," in Entemena Cone A iv 83, which reports a fairly recent answer given by Urlumma to Entemena. When at a much later date Urukagina reports the same event he uses the prefix bí- (Oval Plaque iv 9: bí-du$_{11}$). Very similarly Gudea in relating his dream to Nanshe makes frequent use of -m-mi- since the dream experience is still vivid in his mind and "close" to him, while Nanshe in repeating his statement uses bí- since to her the dream experiences are at a distance; note the parallel statements gi-dub-ba kù-NE-a šu-im-mi-du$_{11}$ in Cyl. A iv 25 but gi-dub-ba kù-gi šu bí-du$_8$-a in col. v 22, dub mul-an-du$_{10}$-ga im-mi-g̃ál in col. iv 26 but dub mul-du$_{10}$-ga bí-g̃ál-la-a in col. v 23, li-um za-gìn šu im-mi-du$_8$ in col. v 3 but li-um za-gìn šu bí-du$_8$-a in col. vi 4, é-a g̃iš-hur-bi im-g̃á-g̃á in col. v 4 and, for a change, é-a g̃iš-hur-bi im-mi-si-si-ge in col. vi 5. In Nanshe's last statement she is apparently reporting what is going on among the gods as she speaks: "he is copying thereon the plan of the house." Note also her use of ù-mi-kúr in Cyl. A vi 6; she foresees action in the near future. The scribe reporting the execution long afterward uses bí-:bí-kúr (Cyl. A vi 13). The prefix is incompatible with infixes of the a-series.

bi/e, mark of location of the occurrence denoted by the verb outside, on the outside border of, the relevant area, not that of the speech situation, "at that region," for example me-a bi-ù-tu-da-me-eš, "where were they born" (*CT* XVI, Pl. 42, line 82).

In functional overlap bi- occurs also as specific indication of third person neuter allative and causative, for example mu-sar-a-ba šu bí-íb-ùr(.re)-a, "who will wipe the hand over (bi-b-ur-e-a) its inscription (to erase it)" (Gudea St. C iv 8), and this has become the normal use of the prefix. It also carries connotation of time "then" as relatively remote (examples given above under mi-).

The prefix bi- is incompatible with infixes of the a-series.

Aspect of Propinquity II (Pr. 22)

The prefixes constituting the rank of Aspect of Propinquity II consist of a consonantal pronominal-adverbial element of place followed by zero mark of collative case. The consonantal element, n, may be assumed to have been syllabic in nature.

n#, mark of propinquity to (zero mark for collative) an autonomous area within that of the speech situation other than those of speaker and addressee. The prefix can occur in functional overlap as replacement for the subject element third person singular transitive active preterit as shown in *MSL* IV 43* and note on p. 106, lines 73–75: sá ba-an-na-du$_{11}$ in third person singular but sá ba-na-du$_{11}$ in first and second person singular.

INFIXES

The infixes cannot begin a form but must always follow a profix or prefix. They denote relations of the occurrence denoted by the verbal root to specific entities explicit or implicit in the conveyed content, case relations such as those in which the verb governs the various indirect objects in a sentence.

In form the infixes are composites of pronominal, nominal, and relater elements joined in that order in partitive parataxis. The pronominal elements occurring or to be understood are singular: first person #, second person -e-, third person -n-, third person neuter -b-; plural: first person -me-, second person -ene-, third person -ne-.[12] The nominal elements are r, d, š, t. The relater elements are .a, "inside of" (illative), .e, "on surface of" (allative), and zero, "in propinquity to" (collative).[13] Depending upon how many partitive parataxis relations they contain, compounds formed from these kinds of components will thus have reference to (1) the whole (pronominal element + zero), (2) a part (pronominal element + relater denoting "inside" or "on surface"), and (3) a part of a part (pronominal element + nominal element denoting some part of it + relater denoting "inside" or "surface" part of the part) of a pronominally indicated entity.

Consonantly with the grammatical categories governing for their components the infixes are ordered in ranks according to person and gender (inherent in the pronominal component), case (expressed by the relater component), and relative quantity or size (conveyed in the nominal component).

The ordering by person establishes in the series of infix ranks three successive points of division, a first person point, a later second person point, and a last third person point. Since the category of person is narrowly applied—to persons as complete entities, to whole persons, not to parts—the ordering affects only infixes in which the primary reference is to the person as a whole, that is, infixes of the form pronominal element plus zero. These infixes distribute into rank classes at the first person singular point comprising the first person singular element zero plus zero, at the second person singular point comprising the second person singular element -e- plus zero, and at the third person singular point comprising the third person singular element n plus zero.

Concurrent with the ordering by person runs a corresponding ordering by case. This ordering also divides the infix series into three: a series of infixes in .a (illatives), a following series in .i (allatives), and a series in zero. The two orders, by person and by case, are so correlated that the a-series follows the first person singular plus zero rank, the i-series follows the second person singular plus zero rank, and the zero series coalesces with the third person singular plus zero rank into one single rank immediately before the root.

The successive series of the ordering by person and case—except the zero series—are further divided according to the gender of explicit or understood pronominal element into a subseries with neuter pronominal reference. As to explicit or understood pronominal reference, it would appear that explicit pronominal reference can only occur with the first of several elements belonging to the same subseries if they occur together in a form; for the others the pronominal reference must be left understood.

Lastly, within the subseries, the various infix ranks are ordered according to relative quantity conveyed by the partitive nominal component. After the ranks of infixes referring to the pronominal element as a whole (pronominal element + zero) and the following rank denoting a part of it (pronominal element + relater a or i) follow the ranks of infixes denoting a part of a part of it, beginning with the rank of infixes with component r, then—presumably in this order—those with component t, those with d, and those with š.

Representing personal pronominal component by "P," neuter by "N," using index figures when a rank has only first, second, or third person pronominal element, and showing the pronominal elements only with the first two ranks of a subseries, we may express in diagram form the ordering here discussed.[14]

a(-CASE) SERIES

Personal (Gender) Subseries

	Erg.	a- Dat.	ra- Dat.	Abl.	Comit.	Dir.
1st p. sg.	P-#	P-a	-r.a	-t.a	-d.a	⟨-š.a⟩

Neuter (Gender) Subseries

	*Erg.	a- Dat.	Elat.	Abl.	Comit.	Dir.
1st n. sg.	⟨N_1-#⟩	N-a	-r.a	-t.a	-d.a	⟨-š.a⟩ (cont.)

e/i(-CASE) SERIES

Personal (Gender) Subseries

	Erg.	All.	Sup.	Delat.	Adcom.	Dir.
2nd p. sg.	P-#	P-i	-r.i	-t.i	-d.i	-š.i

Neuter (Gender) Subseries

	*Erg.	All.	Sup.	Delat.	Adcom.	Dir.
2nd n. sg.	⟨N_2-#⟩	N-i	-r.i	-t.i	-d.i	-š.i (cont.)

ZERO(-CASE) SERIES

Personal (Gender) Subseries

	Erg.	Zero Collat.
3rd p./n. sg.	P-#	P-#

Neuter (Gender) Subseries

	Erg.	Zero Collat.
3rd n. sg.	N_3-#	N-#

———collapsed into———

a-CASE SERIES

Personal Reference Subseries

(1) First Person Singular Ergative (< Decollative) (Pr. 21)

P_1-#, that is, #.#, mark of first personal singular ergative, that is, of first person singular subject of transitive active preterit form. The rank is hypothetical and is postulated for systematic reasons only. For all we know it might be ranked just as well with second or third person singular element; so far no distinctive mark of first person singular ergative has been isolated in any relevant form. Cf. for example in-ꜛnaꜜ-an-ğar:*iš-ku-un-šum*, i[n-n]a-ğar:⟨*aškunšum*⟩, [i]n-na-e-ğar:⟨*taškunšum*⟩ (*MSL* IV 83, lines 118–120).

(2) Personal a- Dative (< Illative) (Pr. 20)

P-a, mark of personal a- dative. Occurring forms are singular first person -e.a-, "for me," second person -e.a-, "for thee," third person -n.a-, "for him/her." The basic, concrete, spatial meaning "into me/you/him/her" is not attested. Instead, the abstract, "grammatical," meaning "inwardly," "emotionally affecting," prevails, so that the rank comes to serve as a *dativus commodi et incommodi* as for example in mu-na-an-ğar:*iš-ku-un-šum*, "he placed for him (mu-na-n-gar)" (*MSL* IV 83, line 136).

(3) Personal ra- Dative (< Elative) (Pr. 19)

P-r.a, mark of personal ra-dative. Occurring forms are singular first person #.ra, "for me," second person e-ra, "for thee," as for example, i-ra-an-ğar:*iš-ku-un-kum*, "he placed for thee (i-(e.)ra-n-ğar)" (*MSL* IV 86, line 211); n-ra, "for him," seems to occur once in a late text: dingir da-ga-na ğar-mu-un-ra-ab:*i-la-am*/*il-šu a-na i-di-šu šu-ku-un*, "place a (personal) god at his side for him (ğar-mu-n.ra-b)" (IV R 17, lines 55–56).

(4) Personal Ablative (Pr. 18)

P-t.a, mark of personal ablative. Occurring forms are so far only singular third person n.ta, "from (out of) him," as for example kù-Lugal-bàn-da tu-ra-ni mu-un-ta-ab-è-dè, "the illness of pure

Lugalbanda left him" (*SEM*, No. 1 iv 24, restored from *OECT* I, Pl. 5, col. i 9).

(5) Personal Comitative (Pr. 17)

P-d.a, mark of personal comitative, contemporaneitive, *potentialis*, etc. Occurring forms are singular first person (e.)da, "with me," second person (e.)da, "with thee," and third person (n.)da, "with him/her." In addition to its use as comitative, "with," for both stationary and moving comitative relation as well as incipient ("to with") and ceasing ("from with") aspects of the relation, the infixes of this rank serve to denote contemporaneitive "under him," "at his time," and, negated, the relation "before," "(when) not yet." They can also serve to denote ability in the subject: "is/were able to." As examples of simple comitative use may serve in-da-ğar:*iš-ku-un-šu*, "he placed with him (i-n.da-(n-)ğar)" (*MSL* IV 82, line 112), and lú na-e-da-du, "no man shall go with you (na-e.da-du)" (Lugalbanda Epic, line 274).

Neuter Reference Subseries

(6) First Person Neuter Singular Ergative ($<$ Decollative)

N-#, that is, ...-#, hypothetical mark of first neuter singular ergative. It must seem possible, though highly unlikely, that Sumerian distinguished a first person neuter singular element for address by animals and things. More likely, but so far not attested outside late grammatical inventories, is a first plural ergative element me#, "we," which may be assumed tentatively to have had this rank. Until further evidence can be adduced this rank must therefore be considered as hypothetical and as posited for systematic reasons only.

(7) Neuter a-Dative ($<$ Illative) (Pr. 16)

N-a, mark of neuter a-dative. Occurring forms are plural first person me(.a), "for us," second person ene(.a), "for you," third person ne(.a), "for them," as for example hé-ne-ab-sum-mu, "may you give to them (he-ne.a-b-sum-e-(n))" (*ITT* II, No. 2751). In illative meaning, presumably the original meaning of the rank, N-a is replaced by N-i/e, which serves for both allative and illative.

(8) Neuter Elative (Pr. 15)

N-r.a, mark of neuter elative. Occurring forms are only singular third neuter (b.)ra, "out of it," as for example ka-a-ki-a-DU-DU-ta a-du$_{10}$ ki-ta mu-na-ra-túm, "from the mouth of the waters flowing in the earth sweet water was brought for him out of it (mu-na-(b.)ra-tum) from below" (Enki and Ninhursag, line 56), umbin-?-ni mu-tur$_x$ ba-ra-an-túm, "dirt from under his nail he brought forth" (Inanna's Descent, line 219). Possible members of this rank—plural first person me-ra, "out of/for us," second person ene-ra, "out of/for you," and third person ne-ra, "out of/for them"—are not to our knowledge attested.

(9) Neuter Ablative (Pr. 14)

N-t.a, mark of neuter ablative, locative, and *instrumentalis*. Occurring forms are singular third neuter (b.)ta, "from it," "in it/them," "by means of it." As example of ablative use may serve lú É-ninnu-ta íb-ta-ab-è-è-a, "the man who will eject it (a statue) from Eninnu (i-b.ta-b-e-e-(e-)a)" (Gudea St. B iv 5–6).

(10) Neuter Comitative (Pr. 13)

N-d.a, mark of neuter comitative. Occurring forms are singular third neuter (b.)da, "with it," as for example, ù-mu-na-da-ku$_4$-re, "when you have entered with it (i.e., a harp) before him (u-mu-na-(b.)da-kur-e(n))" (Gudea Cyl. A vii 2).

e/i-Case Series

Personal Reference Subseries

(11) Second Person Singular Ergative (< Decollative) and Accollative [15] (Pr. 12)

P$_2$-#, that is, e#, mark of second person singular ergative, that is, second person singular subject of transitive active preterit form, as for example in-na-e-ğar:⟨*taškunšum*⟩, "thou didst place for him (i-n-na-e-ğar)" (*MSL* IV 83, line 120).

(12) Personal e-Allative and Causative (Pr. 11)

P-e, mark of personal allative and causative.[16] Occurring forms are singular first person #.e, "on me," second person e.e contracted to e, "on thee," (for occasional third person reference "on him/her" see p. 444, note 12, 3 B), third person n.i., "on him/her." The first person singular allative is usually replaced in functional overlap by the prefix mu-. Examples of allative use are ní mu-e-DU:*ú-par-ri-da-an-ni*, "he terrified me" (K.41 ii [*PSBA* XVII, Pls. I–II] with first person singular allative #.e) munus-e, g̃iš ga-e-du$_{11}$ mu-na-ab-bé, "'woman there, let me cohabit with thee (ga-e.e-dug),' he said to her" (Myth of Enlil and Ninlil; Barton *MBI* No. 4 i 16, restored from unpubl. 3N-T. 294), KA in-ni-g̃á-g̃AR-ar, "he laid claim to him (i-n-n.i-(n-)g̃ar)" (*ITT* III, No. 6439), As example of causative use may serve ninda (gu$_7$-ni-ib, "have him eat (i.e., feed him) bread (gu-n.i-b)" (*VAS* X, No. 204 vi 10).

(13) Personal Superlative (Pr. 10)

P-r.i, mark of personal superlative. Occurring forms are so far only singular second person (e.)ri, "upon you," often also "upon/in it by thee" and in causative forms "caused to...at thee." Examples are du$_5$-na šu-mu sá nu-mu-ri-ib-du$_{11}$:*šal-ṭi-iš qa-a-ti la ik-šu-da-ka*, "my hand relished not seizing you (lit. 'to reach unto you') amain" (Lugal-e XI 41; cf. *JNES* 19 [1960] 110, n. 12), kur-kur ú-sal-la mu-e-ri-nú, "all lands have lain down in pastures under thee (mu-e.ri-nu; lit. 'have lain down on it by thee')" (*TCL* XVI, No. 88 and dupl.), [g]a-mu-ri-ìb-g̃ar:*lu-ša-aš-ki-na-ak-kum*, "let me have (it) put here with you (ga-mu-(e.)ri-b-g̃ar)" (*MSL* IV 80, line 54).

(14) Personal Delative (Pr. 9)

P-t–i, mark of personal delative, "from P." The rank is so far hypothetical; no occurrences are known to us.

(15) Personal Adcomitative (Pr. 8)

P-d.i, mark of personal adcomitative. Occurring forms are singular first person (#.di, "with me," second person (e.)di, "with thee," third person (n.)di, "with him/her," as for example ba-e-di-hu-luh-e, "she shudders at you (ba-e.di-huluh-e(d))" (*CT* XV, Pl. 15, line 14).

(16) Personal Directive (Pr. 7)

P-š.i, mark of personal directive. Occurring forms are singular first person #.ši, "toward me," second person (e.)ši, "toward thee," third person (n.)ši, "toward him/her," as for example in-ši-g̃en:*il-lik-šum*, "he went toward him (i-n.ši-g̃en)" (*MSL* IV 90, line 71).

Neuter Reference Subseries

(17) Neuter Allative-Illative (Pr. 6)

N-i, mark of neuter allative-illative. Occurring forms are singular third neuter n.i, "on/in it (here)," as for example mu-na-ni-in-dù, "he built in it (i.e., in a city) for her (mu-na-n.i-n-du)" (*LIH*, No. 61:40).

(18) Neuter Superlative (Pr. 5)

N-r.i, mark of neuter superlative. Occurrings forms are singular third neuter (b.)ri, "beyond it," "over it," as for example im-mi-ri-bal-bal, "he crossed over it (i.e., a mountain range) over there (i-m-mi-(b.)ri-bal-bal)" (Enmerkar and the Lord of Aratta, line 171).

(19) Neuter Delative (Pr. 4)

N-t.i, mark of neuter delative. Occurring forms are singular third neuter n.ti, "over it/them," as for example in-ti-bal-e-ne, "they were crossing over it (i-n.ti-bal-e-ne)" (Gilgamesh and Huwawa, line 61).

(20) Neuter Adcomitive (Pr. 3)

N-d.i, mark of neuter adcomitative. Occurring forms are singular third neuter (b.)di, "with it," plural third person n.di, "with them," as for example inim-bi-da An-ra ᵈEn-líl-ra kù ᵈNin-in-si-na ki-mah-a-na mu-un-ne-dè-en-ku₄, "with these matters pure Nininsina comes in to An and to Enlil to her high seat (mu-n-ne(.a)-(b.)de-n-kur)" (*SRT*, No. 6 obv. ii 7), An ᵈEn-líl-da bára-gi₄-si-a-na ad mu-un-di-ni-ib-gi₄(!?)-gi₇, "with An and Enlil, seated on her throne dais, she advises (mu-n.di-ni-b-gi-gi)" (*CT* XXXVI, Pl. 28, obv. 14).

(21) Neuter Directive (Pr. 2)

N-š.i, mark of neuter directive. Occurring forms are singular third neuter (b.)ši, "toward it," plural third person ne.ši, "toward them," as for example mu kù-ga-šè PN-ra ba-an-na-ši-g̃ar, "was placed (at disposal) for PN (as security) for the silver (ba-n-na-(b.)ši-g̃ar)" (Reisner, *Telloh*, No. 125), and mu-un-ne-ši-in-hal-hal-la:*i-zu-us-su-nu-ti*, "he (i.e., Enlil) apportioned to them (mu-ñe.ši-n-hal-hala)" (*CT* XVI, Pl. 19, line 62).

Zero-Case (Collative) Series

(22) Third Person/Neuter Ergative (< Decollative) and Accollative (Pr. 1)

P/N-#, mark of singular third person personal and neuter ergative (i.e., subject of transitive active preterit) and of accollative. Occurring forms are singular third person n.#, "he," "in accollative relation to him," third neuter and collective b.#, "it," "they," "in accollative relation to it/them," plural third person ne.#, "they," "in accollative relation to them." As examples may serve in-⌈na⌉-an-g̃ar: *iš-ku-un-šum*, "he placed for him (i-n-na-n-g̃ar)" (*MSL* IV 83, line 118), ki-ta-mu-šè tuš-a-ab:*ti-šab ina ša[p-li-ia]*, "sit down below me" (*KAR*, No. 111 obv. 3 and rev. 3).[17]

THE ROOT (0)

The root has normally punctive singular force. A few roots differ, however, and are on lexical grounds restricted to durative and/or plural meaning. Reduplication of the root or tripling or quadrupling indicates plurality of the occurrence, that is, iterative or plurality of subject or object. A special curtailing reduplication in which the root elides its final consonant (e.g., g̃á-g̃á from g̃ar) serves to lend it durative ingressive force.

SUFFIXES

The suffixes follow the root. They may be subdivided into such as must always close a finite form in which they occur—we may call them postfixes—and such as may close a finite form—we might call these suffixes in the narrower sense—and such as cannot close a finite form—we may call them stem-suffixes since they rank closest to the root. The stem-suffixes serve to denote the relative places in time of the occurrence (the action) and the subject at the moment contemplated by the speaker;[18] the suffixes in the narrower sense serve to denote the person in whom the occurrence is seen as embodied, usually the subject but in transitive active preterit the direct object. The postfix rank, finally, denotes degrees of reality or irreality attributed to the statement. Functionally the stem-suffixes may thus be said to parallel adverbs of time, the suffixes in the narrower sense pronouns in subject and direct-object case, and the postfixes sentence adverbs, adverbs of manner referring to the sentence as a whole.

STEM-SUFFIXES OF TIME

Pre-Actional Aspect (Su. 1)

-ed-, mark of pre-actional aspect indicating prospectiveness of the action as present at the point in time the speaker has in mind. Attention is thus not on the action as future but on its prospectiveness as present. As example may serve ud Gemé-^{d}Lama ba-ug$_6$-e-da-a, "on (-a) the day that (.a-) Geme-Lama will (-e-d.) die" (Falkenstein, *Gerichtsurkunden*, No. 7:15), kur$_6$-bi ú-ul-gíd tukum-bi ì-lá lú-3 kur$_6$-bi ì-lá-a ba-ab-tùmu tukum-bi íb-si Lú-ša-lim-e ba-an-tùmu, "when their fief has been measured if it will prove smaller (i-la-(-ed)) the three men will take (-b-tum-e(d) with third person collective subject infix b.#) their fief which (-a) proved smaller (i-la), if they made it (too) full Lushalim will take (-n-tum-ed with third person singular subject element) it (i.e., that which they had taken in excess)" (ibid., No. 215:3–8), lú...di-kur$_5$-a-ĝá šu ì-íb-bal-e-a níĝ-ba-ĝá ba-a-gi$_4$-gi$_4$-da, "the man...who subverts my judgments or who will (.i-d.) contest (lit. 'come back to') my grants" (Gudea St. B viii 12–20).

Durative Aspect (Su. 2)

-e-, mark of durative aspect. The durative in -e- is often used, much as is the Akkadian "present" or "fientic durative," to denote a simple present/future in which the degree of durative stress is not

DIAGRAM OF THE SUMERIAN VERB

Prefix

Adverbial Mode	Time		Adverbial	Place		
28	**27**	**26**	**25**	**24**	**23**	**22**
V	u	n.ga	u	m#	mu	n# →
de/a,u	a	m.ga	a	1#	ma	
ši/a,u	i		i		mi	
#					ba	
ga/i,u					bi	
he/a,u						
ne/a						
li/a						
nuš						
bara						
nu						

Infix — Pronominal

a-Case Series (Illatives)

Personal					Neuter			
21	**20**	**19**	**18**	**17**	**16**	**15**	**14**	**13**
P₁#	P.a	ra	ta	da	( ) ( ) N.a	ra	ta	da ( )

i-Case Series (Allatives)

Personal						Neuter				
12	**11**	**10**	**9**	**8**	**7**	**6**	**5**	**4**	**3**	**2**
P₂#	P.i	ri	ti	di	ši	( ) N.i	ri	ti	di	ši

Zero-Case Series (Collatives)

Personal/Neuter
1
P₃/N₃#

Root Suffix

	Adv. Time	Pron.	Adv. Mode	
0	**1**	**2**	**3**	**4**
√ (V–) →	ed	e	en	gišen
			en	
			#	
			enden	
			enzen	
			(#)-eš	
			(e)-NE	

Note: The affixes are listed in order of their place in the form. The ranks recognized are numbered from the root backward in the case of the prefixes, forward in the case of the suffixes. Affixes occurring in the same vertical column under a number are mutually exclusive. "P" stands for personal, "N" for neuter pronominal component; P₁ stands for first person, P₂ for second person, P₃ for third person of such component; √ stands for the root.

always clear. As example may serve en-na ba-ug$_5$-ge-a, "until he is dying" or "until he dies" (Enki and Ninhursag, line 219, and Gudea St. B viii 12–20, quoted above under -ed-, where, as Poebel pointed out in *AJSL* 50 [1933/34] 154, the durative -e- and the prospective -ed- stand parallel). More clear is the durative force—again as with the Akkadian present—with use for past action. As examples may serve gaba-ri ì-pà-dè gaba-ri in-pàd, "he was finding (i-pad-e) the answer, he found (i-n-pad) the answer" (Enmerkar and the Lord of Aratta, line 240), and É-ninnu im-ta-sikil-e-NE im-ta-zalag-zalag-ge-eš, "(with tamarisk and...) they were cleaning (i-m-ta-sikil-e-NE) and made it pure (i-m-ta-(n-) zalag-zalag-eš)" (Gudea Cyl B iv. 11–12). In both examples durative presents the action as ongoing process, preterit as complete, as entity. For further examples see note 8 above. Standard is the use of durative—as of Akkadian present—in *verba dicendi* introducing direct quotation since the action of speaking is seen as process enduring throughout the quotation. As example may serve Gù-dé-a alam-e inim im-ma-sum-mu, "Gudea was giving (i-m-ma-sum-e) the message to the statue (as follows:)" (Gudea St. B vii 21–23).

When the durative -e- follows the root directly it may be said to give the form intraactional force; attention is directed to a sequence within the total duration of the action. When the durative -e- occurs after a root modified by the prospective -ed- it serves to stress duration not of the action as such but of the prospectiveness of it and may be said to give the form pending-actional force. As examples may serve munus-e a-na bí-in-ag-e al-gaz-e-dè, "what can a woman do in the matter (bí-) and be under the shadow of being executed" (Nippur Murder Trial; *Analecta Biblica* XII [1959] 135, lines 40–41 [see above, chap. xii]), ma-ab-dù-da-a-ǧá:*ba-a-ni-i*, "(the beard) of my one who is about building for me (ma-b-du-ed-e-a)" (*PAPS* 107 494, line 43; Akkadian gloss: "my builder"), kislah (KI-UD)-zu al-tag é-mu lú ì-buru-dè, "your plot lies abandoned, someone is going to break into (i-buru-ed-e) my house" (Code of Lipiteshtar xiii 25–26).

The difference between √-ed and √-ed-e may be rendered as the one between English "he expects to do" and "he is expecting to do" if "expect" is taken as pure indication of prospectiveness of the action in disregard of its implications for the emotional state of the subject.

Suffixes in the Narrower Sense

Subject and Direct-Object Elements (Collative) (Su. 3)

P/N-#, mark of subject and in transitive active preterit of direct object. Occurring forms are singular first person -en#, second person -en#, third person #.#, plural first person -enden#, second person -enzen#, third person -eš#, and, after durative element -e-, -NE.[19]

Postfixes of Mode

Irrealis (Su. 4)

-g̃išen, mark of *irrealis,* "were it that."

The rank of g̃išen, the last rank in the finite verb proper, is followed by a rank Su. 5 which comprises the nominalizing suffixes a and #[20] and the suffix eše of direct quotation, all of which serve to change the sentence in which the finite verb occurs into a clause which can substitute for a noun and take the various nominal suffixes in their characteristic rank order.

16. Ittallak niāti

OCCURRENCE

The Old Babylonian paradigm du/ĝen, etc.: alākum published by Landsberger in *MSL* IV pp. 88–103 is in general both regular and clear. It rings the changes on the Sumerian and Akkadian verbs for "to go" through number, mood, aspect, stem, and person, and lists for each basic form the variants with directional-dative pronominal complement specifying goal of the going, e.g. (80) [im-m]a-ˈginˈ:it-tál-kam "he came away"...(83) i[m-ma-š]i-gin:it-[t] ál-kaš-šum "he came away (over) to him"...(86) im-mu-[e-ši-gin]:[it-tál-ka]-ˈak-kumˈ "he came away (over) to thee," etc.[1]

Not immediately clear are only two sections, ll. 207–210 and ll. 219–222, which both show verbal forms with accusative pronominal complement rather than, as everywhere else in the paradigm, with directional-datival. The meaning of these accusatives poses a problem inasmuch as none of the established meanings of accusative governed by alākum appears to apply,[2] and inasmuch as the parallel Sumerian forms, which might have provided a clue, show only simple pronominal infix without further overt specification of function. The two sections read:

(207) ba-me-du:	it-tál-lak	ni-a-ti	"he is/was going away...us"
(208) ba-me-du-un:	ta-at-tál-lak	ni-a-ti	"thou art/were going away...us"
(209) ba-e-ne-du:	it-tál-lak	ku-nu-ti	"he is/was going away...you"
(210) ba-e-ne-du-un:	at-tál-lak	ku-nu-ti	"I am/was going away...you"

and

(219) ba-m[e]-gin:	it-ta-lak	ni-a-ti	"he went away...us"
(220) ba-[me-g]in-en:	ta-at-ta-lak	ni-a-ti	"thou went away...us"
(221) ba-[e-n]e-gin:	it-ˈtaˈ-lak	ku-nu-ti	"he went away...you"
(222) b[a-e-n]e-gin-en:	at-ta-lak	ku-nu-ti	"I went away...you"

NOTE: First published in *JNES* 19 (1960) 101–116.

MEANING

In attempting to clarify the meaning of the accusatives in these sections it will be advantageous to consider them in the wider context of parallel constructions in which they occur in the paradigm. This wider context can most simply be presented by a listing in order of the characteristic initial forms of the various sections that go to make it up:

199[–202]	àm- me-du:	*i-il-la-kam*	*ni-a-ši*
203[–206]	àm-ma-me-du:	*it-tál-la-kam*	*ni-a-ši*
207[–210]	ba- me-du:	*it-tál-lak*	*ni-a-ti*
211[–214]	i-im- ⌈me⌉-gin:	*il-li-kam*	*ni-a-ši*
215[–218]	im-[ma-me]-gin:	*it-tál-kam*	*ni-a-ši*
219[–222]	ba- m[e]-gin:	*it-ta-lak*	*ni-a-ti*

As will be seen the paradigm shows here a series of parallel Akkadian constructions each consisting of a form of the verb *alākum* and a following pronominal complement. The verbal form varies as to aspect, the pronoun as to case, and the variations are mutually dependent so that in these constructions the conditions that will produce ventive in the verb (either simple or combined with separative) will also produce directional-dative in the pronoun: *i-il-la-kam, ni-a-ši, il-li-kam ni-a-ši, it-tál-la-kam ni-a-ši, it-tál-kam ni-a-ši,* and such change of conditions as will produce simple separative in the verb will produce accusative in the pronoun: *it-tál-lak ni-a-ti, it-ta-lak ni-a-ti.*

Since thus the conditions which call for ventive aspect at the same time call also for directional-dative case, while the different conditions which call for separative aspect at the same time call also for accusative case, it appears clear that the difference in meaning between the aspects (ventive and separative) must in some manner parallel or equal that between the cases (directional-dative and accusative) which vary concomitantly with them.

Now the difference in meaning between the two aspects is known, it relates to a difference in the motion denoted by the verb; ventive presents the motion as directed "toward" something and limits in addition the something to entities near the speaker; separative presents the motion as directed "from" something, not limiting the something as to location.

As for the difference in meaning between the two cases only the meaning of one of them, the directive-dative, is known: it is direction "toward" something. However, since the difference in meaning between the cases should, as we have seen, parallel or equal that between the aspects, which was "toward":"from" we can set up the proportion:

Aspect			Case	
Ventive	"toward"		Directional-dative	"toward"
————		=	————	
Separative	"from"		Accusative	x

and can posit for the unknown accusative the meaning "from."

The meaning thus found will be seen to satisfy fully every occurrence of the accusative in the sections under discussion:

(207) ba- me-du:	*it-tál-lak*	*ni-a-ti*	"he is/was going away from us"
(208) ba- me-du-un:	*ta-at-tál-lak*	*ni-a-ti*	"thou art/wert going away from us"
(209) ba-e-ne-du:	*it-tál-lak*	*ku-nu-ti*	"he is/was going away from you"
(210) ba-e-ne-du-un:	*at-tál-lak*	*ku-nu-ti*	"I am/was going away from you"

and

(219) ba- m[e]-gin:	*it-ta-lak*	*ni-a-ti*	"he went away from us"
(220) ba-[me-g]in-en:	*ta-at-ta-lak*	*ni-a-ti*	"thou went away from us"
(221) b[a-e-n]e-gin:	*it-⌈ta⌉-lak*	*ku-nu-ti*	"he went away from you"
(222) b[a-e-n]e-gin-en:	*at-ta-lak*	*ku-nu-ti*	"I went away from you"

Since the relation expressed by "from," removal and direction away, is the one characteristically denoted by the ablative case we may, since we are dealing with the meaning of a case, designate the use of the accusative to express this meaning as "accusative in ablative meaning" or briefly "ablative-accusative."

ACCUSATIVE IN ABLATIVE MEANING

Our findings, that the accusative is used with ablative meaning in the sections just discussed, cannot overly surprise, for, while such an accusative is new with the verb *alākum*, it is by no means uncommon elsewhere in Akkadian and its occurrence with words denoting the entity "from which" in expressions of relations of removal and direction away has long been noted by Assyriologists.[3] By meaning and range of occurrence this ablative-accusative can readily be classified as a subclass of a larger class of accusatives which may be termed "prepositional" accusatives since they differ from ordinary accusatives in marking not the direct-object relation but a relation which Akkadian could also have expressed by means of a preposition, and in having their own range of occurrence: (1) as only accusative possible with an intransitive verb, (2) in mutually exclusive distribution with the direct-object accusative with passive verb, and (3) paired with a direct-object accusative in a "double accusative," never alone, with active verb.

In the case of the accusative with ablative meaning its inclusion as a subclass is justified first by the fact that its meaning, ablative, could equally well have been expressed by the preposition *itti* or a corresponding prepositional construction such as e.g. *ina qāti*, secondly by the fact that its range of occurrence may be seen to correspond with that of the "prepositional" accusative generally from the following examples:

(1) *Governed by intransitive verb*. Besides the examples of ablative-accusative with *alākum* discussed above note its occurrence with *maqātum* "to fall" in AO 6770 discussed by Thureau-Dangin in *RA* 33 (1936), 81. The passage in question reads: *qanâm elqe 1 ubānum im-ta-qú-ta-an-ni a-ša[r ig]-ga-am-ra-an-ni 4 ammātum re-iš q[á]-ni-ia mi-nu-um*, "I took a reed (to measure with it). I lost one inch every time (lit. 'one inch repeatedly fell from me'). Four ells was where it was (finally) used up for me (lit. 'away from me'). What was the original length of my reed?" A further example, this time with *halāqum*, offers the Old Babylonian letter *PBS* VII 55.19–21... *as-ba-ás-si-i-ma ki-i-ma ma-am-ma-an la i-šu-ú ih-ta-al-qá-an-ni*, "I seized her, but as I have nobody (to help me guard her) she has got away from me."

(2) *Governed by passive verb*. Exclusive of direct-object accusative. Besides *iggamranni* "it was used up for me" of AO 6770, quoted above, note *hamušta-šu ih-h[a]-as-ba-an-ni-ma*, "a fifth was cut off for (lit 'away from') me" in VAT 7535, Neugebauer *MKT* pp. 294 ff., Thureau-Dangin, *RA* 34 (1937), p. 18.

(3) *Governed by active verb*. Only paired with direct-object accusative. The use of the accusative with ablative meaning as a member of a double accusative was noted early. Thus Delitzsch in his *Assyrische Grammatik* of 1889 observed in discussing the double accusative (§139) that "Besonders beachtenswert ist *mahāru* 'etw. von jem.

nehmen, empfangen'" and Ungnad commenting on the use of this verb in Old Babylonian letters (*VAB* VI, p. 332) stated: "die Person von der man etwas an- oder abnimmt, steht im Akk.: *kaspam mu-uh-ri-šú* Silber nimm (f) ihm ab 152,8 (Wein, etc.) *a-na nikkasim am-hu-ur-ka* nahm ich zur Abrechnung von dir ab 265,5; *ma-ma-an ú-ul im-hu-ra-an-ni* niemand hat (die Sklavin) mir abgenommen 162,24." Further examples of the ablative-accusative may be found in von Soden's discussion of the double accusative in his *GAG* (1952) §145. Among groups of verbs capable of construction with double accusative von Soden mentions in §145e "die Verben des Wegnehmens und des Forderns" and it will be seen that all of these have an ablative-accusative as a member of their double accusatives—natural enough since their meanings inherently tend toward specialization in terms of an ablative object. The many examples of verbs of this group given by von Soden (*eṭērum, ekēmum, našārum, puāgum, šeʾûm, baqārum*) could easily be added to, but we shall restrict ourselves here to the interesting active stative of *habālum*: *kaspa-am ú-ul id-di-nam ù bîtam ha-ab-la-an-ni*, "he did not give me the silver and is wrongfully withholding the house from me" *VAB* VI, 229: 12–13: cf. ibid., line 23 *eqla-am ša ha-⟨ab⟩-lu-ni-in-ni* and also Belili's cry in Ishtar's Descent (*CT* XV 46a 57. Standard Babylonian) *a-hi e-du la ta-hab-bil-an-[ni]*, "Take not unfairly my only brother from me!"

While double accusative including an ablative-accusative is particularly frequent with verbs which, as those singled out in von Soden's group, have a meaning inherently tending toward specification in terms of ablative object, the use is not limited to them. We have already mentioned *mahārum*, which only incidentally will demand ablative specification. Another such verb is *nadānum* "to give," which occurs with double accusative including an ablative-accusative in the rare cases where the direction of the giving is away from the recipient toward a point remote from his normal location. An example furnishes *TCL* VII no. 37.19–22 (cf. Thureau-Dangin *RA* 21, 30–31), where Hammurabi enjoins Shamash-hazir and his associates: *a-na pí-i ka-ni-ki-im-ma šu-a-ti eqla-am id-na-šu-nu-ši-im eqla-am a-šar-ša-ni la ta-na-ad-di-na-šu-nu-ti*, "Give a field to them exactly according to that sealed tablet, do not give a field way off them somewhere else" with which may be compared ibid., 68.21–23, *i-b[a]-aš-ši-i i-na ma-na-ha-ti-šu ú-še-li-šu-ú-ma a-šar-ša-na i-na-ad-di-iš-šu*, "if this is so he would make him lose his labors and give (a field) way off him somewhere else."

The examples of the ablative-accusative here given thus seem to show that this accusative can occur—subject to the general limitations on "pronominal" accusatives—with any verb which in the context is capable of specification in terms of an ablative object. A further observation which may be made is the preponderance of pronominal ablative-accusatives in the examples. Ablative-accusative with nouns does occur but is rare in comparison. It would accordingly seem that the ablative-accusative is tending to lose out in its competition with corresponding prepositional expressions and to be preserved preponderantly in the pronoun. This reminds of the comparable situation with the directional-dative which has completely lost out to prepositional expression with the noun and is limited entirely to use with the pronoun. Generally similar is of course also the restriction of separate dative and accusative forms to the pronouns in languages such as modern English and Danish after these cases had been lost in the noun and replaced there with prepositional constructions.

THE PROBLEM OF *-anni*

The examples of the use of the ablative-accusative given above include not a few instances in which such an accusative of the pronominal suffix first person singular is represented by some part or other of the sequence *-anni*: *imtaqqutanni, ihtalqanni, iggamranni, ihhaṣbanni, imhuranni*, etc. These instances cannot but give pause for reflection for, whereas as traditionally analyzed, *-anni* should consist of a ventive *-am* and a following accusative first person singular pronominal suffix *-ni*, yet in the passages in question no ventive, movement toward first person, can meaningfully be accommodated; it would flatly contradict the following ablative-accusative, movement away from first person, demanded by the context.

We may therefore consider for a moment the bases of the traditional analysis. It was proposed by Landsberger in his classic article on the ventive[4] and was clearly prompted primarily by considerations of form: "Aber auch das Akkusativsuffix der 1.sg. *-anni* muss zerlegt werden in *-am + nī*. Dies lehrt nicht nur die 2. Person sg. fem. + Suffix 1. sg. = *takšudinni* < *tak-šudim-nī*, sondern mit voller Evidenz der Plural: *ikšudūninni* < *ikšudūnim-nī*."[5] Considerations of meaning were less in its favor, rather, they militated against it, for—as Landsberger clearly pointed out—in the context of a direct object accusative first person singular the ventive meaning, so precisely and brilliantly defined by Landsberger in his article as movement toward first person singular, clearly did not apply; the very term ventive was unsuitable: "Freilich will diese Bezeichnung hier nicht passen. Die bisher überall beobachtete Beziehung des Elements -*m* (-*am*) zur 1. Person trifft auch hier zu, aber das Moment der Richtung fehlt."[6] He therefore very finely considered the possibility that in -*anni* a different, possibly older, meaning was present, a locative, suitable with a following direct-object accusative. In following the lines of this suggestion it would seem that we should now, in the light of the forms quoted above, add to this an ablative meaning to go with ablative-accusative pronominal suffix. Since the locative meaning and the here proposed ablative meaning are both restricted to the sequence -*anni*, however, a rather striking contrast between the genuine ventive with meaning "movement toward first person singular" and -*anni* with meanings "locative first person singular" and "movement away from first person singular" becomes apparent, a contrast not easily bridgeable.

Since a development of Landsberger's very acute and fine observations of meaning thus seems to us to lead toward a separation of the sequence -*anni* from the ventive and away from the identification of the two which formal considerations seemed to suggest, a re-examination of these considerations is perhaps in order. One may inquire into the possibilities of further analysis, for instance, to ascertain whether the striking parallel changes in the ventive paradigm: third person masculine singular *ikšudam*, second person feminine singular *takšudīm*, third person masculine plural *ikšudūnim*, and the -*anni* paradigm: third person masculine singular *ikšudanni*, second person femine singular *takšudinni*, third person masculine plural *ikšudūninni* are actually changes in the ventive element or merely changes in other preceding morphological elements, since only if the former were the case would they clearly prove the presence of a ventive in -*anni*. Similarly one might perhaps inquire further into the data for a first person singular accusative pronominal suffix -*nī* since the assumption of such a form seems very largely based on analysis of the difficult sequence *-anni* itself. Questions of such a nature, however, involve a reexamination of the structure of *-anni* in rather broad context and can hardly be dealt with unless we attempt a general morphological analysis of the suffixes found with the prefix forms of the Akkadian verb,[7] however tentative and preliminary such an attempt may have to be.

ATTEMPT AT A MORPHOLOGICAL ANALYSIS OF THE SUFFIXES OF THE PREFIXED VERB FORMS

For purposes of a general morphological analysis of the suffixes of the prefixed verbal forms in Akkadian, an analysis which should obviously seek to establish both the morphological elements themselves and their morphological rank in the form, we may define the term "morphological element" as denoting a significant unit in the expression which can be correlated with a particular feature in the content structure (meaning) so that the occurrence or nonoccurrence of one coincides with that of the other. Correspondingly we can define "minimal morphological element" (morpheme) as the minimal such element reachable by analysis. By the "rank" of a morphological element we shall understand the class into which it will be seen to fall if we begin by gathering together as suffix class 1 su. all morphological elements which are found to occur directly after the root only, in class 2 su. all elements found to occur directly after the root or directly after an element of class 1 su. only, in class 3 su. all elements found to occur directly after the root or directly after an element of class 1 su. or 2 su. only, and so on. By definition the elements of a rank class will thus be mutually exclusive, i.e., any given verbal form can never contain more than one element of any given rank class.

Analyzing on this basis we can set up the accompanying provisional table.

In the table analysis has been carried down to near morpheme level only for classes 1'su., 2'su., and 3'su., with which we are here most directly concerned, and even there it appears likely that class 2'su. on further analysis may prove to divide into two separate successive classes, one containing *n*, the other *i*. In the case of classes 4'su. to 6'su. no attempt to reach morpheme level has been made. To indicate provisional character the numbers of the classes are given with apostrophe and the numbers of the classes 4'su. to 6'su. are in addition placed in parentheses.

Root	1'su.	2'su.	3'su.	(4'su.)	(5'su.)	(6'su.)
√	0				*i*	{*ni*}
	i			{*kum*}	{*ka*}	*ma*
	u			{*kim*}	{*ki*}	*mi*
	a			{*šum*}	{*šu*}	
	ī		{*m*}	{*šim*}	{*ši*}	
	ū		*n̄*	etc.	etc.	
		ni				
	ā					

As mentioned, elements belonging to the same class are mutually exclusive. Accordingly no element in the table can be combined with one occurring above or below it in the same vertical column. Other restrictions found to govern the ability of an element to combine with others are indicated by horizontal lines: an element is freely combinable with any element in a different vertical column unless separated from it by a horizontal line. Thus e.g. *ū* and *ā* of 1'su. can occur with *ni* of 2'su. but *a* and *ī* cannot; *a*, *ī*, *ū*, and *ā* can all occur with {*m*} of 3'su., but 0, *i*, and *u* cannot, etc.

Our use of the symbol zero (0) is limited to cases where a specific meaning within the meaning class of a paradigm is indicated by absence of overt mark in contrast to all other specific meanings within the meaning class. We do not use zero when absence of mark denotes merely that the class meaning as such does not apply.

In cases of allomorphs as, e.g., *š* for *šu* or doubling or lengthening of the initial consonant of a following suffix for *m* etc., we use the convenient mark { } to indicate that the form quoted within the braces stands for the form itself as well as for its allomorphs.

In discussing in more detail the findings of the analysis indicated by the table we shall consider the rank classes in order beginning with the last and shall restrict ourselves in the case of the last three to the brief statement that rank (6'su.) contains the nota relativi *ni* with its allomorph *na*, the particle *ma*, and the particle *mi* of direct quotation (all elements in this class, it will be noted, occur with verbs as well as with nouns), that rank (5'su.) contains the accusative pronominal suffixes (both prepositional and direct-object accusatives), and rank (4'su.) the directional-dative pronominal suffixes. All of these ranks are properly speaking rank groups and would with analysis down to morpheme level each divide into a number of separate successive single ranks.

RANK 3'SU

Rank 3'su. contains first of all the ventive element $\{m\}$, i.e., m or any of its allomorphs, lengthened or doubled initial consonant, n, k, or $š$, of a following pronominal suffix.

The justification for positing the element $\{m\}$ and no more as the ventive element is given with the fact that this element constitutes the only part of expression that is always present with the presence of ventive meaning, always absent with the absence of ventive meaning. Of no other element of the ventive forms does this hold; rather, preceding elements such as -*a*-, -*ī*-, -*ni*- may each, though ventive meaning remains constant, themselves be either present or absent. Moreover, their presence or absence is unrelated to the ventive relation and depends rather on the nature of the subject of the form.

As regards the ventive element m and its allomorphs it is usual to describe the latter as representing an m totally assimilated to a following n, k, or $š$ in contact. Such description is useful and practical but it must not be forgotten that the change involved is a morphophonemic[8] one, the conditions for which are stable in morphological rather than purely phonemic terms. It occurs not only with the ventive m before certain suffixes but also under like conditions with the final m of the directional dative pronominal suffixes when followed by accusative suffixes (see *GAG* §31e). Elsewhere in Akkadian *mn*, *mk*, and *mš* only rarely develop to *nn* or $\bar{n}$, *kk*, or $\bar{k}$, or *šš* or $\bar{š}$ (cf. *amni*, *šamnum*; *amkus*, *amkur*; *amši*, *šamšum*, etc.) and it appears highly doubtful whether the change could ever be satisfactorily accounted for in terms of any particular identifiable phonemic environment alone.

To rank 3'su. belongs also the element preceding a first person singular accusative pronominal suffix in the difficult sequence -*anni*. As mentioned earlier, this sequence is generally analyzed as composed of a ventive -*am* and a following first person singular accusative pronominal suffix -*nī* before which the ventive $\{m\}$ is represented by its allomorph *n*. As also mentioned, however, considerations of meaning militate against assuming that the form contains a ventive element since the contexts in which -*anni* occurs do not allow the ventive meaning "movement toward first person singular" but only "locative first person singular" or the directly opposite ablative meaning "movement away from first person singular." And we have further seen that the ventive element proper is {*m*} only, so that such general similarities between the paradigm of -*anni* and the ventive paradigm, as have been adduced, since they can say nothing about the presence or nonpresence of {*m*} in the former, must be deemed inconclusive. There remains the question of the first person singular accusative suffix for which the traditional analysis assumes a form -*ni*. The existence of such a form for the singular in Akkadian seems, however, open to rather serious doubt.

Unambiguous examples of the first person singular accusative suffixed pronoun in Akkadian, presenting no difficulties of analysis, are furnished by the Assyrian dialect which, unlike the Babylonian, uses this suffix with the endingless indicative. The form shown by these examples is -*i*. Furthermore, the presence of an oblique case first person singular pronominal element of the form *i* in Akkadian is abundantly confirmed by comparison with the first person singular possessive suffix -*ī*, gen. -*ia*, with the independent possessive pronoun first person singular *iāum*, and with the independent pronoun first person singular acc. *iāti*, dat. *iāšim*. And not only is the characteristic first person singular element in all these forms consistently *i*, this element *i* stands as mark of the first person singular in direct contrast within the system to the element -*ni*, which is the distinctive mark of the first person plural. Compare the possessive suffix first plural -*ni*, the independent possessive pronoun first plural *niāum*, and the independent pronoun first person plural acc. *niāti*, dat. *niāšim*.

To assume in the face of this clear picture with its distinctive contrast singular *i*, plural *ni*, a variant singular form *ni* is extremely difficult, the more so since the only basis for assuming such a form seems to be the sequences -*anni*, -*inni* (after second person feminine singular) and -*ninni* (after second and third person plural), which can obviously, consonantly with the attested singular suffix *i*, be analyzed as -*ann-i*, -*inn-i*, and -*ninn-i* just as well as -*an-ni*, -*in-ni*, and -*nin-ni*, and should obviously be so analyzed.[9]

Since on an analysis *-ann-i*, *-inn-i* and *-ninn-i* there is no suffix *-ni* which could have conditioned a ventive allomorph *-n-* we must posit a separate morpheme *-nn-* or *-n̄-* (with length possibly due to stress) identical in rank with {*m*} but different in form and meaning.

As to what the function of the element *n̄* thus posited may have been Landsberger has already, in looking for a suitable spatial meaning consonant with occurrence before a direct-object accusative first person singular, plausibly suggested a speaker-determined locative, "here," and to this general definition may perhaps be added that the occurrence of *n̄* with verbs like *ṣabātum*, *maḫāṣum*, *kašādum*, etc. in *iṣbatanni*, *imḫaṣanni*, *ikšudanni* seems to indicate that not only proximity but actual contact with first person singular is included in the meaning. Contact with first person singular must also be assumed for the ablative meaning in forms like *imqutanni*, "it fell from me," "I lost"; the movement is one away from contact position. As for the range of meaning: "contact," "movement away from contact" compare the similar range of meaning "with," "from with" of the preposition *itti* and "in," "from within" of the preposition *ina*. The assumption of a meaning "here in contact with first person singular" is confirmed rather strikingly by the restrictions on the occurrence of *n̄* in the paradigm of forms with accusative pronominal suffixes. It is found only before first person singular pronominal object, never before second and third. To have a name for *n̄* to distinguish it from the ventive {*m*} we may perhaps call it the visitive and departive *n̄*.

The element of contact with first person singular which we have found to characterize the visitive and departive *n̄* seems to contrast it significantly with the ventive element {*m*} with which it shares a common rank, for the ventive element rather clearly implies mere motion toward first person singular without the idea of contact. A more precise definition of the ventive meaning is therefore probably: "movement toward speaker to a point opposite to him, not in contact with him" and this further precision gives us the means to explain an—otherwise most puzzling—restriction of the use of the ventive in Old Assyrian to forms with second person directional-dative suffix. As Landsberger puts it: "In den kapp. Tafeln treten eigenartigerweise nur die pron. suff. der 2. Person an den Ventiv, die der 1. pl. und der 3. Pers. dagegen an das endungslose Verb."[10] If the ending point envisaged for the ventive movement toward the speaker is *iste* rather than *hic*, however, such restriction on usage must seem a natural one.

In conclusion it may be pointed out that the meanings posited for the two contrasting elements of rank 3'su.: *n̄* "contact with speaker" and {*m*} "direction toward point opposite, not in contact with, speaker" are clearly closely related to the well-known contrast *n*:*m* in the demonstrative pronouns *annīum*, "the one here," and *ammīum*, "the one there, yonder," and their respective cognates, which is one of "near contact" and "near noncontact" with speaker.

RANK 2'su.

The isolation of an element *ni* ranking after the subject elements and before the ventive element is indicated by a comparison of forms such as third person masculine plural indicative *ikšudū* and third person masculine plural ventive *ikšudūnim*. The Assyrian form *imhurūni* "they appealed to me" (CCT II 31 a 9, quoted by von Soden *GAG* §84 e) representing *imhurū-ni-i* serves to show that *ni* can occur outside the ventive before first person singular accusative suffix.

The meaning of the element may be roughly deduced from the limitations on its occurrence. It is limited to speaker-exclusive plural subject (i.e., second and third plural only) and to forms indicating motion or rest determined by reference to the speaker's place (ventive, visitive and departive, and first person singular accusative suffix). From the latter limitation one may conclude to a meaning "mark of plural subject near speaker but exclusive of him."

Basic identity of the *ni* of rank 2'su. with the similarly limited marks *ni*, *na*, *nu* occurring in the speaker-exclusive plurals of the personal pronominal suffixes *kunu*, *kina*, *šunu*, *šina*, etc. appears probable; for the form *ni* compare Old Akkadian *-šuni*.[11] From the variation *ni*, *nu*, *na* in the pronoun one may conclude the composite character of the element, probably two successive morpheme classes, one containing *n*, the other *i*, *a*, *u* are represented.

RANK 1'su.

Into rank 1'su. fall elements usually defined as subject elements and modal elements. The former include first person common singular, second person masculine singular, third person common singular, first person common plural -0; second person feminine singular -ī; second person common plural, third person feminine plural -ā; and third person masculine plural -ū. The latter include the well-known marks: indicative 0 and "subjunctive" u (restricted to first person common singular, second person masculine singular, third person common singular, and first person common plural; with other person, gender, and number identical with indicative). With the modal elements may be grouped also an a occurring in first person common singular, second person masculine singular, third person common singular, and first person common plural, and an -i similarly limited. It may be tentatively suggested that the modus in -a presents the subject as "willing," "approachable," that in i as "under constraint," "forced."[12]

Having thus briefly considered the occurrence of the elements found to have rank 1'su. we may consider next their mutual relations.

As we have mentioned, these elements are traditionally grouped in two separate groups of widely divergent and unrelated function: (1) subject elements indicating person, gender, and number of the subject and (2) modal elements indicating modes. However, if this division had been valid and the functions of the two groups unrelated they should properly have distributed on two different successive ranks, one containing the subject elements 0, ī, ā, ū, one containing the modal elements 0, i, a, u, and a form combining the second person feminine singular subject with, e.g., subjunctive mode should have combined the second person feminine singular mark ī with the subjunctive mark u to a form such as, e.g., *takšud-ī-u* "that you(f.) caught." This, however, does not happen, no forms *takšudīu, takšudāu,* etc., occur; rather, there is only one rank and the distinction of modes, indicative $\sqrt{}$-0: subjunctive $\sqrt{}$-u, found, e.g., in second person masculine singular, becomes inoperative in second person feminine singular $\sqrt{}$-ī, second person common plural $\sqrt{}$-ā, etc. This means that distinctions of person, gender, number are affecting distinctions of mode or vice versa, and that is merely another way of saying that both must be part of a single morphological system expressive of a single system of meaning.[13]

That we are in fact dealing basically with a single system only may be seen also, if we consider the formally distinctive features of the elements which make up rank 1'su, and if we consider the implications for meaning of the grouping of these elements in a single rank group.

The elements which make up rank 1'su. are 0, *i, a, u, ī, ā, ū*. In terms of mutual formal distinctiveness they very obviously form a closed system built around the two axes of vowel quality: zero, *i, a, u* and vowel quantity: zero, short, long, as follows:

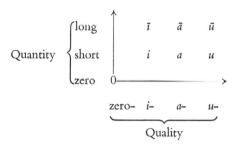

The fact that these elements group into a single rank class, furthermore, has implications for the morphological meanings which they express. We have stated that the principle on which rank classes are set up assures that elements found to belong to the same rank class are by definition mutually exclusive, a given form can contain one of them but never more than one; they are possible replacives of one another. Now in terms of meaning replacives must of a necessity have a common relevance since otherwise they would become meaningless. To the question: "Which color?" the answer might be either "White," "Yellow," "Red," or "Blue." These answers would all be meaningful and thus possible "replacives" of one another; but an answer "Long" or "Short" would not be meaningful since neither "long" nor "short" has relevance when the question is about color. Since they lack a common relevance with "white," "yellow," "red," "blue," etc., they are not possible replacives of them. It follows, therefore, that, since the elements of rank 1'su. are possible replacives of one another, they must have a common relevance, and this again is tantamount to saying that they must constitute a single system of meaning.

As to what this basic system of meaning may have been one would naturally look for clues first to the person-gender-number system, the terms of which are perhaps the clearest. In so doing,

however, one is forcibly struck by the almost total lack of correspondence between the system of mutual distinctiveness of available
meanings and the system of mutual distinctiveness of available marks.

The system of available distinguishable meanings comprises twelve
units [14] and is:

	Sg.		Pl.	
	f.	m.	f.	m.
1 p.	+	+	+	+
2 p.	+	+	+	+
3 p.	+	+	+	+

The system of available distinguishable marks comprises seven
units and is:

Quantity { long $\bar{\imath}$ $\bar{a}$ $\bar{u}$

short i a u

zero   0

zero- i- a- u-

Quality

If the discrepancy in number of units between the meaning and
expression systems is already surprising in itself, a further consideration of the actual correspondence between marks and meanings
achieved is even more astounding. One-to-one correspondence, one
distinctive mark for one distinctive meaning and for that only,
which one would expect of an expression system fitting its system of
content, occurs here only in two cases: the mark $\bar{\imath}$ expresses second
person feminine singular and only that, the mark $\bar{u}$ expresses third
person masculine plural and only that. Otherwise the mark $\bar{a}$ expresses indiscriminately the distinct meanings of second person
masculine plural, second person feminine plural, and third person
feminine plural; and any one of the marks 0, i, a, u, can express
equally indiscriminately either third person masculine singular,
third person feminine singular, second person masculine singular,
first person masculine singular, first person feminine singular, first
person masculine plural, or first person feminine plural.

The lack of correspondence is so glaring that one can only conclude that these two systems were never originally meant for each other, that the meaning system of person-gender-number must have been secondarily and inaptly superimposed upon an older system of marks serving to express an older system of meanings of their own, one for which they were suitable and with which they were functionally congruent. We have attempted to represent the super-imposition and the correspondences in the diagram below.

Nor is it difficult to see from where the intrusive person-gender-number system of meaning would have to come, and why it tended to intrude. The person-gender-number system is germane to the noun and pronoun. Sentences like *šarrum ikšud* or *atti takšudi* reflect earlier syntactical constructions which may be symbolized as *šarrum i kšud* and *atti ta kšudī* and in which *šarrum i* and *atti ta* formed subject and copula,[15] *kšud* and *kšudī* the predicate. A felt need for congruence between subject and predicate would here very naturally lead to reinterpretation of the suffix system of the verbic (*kšud*) in terms of the system of the nominal or pronominal subject.

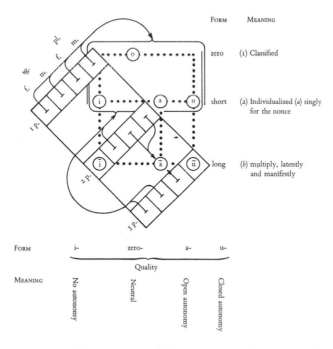

Squares indicate available meanings of the superimposed person-gender-number system of meaning.

Circles indicate available marks of the system of expression.

Arrows indicate the mark by which a given meaning of the person-gender-number system is expressed where that system fails to overlap the system of marks in one-to-one correspondence.

Braces indicate a choice of mark available for such expression.

For the meanings of the marks in the original system given below and to the right of the diagram see the discussion in the following sections.

If, thus, the system of person-gender-number appears to be secondary and intrusive we must, to see what the original single system may have been, turn to the indications given with the other system present, that of the modes. Here, however, we encounter the serious difficulty that the materials on the basis of which the precise meanings of the various modes have to be ascertained are in a great many cases both scant and ambiguous, so that results cannot hope to be either definite or certain, and any suggestions one might attempt must remain in large measure hypothetical. It is therefore subject to this general caution, and very tentatively only, that we venture to suggest that the modal suffixes may have constituted a system of meanings relevant to an assessment of the "manageability" of the subject by the speaker, and operating with the two major categories of generality and individuality (zero: vowel) and, within the latter, the minor categories autonomy of will (vowel quality) and number of manifestations (vowel quantity).

Commenting on details of this proposed system we may begin with the cases in which there is congruence with the person-gender-number system and where we have the relatively clear-cut meanings of that system to guide us. Such a case is $\bar{u}$, restricted to use with third person masculine plural subject, i.e., subject denoting a group of three or more masculina. Asking what particular characteristic the original system may have associated with $\bar{u}$ to make it suitable to denote such a group we may—remembering that the Semitic languages tend to see, as has been said, "alles Gefährliche, Wilde, Mutige, Mächtige, Geachtete, Grosse, Starke als m., alles Schwache, Leidende als f." [16]—first note that a change of the gender of our group to femininum would immediately make $\bar{u}$ unsuitable and bring another mark into play, $\bar{a}$, so that we can conclude that the original $\bar{u}$ quality must lie nearer the pole of the fearsome and formidable than does the original $\bar{a}$ quality. This conclusion is confirmed, and

Modal Suffix System

		No individual autonomy	Neutral as to autonomy	Open individual autonomy	Closed individual autonomy
Predicatively classifiable			0: Undetermined manageability		
Predicatively individualizable	Single instance	*i*: For the nonce compellable		*a*: For the nonce approachable	*u*: For the nonce inapproachable
	Multiple instance	*ī*: Many times compellable		*ā*: Many approachables	*ū*: Many inapproachables

the crucial $\bar{u}$ characteristic more narrowly circumscribed, when we note further that very much less than the drastic change from masculine to feminine will suffice to deprive our group of three or more masculina of its $\bar{u}$ character. If our group, unchanged in all its masculine characteristics, is merely spoken to (second person masculine plural), and thus, however mildly, appears approachable, open to communication, it will just as effectively have been divested of its $\bar{u}$ character—which thus narrows down to something like "unapproachable," "formidable," "forbidding"—and have taken on $\bar{a}$ character, "approachable." In assuming $\bar{u}$ to denote originally "unapproachable," $\bar{a}$ "approachable," we find ourselves significantly close to an earlier result independently arrived at, that the meaning of the modus in -a was "approachability."

Considering next the form $\sqrt{}$ -*i*, which coincided with the second person feminine singular of the person-gender-number system, we note that as $\bar{u}$ could denote only masculinum so $\bar{\iota}$ can denote only femininum, whereas $\bar{a}$, capable of denoting both masculinum and femininum, seems to lie in between. In terms of the gender axis *masculine*: "formidable," "fearsome," *feminine*: "weak," "yielding," we should therefore expect that the meaning of $\bar{\iota}$ will be further away from that of $\bar{u}$, "formidable," "fearsome," "unapproachable," than that of $\bar{a}$ "approachable," and nearer to the feminine pole "weak," "yielding"; and since the weakness inherent in the femininum is with $\sqrt{}$ -*i* at an extreme of being alone (singular) and subjected to the psychological pressure of address (second person) a meaning such as "weak," "yielding," "compellable" suggests itself. Here again we find ourselves significantly close to an earlier result independently arrived at, the meaning suggested for the *i*-modus, which was "compelled."

In our comments so far we have not stressed the different shades of meaning presumably existing between $\sqrt{}$ -*i* and $\sqrt{}$ -*ī*, $\sqrt{}$ -*a* and $\sqrt{}$ -*ā*, and $\sqrt{}$ -*u* and $\sqrt{}$ -*ū*. An obviously valuable clue is given with the fact that in the person-gender-number system $\sqrt{}$ -*ā* and $\sqrt{}$ -*ū* are restricted to plural—their meanings being therefore more precisely "many approachables" and "many unapproachables"—whereas $\sqrt{}$ -*a* and $\sqrt{}$ -*u* are not. This agrees with the use of length of vowel to indicate plurality elsewhere in Akkadian morphology, e.g. in the noun. If, however, length of vowel is a means of indicating plurality a question arises in the case of $\sqrt{}$-*ī*, which is restricted to the singular. The answer is suggested, perhaps, by the use of long vowel elsewhere to denote "latent plurality," "tendency to repeat an action," a usage found, e.g. in the active participle of the base stem, *kāšidum*. For the participle as expressing tendency to perform an action, note particularly its characteristic syntactically determined alternation with the "Gewohnheitsadjektiv" noted in Stamm, *Akkadische Namengebung*, pp. 96–97. If we interpret the form $\sqrt{}$-*ī* as denoting "latent" plurality, a tendency to being repeatedly compelled, we remain within our previous definition of the form as denoting "compellable" and respect the distinction from $\sqrt{}$-*i* which denoted "compelled in a given situation," "compelled for the nonce."

While the distinction between $\sqrt{}$-*a* and $\sqrt{}$-*ā*, "approachable" and "many approachables" (manifest plurality), calls for little comment except for saying that $\sqrt{}$-*ā* in its use for second person feminine plural and third person feminine plural may well have combined latent and manifest pluralic force, the relation between $\sqrt{}$-*u* and $\sqrt{}$-*ū* is less obvious. Taking our clue from the correlation with the third person masculine plural of the person-gender-number system we have defined $\sqrt{}$-*ū* as denoting "many inapproachables" and should accordingly expect $\sqrt{}$-*u* to denote "for the nonce inapproachable." That meaning does, we should imagine, underlie the use of $\sqrt{}$-*u* as *modus jurandi* in the sense of expressing a disinterested, detached, hands-off attitude in the speaker suitable to a form of statement demanding strictly objective presentation. It may be added that the original modal force of $\sqrt{}$-*u* can obviously only be looked for in its use as *modus jurandi*, not in its "subjunctive" use, which is no more than a purely syntactical restriction to use in clauses.

Lastly the contrast of $\sqrt{}$-0 with all the other forms should be mentioned. Here it may be noted that whereas $\sqrt{}$-0 can only serve as verb of a main sentence $\sqrt{}$-*u* can serve both in a main sentence (*modus jurandi*) and in a clause (subjunctive) $\sqrt{}$-*a* likewise both in main sentence and clause (e.g., ventive), while $\sqrt{}$-*i*, so far attested only in main sentence, is likely to have been usable also in clauses. A clue to what is here involved may perhaps be found if we consider that forms like *i-kšud* and *i-kšudu* were originally "nominal" sentences consisting of a pronominal subject and verbic (*kšud*) predicate and so formally comparable to sentences like *šū šarr* and *šū šarrum*.

In the latter case the difference between the sentence with endingless predicate and that with nominative predicate is that in the former, "he is king," the subject is merely predicatively classified, while in the latter, "he is a/the king," it is predicatively individualized.

If the same distinction may be assumed for the endingless verbic $\sqrt{}$-0 as contrasted with $\sqrt{}$-$i/\bar{\imath}$, $\sqrt{}$-$a/\bar{a}$, and $\sqrt{}$-$u/\bar{u}$, it would be understandable why $\sqrt{}$-0 as merely predicatively classifying should be restricted to verbs in main sentences, whereas the individualizing $\sqrt{}$-$i/\bar{\imath}$, $\sqrt{}$-$a/\bar{a}$, and $\sqrt{}$-$u/\bar{u}$ were suitable also in attributive clauses further defining an individualizing noun or pronoun, and also, perhaps, why the detailed assessment of manageability expressed by vowel quality and quantity is applied only in the case of the predicatively individualizing forms, not in the merely classifying one.

17. The Akkadian Ablative Accusative

In an article in this *Journal* entitled *ittallak niāti* (Vol. 19 [1960] 101–116 [see above, chap. xvi]) we suggested that the Akkadian accusative could be used in ablative meaning. This suggestion and a few other points we touched upon have since been discussed by Professor Wolfram von Soden in an article "Zum Akkusativ der Beziehung" (*Orientalia* 30 [1961] 156–162) which, though appreciative of our efforts, comes to the conclusion that our suggestions must be rejected and the problems thought through afresh on a broader basis: "Es ging mir darum zu zeigen, dass die vielen sehr bedeutsamen Probleme, die dort in so tiefschürfender Weise erörtert wurden, noch einmal neu durchdacht werden müssen, weil die bisher geschaffene Basis für den darauf errichteten Oberbau zu schmal ist. Für die notwendige Verbreiterung des Basis möchte dieser kleine Beitrag einige Hinweise geben, die die Diskussion weiterführen sollen" (pp. 161 f.).

It seems only proper to accept this invitation to further discussion and to try to think the problems through afresh, testing with care the reasoning underlying objections raised and the relevancy of new materials adduced.

1. THE INFIXES IN *ba-me-du* AND *ba-e-ne-du*

The first objection raised by Herr von Soden has regard to the absence of overt mark of postpositional function in the infixes -*me*- and -*e-ne*- of *ba-me-du*:*it-tál-lak ni-a-ti*, "he is/was going away from

NOTE: First published in *JNES* 22 (1963) 18–29.

us," and *ba-e-ne-du*:*it-tál-lak ku-nu-ti*, "he is/was going away from you," in the paradigm *MSL* IV pp. 88–99 lines 207 and 209. Speaking of *niāti* and *kunūti* of the Akkadian translations Herr von Soden says: "Diese Pronomina übersetzt J. durch 'from us, from you' was ihren Sinn gewiss gemäss ist. Aber schon die Tatsache, dass im Sumerischen keine Formen mit dem ablativischen Infix -*ta*- entsprechen, zeigt, dass die Babylonier diese Akkusative nicht im Sinn von Ablativen verstanden haben" (p. 157)—a statement which it is for us to evaluate.

Caution seems indicated already by the occurrence of simple -*me*- and -*e-ne*- in the preceding lines 203 and 205. If it were possible to conclude from the occurrence of simple -*me*- and -*e-ne*- rather than of -*me-ta*- and -*e-ne-ta*- in lines 207 and 209 *ba-me-du*:*it-tál-lak ni-a-ti* and *ba-e-ne-du*:*it-tál-lak ku-nu-ti* that the Babylonians did not understand *ni-a-ti* and *ku-nu-ti* in ablative sense, then it would obviously also be possible to conclude from the occurrence of simple -*me*- and -*e-ne*- rather than of -*me-šè*- and -*e-ne-šè*- (or better: -*me-a*- and -*e-ne-a*-) in lines 203 and 205 *àm-ma-me-du*:*it-tál-la-kam ni-a-ši* and *àm-mu-e-ne-du*:*it-tál-la-kam ku-nu-ši* that the Babylonians did not understand the directional datives *ni-a-ši* and *ku-nu-ši* as directional datives, a conclusion that must give pause.

Actually further examination of the paradigm *MSL* IV pp. 88–99 as a whole teaches us that it is the rule in the paradigm that postpositional elements are not shown after plural pronominal infix (-*me*-, -*e-ne*-, -*ne*-) in any indicative form but *are* shown in the imperative (-*me-a*, -*e-ne-a*, -*ne-a*). The occurrence of simple -*me*- and -*e-ne*- rather than of -*me-ta*- and -*e-ne-ta*- in *ba-me-du* and *ba-e-ne-du* is thus normal.

The reasons for the difference of treatment of these infixes in indicative and imperative and for the further difference between the treatment of singular and plural infix are not yet clear. It may be that the writings -*me*-, -*e-ne*-, and -*ne*- represent phonetical reductions of longer forms with postpositional element, reductions which were still phonemically distinctive in the spoken language, or it may be that Sumerian left the syntactical function of plural pronominal infixes in indicative forms to be understood from the context.

In order to leave both of these possibilities open we used careful language in speaking of the forms *ba-me-du* and *ba-e-ne-du*, saying that they "show only simple pronominal suffix without further overt specification of function" (p. 101). As for what that function was we showed—in setting up the proportion on p. 272—that the structure of the paradigm here demands an ablative.

2. MATERIALS FOR THE AKKADIAN ABLATIVE ACCUSATIVE

Herr von Soden's second point is made on the basis of a list of Akkadian accusatives with intransitive or passive verb containing many forms not deemed relevant by us in our discussion of the ablative accusative. As he says: " Während er nun nur Formen von vier Verben aufführt, habe ich entsprechende von elf Verben notiert, wobei ich ebenso wie er zunächst nur Formen mit dem Suffix -*anni* der 1. Person Singularis gesammelt habe, weil in jüngeren Texten nur bei diesem Suffix der Akkusativ eindeutig vom Dativ zu unterscheiden ist " (p. 157). To make sure, therefore, where we are still talking about the same thing, the ablative accusative, it may be well to recall what the criteria of ablative accusative were.

We suggested in our article that a great number of Akkadian accusatives could be grouped together as "prepositional accusatives" since they differ from ordinary accusatives in marking not the direct object but a relation which Akkadian could also have expressed by means of a preposition, and in having their own range of occurrence:[1] (1) as only accusative possible with intransitive verb, (2) in mutually exclusive distribution with the direct-object accusative with passive verb, and (3) paired with a direct-object accusative in a "double accusative," never alone,[2] with active verb.

Under the major group of "prepositional accusatives," as one of the various subclasses that go to make it up, should be counted, we suggested further, the ablative accusative, for the ablative accusative is an accusative the meaning of which could equally well have been expressed by the preposition *itti* or a prepositional phrase such as *ina qati*, and in its distribution it follows the pattern of the "prepositional accusatives." Since our primary concern was with the ablative accusative we did not discuss other subgroups under the "prepositional accusatives" such as, e.g., the *ina* accusative, an accusative the meaning of which could equally well have been expressed by means of the preposition *ina*, the *eli* accusative, an accusative the meaning of which could equally well have been expressed by the preposition *eli*, and so forth.

In the light of the criteria set up for the ablative accusative: (1) meaning which Akkadian could equally well have expressed by the preposition *itti*, "from," or a corresponding prepositional phrase and (2) distribution consonant with the distributional pattern of the "prepositional accusatives" generally, we may then examine the examples added by Herr von Soden.

Three of the new examples we had ourselves considered as probable instances of ablative accusative, but since they were epigraphically not altogether certain we thought it better to leave them out of consideration for the time being and to base our argument only on passages the readings of which were not in dispute. The three examples are: (1) *li-ih-li-iq-šu ṭù(!)-ú-du* "der Weg möge ihm entschwinden," *Bab.* 12 14.1 (Etana Myth), lit., "may the road vanish from him." The uncertainty which existed about the reading of *ṭù(!)* has now been removed by M. Dossin's collation communicated by Herr von Soden. (2) *im-tu-ta-an-ni*, "sie starb mir (weg)," *VAB* VI 162.11, "I lost her by death," lit., "she died from me." This example is not altogether certain. The copy of the text *CT* II 49 (BM 82058) indicates that the first sign of the passage is damaged, a fact duly noted by Ungnad in *VAB* VI 162.11. Ungnad italicized *im* and added a note: "Oder *ih*." Accordingly, though *im(?)-tu-an-ni* seems the more probable reading in the context, a possible reading *ih(?)-tu-ta-an-ni*, meaning perhaps "she infested me with lice," cannot altogether be ruled out. (3) *im-qut(!)-an-ni*, "fiel mir hinunter," Gilg. XII 56 f., 63 f., 70 f. We would translate "(my *pukku*) fell from me (toward the nether world)." The Sumerian version of the tale (*BE* XXXI no. 35 with Kramer's collations *JAOS* 60, 246 f.) has (line 5 f.) GIŠ-LA[G]AB-mu kur-šè mu-da-an-šub, "my *pukku* fell from me toward the nether world."[3]

Among the other examples added one notes a certain number which exemplify not the ablative (*itti*) accusative but a different class of prepositional accusatives, the supra-lative (*eli*) accusative, which expresses the relation "onto."

We may consider first the examples with *ṭiābum*, *ṭābu*, "to become sweet, pleasant." The notational relation holding between the verbal notion of *ṭiābum*, "to become sweet, pleasant," and the person or persons experiencing the becoming sweet, pleasant, could be structured in Akkadian (1) as a supra-lative relation "onto," "upon" (*eli*) *ša e-li-šu ṭà-ba-at*, "that is pleasing unto (lit. onto) him," *ARM* II 90:28, or (2) as a relation of simple direction "to" (*ana*):*ša ip-ša-tu-šu a-na ši-ir* ᵈ*Šamas ù* ᵈ*Marduk ṭa-ba*, "whose deeds are pleasing to (lit. to the flesh of) Shamash and Marduk," *LIH* 57.i.6–8, cf. ii.4–6. Corresponding to this difference in basic notational structure Akkadian could express the relation by means of case in two ways (1) by a supra-lative (*eli*) accusative rendering the notion "onto" or (2) by a directional dative rendering the notion "to," e.g., *na-pí-iš-tum i-ṭi-ib-šum*, "life seemed sweet to him," *VAB* VI 143.30.[4] Examples of construction with supra-lative (*eli*) accusative are OAs. *šu-ma lá i-ṭi-áb-šu-nu*, "if it be not pleasing unto them," *MVAG* 33 No. 7.10, and *ši-i-ri ul ṭa-ba-an-ni*, "my flesh was not pleasing unto me," "I did not feel well," *VAB* II 7.9 (lines 12 and 14 *la ṭa-ba-an-ni*) in Herr von Soden's list. Whether in neo-Babylonian and neo-Assyrian times accusative and dative were still felt as distinct, and if so which is to be assumed in individual examples of the formula *libba-ka/ku-nu lū ṭāb-ka/ku-nu-šú* etc. mentioned by Herr von Soden, seems to us a thorny problem which we need not take up here. In the SB example *mêᵖˡ i-ṭib lib-ba-šu*, "wegen des Wassers erfreute sich sein Herz," Gilg. I col. iv.1 and 5 the accusative is differently used (for that "with which" the heart becomes satisfied) and the notional structure of that relation in Akkadian is not clear to us.

A further supra-lative (*eli*) accusative is the example with *miādum*, "to become many, much," OAss *ú-mu im-ṭi-du-ni-ni*, "die Tage wurden mir nun zu viel, zu lang," *BIN* IV 19.19, since the relation between the verbal notion of becoming (too) much and the person or persons for whom something becomes (too) much is expressible by *eli* "onto" cf. *e-li ṣa-bi-ia i-mi-id-ma*, "is too much for my troops," *ARM* II 21:28 and see Bottéro and Finet, *ARM* XV p. 218 s. v. *mâdum*. Most likely the example *awatum im-qu-ta-an-ni*, "die Sache fiel mir ein," *ARM* II 131:16; V 3:8 quoted by Herr von Soden on p. 157 is also a supra-lative (*eli*) accusative since the becoming conscious of a matter could well have been treated as the becoming conscious of a mental or bodily state which Akkadian can express by *maqātu* with *eli* (see examples in *HW* 424a), but the classification cannot be considered certain.

Under the supra-lative (*eli*) accusative belongs probably also the SB example *ašru šuātu i-mi-ṣa-an-ni*, "diese Baustelle war mir zu klein geworden," Ash. Nin. A V.47. A prepositional expression of the relationship occurs in OBa. *ummânu-um* .... *a-na bu-ni ṣēni*HI.A *mi-iṣ-ṣa[-am]*, "the men are too few for (*lit.* to the (sur-) face of) the sheep and goats," *VAB* VI 57.16. Since the point is the extent of the herds it must seem likely that *bunum*, "face," stands for the upper face, the surface, of the herd, which measures its size, so that *ana buni* expresses very much the same notion, supra-lative, as does *eli*.

Not a prepositional accusative but a normal direct object accusative appears the accusative in MB *ſBēltu-la-te-nin-ni*, "O Mistress! Do not replace me (with another servant)," *BE* XIV 91a.40. Herr von Soden's rendering "Herrin, ändere (dein Geheiss) mir gegenüber nicht!" seems less likely since, according to *ZA* 49 (1949) 162 i 3–4, *qá-bé-e qá-bu-ú-um-ma ú-ul e-ni-a-ak-ki-im at-wa-a-am ma-li ṣa-ab-t[a]-a-ku*, "What is said is said, I did not change for thee a word of what I think," a person to whom a promise, order, or statement is changed, is construed with the dative.

Altogether uncertain appears the example OAkk. *Li-bur-an-ni-*ᵈ*Suēn*, *UET* I 90, which Herr von Soden listed under *buārum*, "in Erscheinung treten, sich offenbaren," and translated as "das Jawort des S. möge..." in *AHw* 108b, and which he now prefers to interpret as "Suēn bestätige sich mir gegenüber!" A third possible rendering would seem to be *Li-bur-il-ni-*ᵈ*Suēn*, "May our personal god (i.e., our good fortune) become manifest, Sîn!" For such rendering the close parallel *Li-bur-i-lí*, "May my personal god become manifest!" (Gelb, *MAD* III 91) could be quoted. It is accordingly uncertain whether the name contains the sequence *-anni* at all and it seems therefore best to leave it out of consideration for the present.

On examination we thus see that Herr von Soden has added to the list of ablative accusatives three examples which probably belong, and a great many that do not belong. The latter, insofar as they can be classed as prepositional accusatives, mostly represent the supralative (*eli*) accusative, which denotes "onto," approach from above.

3. GENERAL AND SPECIFIC MEANINGS

Having thus clarified for ourselves the bearings of the varied materials which Herr von Soden has added we may consider the conclusions which he wishes to draw from these materials. He says: "Unter diesen Formen befinden sich etliche, die eine ablativische Deutung des Suffixes -*anni* ausschliessen und dazu zwingen, diesen Akkusativ als Akkusativ der Beziehung zu verstehen." Underlying his reasoning, it will readily be seen, is an a priori assumption: that all the forms in his enlarged list must have one and the same meaning. It is this assumption that compels to the positing of the very general meaning of "accusative of relation." One does not readily see, however, that there is, or can be, in the evidence anything to justify such an a priori assumption. As we have shown, there are in the list accusatives the meaning of which could equally well have been rendered by the preposition *itti* "from," the ablative accusatives, and there are—added by Herr von Soden—accusatives the meaning of which could equally well have been rendered by the preposition *eli* "onto," the supra-lative (*eli*) accusatives, that is all. There is nothing to indicate that we must obliterate these clear distinctions and demand that the added supra-lative (*eli*) accusatives should be interpretable as ablative accusatives, and to posit that, if they are not then both, they and the ablative accusatives must be accusatives of relation.

The meaning of "accusative of relation" ("Akkusativ der Beziehung"), the mere positing of relation generally, is urged by Herr von Soden not only for the ablative and the supra-lative accusatives in his enlarged list just considered, but also for the accusative which with verbs for taking and taking away marks the person from whom something is taken away, the person who in the situational context stands in ablative relation. He says: "Auch hier dürfte der Akkusativ der Person ein Akkusativ der Beziehung sein, altbab. [*la-*]*a ta-la-qé-šu-nu-ti*, *ARM* IV 68:9, bedeutet also wohl eigentlich 'nimm nicht in Bezug auf sie!,' auch wenn wir zu Recht übersetzen 'nimm nicht von ihnen!'" (p. 159).

In view of this insistence we should therefore perhaps ask ourselves what is, then, this meaning "with relation to" ("in Bezug auf") urged upon us, and why is it that it can be urged at all? The answer cannot be in doubt: it is the general meaning which all cases have in common and which is shared also by the prepositions. As Hjelmslev concluded in his famous study "La Catégorie des Cas," p. 96: "Est cas une catégorie qui exprime une relation entre deux objets."[5]

Once this has been realized it will also be realized that the term "accusative of relation" ("Akkusativ der Beziehung") considered as a term for meaning[6] and denotative of "with relation to" ("in Bezug auf") has a rather curious logical structure. The addition "of relation" does away altogether with the notion "accusative" first posited, which is "limitation to certain specific relations, to accusative relations," and opens the door to any and all relations as suitable meanings. "With relation to" ("in Bezug auf") can be with any kind of case-relation to.

By accepting Herr von Soden's term "Akkusativ der Beziehung" and his translation "in Bezug auf" and by insisting on their general character ("bedeutet also wohl eigentlich 'nimm nicht in Bezug auf sie'") to the point of allowing expression of specific relation given with the situational context the status of gratuitous interpretation only ("auch wenn wir zu Recht übersetzen 'nimm nicht von ihnen!'") we could accomplish only one thing: to blot out all distinctions of individual, specific case meaning.

That this is in fact what Herr von Soden does accomplish is apparent from his treatment of the examples in his enlarged list on pp. 157–158 of his article. Abstracting wholly from the specific meanings of the ablative and supra-lative accusatives, he lumps both together and then proceeds to translate these Akkadian accusatives into German as were they not accusatives but datives: "mir," "ihm."

The abstraction from all distinction of specific case meaning in an "accusative of relation" not only leaves the specific character of the relation present in the situational context unrepresented in the linguistic expression of that context, it also leaves distinctive features of selection in the linguistic expression meaningless and without any function. This may be illustrated from the example cited by Herr von Soden *qí-ša-a-a[t-su-nu la-]a ta-la-qé-šu-nu-ti*, *ARM* IV 68:9, "do not accept from them their presents."

To see clearly which selective features are present in the accusative *-šu-nu-ti* we may compare first a parallel construction with directional dative suffix *-ku-nu-ši-im* such as OBa *kaspam. . . .li-il-qú-ni-[i]k-ku-nu-ši-i[m]*, "may they take the silver to you," *VAB* VI 70.25–27.

It is here clear (1) that the "taking" contemplated has relation to the persons indicated by *-kunūšim*, the taking is "with relation to" you, and this general fact that a relation exists is inherently implied in the likewise general fact that *-kunūšim* is a case form. It is also clear (2) that the "taking" has not only general relation to the persons indicated by *-kunūšim* but specific relation. It is a taking "to" you as distinct from a taking "from" you or a taking in any other relation to "you." This narrowing down of possible relations to the specific one of "to" is implicit in the selection of the directional dative mark from among the available casemarks. Thus general meaning "with relation to" is implicit in the mere occurrence of casemark, the specific meaning "with such and such specific relation to" is implicit in the occurrence of a specific casemark, in casu of directional dative mark, limiting the possible relations to the specific group of directional dative relations.

Exactly correspondingly in *qí-ša-a-a[t-su-nu la-]a ta-la-qé-šu-nu-ti*, the "accepting" or "taking" is "with relation to" the persons indicated by *-šunūti*, and this general fact is implied in the general fact that *-šunūti* is a case form. Herr von Soden wishes us to stop at this point and thus to consider meaningless the further fact that a specific case form, that of the accusative, occurs. We cannot agree with him. We must assume that here as elsewhere the selection of a specific case form is meaningful and indicates the selection of a specific group of relations. The group selected is that of relations compatible only with the accusative[7] and among them is, as we have shown, the ablative relation. An ablative relation is clearly present, moreover, in the situational context, the taking is "from" them. We propose, therefore, that *-šunūti* in *[la-]a ta-la-qé-šu-nu-ti* is an ablative accusative, denotes the ablative relation present in the situational context, and means "from them."

4. ABLATIVE ACCUSATIVE WITH NADĀNUM

In the OBa passage *TCL* VII No. 37.21–22, *eqla-am a-šar-ša-ni la ta-na-ad-di-na-šu-nu-ti* the verb *nadānum* is construed with two accusatives. Thureau-Dangin, who dealt with the text in *RA* 21, 30–31, assumed that the first of these, *eqlam*, was the direct-object accusative and translated: "Un champ ailleurs ne leur livrez pas." We likewise assumed that *eqlam* was the direct-object accusative and considered the second accusative, -*šunūti*, an ablative accusative. We translated: "do not give a field way off them somewhere else." Herr von Soden differs from us. He considers -*šunūti* to be the direct-object accusative and translates: "bezüglich des Feldes gebt sie (die Leute) nicht anderswohin," and cites *VAB* VI 53.10 and other passages in which *nadānum* is used for the "giving" or "assigning" of persons.

Since our present knowledge of Akkadian grammar allows us to say that one of two accusatives with active transitive verb is a direct-object accusative, but does not allow us to say which, a choice between Herr von Soden's interpretation, which makes the passage deal with a transfer of persons and fields, and the interpretations preferred by M. Thureau-Dangin and us, which assume that it merely deals with transfer of fields, can only be made on the basis of general context.

A clear idea of what is involved in a transfer of persons is given by the text *VAB* VI 53 quoted by Herr von Soden. In this text a field has been transferred from one local authority to another by lot. This does not change the status of the man who cultivated it. He has to appeal to the king to be transferred to the same local authority under which the field now sorts. The petition is granted and arrangements are then made for exchanging him for a person from the authority to which he wishes to be transferred so that his present authority will not suffer the loss of a man.

In *TCL* VII No. 37 none of all this is found. There is no mention of different local authorities, no replacing of persons "given" away. Rather the text is exclusively concerned with the reassignment of fields and the replacing of fields reassigned. Interpretation of lines 20–21 as dealing with a transfer of persons, a "giving" of persons from one authority to another, is thus unlikely, and interpretation in terms of reassignment and replacement of fields under a single authority recommends itself. Much the same context is found in *TCL* VII No. 68, which has the similar phrase: *i-b[a]-aš-ši-i i-na ma-na-ha-ti-šu ú-še-li-šu-ú-ma a-šar-ša-na i-na-ad-di-iš-šu*, "if this is so he would make him lose his labors and give (a field) way off him somewhere else." Here too it is a question only of reassignment of, and replacement for, a man's holdings—in fact for part of them merely—not also of his person.

The argument with which Herr von Soden introduces his variant translation is unfortunately not clear to us. He says: "Nur auf Fehlinterpretation beruht J.s Anahme, dass *nadānum* 'geben' im Altbabylonischen bisweilen mit dem doppelten Akkusativ konstruiert werde, wenn es sich um ein Weggeben handle. Gegen die Übersetzung von *eqlam^(am) a-šar-ša-ni la ta-na-ad-di-na-šu-nu-ti* durch 'ein Feld anderswo sollt ihr ihnen nicht geben!,' die in *RA* 21, 31 [1] zu Nr. 37, 21 f. auch Fr. Thureau-Dangin vertrat, spricht doch eindeutig *a-šar-ša-ni eqlam^(am) ta-ad-di-na-šu-nu-ši-im* in Z. 15 f. desselben Briefes; in den Briefen aus Hammurabis Kanzlei werden die Pronominalsuffixe des Dativs und Akkusativs nicht verwechselt!" (p. 159). It must seem unlikely that the point should be that in *TCL* VII No. 37.21–22 *nadānum* is not construed with a double accusative, *eqlam* and *-šunūti*, for it undoubtedly is so construed, or that the passage does not deal with a "Weggeben," for *a-šar-ša-ni*, "elsewhere," shows that it does, or that we should have assumed *-šunūti* to be a dative or a mistake for a dative made by Hammurabi's scribes, for we gave it as an example of an ablative accusative.

It may be noted in passing that Hammurabi in his letter does not right away emphasize the crucial element of "Weggeben" with its implications of unfair hardships on the men who had to cultivate a distant field. In the rhetorical question in ll. 13–16 *a-na mi-nim qá-qá-a[d eq]li-šu-nu te-el-qé-a-ma a-šar-ša-ni eqla-am ta-ad-di-na-šu-nu-ši-im*, "Why did you take their principal holdings and give them a field elsewhere?" it is not yet stressed. Hammurabi keeps the stress for his final injunction in ll. 21–22, where it appears with his choice of ablative accusative for expected dative, which serves to give to the injunction the character of a reproach *eqla-am a-šar-ša-ni la ta-na-ad-di-na-šu-nu-ti*, "do not give a field way off them somewhere else!"

5. THE FIRST SINGULAR COMMON DATIVE SUFFIX *-im*

In our article we analyzed the suffix sequence *-anni* as consisting of a modal element *-a-* (*a*-modus, rank 1'su.), a visitive and departive element *-n̄-* (rank 3'su.), and a first person singular common accusative pronominal element -*i* (rank 5'su.). The same elements are present in the sequence -*inni* except that the modal element of rank 1'su. is -*i*- rather than -*a*-, and they are present also in the sequence -*ninni* which is always preceded by a modal element -*ā*- or -*ū*- of rank 1'su., and which shows a plural subject element -*ni*- of rank 2'su. not found in the other sequences. The element -*ñ*- of these series we named the visitive and departive -*ñ*- and defined its meaning as contact with, or moving away from contact with, speaker, and we contrasted it with the ventive element -*m*- which belongs to the same rank, 3'su., and for which we posited the meaning direction toward point opposite, not in contact with, speaker. We also showed that the ventive element was simply -*m*- (more correctly {*m*}).

Herr von Soden's comments on these results are somewhat difficult to follow in their precise application, since he states himself in terms of largely unanalyzed suffix sequences and since he does not make any clear distinction between dative and ventive. He says: "Auf S. 108 f. vertritt J. die interessante These, dass die akkusativischen Pronominalsuffixe -*anni*, -*inni* und -*ninni* 'mich' nicht aus den Ventivelementen -*am*, -*im*, -*nim* und dem Suffix -*ni* der 1. Person Sing. zusammengesetz seien, sondern aus -*ann*, -*inn*, -*ninn* und dem ausserhalb des Altassyrischen nur genitivischen Suffix -*ī*. Damit wäre ein akkusativisches pronominales Element -*nn*- gegenüber dem dativischen -*m*- konstatiert. Eine Auseinandersetzung mit dieser These wäre nur auf breiter sprachvergleichender Basis sinnvoll und erforderte auch eine eingehende Untersuchung der altassyrischen Sprachgebrauchs über die vorläufige Notiz von J. Lewy in MVAG 35/3, S. 76ᶜ hinaus. Innerhalb des literarisch-archaischen Altbabylonischen macht immerhin das von J. nicht erwähnte, seltene Suffix -*nim* "mir" an Singularformen anstelle des normalen -*am* einige Schwierigkeiten . . . . ; es ordnet sich seinem auf S. 106b gegebenen Schema nicht ein. Weitere Belege dafür bleiben abzuwarten" (p. 160).

If we understand this correctly we should say that it is not exactly what we had in mind, an accusatival datival contrast -*nn*- -*m*- is not our thesis. We posit an adverbial (not a pronominal) element -*ñ*- denoting contact and movement away from contact with speaker, belonging to rank 3'su. and not restricted to occurrence with following accusative. Furthermore, we do not identify the ventive -*m*- with dative, rather, we posit for it adverbial (adverb of place) meaning:

movement to point opposite speaker and not in contact with him.

A discussion of the -*n̄*- on broad comparative basis would of course be welcome, but it must seem doubtful whether it could advance us much beyond Zimmern's cautious statement in his *Vergleichende Grammatik der Semitischen Sprachen*, p. 66 f.: "Das Verbalsuffix -*nī* beruht vielleicht auf Analogiebildung nach der 1. Plur., oder es enthält das Nominalsuffix *ī* nebst einem ursprünglich nicht zur Personenbezeichnung gehörenden *n*." It is the instructive contrast of near contact and near noncontact *n̄*:*m* preserved in Akkadian that suggests original adverb of place meaning for this -*n̄*-.

As for the interesting and important suffix sequence -*nim* to which Herr von Soden calls attention, it creates difficulties and fails to fit into the scheme given by us on p. 106b of our article only because Herr von Soden tends to view it as a ventive sequence ending with ventive -*m* and comparable to sequences such as (-*ū*)*nim* and (-*ā*)*nim* except that it is found with singular forms of the verb where the normal ventive sequences is -*am* or -*im*. As succinctly stated in *ZA* 53 (1959) 217: "Sehr merkwürdig ist das Ventive-Affix des Plurals -*nim* bei der Sing.-Form *aṣ-ṣa-ab-ta-nim*."

All difficulties disappear if the sequence is analyzed as consisting not of -*ni*- (2'su.) followed by ventive -*m* (3'su.) but of visitive and departive -*n̄*- (3'su.) followed by first singular dative pronominal element -*im* (4'su.). Thus analyzed it gives us at long last the expected, but hitherto missing, first singular common dative pronominal suffix -*im*, "for me," which in OBa. usage had become almost completely replaced by simple ventive.

In form the new dative suffix consists of a first singular pronominal element -*i*- followed by a casemark -*m* so that first singular dative -*i*.*m* "for me," is seen to correspond to first singular accusative -*i* exactly as second singular feminine dative -*ki*.*m* corresponds to accusative -*ki*, and third singular masculine and feminine -*šu*.*m* and -*ši*.*m* correspond to accusative -*šu* and *ši*.

As basic meaning of the datival casemark -*m* pro-lative meaning seems likely. That the Akkadian dative meaning contained an element of direction "toward" is indicated by the regularity with which dative relation can be expressed by the preposition *ana*; that in addition it contained an element of "toward the front of" is indicated by the fact that the relation in which the dative object, the recipient of a gift, stands is in Akkadian that of confronting, *mahārum*. The dative object, the one given to, is thus literally "the confronter," For extension of pro-lative to dative meaning cf. Latin "pro," German "für," English "for" etc. If, as seems likely, the dative mark -*m* denotes basically "for," "movement toward position before," it can hardly be separated lexically and in origin from the ventive -*m*- denoting "movement toward point opposite, not in contact with, speaker" and from the -*m*- of *ammîum*, "the one there," "iste"(?), though the three elements are of course distinct morphologically in rank and function.

As for the examples to which Herr von Soden calls attention, the first, *mi-im-ma ša ta-qa-bi-ni-im lu-pu-uš*, "anything which you (feminine singular) say here to me I will do," van Dijk, *Sumer* 13, 99.17, occurs in the address to Irninna by Sargon and may be analyzed as *taqqab.ī.n.im* with suffixes -*ī*- (*i*-modus for second person feminine singular Rank 1'su.) + -*n*- "here" (visitive -*ñ*-. Rank 3'su.) + -*im* "to me," (first person singular dative pron. suffix. Rank 4'su.). The second example, *ki ta-da-am-mi-qú-nim*, "as you prosper for me here," *RB* 59 246. viii.10, which Herr von Soden translates more freely as "wenn es dir (wieder) gut geht" may be analyzed as *tadammiq.u.n.im* with suffixes -*u*- (subjunctive mood. Rank 1'su.) + -*n*-, "here" (visitive -*ñ*-. Rank 3'su.) + -*im*, "for me" (Dative first person singular. Rank 4'su.) The third example, van Dijk, *Sumer* 13, 91.4, von Soden, *ZA*, 53, 216.4, occurs in a passage in which Gilgamesh tells about a dream he has had. Unfortunately the context is not altogether clear. *a-na-ku AM-MEŠ ṣi-ri-im aṣ-ṣa-ab-ta-nim*, "I had caught me here a(?)... of the desert." The suffix sequence may be analyzed as -*a*- (*a*-modus. Rank 1'su.) + -*n*- "here" (visitive -*ñ*-. Rank 3'su.) + -*im*, "for me" (first person singular dative suffix. Rank 4'su.). We attempt no explanation of *AM-MEŠ*.

6. THE *i*-MODUS

An important result of our analysis into ranks was the realization that the modal elements and the elements indicating person, gender, and number of the subject must form but a single system. Herr von Soden does not comment on this as a whole but says: "In der Anmerkung 12 auf S. 110 f. behandelt J. schliesslich noch das in GAG §82c erwähnte, nicht sehr oft bezeugte Affix -*i* des Altbabylonischen und möchte diesem den Sinn 'action under compulsion' unterlegen. Diese Deutung erscheint ihm so gesichert, dass er auf S. 114 f. weitreichende Folgerungen aus ihr zieht" (p. 160). As we remember it we merely said in n. 12 [see above, chap. xvi] that "The suggested force of the *i* modus, 'action under compulsion' is guessed from the context" and we based no conclusions on this guess, restricting ourselves to noting on p. 289 that it agreed with results otherwise arrived at. We also made a cautionary statement on p. 287.

In Herr von Soden's following comments he allows—albeit reluctantly—that the meaning suggested by us for the *i*-modus is feasible in eight out of the nine cases we quoted. Only in the ninth example does interpretation as "action under compulsion" seem to him not possible. The example is *TCL* XVIII 81.5, *um-ma-ka-a ma-ar-ṣa-at-ti*, which we translated as "your mother cannot help being ill" explaining that the statement follows an account of various calamities that have occurred. We should perhaps have expanded our brief statement to say that we did not intend to restrict "ill" to a meaning "suffering from a disease" but used it more broadly to include "ill with worry and grief," a meaning also implicit in *marāṣum*. As compelling agency we assumed the circumstances related, under which the mother "could not help" grieving and worrying herself ill. Herr von Soden observes: "Krank ist doch niemand freiwillig." Perhaps, but that is not the point. The point is whether the speaker wished to stress the compulsory aspect in his context or not, to *present* the condition *marṣat* as unavoidable under the circumstances.

Further examples considered by Herr von Soden are *TCL* XVIII 77.5, *ma-tum e-di-iš-ši-ša na-aq*(!?)-*da-at-ti*, "the land, left alone, is perforce distressed," and *VS* XVI 55.5 ff., *i-de e-ma! a-wa-at-ki-ma ra-bi-a-at-ti i-qá-bu-ki ma-gi-ir*, where we should prefer to read with Kraus, *MVAG* 36/1 97, *i-de-e-ma* and to translate: "I know that *your* word perforce carries weight, they will say to you: 'agreed!'" Next are listed two statements made about gods, *JNES* 14, 15.11 f. cf. 17, 56 note 5 7 *bùr eqlam* ᵈ*Sîn i-ṣí*(!)-*di*, "Sin had to reap 7 bur field," and *VS* X 214 v 30, *i-lu É-a ih-ti-i-ši*, "The god Ea had perforce acted quickly." Also a statement about the draught bull before Ishtar's chariot, not about her herself, *VS* X 214 iv 14–17, *uš-na-ar-ra-aṭ e li-im ki uz-za-ʾzuʾ ri-gi-im-ša i še-er-de la iz-zi-i-zi ú-ṣí i-na du-un-ni-ša*, "She was letting quiver (calling) unto the (draught)bull as she was getting furious her voice; it (the bull) perforce did not wait in the traces, she drove out in her might." Lastly an example provided by Professor Edzard from unpublished tablets from ed-Deir is quoted: *im-du-di*, unfortunately without context.

In the first of these cases, *TCL* XVIII 77.5, as earlier with *TCL* XVIII 81.5, Herr von Soden considers the possibility that *-i* may express "ein Bedauern," a possibility which he rightly rejects already with his second new example, *VS* XVI 55.5 ff., where it does not fit. In the examples dealing with actions of gods he assumes that "In keiner dieser Aussagen kann die Rede davon sein, dass man den Göttern ein Handeln unter Zwang zuschreiben wollte" (p. 161). Why not? The ancient Mesopotamian gods no less than men acted under the compelling force of circumstances, passions, obligations, decisions by other gods (see e.g. the lamentations), etc. We agree with Herr von Soden, of course, when he adds "ebensowenig wollten die Dichter ein Bedauern zum Ausdruck bringen" (p. 161), that was his suggestion. Herr von Soden concludes: "Angesichts der grossen Verschiedenartigkeit der von J. und hier vorgeführten Aussagen, die das *-i* fast immer als Verbalaffix zeigen, sehe ich vorläufig keine andere Möglichkeit als die, dem *-i* eine stark hervorhebende Function zuzuschreiben. Dabei bleibt freilich unerklärlich, warum es so selten gebraucht wird" (p. 161). The objection raised seems to us well taken and conclusive. As may be seen from our translations of the passages involved we experience no difficulties with our suggested interpretation "action under compulsion." In fact a translation "perforce" or "had to" appears to fit remarkably well in all of them. That does not yet prove, of course, that interpretation as "action under compulsion" is the correct one, it merely indicates that so far such interpretation is possible, perhaps even probable.

7. CONCLUSION

We have now come to the end of our reexamination and may try to sum up: (1) In our article we had posited an ablative accusative, that is, an accusative the meaning of which Akkadian could equally well have expressed by the preposition *itti*, "from," and had listed a number of examples of its occurrence. Herr von Soden's first objection was that since in *ba-me-du:it-tál-lak ni-a-ti* the Sumerian infix is *-me-* and not, as he expected, *-me-ta-* the corresponding *ni-a-ti* cannot have been understood as an ablative. As we have seen, however, his form *-me-ta-* may not be expected since it is the rule of the paradigm to show the plural infixes *-me-*, *-e-ne-*, and *-ne-* without overt postpositional mark in all indicative forms.

Herr von Soden's second objection was that ablative meaning would not fit in a number of cases which he had added to our list of occurrences. He thought that this compelled the positing of a more general meaning, that of "accusative of relation" ("Akkusativ der Beziehung"), "with relation to" ("in Bezug auf"). As we have seen, however, there is an altogether different thing at issue in these cases. Herr von Soden's additions to our list are mostly accusatives the meaning of which Akkadian could equally well have expressed by the preposition *eli*, "onto." It is obvious that such accusatives cannot be considered ablative accusatives and so have no business in the list. They are supra-lative (*eli*) accusatives denoting "onto," and they form a distinct group parallel to the ablative accusatives within the larger group of "prepositional accusatives." We also saw that the meaning proposed by Herr von Soden, "with relation to," is a general meaning common to all cases and all propositions. If insisted upon it obliterates all distinction of specific meaning, i.e., of restriction to particular kinds of relations, and that not only between different accusatives but between accusative and nominative, genitive, dative generally.

(2) In our article we had proposed an analysis of the suffixes of the prefixed verbal forms according to rank in the form. Among the suffixes thus isolated and ranked was an adverbial (adverb of place) element *-n̄-* which we called the visitive and departive *-n̄-* and a likewise adverbial (adverb of place) *-m-*, the ventive element. Herr von Soden somewhat differently thinks it possible to see in these two elements a contrast between an accusatival pronominal element *-nn-* and a datival element *-m* but wishes to reserve his opinion about such a thesis. Herr von Soden also raises the objection that the suffix sequence *-nim* found with singular form of the verb does not fit into

our analytic scheme given on p. 278. As we have seen the difficulties arise from Herr von Soden's view that this sequence is a ventive sequence and disappear if it is realized that the sequence contains the visitive -*n̄*- and the long-sought-for first person singular dative suffix -*im*.

(3) In our article we had made a cautious suggestion that the modal suffix -*i* may have denoted "action under compulsion." Herr von Soden, listing a number of additional examples of the suffix, objects that in one of the examples quoted by us and in all those added by him a meaning "action under compulsion" is not feasible. Our re-examination of the examples showed, however, that on a second look the meaning may be said to fit them very well indeed.

It seems to us, accordingly, that we may maintain the positions taken on these various points in our original article.

It remains to thank Herr von Soden for the readiness with which he has entered into a discussion of these interesting problems. A discussion may not always lead to agreement but if only it results in reasoned disagreement it helps to clarify and thus constitutes a step forward; it is also likely to elicit, as this discussion has already done, important new, and important related, materials.

Abbreviations

Notes

Bibliography of Jacobsen's Writings

Lexical Index to Jacobsen's Writings

General Index

Abbreviations

á-a	lexical series
AASOR	*The Annual of the American Schools of Oriental Research*
AHw	Wolfram von Soden, *Akkadisches Handwörterbuch* I, II (incomplete) (Wiesbaden, 1965–)
Ai	*Ana ittišu* (lexical series)
AJA	*American Journal of Archaeology*
AJSL	*American Journal of Semitic Languages and Literatures*
ANET	*Ancient Near Eastern Texts Relating to the Old Testament* ed. James B. Pritchard (Princeton, 1950; 2nd ed. 1955)
Angim	Sumerian epic
AnOr	*Analecta Orientalia* (Rome)
AO	Tablets in the collections of the Musée du Louvre
AOB	*Altorientalische Bibliothek* I (Leipzig, 1926)
AOF	*Archiv für Orientforschung*
AOTU	*Altorientalische Texte und Untersuchungen* (Leiden, 1917)
AR	D. D. Luckenbill, *Ancient Records of Assyria and Babylonia* I–II (Chicago, 1926)
ARM	*Archives royales de Mari* (*ARM* I = *TCL* XXII, etc.)
ArOr	*Archiv orientální*
AS	*Assyriological Studies* (Chicago)
ASKT	P. Haupt, *Akkadische und sumerische Keilschrifttexte*... (Leipzig, 1881–1882)
BA	*Beiträge zur Assyriologie* (Leipzig)
Bab	*Babyloniaca*
Bagh. Mitt.	*Baghdader Mitteilungen,* Deutsches Archäologisches Institut, Abteilung Baghdad. I– (1960–)
BASOR	*Bulletin of the American Schools of Oriental Research*
BAW	B. Meissner, *Beiträge zum Assyrischen Wörterbuch* I and II (= *AS* I and IV)
BE	*The Babylonian Expedition of the University of Pennsylvania* (Philadelphia)
Belleten	*Türk Tarih Kurumu, Belleten*
BIN	*Babylonian Inscriptions in the Collection of J. B. Nies* (New Haven)

BL	Langdon, *Babylonian Liturgies* (Paris, 1913)
BM	Tablets in the collections of the British Museum
BMS	L. W. King, *Babylonian Magic and Sorcery* (London, 1896)
Boson Tavolette	G. Boson, *Tavolette cuneiformi sumere degli archivi di Drehem e di Djoha...* (Milan, 1936)
BRM	*Babylonian Records in the Library of J. Pierpont Morgan* (New Haven)
Bu	Tablets in the collections of the British Museum
BuA	B. Meissner, *Babylonien und Assyrien* I–II (Heidelberg, 1920–1925)
CAD	*The Assyrian Dictionary of the University of Chicago* (Chicago-Glückstadt, 1956–)
CBS	Tablets in the collections of the University Museum, University of Pennsylvania
CCT	*Cuneiform Texts from Cappadocian Tablets in the British Museum* (London, 1921–1956)
CH	Code of Hammurabi
Clavis	A. Howardy, *Clavis Cuneorum* (Leipzig, 1904–1933)
Corpus	E. Sollberger, *Corpus des inscriptions "royales" présargoniques de Lagaš* (Geneva, 1956)
CT	*Cuneiform Texts from Babylonian Tablets in the British Museum* (London, 1896–)
CTC	T. Jacobsen, *Cuneiform Texts in the National Museum, Copenhagen, Chiefly of Economic Contents* (Leiden, 1939)
CTP	*The Cappadocian Tablets in the University of Pennsylvania Museum*
Datenlisten	A. Ungnad, *RLA* II 131–194
DDU	N. Schneider, *Die Drehem- und Djoha-Urkunden...*, *AnOr* I (Rome, 1931)
Diri	lexical series
DP	F. M. Allotte de Fuije, *Documents présargoniques*, Fasc. I–II (Paris, 1908–1920)
Dreambook	A. Leo Oppenheim, *The Interpretation of Dreams in the Ancient Near East*, Transactions of the American Philosophical Society XLVI/3 (1956)
Eames Coll.	A. Leo Oppenheim, *Catalogue of the Cuneiform Tablets of the Wilberforce Eames Collection in the New York Public Library* (New Haven, 1948), Amer. Or. Series XXXII
Erimhuš	lexical series
Fauna	B. Landsberger, *Die Fauna des Alten Mesopotamien nach der 14. Tafel der Serie Har-ra = ḫubullu*, Abh. d. Sächsischen Akad. d. Wissenschaften, Phil.-hist. Klasse 42/VI (Leipzig, 1934)
Fara	E. Heinrich, *Ergebnisse der Ausgrabungen der Deutschen Orient-Gesellschaft in Fara und Abu Hatab 1902/03* (Berlin, 1931)
GAG	Wolfram von Soden, *Grundriss der akkadischen Grammatik*, *AnOr* XXXII (Rome, 1952)
Gerichtsurkunden	A. Falkenstein, *Die neusumerischen Gerichtsurkunden* I–III,

	Bayerische Akad. d. Wissenschaften, Phil.-hist. Klass, Abhand. NF 39–40, 44 (Munich, 1956–1957)
Götterepitheta	K. Tallqvist, *Akkadische Götterepitheta, Studia Orientalia* VI (Helsinki, 1938)
Götterlieder	A. Falkenstein, *Sumerische Götterlieder*, Abh. d. Heidelberger Akad. d. Wissenschaften, Phil.-hist. Klasse, 1959–1960 (Heidelberg, 1959–1960)
GSG	A. Poebel, *Grundzüge der Sumerischen Grammatik* (Rostock, 1923)
GSGL	A. Falkenstein, *Grammatik der Sprache Gudeas von Lagaš* I–III, *AnOr* XXVIII–XXX (Rome, 1949–1966)
Haupttypen	A. Falkenstein, *Die Haupttypen der sumerischen* Beschwörung *literarisch untersucht, LSS* n. F. I (Leipzig, 1931)
HG	J. Kohler et al., *Hammurabi's Gesetz* I–VI (Leipzig, 1904–1923)
HGT	A. Poebel, *Historical and Grammatical Texts, PBS* V (Philadelphia, 1914)
IIh	ḪAR-ra = *ḫubullu* (lexical series)
HiAV	(*Hilprecht Anniversary Volume*) *Assyriologische und archäologische Studien Hermann V. Hilprecht* ... *gewidmet* (Leipzig-Chicago, 1909)
HSM	Tablets in the collections of the Harvard Semitic Museum
HSS	*Harvard Semitic Series*
HT	A. Poebel, *Historical Texts, PBS* IV.1 (Philadelphia, 1914)
IIymnenkatalog	E. Ebeling, *Ein Hymnenkatalog aus Assur* (Berlin, 1922)
HW	F. Delitzsch, *Assyrisches Handwörterbuch* (Leipzig, 1896)
IDB	*The Interpreter's Dictionary of the Bible*, ed. George Arthur Buttrick et al. I–IV (New York, 1962)
IM	Tablets in the Iraq Museum at Baghdad
ITT	*Inventaire des tablettes de Tello conservées au Musée imperial Ottoman* I–V (Paris, 1910–1921)
Izi	lexical series
JAOS	*Journal of the American Oriental Society*
JCS	*Journal of Cuneiform Studies*
JEA	*Journal of Egyptian Archaeology*
JNES	*Journal of Near Eastern Studies*
JRAS	*Journal of the Royal Asiatic Society*
JSOR	*Journal of the Society of Oriental Research*
K	Tablets in the Kouyunjik collection of the British Museum
KAH	*Keilschrifttexte aus Assur historischen Inhalts, WVDOG* XVI, XXXI (Leipzig, 1911, 1922)
KAR	*Keilschrifttexte aus Assur religiösen Inhalts, WVDOG* XXVIII, XXXIV (Leipzig, 1919, 1923)
KAV	*Keilschrifttexte aus Assur verschiedenen Inhalts, WVDOG* XXXV (Leipzig, 1920)
Kich	H. de Genouillac, *Premières recherches archéologiques à Kich* (Paris, 1924–1925)

Kult. Kal.	B. Landsberger, *Der kultische Kalender der Babylonier und Assyrer, LSS* VII/1–2 (Leipzig, 1915)
LAK	A. Deimel, *Liste der archaischen Keilschriftzeichen, WVDOG* XL (Leipzig, 1922)
LIH	L. W. King, *The Letters and Inscriptions of Hammurabi* (London, 1898–1900)
LKA	E. Ebeling, *Literarische Keilschrifttexte aus Assur* (Berlin, 1953)
LKU	A. Falkenstein, *Literarische Keilschrifttexte aus Uruk* (Berlin, 1931)
LRSt	*Leipziger rechtswissenschaftliche Studien*
LSS	*Leipziger Semitische Studien*
Lu	lexical series
Lugale	Sumerian epic
Macm. *Rel. Texts*	K. D. Macmillan, *Some Cuneiform Tablets Bearing on the Religion of Babylonia and Assyria, BA* V/5 (Leipzig, 1906)
MAD	I. J. Gelb, *Materials for the Assyrian Dictionary* I–III (Chicago, 1952–1957)
MAH	Tablets in the collection of the Musée d'Art et d'Histoire, Geneva
MBI	G. A. Barton, *Miscellaneous Babylonian Inscriptions* (New Haven, 1910)
MDP	*Mémoires de la Délegation en Perse* I– (Paris, 1900–)
MJ	*The Museum Journal* (University Museum, University of Pennsylvania)
MKT	O. Neugebauer, *Mathematische Keilschrifttexte* (Berlin, 1936–1937)
MLC	Tablets in the collections of the J. Pierpont Morgan Library
MSL	*Materialien zum sumerischen Lexikon* (Rome)
MVAG	*Mitteilungen der Vorderasiatisch-Ägyptischen Gesellschaft*
NBGT	Neobabylonian Grammatical Texts (*MSL* IV 129–178)
Nabnitu	lexical series
NFT	G. Cros, *Nouvelles fouilles de Tello* (Paris, 1910)
NIK	M. V. Nikolski, *Dokumenty khosiaistvennoi otchetnosti* ... I–II (Moscow, 1908–1915)
N-T	Field numbers of tablets found at Nippur
OBGT	Old Babylonian Grammatical Texts (*MSL* IV 47–128)
OBI	H. V. Hilprecht, *Old Babylonian Inscriptions Chiefly from Nippur*, Parts I–II, *BE* I.1–2 (Philadelphia, 1893–1896)
OECT	*Oxford Editions of Cuneiform Texts*
OIC	*Oriental Institute Communications* (Chicago)
OIP	*Oriental Institute Publications* (Chicago)
OLZ	*Orientalistische Literaturzeitung*
PBS	*Publications of the Babylonian Section, University Museum, University of Pennsylvania*
Pantheon	A. Deimel, *Pantheon Babylonicum* ... (Rome, 1914)
PAPS	*Proceedings of the American Philosophical Society*

Patesis	C. E. Keiser, *Patesis of the Ur Dynasty* (New Haven, 1919)
PSBA	*Proceedings of the Society of Biblical Archaeology*
R	H. C. Rawlinson, *The Cuneiform Inscriptions of Western Asia* I–V (London, 1861–1909)
RA	*Revue d'Assyriologie*
RB	*Revue biblique*
REC	F. Thureau-Dangin, *Recherches sur l'origine de l'écriture cunéiforme* I + Supplement (Paris, 1898–1899)
Recueil	L. Speleers, *Recueil des inscriptions de l'Asie antérieure des Musées Royaux du Cinquantenaire à Bruxelles* (Brussels, 1925)
RLA	*Reallexikon der Assyriologie* (Berlin-Leipzig, 1932–)
Rm	Tablets in the collections of the British Museum
RTC	F. Thureau-Dangin, *Recueil de tablettes chaldéennes* (Paris, 1903)
SA	C.-F. Jean, *Šumer et Akkad, contribution à l'histoire de la civilisation dans la Basse-Mésopotamie* (Paris, 1923)
SAI	B. Meissner, *Seltene assyrische Ideogramme* (Leipzig, 1910)
SAK	F. Thureau-Dangin, *Die sumerischen und akkadischen Königsinschriften*, *VAB* I (Leipzig, 1907)
SAOC	*Studies in Ancient Oriental Civilization* (Chicago)
SBH	G. A. Reisner, *Sumerisch-babylonische Hymnen nach Thontafeln griechischer Zeit* (Berlin, 1896)
SEM	E. Chiera, *Sumerian Epics and Myths*, *OIP* XV (Chicago, 1934)
SF	A. Deimel, *Schultexte aus Fara, in Umschrift herausgegeben und bearbeitet*, *WVDOG* XLIII (Leipzig, 1924)
SGl	F. Delitzsch, *Sumerisches Glossar* (Leipzig, 1914)
SK	H. Zimmern, *Sumerische Kultlieder aus altbabylonischer Zeit* I–II, *VS* II, X (Leipzig, 1912–1913)
SL	S. Langdon, *Sumerian Liturgies and Psalms*, *PBS* X.4 (Philadelphia, 1919)
ŠL	A. Deimel, *Šumerisches Lexikon* I–IV (Rome, 1925–1950)
SLT	E. Chiera, *Sumerian Lexical Texts from the Temple School of Nippur*, *OIP* XI (Chicago, 1929)
SLTN	*Sumerian Literary Texts from Nippur in the Museum of the Ancient Orient at Istanbul*, *AASOR* XXIII (New Haven, 1944)
SRD	W. M. Nesbit, *Sumerian Records from Drehem* (New York, 1914)
SRT	E. Chiera, *Sumerian Religious Texts* (Upland, Pa., 1924)
STA	E. Chiera, *Selected Temple Accounts from Telloh* (Philadelphia, 1921)
STD	C. E. Keiser, *Selected Temple Documents of the Ur Dynasty*, *YOS* IV (New Haven, 1919)
STH	M. I. Hussey, *Sumerian Tablets in the Harvard Semitic Museum* *HSS* III–IV (Cambridge, 1912–1915)
Streck Asb.	M. Streck, *Assurbanipal und die letzten assyrischen Könige bis zum Untergang Ninevehs* I–III, *VAB* VII (Leipzig, 1916)

STVC	E. Chiera, *Sumerian Texts of Varied Contents, OIP* XVI (Chicago, 1934)
TAD	S. Langdon, *Tablets from the Archives of Drehem* (Paris, 1911)
TC	*Tablettes cappadociennes* (I = *TCL* IV, II = *TCL* XIV; III = *TCL* XIX–XXI)
TCL	*Textes cunéiformes*. Musée du Louvre
TD	H. de Genouillac, *Tablettes de Drehem, TCL* II (Paris, 1911)
TD	G. G. Hackman, *Temple Documents of the Third Dynasty of Ur from Umma, BIN* V (New Haven, 1937)
Tell Sifr	C.-F. Jean, *Tell Sifr*, textes cunéiformes conservés au British Museum, réédités (Paris, 1931)
TEO	H. de Genouillac, *Textes économiques d'Oumma de l'époque d'Our, TCL* V (Paris, 1922)
Tr. D	H. de Genouillac, *La trouvaille de Drehem* (Paris, 1911)
TRS	H. de Genouillac, *Textes religieux sumériens du Louvre, TCL* XV–XVI (Paris, 1930)
TSŠ	R. R. Jestin, *Tablettes sumériennes de Šuruppak conservées au Musée de Stamboul* (Paris, 1937)
TU	G. A. Reisner, *Tempellurkunden aus Telloh* (Berlin, 1901)
TuM	*Texte und Materialien der Frau Professor Hilprecht Collection of Babylonian Antiquities im Eigentum der Universität Jena*
UCP	*University of California Publications in Semitic Philology*
UDT	J. B. Nies, *Ur Dynasty Tablets* (Leipzig, 1920)
UE(T)	*Ur Excavations (Texts)* I–VIII (London, 1928–)
UM	Tablets in the collections of the University Museum, University of Pennsylvania
UMB	*The University Museum Bulletin*
VAB	*Vorderasiatische Bibliothek*
VAT	Tablets in the collections of the Staatliche Museen, Berlin
Voc. Zim.	B. Zimolong, *Das sumerisch-assyrische Vokabular Ass. 523* (Leipzig, 1922)
VS	*Vorderasiatische Schriftdenkmäler der Königlichen Musseen zu Berlin*
WF	A. Deimel, *Wirtschafttexte aus Fara, in Umschrift herausgegeben und bearbeitet, WVDOG* XLV (Leipzig, 1924)
WO	*Die Welt des Orients*
YBC	Tablets in the Yale Babylonian collections
YOS	*Yale Oriental Series, Babylonian Texts*
ZA(n.F.)	*Zeitschrift für Assyriologie (neue Folge)*
ZDMG	*Zeitschrift der Deutschen Morgenländischen Gesellschaft*
ZWU	N. Schneider, *Die Zeitbestimmungen der Wirtschaftsurkunden von Ur III, AnOr* XIII (Rome, 1936)

Notes

1. Formative Tendencies in Sumerian Religion

1. On religion and the study of religion generally, see Rudolph Otto, *The Idea of the Holy* (London, 1943); G. van der Leeuw, *Religion in Essence and Manifestation* (New York, 1938); Ernst Cassirer, *Philosophie der symbolischen Formen* II: *Das mythische Denken* (Berlin, 1925).

2. For general orientation, see, e.g., E. Dhorme, *Les Religions de Babylonie et d'Assyrie* (Paris, 1945).

3. Cf. *JNES* 12 (1953), p. 167, note 27 [see below, Chap. V].

4. The credit for first recognizing the true nature of the Mesopotamian cult drama belongs to Sv. Aa. Pallis, *The Babylonian Akîtu Festival* (Copenhagen, 1926). On the nature of the identity involved, see the work of Cassirer cited above in note 1.

3. Ancient Mesopotamian Religion: The Central Concerns

1. See William James, *The Varieties of Religious Experience* (New York, 1902); Rudolph Otto, *The Idea of the Holy* (Oxford, ninth impression, 1943); G. van der Leeuw, *La Religion dans son essence et ses manifestations* (Paris, 1948), §110.

2. It is, of course, in no way our intention to try to reduce religion to fear, or to fear and its counterpart hope; merely to distinguish and try to trace these important components of the human religious response for ancient Mesopotamia. A more comprehensive statement we have tried to give in "Formative Tendencies in Sumerian Religion," *The Bible and the Ancient Near East: Essays in Honor of William Foxwell Albright* (New York, 1961), pp. 267–278 [see above, chap. i]. See also our article, "Assyria and Babylonia. Religion," in the 1963 printing of the *Encyclopaedia Brittannica* [see above, chap. ii]. As particularly characteristic of the ancient Mesopotamian response we tend to see its unreflected apprehending of the numinous as will and power in and for the specific situation in which it was experienced to come into being and be. The numinous was thus experienced not as one but as many different powers, form was attributed to these different powers in terms of the different situations in which they were thought to be encountered, and human values in the situation, whether good or evil, tended to condition the response as

one of allegiance or one of avoidance and defense. It was particularly in this evaluation of situations that the human urge to seek security and salvation became guiding for selective attention and directed primary allegiance toward powers in situations and phenomena recognized as basic for human survival, powers in the basic economies.

General presentations of ancient Mesopotamian religion may be found, e.g., in E. Dhorme, *La Religion assyro-babylonienne* (Paris, 1910), whicn in many respects is not superseded by the same author's *Les Religions de Babylonie et d'Assyrie* (Paris, 1949). See also J. Bottéro, *La Religion de Babylonie et d'Assyrie* (Paris, 1952), and cf. H. Frankfort et al., *The Intellectual Adventure of Ancient Man* (Chicago, 1946; also in Penguin edition as *Before Philosophy*, 1949), and D. O. Edzard in *Wörterbuch der Mythologie*, ed. H. W. Haussig, section I. 1.

3. I.e., Ubaid, Warka, Protoliterate, and Early Dynastic I incl. Generally we may say that in attempting to organize the varied materials for ancient Mesopotamian religion within a meaningful temporal framework we have been guided by the following considerations:

(1) The sources available for the earliest periods down to the later parts of Early Dynastic are almost exclusively archaeological in nature, written sources of some substance begin late in Early Dynastic but flow freely only at two points in time, in the Old Babylonian period and in the Neo-Assyrian and later periods. We are thus rather unevenly informed and must often have recourse from the less well documented to the relatively fully documented periods for understanding. Such recourse, however, very obviously presents problems of method.

(2) Most striking, perhaps, is the case of the earliest periods. Interesting and suggestive as are the materials directly datable to these periods it is quite clear that they do not in fact constitute an autonomous body of evidence interpretable in and of itself; rather, dependence on later evidence is so essential for understanding that if the early materials were left to stand by themselves they would be largely meaningless and incoherent.

(3) While recourse to later evidence is thus necessary for understanding of the earlier materials such recourse must not be had uncritically, for the later materials cannot be considered of a piece but represent a stage of a developing tradition comprising elements directly surviving, elements surviving more or less altered and reinterpreted, and elements that are new developments altogether. Before they can be confidently used they must be carefully analyzed and evaluated, observable differences in basic religious attitude and form must be discerned, internal criteria of relative age considered, and the various strata of tradition distinguished as far as possible. Only thus can they be utilized for the interpretation of older data without obvious danger of anachronism.

(4) As an important criterion in the evaluation of the later materials we consider the observable difference between "intransitive" and "transitive active" view of the gods. All ancient Mesopotamian gods appear to be the power in and for some phenomenon, they are gods, e.g., of heaven, of the storm, of the sweet waters, of the moon, of the sun, of birth, of fertility and yield, of reeds, of barley, of beer-making, etc., etc. However, whereas some of them such as, e.g., the god Dumuzid,

god of fertility and yields, have intransitive character, are mere will and power for their relevant phenomenon to be, others, such as, e.g., Enlil, god of the storm, transcend the limits of the phenomenon with which they are associated in that they will and act beyond it, they are powers broadly active in human life, guiding and shaping human history. For a discussion of these two aspects see "Formative Tendencies in Sumerian Religion," *The Bible and the Ancient Near East*, ed. G. Ernest Wright (New York, 1961), pp. 268 f. [see above, chap. i] and "Toward the Image of Tammuz," *History of Religions* (Chicago, 1961) 1/2, pp. 190–192 [see below, chap. vi].

(5) As for the relative age of these two views of the divine, it may be confidently assumed that the intransitive view is a general and an old feature, for an unmistakable intransitive core is traceable in all figures of the Sumerian pantheon. The active transitive view, on the other hand, applies less generally and—more important— it is always connected with and expressed under inherently late anthropomorphic forms borrowed from human society and its human dignitaries. (On the earlier nonanthropomorphic stage of visualizing the gods see Falkenstein, *Archaische Texte aus Uruk* (Leipzig, 1936), and our "Formative Tendencies in Sumerian Religion," pp. 269 f. [see above, chap. i].) The specific extension of anthropomorphism with which we are here dealing—politicomorphism—can be dated with a fair amount of probability to the middle of the Early Dynastic period since the specific form of political institutions assumed for the gods, primitive democracy with general assembly at Nippur and ruler image close to that of primitive monarchy, can best be accommodated at that point of time (see our discussion in "Early Political Development in Mesopotamia," *ZA* 52 (1957) 91–140, esp. 106–109 and 120 [see below, chap. viii]). It would accordingly appear that materials characterized by transitive character of the gods in politicomorph expression are less suitable for reconstruction and interpretation of evidence from before Early Dynastic than is evidence characterized by an intransitive view and that the overall picture suggested is one of the gods as powers in nature, particularly in its economical aspects, before ca. 3000 *B.C.*; as powers also in history after that date.

4. See generally Frankfort et al., *The Intellectual Adventure of Ancient Man*, pp. 125–128; Robert M. Adams, "Early Civilizations, Subsistence and Environment" in *City Invincible*, ed. Carl H. Kraeling and Robert M. Adams (Chicago, 1960); Jacobsen and Adams, "Salt and Silt in Ancient Mesopotamian Agriculture," *Science* 128, 3334 (1958) 1251–1257; Jacobsen, "Summary of Report by the Diyala Basin Archaeological Project...," *Sumer* 14 (1958) 79–89.

5. Many passages in the later literature testify to intimate knowledge of the terrors of prolonged famine when "the daughter sees the mother go in and the mother does not open her door to the daughter; the daughter watches the balances of the mother, the mother watches the balances of the daughter" and—as the famine continues—"they set aside for a meal, they set aside the child for food" (*CT* XV 49 i 7′–12′).

The importance of communal storage as a means to counteract the precariousness of the early economy and as a prime factor in the achievement of conditions for permanent human settlement has hardly yet received the attention it deserves. It underlies the "temple-economy," which originally most likely embraced not merely a temple or group of temples but the whole community, as it underlies the later palace economy. Significant are the frequent designations of temples as storehouses (é-uš-gíd-da:*arahhu, našpaku, ašlukkatu*; é-gi-na-ab-du₇:*šutummu*; gá-nun:*ganūnu*. Note especially the Gá-nun-mah in Ur with its central cellas and surrounding storerooms) and as places of division of yields (é-zi-ki-šu-p[eš₅] na-ám-mu-lu-a-mu: *bītu ki-i-ni ma-ha-zi šá ni-ši-ia SBH* 31:9 "my good house, my people's place of dividing up the yield"; see further *ZA*, 52, 103, note 19 [see below, chap. viii], but note that šu peš is better understood as "to make the 'hands' three," i.e., to divide (yield) into three parts. (The Akkadian equivalent *šabāšu* is conceivably ultimately derived from the Sumerian expression.) The many-sided goddess Inannak seems originally to have been the personified power of the storehouse (see *ZA*, 52, 108, note 32 [see below, chap. viii]). In the Gilgamesh Epic she promises to store grain enough to feed the people for seven years to alleviate the famine that releasing the bull of heaven will cause. The door of the giparu in Eannak at which she awaits her bridegroom, Dumuzid, is said to be the door of the storehouse (é-uš-gíd-da *TRS* 70 rev. 2–3. Cf. *ZA*, 52, 108, note 32 [see below, chap. viii]). An example of a ruler—a "lord," en, embodiment of magic powers for fertility—alleviating a famine with stored surplus of grain offers the story of Enmerkar and the Lord of Aratta (Kramer, *Enmerkar and the Lord of Aratta* [Philadelphia, 1952]).

6. See "Formative Tendencies in Sumerian Religion," *The Bible and the Ancient Near East*, ed. G. Ernest Wright (New York, 1961), pp. 271–274 [see above, chap. i] and "Assyria and Babylonia. Religion," *Encyclopaedia Britannica*, 1963 printing [see above, chap. ii]. For the cult of Dumuzid and Inannak see also *ZA*, 52, 108, note 32 [see below, chap. viii], Edzard in *Wörterbuch der Mythologie*, ed. H. W. Haussig I, 1, pp. 51–53 and 81–89 and our article "Toward the Image of Tammuz" in *History of Religions* (Chicago, 1961) 1/2, pp. 189–213 [see below, chap. vi].

The name Dumuzid (written ᵈDumu-zi, the final d occurs in writing only when it forms a syllable with a following vowel) is mostly rendered as "the true son" (see, e.g., Edzard, *Worterbuch der Mythologie*, p. 51: "rechter Sohn"). In *JNES* 12 (1953) 166, note 23 [see below, chap. v] we suggested that the element zi(d) most likely represents a factitive nomen agentis from the intransitive stem zi(d) which occurs in the meanings *nêšu* "life," "vigor," "health," and perhaps *napištum* "breath of life." We accordingly translated Dumuzid as "he who quickens the young ones." A phrase written nam-dumu-zi occurs in a hymn to the goddess Manungal in a passage in which that goddess states her capabilities as a midwife but is unfortunately not conclusive for the interpretation of the name Dumuzid. The passage (*SEM* 51.ii.4′–5′ & 53 obv. 5′–rev. 1 & *PBS* I.2 no. 104 rev. 4–5 & 3NT 409, 453 and 675) reads: ᵈNin-tu-rakinam-dumu[-zi-ka mu-da-an-gub-bé-en] gi-dur ku₅-da nam-tar-re[-da KA-sa₆-ga-bi mu-zu] "I assist (the goddess of birth) Nintud at the place of child-quickening, I am experienced in (lit. 'I know') cutting the umbilical cord and in saying (only) nice things (because) of (the possible effect of words spoken at that time on) determining (the) fate (of the newborn child)." The translation here given, "place of child-quickening," assumes that nam-dumu-zi represents nam-dumu-zi(d) and refers to the often crucial task of making the newborn infant take its first breath. However, because of the ambiguities of cuneiform orthography, it is just as possible that nam-dumu-zi represents nam-dumu-zi(g), which might denote either the "extraction of the child" or the "lifting up of the child" (cf. German "Hebamme"), and so would have nothing to do with the name ᵈDumu zi(d).

The name of the goddess Inannak is usually analyzed as a derivation from older nin-an.ak and interpreted "Lady of heaven." The final -k of the name occurs in writing only when it forms a syllable with a following vowel. In *ZA*, 52, 108, note 34 [see below, chap. viii] we proposed a variant rendering: "Lady of the date-clusters" (an:*sissinnu*) and listed evidence in its favor. More recently the name has been discussed by I. J. Gelb in his article "The Name of the Goddess Innin" in *JNES* 19 (1960) 72–79. Gelb presents in compact form extensive and varied materials and makes many important observations. We tend to hesitate, however, in following him in his conclusions that the materials point to a form Innin as the standard form of the name of the goddess, but can here indicate only a few main lines of our different evaluation: the materials, we believe, might with advantage be strictly separated according to Sumerian and Akkadian context and sifted according to whether reference is to standard name of the goddess of Uruk, to one of her epithets, or to other deities or entities altogether. If this is done we believe that (1) the older (i.e., Old Babylonian or earlier) evidence for the reading of the sign-group ᵈMUŠLANU in Sumerian context points to a reading ninnana(k). Note especially the syllabic rendering of the personal name written Ur-ᵈMUŠLANU as ur-ni-in-[na]-na in *MDP* 18, 57 (Gelb, 4), the Eme-sal form ᵈGašan-an-na (Gelb, 14), particularly the writings mu-ge-eb NIN-na-na (AO 4331 + 4335 i 2) and [m]u-ge₄-eb NIN-na-na-ke₄ (AO 4327) in texts of Isin-Larsa date published by Thureau-Dangin in Cros, *Nouvelles fouilles de Telloh*. For the later loss of the initial n there are good parallels (see *ZA*, 52, 108, note 32 [see below, chap. viii]).

That the name ended in a genitive -ak is indicated by numerous cases in which the final k formed a syllable with a following vowel and where accordingly ᵈMUŠLANU occurs with a phonetic complement -ka or ke₄. Incidentally, it may be noted that the consistency with which the phonetic complement is -ka and -ke₄ in older texts, not -na-ka or -na-ke₄, tends to indicate long a before the k so that we should perhaps analyze nin-ana.ak < nin-anāk. (2) When the sign *mušlanu* occurs without divine determinative, i.e., not as sign for the divine name here discussed, it had apparently also a possible value inen (Gelb, 4) and a phonetic value nín (*YOS IV* 43 seal. Gelb, 11). It should also be noted that Sumerian had a separate word in-nin/nin₉ which was used as a honorific epithet for various goddesses, also for ᵈMUŠLANU. The fact that it was once translated by Akkadian *irnina* "Victoria" *Sumer* 13 p. 69.1 see below) suggests perhaps a meaning such as "conqueress." That it is not a phonetical rendering of ᵈMUŠLANU is clearly shown by the fact that it occurs in Sumerian poetry in parallel with that designation and is listed as an epithet of ᵈMUŠLANU in the Old Babylonian god-list *TCL* XV 10 1.203 separated by four other epithets from ᵈMUŠLANU in lines 197 and 198.

(3) The Akkadian materials appear to indicate that only the name Ishtar is used to render Sumerian ᵈMUŠLANU. Akkadian also possesses a number of genuinely

Akkadian names for originally independent goddesses of war, most of whom later came to be considered aspects of Ishtar so that their names will serve as epithets for her. Such names are O. Akk. *Inin* (endingless fi'l of '-n-n) "Skirmishing" (cf. Gelb, p. 76 and no. 2. The recognition that *i-nin* represents a divine name is due to him), *Anūna* (fa'ūl of '-n-n with suffix -*a*) "Skirmish," *Anūnītum* "She of the Skirmish," *Irnina* (-*a* form corresponding to *irnittu*) "Victoria." This name developed by assimilation (see Gelb, pp. 78 f.) to *Innina*. All of these names are good Akkadian formations and so not evidence for the reading of the Sumerian name written ᵈMUŠLANU. We retain, therefore, for the time being the reading of the latter as Inannak.

7. This is not to say that the earlier phases of ancient Mesopotamian religious life had not much more variety than the Dumuzid cults by themselves could suggest, probably they did. However, the Dumuzid cults, with their focus on the death or disappearance of the god, are probably more representative than one would at first think. Features of a similar nature are clearly present in the cult of Enlil at Nippur as shown by the banishment of the god to the nether world in the myth of Enlil and Ninlil, interesting is also the ritual underlying E-ne-ém-mà-ni i-lu i-lu (*SBH* 44, 43, 77 and 69 cf. also *BE* XXX, 1 no. 8 and *CT* XLII pl. 28) which seems to center in a successful appeal to Enlil by Inannak for the dead Dumuzid. An old myth about the god Ishkur shows that also this god was thought to have disappeared to the nether world and had to be rescued (Kramer, *The Sumerians* [Chicago, 1963], p. 169). The near death of the god Enkik in the Tilmun myth also seems to belong; it may well retain memories of rites connected with the low water of summer, seen as a weakening of the god's powers. The myth of Inannak's Descent, finally, also seems to root in the complex of the disappearing and dying god.

8. On Damu and his relations to Dumuzid see Edzard, *Wörterbuch der Mythologie*, ed. H. W. Haussig, I, 1, pp. 50 f. and literature there cited; also our article "Toward the Image of Tammuz," *History of Religions* (Chicago, 1961) 1/2, pp. 202 f. [see below, chap. vi]. The name Damu means "the child" (see Deimel, *Pantheon* 687.2). As a power for fertility and new life the god would appear to have been specifically the power in the life-giving waters as they return in springtime in the rivers, rise in the ground, and enter trees and plants as sap, for when in the cult Damu's mother and sister seek him he has died in the trees and rushes and the search moves through a world that has become the nether world, dry and lifeless. When the god is found and returns, it is from the river that he comes back.

The original setting of the Damu cult would seem to have been the essentially horticultural economy of the settlements along the lower Euphrates south of Uruk. Damu's home town is Girsu (Eme-sal Mersi) on the Euphrates and in the litany characteristic of the Damu laments he is identified with a number of neighboring deities—all chthonic in character—such as Ningishzida ("Lord good tree" married to ᵈÁ-zi-mú-a, "Well grown branch") of Gishbanda, Ninazu of Enegir (cf. van Dijk, *Sumerische Götterlieder* (Heidelberg, 1960) 2: pp. 57–80), Sataran of Etummal, Alla, lord of the net, of Esagik, etc. Also identified with Damu in the liturgy is every single dead king of the Third Dynasty of Ur and many of those of the following dynasty of Isin. For each—as for Damu and the gods identified with him—the litany makes a point of specifying where he "lies," i.e., where his grave is. It would seem, therefore, that we are here in direct continuation of very early concepts of the ruler as a magic source of fertility and able to exert that power from the earth, from his grave after death. The same early concept underlies the cult of the dead en's for which see Deimel, "Die Listen über den Ahnenkult aus der Zeit Lugalandas und Urukaginas," *Orientalia* 2 (1920), and Penelope Weadock, *The Giparu at Ur* (unpublished Ph.D. dissertation, Chicago). Note also the listing of En-me-en-lú-an-na and En-me-en-gal-an-na with ᵈDumu-zi siba, "Dumuzid the shepherd," as antediluvian kings of Badtibira and of En-siba-zi-an-na as antediluvian king of Larak in the Sumerian King List (see *AS* XI, 71–74). These names occur also as forms of Dumuzid in the god-lists (*CT* XXIV 9, K. 11038, restored by pl. 19 ii) and in the Dumuzid laments (e.g., *BE* XXX 12 ii 14–15, K. 5044, unpublished copy by Geers mentioning ᵈAm-me-lu-an-[na...] ᵈAm-me-gal-an-[na] [...] ᵈAm-me-siba-[zi-an-na...], *CT* XLII 28 ii 22, and AO 4346 obv. in Cros, *Nouvelles fouilles* p. 211 1′–2′ Am-me-[lú]-[an-na...] Am-me-gal-an-na...). They are most likely names of early rulers, en's, who embodied Dumuzid in the cult rites and were worshiped as powers for fertility after their death.

9. *CT* XV 25 1–21 cf. *TRS* 8 64–75. Particularly helpful is Falkenstein's treatment *ZA* 47 (1942) 197–200, cf. his comments *AOF* 16 (1952) 60–65. See also his translation in Falkenstein and von Soden, *Sumerische und akkadische Hymnen und Gebete* (Zürich, 1953), pp. 185–186. The passage is preceded in *TRS* 8 by a praisehymn for Damu and a probably secondary section dealing with a divine sentence passed upon Uruk (the section may have come from the enemmani ilu ilu lament, see above, note 5). It is followed by sections dealing with the search for the god. His mother asks for him from his nurse with whom she had placed him, probably a tree, moves on in the search to the rushes and finally to the desert. The last part of the composition consists of hymns of praise for Damu as the one who comes out of the river; they have the character of processional hymns.

10. ki-bad-du-ke₄ (var. *TRS* 8 ki-hé-da-ke₄) i-lu na-ám-er-ra (var. *TRS* 8 nam-mir-ra). The line allows of a great many possible interpretations and a choice between them is not easy. We analyze ki-baddu(.a)k.e "for (.e) him of (.ak) the faraway places" ilu na(.a)m.err.O.a "the wail (ilu) that (.a) he (.O) may not (na.) travel (err) hither (.m.)." For er:*alāku* see Falkenstein, *Gerichtsurkunden* III, p. 108. The verb is attested in Eme-sal context also in the meaning "to bring" (*wabālu*, see Deimel ŠL 232: 2), which would furnish "be brought" for "go," "travel." The element na- we interpret as the negative equivalent of hé-, assuming that as hé-can denote both "may be" (positive wish) and "he may" (positive possibility) so na- can denote both "may he not" (negative wish) and "he may not" (negative possibility). An advantage of this interpretation is that it allows na- to have the same meaning throughout the passage.

11. The term gudu (ᴜʜ + ɪšɪʙ), Akkadian *pašīšu* "the anointed one" denotes a class of priests or cult personnel. It is frequent as a designation of Damu in the Damu texts. Its original connotation is seen most clearly, perhaps, in passages such as *utukkê limnûte* 5 (*CT* XVI pl. 12) ii.1 (cf. 4. v. 60 on pl. 11): uh-tuku (var. tag-ga)-a-mu-dè ià ga-ba-da-an-šéš hé-me-en, "Be you a (man who begged:) 'Plagued

with lice as I am (lit. in my lousiness) let me anoint myself with you,'" which show that anointing served specifically as a means to rid oneself of lice; conceivably the oil used contained petroleum or some other effective bituminous ingredient. That this connotation of delousing underlies the term gudu: *pašišu* "the anointed one" may be seen from the writing of the word gudu, UH + IŠIB which consists of the sign uhu "louse" (*uplu*) and the sign išib, "anointed," (*pašišu* K. 4148.6 *CT* XI 38) and "clean" (*ellu* K. 4148.3 *CT* XI 38). Most likely this writing renders an old word uhu-išib, "lice-cleansed," which went out of use and was replaced in the language by later gudu. For such cases of old lost words retained in the writing but replaced in reading by later synonyms see the series Diri-*siiaku-watru*. Further indication of the gudu's concern to keep himself free of infection with lice is probably the sterotype line about the gudu in laments for a destroyed temple: gudu-bi hi-li-a ba-ra-mu-un-du, "its gudu-priests no longer go about in wigs" (Lament for Ur. 1. 348), gudu-bi hi-li-ta ba-ra-è:*pa-ši-is-su ina ku-uz-bi it-ta-ṣi* "its gudu-priest has left (lit. gone out from) the wig" IV R. 11.33, for they suggest that the gudu typically kept his head shaved to avoid lice and wore a wig. For personal cleanliness as characteristic of the gudu generally see Gudea Cyl. A XXIX. 5–6 where é-gudu-kù a nu-šilig-ge-dam, "a pure gudu-house never wanting for water," is used as a metaphor and *HGT* 76. vi gudu šu-sikil-ge$_{18}$, "like a gudu clean of hands."

The term gudu: *pašišu* "the anointed one" would accordingly seem to be in origin a term of personal cleanliness which has been specialized to denote the ritual purity of priests so that "the anointed one" became a term for a class of priests or cult personnel for whom such personal cleanliness was mandatory. From such specialized connotation of ritual purity derives presumably also the symbolic use of anointing as a sign of consecration of priests and of sacred rulers in the Old Testament and elsewhere. In the case of the god Damu the use of the term gudu may be assumed to have essentially its basic connotation of cleanness shading perhaps into sacred purity rather than that of membership in a specific class of priests.

12. For the close connection of Damu with the cedar, note also the following passage *CT* XV. 27.4–6 where his mother addressing his nurse in her search identifies herself as a cedar: zag-mu ^{giš}erin-àm gaba-mu ^{giš}šu-úr-men$_5$-àm e-me-da zag-si-mu ^{giš}erin-duru$_5$-àm ^{giš}erin-duru$_5$-àm ha-šu-úr-ra-ka, "my sides are cedar, my breast is cypress, O nurse! my limbs(?) are sappy cedar, are sappy cedar, are of the hashur cedar." See also the duplicate of pl. 30 obv. 8–10 and cf. for the general context *TRS* 8 ki-ru-gu 6. The mother complains to the "cut down nurse" (um-me-da-gur$_5$-ru-mu) that she entrusted Damu to her (me-e za-ra dumu i(!?)-ri-in-tuš "I let the child dwell with you") and that now he lies dead within her (za-e dumu-bi šà-za ní-ta bar-za ní-ta, "You! that child lies (dead) in your marrow, lies (dead) in your bark").

13. We omit lines 11–12 as probably secondary. They fit badly into the general pattern.

14. *SK* 26 vi. 14–20. The text is an early version of Edinna usagga.

15. *SK* 27 v. 12′–15′. Also an early version of Edinna usagga.

16. *SK* 35 iii. 6′–9′. Our term "priestess-bride" renders Sumerian en. The

composition to which this text belongs would seem to come from the Damu cult at Ur. A partial duplicate is the Harvard text HSM 7527 published by Edzard in *JCS* 16 (1962) 80. A further duplicate, found in Ur itself, will be published by Gadd and Kramer. We owe the reference to it to Dr. Kramer. To the cult of Damu at Uruk may be assigned, on the other hand, the composition represented by *TRS* 8 and *CT* XV pl. 26 f. and pl. 30, in which Uruk and Eannak seem to play a major role. On the basis of these texts we may visualize the Damu rites in Uruk as consisting of laments for the dead god, a search for him by his mother that takes her to various trees and rushes and into the desert, and then a finding of the god who comes out of the river and is escorted back in triumphal procession. In Ur the search seems to have continued into the land of the dead, where Damu's sister at last finds him. They return together to Ur by boat, probably down the Euphrates.

The texts here mentioned appear to represent the Damu cult in its pure form. As the cult spread northward it seems to have incorporated into its ritual and litany many features of the generally similar cult of Dumuzid the shepherd. To such a blending of Damu and Dumuzid materials testify the preserved versions of the composition Edinna usagga (edin-na ú-sağ-ğà, "In the desert in the early grass") which identify Dumuzid and Damu and contain materials from both cults. This lament—or perhaps better the ritual to which it belongs, lament in the desert for the dead Dumuzid—is first mentioned in economic texts from the period of Ur III (see, e.g., Jean, *SA* CL.XIII. 29 1 udu-ú ^{d}Nin-ği$_6$-par ú-sağ-šè è, "one grass-fed sheep (for) Ningiparak going out to the 'early grass' rite." Cf. also *TEO* 5672.iii.22, Keiser *STD* 207.iii.46–47 all from Umma. In texts from Ur ìr ú-sağ- á "the lament 'In the early grass'" is mentioned in *UET* III 472.9. Cf. also 273, which mentions ú-sağ ^{d}Nin-[...] and ú-sag ^{d}Nin-AN-[....]). Our earliest versions of the lament— already blending Dumuzid and Damu features—are of Old Babylonian date. They are *SK* 26, *SK* 27, *SK* 45, and Genouillac, *Kich* nos. D 41 and C 8. Later versions are represented in IV R 27.1, *OECT* VI pl. XV K. 5208, K. 4954 (unpublished copy by Geers), *ASKT* 16 Sm. 1366, Frank *ZA* 6 p. 86 Rm. 220, *TCL* VI.54, *LKU* 11, *BA* V p. 681, K. 6849, IV R 30.2, K. 4903 + Sm. 2148, *SBH* 37, Macm. *Rel. Texts* 30, *SBH* 80, Meek *BA* X p. 112, K. 3311. The composition begins with a lament for the dead god and moves into a description of his mother's search for him. The search takes her to the canebrake and to the desert and she tells how her son was taken from her by the "reve" (gal$_5$-la) in Girsu on the Euphrates, how she intends to stand by the gate of the "constable" (libir)—probably the reve's superior— to demand him back, and how she eventually takes the road to the nether world— where these officials presumably came from—to seek her lost son there.

Still not clarified is the relation of Damu to the god or goddess of the same name who was worshiped in Isin and was considered a child of the goddess of Isin, Nin-insinak. Most likely we are here dealing with a quite distinct figure, a divine leach, who was secondarily identified with the southern Damu. A text blending features of the southern cult with elements of the Isin cult offers *BE* XXX no. 2 (also published *PBS* I.1 as no. 5).

17. I.e., Early Dynastic II, III, Agade, Gutium, Ur III incl.

18. Cf. *ZA*, 52, 112–113 and 120 [see below, chap. viii].

19. Cf. *ZA*, 52, 110–120 [see below, chap. vi].

20. Some of the implications of "applied to the gods" may usefully be spelled out:

I. *Role of Metaphor.* As Rudolph Otto rightly insists (*The Idea of the Holy*, Chapter II, "Numen" and the "Numinous," pp. 5–7), the numinous eludes apprehension in terms of concepts and cannot be described, only "evoked" in the mind. Concepts taken from general experience, if applied to the numinous, serve therefore essentially this function of "evoking," they are properly metaphors or "ideograms" only. The number of such effective, evocative metaphors available to individuals or communities is always limited, and the more so the more limited the general experience of the individual or community has been. New general experience may therefore lay to hand new concepts which may prove powerful metaphors for evoking the numinous more fully and may direct and deepen religious understanding. As such a new concept, shaped by the political development at the turn of the third millennium *B.C.* and laying to hand a powerful religious metaphor, we consider the concept of the ruler, of the lord and king.

II. *Specific Applicability.* In two ways in particular was this new metaphor capable of extending and deepening the evocation of the numinous: in its suggestiveness of the element of "majestas" and in its suggestiveness of the element of "energy" which are components of "Tremendum" (see Otto's analysis of "Tremendum," *The Idea of the Holy*, pp. 12–24, especially pp. 20–23, "majestas," and pp. 23–24 ("Energy.")

II. A. "*Majesty.*" The experience available in a small homogeneous community is not generally conducive to the development of attitudes of deep respect and reverence. This must have been so also in the early Mesopotamian communities, and correspondingly feelings of real awe and reverence toward the divine are almost conspicuously lacking in old cults such as that of Dumuzid (see our analysis in "Toward the Image of Tammuz," *History of Religions* [Chicago, 1961]) 1, pp. 207–212 [see below, chap. vi]. With increasing social differentiation of the human community such attitudes of respect and reverence are, however, likely to develop, especially in connection with the growing power, authority, and distance of the ruler, so that the new concept of the ruler can offer for the first time an evocative metaphor or "ideogram" for the element of majesty in the numinous. A striking example is the well-known prayer of Gudea toward the end of the third millennium, utterly different in its divine image from the Dumuzid materials (Cyl. A viii.15–ix.4):

O my master Ningirsuk, lord, (flood-)water angry-red poured forth,
Good lord, (seminal) water emitted by the great mountain (Enlil),
Hero without challenger,
Ningirsuk, I am to build you your house,
But I have nothing to go by!
Warrior, you have called for "the proper thing"
But, son of Enlil, lord Ningirsuk,
The heart of the matter I cannot know,
Your heart, rising as (rise the waves in) mid-ocean,
Crashing down as (does the falling) ushu-tree,

Roaring like the waters pouring out (through a breach in a dike),
Destroying cities like the flood wave,
Rushing at the enemy country like a storm,
O my master, your heart, an outpouring (from a breach in a dike) not to be stemmed,
Warrior, your heart, remote (and unapproachable) like the far-off heavens,
How can I know it?

We base our interpretation of a-huš-gi₄-a as "(flood-)water angry-red poured forth" on a-gi₄-a : *šanû* "to pour waters out over," "to flood," and *naqāru ša âli*, "to devastate a town by flooding" (see Deimel, *ŠL* 579.287). The enigmatic níg-du₇-e "the proper thing," which is a major concern in the early parts of Cylinder A, was finally successfully produced by Gudea in Cyl. A xiii.26. The passage shows that "the proper thing" refers to the brick to be used for building the temple, Eninnu. This designation of the brick as the "proper," "befitting" thing can hardly apply otherwise than to a magical affinity with, a "participation" in, the particular essence of the temple and the god, for to know the innermost core of "the proper thing" (šà-bi "its heart" viii.22 referring back to níg-du₇-e viii.20) is tantamount for Gudea to knowing the innermost core of the god's being (šà . . .-zu "your heart, . . ." viii.23 resumed by šà-zu ix.1 and šà. . .-zu ix.2). Only thus, moreover, will Ningirsuk's answer to Gudea (Cyl. A. ix.7–xii.11) make sense at all, for it consists precisely in the requested authoritative statement of his own nature and the nature of his temples, among them Eninnu. That the brick in fact participated in the essence of Aninnu—and of Ningirsuk—is also signalized by the fact that Gudea stamped it (A. xiii.21–22) with the image of the Imdugud, emblem and older form of Ningirsuk himself. The identity of Eninnu with Ningirsuk was specifically revealed in Ningirsuk's answer (Cyl. A. xi.1–4).

II. B. "*Energy.*" Essential in the new concept of the ruler as it developed was, furthermore, unique and unprecedented power to act. The ruler embodied in his person the initiative of the community, he was the will energizing and directing it in concerted action. Because of this essential element of energy and action the new ruler-concept was able as a religious metaphor to evoke also the element of "energy" in the numinous, and thus to broaden and deepen further the religious understanding. As we have already mentioned (see above, note 3 section [5]) the awareness of the element of "energy," of active transitive character of the divine is, when it goes beyond the particular natural phenomenon with which a god is associated, always connected with and expressed under a politicomorph form borrowed from the human ruler-image in one or another of its aspects. In the application of the metaphor of the ruler to the divine a degree of dynamic tension between metaphoric and everyday reference can hardly have been avoided and hopes for divine help must almost unavoidably have taken direction and color from what was expected of the human ruler: protection against external foes, justice and security within the community.

III. *Context.* For the sake of clarity we have spoken here of the new concept of the ruler as if it were a constant that could be isolated. Actually this is an over-simplification. The concept of the ruler that proved such a powerful metaphor for the numinous was a concept in the process of evolving in fusion of the types of the "lord" en, manager with magic powers to make things thrive under his hand, and "king," lugal, originally the young leader in war and righter of wrongs internally. Nor was it ever applied in isolation, always in and with the whole political matrix in which it was imbedded. The ruler metaphor is indissoluble from a total view of existence, of the cosmos as a state in which the gods form the politically active ruling aristocracy. Human allegiance to the numinous and dependence on it is thus guided into channels parallel to those developed for dependence in human society and comes to be understood very largely in similar terms.

IV. *Point of Growth.* As the point of growth of this whole development we may with some plausibility posit the ritual drama of the older periods such as, e.g., the sacred marriage rite of the Dumuzid cult and perhaps the rites of lament of the Damu cult. In these ritual dramas—as we know directly from later texts and by inference from early representations such as that on the Uruk Vase—the leader of the human community the "lord" (en) became the embodiment of the god, was him and acted as him. Here, accordingly, was a theophany in which the numinous was encountered not only in human form but in a human form socially defined and recognizable, that of "lord" (en) and leader of the community generally. The appropriateness of the form of the ruler as a form of the divine, occurring as it did in a dramatically pregnant, recurrent, central and authoritative theophany, could therefore hardly have been questioned. As the form itself around the turn of the third millennium developed a new content of majesty and energy, allowing more full and profound understanding of the numinous, and as human attention focused ever more on hopes for protection and justice which it and the institutions for collective security in which it was embedded held out, the road to the development we have suggested above was open.

21. The divine initiative responsible for Urukaginak's reforms is stated as follows in Cone B + C vii.29–viii.13: u_4 dNin-ğír-su ur-sağ dEn-líl-lá-ke_4 Uru-ka-ge-na-ra nam-lugal Lagašaki e-na-sum-ma-a šà-lú-36000-ta šu-ni e-ma-ta-dan_5-ba-a nam-tar-ra u_4-bi-ta e-šè-ğar inim lugal-ni dNin-ğír-su-ke_4 e-na-du_{11}-ga ba-dab_5, "When Ningirsuk, the warrior of Enlil, had given to Urukaginak the kingship of Lagash and his hand had picked him out from among 36,000 men he set aside the former laws (decrees). The command which his master Ningirsuk gave him he grasped..." Cf. *ZA*, 52, 102, note 13 [see below, chap. viii].

The covenant protecting orphans and widows is mentioned in Cone B + C xii.24–28 nu-síg nu-ma-su lú-á-tuku nu-na-ğá-ğá-a dNin-ğír-su-da Uru-ka-ge-na-ke_4 inim-bi KA e-da-KÉŠ, "That he deliver not up the orphan and the widow to the powerful man, this covenant Urukaginak made with Ningirsuk."

22. An interesting aspect of the function of the gods as upholders of law and order is the possibility of seeking legal redress against demons causing disease and other evils which it opened up. The form of the lawsuit in which the god Enkik (Ea), god of the cleansing power of water, undertakes the responsibility for execution of the judgment and sends his messenger (the incantation priest) with the human plaintiff to the law court of the divine judge Utu (Šamas), the sun-god, who hears the complaint and gives judgment in an assembly of gods, is a common form in incantations. A following lustration ritual represented Enkik's execution of the

judgment. Particularly striking is the use of this form in the bit rimki ritual (see J. Læssøe, *Studies on the Assyrian Ritual and Series bît rimki* (Copenhagen, 1955), esp. pp. 86–89), where the formal presentation of the case to the divine judge is designated by the term ki-ᵈUtu-kam, "Being at the place of the Sun-god," and has reference to the fact that the lawsuit ritual was performed before the sun at sunrise. The earliest references to this ritual are, as far as we know, mentions in the economic texts of the Third Dynasty or Ur (see Schneider, "Die Götternamen von Ur III," *AnOr* 19 [Rome, 1939] pp. 41–42 no. 41, section 5). In general see *The Intellectual Adventure of Ancient Man*, pp. 206–207.

23. For details of the form which application of the ruler metaphor to the divine took in Mesopotamia and the politicomorph understanding of the cosmos in terms of a state in which it is embedded see *The Intellectual Adventure of Ancient Man*, Chapter V: "Mesopotamia: The Cosmos as a State," pp. 125–201 and cf. "Primitive Democracy in Ancient Mesopotamia," *JNES* 2 (1943) 159–172 [see below, chap. ix]; "Early Political Development in Mesopotamia," *ZA*, 52, 99–120 [see below, chap. viii]; "Formative Tendencies in Sumerian Religion," *The Bible and the Ancient Near East*, ed. G. Ernest Wright (1961), pp. 274–277 [see above, chap. i].

24. S. N. Kramer, "Lamentation over the Destruction of Ur" (*AS* XII (1940)) pp. 26 and 28 lines 99–112. For translations see Kramer, "Lamentation over Ur," pp. 27 and 29, our translation in *The Intellectual Adventure of Ancient Man* (1946), pp. 196–197, Kramer in *Ancient Near Eastern Texts*, ed. J. B. Pritchard (1950), p. 457, Falkenstein, *Sumerische und akkadische Hymnen und Gebete* (1953), pp. 192–213, and cf. Witzel, *Orientalia* NS 14 (1945) 185–234, and 15 (1946) 44–63. The translation here given is that of *The Intellectual Adventure of Ancient Man*. The following comments may be offered: *Line 99*. The translation assumes anticipatory genitive construction with loss of the genitive mark as frequent in later texts. An alternative interpretation is as conjunctive parataxis: "dread of the storm and its floodlike destruction." ha-ma-lá-lá means literally "was verily tied and tied to me." The translation has in view the frequent use of this verb for tying on of burdens, but connotations of inability to get rid of something: "cleaved to me," "haunted me" are also possible. *Line 100.* u₄ [TUR]-bi-šè is restored on the basis of line 101. It seems to mean "in the manner of (-šè) the fewest days" (see for the adverbializing force of -šè Poebel *GSG* §389 and cf. §394–95). Besides the meaning "of a sudden" also "shortly," "soon" might be considered. ki-ná-mi-ù-na-mà means literally "on my couch of night." LUL denotes "false," "illusory." The translation assumes that it here refers to dream phantasies. Better is, perhaps, a reading lib, Akkadian *kūru* (k-r-' cf. Arabic kariḭa "to slumber") which seems to denote a state of losing consciousness as in dozing off or in being completely dazed by grief. In igi-lib: *dalāpu* "to be sleepless," "to be awake at night" the basic connotation is probably that of weariness of the eyes, drowsiness. *Line 101* GIŠ-l[á-a-bi] nu-ši-in-ga-ma-ni-ib-túm "and (-n-ga-) its (i.e., the couch's tranquility) was not brought me thereon." The translation given above assumes that the tranquility (GIŠ-lá : *qûltu*, "deep quiet of the night") of the couch has reference to sound dreamless sleep, oblivion, and that the prefix nuš-, which is rendered lu-ma-an AN-TA and ú-ul AN-TA in *MSL* VI: p. 149.15–16 is here used in the second of these senses, as simple

negation. A possible variant translation might be: "And of a sudden on my couch that (-bi) night-stillness (mu-us-lá-a), on my couch that night-stillness, could it but (nu-š) also (-n-ga-) have been transmitted (lit. 'brought' 'conveyed') to me there." *Line 102.* ba-ma-al-la-ke₄-eš lit. "because...was established for it." For gál/mal: *šakānu* see Deimel *ŠL* 80.22 and 342.860. *Lines 103–104.* The translation of these lines is uncertain, "scoured the earth" for ki šu—ag was a guess from the context and the deletion of ní(?) in line 104 may be too audacious. A better rendering, but also not certain, is perhaps: "even had I—as a cow the calf—tried to help it on the ground (ki-e) I could not have retrieved my land from the mire (imi(.ta)imi is wet clay, mire, for the loss of -ta, cf. *GSG* §363). For šu—ag : *a-za-ru* "to take pity on," "to help," see Deimel *ŠL* 354.165 and von Soden *AHw* sub voce *azāru*. The underlying image would then be that of a cow (the goddess) trying to help its calf (her land) as it sinks deeper and deeper down in wet sticky clay. *Line 105.* du-lum would seem to be a loan from Akkadian *dullum*. *Line 106.* Literally: "even if like a bird of heaven I had beat my wings in the direction toward it." *Line 108.* hé-en-ga-mu-da(!)-gul literally: "would surely also/yet have been destroyed for (lit. 'from with') me." *Line 110.* For an-ta—gál : *našû*, *šaqû*, see Deimel *ŠL* 13.63 and note the cone of Entemena vi.24–25 šu-mah-gir-mah-ni an-ta (hé-gá-gá, "may he (i.e., Ningirsuk) raise his exalted hand and exalted foot" (and after he has made the people of this city ferocious toward him may he crush him in the midst of this city). The form gá-gá is reduplicated present (*GSG* §446c) of gál with the characteristic reduction.

25. Kramer, "Lamentation over the Destruction of Ur," *AS* XII (1940), pp. 38 and 40, lines 211–218. Translations in the works cited in note 24. The translation here given is that of *The Intellectual Adventure of Ancient Man*, p. 142. The following comments may be in order: *Line 211.* The rendering seeks to convey the essentials of meaning clearly. Literally the line reads un-bi sika-kud-da-nu-me-a bar-ba ba-e-si, "Its (i.e., Ur's) people who are not potsherds filled its outsides." See *AJSL* 58 (1941) 223. For the 3n. locative -e- of ba-e-si resuming the -a of bar-b(i).a see *ZA*, 52, 101, note 11 end [see below, chap. viii]. *Line 212.* "The walls were gaping," literally "in its wall breaches (*ŠL* 106.173) had been made," cf. *AJSL* 58, 224. *Line 213.* Literally: "In its exalted gates and roads (gir-gál-la: *daraggu ŠL* 444.37) bodies were piled." *Line 214.* sila-dagal-ezem-ma (var. -gim)-dù-a-ba "in its broad streets filled on (var. 'like') the festivals." For dù : *malû*, see *ŠL.* 230.21. *Line 215.* "lay," more precisely "were piled." *Line 216.* Literally: "in its places where the dances of the land were (i.e., 'took place')." *Line 217.* "like metal" literally "like copper and tin." The words "in a mold" are added for clarity. u-mu-un-kalam-ma-ke₄ seems to demand a transitive verb, so ba-gar-gar represents perhaps gar : *rahāṣu* "to flood," *ŠL* 597.38. The variant ba-ni-in-túm-eš may be interpreted as "(crevices/holes) guided (túm : *warû*)" the blood of the land (-e locative, governed by túm). *Line 218.* "Bodies" more precisely *ad*ₓ (LU × BAD *MSL* II 626)-bi "its bodies" i.e., the dead bodies from which the blood had come. uzu-ì-udu is specifically "sheep-fat." For u₄-da : *ṣētu* "in the sun" see *CAD* XVI p. 150 ff.

26. I.e., Isin-Larsa, Old Babylonian, and Cassite periods.

27. For the concept of the personal god see *The Intellectual Adventure of Ancient*

Man, pp. 203–207 and cf. "Formative Tendencies in Sumerian Religion," p. 270 [see above, chap. i].

28. S. N. Kramer, "Man and his God," Supplement to *Vetus Testamentum* edited by the board of the quarterly (Leiden, 1955), pp. 170 182.

29. Ibid., 26–30 (26) guruš-me-en zu-me-en [níğ-]zu-mu si nu-mu-da-sá-e (27) zi-du₁₁-ga-mu lul-šè í-kur₅ (28) lú-lul-la-ke₄ u (GÁL)-lu mu-un-dul šu-kin mu-un-na-díb (29) á-nu-zu-mu ma-ra-pe-lá-en (30) du-lum-ma-ki-bíl-bíl-la-bi sağ-e-eš mu-e-rig₇, "I am a young man, I am knowledgeable, but what I know does not come out right with me, (27) what I truthfully say turns into a falsehood, (28) the wrongdoer hoodwinks me (lit. 'covers me with a cloud'), I (innocently) lay hold of the handle of the sickle for him (i.e., 'do his dirty work for him'), (29) my arm all unknowing sullies me in your eyes (lit. 'for you') (30) and you bestow on me the most burning of sorrows."

30. Ibid., lines 35–39: (35) du₁₀-sa-mu inim-[ge]-[na]-[na] ma-ab-bé (36) ku-li-mu inim-zi-du₁₁-ga-mu-[uš] (var. om. -uš) lul (var. lul-kam) ma-ši-ğá-ğá (37) lú-lul-e (var. lú-lul-la-ke₄) inim-ur mu-un-du₁₁ (38) dingir-mu nu-mu-na-ni-ib-gi₄-gi₄-in (39) umuš-mu ba-an-ta túm un, "my friend speaks to me words not reliable" (for the suffix -na, cf. *RA* 11, 155.15: níğ-sì-sì-ki-da-na:*šá la um-daš-šá-lu*), (36) my companion imputes falseness (var. direct quotation: 'It is of falseness!' For the predicative use of the genitive cf. Poebel *JAOS* 58 [1938] 148–150) to words I truthfully speak, (37) the liar (var. 'the wrongdoer') speaks upsetting words to me (38) but you, my god, do not answer them back (for the common contraction of third person dative infix-ne-a- to -na-, cf., e.g., Sollberger, *Corpus*, Ent. 45–73 mu-ne-dù, var. mu-na-dù; mu-na-du₁₁ var. me-ne-du₁₁ and Descent of Inannak lines 264 and 265 mu-na-ba-e-NE "they (tried to) give to them" etc. etc.) (39) you take away my wits."

31. Ibid., line 98: en-na-me-[šè] en-mu nu-tar-re-en ki-mu nu-kin-[k]in-en, "How long will you not ask for me, not seek out where I am (lit. 'my place')."

32. Ibid., 101–103: (101) mi-ni-ib-bé-NE šul-gal-an-zu-NE inim-zi-si(?)-sá(?) (102) u₄-na-me dumu-nam-tag-nu-tuku ama-a-ninu-tu-ud (103) kúšla-ba-sá erín-nam-tag-nu-tuku ul-ta nu-ğál-la-àm, "(101) men greatly experienced say a word true and right: (102) "The child without faults, not ever did its mother give birth to it!" (103) the toiler attains it not, a worker without fault never was from oldest time."

33. Ibid., lines 111–113: (111) dingir-mu...nam-tag-mu igi-mu ù-mi-zu (112) ká-unkin(?)-ka ha-lam-ma-bi dili-bad-bi ga-am-du₁₁ (113) guruš-me-en KA-TAR nam-tag-mu igi-zu-šè ga-si-il, "(111) O my God...when you have let my eyes recognize my faults (112) in the gate of the assembly(?) those of them that have been forgotten and those of them that are (still) mentioned I shall tell (113) I young man shall publicly declare my faults before you."

34. *PBS* I. no. 2 ii.35′–40′: (35) *Eš₄-t[ár] [m]a-a[n]-nu-um e-la-ki ur-ha-š[u ú-pe-et-te]* *še-em-me-e-ma te-es-li-ta-šu[...]* (36) *i-ni-ih-ki-im-ma aš-ra-ki i-š[e-i] warad(?)-ki* *i-gu-ú ri-ši-šum re-[e-ma-am]* (37) *ik-nu-uš-ma ir-gu-um ut(!?)-ni-in-n[a-ak-ki-im]* *a-na* *gi-il-la-at i-pu-šu i-ša-á[s-si ši-ga-a-am]* (38) *i-ma-an-nu ma-la-iš dum-qa-at Es₄-t[ár]* *ša ha-as-su ù im-šu-ú i-uš(?)[...]* (39) *ih-ti mìm-ma-ma al-ka-ta-šu i-p[a-aš-ša-ar]* (40)

in-hu i-na-hu ú-ša-an-n[a-a] ú-gal-il-mi gi-il-la(!?)-[at e-pu-šu] Eš₄-tár ú-dam-mi-qá-am a-b[ak]-ki ṣ[ar(!?)-pí-iš] (41) *ú-ul ak-ku-ud* Es₄-tár... etc.

35. *Ludlul bêl nêmeqi.* Lambert, *Babylonian Wisdom Literature* (Oxford, 1960), p. 40, lines 34–38. The translation here given is with a few changes that of *The Intellectual Adventure of Ancient Man*, p. 215.

36. See generally "The Good Life," in *The Intellectual Adventure of Ancient Man*, pp. 202–219; W. von Soden, "Religion und Sittlichkeit nach den Anschauungen der Babylonier," *ZDMG* 89 (1935) 143–169; Kraus, "Altmesopotamisches Lebensgefühl," *JNES* 19 (1960) 117–32; Lambert, *Babylonian Wisdom Literature* (Oxford, 1960), pp. 1–20.

5. *The Myth of Inanna and Bilulu*

1.–2. Notes 1 (listing abbreviations) and 2 (referring the reader to Kramer's appendix) are omitted.

3. It should be realized that in large sections the text is so damaged that unavoidable margins of subjectivity shade the certainty of the readings and thereby in part that of the overall conception of the story. We mention this specifically since long concern with the text and its problems seems to us to have given a certain surface smoothness to our transliteration and translation which should not mislead the reader.

4. We use the term "possible" rather than "probable" advisedly. It must be kept in mind that the first part of the sequence, (lyrical) lament to narrative, is a standard compositional feature of Sumerian laments, especially of the Dumuzi laments, and that the crucial identification of the last section as a paean of victory is not beyond question, owing to the broken state of the text. Furthermore, even if it were certain the relation of this paean to the traditional ershemma would yet have to be clarified.

The term *ù-líl-lá* itself, since its basic meaning is obscure, adds nothing to the definition of the genre for which it stands. The writing *ù-líl-lá* and the final a of the word militate against combining it with *ù-li-li* "(cry of) woe" but it is possible that its latter parts are the same as those found in *e-líl:e-li-lu* "song of joy" and *e-líl-lá:me-ku-ú* listed in *izi:išatu* (VAT 11516). Unpublished. I owe the reference to these words to Professor Landsberger). Cf. also II R, 30, 18, c and d *é-líl-lá:*MIN(= *e-li-lum*). The complete word *ù-líl-lá* may occur, finally, in *ù-líl-lá-en-na:⌈a⌉-pu-u*, the name of an insect mentioned between *nappilu, napu, qarrišu ša eqli,* and *ṣaṣiru, ṣarṣaru* "cricket" in *CT*, XIV, 9, K.4373, ob. ii, 5. Cf. Landsberger, *Die Fauna des alten Mesopotamien nach der 14. Tafel der Serie* HAR-ra = *hubullu* (Leipzig, 1934), p. 43 l. 72a. If this insect represents a kind of cricket the various terms for the latter connecting it with wailing and music, e.g., *lallartu* and *timbut eqli* (cf. Landsberger, *Fauna*, pp. 104 f.), are relevant. Doubts are raised, however, by the divine name ᵈLíl-lá-en-na (Deimel, *ŠL*, 313; 17), which suggests a possible variant derivation.

5. Our inquiry into the strophic pattern of the composition—undertaken at the suggestion of Landsberger—gave the following results: the basic strophic unit seems to be the stanza. As stated above, it consists of a strophe and an antistrophe (distich) or of a strophe and two antistrophes (tristich). A characteristic form of the

stanza is the "particularizing stanza" in which a person or thing is mentioned under a general term in the strophe to be then particularized in the otherwise identical antistrophe. As an example may serve the distich in ll. 47–48, in which "My-lady" (nin-mu) of l. 47 is particularized to "Holy Inanna" (kù dInanna ke₄) in l. 48. The corresponding type of tristich may be illustrated by ll. 72–74, where "the shepherd" (siba) of l. 72 is particularized to "Dumuzi" in l. 73 and to "Ama-ushumgal-anna" in l. 74.

The stanzas appear to be grouped in the larger units we have called "megastrophes." Two megastrophes of the same number of stanzas in the same order combine to form a couplet consisting of a megastrophe and an antimegastrophe. As a particularly clear example may serve ll. 105–26 in which the megastrophe—consisting of three distichs followed by a tristich and a distich—describes the curse which Inanna pronounced on Bilulu and her household (ll. 1–5–115) while the antimegastrophe, built up in the same manner, tells how the curse took effect (ll. 116–26). Whether triplets consisting of three megastrophes occurred besides the couplets cannot, owing to the broken state of the text, be decided with certainty. It seems likely, however, that they did.

A peculiarity of the megastrophes is their regular increase in length from one couplet (or triplet?) to another as the story moves forward. Only the last couplet of the composition, which represents a descent, begins a decrease of the megastrophes by one stanza. This last couplet is also irregular by the fact that it has a tristich as ante-penultimate stanza in the megastrophe, as ultimate in the antimegastrophe. In all other cases megastrophe and antimegastrophe are built alike and tristichs occur only as penultimate members. The pattern such as we believe we discern it may best be set forth in a diagram. We symbolize strophe, antistrophe, and second antistrophe of the various stanzas by a, b, and c. The corresponding larger units megastrophe, antimegastrophe, and second antimegastrophe by A, B, and C. These symbols have also been used in the margin of the translation to indicate the strophic pattern.

Lines	Unit	Pattern
30– 35	B(?)	ab + ab
36– 41	A	ab + ab + ab
42– 48	B	ab + ab + ab
49–		
72– 79	A	ab + abc + ab
80– 87	B	ab + abc + ab
88– 96	A	ab + ab + abc + ab
97–107	B	ab + ab + abc + ab
108–119	A	ab + ab + ab + abc + ab
120–130	B	ab + ab + ab + abc + ab
131–140	C(?)	
141–152	A	ab + ab + ab + ab + ab + ab
153–164	B	ab + ab + ab + ab + ab + ab
165–175	A	ab + ab + abc + ab + ab
176–186	B	ab + ab + ab + ab + abc

6. By the Bad-tibira tradition we understand a group of Dumuzi texts which can be singled out on the basis of internal criteria, chiefly epithets and titles used for Dumuzi, and which in its topographical outlook points toward Bad-tibira. Examples of such texts are *BE* XXX 6, *CT* XV 18, *SK* 34, *SK* 32, and *BE* XXX 5. Especially significant among the Dumuzi names in these texts are ù-mu-un-e Bàd-tibira^ki and ù-mu-un-e É-mùš. The latter represents the Eme-sal form of the name under which Dumuzi was worshiped in Bad-tibira, Lugal-É-mùš (See Falkenstein, *ZA* n.F. 11 [1939] 181 and 186).

To the Bad-tibira tradition we would assign also the pastoral passages in Edin-na ú-sag-gá, which is in part a Damu, not a Dumuzi, text. With the important distinction between Dumuzi and Damu—identified with each other in the later Dumuzi tradition—we hope to deal in detail elsewhere. That Dumuzi and Damu are originally distinct figures was seen independently of me, and at an earlier date, by Landsberger. See now also Kraus, *JCS* 3 (1951) 80–81.

7. See *CT* XV 18 and cf. *BE* XXX 6. In the latter text it is possible that captivity takes the place of death or is a euphemism for it.

8. The author would thus use the effective literary device of beginning and ending his composition with the same motif. The outstanding example of this device in ancient Mesopotamian literature is the Gilgamesh Epic. See A. Heidel, *The Gilgamesh Epic and Old Testament Parallels* (Chicago, 1946), pp. 15 f.

9. It is possible that we should imagine the relation between Dumuzi and Inanna as that of a marriage which, while concluded, has not yet been consummated, and which is to be consummated only when Dumuzi can lead Inanna from her father's house to his own. The terms used in the text—ki-sikil for Inanna, guruš, nitalam, and mu-ut-na for Dumuzi—are, however, not yet sharply defined enough to allow a decision. It should be specifically noted that the term nitalam is so far only attested in connection with the consummation of marriage (see n. 41 below), a fact which enjoins caution against assuming either a betrothal or a "concluded" but not "consummated" marriage. On the form and nature of Sumerian and Akkadian marriage —a question which at the moment is in a more opaque state than ever—see A. van Praag, *Droit Matrimonial Assyro-Babylonien* (Amsterdam, 1945) and the literature there listed. Add Koschaker, *ArOr* 18, 210–296, and *JCS* 5 (1951) 104–122.

10. Deduced from the term lugal-mà "of my master," which the speaker uses in referring to Dumuzi. Identity of this speaker with the "partridge(?)," mentioned later on in the text, may be considered; it would lend more unity to the composition.

11. See n. 28 below.

12. See n. 65 below.

13. See n. 77 below.

14. The name of Dumuzi's mother is usually written ^dBU-du in Eme-ku, ^dZé-er-tur in Eme-sal. That the Eme-ku writing should be read Dur_x-du (< Durdur) is indicated by the Akkadian form of the name, *Dutturum* (< *Durturrum*), occurring in Reisner, *SBH*, 82, obv. 16/17, [^dZ]é-er-tur-raama siba-da-[r]a i-bí-bi-ta ba-an-[. . . .]: *ana Du-ut-tu-ur-ra um-mi re-é-i*[. . . .], by the writing Tur-tur in *SK*, 2, rev. i. 9, and, perhaps, ⌈Tu⌉-ur-tu-ra in *SLTN*, 35 iv. 10'. As for the nature of the two dentals in the name little can be said with certainty except that they

were hardly identical since the first changes to z in Eme-sal, the second does not.

A value dur$_x$ or (d/tur$_x$) for BU which corresponds to zé-er in Eme-sal seems to occur aslo in me-zé-er : mu-BU:ur-ru-[šum], ASKT, p. 113, No. 13b (K 5341 + K 4410) col. ii. 42 (var. me-zé : mu-BU:ru-šum, VR, 11 ii 49), in TÚG-SIG$^{mu-ud-ru}$ BU : a-ra-šu, CT, XII, 34 f., i. 38, and in TÚG mu$^{mu-ud-ra}$ BU : ṣu-bat a-riš-ti, ibid., i. 42; cf. the Akkadian loanword mudru, HW, 394a. It may be noted that already Hommel, Sumerische Lesestücke, p. 51, read the name of Dumuzi's mother as Dur(or sur)-tur. His reasons for this reading are unknown and the reading was—correctly—rejected by Zimmern in his Der babylonische Gott Tammuz, p. 712, n. 1, as "wenig begründet."

Besides the phonetic writings ^{d}Dur$_x$-du, ^{d}Zé-er-tur, etc., mentioned above, also the writing ^{d}u$_8$ occurs, see CT, XXIX, 46, No. iii, 17: ⌜zé⌝(!)-er-du:^{d}⌜u⌝$_8$ (I owe the reference to this passage to Landsberger). This writing is important as a clue to the nature of Duttur; she is the deified ewe. That the goddess of the ewe, source of the (sheep-)milk, should figure as mother of Dumuzi, who is a personification of milk and its powers, is, of course, entirely appropriate. Cf. below pp. 56 f.

15. See above nn. 6 and 7. The myth referred to in n. 19 below may serve as an example of the Uruk tradition.

16. To avoid misunderstanding it may be specifically stressed that Dumuzi is the divine *power* in and behind milk and may not simply be identified with milk as concrete matter. See to this point G. van der Leeuw's discussion of "naturisme" as a hypothesis in the study of religion in his La Religion dans son essence et ses manifestations (Paris, 1928), §5, and especially his caution: "mais ce que l'on adore, ce n'est jamais la nature ou le phénomène naturel comme tel, c'est toujours la puissance qui lui est inhérente, ou sous-jacente" (pp. 40 f.). This distinction in the case of Dumuzi seems to be explicitly made in SK, No. 2, iii, 19–20, which comments on Dumuzi's death with the words: u$_5$ nu-me-en-na u$_5$ ba-an-da-bala-a ga nu-me-en-na ga ba-an-da-naga$_x$ (GAZ), "you who are not the cream were poured out with the cream, you who are not the milk were drunk with the milk." On the reading naga$_x$ for GAZ cf. MSL II p. 76, note to l. 607. Note that this phrase, which is a stereotype, seems to have been variously understood, for it occurs in widely different wordings and meanings. Our interpretation here has therefore reference only to the sense in which the scribe of SK, No. 2, appears to have used the phrase and to which he or an earlier copyist adapted its wording. The older version of the text, Scheil, RA, 8, 162 ff., differs.

17. See above n. 14.

18. K 11038 (CT, XXIV, 9) line 3 restored by K 4338 B (ibid., 19) ii 2. Cf. Zimmern, Der babylonische Gott Tammuz, p. 705, n. 1.

19. The text of this myth is contained in UM 8318 (unpublished), de Genouillac, Kich, II D 53 and C 45, SLTN 36, BE XXX 2, and SEM 88. To these add now 3N-T.368, 3N-T.555, and 3N-T.661, all unpublished recent finds at Nippur.

20. UM 8318, iv 9'–11': 5-kam-ma amaš-tùr-šè tu-r[a-ni...], DUK šakir ì-KU-KU ^{d}Dumu-zi nu-un-t[i] [a]maš líl-lá-aš al-dù. Cf. de Genouillac, Kich, II D 53, rev. 11–12, DUK ⌜šakir⌝ ì-KU-KU ga nu-mu-da-dé an-za-am ì-KU-KU ^{d}Dumu-zi

[n]u-mu-un-til-le ⌜amaš⌝ lí[l-lá]-aš ba(?)-an-dù. The latter passage is from Dumuzi's dream, the former from its fulfillment. The translation of DUK šakir as "churn" I owe to Landsberger, who refers to *RA*, 28 132–133, K 242, rev. 46, restored by V R, 32, No. 4, iv (cf. *SGl*. p. 258 *sub voce* šakir. As Landsberger has noted, Delitzsch placed the third column one line too high in his restoration—DUK^sa-ki-ir šakir:šu: *n[a-ma]-ṣu šá šiz-bi*, "milk churn." On *mâṣu*, "to churn," see Landsberger, *MSL* II, p. 146, l. 38 and his reference to *SBH*, I, obv. 12 f. [Landsberger, *MSL* II, p. 117, section 4] umun ^dMu-ul-líl-lá ga nu-du₉-du₉ DUK šakir-rai-DÈ-in-dé:*be-lum II ši-zib-bi la ma-ṣi ina ša-ki-ri ta-aš-pu-uk*, "Lord Enlil, milk which will not churn you have poured in the churn.") For an-za-am see HAR-gud A, tablet 2, 92 = B, tablet 2, 297(?) (Landsberger's MS edition):

$$[\text{duk.}]\text{an.za.am} = az\text{-}[za\text{-}mu\text{-}u]$$
$$= mu\text{-}ṣa\text{-}riš\text{-}tum$$
$$[\text{duk.}]\text{an.za.am.kaš} = zar\text{-}ba\text{-}[bu \ šá \ \text{BI}]$$
$$= [ka\text{-}a\text{-}su]$$
$$\text{duk.níg.lú.gàl.lu} = mu\text{-}ṣar\text{-}riš\text{-}tum$$
$$= k[a\text{-}a\text{-}su]$$
$$\text{duk.a.nak} = \text{šu.}kum$$
$$= ka\text{-}a\text{-}[su]$$

The text is composed from K 4411 + 4602 + Sm. 21 (*RA*, 28, 130/31) and K 16147 (unpublished. Copy B.L.). For occurrences of *azzamu/assammu* see von Soden, *Göttinger gelehrte Anzeigen* (Dec. 1938), p. 519, n. 3. A detailed description of an an-za-am of calcite is given in *UET*, III, Nos. 436, 440, and 1498, obv. v. 28–30. According to de Genouillac, *Kich* II D 53, rev. 5, the an-za-am normally hung on a peg.

21. *BE*, XXX, 2, 11 and *SEM*, 88, ii, 6′ du₁₀ kù-ge du₁₀ (var. *SEM*, 88: kù) ^dInanna-ke₄ e-ne-di du₁₁-ga-me-en, "I am he who dances on the holy knees, the knees of Inanna (var. *SEM*, 88, om. "the knees" and adds "holy" before Inanna). The verbal phrase e-ne-di...du₁₁ is formed from the core e-ne-di by means of the auxiliary verb du₁₁, on which see Poebel, *AS*, X, 100–101. The verb of the core phrase, di, is a present/future stem to which corresponds the preterite stem du₁₁. With the preterite stem, as e-ne-du₁₁, the phrase is given in Voc. Ass (*SGl*. pp. 274 f. *sub voce* ešemen) as corresponding to *me-lu-lum*, *sa-a-rum*, and *ra-a-šu*, "to dance," and as e-ne-du₁₁-du₁₁: *me-lu-lu*. Note also Fragment R iii (Delitzsch, ibid.) e-ne-du₁₁-du₁₁: *mu-um-mi-rum* listed between *zammirum*, "singer," and *raqqidu*, "dancer," We translated this term, which occurs below in l. 152, as "foredancer," the person who leads the dance and the singing. On *malālu, "to dance," cf. von Soden, *Orientalia*, NS 20 (1951) 265 f. With the present/future stem di the phrase occurs in ki e-ne-di (for which the synonym ešemen could also be read) translated as *kip-pu-u* and as *me-lul-tú*, "play, sport, dance," in K 82, 8–16, 1 col. iv. 7 (*SGl*. p. 37 *sub voce* ešemen).

22. See J. J. Hess, *Von den Beduinen des Innern Arabiens* (Zürich, 1938), p. 115.

23. We consider dumu to be the direct object of the following zi(d) and see in the latter a factitive *nomen agentis* of the stem zi(d) "to quicken," "make vigorous," which occurs in nonfactitive meaning in zi(d), *nêšu*, "life," "vigor," "health,"

and perhaps also in zi(d), *napištum*, "breath of life," zi(d), "right (i.e., potent, effective) hand," and zi(d), "true" (i.e., effective, able to maintain itself, in contrast to the lie or falsehood [lul] which is fleeting). Whether Dumuzi, as the power that caused the milk to flow, was also considered as the power that quickened the child in the womb, or whether his name refers only to the nutritive power in milk is yet to be decided. We hope soon to present evidence favoring the former alternative.

24. As a form of Ishkur/Adad Enbilulu is mentioned in *KAR*, 142, rev. iii, 19: ^d*En-bi-lu-lu* ^d*Adad ša* TIN-TIR^{ki}, "Enbilulu, Adad of Babylon." For other references see Tallqvist, *Götterepitheta*, and Deimel, *Pantheon*. Of importance for the reading of the name is the writing ^dEn-bí-lu-lu kù-gál íd-da-ke$_4$, *SEM*, 78, iii, 24 (recognized as a variant proving the reading ^dEn-bi-lu-lu by Chiera in his handwritten index of Sumerian passages in the Oriental Institute). Note also the plant ú-bi-lu-lu : *išbabtu*, "Riedgrass" (Landsberger, *Fauna*, p. 66) and the snake muš-bi-lu-lu, also translated, as *išbabtu*. See Landsberger, ibid., and Del. *SGl.* p. 69.

25. See v. Soden, *ZA*,(n.F.), 13 (1947), 10–13.

26. On *gugallu*, see Landsberger, *WO*, 1, 375, n. 84 and literature there quoted.

27. ^dIm-dugud^{mušen} is the thunder cloud personified. The mythopoeic imagination saw it as an enormous vulture floating with outstretched wings in the sky. Because its roar, the thunder, is like the roar that issues from the lion's mouth it was imagined with the head of a lion. The name Im-dugud seems to be composed of imi, "rain" (*CT*, XI, 31, 30a, i-mi:IM:*zu-un-nu*) and dugud, "cloud" (*JNES* 2, 119, and negatively Falkenstein, *GSGL*, I, 8, n. 1). The Akkadian translation of im-dugud was *imbaru*, "thundershower" (Deimel, *ŠL*, 399, 209a. On *imbaru* see the materials collected and discussed by Schott, *ZA*,(n.F.), 10, 170–177. They support, in our opinion, the traditional translations, "*Gewittersturm*," *HW*, 79a, "*Gewitterregen*," Bezold, *Babylonisch-assyrisches Glossar* [Heidelberg, 1926], p. 39a, "*Wetterwolke*," Jensen, *Keilinschriftliches Bibliothek* VI$_2$, p. 99, against the proposed "*Nebel*").

The identity of Imdugud with Ninurta/Ningirsu is given with the fact that the "emblems" of the Sumero-Akkadian gods are as a rule older, preanthropomorphic forms (cf. the sun disk of Utu, the crescent of Nanna, the *marru* of Marduk, etc.); it is specifically supported by the macehead of Bára-ki-ba (BM 23287, Frankfort, *AnOr*, XII (1935), 105 ff. and figs 5–8), which is dedicated to Ningirsu (see the inscription *CT*, V, Pl. 1, cf. *SAK*, p. 31 c) and shows the adorant before the lion-headed bird; by Gudea's dream in which he saw Ningirsu with wings like Imdugud, i.e., still partially in bird shape (Cyl. A iv 17. For this semi-human shape cf. representations on seals such as Frankfort, "*OIC*," 19, fig. 33, and Heinrich, *Fara*, p. 54. See Frankfort's discussion, "*OIC*," 19, p. 31), and by the complete coincidence of the functions of Imdugud, son of Enlil, decider of the fate of the Tigris, etc., in the Lugalbanda epic with those of Ningirsu.

28. edin-líl-lá, the "desert of the wind," seems to be conceived of in the text as a proper name denoting the home of Bilulu and Girgire, and we should, therefore, perhaps assume that it referred both to a particular desert region and to a house, estate, or village situated in it. The conception of Edin-líl-lá as a house or abode rather than as a desert region is met with also in K 4355 + Sm 1981 (Langdon, *Babyloniaca*, IV, Pl. IV opp. p. 189) col. iv(?) 2–3 where ki-sikil Edin-na-líl-lá seems

to be translated as *ar-da-tu ša Bît-za-qí-qí*, "the maid of the house of the wind"; cf. also Sm 10 (Meek, *RA*, 18, 176), vi 1–3, which belongs to the later part of the same incantation, . . .ki-sikil líl-lá Edin-na-líl-lá : . . .*ar-da-tu ša ina Bît-za-qí-qí*. ., "the maid who in/from the house of the wind. . ." Unfortunately the text of the two passages is not clear and seems to have suffered corruption.

To be distinguished from Edin-líl-lá—even though it might on occasion also be translated as *Bît zaqîqi*—is apparently the Sumerian É-líl-ʳláˀ, "House of the winds." The latter occurs in a ritual from Uruk (*TCL*, VI, 49, obv. 9) and is perhaps to be sought in one of the chapels in the *Riš* sanctuary in that city (Falkenstein, *Topographie von Uruk*, p. 17). One of the goddesses worshiped in É-líl-ʳláˀ was [ᵈBe-l]i-li, near whose major sanctuary, the É-ᵈBe-li-li (see below n. 35), the body of Dumuzi seems to have been found in our myth (see l. 73). Since É-ᵈBe-li-li is in all probability to be thought of as located in the proximity of Edin-líl-lá it is of course possible that the naming of Belili's sanctuary in Uruk was determined by that fact. The ritual which mentions É-líl-ʳláˀ and [ᵈBe-l]i-li refers also to an É-ᵈlamma-edin-na, "the temple of the lamma of the desert," i.e., of the *numen* into which Bilulu in our myth was changed by Inanna. Since both [ᵈBe-l]i-li and the deities of the É-ᵈlamma-edin-na of the ritual belong to the circle around Inanna (cf. Falkenstein, *Topographie*, p. 36) these temple names in Uruk and our myth presumably draw on a common mythological background of Inanna-Dumuzi lore.

Lastly, the interesting occurrence of edin-líl-lá in *ASKT*, No. 21 (p. 128), rev. 7, may be mentioned. Inanna there states: gašan-mèn sa-bàr-maḫ [edin]-líl-lá dúr (!Text:ṣu)-ru-na-mén:*be-le-ku sa-pár-ra ši-i-ri ina ṣe-e-ri za-qí-qí šur-bu-ṣa-at ana-ku*, "I am a (noble) lady (and) I am a net lying stretched out in the desert of the wind." It seems possible that this too has reference—if not directly to Inanna's curbing of Bilulu in Edin-líl-lá as told in Ist. 4486—at least to mythological lore of a similar or related kind.

29. The course of the headache demon is unpredictable "like that of the heavy *imbaru*" (*CT*, XVII, 19, 27/30). On *imbaru* see above n. 27. That Imdugud/Zû as the thunder cloud has power to move against the wind, i.e., against his father, Enlil, is likely to be behind the notion that he once stole the tablets of destiny, which represent authority over the universe, from Enlil.

30. Cf. gíri, "lightening," (*birqu*), gír-gíri, "to flash" (*barāqu* IV 3), *SGl.* p. 94.

31. See n. 28 above.

32. Rainer Maria Rilke, "Gesammelte Werke," I (Leipzig, 1927), 353. See also the illuminating discussion by G. van der Leeuw, *La Religion dans son essence at ses manifestations* (Paris, 1948), §3, Chose et Puissance, who quotes Rilke's lines.

33. We have emphasized the attitude of the myth to nature and its forces as a major stumbling block to the modern reader. Actually it is only a specific instance of the difficulties arising from the fact that any work of art creates—or better: induces its reader, spectator, or listener to recreate—a complete world of its own. "Before we begin to read the *Ancient Mariner* we know that the Polar Seas are not inhabited by spirits, and that if a man shoots an albatross he is not a criminal but a sportsman, and that if he stuffs the albatross afterwards he becomes a naturalist also.

All this is common knowledge. But when we are reading the *Ancient Mariner*, or remembering it intensely, common knowledge disappears and uncommon knowledge takes its place. We have entered a universe that only answers to its own laws, supports itself, internally coheres, and has a new standard of truth." (E. M. Forster, *Anonymity* [London, 1925], pp. 13–14). The ease and precision with which we can recreate and enter the particular universe of a given work of art depends obviously on the suggestive power of the artist and on our own ability to respond: to free ourselves from bondage to "common knowledge" and to summon up experience transmutable into the "uncommon knowledge" of the work. Apart from a few outstanding exceptions ancient myths were probably never as good art as even the *Ancient Mariner*. And the experiences they call upon are experiences in a mode to which we are not accustomed, to which we normally deny validity, and which we therefore usually suppress before these experiences can ripen into insights.

34. Translated from the preface to *Fire opbyggelige Taler*, Søren Kierkegaards samlede Værker udgivne of A. B. Drachmann, J. L. Heiberg, og H. O. Lange, 2d ed. IV (Copenhagen, 1923), p. 7.

35. In the line count half-lines are counted as separate lines in order to achieve uniformity with the estimates of length of lacunas.

36. The text is broken at the top. The first preserved traces appear to belong to the latter part of a line so long that it had to be written as a line and half-line. Since the scribe is consistent in abbreviating repetitious matter we may assume that this very long and full line represented the beginning of the text.

37. The restorations offered for ll. 1–6 are based on ll. 179–183, which, though not identical with them, seem very close in wording. For the restoration and reading of the place names see also the litanies of the texts of the Bad-tibira group quoted above in n. 6. The reading [i-lu] ⌈balag⌉(?)⌈mu⌉- in l. 2 is based on a photo which became available to the authors after the original MS was completed and which bears out Kramer's objection to an earlier reading [i-l]u ⌈mu⌉-. See Appendix. With ki(!?)-nam-siba(d), (not kinam-sibad-a[k]) in l. 6 cf. ki-nam-erím, Gudea St. B, v. 8, ki-nam-sukkal, Delitzsch, *Assyrische Lesestücke*⁴, p. 119. Sm. 61. 19. The reading of the first sign in l. 7 as amaš is due to Kramer (See Appendix. The original MS restored SIG₇-A[LAM]), it is clear in the photo.

38. See below n. 78.

39. See below n. 41.

40. On the question of the reading of Ù in this verb see Falkenstein, *ZA*,(n.F.), 11, 30, n. 2 and the literature there quoted. As for the meaning, the Sumerian passages suggest—besides the meanings "to tire" and "to labor (physically and mentally)"—a *verbum dicendi*. Because of the frequent qualification "tearfully" we translate "to sob." The question whether a basic meaning "to breathe in gasps" can be established for kúš and Akkadian *anāhu* may well be left an open question for the time being.

41. The epithets used by Inanna in these lines, especially guruš (? Uncertain. Kramer reads DAG [See Appendix]. We are not able to identify the sign definitely from the photograph and retain provisionally ⌈guruš⌉[?]), nitalam, and umun, call for comment since they are important for the question of how we should visualize the relations between Inanna and Dumuzi (See above n. 9). We have

therefore given briefly below the considerations underlying our translations without, however, in any way intending a full treatment of these terms, desirable as such treatment would be.

kakùigisa$_6$-sa$_6$. The phrases kakù and igi-sa$_6$-sa$_6$, consisting respectively of substantive + adjective, and of substantive + reduplicated intransitive *nomen actionis* may be compared with English adjectival compounds such as "blue-eyed," from which they differ mainly by the absence of an external formative element. As all Sumerian "adjectives" they can be used both as primaries and as secondaries (Jespersen's terminology). An example of the former may be found in l. 30. As other examples of such compounds we may quote saggi$_6$-ga "black-headed," used both as primary and as secondary, išib šu sikil, "pure-handed *ishippu* priest" (e.g., *SAK*, p. 204, 1, b), en gišgal-an-na: *be-lum man-za-zu ša-qu-ú*, "lofty-throned lord" (Lugal-e, I, 24). As for the meaning of ka kù, the context—a lovelorn girl's complaint—hardly favors the traditional rendering "pure" or "holy" mouth. Assuming that the concept underlying the expression is that a mouth gets defiled by rude and harsh language (cf. English "foul," "dirty," mouth) we have rendered it "fair (-spoken) mouth." This places the expression on a line with the following igi sa$_6$-sa$_6$, literally "(of) pleasant mien/eyes," which connotes "friendly," "benevolent" (cf. e.g., Samsuiluna, *YOS*, IX, Nos. 36 and 37 (Dupl. *PBS*, V, 101, *OECT*, I, Pl. 31, *PBS*, XIII, 57, Akk. *CT*, XXXVII, 1–4, S. Smith, *RA*, 21, 1–11, edition by Langdon, *RA*, 31, 119 ff.), i, 1–5 u$_4$ ^{d}En-líl-le lugal dingir-re-e-ne en-gal-kur-kur-ra-ke$_4$ ^{d}Utu-ra igi-sa$_6$-ga-na mu-un-ši-in-bar-ra-àm:*i-nu* ^{d}*En-líl šarrum ša i-lí be-lum ra-bi-um ša ma-ta-tim a-na* ^{d}*Šamaš in bu-ni-šu el-lu-tim ip-pa-al-su-ma* and cf. ú-du$_{11}$ igi-sa$_6$ ^{d}lamma igi-sa$_6$-ga bar-še im-ta-an-gub, *TRS*, I, Pl. 38, 4–6, etc. The form with reduplicated sa$_6$ occurs—once more as term of endearment—in *SRT*, 31, 26, i-bí-sa$_6$-sa$_6$-mu.

The reduplication of sa$_6$ probably denotes repeated action: "ever kind." The writing igi-sa$_6$-sa$_6$ in the text should be noted; one expects i-bí since the text quotes Inanna directly. The treatment of Eme-sal passages seems, however, to be rather loose throughout the text. Note nitalam in l. 38 for expected mu-ut-na, dumu in l. 47 for ṭu-mu, ^{d}Dumu-zi in lines 34, 84, etc., for ^{d}Ṭu-mu-zi, ba-ug$_5$-ge-en in line 108 for ba-ub-bé-en, na-nam-ma-àm in line 108 for na-na-ám-ma-àm, ku$_6$-lam-e in the same line for gillem-e, etc.; the whole of Inanna's curse from line 108 to line 119 is written in Eme-ku.

guruš. Our translation "lad" takes into consideration that guruš:*eṭlu* seems to denote essentially the young adult man of marriageable age and particularly fit for military service (cf. *OIP*, LVIII, 297). A key passage is *ana ittišu*, 7, iii, 20–21, sa te-na bí-in-SAR dam in-ni-in-tuk, "he (i.e., the stepfather) let beard grow (i.e., supported him until beard grew) on his cheek and had him take a wife," translated *ú-uṭ-ṭi-il-[šu] aš-ša-tum ú-ša-ḫi-i[s-su]*, "He let him become (i.e., supported him until he became) an *eṭlu* (Landsberger: "*machte ihn mannbar*") and had him take a wife." While the "young" guruš, the adolescent boy, (guruš tur:*baṭūlu*) is typically single (cf. Arabic بتل) the guruš as such may be either single (guruš sag dili), betrothed(?), or married (cf. dam-guruš:*al-ti eṭ-li*). The wife of the married guruš can (typically?) remain in her paternal home as seems to be the case with Inanna in the present text. The married guruš would appear to differ from the lú:*awīlum* chiefly through the fact that the latter heads a family for which he has full economic and other responsibilities. Note the gloss *za-ni-in* to lú in *CT*, XXXVI, 27, 12, and the instructive enumeration in *SEM*, 58, obv., 22–26, ninda-ba lú dam-tuku 2-àm ì-gá-gá ninda-ba lú dumu-tuku 3-àm ì-gá-gá ninda guruš sag-dili 1-àm ì-gá-gá ᵈMar-tu didli-ni 2-àm i-gá-gá, "the bread-portion of the married man (lú) she set as 2, the bread-portion of a man (lú) who had a child she set as 3, the bread of the single guruš she set as 1, for Martu, though he was single, she set it at two."

nitalam:*hāwirum/hīrtum* was rendered as "Freier, junger Ehemann" by Delitzsch in his *SGl*, p. 133. This seems essentially correct though clear evidence for "Freier" is not known to us. The term is applicable after the groom has led the bride from her parental home (*SLTN*, 3, 5, iii. 9) and immediately after the consummation of marriage (*SRT*, 1, vi. 5). To judge from *TCL*, VI, 51 (Elev. of Inanna), obv. 17–20, its bestowal upon the ki-sikil with whom a man had fallen in love represented equality of status with him as full partner in marriage. The code of Lipit-Eshtar (Steele, *AJA*, 52 (1948), 425–450) uses the term to denote the first and chief wife of a man. It is not, as the more general term dam, qualified (cf. dam-tab-ba, etc.) to denote lower status, but serves itself as a qualification of dam in the sense stated above.

umun and its Eme-ku equivalent en are translated in Akkadian by *bēlum* or, when they denote the human spouse of a deity, by *ēnu/ēntum*. The traditional English rendering, "lord," would be happier if it had preserved overtones of its original meaning, "breadkeeper" (hlaford), for the core concept of en is that of the successful economic manager. The term implies authority, but not the authority of ownership, a point on which it differs sharply from *bēlum* (Sumerian has no term for owner but has to make shift with lugal and constructions with -tuku), and it implies successful economic management: charismatic power to make things thrive and to produce abundance. As passages that throw light on the concept of the en we may quote *Enuma elish*, Tablet VI, ll. 99 ff., in which Marduk is given the *enūtu* after he has created man to relieve the gods of their toil and has organized the gods assigning them their duties. Ll. 103–108 emphasize the aspect of authority in the *enu*-ship:

"His utterance........
His command be forsooth surpassing.....
Exalted be........
His *enu*-ship be surpassing, let him defeat his enemies,
Let him exercise the shepherdship over the black-headed (people), his creatures,
To the end of days without forgetting let them be mindful of...."

In the following ll. 109–111 the aspect of the provider and good manager is stressed:

"Let him make constant for his fathers great food-portions,
Let him undertake their upkeep, take charge of their sanctuaries,
Let him cause incense to be burned, let him....their...."

These same functions of authority and providing he will exercise on earth (l. 112):

"Exactly corresponding to what he does in heaven (let him do) on earth"

he is to inspire authority (ll. 113–115):

"Let him instruct the black-headed people to fear him,
Let the subjects be mindful of their gods and goddesses,
And let them hearken to his utterances as (one hearkens to) that of one's goddess"

and he is to look after the economic interest of the gods (ll. 117–121):

"Let bread-portions be brought; their god and goddess
Let them not forget, let them uphold(?) their god
Let them cause their (god's) lands to appear splendidly, let them make their throne daises.
May the black-headed (people) stand (in attention on) the gods
As for us—as many as we are—he is our god."

The same two basic aspects of the *enu*-ship, power to make things thrive and authority are stressed in the paean to Enlil as en, which closes the myth of Enlil and Ninlil (Kramer, *Sumerian Mythology*, nn. 47 and 48):

> en ⌜za⌝-[e-me-en....]
> ᵈEn-líl ⌜en⌝ [za-e-me-en....?]
> ᵈNu-nam-nir en ⌜za⌝-[e-me-en]
> en ɢìʀ-ma en erìn-na[..?]
> ⌜en⌝ še(var. numun) mú-mú en gu mú-mú za-⌜e⌝-[me-en]
> ⌜en⌝ an-na en hé-gál en ki-a za-e-[me-en]
> ⌜en⌝ ki-a en hé-gál en an-na za-e-[me-en]
> ᵈEn-líl an-na (var. e[n-àm]) ᵈEn-líl lugal-[àm]
> ⌜en⌝ níg-ka-ba-a-ni (var. du₁₁-ga-ni) níg-nu-kúr-ru
> du₁₁-ga-ni sag-dù[-dù-a] šu nu-bala-e-d[è]

The text as here given is that of *SLTN*, 19, rev. 1′–10′ with variants from *MBI*, 4, iv, end (Pl. xxxiii). (*Provider:*)

"Thou art en......
Enlil, thou art en........
Nunamnir, thou art en,
en of the...., en of the storehouse
the en who makes the grain (var. 'seed') grow, the en who makes the flax grow,
    art thou,
the en of heaven, an en of bounty, and en of the earth art thou
the en of the earth, an en of bounty, and en of heaven art thou,

(*Authority:*)

> Since Enlil is en (thus with variant!), since Enlil is king
> is Enlil's utterance (var. 'word') unalterable,
> can his impetuous word not be changed."

The context in which Inanna uses umun of Dumuzi suggests, of course, that she is thinking of him as the good provider. The epithet follows therefore naturally on nitalam.

The term zú-lum, "date," which closes the series of epithets and in which the series comes to a climax, does not to our knowledge occur elsewhere as a term of endearment. One might therefore consider whether perhaps it is specially conditioned: a traditional term, at home in the cult of Ama-ushumgal-anna, who, as we hope to make plausible elsewhere, was a deity closely connected with the date palm and originally distinct from Dumuzi. The final e of ᵈDumu-zi-dè we interpret as the vocative suffix -e discussed in *JNES*, 5, 132, n. 9 [see below, chap. vii].

42. The reading of the signs as lú-gar-ra here and in the following line is not entirely beyond doubt. The term is not known to us from elsewhere.

43. The copy shows a slightly damaged GURUŠ. Kramer (see Appendix) reads DAG. Our own inspection of the photo as well as considerations of meaning make us tentatively suggest the reading ama$_5$.

44. The term a-ra-zu:te-eš-li-tu "supplication" is well known. The original meaning would appear to have been "report"; cf. *CT*, XV, 28, 12: amaš kù-ga-mu a rá-bi ga-me-ši-zu, "I will inform (zu) you about the state (a-rá, lit. 'going') of my pure fold." The preceding e is difficult. On the strength of parallels such as *SRT*, 6, ii, 5 siskur$_x$ a-ra-zu-a mu-na-an-su$_8$-su$_8$-ge-eš, "in prayer and supplication they stood before her," one expects a term for prayer or possibly for assent. The DU$_9$-DU$_9$ which follows a-ra-zu is also unexpected. Could it represent an old miscopying of DU$_9$-na(!)-bi(!) through a damaged intermediary?

45. The reading of this sign as dib was suggested to us by Landsberger. On the use of ga- and da- as cohortatives (On da- see Poebel, *GSG*, §666; Falkenstein, *GSGL*, I, 219, n. 5) in the same sentence cf. the use of ga- and dè- together, IV, R, 21, No. 2, obv. 23–25 (Poebel, *GSG*, p. 266).

46. Cf. Kramer's comment in the Appendix. The photo seems to us to show a clear ga-.

47. The suggested rendering is highly tentative and is given with every reserve. For bu$_7$:nu-rum and na-pa-ḫu-um see *MSL*, II, p. 151, 29–30. For napāhu used of the lighting up of stars and of the moon see *HW*, 474a. The assumed extraordinary use of ma-ra- as a dative 1 p. finds a parallel in *TRS*, I, 12, 72 ma-ra-an-sì, "he gave to me."

48. See the Appendix. The sign seems, with Kramer, to be bi.

49. The "House of Be-li-li" is mentioned also in the "Myth of Dumuzi's Dream" (see above n. 19). It was located in the town uru-sig$_4$-é-Be-li-li (cf. uru ši-bi-Bi-li-li-šè, *SK*, I, iii, 14, uru-še-eb É-Be-li-li-šè in *SK*, 27, ii) and seems to have been a sanctuary in the vicinity of Bad-tibira. A local chapel for her in Uruk was called É-líl-˹lá˺. See above n. 28. The goddess Belili occurs in the genealogy of An (*CT*, XXIV, Pl. 1, 17 and elsewhere) and is mentioned as the sister of Dumuzi in the Akkadian myth of the Descent of Ishtar, *CT*, XV, Pl. 47, 51–55, dupl. ibid., 48 (K 7600 + *CT*, XXXIV, 18(A) and *KAR*, No. 1, cf. p. 321 (B). On Belili in general see the literature quoted by Ebeling, *Reallexikon der Assyriologie*, I, 479 (Whether the goddess ᵈBe-lí-lí mentioned in *KAV*, 50, iv, 5 may be identified with ᵈBe-li-li,

the sister of Dumuzi, appears extremely doubtful). The line and the problems it raises are discussed by Kramer in the Appendix. His interpretation differs widely from ours.

50. mu-lu ná, literally "lying man," is used typically of a person asleep, cf. *RA*, 8, 162 ff. (dupl. *SK*, 2) ll. 41–42, ì(gloss: i)-lum mu-lu ná-a ù-a mi-[ni-in-zi-zi] ᵈDumu-zi mu-lu ná-a ù-a mi-ni-[in-zi-zi] dam kù Ga-ša-an-an-ka mu-lu ná-a ù-a m[i-ni-in-zi-zi], "He (a *gallû*) woke up the noble, who lay asleep, woke up Dumuzi, who lay asleep, woke up the husband of holy Inanna, who lay asleep." Cf. also ná-a-ra, "to the sleeping one," in the account of the dream of Eannatum (St. of Vult., ob., vi, 26) and Gudea (Cyl. A, ix, 5). The phrase is also employed, however, as a euphemism for those who sleep the "treacherous" sleep (ù-lul-la) of death. Note e.g., *CT*, XV, 18, am-e a-ge₁₈ ná-dè-en ⌈u₈⌉ silá-bi ù-bi a-ge₁₈ bí-ᴋᴜ, "O wild bull, how (fast) you sleep, how (fast) sleep ewe and lamb" (cf. Falkenstein, *Archiv für Orientforschung*, 14, 123. On the prefixless finite form see, besides the examples noted by Kramer and Falkenstein, perhaps also ù-tu-dè-en in the *Allu*-myth, ll. 26–27). The lines follow a Dumuzi litany lamenting that he "lives no more (nu-un-ti)." Cf. Langdon, *Babylonian Liturgies*, pl. VIII, Edin. 09.405–26139, ᵈDumu-zi mu-lu am-ge₁₈ ná-a-ra mu-tin-mèn ù ⟨nu-ᴋᴜ-ᴋᴜ⟩, and see also the well-known Damu litany of edin-na ú-sag-gá listing the "resting places" (i.e., the tombs) in which various incarnations of the god (including the rulers of the Third Dynasty of Ur and the First Dynasty of Isin) had lain down to rest (àm-ná-a-ba) (*SK*, 26, vi, *SK*, 27, ii, de Genouillac, *Kich* II, D, 41, ii): Ibbi-Sîn is said to lie in Anshan, Ishbī-Erra in Isin (?). Cf. also am ù-lul-la ná of the Enlil litany.

51. Contracted from mu-e-gub. Cf. Poebel, *GSG* §656. The argument from the order of rank is, as we hope to show elsewhere, not compelling.

52. The traces preceding ᵈutu-da and ge₆-da in the copy appear from the photo to belong to col. i.

53. The suggested reading si₈ and the tentative assumption that this is a phonetic writing of si₆:*immerum* (Yale Syll., iii, 163) has perhaps too much temerity. If the text were careful in distinguishing eme-ᴋᴜ and eme-sal one would expect e-zé here.

54. With this paean to Dumuzi as shepherd compare in general *BE*, XXXI, 46, i ff.

55. The term um-ma, translated as *šibtu* and *puršumtu* (see Delitzsch, *SGl* p. 52) denotes primarily the wise and skilled woman and can be used without implication of advanced age; cf. de Genouillac, *Kich* II, D, 53, 23–23a (written on edge) um-ma šà-ma-mú-da-zu-mu tù-mu-un-zé-en nin-mu tù-mu-un-zé-en lú-bàn-da šà-inim-ma-zu-mu tù-mu-un-zé-en nin-mu tù-mu-un-zé-en, "Bring to me the wise woman who knows the meaning of dreams, my sister bring to me, bring to me the young child who knows the heart of matters, my sister bring to me!"

56. On lú-dili-àm cf. Voc. Zim., i. 60, di-li:ᴀš:*e-du-um*:*gít-ma-lu*. We assume the term to be used in the sense of *gitmalum* because of the parallel lú ì-zu-àm in the next line. This is, of course, not compelling. Landsberger prefers the reading lú-aš-àm, "an only son," and refers to *PBS*, V, 154, vi, 9, á (gloss: a)-lú-ša:*a-hu-lap we-di-im*, for the reading of ᴀš as aš in the meaning *wēdum*.

57. For ul₄-ul₄-e àm-túm, "he is worthy of (-e) directing," cf. ul₄:*šu-te-šu-ru*, Deimel, *ŠL*, 10, 23. The coincidence of the writing of this word and of ul₄-ul₄-la in

l. 92 with that of the name of Girgire is rather striking. It may be due to a graphic play on the name. Landsberger would read the name Gír-gír-e in this passage rather than ul_4-ul_4-e.

58. On lú ì-zu-àm cf. V R , 43, rev., 34, dingir ì-zu:$^d Nab\bar{u}$ ilu mu-du-u.

59. Instead of dab_5-ba one expects—as Landsberger points out—a word for "sheep" to justify the mention of amaš besides tùr in the following, and because of the expected parallelism of gu_4 DAB_5-ba-ni with gur_7-du_6-ra-ni in l. 93.

60. Compare Lugal-e, VIII, 30 (*BE*, XXIX, 2, 30 and 3, 30, *SEM*, 35, *SRT*, 18, and *SBH*, 71, rev. 13–14): gur_7-du_6-dè (var. *BE*, XXIX, 2, 30 and perhaps *SBH*, 71, 13:-re) gú im-mi-in-gur-gur (var. *SBH*, 71, 13: mi-ni-in-gar) translated (in *SBH*, 71, 14) as [*ina ka-re-e ù*] *ti-li u-gar-ri-in*. Other passages in which gur_7-du_6 occur are Gudea Cyl. B, XV, 3; *TRS*, 29, 18; 2N-T. 226 (unpublished), and *SEM*, 115, obv. 2'. Most of the passages were quoted by Falkenstein, *ZA*,n.F. 14 (1948), 83, in his discussion of gú-gur, which see. (Is Falkenstein's reading du_6-la of *SBH*, 71, rec. 13 based on a collation? The copy seems to be compatible with a reading -⌜re⌝.) The present passage is valuable as one more indication that du_6(r), "pile," ended in -r. Note also *TRS*, II, 70, obv. 9, du_6-ra gaba-bi-a za-gìn-na bí-ib-ri-ge, "at the edge (or "surface") of the pile he gathers lapislazuli." For the restoration of the Akkadian translation in *SBH*, 71, rev. 14, cf. *Enuma elish*, Tablet VII (v. Soden, *ZA*,n.F. 13 [1947], 12), l. 18: $^d Gil$ $mu\check{s}$-⟨tap⟩-pi-ik ka-re-e ti-li bit-ru-[ti].

61. On ri-ig : GÁ-GIŠ : *ka-ak-ku* see *Voc. Zim.*, i. 33 and references, p. 28. The form of the sign, which derives from GAG-GIŠ (*REC* 318), seems late, but the flare of the two horizontals in GÀ may have been slightly more pronounced in the original than in the copy. [The photo bears this out.]

62. dumu-ni is probably a mistake for dumu-na, cf. ll. 102, 109, and 120, which all have -na. On this suffix, which seems to mean: "who/which is not" cf. *TCL*, VI, 51 (Elev. of Inanna) obv. 29/30, níg-sì-sì-ki-da-na: *ša la um-daš-ša-lu*, "which is not something that can be imitated" = "inimitable," and *ASKT*, No. 14 (pp. 115–116), K 101, rev. 1–2, za-e-na dìm-me-er s-sá nu-tuku-àm : *e-la ka-a-ti i-lim muš-te-še-ru ul i-ši*, "a guiding god who is not you I do not have," i.e., "I have no guiding god but you." Cf. the similar use of nu, Poebel, *GSG*, p. 259, n. 1, Falkenstein, *GSGL*, I, 47, a, 3.

The statement dumu-na ku-li-na, "who is no (one's) child, who is no (one's) friend," may characterize sìr-ru Edin-líl-lá as an outcast without family and friends. Cf. the frequent descriptions of the wind demons as without family ties: dam-nu-tuku-me-eš dumu nu-tu-ud-da-me-eš, "they are (beings) who have no spouses, to whom children are not born" (*CT*, XVI, 15, v. 6.).

63. We prefer to analyze the phrase as "what (ana) was the lady (nin-e, subj. of trans. active verb) carrying (am-tum) on/in her heart (šag-an(i)-e)," thus allowing reflexive datival meaning to the prefix na-. The alternative, assuming that ana is the subject of a passival verbal form, nin-e a dative, appears most unattractive. The copy shows two small wedges after túm which are perhaps accidental scratches. If that is not the case we may have to read am-tumu-a < am-tumu-e, cf. Poebel, *GSG*, §476. On the phrase šà-túm see Falkenstein, *ZA*,n.F. 13 (1947), 191. To the materials there adduced add *SEM*, 48 (Desc. of Inanna), rev. 10.

64. It occurred independently to both Landsberger and us that ù-mu-un in this line might be a scribal mistake for um-ma, perhaps misheard in dictation. This is particularly likely since an eme-sal form is quite uncalled for here. The mistake may have been conditioned by the name of Bilulu in her male aspect, En-bilulu, to which should correspond an eme-sal form Umun-bilulu.

65. The phrase ki-nú-du$_{10}$ seems to mean "to rest comfortably"; cf. Gudea Cyl. B., xvii, 2–3 ama ^{d}Ba-ba$_6$ en ^{d}Nin-gír-su-da ki-nú mu-da-ab-du$_{10}$-ge," (on its [i.e., the bed's] pure surface [For bar as a term for the part of the bed on which the bedspread is spread cf. *HiAV*, 2, 32; *SRT*, 1, V, 25] spread with clean hay) Mother Baba rested comfortably with the lord Ningirsu" (Cf. Falkenstein, *GSGL*, I, 24) and *SRT*, 6, iii, 27–28 = 7 obv., 38–39, nitalam-mu en ^{d}Pa-bíl-sag dumu ^{d}En-líl-lá-ke$_4$ šà-ba e-ne AD-bi mu-da-an-ná ki-nú mu-ni-ib-du$_{10}$-ge, "My (i.e., Nin-insinna's) young husband the lord Pabilsag, son of Enlil, lies with me therein (i.e., in Nin-insinna's temple) in......fashion, rests comfortably." Note also ki-nú (gloss: nu), ki-nú-du$_{10}$, and ki-nú-du$_{10}$-ga, all translated simply a-šar ma-aįa-lim in VAT 9714 (Meissner, *MAOG*, XIII^2, 31 ff.) ii, 7–9. The implications of the phrase in the present passage—whether it is by avenging him or by furnishing him with proper burial that Inanna is to make Dumuzi rest comfortably—is not clear. On the importance of the funeral couch of Dumuzi in the cult in later time see the incantation Ebeling, *Tod u. Leben*, p. 49; cf. v. Soden, *ZA*,n.F. 9 (1943), 258 f., according to which the twenty-ninth of Dûzi was the "day on which the couch (*maįaltu*) of Dumuzi was set up."

66. The form nam-túm contains a modal prefix na- distinct from the na- of negative wish. That such a prefix (or that such prefixes?) na-, introducing verbal forms of positive rather than negative statement, occur relatively frequently in Sumerian was conclusively demonstrated by Falkenstein's thorough study in *ZA*, n.F. 13 (1947), 181–223. While the general contexts of some of the forms in question suggest dative force for the initial na- there are a great many cases in which na- is not so easily tagged. Falkenstein, who has dealt with the question again in his *GSGL*, §§60, 72, 115, and 128 proposes a distinction between a dative prefix ("Präfix") na-, to be recognized in the cases where dative meaning is clearly suggested by the context, and a "Präformativ" na-, which has affirmative, i.e., emphatic force, and which is to be found in the other cases where a na-form of positive statement occurs. While we would agree with Falkenstein that a dative prefix na- exists (see our remarks, *JNES*, 5, 135, n. 12) [see below, chap. vii] and that other positive forms with na- occur, forms in which a dative force is not—or at least not yet—immediately recognizable, we are less certain that emphatic force can be ascribed to na- in these latter cases. Our hesitation (which means that to us the question of the precise meaning of na- in these cases is still an open one) is based on the following considerations: (1) The emphatic shade of meaning is a particularly elusive one; in very few cases, if any, can we in our present stage of knowledge of Sumerian decide for certain that e.g., a translation "he went" is correct, a translation "he went forsooth" impossible or *vice versa*. This means that examples which would prove, or at least make probable, an emphatic meaning for na- must be particularly pregnant and free of ambiguity. (2) Such is very far from being the case. The

occurrences collected by Falkenstein do not—at least to our feeling even suggest emphatic force. In fact Falkenstein's translations, which do not attempt to render the assumed emphatic force of the forms with na- at all, read very well as they stand and would not be improved by the addition of "fürwahr." (3) The section of the grammatical text AO 17602 (*RA*, 32, 90–91) which deals with the emphatic verbal prefixes in eme-ku is preserved in its entirety (Col. vii, 15–20). It lists first ga-, then hu-, ha-, hé-, then ša-, ši-. It does not list na-.

The form nam—túm above seems to belong to the examples of na- with datival force, more particularly to that group of examples which comes from expressions for mental states as e.g., šà—túm, geštú—gub, etc., in which na- serves to limit the relevance of the verbal state or action to a particular person.

67. Since Inanna is here the subject of an intransitive verb one expects the form ᵈInanna, not ᵈInanna-ke₄. It seems possible, therefore, that ke₄ is an old misreading for é, or that we are dealing with *sandhi* for ku(g) Inanna-ak e eš-dam-a.

68. The term (é) éš-dam, "inn," "alehouse," Akkadian (*bît*) *aštammi*, has been widely discussed, see e.g., Holma, *Körpert.*, p. 172, Langdon, *OECT*, I, p. 27, n. 3, Ebeling, *Hymnenkatalog*, p. 28, Weidner, *AOB*, I, p. 91, n. 3, Landsberger, *OLZ* (1931), p. 135a, *Belleten*, XIV, No. 53, 240, and Oppenheim, *Eames Coll.*, p. 112, M19a. The meaning is, with Landsberger, probably "Gasthaus mit Herberge" rather than the very specialized one of "Bordello" even though the (é) éš-dam was typically frequented by and owned by the kar-ke₄:*harimtu* (cf. *SBH*, 56, 49–50, *BE*, XXXI, No. 12, rev. 10, *ana ittišu*, 7, ii. 25). As for reading, the commonly accepted éš-dam—clearly indicated by the Akkadian *aštammu*—is probably correct even though some older texts, (cf. Langdon, *OECT* I), seem to have (é) TÚG-dam, as here, not (é) éš-dam.

In the translation we have assumed that the éš-dam represents the social center of the estate or village of Edin-líl-lá, a place in which the inhabitants would typically gather for talk and recreation after the end of work (the harvest was just in!) as in a modern coffeehouse or village inn. Such a meaning would agree well with the passage from the Nergal hymn cited above (ll. 16–19. Only the more important variants are noted): ù-mu-un é-kaš-a-ka na-an-ne-tu-tu : *be-lum a-na bît ši-ka-ri la ter-ru-ub*, um-ma zà kaš-e tuš-a-ra ág nam-mu-un-gi₄-gi₄ : *pur-šum-tam ša ašar ši-ka-ri [aš-] bat la ta-da-ak*, ù-mu-un éš-dam-ma-ka (var. aš-te-ba) na-an-ni-tu-tu: *be-lum a-šar ši-tul-ti* (translates the variant aš-tc-ba) *la ter-ru-ub*, ab-ba enem-zu-bi tuš-a-ra ág nam-mu-un-gi₄-gi₄ : *ši-i-bu mu-de-e a-ma-ti ša aš-bu la ta-šab-bi[t]*, "Lord, enter not the alehouse, smite not the old woman who sits beside the beer (to serve it), Lord, enter not the *aštammu*, smite not its old man wise in lore(?)." Inanna presumably goes to the éš-dam as the place where she is likely to find the people gathered.

Landsberger, referring to the Nergal passage quoted above and to the epithets um-ma and bur-šu-ma used of Bilulu in ll. 88–89 of the text, would consider going a step further and viewing Bilulu under the type of *sabîtum* "innkeeper." Such a role would indeed be quite in keeping with her aspect of agricultural deity; note that Imdugud/Ninurta's mother in the Lugalbanda epic (ll. 15–23) is Ninkasi and note the emphasis placed on her role as dispenser of beer (*ibid.*). For the parallels in nature between Bilulu and Imdugud/Ningirsu see above note 20.

69. KUŠ A-EDIN-LÁ : *nādu*, "water skin," see Deimel, *ŠL*, 579,219. The following A MÙŠ DI we read as a še$_x$-di, "cold water," assuming that also the simple sign MÙŠ had the values še and šedi, "to be cold," pertaining to the various compounds MUŠ × A MUŠ × A-DI, ZA-MÙŠ-DI, A-MÙŠ-DI (cf. *ZA*,n.F. 8, 149, etc. Note a MÙŠ ì-dé, Gudea Cyl. A, ii, 8, "he libated cold water," and a MÙŠ dé, "libation of cold water," *TEO*, 5672, iii. 19. This is the normal older orthography. For the use of the KUŠ A-EDIN-LÁ : *nādu*, cf. the Sennacherib passage *me*$^{me-eš}$ ^{kuš}*na-a-di ka-ṣu-te a-na šu-um-me-ia lu áš-ti*, "for my thirst I drank the cold water of the water skin" (Luckenbill, *Annals of Sennacherib*, IV, 8–9). The statement a ub-ta-an-bal-bal zì ub-ta-an-dub-dub, "when water has been libated from it, flour poured from it," seems to presuppose that both water and flour could be carried in a KUŠ A-EDIN-LÁ. This does not agree with other references according to which flour was carried in a KUŠ A-GÁ-LÁ : *naruqqu*, see e.g., the ancient myth, Barton, *MBI*, No.1, iv, KUŠ A.GÁ-LÁ-ke$_4$ zì a-ba-ta-si-ge KUŠ A.EDIN-LÁ-e a a-ba-ta-dí, "when he(?) has filled the *naruqqu* with flour, when he has poured water in the water skin." Note also *BE*, III, 76:3, a reference which I owe to Dr. Geers, and *PBS* I.1, No. 3, i, 4–5 and 11–12. The latter passages suggest the word may have ended in -d. On the ^{d}lamma-edin-na into which Bilulu is changed, cf. the temple É-^{d}Lamma-edin-na referred to above in note 21. Landsberger calls my attention to the double meaning of Hebrew אוֹב; "water skin" and "ghost," as possibly relevant to the status of Bilulu as both water skin and lamma of the desert after she has been killed.

70. The combination of ŠID/SANGA with zì, "flour," suggests that it is to be taken in the meaning *lâšu*, "to knead," Deimel, *ŠL*, 314, 12. After we had considered this possibility but had given preference to the vague "keep count of" (because it seemed difficult to us to connect an acceptable meaning with "may he stand [or "wander"] in the desert and knead flour"—especially since the pouring of the flour from its container is not mentioned until the next line), Landsberger independently urged the same translation. It may well be the correct one, the seeming difficulties of meaning arising out of our failure to visualize the precise situation to which the line has reference.

71. The identity of the "lad wandering in the desert" poses a problem. Three possibilities present themselves: (1) Since guruš is a stereotyped epithet of Dumuzi one may think of him or rather of his shade. Cf. for this especially *SK*, 123, ii, 16′, guruš edin zé-ba, "the lad in the pleasant desert," and guruš-e edin-na, "the lad in the desert," of lines 8′, 9′, 14′, 15′, and 16′ (cf. Falkenstein, *ZA*,n.F. 11 (1945), 186). This is the interpretation we have adopted in the translation; it accords exceptionally well with the implications of the following kisa-ḫa (see n. 57) and in its favor is the further consideration that it adds point to Inanna's vengeance that Bilulu and her son should serve Dumuzi, whom they have killed. (2) guruš might stand for any young traveler in the desert making an offering at any time. If so, the precise meaning of the following passage remains obscure. (3) Landsberger suggests to us that the guruš edin-na DU is identical with SÌR-RU Edin-líl-lá, of whom the preceding line has stated, edin-na hu-mu-ni-DU, "let him stand/wander in the desert." Landsberger would consider him the subject of the following verbs and would assume that the passage prescribes how he—who alone is left alive of Bilulu's

household—is to provide offerings for Bilulu and her son in their new forms of lamma and utukku of the desert. If Landsberger is right, *CT*, XXV, 6, 23–24, ᵈGURUŠᵇⁱ⁻ⁱʳ⁻ᵈᵘEDIN : *Bi-ir-du*, ᵈGURUŠˢᵃ⁻ʳᵃ⁻ᵇᵘ EDIN : *šar-ra-bu* and ibid., line 28, ᵈGURUŠ MIN EDIN:MIN (= *i-lu ki-la-la-an*), may be relevant even though our text gives no indication that the guruš edin-na DU was thought of as one of a pair. We have read ᵈGURUŠ in these passages rather than ᵈLamma since male deities seem to be involved. On *šarrabu* see Landsberger, *Archiv für Orientforschung*, X, 141, n. 3.

72. Doubtful. See Kramer's comment in the Appendix.

73. We read originally sa(?)-lah-ha-[a]-na, on which see Kramer in the Appendix. The reading ki-sa-ha-[a]-na seems to have the support of the photo. For ki-sa-ḫa here and in l. 125 see Legrain, *UET*, III, 897:5 sìla eša 5 sìla šikₓ ½ sìla zì-še níg-ki-sa-ḫa-še a-šà GABA-GUG(?)-še, etc., "5 'cups' *šasqu* flour, 5 'cups' *hišletum* flour (see Oppenheim, *Eames Coll.*, p. 137) ½ 'cup' *tappinu* flour as offering materials for the ki-sa-ḫa for the field GABA-GUG(?), etc." Landsberger convincingly connects this ki-sa-ḫa with the well-attested term of offering níg-ki-zahaₓ-(A×HA. See his *Der Kultische Kalender*, p. 75, Schneider, *Orientalia*, 18, 69, Oppenheim, *Eames Coll.*, p. 43, to E 3, e. Since originally A and ZA were merely graphic variants of the same sign A×AH represents a writing sà.ḫa. We have therefore no hesitation in positing a value saḫaₓ besides zàh). The writing of the term as ki-sahaₓ suggests a meaning "place from which he/she/it has disappeared/fled." Such a meaning makes excellent sense in the passage under discussion where ki sa-ha-a-na, "in the place from which he disappeared," stands parallel to edin-na, "in the desert." The import of Inanna's instructions is then that Bilulu and Girgire, who have been made the lamma and utukku of the desert, have a duty to call Dumuzi whenever an offering to him is made in the desert, which he once frequented but from which he has now disappeared, in order that he may enjoy the offering.

As a general cultic term nig-ki-sahaₓ, "offering-materials for the place from which he/she disappeared," may be assumed to refer to offerings to deities who, like Dumuzi, were thought to be alive, or at least present, only for a part of the year; offerings made at the place where they were typically present when alive. In favor of such an interpretation is the frequent occurrence of these offerings in the cult of the goddesses *Belat-šuknir*, *Belat-Tiraban*, and their group, (on these deities, imported from the Kirkuk region, see *OIP*, XLII [1940], 143–144) deities in whose cult, as in that of Dumuzi, rites of lamentation played a major role. Note also Ḫḫ, xiii. 155 (Oppenheim and Hartmann, *JNES*, 4 [1945], 164) where udu ki šà (emend to zàh?)-ḫa:šu-u is listed with udu ki-sì-ga : II (= *immer*) ki-is-pi "sheep for a funereal sacrifice." On the use of zàh for recurrent absence such as that of the gods of vegetation and of the milk, see *BE*, XXXI, No. 50, obv. 7'–11' and dupl., *SRT*, 26, ii, 3' = 7', in which the hoe chides the plough: íl-la-zu tur-ra-àm a-rá-zu mah-àm u₄ zag-mu itu 12-àm u₄-gub-ba-zu itu 4-àm u₄-saḫaₓ-zu itu 8-àm gub-ba-zu-ge₁₈ min-àm ba-du-un, "your turning up is (of) short (duration, lit., 'little') your going (away) is long (lit., 'huge') at year's end are twelve months; the time you have been present is four months, the time you have been absent is eight months, you are gone twice as long as·you are present."

74. This line is one of the stereotypes of Sumerian literature, occurring in slightly

varied form as introduction and/or close of sections relating that a divine "determining of fate" took effect (cf. Landsberger, *WO*, 1, 364, n. 19). A particularly close parallel offers the myth of Enki and Ninhursaga (Uttu myth) in the section relating how Enki's divine orders that Dilmun be provided with fresh water took effect. The passage is introduced with the lines (Kramer, *BASOR*, Suppl. St., 1, ll. 52–53) i-bí-éš ᵈUtu u_4-ne-a ᵈUtu an-na gub-bi-e, "immediately, on this day and (position of the?) sun, the sun (still) being up (lit. standing in heaven)"; then follows an account of the fulfillment of Enki's words, and the passage closes with the line (ibid., l. 64) i-bí-éš ᵈUtu u_4-ne-a ur_5 hé-na-nam, "immediately, on this day and (position of the?) sun it verily became thus." We interpret u_4-ne-a as "on (-a) this (-ne)day (u_4)" and assume it to stand asyndetically with the preceding ᵈUtu. On u_4-ne, "this day," cf. Falkenstein, *GSGL*, I, p. 55. In ᵈUtu, "sun-god," we see a variant and more poetic expression for "day." Another possibility would be that the expression is short for "(position of the) sun-god," in which case it would correspond roughly to "hour." ᵈUtu an-na gub-bi-e is difficult and allows of various interpretations, the simplest is perhaps "on/at its (i.e., the day just mentioned) Sun (ᵈUtu) standing (gub) in heaven (an-a)," an elaboration of the element ᵈUtu of the preceding phrase. Other parallels to the phrase as a whole offer Lugal-e in the section in which Ninurta determines the "fate" of the various stones. There the phrase comes at the end and takes the form: i-bi-éš nam-tar-ra ᵈNin-urta-ka-ta u_4-da kalam-ma....... ur_4 hé-na-nam-me, "immediately through the determining of fate by Ninurta and (now) today in the land......thus it verily is" (see Landsberger, *WO*).

75. For the expression šu-dù-a used of the dead Dumuzi see *BE*, XXX, 1, iii, 15–16, and *CT*, XV, 20–21, obv. 28–29. Cf. Falkenstein, *ZA*,n.F. 11, 24, and 13, 207.

76. Thus with Kramer (see Appendix) who on the basis of the photo rightly rules out our original reading bi(?)-.

77. The reading must count as uncertain. Another possibility would be to read $buru_5$-darᵐᵘˢᵉⁿ translated as *burrumtu* and *tarru*, Deimel, *ŠL*, 79a, 15. The $buru_5$-darᵐᵘˢᵉⁿ which—as Landsberger noted—would have been particularly appropriate in this passage since it is known as a lamenting bird (see Kramer, *BASOR*, Suppl. St., 1, p. 22, n. 34a). On the $buru_5$-habrudaᵐᵘˢᵉⁿ, Akkadian *iṣṣur hurri*, see Ehelolf, *Boghazköi-Studien*, X (1924), 59 ff. Ehelolf argues convincingly for a meaning "*Steinhuhn*." In view of the damaged condition of the text a decision as to which bird is meant in the present passage can hardly be made until a duplicate is found.

78. With ll. 149 and 150 compare *CT*, XVI, 9, i, 32–35, tuᵐᵘˢᵉⁿ ab-lal-bi-ta ba-ra-an-dib-dib-bi-ne:*su-um-ma-ti ina a-pa-ti-ši-na i-bar-ru*, $buru_5$ á-búr-bi-taba-ra-e_{11}-ne : *iṣ-ṣu-ru ina ab-ri-šú ú-še-el-lu-ú*. On ab-lál cf. also *PBS*, X.2, No. 2, obv. 14. We can offer no parallel for the construction ad-e-éš-gi_4, which also occurred in l. 29 above. It seems not to differ essentially in meaning from the more usual ad-gi_4.

79. See Kramer's comment in the Appendix.

80. We read ṭu- here and in ll. 171, 176, and 183 and assume that it developed from the Eme-sal optative elements 1 p. da- (see Poebel, *GSG*, §666) by assimilation to the following -mu-.

81. It is possible that these lines should be completed on the pattern of ll. 165–166. For a convincing restoration see Kramer in the Appendix.

82. Restored on the basis of l. 184. We would analyze ne-nam as consisting of nen : *kiam* and the enclitic -àm. With the line as a whole compare *TCL*, VI, 31 (Elev. of Inanna), obv. 19–20, Ki šár nitalam(gloss: ni-it-la-am) e-da-di ḫé-na-nam: *lu-ú An-tum ḫi-ir-tum šun-na-at-ka ši-ma.*

83. -ra is very doubtful. See Kramer's comment in Appendix.

84. Perhaps meant to be completed on the pattern of l. 176.

85. Little effort has been made to distinguish translations of restored passages or to separate what is uncertain from what is even more uncertain in the translation. The *whole* of the translation must be considered tentative in a very high degree.

7. Sumerian Mythology: A Review Article

1. S. N. Kramer, *Sumerian Mythology: A Study of Spiritual and Literary Achievement in the Third Millennium B.C.* (Philadelphia, 1944).

2. In painstaking exactitude of copies, translations, and interpretation, nobody surpasses Poebel, but he has published relatively little in this field. Radau's copies and translations are very commendable, his interpretations less so. De Genouillac and Langdon will be gratefully remembered by workers in this field chiefly for the large volume of materials which these two scholars made available.

3. We have in mind especially the results embodied in the introduction to *SRT*, *SEM*, *STVC*, and in the article *JAOS*, 54 (1934) 407–420. Dr. Kramer, who edited all but the first of these after Dr. Chiera's death, deserves great credit for having made these important studies of Chiera available.

4. *Sumerian Mythology*, p. 65.

5. S. N. Kramer, "Sumerian Literary Texts from Nippur in the Museum of the Ancient Orient at Istanbul," *AASOR*, Vol. XXIII (New Haven, 1944).

6. Or do the texts in question actually have ku-gál? We would not so expect.

7. We restore the text (Langdon, *Le Poème sumérien du Paradis, du Déluge...* [Paris, 1919], Planche I, 1–4) as follows:

> [ki sikil]-àm e-ne-ba-àm me-en-zé-en
> [kur] ⌈Tilmun⌉ ki kù-ga-àm
> [ki kù]-ga e-ne-ba-àm me-en-zé-en
> ⌈kur Tilmun⌉ ki kù-ga-àm

and derive e-ne-ba-àm from ba. Akkadian *zâzu*, "to divide." "to receive as one's portion in the division into severalty of property held in common." The form offers a welcome example of the second person plural preterite active of the a- theme of the Sumerian verb. The mark of this theme, the prefix a- (contracted with following e in the second person singular and plural preterite active), has hitherto been considered a mere phonetic or dialectical variant of the prefix e-/i-, and the difference in meaning of the two prefixes has been largely overlooked. This difference may be defined—provisionally—as similar to the difference in tempo between aorist (e-/i-) and imperfect (a-) as described by Jespersen, *Philosophy of Grammar*, p. 276: "The Aorist carries the narrative on, it tells us what happened next, while the Imperect lingers over the conditions as they were at that time and expatiates on them with more or less of prolixity." The lingering force of the a- theme occasions a significant shift of tenses in Akkadian renderings of its forms: Sumerian "present" and "preterite" active are both rendered as "present" (i.e., fientic durative?) in Akkadian, while Sumerian "present" and "preterite" passive are rendered, respectively, by present IV.1 and permansive I.1 in Akkadian. We hope to treat of the a- prefix in wider context elsewhere and refer for the time being to Poebel, *PBS*, VI, 115 (preterite active), and *AJSL*, L (January, 1934), 147 (passive) for its morphology; Poebel's term for the preterite active, "active permansive," shows that he recognized the basic meaning of the theme quite clearly at the time. The enclitic -àm at the end of the form serves here to mark circumstance of time—a frequent usage. [After the above was written, Dr. Kramer's study, *BASOR*, "Supplementary Studies No. 1," has become available. The transliteration and photograph there published favor a restoration [ki kù-g]a "The pure earth" in line 1.]

8. The introductions to Sumerian tales bid for the listener's attention and therefore make use of a great variety of stylistic devices. This does not always stand out in Dr. Kramer's renderings. The story of Martu's marriage, for instance, purports to be an account given by a hoary old tree which had lived in primeval times and could therefore tell what had then happened. It begins (*SEM* 58, 1–9; Dr. Kramer deals with it on p. 100 of his book):

> "When Ninab was (but) Aktab was not (yet),
> When the pure crown was (but) the pure tiara was not,
> When the pure herb was (but) the pure cedar was not,
> When the pure salt was (but) the pure potash was not,
> When cohabiting and conception were,
> When pregnancy and birth-giving were,
> I, the. . . . of the pure cedar, was; I, the forebear of the *mesu*(?)-tree,
> I, the parent of the white cedar, the kinsman of the Hashuru-tree, was.
> In those days. . . . etc. . . . . ."

We restore lines 5–6 as follows: gìš-du₁₁-du₁₁-ᵣgaᵀ š[à-ga šu-ti-a] ì-me-a šà-ᵣtuᵀ-šà-tù-ma ᵣtu-daᵀ ì-me-a. Note that, syntactically, ì-me-a and nu-me-a can be used with participial force: "being," "not being"; "when. . . . was," "when. . . . was not." For an especially clear instance see *SRT*, Nos. 6 and 7, l. 94.

Another interesting example is the introduction to the myth of Enlil and Ninlil (dealt with by Dr. Kramer on p. 43):

> Dur-an-ki uru na-nam àm-dúr-ru-dè-en-dè-en
> Nipru^{ki} uru na-nam àm-dúr-ru-dè-en-dè-en
> Dur-ᵍⁱˢgišimmar uru na-nam àm-dúr-ru-dè-en-dè-en
> íd sal-la íd kù-bi(!?) na-nam
>
> "In Duranki, in that very city we are living,
> In Nippur, in that very city we are living,
> In Durgišimmar, in that very city we are living,
> None but the Idsalla was its pure river, ..."

The narrator is telling his listeners that the scene of the ancient tale which he is going to narrate is none other than their own town of Nippur, thus bidding fair to interest them.

The word na-nam does not mean "behold," as Dr. Kramer translates it but has identifying and restrictive force: "It is/was . . . and none other" (or: ". . . . and no more"; or: ". . . . and no less"); it is therefore often rendered in Akkadian by -*ma*. In the sentences under discussion it seems to be used parenthetically: "Duranki—it and no other was the city (in question)—we inhabit," i.e., "We are living in that very city, (in) Duranki." The text Barton, *MBI* 4, varies from the one quoted above (Pinches, *JRAS*, 1919, p. 190) by seemingly reading [uru^ki n]a-nam instead of Dur-an-ki (thus apparently also the catalogue published by Dr. Kramer in *BASOR*, No. 88, pp. 10–19, ii.5), by adding the determinative KI after uru, and by introducing the verbal form with the datival na- (see n. 12 below): na-an-dúr-ru-dè-en-dè-en. This dative seems to have reference to Enlil, and its force is best rendered by a possessive pronoun: "In his very city, in his very city we are living." The Akkadian translator (*JRAS*, 1919, p. 190)—perhaps not a Nippurian—disassociates himself from the Sumerian narrator and his public, reporting rather than translating the meaning of these lines. He has: *ina II* (i.e., *Dur-an-ki*) *āli-šu-nu šu-nu ú-ši-ba*, "They (i.e., the Sumerian narrator and his audience) dwelt in their (i.e., Enlil and Ninlil's?) city Duranki." In the third line we read Dur-^gišgišimmar, following Pinches (*JRAS*, p. 190) and Van der Meer (*Iraq*, 4 [1937], 144 ff., No. 88 i) rather than Langdon (*RA*, 19 [1922], 68, n. 7). The reasons underlying Dr. Kramer's rendering "the 'kindly wall'" are not clear to us.

9. The relevant section reads:

> ^dEn-líl Ki-ùr[1] im-ma-ni-in-DU-DU
> ^dEn-líl Ki-ùr[1] dib-dib[2]-da-ni
> dingir gal-gal ninnu-ne-ne
> dingir nam-tar-ra imin-na-ne-ne
> ^dEn-líl Ki-ùr-ra im-ma-ni[3]-dab-bé-ne[4]
> ^dEn-líl ú-zug[5]-e[6] [uru-ta ba-ra-è][4]
> ^dNu-nam-nir ú-zug[5]-e[6] uru-ta ba-ra-ˈeˈ[7]
> [7]^dEn-líl níg-nam-ma[8] nam[9] mu-un-tar-ra-šè
> [7]^dNu-nam-nir[10] nam-šè nam[9] mu-un-tar-ra-šè
> ^dEn-líl ì-du . . . . etc. . . . . .

The text is based on Barton, *MBI* 4 ii 11–13 for its first three lines; from then onward on Pinches, *JRAS*, 1919, 190–191. Variants are: [1]*SEM* 77: + -ra. [2]*SEM* 77: + -bé-, [3]*SEM* 77: + -in-. [4]Thus *MBI* 4. [5]*MBI* 4: KA + SAR. [6]*MBI* 4 and *SEM* 77: ge. [7]*MBI* 4: omits this line. [8]*SEM* 77: -šè. [9]*SEM* 77: omitted. [10]*SEM* 77: + níg-.

> "Enlil came walking into Kiur
> And while Enlil was passing through Kiur
> The fifty senior gods
> And the seven gods who determine destinies

Had Enlil arrested in Kiur:
"This sex-criminal Enlil will leave the town!
This sex-criminal Nunamnir will leave the town!"
Enlil, in accordance with that which had been decided as destiny,
Nunamnir, in accordance with that which had been decided as destiny,
Enlil (did) go (away)....etc....."

The Akkadian translation reads, beginning with the fifth line:

MIN (i.e., ᵈ*En-líl*) *i-na* MIN(i.e., *Ki-ùr-ra*) *ú-šá-ḫa-zu-ú*
MIN (i.e., ᵈ*En-líl*) *mu-su-uk-kum i-na a-li li-si*
MIN (i.e., ᵈ*Nu-nam-nir*) *mu-su-uk-kum i-na a-li li-ṣi*
MIN (i.e., ᵈ*En-líl*) *a-na šim-ti šá ta-ši-mu*
MIN (i.e., ᵈ*Nu-nam-nir*) *a-na šim-ti šá ta-ši-mu*
MIN (i.e., ᵈ*En-líl*) *il-la-ak....etc.....*

The word ú-zug (borrowed by Akkadian as (*m*)*usukku*, fem. (*m*)*usukkatu*), denotes a person who is sexually unclean, who is dangerous to the community because he is under a sexual taboo. This term may be used of a menstruating woman or—as here— of a person who has committed a sex crime, rape. The -e which follows the word we interpret as the demonstrative -e, "this" (see Poebel, *GSG*, §§223–226). Related to the latter is probably a "vocative" -e which occasionally occurs. Examples are IV R, Pl. 9, obv. 5: aia-ᵈNanna-umun-an-gal-e nir-gál dìm-me-er-e-ne/*a-bu* ᵈ*Na-an-nar be-lum* ᵈ*A-num rabu-u e-til-li* ili^{me-eš}, "O father Nanna, lord, great Anu, respected one among the gods"; the first line of Lugal-e: lugal-e u₄ me-lám-bi nir-gál, "O king, storm whose sheen inspires respect"; and Exaltation of Inanna (*RA*, 11 [1914], 144, obv. 5): lugal dìm-me-er-e-ne-ke₄, "O king of the gods!" Cf. also Frank, *ZA*,n.F. 7 (1933), 195, obv. 9 and 2; S. A. Smith, *Miscellaneous Assyrian Texts*, Pl. 24, ll. 18 and 22, etc. For the semantic range involved, cf. the similar use of Egyptian *pw*, "this," in vocatives. See Gardiner, *Egyptian Grammar*, §112.

10. The Sumerians, it would appear, considered it possible for a woman to continue to conceive though already pregnant.

11. The words a lugal-mu (representing a lugal(-ak)-mu) appear to contain an intentional ambiguity which is not easily rendered in English. The words may— and thus Ninlil is meant to interpret them—be understood to contain the possessive suffix first person singular in its caritative meaning: "my (beloved) seed (i.e., offspring) of the king," i.e., "my (dear) prince." They may also, however, be understood as containing a genitive of characteristic followed by the possessive suffix first person singular in its possessive meaning "my 'king's seed,'" i.e., "my royal offspring, engendered by me, a king, and thus of royal essence." With this genitive of characteristic compare the similar genitive in a nun-ak-ene, "the athelings," literally: the "magnate's seed", describing the gods as those of noble lineage. In their first sense these words could be fittingly spoken by a gatekeeper, a servant of Enlil; in the second sense they fit Enlil in his true identity.

On the use of -ge₁₈ (< gimin; see Poebel, *MVAG*, 1921, 1, p. 15) in the sense of "as equivalent of," compare *PBS*, VIII.2, No. 162, munus šu-gi munus kaš-ši-tum

5 gín-guškin-gimi-nam. "One old woman, a Kassite, being the equivalent of 5 shekels gold"; and see also Lugal-e Tablet X.1 ff., where -ge₁₈ (translated ki-i) in Ninurta's verdicts serves to connect crime with punishment: "in recompense, retribution, for (that)."

12. The text is based on SRT 19, SEM 34, PBS, X.2, p. 16, SK 207, and TRS 72 as follows: First line. Restored on the basis of SRT 19: uzu-è ᵍⁱˢal-a-[ni.....] and SEM 34: [...mi-n]i-in-dù. TRS gives [uz]u-mú-a ᵍⁱˢ⁽!?⁾al(!?) (read thus for SAG-NU) gá-gá-dè, "When the pickax was being applied in Uzumua"; SK 207 retains [...]ᵍⁱˢal[...]; PBS, X.2, p. 16 (perhaps only Langdon's copy?) omits the line. Second line. Preserved in part by PBS, X.2, p. 16, and SEM 34, fully by TRS 72. SEM 34 has -gál, "was," TRS 72 -gar, "was situated," as the last sign; the last mentioned text also writes the determinative GIŠ before ù-šub-ba. Third line. Preserved in full by PBS, X.2, p. 16, and TRS 72 (read kalam-ma-ni(!?) ki mu-un(!?)-ši(!?)-in-dar-re), in part by SEM 34 and SK 207. The latter reads [kala]m-ma-na ki KU mu-un-dar⌈a⌉. We consider the present form of the verb—as given in TRS 72—the better text. It should be noted that the present tense is often used in Sumerian—as it is in Akkadian—to express attendant circumstance. It is then to be rendered by a participle or a durative past ("....ing" or "was....ing") in English. Cf. PBS, X,2, p. 14, rev. 8 ff.: ᵈEn-líl lugal kur-kur-ra-ke₄ igi-zi-ti-la sag-ki-zalag-ga-ni mu-un-ši-in-bar ᵈIš-me-ᵈDa-gán-na nam mu-ni-íb-tar-re.... ᵈEn-líl-le nam-šè mu-ni-in-tar, "Enlil, the king of all countries, looked with a true eye of life and with a clear brow at him. Determining destiny for Ishme-Dagān.... such and such things....did Enlil determine for him as (his) destiny." Cf. also HiAV, 6, 12, u₄-ba ᵈEn-ki-ke₄ ᵈEn-líl-ra gù mu-un-na-dé-e, "At that time Enki was saying to Enlil," where u₄-ba clearly shows that no "present" or "future" tense (in the strict sense of that term) is intended. The usage is parallel to Akkadian usage, e.g., in A pâ-šu ipuš-ma iqabbi izakkara ana B, "A opened (lit.: 'worked') his mouth speaking (the reference is primarily to articulate sound), saying (more precisely 'calling to mind,' 'calling up images, concepts'; the reference is primarily to meaning) to B." As for the meaning of ki....dar, cf. dar, litû, "to cleave," "to spit," Deimel, ŠL, 114.9; and ki-in-dar, nigiṣṣu, "crack (in the earth)," ibid., 461.101. We know of no such meaning as "to clothe" for ki....dar. Fourth line. SEM 34 reads mu-ši- for nam-mi-; TRS 72 seems to read the verb as mu-un-pà, but de Genouillac's copy may be doubted (mu-un-ši-bar(!?)). SK 207 omits the line.

The verbal form nam-mi-in-bar shows the datival prefix na- (or rather the datival verbal element (-)na- in initial position?): "toward his black-headed ones the eye was opened in trusty fashion for him." The datival force of this relatively frequent "prefix" (see already above, n. 8) may be demonstrated most clearly, perhaps, by a comparison of two variant forms of Eannatum's name quoted in the "Stele of the Vultures." In obv. v. 20 ff., the author of that inscription tells about the name which Ningirsu gave Eannatum as follows: É-an-na-tù á(!?)-tuku-e kur-a du₁₇-éš na-e É-an-na-tù-ra mu ᵈInanna-ke₄ e-ni-sa₄-a-ni É-an-na-ᵈInanna-ib-gal-ka-ka-a-tù mu m[u]-ni-[sa₄], "He (i.e., Ningirsu) named Eannatum—(this being) his name (by) which Inanna had named him: 'The one worthy of the Eanna of Inanna of Ibgal'— (by) the (new and longer) name: É-an-na-tù-á-tuku-e-kur-a-du₁₇-éš-na-e (i.e.,

Eannatum, the possessor of strength, will sound for him [i.e., for Ningirsu] the battle cry in the enemy land').'' Shortly afterward the author of the "Stele of the Vultures" again refers to this new name (vi.1 ff.), but now he quotes Ningirsu's actual words in naming Eannatum. Here na-, "for him," is replaced with mà-, "for me": á-tuku-e mu-pà-da ᵈNin-gír-sú-ka-ke₄ É-an-na-tù-me kur-a du₁₇-éš m[à-e] níg-ul-lí-a-d[a] gù nam-mi-dé. "'The possessor of strength, the one made known by name by (me) Ningirsu, Eannatum, will sound for me the battle cry in the enemy land' he called out unto him alongside the original one (i.e., the original name, É-an-na-tù).''

Further instances of (-)na- used initially are the well known: X. na-a-e-a, "what X. is saying unto him," in the introduction to letters; the introductory line of Inanna's Descent (we quote 1. 3), ᵈInanna an-gal-ta ki-gal-šè geštu-ga-ni na-an-g[ub], "(As for) Inanna her mind was turned (lit.: 'was set') for her away from the great(er) heaven and toward the great(er) earth." Cf. also Elevation of Inanna (*RA*, 11 [1914], 144–145, l. 13): An-na-ra i(nim)-bala bar-zé-eb-ba-ke₄ ḫúl-le-eš nam-mi-in-gar, *ana* ᵈ*A-nu na-pa-le-e ṭu-ub ka-bat-ti ḫa-diš iê-ša-kin-šum-ma*, "For Anu was joyfully established rejoinder of good(ness of) liver," i.e., "A pleasant answer joyfully suggested itself to Anu"; and Gudea, St. B, vii.4: na-mu-dù, "He built it for him." (The existence of a datival prefix na- has often been assumed. For recent views of this na- and its meaning see Falkenstein, *ZA*,n.F. 11 [1939], 183, and literature there quoted. The passage on which Falkenstein comments contains, in our opinion, the na- of negated wish.)

Just as a dative element (-)na- is found both initially and medially (as "prefix" and as "infix") in the Sumerian finite verb, so corresponds apparently the element (-)ba-, "for it," which occurs as infix in Urukagina Oval Plaque (cf. ii. 7, nu-na-sì-mu, "He was not giving unto him," i.e., unto the royal archer, with ii.9, nu-ba-sì-mu, "He was not giving unto it," i.e., unto the archer's donkey; cf. also Eannatum, Mortar iv.8), to the better known "prefix" ba- (on its use with nonpersonals see Falkenstein, *OLZ*, 1933, Sp. 303–304). Similarly, the "prefix" bé-/bí-, "at it," "on it," has a corresponding "infix" -be₆- (cf. Poebel, *AS*, II, pp. 16–19; we would prefer to assume that the meaning "with them" derives from a locative "at it/them"). We hope to return elsewhere to these correspondences, to the question of difference of grammatical function in different position, and to their general implications for the structure of the Sumerian verb.

13. Uzumua is mentioned also in *KAR* 4, obv. 24, and in *CT*, XV, 31, 4 ff. Dr. Geers calls my attention to Van der Meer, "Tablets of the ḪAR-RA = ḪUBULLU Series....," *Iraq*, 6 (1939), 144 ff., No. 88, i.15, where it is explained as (a part of, or a term for) Nippur. See also Heidel, *Babylonian Genesis*, p. 57, n. 40, and literature there cited. We assume uzu-mú-a to have been abbreviated from a longer form: ki-uzu-mú-a, "the place where flesh sprouted forth" (on construction cf. *GSG*, §718), but other etymologies seem possible and may prove preferable.

14. Dr. Kramer, who treats of this passage on p. 62 of his book, translates:

> "After the water of *creation* had been decreed.
> After the name ḫegal (abundance), born in heaven,
> Like plant and herb had clothed the land, ..."

But a-ri-a—which we have rendered "(all) engendered things"—means actually "seed," "offspring" (lit.: "ejaculated *semen virile*"), Akkadian *riḫūtu*, not "the waters of creation"; nor does nam....tar have the connotation of "decreed" as here used. It means to decree a "fate," the form or *modus* under which something is to exist, not to call that something into existence. On ki....dar see n. 12 above.

15. On the meaning of ù-šub, or rather of its Akkadian counterpart *nalbantu*, see von Soden, *ZA*,n.F. 11 (1939), 64, n. 3. Von Soden shows that *nalbantu* denotes a cavity shaped like an inverted truncated pyramid of square ground plan. He translates it "Ziegelgrube." In our passage—as indicated above—the word apparently refers to the hole left by the clod broken off by Enlil's pickax.

16. On búru (presumably ⟨bura with a⟩ u after r; cf. Poebel, *GSG*, §§723 and 470, also *JAOS*, 57 [1937] 51 ff.), "fissure," "gash," cf. my remarks in *OIP* XLIII, 170–171, No. 42, n.†.

17. The element nanga-, namga- (on *n* > m before g see Poebel, *GSG*, §63), which introduces the finite verb of this and several of the following lines, is an element of relatively frequent occurrence. (Note apart from this passage *PBS*, X.2, p. 6, rev. i.18–19; *BE*, XXIX.1, No. 2.34 [cf. p. 70]; Lugalbanda epic, 167–169; *TRS* 12, 104–106; *SRT* 3, iii.18; *SRT* 6.81–82; vase inscription of Enshakushanna, *RA*, 14 [1917], 152, and *TRS* 50, 57–58. The latter passage is not clear.) Its place in the verbal chain—always at the beginning before the prefix—classes it with the modal elements such as optative ḫé-/ḫa-, cohortative ga-, negative nu-, negating wish na-, etc. The force of the mode marked by nanga-, namga- is suggested by the Metropolitan Syllabary (Langdon, *JSOR*, 1 [1917], 22–23, obv. i.12–15), which translates nam-ga- as *tu-ša-ma*, *mi-in-di*, *ap-pu-na*, and *pi-qá-at*, and by *BE*, XXXI, No. 46, i.2 (cf. Kramer, *JAOS*, 60 [1940], 251), which translates ra(?)-i-ma. Basic in these words is an appeal to the listener's own judgment and experience; they present a fact or conjecture as "evident," "obvious," as a necessary inference from the premises, but they tend to shade off into the more general, affirmative meaning "surely," "verily." (Cf. the translation of these words suggested by Landsberger, *ZA*,n.F. 9 [1936], 73, and by Thureau-Dangin, *RA*, 30 [1933], 30, and *Analecta Orientalia*, XII, 308. Ra-i-ma may be considered permansive I₁ of a root r-ʾ-i, "it is seen" [cf. رَأَى], followed by -ma: "it is seen that," "it is evident that" > "surely," "verily"; cf. the material on raʾi collected by Ungnad in *ZA*,n.F. 4 [1929], 71.) We may therefore tentatively define the mood marked by nanga- as an inferentative-affirmative mood. Its force may be rendered approximately by "obviously" and by "verily."

18. Very doubtful. We tentatively restore ᵍⁱˢal-⌜sa(!?)-lá(!?)⌝-a-ni. Dr. Kramer seems to read ᵍⁱˢal-é (or gá)-a-ni, but "the pickax of his house" would be ᵍⁱˢal-é-(or gá)-a-na.

19. Our rendering of si as "bastion" is based on si-bàd (.ak), *situ*, "bastion." The comparison seems to be with bastions of a very long and narrow type such as found e.g., in Agrab (*OIP*, LVIII, 221, Fig. 170). *TRS* 72 has ù-tu-da, "born of," instead of è-a, "projecting from." This variant would appear to render Dr. Kramer's interpretation of the line less likely.

20. The Sumerian word me, here rendered as "modus operandi," means

approximately "set, normative pattern (of behavior)," "norm." Etymologically it may be considered as the noun ("being" = manner of being) which corresponds to the verb me, "to be." It is used characteristically of the totality of functions pertaining to an office or a profession (cf., e.g., Gudea, Cyl. B, vi.23, vii.11, 23, etc.), of rites, and of mores (cf., e.g., Kramer, *AS*, XII, p. 24, l. 70; *PBS*, X.2, p. 1, obv. iii.12–13; see n. 23 below). Instructive also is me-te, "approaching the norm" = "proper," "fitting" (Akkadian (*w*)*asmu*). Landsberger, to whom the clarification of this term is largely due, translates "Göttliche Ordnungen von ewiger, unveränderlicher Geltung" (*Islamica*, 2 [1927], 369). In his earlier, detailed study of the word (*AOF*, 2 [1924], 66) he proposed "'specifisch göttliche Gewalt (Funktion)' oder 'heilige Macht.'"

21. The Yale Syllabary (*YOS*, I, Pl. 53.57–60) and the duplicate text *CT*, XXXV, 1, i.46–49, list four meanings of the sign with their reading. The meanings seem to be arranged in pairs comprising first a name of an entity, then the name of the deity of that entity:

i	ENGUR	*na-a-ru*	"river"
i-id	ENGUR	ᵈ*Íd*	"the god (of the river) Id"
en-gur	ENGUR	*ap-su-u*	"the *apsû*"
nam-mu	ENGUR	ᵈ*Nammu*	"the goddess (of the *apsû*) Nammu"

A further reading—originally perhaps pertaining to a separate sign which in time became merged with ENGUR—is gi-lu-gu (Meissner has suggested the emendation zi(!)-ku(!)-um(!), "heaven," Akkadian *šamû* [see *SAI*, 7737 and Deimel, *ŠL*, 484.8]). As translation of engur occurs also *engurru*, which is merely the Sumerian word itself in Akkadian garb (see Deimel, *ŠL*, 484.2).

The reading with which we are here concerned is engur, translated as *apsû*, and forming a pair with the divine name Nammu. There can be little doubt about its basic meaning. Its Akkadian counterpart, *apsû*, denotes the sweet waters of the underground water-bearing strata of Mesopotamia, waters which may be reached when one digs down deep to lay the foundations of a temple, but which also appear in pools and marshes where the surface of the plain naturally dips down below the water table (see the current dictionaries *sub voce* and Jensen, *RLA*, I. 122–123).

As *apsû* is used in Akkadian so is engur and its approximate synonym abzu (from this word derives Akkadian *apsû*) in Sumerian. Gudea tells us that the subterranean *temennu* (lit.: "*temennu* of the abzu") of the temple Eninnu in Lagash "consults together" with Enki down in "the house of the engur" (é-an-gur₄-ra-ka, Cyl. A, xxii. 11–13; cf. *JNES*, 2 [1943], 118). Here, accordingly, the engur is deep down in the ground. Ur-Nanshe, on the other hand, invokes the reeds of the marshes as "reed-of-the canebrake of the engur" (gi.giš.gi engur(.ra), Diorite plaque i.2; cf. *JNES*, 2 [1943], 118) and states that its root is in one place with Enki. Here, accordingly, the engur is the subterraneous waters as they come to the surface in the marshes.

Although the notion underlying the words engur, abzu, and *apsû* is thus in itself both clear and well defined, one might, of course, raise the question whether occasionally one or the other of these terms might not have been used more loosely to include also the other large body of terrestrial water, the sea. On the whole, we believe, the answer must be in the negative.

The Akkadians—as shown by *Enūma elish*—distinguished quite clearly *Apsû*, conceived as male, from his spouse *Ti'āmut*, the sea, conceived as female. Nor are engur or abzu ever translated as *tâmtu*, "sea," in Akkadian; this translation pertains to ab and a-ab-ba. But also the Sumerians treat engur and abzu as distinct in meaning from a-ab-ba, "the sea." We need quote only the passage which describes Enki's departure for Nippur in the myth of Enki and É-engurra (Dr. Kramer's translation may be found on p. 63 of his book):

> ᵈEn-ki zi-ga-na (var. -ni) ku₆ i-zi (var. izi) šu na-zi
> ab.zu-e (var. -a) u₆-e àm (var. nam)-ma-gub (var. lá-a)
> engur-ra ḫúl-la mu-ni-ib (var. -ib)-túm
> a-ab-ba-ka (var. -a, -ge₁₈) ní mu-un (var. om.)-da-gál
> íd-maḫ-e (var. -ge₁₈) su-zi mu-un (var. om.) -da (var. + -an) -ri
> íd-Buranun-na(!) lu (var. tu₁₅-ulú) súr mu-un-da-an-zi

"When Enki rose the fishes rose, raised (their) hands (in prayer) to him —
He stood, a marvel unto the *Apsû*,
Brought joy to the Engur.
To the Sea (it seemed that) awe was upon him,
To the Great River (it seemed that) terror hovered around him,
While at the same time the south wind stirred the depths of the Euphrates."

The variants affecting the sense are: "He floated" or "hung suspended" instead of "He stood" in the second line: "Awe was upon him as (it is upon) the sea" and "Terror hovered around him as (it hovers around) the great river" in the fourth and fifth lines. Besides the translation of ll. 2–6 given above, one might also consider: "He stepped—a marvel to behold—up to the *apsû*, was carried in joy into the engur. In the sea awe was upon him, on the great river terror hovered around him, in the Euphrates the south wind stirred the depths when he arrived thither (lit.: 'with him')." On any translation the engur and the "sea" (a-ab-ba) are different entities. Another passage which shows the two words to represent distinct entities is *AO*, 4331 + 4335, iv, 1–2; *NFT*, p. 206; Poebel, *ZA*,n.F. 3 (1927), 162.

In favor of a less strict usage we could at best quote passages like *TC*, VI, 47, l. 2, which points up a resemblance between Ea and Ereshkigal as follows: *a-me* ᵈÉ-a *ki-i* ⌈ap⌉-*su-ú ap-su-ú tam-tim tam-tim* ᵈ*Ereš-ki-gal*, "Ea resembles the *apsû*, the *apsû* the sea, the sea Ereshkigal." However, as anyone conversant with theological texts of the type of *TC*, VI, 47 will know, such associations are important rather for what they tell about Mesopotamian speculative thought than as precise contributions to lexicography.

Little is gained also from V R, Pl. 51, iii.77–78: ᵈNammu nin ab-gal-l [a...], ᵈMIN *be-el-tu šá ina tam-tim* [...], for the lacuna in the text leaves the exact relations between Nammu and the sea or lake undetermined: "Nammu, the lady who in(to)/ from the/a great sea/lake [...]." That etymologically the term abzu and the terms for sea, ab and a-abba(k), may be related, and that correspondingly in a remote past the Sumerians may have distinguished the bodies of water involved less sharply, is possible (a suggestion to that effect has been made by Poebel; see *ZA*,n.F. 3 [1927], 258, and *apud* Jensen, *RLA*, I, 122) but is not, of course, immediately relevant to the usage of historical times.

Under these circumstances the likelihood that in historical times engur, abzu, and *apsû* were used—even occasionally—to include also the sea appears rather problematical. To set aside their clear and well-established meaning, "sweet waters of the subsoil and of pools and marshes," and to assume instead this questionable meaning, "sea," to be their primary and basic connotation seems decidedly un-advisable, the more so since the deities connected with the engur and the abzu/*apsû*, Nammu and Enki, played a very prominent role in Mesopotamian religious thought, as did the sweet waters of the subsoil, of rivers, wells, canals, and of the marshes in the life and outlook of the Mesopotamian himself. The sea, on the other hand, was an almost negligible factor in his life. It would be very strange indeed if he had chosen it and the divine powers manifest in it as his most popular object of worship.

22. See V R, Pl. 50 line 5. Cf. Jensen, *RLA*, I 122.

23. Enki touches first on Shumer's cultural leadership: it sets the norms, the standards of right behavior. Utu-è-ta utu-šú-uš ukù-e me sì-mu cannot—for reasons of grammar—mean "the people from sunrise to sunset obedient to the divine decrees" but must be rendered: "(Thou Shumer) who dost set (lit.: 'give') norms for the people from sunrise to sunset," i.e., from the farthest east to the farthest west. He then mentions Shumer's powers as "kingmaker": it has authority to confer the high offices of "king" and "*enu*." The relevant lines—which belong closely together —have been separated by Dr. Kramer and distributed to two of the sections into which he divides the text. They read:

> umun$_9$-zi-ki-dingir-ù-tu-za an-ge$_{18}$ šu nu-te-gá
> lugal ù-tu suḫ-zi-kés-di
> en ù-tu sag men gá-gá

> "Thy true matrix, the place which gives birth to gods,
> is untouchable like heaven,
> It gives birth to kings, ties(?) rightly the pectoral(?),
> It gives birth to *enu*'s, sets the crown on(?) (their) heads."

The crown and pectoral(?) are symbols of office; the phrase "which gives birth to gods" may have reference to deified rulers.

24. Another form of the tradition is preserved in *KAR* 4. This text also mentions the separation of heaven and earth: u$_4$ an ki-ta tab-ge-na bad-a-ta bà-a-[ba]. "When heaven from earth—from the far-removed trusty twin—had been parted," and proceeds to tell of a divine decision to create man in Uzumua (obv. 24–25). But the decision is taken at an assembly of all the gods, and man is to be fashioned from the blood of the two Lamga gods who are to be slain for that purpose.

25. One might guess—but it could be no more than a guess—that the myth aimed at explaining how Enki, the sweet waters in the ground, came to occupy his present position (see n. 28 below) separating the earth above (ki) from the underworld

(ki-gal, "the great(er) earth") below. It is only fitting, before leaving the passage with which we have been dealing, to call attention to Dr. Kramer's earlier—and far more cautious—treatment of it in *AS* X, pp. 3 and 34 ff.

26. Langdon, *OECT*, VII, No. 99.

27. Deimel, *Schultexte aus Fara* (Leipzig, 1923), Nos. 1.i.4, 5.i.2, etc.

28. The assumed connection of Enki with the sea and the translation of the name of his temple in Eridu, É-engura(k), as "seahouse" (p. 79 *passim*) are largely based on the belief that abzu and engur denote "sea," which we have discussed in n. 21 above. Concerning É-engura(k) in Eridu it should be noted that the "sea" on which Eridu was situated was in reality an inland lake, as shown by R. Campbell Thompson's finds of freshwater shells on the site (*Archaeologia*, 70 [1920], 124–125). Both Akkadian *tâmtu* and Sumerian a-abba(k) could be used for "lake" as well as for "sea" (cf. Jensen, *RLA*, I, 123; Unger, *RLA*, I, 404–405). The flora and fauna of its immediate surroundings (Myth of Enki and Eridu, ll. 75 ff.: reed thickets, fruit-bearing orchards, birds, and fishes; cf. Kramer, p. 63) are those of a freshwater lake, not of the sea. The engur, from which the temple is named, is therefore the water-bearing strata at the lake bottom from which water seeps into the lake from the surrounding soil and, cosmically conceived, the "house of the engur" stretches underground with the water table to Lagash, where the substructure of É-ninnu reaches down into it (see n. 21 above). Thus we also understand the description in the legend of the Kishkanû (*CT*, XVI, 46–47, 187–192): Enki, the god of the sweet waters in the earth, lies in the chambers of Nammu, goddess of the water-bearing strata; these chambers are down in the earth just above the "surface of the underworld" (ḫi LIB written IGI-KUR(.ra), i.e., "surface of the underworld"; see Deimel, *ŠL*, 449.174).

ᵈEn-ki-ke₄ (var. + ki-) du-du-a-ta Friduᵏⁱ-ga ḫé-gál si-ga-àm
ša ᵈ*É-a* (var. ᵈBE) *tal-lak-ta-šú ina E-ri-du* (var. *Eri-du₁₀*) *ḫé-gál ma-la-a-ti*
ki-dúr-a-na ki ḫi LIB-àm *šu-bat-su a-šar ir-ṣi-tim-ma*
ki-ná-a itim ᵈNammu-àm *ki-iṣ-ṣu-šu* (var. -*šú*) *ma-aia-lu* (var. -*al-ta*(?)) *šá* ᵈMIN.

> "The haunts of Enki in Eridu are full of bounty,
> Where he sits is the surface of the underworld,
> Where he lies is the chamber of Nammu."

Literally translated, the last lines read: In his place where he is sitting is the place (of the) surface of the underworld, in the place where (he is) lying is the (bed)chamber (of) Nammu (the Akkadian version seems to reverse "place where (he is) lying" and "chamber").

29. Haupt, *ASKT*, No. 10, p. 80 lines 25–26; J. 5326 (Geller, *AOTU*, I.4, p. 279); and Kramer, *SLTN* 6 rev. The reading en-na of *SLTN* 6 is preferable to en given by *ASKT* 10 (and by J. 5326?). The damaged signs at the end of line 25 in *ASKT* 10 are undoubtedly to be read with J. as geštu mi(!?)-ni-i[n-...]. The first sign of ba-[*šá-a*] is preserved in J. alone.

30. On *Asakku* see, e.g., Ebeling, *RLA*, II 108–109.

31. Á-sàg, literally "the one who smites the arm," corresponds to Akkadian *kamû*, "the one who binds," "the one who lames" (cf. Deimel, *ŠL*, 334.104).

32. In view of the intrinsic interest of the subject, a few words may be said of "biblical parallels." As some relationship—indirect—may reasonably be assumed to exist between the Sumerian and the biblical deluge stories (p. 97), so one would not a priori reject the possibility that Sumerian dragons—though not Kur—may be remote cousins, less likely ancestors, of Leviathan and similar monsters of a later day (pp. 13 and 76 ff.). Much painstaking work must yet be done, however, before the Mesopotamian concepts are so far clarified that the problem can be at all fruitfully attacked or even formulated. Generalities such as the mere belief in "a" dragon and "a" dragon-slayer mean practically nothing, for in all questions of cultural influence it is not the abstract and the simple but the particular and the complex which furnish reliable evidence.

This must be kept clearly in mind when one evaluates the implications of even such attractive suggestions as that the Sumerian lamentations are forerunners (p. 14) of the "Book of Lamentations." (Forerunners in the sense of compositions of an earlier age treating of similar subjects? Yes, certainly. Forerunners in the sense that the "Book of Lamentations" stands in a Sumerian literary tradition from which it derives literary patterns and phraseology? Surely not until it has been shown that the extant similarities go beyond what similar subject matter and similar situations will naturally suggest to any good poet.) It is far more imperative with remarks such as that on p. 82 that the passage giving Ninurta's verdicts on the stones "in style and tone, *not in content*, is very reminiscent of the blessing and cursing of Jacob's sons in the forty-ninth chapter of Genesis." Here the reader who is intent on "parallels" must make clear to himself that the similarities pointed to are on such a high level of abstraction that they can have no bearing on questions of cultural (stylistic) influence: they will hold equally with any series of motivated blessings, curses, or verdicts in any literature anywhere at any time. Similarly with the "Cain-Abel motif" (in Pan-Babylonistic parlance this used to mean "*Brudermord*"), which is mentioned whenever a Sumerian myth treats of the rivalry between shepherd and farmer (pp. 49, 53, 101). Here again the reader should note that Dr. Kramer does not speak in terms of cultural influence. The contrast and rivalry of two ways of life, of the desert and the sown, goes through all Near Eastern history: it is of a nature to seek literary expression spontaneously, independently at varying times and places. That the Hebew and the Sumerian stories have as their theme this ever present social and economic contrast is not significant; what *is* significant is rather the utter difference of treatment and of underlying emotional attitude in the two cases. The shepherd-farmer problem and its literary formulation must be different in a near-tribal community from what it is in a highly integrated state. It is not likely that any of the Sumerian stories ever influenced that of Cain and Abel; that we are, in any sense, dealing with the borrowing of a literary motif.

Indeed, the great problem which the Sumerian material raises is not a comparative problem; it is rather to understand, first and foremost, that literature in its own Sumerian setting—to interpret it as the expression of Sumerian culture itself. When that has been done, and only then, will it be possible to make valid comparisons and to test Dr. Kramer's extremely bold dictum concerning the Sumerian compositions that "the form and contents of the Hebrew literary creations and to a certain extent even those of the ancient Greeks were profoundly influenced by them" (p. viii).

For the time being side glances seem more likely to distract. Thus we would suggest that the text which serves as frontispiece and which is said to describe the state of man "before the 'confusion of tongues'" and to be "very reminiscent of Genesis XI:1," would have been differently interpreted by Dr. Kramer if he had sought Mesopotamian rather than biblical parallels for its phraseology. The passage which interests us reads:

"In those days the land Shubur (East), the place of plenty, of righteous decrees,

Harmony-tongued Sumer (South), the great land of the 'decrees of princeship,'

Uri (North), the land having all that is *needful*,

The land Martu (West), resting in security,

The whole universe, the people *in unison*

To Enlil in one tongue *gave praise*."

A key term of this passage, eme-ha-mun, which Dr. Kramer translates "*harmony-tongued*," occurs also in an address to the divine judge Utu in VR, Pl. 50, i.69–70 (cf. IV R, Pl. 19.2, 45–46):

eme-ha-mun mu-aš-ge$_{18}$ si ba-ni-íb-sá-e

li-šá-an mit-hur-ti ki-i iš-tin šu-[me tuš-te]-šir

"Mutually opposed testimonies thou dost straighten out as (were they but) one single statement."

The reference is to the judge's task of finding the facts of a case. In the phrase *lišān mithurti* (*lišān*, sg. with collective force [see Delitzsch, *HW*, p. 386], is in the construct state before the genitive of characteristic *mithurti* [Inf. I.2 of *m-h-r*; the -*t*- has reciprocal force]), the word *mithurtu* is used in its original meaning of "being mutually opposed" and not in its derived meaning of "matching one another," "corresponding to one another" (this latter shade predominates in the related adjective-adverb *mithāru* and *mithāriš*), as may be seen from its Sumerian counterpart ha-mun, which denotes "conflicting," "mutually opposed" (cf. ri-ha-mun, "whirlwind" [Akkadian *ašamšutu*, Deimel, *ŠL*, 86.103], literally "(a) mutually opposed blowing" [cf. ri, translated as *zíq šári*, ibid., 86.16], a clashing of two winds blowing in opposite directions).

On this basis, then, eme-ha-mun in the passage under consideration would seem to mean not "harmony-tongued" but "(of) mutually opposed tongues" in the sense of "comprising people of widely different opinions." In corresponding sense, as equivalent to "expression of opinion," one will naturally interpret "tongue" also in the last line of the passage and translate: "to Enlil *with* one tongue gave praise." The line then expresses that on one thing the motley of countries and people mentioned could all agree: praise to Enlil. It is unity of mind, not unity of language, with which the ancient poet is concerned.

33. *Maqlû*, II, 104–108. Cf. G. Meier, *Die Assyrische Beschwörungssammlung Maqlû* Berlin, 1937), pp. 16–17.

34. [For Kramer's rejoinder see *JCS* 2 (1948) 39–70. Ed.]

8. Early Political Development in Mesopotamia

1. The following inquiry was presented as a lecture in the Seminar on Comparative Law at the University of Chicago Law School, Spring Quarter, 1956, given jointly by Professor Karl N. Llewellyn, Professor Max Rheinstein, and the writer. Thanks are due to the members of the seminar who participated in the discussion and very particularly to Professor Rheinstein, whose courses on "Legal Regulation of Society" years ago first stimulated our interest in ancient Mesopotamian governmental forms and opened up to us fruitful avenues of approach.

A few words may be said about the basic assumptions underlying our transliterations:

(1) *Orthography*. The history of Sumerian writing is one of progressively ever greater but never quite attained adjustment to Sumerian speech. Three major stages may be recognized: (A) *Ideographic Stage*. Sumerian writing goes back to an ideographic stage in which a sign might stand for any one of a group of words related through association of ideas, and for any grammatical form of that word. (B) *Semiphonetic Stage*. Phonetic writings, based on the rebus principle, first appear, as Falkenstein has shown, at the end of the Protoliterate period (Jemdet Nasr period). Conditioning for the further development of the writing were, however, less the straight phonetic renderings now possible, than the "hybrids," i.e., writings in which an ideogram was associated with a phonetic sign indicating one or more syllables of the word the ideogram was intended to represent and serving as a "phonetic complement." At this, as at the preceding stage, the signs were generally arranged in "cases" within which their order remained arbitrary. (C) *Phonetic Stage*. When the writing eventually became fully phonetic (this change in viewpoint is indicated by the related change from arbitrary to phonetic order of the signs and took place at the time of Eannatum) hybrid writings such as ğeš + EAR for ğeštug "ear" were felt as incomplete and were completed either by further addition as e.g., ğeš + EAR + túg, which left the original ideogram as a kind of "determinative," or by giving the ideogram such phonetic value as would complete the reading, e.g., YOUNG + da for banda "young," "vigorous," was conceived of as representing bàn-da. Purely ideographic writings such as YOUNG were likewise phonetically reinterpreted, the ideogram YOUNG being given the phonetic value bànda. Since, in order to minimize the ambiguities inherent in the writing, phonetic complements were usually chosen so that they would cover, and thus fix, the part of the word which tended to vary most grammatically, i.e., the beginning of a finite verb, the end of a noun, the phonetic values left to be covered by, and eventually assigned to, the old ideograms were on the whole the invariant parts of the words, the stems and their immediate surroundings.

At the time of Eannatum, however, this process of assigning phonetic values to original ideograms was still in flux and the operative principle may be stated as follows: "The *possible* phonetic range of a sign or sign group extends by syllabic steps virtually, dependent upon the volition of the scribe, to the *complete forms* of the word (inclusive of grammatical elements) of which it would normally indicate merely a basic part" (*OIP* LVIII p. 292 and see the proofs there given). From the point of view of the somewhat later reduction of this flexibility of the signs to fixed short values such as are given in the syllabaries (approximately what we called "basic part" above, the value of an invariant stem) the earlier writings appear "elliptic." In our transliterations of the older texts, in order to harmonize them with the later, more rigidly ordered, and phonetically more explicit, orthography, we have used the following symbols: Hyphen, -, to indicate written and read order. Colon, :, to indicate written order only. Period, ., to indicate order adjusted to reading order. Parentheses, ( ), serve to harmonize the "elliptic" older orthography with the more explicit later one and enclose, divided by periods, signs which would presumably have been added in the latter. In addition comma serves as line divider in consecutive transliteration of Sumerian passages, colon to separate Sumerian from its Akkadian translation.

(2) *Phonemics*. (a) *Final Consonants*. As shown conclusively by the Akkadian loans from Sumerian, final consonants were hardly ever lost in spoken Sumerian. Such consonants were, however—probably for reasons connected with the syllabification of Sumerian—rarely indicated in writing until the time of Ur III (at this time writings of the type -a-ni-ir for -anir regularly begin to replace the older orthography -a ni for -anir) and they were never completely and consistently rendered by the writing (the final k of the genitive -ak, for instance, was omitted to the last. Cf. *AS* VI p. 16–19). In quotation of Sumerian names in English context we accordingly give the complete form as far as it can be ascertained. We write, thus, Shulgir, not Shulgi, Ningirsuk, not Ningirsu.

(b) *Voiced and Unvoiced*. As shown by the fact that the Akkadians, when they took over the Sumerian writing, found no means in it for rendering their phonemic distinction between voiced and unvoiced stops, sibilants, etc. the distinction voiced: unvoiced, if it existed in Sumerian, was at any rate not phonemic. Sumerian had, however, a different, as yet not certainly identified, other phonemic distinction which may have been one of rounded (i.e., pronounced with rounded lips) and unrounded. We render the two series conventionally by b, d, g, z, š for the rounded (?) stops and sibilants, p, t, k, s, for the unrounded(?), without prejudice to what may have been the actual pronunciation.

(c) *Nasals*. Besides the rounded nasal m and the unrounded n Sumerian possessed a nasalized velar pronounced with rounded lips (nasalized labio-velar), approximately $\check{c}_w$. It is rendered in Akkadian as *g*, *k*, *ḫ* (in transliterations from Susa), *m*, and (as final only) *n*. We symbolize it conventionally as $\tilde{g}$ in Eme-KU (except in the pronouns and pronominal suffixes where we somewhat inconsistently retain m) and as m in Emesal.

(d) *Other*. The two different l's in Sumerian contained in lá and la respectively we do not distinguish, rendering both as l. A special r may underlie the sign rá(DU) as over against ra. It occurs in sù-DU varying with sù-ud-ra in later writings.

2. *The Timaeus*, A. E. Taylor's translation. Quoted from A. N. Whitehead, *Adventures of Ideas*, Mentor edition (New York, 1955), p. 110.

3. The contemporary form of the name would seem to have been more like Naram-Suen. For the reading of the divine name written ᵈEN:ZU as ᵈSuen in older Akkadian contexts note the writings *Sú-en* and *Sú-in* common in Old Assyrian and

sú-e-ni-in = *sū'ēnēn* in the Irishum inscription published by Balkan and Landsberger, *Belleten* 14 (1950) 248. Note also the early writings *sú-en* in *Sú-en-šàr YOS* IX no. 1. 1 and *Ṣi-lúm-*ᵈ*Sú-en UET* I no. 11. 2. It is possible, therefore, that in Akkadian context the writing ᵈEN:ZU was viewed as an anagram comparable to e.g., GAL:LÚ for lu.gal, ZU:AB for ab.zu and was read ᵈ*Sú.en.*

In Sumerian context, however, ᵈEN:ZU seems to have been read as written and to have served as an elliptic writing for fuller Enzun (pronnunced Ensun). For evidence of final -n see e.g., bala-bala-e ᵈEN:ZU-na-kam *SRT* no. 9. 82, also *PBSA* XL pl. 11. 45 and elsewhere. This -n—if we are not simply dealing with a nasalized vowel: -zū—seems to have had firm juncture with the preceding vowel so that if a further vowel was added the syllable division would tend to fall after the -n (as e.g., in the writing ᵈEN:ZU-e = ᵈEnzun-e, Gudea Cyl. B xiii. 5, *SRT* 9. 59, *TRS* 12. 44) less often in the consonant (as e.g., in *SRT* 9. 82 quoted above).

As evidence for the reading Enzu(n) may be listed the glosses in *CT* XXIX 46 26–28

na-an-na	ᵈŠEŠ + KI	ᵈ[Sin]
en-zu	ᵈEN-[ZU]	[,,]
si-in	ᵈ[EŠ]	[,,]

and the passage Diri III 48, [tu-un]-gal : GIŠ-ᵈEN-ZU : MIN(= giš)-*e-zi-na-ku* : *tùn-gal-lum*, where the sign-name of ᵈEN:ZU is given as *ezin.*

As to the relation between Sumerian Enzun or Ensun and Akkadian *Suen*, later. *Sín*, it may be that both derive from an original en Suen "Lord Suen" at a time when the initial en was still felt as a title rather than as an integral part of the name.

4. In our conception of history and its essential nature we follow the acute analysis given by Michael Oakeshott, *Experience and its Modes* (Cambridge, 1933), pp. 86–156. For a brief resumé see also R. Collingwood, *The Idea of History* (Oxford, 1946), pp. 151–159 (Where Collingwood goes beyond Oakeshott, assuming a "living past," we are unable to follow). According to Oakeshott "the historical past is a world of ideas" (p. 110), an "organization of the totality of experience *sub specie praeteritorum*" (p. 111). By "a world" Oakeshott understands "a complex integrated whole or system" (p. 28), by "ideas" he has in mind that "an event independent of experience, 'objective' in the sense of being untouched by thought or judgment would be an unknowable" (p. 93), so that "in so far as history is a world of facts (which will scarcely be denied), it is a world of ideas" (p. 93). It follows that the historical past is in reality a present: "The past in history is, then, always an inference; it is the product of judgment and consequently belongs to the historian's present world of experience. All he has is his present world of ideas, and the historical past is a constituent of that world or nothing at all" (p. 108 f.). The truth of this "world" that is the historical past depends on "the degree of its coherence" (p. 93) and "the relation *between* events is always other events and it is established in history by a full relation *of* the events" (p. 143). The purpose of history, finally, is clarification: "in history what is attempted is to give a rational account of the world" (p. 125).

Elaborating briefly on Oakeshott's views here summarized we may perhaps state that history is the historian's evidence weighed and organized in his mind on the basis of his own total experience, it is "what the evidence obliges us to believe" (ibid., p. 107). As such it must always remain closely conditioned by the historian's present, for his judgment and experience is shaped and conditioned by the culture in which he himself stands. He may—indeed must—use this judgment immediately in determining what is believable and what is important in his sources as far as events are concerned. He may use it immediately only in so far as he seeks to understand ancient meaning and motivation; for these are given with, and determined by, a system of their own, the ancient culture, which the historian must first clarify, then interpret, in modern terms. "The *differentia* of the historical past lie in its very disparity from what is contemporary, the historian does not set out to discover a past where the same beliefs, the same actions, the same intentions obtain as those which occupy his own world" (Ibid., p. 106). If he disregards this either by interpreting without allowing for cultural refraction or by not interpreting, merely presenting monolithic blocs of ancient sources, the "world of ideas" he constructs will prove false by its lack of all real coherence.

On the insufficiency of such "history" in the Mesopotamian field see the timely remarks by R. F. Kraus in his "Nippur and Isin . . .", *JCS* 3 (1951), 1.

5. Oakeshott, *Experience*, p. 107.

6. "Reasonable" as here used has reference primarily to practical judgment based on everyday experience. For purposes of the subject of the present inquiry, however, judgment of what may and may not be reasonable should preferably be based on a modicum of knowledge of human political forms in primitive as well as more complex societies over and beyond those of the modern Western states of everyday experience.

7. The description given in this paragraph embodies results of an archaeological survey of southern Mesopotamia undertaken by Mr. Faud Safar, Mr. Vaughn Crawford, and the writer in 1954. The results of this survey, which was sponsored jointly by the Baghdad Schools of the American Schools of Oriental Research and the Iraq Department of Antiquities, are at present being prepared for publication. They include the identification of Zabalam with Bseikh, of Bad-Tibira with Tel Medina, and of Bagara with remains in the northern parts of Al Hibba. The course of the canals here called the Iturungal and the Sirara was determined from the distribution of ancient mounds along their banks. The identifications proposed will be argued in detail in the coming publication.

8. Deep trenching at Tel Asmar, Kish (at Hursagkalamma), Fara, and at Jemdet Nasr, reached virgin soil with the later part of the Protoliterate period (Jemdet Nasr period). See Frankfort, *OIC* 20 Chronological Table (at end) and *SAOC* No. 4, p. 50 and Table I. Similar results were reached for Nippur in recent trenches within the sacred area of the town. For a detailed discussion of these data and their interpretation see a forthcoming study of the Protoliterate period by P. Delougaz.

9. The concept of gradual destruction of the arable soil in the course of continuous cultivation as a major factor in Mesopotamian history was developed in discussions with the members of the survey mentioned in note 7, especially Faud Safar. The emphasis on unavoidable gradual salting of the soil as the main cause owes much to

talks with Professor Russel of the Agricultural College in Baghdad, who is engaged in a special study of this problem. The total concept is based on our findings in the regions surveyed that ancient, Hellenistic, Islamic and modern occupation areas hardly every significantly overlap, suggesting that old cultivated areas could not be reclaimed.

10. See "Primitive Democracy in Ancient Mesopotamia," *JNES* 2 (1943) 159–172 [see below, chap. ix]. To avoid as far as possible misunderstandings of the term we repeat our definition (Ibid., p. 159): "We shall use 'democracy' in its classical rather than in its modern sense as denoting a form of government in which internal sovereignty resides in a large proportion of the governed, namely in all free, adult, male citizens without distinction of fortune or class. That sovereignty resides in these citizens implies that major decisions—such as the decision to undertake a war— are made with their consent, that these citizens constitute the supreme judicial authority in the state, and also that rulers and magistrates obtain their positions with and ultimately derive their power from that same consent. By 'Primitive democracy,' furthermore, we understand forms of government which, though they may be considered as falling within the definition of democracy just given, differ from the classical democracies by their more primitive character: the various functions of government are as yet little specialized, the power structure is loose, and the machinery for social co-ordination by means of power is as yet imperfectly developed. We should perhaps add that the contrast with which we are primarily concerned is the one between 'democracy' as defined above, on the one hand, and 'autocracy,' used as a general term for forms which tend to concentrate the major political powers in the hands of a single individual, on the other. 'Oligarchy', which so subtly merges into democracy and which so often functions in forms similar to it, can hardly, at the present stage of our knowledge of ancient Mesopotamia, be profitably distinguished." For examples of the types of government we have in mind as comparable see especially the section "Conclusions" (Ibid., p. 172) and the literature there quoted. For comparison with the much more developed classical democracy see e.g., J. A. O. Larsen, "Cleisthenes and the Development of the Theory of Democracy at Athens" in *Essays in Political Theory Presented to George H. Sabine* (1948), pp. 1–16; V. Ehrenberg, "Origins of Democracy," *Historia* I (1950), 515–548; J. A. O. Larsen, "The Judgment of Antiquity on Democracy," *Classical Philology* 49 (1954) 1–14.

11. Falkenstein, *Cahiers d'Histoire Mondiale* I, 4 (Paris, 1954), p. 801, argues that the assembly had advisory powers only: "Par contre je crois qu'il ne faut pas exagérer l'importance de l'Assemblée' des citoyens libres ('unken,' appelée plus tard 'pu-úh-rum,' d'un terme emprunté à l'akkadien): il s'agissait là d'une institution qui n'était guère un organe de contrôle et encore moins de commandement, mais qui exerçait probablement des fonctions consultatives." Such a position seems to us difficult to maintain in view of the clear evidence that the assembly had and exercised the power to elect the king (see e.g., Enuma elish, the election of Marduk, and for historical periods *RA* 16 [1919] 151 f., cf. Poebel, *AS* XIV 23–42) as well as that of deposing a king (see e.g., *STVC* 25 obv. 14 rev. 23 and the Lament for Ur, *AS* XII lines 152–164, both passages discussed in *JNES* 2 171 f. [see below, chap. ix], as also

the assembly instituting the rebellion against Naram-Sîn, *RA* 16 [1919] 157 ff. quoted above. Cf. also Gilgamesh and Agga, see below note 55).

Falkenstein adduces two specific arguments. First that "Dans cette 'Assemblée des anciens de la ville' les choses devaient se passer à peu près comme dans le conseil des dieux dont la description s'inspirait certainement du modèle terrestre: dès que des dieux suprêmes, maîtres du destin, avaient prononcé leur sentence, toutes les autres divinités présentes répondait aussitôt: 'Ainsi soit-il.'" This is quite correct and corresponds to what we know of the workings of similar primitive assemblies elsewhere. The parallels show, however, that one may not—as Falkenstein appears to do—deduce from the smooth workings of an assembly a onesided submission by the members to one or two supreme wills; rather, comparison with similar assemblies elsewhere (see e.g., Georg Jacob, *Altarabisches Beduinenleben* (Berlin, 1897), p. 223 on the leader of a Beduin camp: „Der saijid darf Niemanden im Stamme Befehle erteilen. . . . . . Im Namen des Stammes wird er nur dann handeln, wenn er sich mit demselben derselben Ansicht weiss und in wichtigen Angelegenheiten stets die Stammesversammlung befragen, in der er teils durch Autorität, teils durch Rede-gewandheit die Differenzen beilegt" See also K. N. Llewellyn and E. A. Hoebel, *The Cheyenne Way* (Norman, 1941), p. 98) indicates that a mutual adjustment is involved. A leader—if he is not to loose his leadership—must take great pains to propose only what will meet with general approval; his task is to find and urge consensus. Successful leadership, such as that furnished in the divine assembly by An and Enlil, consists precisely in reflecting and crystallizing the public will. The psycho-logical pressure on the leader to be representative is *the* basic technique through which a primitive assembly exercises effective control.

Falkenstein's second point, "Que dans le poème épique de la lutte de Gilgameš contre Agga de Kiš 'l'assemblée des anciens de la ville' oppose à l'appel funeste de Gilgameš au combat, une proposition de se soumettre, ne contredit guère notre opinion. Car, Gilgameš ne s'en tient nullement à l'avis du conseil: il fait aussitôt appel à la jeunesse de la ville et obtient son appui" overlooks the formal character of the proceedings; we are dealing with a plebiscite. The important point is not that Gilgamesh can disregard the opinion of the assembly of the elders, but that he can do so only with the formal consent of the citizens generally, especially those capable of bearing arms, the guruš—therefore the appeal from the assembly of the elders to the assembly of the guruš. Without specific authorization from a popular assembly the king is powerless to act, he is as yet a leader only, not a power.

An unambiguous instance of a ruler frustrated in his designs by opposition from his assembly furnishes the—as yet largely unpublished—story of Enmerkar and En sukeshdanna of Aratta. After the latter has sent messengers to Enmerkar demanding his submission and Enmerkar has emphatically refused, Ensukeshdanna is censured for his action in the assembly of Aratta:

ukkin gar-ra si-sá na-mu-na-ni-ib-gi₄-gi₄
za-e-me-en ⟨en⟩ Unu^ki-ga-šè dub-sag-ta
níg-gal-gal En-me-er-kár-ra kin-gi₄-a-aš ba-e-gi₄
En-me-er-kár la[-ba-an]-dù-e za-e-me-en ba-e-dù-e
gib-gi₄-ba šà-zu [níg-na]-me na-an-tum₄ en-na ba-e-zu-zu

"After an assembly had been established it straightforwardly answered him:
'You yourself first sent to the lord of Uruk
arrogant message (lit, 'grandiose things as message'), to Enmerkar.
It is not Enmerkar's doing, it is your own doing,
your wicked heart prompted everything as far as can be known.'"

Thus denied support Ensukeshdanna is reduced to seeking his goal by magical means suggested by a *mašmaššu* priest at his court, and when that fails he himself recognizes Enmerkar's superiority. (With the 3n. locative element -e- in ba-e-dù-e and ba-e-zu-zu we hope to deal elsewhere, cf. note 49).

12. The term "vote" is here used in the sense of "A formal expression, an indication by some approved method, of one's opinion or choice on a matter under discussion; an intimation that one approves or disapproves, accepts or rejects, a proposal, motion, candidate for office, or the like" *NED* 19 p. 313. "Vote" Sense 5. It is to be noted that the technique of reaching decisions by count of votes was not in use in Mesopotamia (on the origins of this important technique see J. A. O. Larsen, "The Origin and Significance of the Counting of Votes" *Classical Philology* 44 (1949) 164–181).

13. nam—tar, Akkadian *šîmtam šâmu* "to decree," "to command with absolute authority and effectivity" is used of the sentence imposed by a judge (e.g., of the sentences imposed by Ninurta on the stones in Lugal-e) or by an assembly (e.g., the sentence imposed on Enlil by the divine assembly in Nippur when he had raped Ninlil in the myth of Enlil and Ninlil). It may be used not only of specific orders by such authoritative persons or bodies, of "sentences," but also of general orders by them and denotes then approximately "law." In Cones B + C of Urukagenak practices constituting traditional "common law" in Lagash, having existed from the beginning (u₄-ul-ì-a-ta numun-è-a-ta "Since the bud was put forth. since the seeedcorn sprouted forth" iii. 3–4. For ul "bud" cf. *CT* XV 23. 1 ul-e pa-pa-al-ta ír àm-da-n[i-šeg-šeg] "The bud wept from the young shoot") and defined as pi-lug-da "mores," "customary law" (pi-lug-da u₄-bi-ta e-me-am₅ "was the former common law/mores" vii. 9–11. u₄-bi-ta "former," a postpositional phrase used as a noun in the genitive, seems to denote "of from that day [backwards in time]") are called nam-tar-ra u₄-bi-ta "former decrees" later on in col. vii. 20–21: u₄ ᵈNin-ĝír-su ur-saĝ ᵈEn-líl-lá-ke₄ Uru-ka-ge-na-ra nam-lugal Lagašaᵏⁱ e-na-summa-a šà lú 36,000-ta šu-ni e-ma-ta-dab₅-ba-a nam-tar-ra u₄-bi-ta e-šè-ĝar "when Ningursuk, the warrior of Enlil, had given unto Urukagenak the kingship of Lagash and his hand had picked him out of 36,000 persons he set aside the former laws (decrees)" vii. 12–22. For the meaning "set aside" of e-šè-ĝar cf. ibid. xii 5–14: šà mu-ba-ka íd-dumu-Ĝír-suᵏⁱ-ì-tuku-a ᵈNin-ĝir-su-ra al mu-na-dù mu-u₄-bi-ta e-šè-ĝar ᵈNin-ĝír-su Nibruᵏⁱ-ta nir-ĝál Uru-ka-ge-na-ke₄ mu mu-na-sa₄ "Within that year he dredged for Ningirsuk the canal Id-dumu-Girsu(k)-itukua, its former name he set aside, Ningirsu(k)-Nibruta-nirgal Urukagenak named it for him."

The absolute authority and effectivity involved in nam-tar is clearly expressed in Enuma elish where the gods, having conferred it upon Marduk, test it by asking him to command that a cloth be and not be and rejoice when his command proves effective (cf. *JNES* 2 169 f. [see below, chap. ix]). Since in the assembly nam-tar cannot have reference to the deliberations, which were not binding, and since the power belongs to a small group within the assembly only, we must assume that it has reference to the formulating and official announcement of the assembly's decisions which would give them the force of law. Such final formulation and announcement would naturally be the task of a smaller specially qualified group, a "committee" so to speak.

Another term, besides nam-tar, for the formulated and announced decision of an assembly was inim, "verdict," well-known from the so-called inim-hymns, which are often fond of spelling it out as the inim of all the various individual divine members of the assembly whose assenting votes it represents. Cf. also *PBS* V no. 1 iv 9–10 di-til-la inim pu-úh-ru-[um dingir-re-ne-ka] du₁₁-du₁₁-ga An ᵈEn[-líl-lá-ta] "According to the decision, the verdict of the assembly of the gods, and the (executive) command of An and Enlil," referring to the decision to send the Deluge.

14. See JNES 2 168, note 50 [see below, chap. ix]. The dingir-gal-gal-e-ne of the divine assembly correspond probably to the *rabiūtu* "seniors" of the Old Assyrian assembly, where they contrast with the *ṣehrūtu* "the juniors" (Ibid., end) and may also correspond roughly to the group known as ab-ba "elders" (ibid., p. 166, note 44), which seems to have handled the normal run of affairs when the calling of a larger general assembly was not deemed necessary. Besides the translation "seniors" for gal here suggested a connotation "head of a large household" might also be considered.

15. See *JNES* 2 171, note 68 [see below, chap. ix].

16. Cf. e.g., the trial of Kingu in Enuma elish and that of Enlil in the myth of Enlil and Ninlil. Further materials *JNES* 2 169 [see below, chap. ix].

17. Cf. the conferring of the "lordship" on Marduk in a divine assembly after he has shown his organizing abilities. Enuma elish VI 99 ff. (cf. *JNES* 12 181 [see above, chap. v]) and the eclipse myth, *CT* XVI pl. 19 f. 25–28, where the arrogants and licentious behavior of the king's messengers is checked by the appointment of three children of Enlil, Nanna, Utu, and Inanna, to the "lordship" (nam-en-na kiši an-na-ke₄:*be-lu-ut kiš-šat šame-e*) that they may exercise police functions. For this passage see also note 51 below.

18. For the character of the office of the en see *JNES* 12 180–182 [see above, chap. v].

19. Cf. e.g., Marduk in Enuma elish, approached through his father, Ea, and without a house of his own. Also Ninurta in the Zu myth *RA* 35 14 ff. is approached through his mother, Nanshe, after she has been asked to do so by the asembly and has agreed. Note likewise Sharur's description of the Asakku in Lugal-e I 33 lugal-mu lú uru-a-ni-šè gur-ra ama-a-ni-šè ag-a-ab:*be-lum ša ana a-li-šú ta-a-a-ra ana um-mi-šú ep-pe-šu*: "O my master, one who is merciful toward his city, diligent toward his mother" i.e., who through his industriousness is a good support for his mother in the running of her estate, a phrase suggestive of a son living at home. Ninurta, himself, corresponding to the slightly more advanced stage of kingship represented in Lugal-e (see below sect. IV) already has his own house É-šu-me-ša₄. On the reading cf. the variants ki-šu-me-DU na-ám-lú-lu₇ (GIŠGAL)-mu *PBS* X. 2 no. 15 i. 12, ki-šu-me-eš na-ám-lu-lu-m[u] *STVC* 30 ii. 5, and é-zi ki-šu-p[eš₅](ŠU +

[KAD]) na-ám-mu-lu-a-mu:*bîtu ki-i-ni ma-ha-zi šá ni-ši-ia* SBH 31. 9. The name É-šu-me-ša$_4$ would thus appear to mean "House (in which) hand is spread (upon abundance)" cf. Gudea, Cyl. A xi. 9 un-e hé-ğál-la šu hé-a-da-peš-e "the Nation will spread the hand upon abundance under you," or possibly "House (in which) hand is (put) repeatedly (upon abundance)." Whether also Akkadian *mahāzu* means "place of receiving (rations)" and is to be derived from *ahāzu* we leave undecided.

With the division of function between an administrator (en:*bēlu*) and a young war leader (lugal:*šarru*) should be compared the similar division among the Arab bedouins between the sheikh, older sayyid, and the 'aqîd cf. Georg Jacob, *Altarabisches Beduinenleben* (Berlin, 1897), pp. 224 f. "Kehren wir zu den rein-arabischen Verhältnissen zurück so ist vor allem zu beachten, dass den Stamm selten ein saijid ins Feld führte s. Nallino a. a. O. s. 619, dem wir den Nachweis verdanken, dass im Kriegsfalle ein raîs order qâid, dem heutigen 'aqîd entsprechend als Feldherr fungiert." The 'aqîd was chosen by the tribal assembly from certain families which had the right to provide such a war leader.

20. Note that the assembly called to elect Marduk "king," i.e., "war leader" in Enuma elish is too local to confer on him the powers of authoritative decree (*šîmtam šâmu*) which he has demanded, and that a second assembly of larger scope therefore has to be called.

21. On bala see *JNES* 2 170, note 61 [see below, chap. ix].

22. On the hierarchy of power structures in a society see generally Timasheff, *An Introduction to the Sociology of Law* (Cambridge, 1939), pp. 231 f.

23. Only a few of the many references to the appointment of the king can be mentioned here. In the Shulgir hymn *TRS* II no. 86 (dupl. *BE* XXXI 24) we are told that Shulgir was received in audience by Nanna (lit. "went in to him") and discussed with him the restoration of the cult (me-e šu-bi gi$_4$-gi$_4$[húl]-la-da na-du$_{11}$-du$_{11}$ "to restore the cult he (Shulgir or Nanna?) joyfully promised)." Thereupon Nanna journeyed to Nippur and recommended Shulgir to Enlil. His proposal having been favorably received he then returned to Ur to inform Shulgir that Enlil had given him complete power in the country. An even clearer picture is given by the Ur-Ninurtak hymn *CT* XXXVI 28–30 treated by Falkenstein in ZA, 49, 106–113. Inannak favors Ur-Ninurtak for the kingship, takes him by the hand and leads him into Ekur, where the gods are in council. She proposes his name to An and Enlil in a nominating speech, which sets forth his various qualifications. An and Enlil, in separate speeches, then give their verdict appointing Ur-Ninurtak king, and all of the assembled gods confirm it by their assenting votes of heam "let it be!" Cf. also the Lipit-Eshtar hymn *SK* 199, where An himself chooses Lipit-Eshtar, then appoints him king in the assembly of the gods. His speech of appointment indicates that the other major gods join him in the appointment and add their special gifts of authority.

24. *JNES* 2 171 f. [see below, chap. ix].

25. Cf. *JAOS* 59 (1939) 487, note 11 [see below, chap. xi].

26. Vase inscr. of Lugalzagesi ii 21–22.

27. See above note 8.

28. See below sect. V. 1.

29. Falkenstein, *Archaische Texte aus Uruk*, sign no. 153. The meaning of the sign, "assembly," is clear from its occurrence in the school text no. 340 obv. ii in the combination gal.ukkin "usher(?) of the assembly" (Akkadian *mu'irrum*) among other terms for officials, and from the fact that the text no. 340 lies in an unbroken tradition which can be followed over *UET* II no. 14 down to unambiguous Fara texts, Deimel, *SF* nos 33, 75, and 76. See Falkenstein, *Archaische Texte*, pp. 44 f.

30. Falkenstein, *Archaische Texte*, sign no. 383.

31. Burrows, *Archaic Texts*, *UET* II sign no. 236, ref. for lú-gal and p. 16 (24).

32. Ibid., p. 14 L ii, ref. for é-gal. It has been suggested, Falkenstein, *Cahiers d'Histoire Mondiale* I. 4 p. 798, that the ruler originally lived in the temple as priest of the city-god or goddess and that the establishment of a separate palace, the é-gal, was part of a move on the part of the ruler to free himself from the temple. We are inclined to see the development as rather more complex and to stress the original differences between the "lord," en, and the "king," lugal, as determinants.

In the case of the en the political side of the office is clearly secondary to the cult function. The en's basic responsibility is toward fertility and abundance, achieved through the rite of the "sacred marriage" in which the en participated as bride or bridegroom of a deity. In cities where the chief deity was a goddess, as in Uruk and Aratta, the en was male (Akkadian *ēnum*) and attained, because of the economic importance of his office, to a position of major political importance as "ruler." In cities where the chief deity was male, as in Ur, the en was a woman (Akkadian *ēnum* or *ēntum*) and therefore, while important religiously, did not attain a ruler's position. Whether male and politically important as ruler, or female and only cultically important, the en lived in a building of sacred character, the *Giparu*. Where the en was male and a ruler that building in time took on the features of an administrative center, a palace (see the epics of "Enmerkar and the Lord of Aratta" and of "Enmerkar and Ensukeshdanna"). Where the en was female this did not happen (Ur).

The "king," lugal, in contrast to the en was from the beginning a purely secular political figure, a "war leader." His residence, the é-gal, "great house" has no ties with the temple but is merely his own large private manor which, because of his office, comes to take on the public aspects of a "palace."

The original nature of the *Giparu* in which the en resided is indicated by the interesting text *TRS* 60 rev. 2–3 ᵍⁱˢig naₐ-za-gìn-na G̃i₆-parₓ (KISAL)-ra gub-ba en gaba na-mu-ri, ᵍⁱˢig-sal é-uš-gíd-da É-an-na-ka gub-ba ᵈDumu-zi gaba na-mu-ri "At the lapis-lazuli door which stands in the *Giparu* she (Inannak) met the en, at the narrow(?) door of the storehouse which stands in Eannak she met Dumuzid." Here, as will be seen, the *Giparu*, mentioned by name in line 2, is referred to as "the storehouse" (Cf. Diri V 283–284 [a-ra-a]h:É-UŠ-GÍD-DA:*a-ra-ah-hu*, *na-áš-pa-ku*; the text seems to use the older term é-uš-gíd-da rather than the later arah, which had replaced it when Diri was composed) in the parallel line 3.

The connection between the en and the *Giparu* storehouse are made clear by the text as a whole, which, dealing with the "sacred marriage" shows it to be a rite celebrating the bringing in of the harvest. It describes first how Inannak, the bride, is decked out for her wedding with freshly harvested date clusters, which represent her jewelry and personal adornments. She then goes to receive her bridegroom, the en, Dumuzid, at the door of the *Giparu*—this opening of the door for the bridegroom by the bride was the main symbolic act of the Sumerian wedding, see *BASOR* 102 (1946) 15—and has him led into the *Giparu*, where the bed for the sacred marriage is set up.

As for the participants in the rite the bridegroom, who is led into the storehouse, Dumuzid or Amaushumgalannak, is easily seen to be the date harvest. His name ama-ušum-gal-an-ak means "the one great source (lit. "mother") of the date clusters (an:*sissinnu*)," which can only refer to the single huge bud of the date palm, the so-called "date cabbage" or "heart" of the date palm, which is its point of growth and fertility. This is confirmed by *PBS* X. 4 12 obv. i 5, where the "heart of the date palm" is identified as Dumuzid (^{ɡⁱˢ}šà-ɡišimmar: ^{d}*Dumu-zi*). He is thus a natural representative of the productivity of the date palm and so of its produce. As to his title, en, note that the Sumerian word for "crops," buru$_x$ (*MSL* II 417), earlier ebur(u) (shown by the Akkadian loan *ebūrum*), apparently goes back to *en-bur(u) < *en-ɡur(u) "carrier (of) the en" (shown by the writing which is en.ɡur(u)$_6$). On the alternation ɡ/b cf. the values ɡá, mà, and ba$_4$ of the sign MÁ.

As for the bride, Inannak, her name, developed from Nin-an-ak (Cf. *MDP* XVIII 57 in which Ur-^{d}INANNA is spelled out as ur-ni-in-[na]-na and the variant forms Nin-Šušinak/In-Šušanak, Nin-urta/Inušt), would appear to have meant originally "The lady of the date clusters" (an:*sissinnu*, later reinterpreted as an:*šamû*). The date clusters—her bridal ornaments in *TRS* 70—are, of course, if to be seen as ornaments, not properly the ornaments of a person but properly those of a storehouse for dates. The basic identity of Inannak with the storehouse thus suggested is further indicated by early representations of the "meeting at the gate" of the "sacred marriage" rite (see Mrs. van Buren, "The Ear of Corn," *Orientalia* 12 [1935] 327–335), where the motif of a man carrying an ear of grain (and therefore representing the harvest) and walking toward a woman waiting at a gate, the storehouse, allows of variants in which the woman and the gate are replaced by the symbol for the gate alone, suggesting that woman and gate were identical. This identity is confirmed by the fact that in the script the gate symbol in question serves as the sign for Inannak.

Summing up we may thus say that—at least in Uruk—the en lives in the storehouse, the *Giparu*, because the crops are in the storehouse and the en is the human embodiment of the generative power, Dumuzid or Amaushumgalannak, which produces and informs them.

33. Burrows, *Archaic Texts*, no. 371.

34. Ibid., no. 366 i.

35. Legrain, *Archaic Seal-Impressions*, *UE* III, pl. 21–24 and, with occasional reservations, Legrain's comments in the catalogue to nos. 400 ff. As examples the group Keš, Adaba, Urí(m) on nos. 400–401 and Nibru (upper register), Adaba, Urí(m), X, Keš(?), and Zarar(im) on no. 429 may serve.

Collective seals such as those to which the fragments of impressions published by Legrain attest are most easily understood as used for sealing deliveries from a common fund of goods, created for a common purpose by individual contributions from the cities collectively sealing, i.e., league funds. Whether such collective seals would normally have all the names of the members of the league, or only the names of a group contributing e.g., during a certain period of the year, or to a specific point, is not clear from the evidence.

On the later bala deliveries from various cities to the king's sacrifices to Enlil and other gods in the Ur III period see *AJA* 57 (1953) 126 b. Note especially the schedule of such deliveries during the year Radau, *Early History of Babylonia*, p. 299 (E. A. Hoffman Collection, No. 134).

36. The question which common danger may have been great, clear, and present enough to force all of Sumer to unite is a legitimate one, but any attempt to answer it must remain strictly conjectural. As one possible conjecture we would suggest pressure from Semitic nomads, the Akkadians. If, as the traditional tie of the "king-ship" over Sumer with Ur seems to suggest, the danger point was in the South, we may assume that the formation of the Kengir League succeeded in withstanding and in diverting the pressure to the less well defended North, Uri. The cities of the North were, to judge by archaeological evidence (see above note 8), founded or grew to city size in late Protoliterate times (Jemdet Nasr period). To judge by city names, names of chief temples, and names of chief deities, they were, furthermore, Sumerian. Cf. e.g., Èš-nun-ak ("The manor of the prince") with chief temple É-sikil ("The pure house") and chief god Nin-azu ("The lord leach"), and Hursağ-kalammak ("The mountain of the nation") with chief goddess (N)in-an-ak ("The lady of the date clusters," see above note 32) etc. Evidence of Akkadian occupation occurs in the Diyala region with Early Dynastic II (see *OIP* LVIII p. 291, nos 4, 6, 7, and 10) and a dating of their first appearance in force to the preceding period of Early Dynastic I—the period we have suggested for the Kengir League—is thus not implausible.

37. On the nature of power and on the means of defending it (power defense) see generally N. S. Timasheff, *An Introduction to the Sociology of Law* (Cambridge, 1939), Part II, pp. 171–242.

38. Cf. Lugal-e Tablet I 12 ^{d}Nin-[urta] lugal dumu ^{d}En-líl-lá ní-te-na diri-ga ^{d}MIN *šar-ru ma-ru šá* ^{d}*En-líl ina ra-ma-ni-šú ú-šá-ti-ru-šú* "Ninurta, the king, the son, whom Enlil made greater than (he) himself (is)," and ibid., 16 ^{d}Nin-urta lugal dumu-a-ni sù-ud-bi-šè KA-šu-ğál:^{d}MIN *šar-ru ma-ru šá a-bu-šú ana ru-qé-e-tim ap-pa ú-šal-bi-nu-šú*, "Ninurta, the king, the son, whom his father caused to be saluted far (and wide)." For the meaning of KA-šu—ğál:*labān appi* as denoting a gesture of greeting consisting in holding the hand before the mouth, the fingers touching the nose, see *OIP* XXIV p. 38, note 46. The gloss zi-par to KA in KA^{zi}-p^{ar} šu-ğál:ba-la-su, *TCL* VI no. 35, 4, 21, suggests that KA in this phrase has the reading zipar, a reading which it may also have had in UD-KA-BAR, zabar, "bronze." As shown by the Akkadian *siparrum*, Sumerian zabar has developed by vowel assimilation from an older form zibar, and while the precise role of UD in UD-KA-BAR is not yet clear the following KA and BAR are likely to represent zipar and a phonetic complement -bar, respectively.

39. Lugal-e I 17–19 ^{giš}gu-za bará-mah tuš-a-na ní-gal ğùr-ru-na:*ina ku-us-si-e pa-rim*(?)*-ma-hi ina a-šá-bi-šú nam-ri-ir-ri ina na-še-e-šú*, ezen ğar-ra-na húl-la-na dağal-a-bi tuš-a-na:*ina i-sin-ni šak-nu-uš ha-diš* (var. + *rap-šiš*) *ina a-šá-bi-šú*, An ^{d}En-líl-da zag-di-a-na kurun-nam du$_{10}$-ga-e-da-na:*it-ti* ^{d}*A-nim u* ^{d}*En-líl ina šit-nu-*

ni-šú ku-ru-un-na šu-ṭub-bi-šú, "As he sits on the throne (on) the exalted throne dias, as he is full of awesome splendor, as he sits broad and happy at the feast he is giving, as he vies with An and Enlil, as he mixes the wine."

40. Lugal-e I 20–21 ᵈBa-ba₆ a-ra-zu lugal-la-ke₄ ù-gul g̃á-g̃á-e-da-na:ᵈMIN *tas-li-ta ana šar-ri ina ut-nin-ni-šú,* ᵈNin-urta en dumu ᵈEn-líl-lá-ke₄ nam-tar-ra-e-da-na:ᵈMIN *be-lum mar* ᵈMIN *šim-ta ina šá-a[-mi-šu],* "As Baba is about to urge (upon him) the petitions to the king, as Ninurta, the lord, the son of Enlil, is about to pronounce sentence."

41. The section Lugal-e I 22–45 contains a report to Ninurta by his weapon Sharur about developments in the mountains, which precipitates the following events. It is rather difficult because of the many vocatives "O Ninurta!" and "O my master" with which Sharur interlards his narrative. As far as can be seen Sharur reports that a certain mighty being, the Asakku, was born by the Earth after it had been impregnated by the Sky (lugal-mu An-na Ki sig₇-ga g̃iš(!) im-ma-ab[-du₁₀]: *be-lum* ᵈ*A-nu er-ṣe-ta ba-ni-tum ir-he-e-ma,* ᵈNin-urta ur-sag̃ ní nu-zu Á-sàg mu-un-ši-in-tu-ud:"*ana*" ᵈMIN *qar-ra-du la a-di-ri A-sak-ku ú-tal-lid-su* I 26–27. "O my master! An impregnated the fair Earth and, O Ninurta!, a fearless warrior, the Asakku, she bore unto him." Already the Akkadian translator seems here to have missed the vocative and to have construed: "one who is unafraid of the warrior Ninurta"). After a detailed description of the Asakku's qualities Sharur then reports that the Asakku has had the interior parts in the mountains climbed and has sown them. In consequence the plants have unanimously chosen it king and the various stones—both plants and stones are closely associated with its mother, the Earth—are its warriors, who issue forth from the kingdom of the plants to raid the cities for them. It competes directly with Ninurta by "judging" in the country and this is the point to which Sharur has been leading up: ᵈNin-urta en za-gim Kalam-ma di-bi ši-in-tar-re:ᵈ*Nin-urta bêlu ki-ma ka-ta di-in ma-a-ti i-da-[an],* Á-sàg me-lám-ma-bi a-ba šu-mi-ni-ib-tu-tu:*A-sak-ku me-lam-mi-šu ma-an-nu i-mah-har-šu* sag̃ ki-bi-gal-gal-la-bi-šè a-ba ib-ta-an-g̃á-g̃á:*a-na šak-ki-šu rabûti man-nu -i'a-[ar-ru]* I 42–44, "O lord Ninurta! On its own (ši-) it judges as you the cases of the nation, who can stay the Asakku's awesome splendor, who can go against all its great ordinances(?)"

42. See the section Lugal-e Xff., the sentences pronounced upon the stones.

43. See e.g., Enmerkar's threat against Aratta, Kramer, *Enmerkar and the Lord of Aratta* 115–120 and 188–193, cf. 488–491: uru-bi KAS-sag̃ᵐᵘˢᵉⁿ-gim g̃iš-bi-ta na-an-na-ra-ab-dal-en, mušen-gim gùd-ús-sa-bi-a nam-bí-ib-dal-le(?)-en, ki-lam-g̃ál-la-gim na-an-si-ig-en, uru-gul-gul-lu-gim sahar nam-bi-ib-ha-za-en, Arattaᵏⁱ á-dam ᵈEn-ki-ke₄ nam ba-an-tar, ki bí-in-gul-la-gim ki(?) nam-ga-bí-ib-gul-e, "Lest I make (the people of) that city fly up for him like a wild dove from its tree, lest I make it fly (around in fear) like a bird in the vicinity of its nest, lest I dispose(?) of it (as slaves) at the current market rate, lest I gather dust in it as (in) an utterly destroyed city, and lest, moreover, I destroy Aratta as (thoroughly as) a settlement which Enkik has cursed and whose site he has destroyed," For KAS-sag̃ᵐᵘˢᵉⁿ: *arašānum* "wild dove" cf. Deimel, *ŠL* 166. 3, Meissner *BAW* II 22. For the custom of gathering dust from a city as symbol of its utter destruction cf. e.g. Sennacherib

KAH II 122. 46–47, *V* R 6. 96–100, *KAH* I 13.ii.10–13. The comparison to a settlement destroyed by Enkik, god of rivers and marshes, refers probably to instances of destruction of arable lands by flooding of low-lying fields which cannot be drained and so salt up. For an example of such destruction at the end of Early Dynastic II the region around Al Hibba may serve. Cf. above note 9.

44. This seems attested already in the myth Lugal-e, where Ninurta after his victory built a dam of stone to redirect the waters which hitherto had flowed into the vanquished "mountains" into the Tigris, so that they would benefit Sumer instead. See Lugal-e VIII.

45. See my note to lines 5–7 and 28 of Gilgamesh and Agga, Kramer, *Gilgamesh and Agga*, *AJA* 53 (1949) 17, and also Kramer *Enmerkar and the Lord of Aratta* 48–56 and 78–87: Aratta^{ki} [Unu^{ki}-šè] gú ĝiš ha-ma-[ĝá-ĝá], nam-lú-u$_x$-lu [Ar]atta^{ki}-[ke$_4$], na$_4$ hur-saĝ-ĝá kur-[bi] ha-ma-ab-e$_{11}$, Iri$_x$-gal ha-ma-dù-e u[nù]-gal ha-ma-ĝá-ĝá, unú-gal unú-[dingir-re-e-ne-ke$_4$ pa]-è [ha]-ma-ab-ag-e, me-mu Kul-aba^{ki}-[a] si ha-ma-ni-ib-sá-e, Ab.zu kur-kù-gim ha-ma-ab-mú-mú, Eridu^{ki} hur-saĝ-gim ha-ma-ab-sikil-e, èš Ab.zu kù ki-in-dar-ra-gim pa-è ha-ma-ab-ag-e, "Let Aratta put (its) neck under the yoke for me in Uruk, let the population of Aratta bring down stones of the mountain from their highland for me, let them build the Irigal for me, set out great feasts for me, great feasts, feasts for the gods, let them produce, let them make my rites in Kullab right for me; let them (as builders) have the Apsu temple grow and grow like a pure mountain, make Eridug clean as a mountain range, have the manor house, the Apsu temple, appear like silver in the lode." For the reading Irigal see Falkenstein, *Topographie von Uruk*.

46. On the institutionalization of power generally see Timasheff, *Sociology of Law*, pp. 229 ff., §4: Tendencies in the Development of Power Structures.

47. As such a provincial palace of the king of Kish we should probably envisage Gilgamesh's palace in Uruk in the story of Gilgamesh and Agga. See the comments below note 55.

48. See the inscription of Anam, *SAK* 222 no. 2b.

49. Gudea, Cyl. B xii. 19–25 uru-dù-a-da ki-tuš ĝar-ra-da, bàd uru-kù-ga en-nu dù-a-da, dingir uku-uš dág-ga-na-bi, Šitá-saĝ-mah-^{ĝiš}erin-babbar-babbar-ra, é-e dub$_x$(URUDU)-ba-da, ^{d}Lugal en-nu uru-kù-ga-kam, en ^{d}Nin-ĝír-su-ra me-ni-da mu-na-da-díb-e, "That the city be built up, that (new) dwellings be established, that the wall of the 'sacred city' be guarded, that its sergeant (of the guards) of the harem, 'Huge-Mace-head(-with-shaft)-of-White-Cedar-Wood,' patrol (lit. 'go around') the temple, he (i.e., Gudea) let Lugal, the guardian of the 'sacred city' in person, go about his duties for the lord Ningirsuk." For an only slightly different rendering see Falkenstein, *Sumerische und akkadische Hymnen und Gebete* (Zürich, 1953), pp. 175 f. The first line may be interpreted to mean that the security of a well-guarded city encourages its growth, uru-kù "the sacred city" seems to be a general term for the quarter of a city in which the main temples clustered. The Uru-kù *kat exochen* of the Lagash region, the surviving "sacred city" of Al Hibba (Lagash?), is hardly intended here, the context suggests the sacred quarter of Girsu (Telloh) in which Eninnu was located. The phrase en-nu dù in the approximate meaning of "to guard" occurs also in the tale of the catastrophe which befell Akkade

under Naram-Sîn *PBS* XIII 43 obv. 22–33 and dupl. *STVC* 94 12–13: ganá(?) gú-sağ(!?) en-nu-un ba-e-dù, har-[ra-an]-na lú-sa-gaz ba-e-tuš, "watch was kept over fields and riverain territories(?), on the highways bandits dwelt" (For the 3n. locative infix -e- we refer to a future treatment cf. note 12). The full form of en-nu is ennuğ, as may be seen from the genitive form en-nu-ğá (*SAK* 202 Šu-Suen Doorsocket B 11) and the explicit writing en-nu-uğ$_x$ (BÀD) in the olives (actually tags for baskets with profane or cult-deliveries) of Urukagenak cf. e.g., Sollberger, *Corpus* Ukg. 28 en-nu-uğ$_x$(BÀD), Amar-ezen, ugula Lú-IGI "(Delivery for) the watch, (to) Amar-ezen (who is under) the lieutenant Lú-IGI." For the translation "harem," i.e., the private quarters of a house in which the family lived cf. the Nergal hymn edited by Zimmern *ZA* 31 112–117, line 27, dakan-na mu-lu dam-tuk-ke₄(!?) tuš nam-bí-ğá-ğá:*ina tak-kan-ni it-ti al-ti a-me-lu la tu-uš-šab*, "Do not (Nergal) take up your residence in the harem with (Sum. *dativus incommodi* -e, Akk. *itti*) the married man (Akk. 'the wife of a man')." The proper name Šitá-sağ-mah-ᵍⁱˢerin-babbar-babbar-ra we analyze as šitá with sağ in partitive apposition, 'mace head,' qualified by the adjective mah, and followed by a genitive, ᵍⁱˢerin-babbar-babbar-a(k), which denotes a close relation short of identity (thus not form and material!). The context indicates the relation between mace head and shaft of the mace. On dub$_x$(URUDU) see Poebel, *AOF* 9 283 ff. We follow his suggestion in note 91 and assume a meaning "to go around," "to distribute around (in) something" for Cyl. A. xxiii. 4, xxix. 1 as well as here.

50. Kramer, *AS* X, pp. 1–10. Professor Kramer informs us that a new text in Jena shows that Inannak first appeals to Utu and is referred by him to Gilgamesh, i.e., the ruler acts here as the executor of a judgment. It is to be noted that the originally rather amorphous role of the ruler with respect to justice: as judge (e.g., Lugal-e, stone section), as "judge" in the sense of adviser in trouble (e.g., Gilgamesh and the trapper in the Gilgamesh Epic. Cf. with this the manner in which Shamash discharges his office as judge in the Etana story: by judging and then advising the plaintiff how to get the accused into his power through a trick), and as executor of judgments (Gilgamesh and the Huluppu Tree), crystallized in time into one of referring cases to extant courts and—presumably—of executing judgments. See Lautner, *Die richterliche Entscheidung* . . . . (*LRSt.* 3) p. 74 ff.

This particular role seems dictated by the difficulties in less developed legal systems of persuading courts to accept cases in which there was no guarantee of execution if the court found for the plaintiff. It is this need for a guarantor of execution which the king meets (note that in the lawsuits against demons before Utu, e.g., *Bît rimki*, 3rd House, *V* R 50 + 51, 81–88, Enkik usually accepts the role of guarantor and sends his messenger to court with the plaintiff to urge that his case be accepted. The execution of Utu's judgment by Enkik takes place in the lustration rite in which the water [Enkik] drives away the demon).

51. The nearest thing to a systematic account of the later Sumerian kingship is the self-praise of Lipit-Eshtar *TRS* II 48 and its duplicates. The organization of the text is made clear by a recurrent refrain referring to Lipit-Eshtar by name which divides the various sections of which the text is composed. The aspects under which the king is viewed in these sections are I. Personal qualities (noble birth, valor, etc.),

II. King of divine grace (political titles and titles expressing his favor with individual gods), III. Producer of wealth, IV. Pious supporter of the cult, V. War leader, VI. Circuit judge, VII. Home life as spouse of Inannak.

The basic division into features going back to the en: responsibility for fertility (III and IV) and those going back to the lugal: war leader and righter of wrongs (V and VI) stands out clearly.

52. Cf., e.g., the tale of Enmerkar and the Lord of Aratta in which Inannak's preference for one of her *ēnus*, Enmerkar, makes her willing to withhold rain from the other, the *ēnu* of Aratta, in order to force him to submit to Enmerkar.

53. From the reply by the assembly of the guruš to Gilgamesh in Gilgamesh and Agga. See Kramer, Gilgamesh and Agga, *AJA* 53 (1949) 8, lines 30–35. The words are clearly a formula for granting rulership.

54. See above section III. 3.

55. The key to a correct interpretation of the story of Gilgamesh and Agga is, we believe, to be found in its concluding section. Gilgamesh and Enkidu make a successful sortie from beleaguered Uruk, penetrate to the boat camp of the attackers and take the leader Agga of Kish captive:šár-ra ba-an-šub-uš šár-ra ba-an-zi-ge-eš, šár-ra sahar-ra ba-an-da-šár-re-eš, kur-kur dù-a-bi ba-an-da-šú, ka ma-da-ka sahar-ra ba-da-an-si, si ⁿⁱˢmá-gur-ra-ke₄ ba-ra-an-kud, Ag-ga lugal Kišiᵏⁱ šà erín-na-ka-ni šaĝaₓ(LÚGANA*tenû*)-a ba-ni-in-ag 94–99, "In the throng he cast them down, in the throng he tore them out, in the throng he was able to roll(?) them in the dust, all of the highlanders he was able to overcome, the steppe dwellers he made bite the dust, away he cut to the prow of the longboat, Agga, king of Kish, at his (place in the) center of the army he took captive." Having captured Agga, Gilgamesh addresses him: Gilgameš en Kul-abaᵏⁱ-ke₄, Ag-ga-a gù mu-na-dé, Ag-ga-a ugula-a-mu Ag-ga-a nu-bànda-mu, Ag-ga šagub-erín-na-a-mu, Ag-ga mušen-kar-ra še bí-ib-si-si, Ag-ga zi ma-an-sum Ag-ga nam-ti ma-an-sum, Ag-ga lú-kar-ra úr-ra bí-in-túm-mu, Unuᵏⁱ ĝiš-kin-ti dingir-re-e-ne-ke₄, bàd-gal bàd An-ni ki-ús-sa, ki-tuš-mah An-ni ĝar-ra-ni, saĝ mu-sum za-e lugal ur-saĝ-bi, saĝ hum-hum nun An-ni ki áĝa, igi ᵈUtu-šè šu-u₄-bi-ta e-ra-an-gi₄, Ag-ga Kišiᵏⁱ-šè šu ba-ni-in-ba, Gilgameš en Kul-abaᵏⁱ-ke₄, za-mí-zu du₁₀-ga-àm (100–115). Gilgamesh, lord of Kullab, said to Agga: "O Agga, O my lieutenant, O Agga, O my colonel, O Agga, my general of the army! Agga, you sated the fleeing bird with grain, Agga, you spared my life, brought me back to health, Agga you took the fugitive in your lap! This (-e) Uruk, the handiwork of the gods, the great wall, the wall founded by An, his (i.e., An's) exalted abode established by An, is entrusted to you, you are its king and defender, the bruiser of heads, the prince beloved by An! Before Utu! I have (now) repaid you the former benefaction! He let Agga go free to Kish. O Gilgamesh, lord of Kullab, your praise is sweet."

As will be seen from this, Gilgamesh owed Agga a debt of gratitude (šu-u₄-bi-ta: *tahanatum*, "previous benefaction," Howardy, *Clavis* 331. 229); he had at some time previous to the events told about in the story been forced to take refuge with Agga in Kish, Agga received him kindly, nursed him back to health and—we may assume —eventually placed him in the trusted position of Agga's vassal ruler in Uruk. This latter assumption may find some support from the difficult term lú-še by which

Agga twice (69 and 91) refers to Gilgamesh. It is undoubtedly to be connected with the element -še occurring in grammatical texts (see Landsberger *MSL* IV, index). The clearest passage, which we owe to Landsberger, is perhaps the unpublished VAT 9528 i. 11'–15'

[lú-š]e	a-nim-ma-mu-ú	"anyone from here"
[lú-e]-meš	an-ni-ú-tum	"they are these"
[lú-še]-e-meš	a-nim-ma-mu-tum	"they are some from here"
l[ú-l]ú-a-meš	a-nim-ma-mu-tum	"they are everyone from here"
lú-[še]-ne-meš	a-ni-ú-tum-ma-an-nu	"which ones from here (Akk. 'these') are they?"

For the translation of *animmamû* as "anyone from here" cf. on the one hand *animmû* "the one from here" (e.g., *VS* XV 148. 13 KÙ-BABBAR *an-ni-im-mi-a-am*, "silver from here," ibid., 160, lines 27–29 *aš-šum a-gi-ir-tim a-ni-mi-tim*, "as for the hired woman from here," and ibid., 160 line 22 *ù* 2 LÚ-ME + EŠ *a-hu-tim a-ni-mu-ti-in tu-ri-im-ma* "and give me back two other men from here") and for the infixed *-ma- mimma* "anything" *mamma* "anybody" as compared with *mīnu* and *mannu*. A translation of arad lú-še lugal-zu-ù as "Slave! Is your master anyone from here?" in lines 69 and 91 of Gilgamesh and Agga (In the answer lú-še must be considered "quoted speech") would fit the context very well if Gilgamesh had been set over Uruk as one of Agga's men. We should now prefer to separate *animmû* "the one from here" from *animmamû* (< *anim + am + iu(m)*) and to translate the latter, and Sumerian-še, as "the one here (hailing) from there." On such a supposition also the remainder of the tale becomes clear. Gilgamesh, smarting under the fact that he owes his position to the favor of Agga rather than to his own prowess, inveigles Uruk to rebellion against Kish. When Agga arrives to suppress the rebellion Gilgamesh is able to prove himself the better warrior by taking Agga captive in battle. Having thus satisfied his heroic pride he then satisfies the heroic code of loyalty. He sets Agga free and voluntarily reacknowledges him as his liege lord. He has now paid his debt to Agga and can serve him without detriment to his self-respect.

As the assembly—both that of the elders and that of the guruš—serves in the Gilgamesh and Agga tale as an instrument for obtaining approval for a rebellion, so it serves in the Naram-Sîn text, *RA* 16 (1919) 157 f. (cf. *JNES* 2, 165 [see below, chap. ix]. Poebel *AS* XIV 23–42), where Kish, rebelling against Naram-Sîn, assembles in Ugar-Enlil to choose its own king.

To the discussion of the tale of Gilgamesh and Agga earlier in this note may be added that the warrior who, before Gilgamesh, attempted a sortie from beleaguered Uruk was the zabar-dab₅ of Uruk, i.e., the official in charge of the bronze (tablewares, cups, knives, etc. of a large establishment, and possibly of the bronze weapons as well). The word was borrowed into Akkadian as *zabardibbu*. Professor Kramer's rendering of the term as a proper name in *AJA* 53 (1949) 16 and 17 in stating my view was due to a misunderstanding of my too brief comment. The name of his slave BIR-HUR-TUR-RA is probably to be interpreted in the light of the reading giriš "butterfly" for BIR and of HUR-dúr-ᵈᵘ-ra:*tul-tum*, HUR-dúr-ra:*mu-bat-ti-rum* in Izi:*išātum* J ii 4–5; so Giriš-hur-du₁₃-ra, "Butterfly larva," "Caterpillar."

56. Cf. Gilgamesh and Agga 48–50. After Uruk's decision to rebel u_4-nu-5-àm u_4-nu-10-àm, Ag-ga dumu En-me-bara-gi$_4$-e-si Unu^{ki} zag-gaba-an-díb-bé-eš Unu^{ki}-ga dím-ma-bi ba-suh, "In less than five days, in less than ten days, Agga son of En-me-bara-gi$_4$-e-si enveloped (? lit. 'seized them at the side?') the Urukeans. Uruk panicked (lit. 'the reasoning ability of Uruk became confused')." On the earlier kingdom of Kish see *AS* XI p. 155 and 181–182 and Falkenstein, *Cahiers d'Histoire Mondiale* I. 4 (1954), p. 805.

57. Note that already in the myths there is an example of an important appointment of officers ("lords") by arrangement between An, the king, and two powerful nobles of the realm, Enlil and Enkik, without recourse to a general assembly. See the eclipse myth, *CT* XVI pl. 19 ff.

58. On the basic meaning of lú as "head of a household" see my note on guruš *JNES* 12 (1953) 180 [see above, chap. v].

59. See Kramer, The Death of Gilgamesh, *BASOR* 94 (1944) 4–6 and 8 B 1–7. For ĝìr(?)-kug-ga in l. 5 read ĝìr-sì-ga. For the origins of the royal administration in the household relation cf. also the titles of the highest administrative officers in later time, the "vizier" (sukkal-mah, "chief page-boy"), the "general" (šagub, originally, to judge from the writing, likely "donkey tender," cf. mareschal, marshal), "cup bearer" (SILA-ŠU-DU$_8$, for reading sagi, loan from Akkadian *šāqium*, see the variant É-sa-gi zabar-tur-ra-ka, Genouillac, *Kich*, II D 41 i 28′ to É-SILA-DU$_8$-a zabar tur-ra-ka *SK* 26 vi 36′ and ibid., ii 3′) etc., and also the highly significant fact that all administrative officials are "slaves," ir, of the king on their seals.

60. On the erín as "serfs of the crown" in Ur III see my remarks *AJA* 57 (1953) 127 f. The word is a collective denoting a team in which the members adjusted the obligation of service between themselves. On this see Landsberger, *JCS* 9 (1955) 121–131.

61. See Falkenstein, *Cahiers d'Histoire Mondiale* I. 4 (1954), p. 807.

62. See *AS* XI p. 187 ff.

63. See especially the lists of rations for the dumu-dumu šà é.gal(.la) "juniors, palace servants," Deimel, *WF* 65, 66, 99, 104, Jestin, *Tablettes Sumeriennes de Šuruppak* (Paris, 1937), pp. 45, 245, 574.

The numbers of various types of servants given above are based on Jestin, *TSŠ* no. 245. This text is of particular interest in that it shows the palace servants to belong to 7 "clans" im-ru(.a) with which the im-ru-a of Gudea Cyl. A xiv 13 may be compared. In view of the frequent variation between ru and ri we consider it almost certain that the word is identical with later im-ri-a "clan," "family." It is highly likely, furthermore, that this early principle under which each of the various kinds of palace servants were recruited from one or more special families carried in unbroken line down to Old Babylonian times, when a royal retainer's special function as e.g., "cook" (muhaldim:*nuhatimmum*), was determined by his ancestry (*dûr-šu*) cf. *VAB* VI 35. 18; 39. 11, 16, 22.

64. W. Andrae (editor) and E. Heinrich, *Fara* (Berlin, 1931) pp. 14–15, house in trench XIII f. In this house large numbers of tablets were found. A less likely candidate for the palace is the house in trench III a–c ibid., pp. 12–13 and plate 5.

65. Jestin, *TSŠ* 782 ii mè(.še)g̃en and mè.tag̃en.

66. Deimel, *WF* 95 subscribed gú-an-še 680 guruš mè "total 680 men; the battle," and ibid., 101, 670 guruš mè(.šè)g̃en "670 men going into battle."

67. Jestin, *TSŠ* 782 ii.....10 še-gín DÍM.gal Kiši^ki Utu.ur.sag̃ ba.zi maškim "10 measures of varnish (for) the chief builder of Kish. Utu-ursag paid it out (and was) comptroller."

68. Jestin, *TSŠ* 881 F vi amounts for Si:ab:g̃ar Zimbir^ki lugal "Si:ab:g̃ar, a Sipparean (belonging administratively under) the king."

69. Cf., e.g., Deimel, *WF* 70 subscribed gú.an.šè guruš 94 dub uru(.šè)g̃en dub nimgir(.ra) "Total 94 men, tablet dealing with visitors to the city, tablet of the constables." The cities from which the visitors hail are Nibru, Kullab(? = GIŠ: NUMUN:AB), Uruk, URU × UD-ZA:GÚ, Adaba, and Lagasa. Entries listing visitors are quite common, see e.g., Deimel, *WF* 72 vii, 73 ii, Jestin, *TSŠ* 150 xi etc.

70. Deimel, *WF* 92: 192 guruš, Unug^ki, 192 Adaba^ki, 94 Nibru^ki, 60 Lagasa^ki, 56 Šuruppak^ki, 86 Umma^ki, lú ba.dúru.duruna, Ke.en.gi, Du-du šu sum-(.ma) *rev.* šu-nigín, 670 guruš, lú ba-dúru.duruna "182 men, Urukeans, 192 Adabeans, 94 Nippureans, 60 Lagasheans, 56 Shuruppakeans, 86 Ummeans, people stationed elsewhere (ba-)." The very similar text Deimel, *WF* 94 is subscribed gú.an.šè 640 guruš, lú-duruna Ke.en.gi "Total 640 men, people stationed, Kengir (troops)." Due to the ambiguities of the Fara orthography the readings here given must remain tentative. We have been guided in our interpretation by *ITT* 1100 of Akkade date. While a reading lú dab₅.dab₅.ba "seized people" is entirely possible it lends itself less well to interpretation. If one thinks of apprehended deserters the numbers seem improbably high, if one thinks of captives taken in battle the inclusion of Shuruppakeans suggests enemy records, which is hardly consistent with the archive as a whole.

70a. See above note 55.

71. The title ensik, Akkadian *iššakkum*, is rare in both myths and epics (we can refer only to the ensik of Ninab in the Martu myth, *SEM* 58, and to passing references to the "ensiks of all the sovereign countries" in the epic tale of Enmerkar and Ensukešdanna), but it gains wide currency by the time of the earliest historical texts. It seems to denote specifically the ruler of a single major city with its surrounding lands and villages, whereas both "lord" (en) and "king" (lugal) imply ruler over a region with more than one important city.

As for the origins of the office, the ensik seems to have been originally the leader of the seasonal organization of the townspeople for work on the fields: irrigation, ploughing, and sowing. It is not difficult to see how the leader of such important and inclusive an organization of the townsmen could attain to the high political influence and power in the town which the ensik wields in Early Dynastic times. In favor of such origins for the ensik is the term itself: en-sig/k < *en-si-ak (cf. the early Akkadian loan *iššakkum*) "manager of the arable lands" (cf. si-i: [SI]: *si-su-u*:....., *mi-ri-šu* "plough-land," "cultivated land." á—A III. 4 166). It has the support of the allotment of the month gu₄-si-su (*Aiiar*), the month of preparing the fields, to "the warrior and chief ensik of Enlil, Ningirsuk," whose close connection with ploughing and irrigation is well known; see *KAV* 218 A i. 12–25; ^iti gud mul-

mul ᵈImin-bi, dingir-gal-gal-e-ne, ki-pad-du gu₄ si-sá-e-dè, ki-duru₅ gal-kid-kid, ᵍⁱˢapin dur-dur-ru-ke₄, iti ᵈNin-ĝír-su, ur-saĝ ensik-gal ᵈEn-líl-lá-ke₄: ᵃʳᵃʰGUD za-ab-bu IMIN-BI DINGIR-ME + EŠ GAL-ME + EŠ, pe-tu-ú r-ṣe-ti, GUD-ME + EŠ ul-te-eš-še-rù, ru-ṭu-ub-tu up-ta-ta, ᵍⁱˢAPIN-ME + EŠ ir-ra-aḫ-ḫa-ṣu, ITI ᵈNin-ĝír-su, iš-ša-ak-ki GAL-i ša ᵈEn-líl "Ayyar, the Pleiads, the great gods (known as) The Septad. Breaking (of) the soil, the oxen to be (Akk. 'are') yoked (to the plough), the soaked ground to be (Akk. 'is') opened up, the plough of the soaked (ground) (Akk. 'the ploughs are flushed'). Month of the warrior (Akk. om.), the chief ensik of Enlil, Ningirsuk." See Landsberger's discussion of the passage in *JNES* 8, 277 f. (For the reading iti "month" "moon" see *MSL* II 161 and note the phonetic rendering ì-ti in Gudea, Cyl. A xi 24–27 kalam-e zi-ša-ĝál ù-ma-sum, lú-dili lú-min-da kin mu-da-ag-gé, ĝe₆-a-na ì-ti ma-ra-è-è, e-ne-kára u₄-ma-dam ma-ra-è-è "when it (a north wind) has revived the nation a single man will work as much as (lit. 'with') two, during the night the moon will always rise for you, during the day plentiful daylight (see Kramer *AS* XII p. 86) will come forth for you," xxi. 12 É-ninnu ì-ti u₄-zal-la kalam si-àm "Eninnu is the moon of evening lighting up the land," Cyl. B iii 10–11 ì-ti sa-sa im-è, kalam-ma u₄ mu-ĝál "(Ningirsuk coming from Eridug) emitted brilliant (? For sa(h)-sa(h) cf. sa-sa-ha Gadd, *Iraq* 13 (1951) pl. XIV i. 6) moonlight and illuminated the land," ibid., iv. 22–24 u₄ siskur₍ₓ₎(AMAR + ŠE-AMAR + ŠE)-re ĝe₆ šud₍ₓ₎(KA + ŠU)-dè, ì-ti ní[ĝ]-u₄-zal-la-ke₄, lugal-bi mu-um-mà-e "saluting the day (in bidding it farewell), greeting the night, at the (time of the) evening moon its (i.e., the temple's) owner was ready to alight.")

An original meaning "manager of the arable lands," for ensik is borne out, finally, by the fact that the Akkadian loan from it, *iššakkum*, continued in use in much this meaning to Old Babylonian times (approximately "leader of a ploughing outfit") after it had become obsolete as a political term.

Whether the various writings ù-mu-un-níĝ-[sì-ga]:*be-el na-ás-pa*[*n-ti*] Haupt, *ASKT* 16 obv. 3′, ù-mu-un-si-ga:*be-el na-as-pan-ti* ibid., rev. 1, and ù-mu-un-si-ka, ù-mu-un-saĝ-ke₄, níĝ-sì-ga *TCL* VI 54 rev. 15–16 (seemingly variants of one original text) and the translation *bēl naspanti* can be utilized for the original meaning of the word is not clear to us but seems likely.

The term ensik is usually written PA:TE:SI. The establishing of the reading ensi(g) is due to Falkenstein, *ZA*, 42, 153 f. For final -k rather than -g see Uruka-genak, Oval Plaque ii. 17 PA:TE:SI-ke₄ and comes B + C iv. 17 PA:TE:SI-ka "(in the good fields of the gods were garlic and cucumber plots) of the ensik." New evidence as to the reading is given by the unpublished text IM 53977, a copy of which the late Professor F. W. Geers kindly placed at our disposal. This text, an Old Babylonian bilingual copy of an inscription of Shulgir, which uses a phonetic orthography, writes ni-in-si:*i-ši-a-ku-um*. The form ninsi rather than ensi(k) may be due to a secondary nazalization of the initial vowel since ensi(g/k) has the support both of the Eme-ᴤᴀʟ form umun-si(k) and of the Akkadian loanword *iššiakkum, iššakkum*. For the Akkadian *iššiakkum* see besides IM 53977 also the Irishum inscription published by Balkan and Landsberger, *Belleten* 14 (1950) 224 line 4 *i-ši₄-a-ak A-šir* and comment ibid., p. 230. Note finally the curious "misspelling" nu-PA:TE:SI i.e., nu-ensik, nu-iššak, for nu-èš i.e., nu-eš-ak, nisak in Prec. of Lú:*amēlu* Landsb. MS., 48. 208.

72. We still consider insufficient the proofs adduced for a reading sur of UR in proper names such as UR-ᵈNanše etc. See *OIP* LVIII p. 293, note to no. 4 line 1. The difficult passage of the Entemenak inscription *UET* I no. 1 v. 1 recently adduced by Sollberger (*JCS* 10, 1956 11, note 4) reads in context (*UET* I l. v–vi, Sollberger, *Corpus* p. 32):25 (bur) iku En-an-na-túm sur ᵈNanše e-ta-e₁₁, 10 (bur) iku im-saǧ zukum, ganá zug Ninaᵏⁱ-ka, e-kù-ge-ús-sa, 60 (bur) iku ᵈEn-líl, ganá Gú-edin-na-ka, En-te-me-na, ensig, Lagasaᵏⁱ-ke₄, ᵈEn-líl, É-ad-da-ka-ra, ǧír e-na-dù "25 bur (belonging to) Eannatum—Nanshe had ceded rights in (lit. "gone up from") the rushes—and 10 bur im-saǧ, zukum-rush, (constituting) fields of the marsh of Ninâ adjoining the 'Pure-Dyke'; and 60 bur (belonging to) Enlil, (constituting) fields of the Guedenak; did Entemenak ensik of Lagash assign(?) to Enlil of Eadda." We assume that the names En-anna-tum (v. 1) and En-lil (v. 5), standing absolutely, refer to the original ownership of the plots in question. sur is translated *urbatum* "rushes" (Howardy, *Clavis* 114. 37) and *zu-uk-*[...] (ibid., 41), with which cf. Sumerian zukum (See *MSL* II 456 and notes to lines 456 and 454–456), apparently a kind of rush. Why Urnanshek should be mentioned in this passage and listed after Enannatum, Entemenak's father, and why the scribe should have changed his orthography from UR-ᵈNanše in i. 14 to Sur-ᵈNanše in v. 1 is not readily apparent.

73. The problem of relative dating within the latter half of Early Dynastic III is still full of difficulties. The attempt made in *AS* XI table II relies, we now believe, too much on its schematic reconstruction of thirty and twenty years for unknown reigns and goes probably too far in some of its attempts to identify rulers of the list with rulers known from inscriptions. We hope at a later date to review the problem in the light of more recent evidence and to discuss on that occasion the very valuable article by Kraus, Zur Liste der älteren Könige von Babylonien, *ZA.* 50 (1952) 29–60 and the various points raised by him. For the present we would merely state that we tend to maintain our overall analysis of the list into separate sources as also our dating of its first composition to the time of Utuhegal. In the present article the relative chronology must be considered tentative throughout. We have used as fix point the change from a highly elliptic orthography with more or less arbitrary sign-order to a more explicit orthography with the signs written in the order in which they were to be read. This change took place in Lagash with Eannatum. Since it is fully established in the inscriptions of Aannepada we assume that he and Eannatum were approximately contemporaneous. For further assumptions bearing on the relative chronology of the rulers see the following notes.

74. Urnanshek takes the title lugal Lagasaᵏⁱ regularly (Sollberger, *Corpus* Urn. 1 ff.) his son Akurgal is given this title on the Stele of the Vultures ii 8–9, but does not take it in his own inscription (Sollberger, *Corpus* Akg. 1). In Ur. Mes-kalam-du₁₀ and A-kalam-du₁₀, who preceded the First Dynasty of Ur, take the titles lugal (*UE* II p. 316, U 11751) and lugal Urí(·ᵏⁱ.ma) (*UE* II p. 316, U 11825) respectively. In Umma É-ab.zu is lugal Ummaᵏⁱ(*SAK* 150 II. 1). In Adab we have inscriptions of Me-dur.ba ("The functions in their totality"?) lú.gal.Adaba (*OIP* XIV nos. 8 and 9) and Lugal-da-lu lugal Adabaᵏⁱ (Banks *AJSL* 21 59).

75. Reasons for assuming that Enshakushannak ruled in Uruk have been given by Poebel *PBS* IV. 1 p. 153. The first occurrence of the title lugal Unu^{ki}(.ga) is in the inscription of Sá-lah published by Thureau-Dangin in *RA* 20 (1923) 3–5, where it is given to Lugalkisalsi.

76. The inscription of Ur-zag-è, *OBI* 93, may tentatively be rendered as [^dEn-líl], lugal kur-ku[r]-ra, ^dNin-líl, nin Ki.dingir-ra šilam(!?) niĝan(ŠE)-na-ni, dam ^dEn-líl(.lá)-ra, Ur-[zag]-è, lugal Kiš^{ki}, lug[al Ki.dingir-ra] gap. "To Enlil, king of all sovereign countries, and to Ninlil, queen of Ki-dingir, his (i.e. Enlil's) fattened cow, the wife of Enlil, did Ur-zag-è, king of Kish, king of Ki-dingir" etc. Ki-dingir is mentioned with Umma in the Rimush inscription *PBS* V 24 xxi end + *PBS* XV 41 xxi beginning.

77. The damaged cartouche C on the Stele of the Vultures (Sollberger, *Corpus* p. 16) is possibly to be restored as [Kà]-al-b[um], lug[al] Kiš[i]^{ki} with the sign kà in the upper right hand corner to allow room for the large signs al and bum. See further below note 90. The next king of Kish proper known from contemporary inscriptions is Enbi-Eshtar (Poebel, *PBS* IV. 1 p. 151). A king of Akshak, Zuzu, is mentioned by Eannatum on Boulder A v 4–5.

78. Note for the granting of the ensikship of Lagash En-anna-tum I, Brick B (Sollberger *Corpus* p. 27), ii 8—iii 1. u₄ Lugal-URU × GANAtenú^{ki}-ke₄, En-an-na-túm-ra, nam-[PA]:[T]E:[SI], ŠIR:LA:[BUR], mu-na-sum-ma "when Lugaluruk had given unto Enannatum the ensikship of Lagash." For the kingship of Lagash, Entemenak, Doorsocket E (Sollberger, *Corpus* p. 36), 13–16 u₄ ^dNanše, nam-lugal, Laga^{ki}-sa(!?) (ŠIR:LA:KI:BUR-sa), mu-na-sum-ma-a "when Nanshe had given him (Entemenak) the kingship of Lagash," and Urukagenak Cone B C vii 12–19 u₄ ^dNin-ĝír-su, ur-saĝ ^dEn-líl-lá-ke₄, Uru-ka-ge-na-ra, nam-lugal, Lagasa^{ki}, e-na-sum-ma-a, šà lú-36000-ta, šu-ni e-ma-ta-dab₅-ba-a "when Ningirsuk, the warrior of Enlil, had given unto Urukagenak the kingship of Lagash and his (i.e. Ningirsuk's) hand had picked him out of 36,000 persons." For the kingship of Kish, Eannatum, Boulder A, v 23–vi 5 É-an-na-tum, ensik, [Lagasa]^{ki}-ra, ^dInanna-ke₄, ki an-na-áĝ-ĝá-da, nam-ensik, Lagasa^{ki}ta, nam-lugal Kiš^{ki}, mu-na-ta-sum, "To Eannatum, ensik of Lagash, Inannak gave, because she loved him, over and above the ensikship of Lagash the kingship of Kish."

79. Cf. e.g. the border war of Lagash and Umma for Ningirsuk's fields in the Gu-edinnak.

80. See e.g., the description of Eannatum's birth in the Stele of the Vultures obv. iv 9 ff., cf. *JNES* 2 (1943) 119–121, and see generally Frankfort, *Kingship and the Gods* pp. 299–310, Labat, *Le caractère religieux de la royauté assyro-babylonienne.* (Paris, 1939). For possible concrete facts underlying the idea of divine conception and birth of the king note the interesting passage in the Shulgir hymn *CT* XXXVI pl. 26, 13–20 É-kur lú-zi-dè ì-dù-e mu-da-rí-kam, dumu lú-zi-da-ke₄ ĝištur mi-íb-sù-du ^{ĝiš}gu-za-bi nu-kúr, nam-bi-éš É-kur-ra SIG₇ mi-ni-ĝar ^dAš(!?)-im₄-babbar-re, a-a-ni ^dEn-líl inim-ma bí-sì ama sá-da mi-ni-in-gub, é-du₁₀-ga ^dNanna dumu-nun-ni niĝ al ba-ni-du₁₁ (gloss: [*um-te-a-ar*]), en-ni šà-tur-šè-ĝál-la-na lú-zi mi-ni-ù-tu, ^dEn-líl siba á-kala-ga-ke₄ mes-e pa bí-è, dumu nam-lugal bára-gi₄ hé-du₇ ^dŠul-gi lugal-àm, "(If) a good householder will rebuild Ekur, becoming (a man) of lasting

'name' (i.e. progeny): a son of the good householder will long (wield) the scepter, their (i.e. father and son's) throne not changing (hands). To that end Ash-im-babbar put on beauty in Ekur, formed a mental image of his father, Enlil, and made a comparable mother step up; in the bedroom the thing was requested (Akk. gloss perhaps: 'was being commanded' 3. Pres. II. 2 of *ma'āru*) of the princely son, Nanna, and the *entu* gave birth to a good householder from what he (i.e. Nanna) placed in her (lit. 'the') womb. A (little) Enlil, a shepherd of strong arm, a hero, she made appear, a child suitable for kingship and throne-dais—it was king Shulgir." This would seem to mean that Ur-Nammuk by efficient stewardship culminating in the rebuilding of Ekur had established a claim to progeny, to a lasting line of sons to succeed him, so that his throne would not pass to another line. Nanna/Ash-im-babbar-accordingly took steps to engender a worthy son for him, Shulgir. Since Nanna intended the child to be a "(little) Enlil" he first "formed a mental image of his father, Enlil," then chose a mother for the child comparable to that august concept, the *entu*. With a-a-ni ᵈEn-líl inim-ma bí-sì lit. "he made his father Enlil like unto a word/concept," "he thought of his father, Enlil," confer Eannatum's title lú inim-ma sì-ga ᵈNin-g̃ír-su-ka-ke₄ "the householder thought of by Ningirsuk" Boulder A vii 15 and passim, see below note 90. and a-a inim-ma ì-sì-ga-ni "the one whom (his) father thought of" i.e., had in mind, wished for as a son. *SRT* 8 rev. 26–27. Note also the phrase inim—sì "to make words like (unto something)," "to think out," "to formulate in words" Lugalbanda Epic 6–7 lú-inim-šà-ga-na-ke₄ nu-um-mi-íb-sì-ge, šà-ní-te-na-ka inim àm-mi-íb-sì-ge. "No confidant of his was thinking it out, in his own heart he thought it out" (text based on *PBS* V no. 18 and *SEM* no. 1. The younger duplicate *CT* XV pl. 41 reads inim-ma-àm mi-ni-i[b- for inim àm-íb- in line 7 and translates the two lines as: *šá a-mat lìb-bi-šú a-mat u[l uš-ta-bal] i-na lib-bi ra-ma-ni-šú a-mat u[š-ta-bal]*) and ᵈIm-dugudᵐᵘˢᵉⁿ-dè har-ra--an šeš-mu-ne inim hé-im-mi-íb-sì-sì-ge "The Imdugud bird may describe (lit. 'may make words like unto,' 'may put into words') the road of (i.e. taken by) my brethren," *SEM* no. 1 i 27.

The following part of the passage, describing Shulgir's conception and birth, one is led to interpret as meaning that Shulgir was engendered on an *entu* priestess of Nanna in Nippur, presumably during the celebration of the "sacred marriage" between Nanna and the *entu*, in which Ur-Nammuk as king embodied the divine bridegroom, Nanna. Note also in this connection the epithet given to Shulgir later in the text (rev. 9) ama-tu É-kur-ra "houseborn slave of Ekur." For comparable Egyptian concepts see *JNES* 2 (1943) 119–121 quoted above.

81. Entemena, Cone A (and B) iii 5–14.

82. *OBI* II no. 86 pl. 37, *SAK* p. 156 c. It is possible, however, that this, the latter part of *OBI* 86, represents a separate inscription to be restored from *OBI* 89 as: . . . . . . ᵈEn-líl, lugal kur-kur(.ra)-r[a], Lugal-kisal-s[i], d[umu]-[sag̃], Lugal-ki-gen-né(.éš)-du₇-du₇, lugal Unuᵏⁱ-ga(.ka)-ke, etc., in which case we may be dealing merely with a separate inscription of Lugalkisalsi. The inscription *UET* I no. 3, a votive inscription by a merchant of Lugal-kigennesh-dudud for the life of a certain Nin-tur and Lugalkisalsi is more likely to refer to Lugalkisalsi (and his mother?) when a minor than to him as co-regent with his father, although the latter is possible. The

royal name which we have rendered above as Lugal-kigennesh-dudud occurs in the writings (1) undeclined: Lugal:KI-NI:ŠÈ:UL:UL, *UET* I no. 3 and Entemenak Clay-nail B (Sollberger, *Corpus* p. 34). One variant of the latter text has Lugal:KI: NI.UL:UL, which also occurs on *OBI* 86b. (2) With dative suffix-ra· Lugal:KI: DU.NI:UL:UL-ra *OBI* 86. 3 and (3) With subject -e:Lugal:KI:DU:NI:UL: UL:dè:ŠÈ *OBI* 23 (var. no. 22 has Lugal:KI:DU:NI:UL:UL) and Lugal:KI:NI: UL:UL:dè *OBI* 86. 15. As the form most probable to underlie these in part elliptical and anagrammatical writings we suggest Lugal-ki- g̃en(.a)-né-éš-du₇-du₇ representing Lugal ki-g̃en-ani-š du-du-(e)d "King ever butting in the direction of the place against which he is marching" with possible contraction of ki-g̃en-ane-š to kig̃neš in rapid speech to account for the writings Lugal-ki-né-éš-du₇-du₇.

83. The list is Urnanshek—Akurgal (son)—Eannatum (son)—Enannatum I (brother)—Entemenak (son)—Enannatum II (son). If Gunidu and Gur-šár, the father and grandfather of Urnanshek, were rulers, not five but seven generations are attested.

84. The code of Ammizaduga is usually designated as a Seisachtheia rather than as a code. For an evaluation of the Code of Hammurabi as a royal reform decree and an informative discussion of archaic codes generally see W. Seagle, *The Quest for Law* (New York, 1941), pp. 102–117.

85. Entemenak, Clay-nail B (Sollberber, *Corpus* p. 43) ii 4–10.

86. Eannatum, Boulder A v 23–vi 5.

87. The reading Me-salim rather than Me-silim is suggested by the writing Me-sá-lim in the Obelisk of Manishtusu Face B v' and was to be expected since the vowelassimilation of salim (borrowed from Akk. *šalim*) to silim could hardly yet have taken place at that early period. For literature on Mesalim see Edmund I. Gordon, "Mesilim and Mesannepadda—are they identical?" *BASOR* 132 (1953) 27–30. The question of identity with Mes-anne-pada raised by Gordon we should answer in the negative since the replacing of the name Mesalim with that of Mesannepada in the proverb discussed by Gordon is naturally explained by the fact that Mesalim had no place in the historical tradition of Isin-Larsa time, whereas Aannepada = Nanna, also mentioned in the proverb, was known from the History of the Tummal and possibly from the King List too. It was therefore natural for a scribe to replace the name Mesalim, which conveyed nothing to him, with Mesannepada, that of Nanna's father, known to him from the King List. Epigraphical considerations also favor keeping the two rulers apart.

88. *UE* II 312 f. Cf. *AS* XI p. 181, note 31.

89. Aannepada and Meskiagnunnak both take the title "king (lugal) of Ur." For inscriptions of these rulers and for the variant forms of their names in later tradition see *AS* XI p. 93, note 145 (add Gadd, *JRAS* 1928 626–628) and 94, note 146. That they controlled Nippur is suggested by their building activities there, recorded in the History of the Tummal (*PBS* V nos. 6 and 7, *PBS* XIII no. 48) ii. 2. See also Poebel, *PBS* IV 143 ff., our remarks in *JCS* 7 (1953) 38, note 11 [see below, chap. x] and Gordon, *BASOR* 132 29, note 18, the reading Tummal rather than Ebmal has been proved by Gordon and Kramer. Note that *SK* no. 5, quoted by them for the variant Tu-ba-al (obv. ii. 24), also proves the reading Numun_x-bur (see ki

Nú-mu-un-bur *SK* 5 obv. ii. 9) for the $\frac{ZI}{ZI}$ + NIGÍN-BUR mentioned as built by Gilgamesh in the History of the Tummal. Our suggestion *AS* XI p. 89, note 128, that a variant writing for the term $\tilde{G}i_6$-pàr was involved was accordingly incorrect. On the reading numun for $\frac{ZI}{ZI}$ + NIGÍN see *MSL* II 455.

90. The chronology of Eannatum's reign has been discussed by Poebel, *PBS* IV 159–169. We have based our ordering of the sources on the changes in Eannatum's religious titles during his reign. Assuming that the titles given at the beginning of an inscription (exceptionally also later as e.g. St. of V. rev. iv 42 ff.) represent those used by the ruler at the time of the particular achievement for which the inscription was composed, whereas titles occurring in the body of the text, in the resumé of earlier achievements, are such as he used at the time when these achievements were accomplished, we can set up the following sequence:

(1) lú inim-ma-sì-ga ᵈNin-ğír-su-ka. In the body of boulders D and G connected with the gaining of primacy: kur-kur-šè, á ᵈNin-ğír-su-ka-ta, lú-u$_x$ (GIŠGAL) gaba mu-ru-da, nu-tuk[u-am$_5$] "(Eannatum) was one who, in the direction toward all sovereign countries, through the strength of Ningirsuk, had none who could oppose him." In the body of later inscriptions the title is connected with the destruction of A-rù-a^{ki} (Br. B vi. 5–11), the building of the House of Tirash (Boulder A vii. 14–20), and with the conferring upon Eannatum of the kingship of Kish by Inannak (Boulder A v. 20–vi. 5).

(2) kur-gú-ğar-ğar ᵈNin-ğír-su-ka. As only main title Boulders D and G. Connected with the subjection of Adamdun: [ELAM]-dun^{ki} [g]ú mu-na-ğar (Boulder D ii. 2–3) "he (Eannatum) subjected to him (Ningirsuk) Adamdun" (for the reading ELAM-dun i.e. (H)a(l)tam-dun cf. Poebel, *AJSL* 48 (1931–32) 20–26 and the equation *A-da-an-tú*:MIN (= *E-lam-tum*) in *Malku-Šarru* I 222. The reading was first proposed by M. Lambert in *RA* 45 (1951) 60, note to 6. 64 and is undoubtedly correct as against the traditional reading Elam Šubur^{ki} "Elam and Subartu." and with the completion of the House of Tirash (É-Ti-ra-ás-sá mu-na-dù pa mu-[na]-è Boulder D ii. 4–6, Gi. 1′–ii. 1). In the body of later inscriptions it occurs on Boulder A vi. 12–16, likewise connected with the defensive victory over Adamdun (ibid., 17). The passage as a whole, however, (vi. 12–vii. 2) constitutes a later summary of defensive victories on the eastern and western borders of Lagash and refers therefore also to events of much later date than the victory over Adamdun which begins the enumeration and so determined the choice of title.

(3) šà-kù-ge-pà-da ᵈNanše nin en (.na), kur-gú-gar-gar ᵈNin-ğír-su-ka. As main religious titles small column 6–10. Connected with repulsion of Umma and the return of Guedinnak and border districts of Girsu.

(4) á-sum-ma ᵈEn-líl(.lá)....šà(.ge)-pà-da ᵈNanše nin-en(.na) [kur-g]ú-[ğar-ğar] ᵈN[in-ğír-su-ka] etc. Stele of the Vultures rev. v. 42–vi. 1 and Fragment B (Sollberger, *Corpus* p. 26). In both inscriptions Eannatum styles himself lugal Lagasa^{ki} rather than ensik Lagasa^{ki}. Connected with the repulse of Umma and the return of the Gu-edinnak (main event of inscription) and introducing a list of earlier victories over ELAM-dun ("a country [which had taken as spoil] the possessions [of Lagash]"?),

..., Susa (Su-sín^ki-na), Urua, ..., Arua, Šu-è("a Sumerian..."),..., Ur,...(St. of V. rev, vi. 10–ix. 2').

(5) á-sum-ma ^dEn-líl(.lá)-ke₄,... mu-du₁₀-sa₄-a ^dNanše-ke₄, kur-gú-g̃ar-g̃ar ^dNin-g̃ír-su-ka-ke₄ Boulder E iv. 1–12, F iii' 3–iv.' 1. (To be considered titulary at time of inscription.) Connected with repulsion of Umma and the return of the Gu-edinnak.

(6) á-sum-ma ^dEn-líl(.lá)-ke₄...mu-pà-da ^dNin-g̃ír-su(.ka)-ke₄, šà(.ge)-pà-da ^dNanše-ke₄. Brick B i l–11. Connected with the construction of a well for Ningirsuk, the event causing the inscription, and with a list of earlier victories over Elam (kur Elam^ki), Urua, Umma, and Ur, which seems to summarize that of the Stele of the Vultures adding Umma, which was the main event in that inscription. In the body of Brick A (v 9–vi 4), Boulder B + C (v 5–9), and Boulder A (iv 20–24) the title mu-pà-da ^dNin-g̃ír-su-ka is associated with a general attack on Eannatum (kur-kur-ré sag̃ e-dab_x(URUDU)-sìg "all sovereign countries locked horn (lit. 'butted,' 'smote (with) the head') with him." It seems probable that also the defeat of an invasion by Zuzu of Akshak, which follows immediately in Boulders B[+ C] v 10–vi. 5, Boulder A iv 25–v 8, and the digging of the canal LUM-ma-ge₁₈-HI, Boulders B + C vi 6–10, Boulder A v 9–19, are to be placed at the time when Eannatum used this title. The use of mu...-a-a "in the year that" (Boulder A iv 25, Boulder B v 10) suggests, however, that these events were later than the general attack just mentioned. The canal LUM-ma-ge₁₈-HI, "...like LUM-ma," is named, as Poebel was the first to point out, from Eannatum's G̃ÌR-G̃ÌR name, LUM-ma, mentioned in Boulder A v 9–17:u₄-ba, É-an-na-túm-ma, É-an-na-túm, mu Ú-RUM-ma-n[i], mu G̃ÌR-G̃ÌR-ni, LUM-ma-a, ^dNin-g̃ír-[s]u-ra, a-gi[bil], mu-na-dun, "At that time Eannatum, whose Ú-RUM name is Eannatum, whose G̃ÌR-G̃ÌR name is LUM-ma, dug a new canal for Ningirsuk." See Poebel, *PBS* IV p. 166, note 2, *ZA* 36 (1925) 8, and *Paul Haupt Anniversary Volume* (Baltimore, 1926), p. 235, note 2. Besides the reading of G̃ÌR-G̃ÌR as Tidnum and the corresponding completion of the traces Ú-RUM to kalam there proposed, we would admit as deserving consideration also the readings g̃ìr-g̃ìr and ú-rum respectively. While the readings Tidnum and kalam yield a contrast between Eannatum's Amorrite name LUM-ma and his "national," "Sumerian" name Eannatum, g̃ìr-g̃ìr and ú-rum would contrast his "battle" name, Hum-ma (lit. "bruiser"-name, cf. g̃ìr-g̃ìr:MIN (= [hum-m]u-[šu]) "to bruise," Nabnitu H 75, the term for an athlete, *ša hummuši*, CAD Ḫ p. 235 b "bruiser"; "boxer" (not "wrestler"), and the translation *mugdašru* "supremely valiant" of g̃ìr-g̃ìr-re in IV R 21 no. 1 B rev. 13. Note also that the name so qualified, Hum-ma, itself means "to bruise" cf. LUM^hu-um -ma:ha-ma-šum Erimhuš V 221) with his "domestic" name, more precisely, his name as servant of Inannak, attached to her temple Eanna (for the meaning of the full form of the name Eannatum:É-an-na-^dInanna-Ib-gal-ka-ka-túm "worthy of the Eannak of Inannak of Ibgal" see Poebel, *OLZ* (1911) 198–200. For ú-rum "property," person or thing belonging to somebody's "dominium" see Deimel, *ŠL* 318. 17 and cf. *CT* XXXVI 26–27 rev. 9 where Shulgir is called níg̃-ú-rum ^dNanna ama-tu É-kur-ra "property of Nanna, house-born slave of Ekur"). The latter contrast between "battle name" and "domestic name" would make it easy

to understand Eannatum's preference for the name Humma in naming monuments: he wished to be remembered as warrior.

(7) mu-pà-da ᵈEn-líl(.lá)-ke₄ á-sum-ma ᵈNin-g̃ír-su-ka-ke₄, šà(.ge)-pà-da ᵈNanše-ke₄. (A) Brick A i 2–ii 1. Inscription commemorating the rebuilding of Girsu and Ninâ. List of victories over "the Elamites in the Uga mountain range (Elam Hur-sag̃-u₆-ga)," Urua, Umma, Uruk, Uru-za, and Mishime, in part—e.g. Urua and Umma—dating back to before the Stele of the Vultures was written. (B) Boulder B + C i 7–ii 4: Occasion for inscription not clear, perhaps the building of the wall of Lagash and a covenant with Nanshe (i 1–4). Restoration of Girsu, and rebuilding of the wall around its (?) sacred quarter, rebuilding of Ninâ (iii 3–10). List of earlier victories as in Brick A but with addition of Ur and Ki-Utuk after Uruk, Arua after Mishime. Arua dates back to the earliest part of Eannatum's reign, Ur is already mentioned on the Stele of the Vultures. (C) Boulder A i 2–9. Inscription probably commemorating the building of a reservoir for the canal Hum-ma-ge₁₈-HI, introduced by mention of the title á-sum-ma ᵈNin-g̃ír-su-ka-ke₄ in vii 7–13. Restoration of Girsu, building of the wall of its (?) sacred quarter, rebuilding of Nanâ. List of earlier victories as in Boulder B + C. The section vi 12–vii 6 contains a geographically arranged summary of defensive victories against invaders from the East and the West (see above under 2) followed by an account of the paving of the bottom of the Hum-ma-ge₁₈-HI canal and the dedication of it to Ningirsuk. This summary, which includes repulsion of Adamdun and Urua from the canal Asuhur, and of Kish, Akshak, and Mari from the Antasurra, dates probably, like the repairs on Hum-ma-ge₁₈-HI, from the time of the title á-sum-ma ᵈEn-líl (.lá)-ke₄... mu-pa-da ᵈNin-g̃ír-su(.ka)-ke₄ (above 6) or early in the period of mu-pà-da ᵈEn-líl(.lá)-ke₄, á-sum-ma ᵈNin-g̃ír-su-ka-ke₄ (7). Of the victories mentioned, those against Adamdun and Urua predate the Stele of the Vultures, and that over Kish may likewise be early. The victory over Akshak seems to belong with title (6), that over Mari is likely to be the latest (late in 6 or early in 7) and to have prompted the summary. This accords generally with a similar summary in vi 6–11, which looks like an earlier version of the same idea: É-an-na-túm-da Elam sag̃ e-dabₓ (URUDU)-sìg Elam kur-ra-na bé-ge₄ Kišiᵏⁱ sag̃ e-dabₓ(URUDU)-sìg lugal Akšakᵏⁱ kur-ra-na bé-ge₄, "With Eannatum the Elamites locked horns and he repulsed the Elamite into his (own) land; Kish locked horns with him and he repulsed the king of Akshak into his (own) land." The parallelism suffers under the inclusion of an old victory over Kish with the recent one over Zuzu of Akshak, which seems to have prompted the summary. With a dating to the period of title (6) agrees the use of the phrase "locked horns" and also the fact that Mari is not yet mentioned.

Summing up we may state, then, that to the early part of Eannatum's reign belong probably the victories over Adamdun and Arua and a bid for the kingship of Kish, possibly subsequent to a victory over its armies (1). There followed a series of engagements with Ur, Uruk, and other city-states, culminating at the middle of the reign in the great victory over Umma. After that Eannatum seems to have been forced into the defensive through attacks first by "all the sovereign countries," later by Zuzu of Akshak (6). Though Eannatum rode out the storm, extensive rebuilding of major cities appears to have become needed shortly afterward (7), and likewise defense against a new attack by Mari.

A last comment on Eannatum's relations with Kish may be made. In the Stele of the Vultures in the section in which Ningirsuk in a dream encourages Eannatum to resist Umma (obv. vi 22–vii 12) he promises that Kish will take no part in the engagement (obv. vii 1–5): Umma^{ki} Kiši^{ki}-am₅ šu šè-dág-ge libiš-ge dab₅-ba-ta nam-[m]a-da-gen, "Kish itself will let Umma roam on its own (ši/e-) and out of anger it will not come with it." Correspondingly Kish is nowhere mentioned in the account of the battle as we have it. In apparent contradiction to this is the battle scene depicted on the stele in which a fallen enemy threatened by Eannatum's spear is labelled [Kà](?)-al-b[um](?) lugal Kiši$^{[ki]}$. However, it is by no means certain that this scene depicts an incident from the battle with Umma; in fact, since Eannatum on that occasion was seriously wounded and had to temporarily withdraw from the battle, that engagement hardly lent itself to purposes of pictorial glorification (cf. Stele of the Vultures obv. ix 2–7: É-an-na-túm-ra, lú ti mu-ni-ra, ti-ta c-ta-si, mu-haš, igi-ba [li]-bí-KA × [ERÍN]-KA × ERÍN(!?), lú e-líl, [. . . . .] "Against Eannatum a man shot an arrow and he grew weak from the arrow; he broke it off, but could not continue fighting in the front rank (lit. 'before them'). The man [burst into] a triumphal song. . . . ." It was probably on this occasion, pleading for Eannatum's life with the powers that be, that Eannatum's personal deity shed the "effective tears" mentioned in xi 17–18; our interpretation in *JNES* 2 121 is accordingly to be modified. It is therefore a likely thought that Eannatum should have chosen to be depicted on the stele at an earlier moment of supreme glory, an occasion on which he vanquished, and perhaps killed, a king of Kish in person. Such an early victory over an invading king of Kish may possibly be inferred from brief references in his later texts (see above to Boulder A vi 6–11 and vi 12–vii 6) and could plausibly underlie his surprising claim to kingship of Kish early in his reign (see above, title 1). Whether—if this is so and the king of Kish in question was the Kalbum of the King List—the thwarting of Eannatum's ambition was due to Kalbum's successor Šè-e (or Šù-e) and whether reference to the latter is to be found in Šu-è Ke-en-gi "Shu-e, a Sumerian. . ." Stele of Vultures rev. viii 4′–5′, we dare not decide.

91. Major independent operations in southern Babylonia by Akshak, such as Zuzu's attack on Lagash (see above note 90), are hardly imaginable unless the power of Akshak's neighbor, Kish, had lessened considerably.

92. See above note 90 under title (7).

93. *AS* XI p. 102–103 and note 189. We have here tentatively adopted Landsberger's proposal, *OLZ* 1931. 127, to read the name *Ìl-sù*.

94. *UET* I no. 12.

95. See Poebel, *PBS* IV pp. 151–156. On the final -k of the name En-šà-kúš-an-na "*Enu*-priest setting at rest the heart of the date clusters(?)" see Speleers, *Recueil* no. 14 4–5 [nam]-ti, En-šà-kúš-an-na-ka-šè, "for the life of Enshakushannak."

96. Poebel, *PBS* IV p. 154.

97. On the reading of the name of Lugal-kigennesh-dudud see above note 82. On the rendering of the name Entemenak with final -k see Entemenak, Brick A ii. 10

En-te-me-na-ke₄ (subject of active, transitive verb). On the covenant with Lagash see Sollberger, *Corpus* p. 43 Ent. 45–73 ii 4–10, on the joining of the "lordship" and the "kingship" see *OBI* 86. In a newly found vase inscription from Nippur, Lugal-kigen-nesh-dudud takes, as Professor Goetze kindly informs me, the title king of Kish. Cf. also *AS* XI p. 172, note 8.

98. According to *PBS* V 34 vi 34′–35′ the fatal battle was fought *in Ug(?)-bànda*ki *ugar(A?-QAR?)-rí A-kà-dé*ki "in Ugbanda, the commons of Akkade" i.e., on or within the borders of the territory of Akkade itself. It seems therefore to have been a defensive victory by Sargon against invading forces.

99. Cones A and B of Entemenak (Sollberger, *Corpus* p. 37) i 1–12.

100. The later proverb CBS 14139 obv. ii 3–4 published by Edmund I. Gordon in *BASOR* 132 (1953) 27–30 mentions an É-babbar—probably the one in Larsa—as built by Mesalim. Vase inscriptions of his from Adab are *OIP* XIV no. 1 and 5. For the latter see also Luckenbill's earlier copy in *AJSL* XXX (1914) 221 and comment on 219. In *OIP* XIV no. 1 the less deeply cut lines are omitted. We read: Me-salim, lugal Kiši(ki.ke₄), É.sar(.ra), bur mu-gi₄, Nin-kisal-si NÍĜ:PA:TE:SI Adaba-kam(!?) "Mesalim, king of Kish, offered the *burgû*-offering in Esharra. Nin-kisal-si was ensik of Adab." For bur—gi₄ as a technical term for the offering of a special kind of offering (lit. "to bring a stone bowl back [filled with food]"?) cf. . . . .] é-mah-bi, Kar-Ká-sur-ra-ka, íd-da, a-a su-su-da-bi, nar á-lá igi-šè ba-du, 1 gud 4 udu 1 máš ba-sa₆ mí ì-e, bur-gi₄-a-bi, 1 gud 4 udu 1 máš, MÁ-GIN-GA[L], . . . "When the exalted cabin [of the boat] was to be lowered into the water in the river at the Kasurra-quay a lyre singer walked in front, he offered up to it 1 ox, 4 sheep, and 1 kid and sang the praise-hymn. This *burgû*-offering, 1 ox, 4 sheep, and 1 kid, the . . . . ." Gudea, St. L iv. 1′–11′, mu bur-gi₄-a-ni "his name used in connection with the *burgû* offering" *PBS* V 76 vii. 23 and the loanword *burgû* (Streck, *Assurbanipal*, glossary p. 453 *sub voce*). In Girsu, Me-salim presented a mace head to Ningirsuk. Dec. Pl. 1*ter*, *SAK* 160 f.

101. See Burrows, *UE* II p. 321 f.

102. Lugalzagesi, Vase inscription i. 36–ii. 25. The doubtful sign in ii. 25 is proved to be GAM by a new fragment found at Nippur. Our translation of me nam–nun–ak as "arbitral office" seeks to bring out the essence of the term nun, usually translated "prince," as one of authority based on respect only, settling disputes without recourse to force.

103. Such a garrison or police post was found by Mallowan in Tell Brak. It is, from finds of Akkade inscriptions there, likely that there was one in Nineveh also. The records of the Akkade period from Telloh and Susa come—a point not always taken into consideration—likewise from the Akkadian garrisons in these cities and show that the garrisons were largely made up of Akkadians. No general conclusion about the ethnic and linguistic picture at Girsu and Susa at this period can therefore be drawn on the basis of them.

104. See particularly the inscription of Sargon, *PBS* V 34 + *PBS* XV 41 cols. i–iv. (Note that like *PBS* V 34 iv 48–50 so also *PBS* V 34 X 4′–32′ is probably to be considered an epigraph to the representation of Lugalzagesi on a monument of Sargon's.) The policy of destroying city-walls does not seem to have been Sargon's

original policy. His inscriptions may be grouped on the basis of his titles into three successive groups (1) Those with "king of Akkade" as main title. (2) Those with "king of Kish" as main title, and (3) Those with "king of the Nation" as main title. To the first group belong the original conquest of Sumer, to the second the conquest of Elam and Syria. The third was written, we believe, after a reconquest of Sumer following a serious rebellion. In the early descriptions, especially *PBS* V 34 vi 29'–37 + *PBS* XV 41 vii, which belongs with the second group of inscriptions, the conquest was achieved in a few major battles with no destruction of cities. In the later sources of the third group the account seems to have been worked over and reedited to cover the later punitive campaign of reconquest as well.

105. Cf. *PBS* XV iv 4'–10'.

106. See above note 103.

107. The occurrence of *Uru-ka-ge-na* DUMU *En-gil-sa išŝiak Lagasa*^{ki} as a citizen of Akkade on the Obelisk of Manishtusu Face A xiv is difficult to account for on any other assumption. On the identity of this Urukagenak with the author of the reform texts and opponent of Lugalzagesi see Deimel, *Orientalia* 2 (1920) p. 3.

The chronological implications of the identification would seem to be a drastic shortening of Sargon's rule over Sumer to a relatively few years.

108. *il A-kà-de*^{ki} *RTC* 165 and 166 i 3. *SAK* 168 k. It should be noted that both in Akkadian and in Sumerian the words *ilum* and dingir, "god," if followed by a genitive or possessive pronoun, always denote the "personal god" of the person or other entity in question. This is of basic importance for the evaluation of the deification of rulers in Mesopotamia, the deified king is not a "god" generally; he has the specific relation to the country that a personal god has to his ward. The personal god, as may be seen from the phrase *ilam rašû*, is basically a personification of a man's "luck," in older Akkadian texts such as e.g., the Old Assyrian texts from Cappadocia one frequently has the impression that the personal god is still unidentified, known only through his or her effects on the fortunes of the individual. From the personal god comes all successful and fruitful ideas and impulses to successful action. It is in this sense that the king, as leader of the country and originator of policy, is the "personal god" of his realm. The deification of rulers in Mesopotamia is accordingly to be understood not in terms of the qualitative contrast human:divine, mortal:immortal, etc., but in terms of function of the king, he is the "genius" of the country.

109. The Gutian domination is most easily understood as a continued push by nomads from the mountains on the northern Diyala down across the Tigris to Nippur and the region of the Iturungal down to Umma. The Lagash region on the Sirara seems to have been relatively little affected and the same seems true of the southern part of the Euphrates with Uruk and Ur. A major object of the Gutians, besides plunder, was probably the grazing in the Edin. Note that the shepherd-god Dumuzid seems to have counted as god of the Gutians; his assent to the campaign of liberation of Utu-hegal is therefore not overly enthusiastic. Cf. Utuhegal's statement to his troops in the inscription *RA* 9 (1912) 112–113 col. ii 35–41 Gu-ti-um^{ki}, ^dEn-líl-le ma-an-sum, nin-mu ^dInanna, á-tah-mu-um, ^dDumu-zi, Ama-ušumgal-an-na-ke$_4$, nam-mu bí-du$_{11}$ "Enlil has given Gutium (into my hand), my

mistress Inannak is my helper, Dumuzid-Amaushumgalannak has said 'Never mind!' about it." The economic disaster which shook the country under Naram-Sîn and opened it to the Gutians is reflected in the tale of the Fall of Akkade, which has been largely completed by unpublished texts from Nippur and Jena. See also my discussion *AS* XI p. 205 f.

110. Keiser, *Patesis of the Ur Dynasty* (New Haven, 1919), p. 14.

111. See Keiser, *YOS* IV no. 208 and *UET* III no. 50. See *AJA* 57 (1953) 128, note 7.

112. See *JCS* 7 (1953) 36 ff. [see below, chap. x].

113. Cf. Meissner, *Babylonien und Assyrien*, I (Heidelberg, 1920), p. 28.

114. E. T. A. Olmstead, "Assyrian Government of Dependencies," *American Political Science Review*, 12 (1918) 63.

115. The cultural consequences of Alexander's conquest and the confrontation of Greek and Oriental thought which it inaugurated need not be stressed here. Only a remark in passing: How quite close, and how very far apart, were those two worlds is well shown by a passage in Plutarch's Lives. Having told how Alexander returned to Babylon amidst a variety of disquieting signs and portents just before his death Plutarch continues: "And one day after he had undressed himself to be anointed, and was playing at ball, just as they were going to bring his clothes again, the young men who played with him perceived a man clad in the king's robes with a diadem upon his head, sitting silently upon his throne. They asked him who he was, to which he gave no answer a good while till at last coming to himself, he told them his name was Dionysius, that he was of Messenia, that for some crime of which he was accused he was brought thither from the seaside, and he had been kept long in prison, that Serapis appeared to him, had freed him from his chains, conducted him to that place, and commanded him to put on the king's robe and diadem, and to sit where they found him, and to say nothing. Alexander, when he heard this, by the direction of his soothsayers, put the fellow to death, but he lost his spirits, and grew diffident of the protection and assistance of the gods, and suspicious of his friends." (Plutarch, *The Lives of the Noble Grecians and Romans*, translated by John Dryden and revised by Arthur Hugh Clough [The Modern Library, New York], p. 852). It is clear that what the young ballplayers blundered into was the ancient Mesopotamian ritual of the "substitute king," apparently still fully alive at the time.

9. *Primitive Democracy in Ancient Mesopotamia*

1. The substance of this article was presented in a paper read at the meeting of the American Oriental Society held in Chicago in April, 1941. Since then Professor E. A. Speiser has touched on the subject in a paragraph of his paper, *Some Sources of Intellectual and Social Progress in the Ancient Near East* ("Studies in the History of Culture" [Philadelphia, 1942]), p. 60. Speiser's views agree with ours in important points; the term which he suggests, "politocracy," seems, however, less expressive than "primitive democracy" and tends in addition to sever the close ties which connect the Mesopotamian forms with similar primitive forms of government elsewhere, many of which were flourishing in a predominantly tribal, not urban, setting.

2. The beginning of history proper in Mesopotamia may be placed approximately at the time of Urnanshe. As his date we gave ca. 2800 B.C. in *The Sumerian King List* (*O.I.C.*, No. 11), Table II. Since then, however, new material and treatments have appeared, making it highly probable that the date of the First Dynasty of Babylon, upon which all absolute dates in the earlier periods depend, must be radically lowered. Although the various new chronologies which have been proposed are undoubtedly in general nearer to the truth than was the old, high chronology, the material does not, in our opinion, permit us to fix on any of the available possibilities. We are therefore leaving the question open, accepting provisionally the date for Hammurabi proposed by Sidney Smith (*Alalakh and Chronology* [London, 1940], p. 29), 1792–1750 B.C. This means that the scale of time given in *The Sumerian King List* should be shifted downward by 275 years.

3. The major part of the legislative activities of early Mesopotamian rulers falls within the province of "special law" in the sense of commands issued by the state, enforced by its authority, and aimed at some immediate and specific situation. Here belong orders initiating the building and rebuilding of specific temples at specific times and places, repairs and digging of canals, waging of wars, etc. For such achievements the ruler gets—or takes—sole credit in the inscriptions. The main body of the "general law" which regulated Sumero-Akkadian society was presumably unwritten common law. Here too, however, the ruler may intervene, as is evidenced by Urukagena's sweeping changes in the existing legal order (see his Cone B + C and Oval Tablet). The ruler's powers, however, though autocratic, were not absolute. The authority for new special law as well as for new general law was the will of the god of the state as communicated to the ruler through dreams and omens. A detailed description of the genesis of a special law, that initiating the rebuilding of the temple Eninnu in Lagash, is given in Gudea Cyl. A i 1–xii 20. The divine orders leading to Urukagena's reforms are referred to in Cone B + C vii 20–viii 13.

4. Urukagena Cone B + C xii 23: nu-síg nu-ma-su lú-á-tuku nu-na-gá-gá-a ^{d}Nin-gír-su-da Uru-ka-ge-na-ke₄ inim-bé ka e-da-sir: "Urukagena contracted with Ningirsu that he (i.e., Urukagena) would not deliver up the orphan and the widow to the powerful man."

5. See, e.g., Eannatum's Stele of the Vultures obv. ix 1–x 4 and the pictorial representations on that monument; also the account of the wars between Lagash and Umma in Entemena's Cone A (on one occasion, the battle in iii 5 ff., the son of the ruler of Lagash seems to have been in command), the inscription of Utuhegal, *RA*, 9, 111–20, and 10, 98–100, and many others.

6. See Deimel in *AnOr* II, p. 80.

7. There is reason to believe that successful attempts to unify southern Mesopotamia were made very early. See my remarks in *JAOS* 59 (1939) 489, end of note 11 on 487 [see below, chap xi].

8. See for the time being my remarks ibid., 495, n. 26 [see below, chap. xi].

9. We are employing for the historical periods the terms proposed in *The Sumerian King List*, Pl. II.

10. That is, the period of the Old Babylonian kingdom. For the later fate of these

democratic strands and of the institutions in which they were embodied see Olmstead's chapter, "The Imperial Free City," in his *History of Assyria*, pp. 525–541.

11. For general discussion see Landsberger, *Assyrische Handelskolonien in Kleinasien
aus dem 2. Jahrtausend* ("Der Alte Orient," XXIV, 4 [1925]); A. Götze, *Kleinasien*
(München, 1933), pp. 64–76; and I. J. Gelb, *Inscriptions from Alishar and Vicinity*
(Chicago, 1935), pp. 1–18. For the textual material see Eisser and Lewy, "Die
Altassyrischen Rechtsurkunden vom Kültepe" (*MVAG*, Vols. 33 and 35, No. 3).

12. Since the name of this assembly is important for the light it throws on its
character and composition, it may be considered in more detail. The elucidation
of the word *kārum* (also *karrum*) is due to Walther, *Das altbabylonische Gerichtswesen*,
LSS VI (1917), pp. 70–80, and to Landsberger, *ZA*,n.F. 1 (1924), 223–225. A
loan word from Sumerian kar, *kārum* originally denoted "quay," "harbor,"
"emporium." By a natural extension of meaning, however, it came to designate
also the people who had their business on the quay, then their organization, "the
merchant body." While in most settlements the merchants and their organization,
the *kārum*, can have formed only an entity within the organization of the community as a whole (the "town" [*âlum*] or the "(general) assembly" [*puhrum*]), the
kārum would, in settlements of certain types such as merchant colonies or towns
grown out of emporia, either embrace the whole population or stand apart from
the community as an autonomous unit. When reference is made to a settlement of
such a type—e.g., to one of the Assyrian merchant colonies in Asia Minor—*kārum*
is therefore best rendered, with Landsberger, as "the colony."

The qualification *sahir rabi*—literally "small and great"—renders, as Landsberger
has pointed out, the idea of totality (*ZA*,n.F. 1, 224). Since *sahrum* and *rabium*
when used of persons usually refer to age rather than to size (cf., e.g., *maru-ú se-eh-ru*,
"the younger son," as opposed to *mar'u rabu-ú*, "the older son," in *KAV* 2 ii 10–11
and likewise Latin *minor* and *major*), we are perhaps justified in assuming that the
categories under which totality in this case was viewed were those of age and youth.
The *kārum* would thus exhibit the well-known grouping into elders and youths
which underlies so many and so widespread forms of political organization and
which—as we shall presently see—appears also in Babylonia. It should be noted,
however, that the degree to which this grouping had become institutionalized in
the organization of the *kārum*, as also the relation of the elders (*rabiūtum*) to the
group of seven which could represent the *kārum* when it sealed documents (see
G. Eisser in *Festschrift Paul Koschaker*, III [Weimar, 1939], 99) is not yet entirely
clear. See also below, n. 41.

13. CTP 19 obv. 2–14 (Stephens in *JSOR*, 11, 122; transliteration and translation,
ibid., 102 f.). We follow Lewy's translation (*MVAG*, 33, 336; cf. ibid., 35, 191 f.)
more nearly than the more recent rendering by Driver and Miles in *The Assyrian
Laws*, p. 378. The relevant portion of the text reads: . . . .^{2}*a-ua-sú-u* [*ú-lá i-pá*]-*šu-
$^{\ulcorner}$ru$^{\urcorner}$*(!?) ^{3}*ša sahir rabi pá-$^{\ulcorner}$hu-ri$^{\urcorner}$-im i-na* ^{4}*pu-úh-ri-šu-nu a-na tupšarrim* ^{5}*i-qá-bi$_{4}$-ú-ma
sahir rabi tupšarrum* ^{6}*ú-pá-ha-ar ba-lúm a-ui-li* ^{7}*rabi-ú-tim nam-e-dim ue-dum* ^{8}*a-ui-lúm
ša ník-ka-sí a-na* ^{9}*tupšarrim ú-lá i-qá-bi$_{4}$-ma* ^{10}*sahir rabi ú-lá ú-pá-ha-ar* ^{11}*šu-ma
tupšarrum ba-lúm a-ui-li* ^{12}*rabi-ú-tim i pì-i ue-dim* ^{13}*sahir rabi up-ta-hi-ir 10 šiqlē
kaspam* ^{14}*tupšarrum i-ša-qal*: "[if] they (i.e., the seniors) do not solve their case, they

will in their assembly give orders to the clerk concerning assembling young and old, and the clerk will assemble young and old. One single man may not without (the consent of) a majority of the seniors give orders to the clerk concerning settling of accounts, and the latter may not assemble young and old. If the clerk without (the consent of) the seniors at the bidding of single (man) has assembled young and old, the clerk shall pay 10 shekels (of) silver." Our rendering assumes that this ordinance sets forth the procedure to be followed when a difficult case dealing with the settling of accounts was transferred from a lower court (that of the *rabiūtum* alone?) to "the colony young and old," and a meeting of the latter body was to be called. For our reading and restoration of 1. 2 compare *TC* 112 rev. 1′–6′ (see Lewy in *MVAG*, 33, 334–336, No. 289, and Driver and Miles, *The Assyrian Laws*, pp. 376 f.), which appears to deal with a similar transfer: ¹′*i-za-su-ni*[. . . .] ²′*ṭupšarrum a-na* [*šál-ši-šu*] ³′*i-zu-a-sú-nu* [*a-ṃa-tám*] ⁴′*i-pá-šu-ru a-š*[*ar(?) a-ṃa-tám*] ⁵′*ú-lá i-pá-šu-ru*[*ṣaḫir*] ⁶′*rabi i pá-ḫu-*[*ri-im*. . .]: "they shall stand. . . ., the clerk shall divide them into three and they shall solve the case. Where they cannot solve the case (they shall) on assembling young and old. . . . ."

Our translation of *ša ník-ka-sí*, "concerning settling of accounts," takes it as a construction parallel to *ša ṣaḫir rabi paḫḫurim*, "concerning assembling young and old," in l. 3; but Lewy may be right in taking it to denote a person (*MVAG*, 33, 336 ff.), so that we should translate: "a single man in charge of the account may not . . . .give orders to the clerk and the clerk may not etc."

14. See *CCT* 49*b* and Landsberger's discussion in his *Assyrische Handelskolonien* . . . ., p. 11. Cf. Eisser and Lewy in *MVAG*, 35, No. 3 (1930), 164–165 and p. 145.

15. Thus Koschaker, "Cuneiform Law" (art.), *Encyclopaedia of the Social Sciences*, IX (1933), 214, and Landsberger in *Studia et documenta ad jura orientis antiqui pertinentia*, II, 234.

16. See Lautner, *Die richterliche Entscheidung und die Streitbeendigung im altbabylonischen Prozessrechte* ("Leipziger rechtswissenschaftliche Studien," Vol. III), pp. 78–83. On *ṣimdat šarrim* as "legal practice of the king" see Landsberger in *Studia et documenta ad jura orientis antiqui pertinentia* II (Leiden, 1939), p. 120.

17. See Landsberger, *Studia et documenta*, p. 227.

18. "The town" (*ālum*) and "the elders" (*šíbūtum*) must—as urged by Koschaker—be kept distinct. Walther (*Das altbabylonische Gerichtswesen*, pp. 45–64; see esp. pp. 55 and 64) was inclined to identify "the assembly" (*puḫrum*), "the town" (*ālum*), and "the elders" (*šíbūtum*), and Cuq had earlier voiced the opinion (*RA*, 7 [1909–1910], 87 ff.) that "the assembly" and "the elders" were identical. While Walther's identification of assembly and town is undoubtedly correct (see below; Koschaker in *HG*, VI, 148, follows Walther on this point), the letter which he quotes as indicating identity of town and elders (*CT*, VI, 27*b*) gives no basis for such a conclusion; it merely states that "the town" had given the writer a field, half of which "the elders" have now taken away from him.

That town and elders are not the same thing is clearly shown, on the other hand, by the texts cited *HG*, VI, 148 by Koschaker, *HG*, III, 715 (= Jean, *Tell Sifr* No. 58), and *HG*, V, 1194 (= *TCL*, I, 232), which mention them as distinct entities: *ālum ù šíbūtum*, "the town and the elders." To these texts may now be added *VS*,

XIII, 20, *TCL*, VII, 40, and Lutz, *Legal and Economic Documents from Ashjâly*, No. 107.

Though distinct entities, "the town" and "the elders" could, of course, function together as one tribunal. The texts just quoted suggest that they frequently did so; and in a wider sense "the elders" formed naturally part of the "town."

19. See Walther, *Das altbabylonische Gerichtswesen*, pp. 49–51. The text reads: ¹*i-na pu-ḫur Dil-bat*ki ²m*A-píl-i-lí-šu* ³*ù E-ri-ba-am* ⁴*ki-a-am iq-bu-ú um-ma šu-nu-ma* ⁵*mi-im-ma nu-ma-tum* ⁶*ma-la ḫa-al-qá-at* ⁷*ma-ḫar* d*Ip-te-bi-tam* ⁸*ú-ul i-li-a-am* ⁹*i-na-an-na nu-ma-tum* ¹⁰*i-ta-li-a-am* ¹¹*ki-ma Dil-bat*ki *iq-bu-ú* ¹²*nu-ma-at 1* GAR ¹³⌈*a*⌉*-na ki-iš-ša*(!)*-a-tim* ¹⁴[*ša*] d*Nin-urta-ma-an-si* ⌈*kalêm*⌉ ¹⁵*iz-iz-iz-ma* ¹⁶m*Nu-úr-*d*Šamaš* ¹⁷md*Sú . en-eriš rakbum* ¹⁸md*Sú . en-ma-gir mār Ka-ma-nu* ¹⁹m*Im-gur-*d*Sú . en ra-bi-a-nu* ²⁰m*Iš-*[*m*]*a-tum mār Ṣíl-lí-*d*En-líl* ²¹m*A-píl-i-lí-šu šangû* ²²*ša ú-ša-am-nu-ši* ²³m*E-ri-ba-am mār Ḫa-bi-it-Sin* ²⁴*ša a-na ra-bi-iṣ-tim* ²⁵*iš-ša-ak-nu-ši* ²⁶⌈*ú*⌉*-ta-ar-ši*, "In the assembly of Dilbat did Apil-ilishu and Erîbam speak thus: 'None of the property that had disappeared turned up before (the god) Ipte-bîtam. Now the property has turned up!' As Dilbat commanded, the property was put (lit. 'took (its) stand') at the disposition of Ninurta-mansi the *kalû* priest, but so that (*-ma*) Nûr-Shamash, Sîn-erish the *rakbu*, Sîn-magir the son of Kamânu, Imgur-Sîn the mayor, Ishmatum the son of Ṣilli-Enlil, and Apil-ilishu the *shangû* are the ones who will have it counted. Eribam the son of Habit-Sîn, who was made commissary for it, will take it back (namely to Ninurta-mansi after it has been counted)." Our translation of *-ma* as "but so that" is based on fact that *-ma* after a verb frequently serves to give the following clause adverbial character, defining more precisely the manner or nature of the action expressed by the verb. Cf., e.g., CH xxxiv 6–8: *im-ta-ḫa-aṣ-ma sí-im-ma-am iš-ta-ka-an-šu*, "has struck so as to give him a wound"; ibid. xxi 28–29: *ú-ba-nam ú-ša-at-ri-iṣ-ma la uk-ti-in*, "has pointed the finger but so that he has not been able to prove it"; etc. Dr. A. Sachs, with whom we discussed this usage, suggested the term "*-ma* of specification."

20. Cf. also Jean, *Tell Sifr* No. 42 (= *HG*, III, 711): *daịānum* (DI-KUR₅) *a-lum ip-ḫu-ur-ma*, "the judge assembled the city," where *a-lum* seems a mistake for *a-lam* (cf. Walther, *Gerichtswesen*, p. 46). There were naturally other "assemblies" besides the one here considered, that constituted by "the town." *Puḫrum* is a general word for "gathering," "assembly," and is used in other phrases such as *ina puḫur aḫḫēịa*, "in the assembly of my brothers," and *puḫur ummâni*, "the collegium of scholars." The elders likewise, when they gathered for deliberation, formed a *puḫrum*, "an assembly"; note, e.g., the words of the elders in the Gilgamesh Epic (Tablet III 11): *i-na pu-uḫ-ri-ni-ma ni-ip-qí-dak-ka šarra*, "in our assembly have we entrusted the king unto thee," and the letter *YOS* II 50:8:: *20 ši-bu-ut a-lim ú-pa-aḫ-ḫi-ir-šum-ma*, "twenty elders of the city I gathered on his account." In an omen text, *KAV* 218 A iii 19 (cf. K 2920 [*BA* V 705] rev. 10; Weidner, *Handbuch der babylonische Astronomie*, pp. 85 ff. iii 19), we are told that *ši-bu-ut âli ana puḫri uṣ-*[*ṣu-ni*], "the elders of the town will go out to the assembly," a statement which might refer to a normal session of the elders but more likely has reference to a joint session with the general assembly of the townspeople as "the town and the elders."

21. Note, e.g., the *a-ụi-il-tum mārat I-da-ma-ra-aṣ*ki, "lady, citizen of Idamaraṣ," mentioned in *VS*, XVI, 80.

22. We cannot be certain. Note in this connection that the *puḫrum* of the gods was open to goddesses. In the Gilgamesh Epic (Tablet XI, 116 ff.) Ishtar reproaches herself for having advocated the flood in the assembly of the gods, and in the Old Babylonian hymn *RA*, 22 (1925), 170–171, rev. 33–35, we hear that: [33]*pu-uḫ-ri-šu-un e-te-el qá-bu-ú-ša šu-tu-úr* [34]*a-na An-nim šar-ri-šu-nu ma-la-am aš-ba-as-su-nu* [35]*uz-na-am ne-me-qé-em ḫa-si-i-sa-am er-še-et*, "in their (i.e., the gods') assembly her word is highly esteemed, is surpassing; she sits among them counting as much (with them) as Anum, their king. She is wise in (terms of) intelligence, profundity, and knowledge." (The translation of l. 34 follows a Von Soden manuscript in the Oriental Institute.) Similarly Gudea calls on Inanna to curse in the assembly (ukkin) the man who would remove his statue and destroy its inscription (Gudea Statue C iv 9–12), and several other passages could be cited. Noteworthy parallels for participation of women in political assemblies furnish ancient Israel (see A. Menes, *Die vorexilischen Gesetze Israels* (*Zeitschrift für alttestamentliche Wissenschaft*, Beiheft L. [Giessen, 1925], p. 89) and the Manchus. Among the latter the women formed an assembly parallel to that of the men, but questions of importance to men and women alike were dealt with in a special assembly of both sexes (see Thurnwald in Ebert, *Reallexikon der Vorgeschichte* X (Berlin, 1927–1928), 215.

23. K. 8282 obv. i 25–29 (*PSBA* [1916], pl. VII opposite p. 132) restored by K. 3364 (*CT*, XIII, 29). Cf. Langdon's transliteration and translation, *PSBA* (1916), pp. 132 E and 113 E. The relevant lines read:

> [25]*[ina pu]-uh–ri e ta-'i–ir ú–zu–uz–za*
> [26]*[a-šar ṣal-t]im–ma e tu–ut–tag–ge–eš*
> [27]*[ina ṣal-tim]–ma i–ra–áš–šu–ka šim–ta*
> [28]*[ù at-ta] a–na ši–bu–ti–šú–nu taš–šak–kin–ma*
> [29]*[a–na la di]–ni–ka ub–ba–lu–ka a–na kun–ni*

24. *Uzuzzu*, "to stand," and *uašābu*, "to sit," are technical terms for participating in the *puḫrum*. On *uzuzzu* cf., e.g., Sidney Smith, *Babylonian Historical Texts*, Pl. VIII v 8: *izza-zu ina puḫri ú-šar-ra-ḫu ra-[ma-an-šu]*, "he (i.e., Nabonidus) stands in the assembly and lauds himself"; cf. Landsberger and Bauer in *ZA*,n.F. 3, 92. The same usage occurs with "town and elders" in *TCL*, VII, 40:[md] *Šamaš-ḫa-ṣí-ir a-lum ù ši-bu-tum iz-zi-zu*, "Shamash-ḫāṣir, the town, and the elders 'stood,'" i.e., "took their place in the assembly." A different, essentially oligarchic, picture of the Old Babylonian assembly is given by Leo Oppenheim in *Orientalia*, 5 (new ser., 1936), 224–228. Oppenheim thinks the assembly was limited to "elders" and "nobles." His evidence for this is primarily the omen passage Clay, *BRM*, IV, 15, 24–27 (duplicate ibid., 16, 22–25) which he renders as "Die 'Patrizier' werden zusammentreten und das Land (nicht) regieren.....Die 'Ältesten' werden zusammentreten und das Land (nicht) regieren." Such a rendering is, however, not tenable. We must—in view of the variant text presented by the duplicate—translate: "Kings (var. "Two kings") will team up and will (will not) dominate the land..... Elders will team up and will (will not) dominate the land." The term used, lugal-e-ne, means "kings," never "nobles," "patricians." The reference is apparently to

conditions such as prevailed, e.g., in the early years of Hammurabi when a number of kinglets played for power in Babylonia through systems of alliances (cf. the letter quoted by Dossin in *Syria*, 1938, p. 117). The "land" is presumably the land of the person receiving the omen, it may become dominated by a coalition of foreign kings or by a group of influential elders in the council of its own ruler.

25. See Walther, *Gerichtswesen*, pp. 45 ff., and Koschaker, *HG*, VI, 148.

26. *HGT* 100 iii 35–38.

27. *BE*, VI, 2, No. 10.

28. *BE*, VI, 2, No. 10:16–17: pu-úḫ-ru-um Nibru^{ki}-ka inim-inim-ma igi bí-in-du₈-eš-ma, "In the assembly of Nippur they examined the statements." For the meaning of the phrase *igi-du₈*, Akkadian *amārum*, cf. *HGT* 100 i 36–38 *a-ya-ti-šu-nu i-mu-ru ṭup ni-iš ilim ma-aḫ-ri-a-am iš-mu-ú ši-bi-šu-nu i-ša-lu*, "They examined their statements, listened to the document concerning the earlier oath by a deity, asked their witnesses."

29. *HGT* 100 iii 39 ff.

30. E.g., bí-in-bé-eš, "they commanded" (*BE*, VI, 2, No. 10:19). Cf. *ki-ma Dil-bat^{ki} iq-bu-ú* in *VS*, VII, 149:11; see above, n. 19.

31. Civil cases are *BE*, VI, 2, No. 10, dispute about ownership of house and garden; *HGT* 100, case about disputed paternity; *VS*, VII, No. 141, disposal of lost property (?); *CT*, VIII, 19, Bu 91–5–9, 650, nullification of contract entered into under duress. Criminal cases are *CT*, IV, 1–2, BM 78176 obs. 19 ff., seditious utterances; *PBS*, VIII, 2, No. 173, murder.

32. *PBS*, VIII, 2, No. 173.

33. CḤ §5.

34. *CT*, IV, 1–2, BM 78176 obv. 19 ff.

35. Boissier in *RA*, 16 (1919), 163 lines, 7–12: cf. ibid., p. 206. The lines in question read: ³⁵*i-na Ugar-*^d*En-líl* (or ^d*Sú.en*? Thus Professor Gelb) *bi-ri-i-it* ²⁶*É-sa-bad bít* ^d*Gu-la* ²⁷*Kiši^{ki} ip-ḫu-ur-ma* ²⁸*^mIp-ḫur-kiši^{ki} ayil Kiši^{ki}* ²⁹*mār*(?) *ma* ⸢*ar* (?)⸣ *sa*(?) ⸢*at*⸣ *eš₄-tár za ar ri iḫ tim* ³⁰*a-na ša*[*r*]-⸢*ru*⸣-[*t*]*im iš-šu-ma*. A valuable discussion of the text is given in *ZA*,n.F. 8, (1934), 77–79, by Güterbock, who probably underrates the historical element in the tradition. The name Ipḫurkish to which he objects as "künstlich" is now attested in an unpublished literary tablet from Tell Asmar (As. 31:T.729) of Agade date.

36. *PBS*, X, 2, No. 5; *SEM*, No. 29; *SRT*, No. 38; Fish in Johns Rylands Library (Manchester), *Bulletin*, 19 (1935), 362–372. The text was edited in unsatisfactory transliteration and translation by Witzel in *Orientalia*, 5 (new ser., 1936), 331–346. We refer, following Witzel, to the Johns Rylands text as A, to *PBS*, X, 2, No. 5 as B.

37. ⸢^d⸣Giš-BIL-ga-mes igi ab-ba uru-na-ka [KA] ba-an-gar.... A obv. i 3–4.

38. [é-gal] Kiši^{ki}-šè gú nam-ba-an-gá-gá-an-dé-en ^{giš}tukul ga-àm-ma-síg-en-dè-en A obv. i 8.

39. [ukkin]-gar-ra ab-ba uru-na-ke₄ ^dGiš-BIL-ga-mes-ra mu-na-ni-⸢íb⸣-gi₄-gi₄ A obv. i 9–10.

40. ^dGiš-BIL-ga-mes en Kul-aba^{ki}-ke₄ [....] nir-gál-[la-e] inim ab-ba uru^{ki}-na-ke₄ šà-ga-ni al-ḫúl ur₅-ra-ni ba-an-sig₅ A obv. i 15, B obv.

41. min-kam-ma-šè ᵈGiš-ʙɪɪ-ga-mes igi ⌈guruš⌉ [uru-na-ka] ᴋᴀ ba-an-gar .... B obv. 3′–4′.

42. The text, B obv. 14′, has nam-ḫa- for expected gá-am, presumably by dittography from the preceding form.

43. u₄-bi-a ᵈGiš-ʙɪʟ-ga-mes en Kul-abaᵏⁱ-ke₄ [inim guruš uru]⌈ᵏⁱ⌉-na-šè šà-ga-ni an-ḫúl ur₅-ra-ni ba-an-ša₄ B obv. 25′ rev. 1.

44. Other evidence contributes in some measure to the picture of the two groups which the above text presents.

The elders were, to judge from the Sumerian terms abba, literally "father," and abba uru, "town fathers," originally the heads of the various large families which made up the population of the town. Assembled they would therefore represent an aggregate of the *patria potestas* in the community. Their relation to the king appears to have been that of counselors. In the Gilgamesh Epic they are once explicitly so named: *iš-me-e-ma* ᵈGiš *si-ki-ir ma-li-[ki]-šu*, "Gilgamesh listened to the words of his counselors" (Old Babylonian version, *YOS* IV 3 v 20). Being at first opposed to letting Gilgamesh set out against Huwawa, they are later, it seems, won over to the plan so that he leaves with their blessings and much paternal advice as to how one should behave on a long journey (*YOS* IV 3 iv 19 ff.). Truly paternal is also the solicitude for the young king which inspires their words to Engidu, who is to guide and guard Gilgamesh: "In our assembly we have entrusted the king to thee, thou wilt entrust the king to us again" (*i-na pu-uḫ-ri-ni-ma ni-ip-qí-dak-ka šarra tu-tar-ram-ma ta-paq-qí-dan-na-ši šarra*, Tablet III 11–12). They appear once more in the Gilgamesh Epic when Gilgamesh gives vent to his sorrow over Engidu's death to them (Tablet VIII ii 1 ff.), and Utanapishtim refers to them in the flood story when he asks Ea what explanation he shall give for building his big ship: "What shall I answer the town, the craftsmen and the elders?" [*mi-na-m*]*i lu-pu-ul âlu um-ma-nu ù ši-bu-tum* (Tablet XI 35. For a daring and interesting, different, interpretation of this line see Speiser's paper quoted in n. 1 above).

The "assembly" to which Gilgamesh turns after he has obtained the consent of the elders is composed of the "men" of his town. The Sumerian word used, guruš, is in the older inscriptions the usual designation of an individual as a unit in the apparently identical labor and military organization of the city-state (see *O.I.P.* LVIII, P. 297), and since the assembly has been convened to consider a line of action which will almost certainly lead to war it is not unlikely that we should view it as essentially a gathering of the male population bearing arms (parallels for "the male population bearing arms" as the original nucleus of legislative assemblies are many; we may mention the Roman *comitia* as an example). In the same direction points also another term which can be used to designate the members of the assembly, namely mes "man," "hero." This term, which like guruš is rendered as *eṭlum* in Akkadian, occurs in the compound ukkin-mes (Deimel, *ŠL*, 40:7) "assembly man" (the connotations of age suggested by the Akkadian translation *puršumu*, "old man," and *abu*, "father," "elder," cannot be original, for in Sumerian mes denotes the man in his prime). It appears also—as loanword in Akkadian—as *mēsum* in *Enûma eliš* Tablet VI 166–167 *u-ši-bu-ma ina ukkin-na-šu-nu i-nam-bu-u ši-ma-a-šu ina mé-e-si nag-ba-šu-nu u-zak-ka-ru-ni šum-šu*, "they (i.e., the gods) sat down in their assembly to proclaim his destiny, in the gathering of all the (staunch) men they were mentioning his name." Lastly we may point to the use of *puḫrum*, "assembly," for "army," a usage which is especially frequent in Assyrian sources (for this use of *puḫrum* see *HW* 520b *puḫrum* 1 a).

45. See *CT*, XV, 3 i 7: ᵈ*En-líl pa-šu i-pu-ša-am-ma i pu-uḫ-ri ka-la i-li iz-za-ak-kà-ar*, "Enlil opened his mouth and spoke in the assembly of all the gods."

46. See above, n. 22.

47. *Enûma eliš* Tablet III 130–132. See, e.g., R. Labat, *Le Poème babylonien de la création* (Paris, 1935), A. Heidel, *The Babylonian Genesis* (Chicago, 1942). Compare also the older English translation by Langdon, *The Babylonian Epic of Creation* (Oxford, 1923).

48. *Enûma eliš* Tablet III 133–138. See the literature quoted in n. 47. We have quoted the passage in Heidel's rendering.

49. With the banquet which here serves as introduction to the session of the assembly of the gods may be compared the banquet with which each session of the Greek *Boulē* commenced in Homeric times (see Glotz, *The Greek City and Its Institutions* [New York, 1930], p. 47). An even more striking parallel, to which Professor Cameron called our attention, is furnished by the Persian customs described by Herodotus i. 133. See, furthermore, the article, "Mahlzeit und Trinkgelage," §6 in O. Schrader, *Reallexikon der indogermanischen Altertumskunde* (2d ed.; Leipzig, 1929), II, 30, which quotes also the Germanic parallels (Tacitus *Germ.* 22).

50. The two groups which stand out from the ordinary members of the *puḫrum*, the *ilū rabiūtum* and the *ilū šīmāti* or *mušimmu šīmāti*, are mentioned already in the myth of Enlil and Ninlil (Barton, *MBI* No. 4 ii 13–14; Chiera, *SEM* 77 ii 5′–6′; Pinches in *JRAS*, 1919, pp. 190 f. rev. 1–2) as dingir gal-gal ninnu-ne-ne dingir nam-tar-ra imin-na-ne-ne, "all the fifty senior gods and the seven gods who determine fates." *Enûma eliš* mentions them in Tablet III 130: *ilāni rabûti ka-li-šu-nu mu-šim-mu šīmati*, "all the senior gods, the determiners of fates," and again in Tablet IV 80: *ilū rabûti ḫa-am-šat-su-nu u-ši-bu-ma ilū šīmāti sibitti-šu-nu a-na* [ᵈ*Marduk šīmāti*] *uk-tin-nu*, "The fifty senior gods sat down, and the seven gods of fates fixed fates for Marduk." The assembly described in Tablet III is convoked with the express purpose of giving Marduk power as a determiner of fates, whose word is decisive.

We have little evidence concerning the mutual relation of "the senior gods" and "the seven gods who determine fate." The language of the texts just quoted would seem to indicate that they were separate and parallel groups. Yet it is possible —and to us more likely—that the seven gods who determine destiny formed merely a part of "the senior gods."

The functions of "the seven gods who determine destinies" may be deduced from the term itself. The concepts underlying that expression are clear from the account in *Enûma eliš* (cf. the literature quoted in n. 40), Tablet IV. They belong with ideas such as "le verge créateur" and the "wish come true." The god who can "determine destiny" possesses a power, a magical and absolute authority, over all things in the universe, whereby anything he may order immediately comes true. Reality so to speak automatically conforms itself to his command. When the gods have conferred this power on Marduk by word of mouth, they test it—an early instance of the "experimental technique"—by bringing a garment and having Marduk command that it be destroyed, which comes true, then that it again be whole, which also comes true.

Translating these mythical concepts into "political" terms, we must define the seven gods "who determine destiny" as gods whose words are "authoritative" or "decisive."

With the group of "senior" gods should undoubtedly be compared the "seniors" (*rabiūtum*) in the *kārum* of the Assyrian merchant colonies, while the seven deciding gods may well have their counterpart in the group of seven which, as Eisser has shown (see above, n. 12), could represent the *kārum* when it sealed documents.

51. Cf. *RA*, 22, (1925), 169–177, rev. 33 f.: quoted in n. 22 above.

52. *KAR* No. 80 (cf. the duplicate BM 78242 published by Langdon in *RA*, 26, 39–42) says of Shamash (obv. 21): *ina puḫur ilī rabûti* (DINGUR-MEŠ GAL-MEŠ) *ši-ma-*[*a*]*t qì-bi-su*, "In the assembly of the senior gods his utterance is listened to"; note also King, *BMS*, No. 19, where a man prays: *ina puḫri lu še-mat qí-bi-ti*, "Let my word be listened to in the assembly."

53. The terms are: *šitūlum*, "to ask one another" (cf. Meissner and Rost in *BA* III 331, Bu 88–5–12, 78 viii 12′: *ina Ub-šu-⌜ukkin-na-ki⌝ ki-sal puḫur ilâni* (DINGIR-MEŠ) *šu-bat ši-tul-ti*, "in Ubshuukkinna, the court of the assembly of the gods, the abode of discussion," and the Agushaia song, *VS*, X, 214 rev. i 14: *ip-ta-aḫ-ru iš-ta-lu*, "they gathered and discussed"), and *šutāu̯ûm*, "to talk with one another" (e.g., King, BMS 1 obv. 15 *izzazū* (GUB-BU) *pu-ḫur-šu-nu uš-ta-mu-ú ina šapli* (KI-TA)-*ka*, "They stand (in) their assembly and discuss under thee"). A vivid account of a discussion between An, Enlil, and Shamash is preserved in the Hittite version of the Gilgamesh Epic; see Friedrich in *ZA*,n.F. 5, 16–19.

54. Gilgamesh Epic, Tablet XI 116. We have quoted Leonard's rendering (*Gilgamesh, Epic of Old Bablyonia, a Rendering in Free Rhythms*, by Ellery Leonard [New York], pp. 64–65).

55. See n. 50 above.

56. Chiera, *STVC* 25 obv. 18–19 (see below, p. 168); also *HGT* 1 iv 9–10: di-til-la inim pu-úh-ru-[um dingir-re-ne-ka] du_{11}-du_{11}-ga An ^{d}En-[líl-lá-ka-ta].

57. In the *Lamentation over the Destruction of Ur* (*AS* XII), lines 171 ff. it is Enlil who gives the detailed orders concerning the destruction.

58. Meissner and Rost in *BA* III 331, Bu 88–5–12, 78 viii 12′ ff. (cf. Luckenbill, *AR* II §658): *ina Ub-šu-⌜ukkin-na-ki⌝ ki-sal pu-ḫur ilani* (DINGIR-MEŠ) *šu-bat ši-tul-ti a-mat-su li-lam-min*$_4$*-ma u*$_4$*-mu ište-en la ba-laṭ-su liq-bi*, "May he (i.e., Marduk) in Ubshuukkinna, the court of the assembly of the gods, the abode of discussion, make bad his case; may he order that he live not a full day."

59. Related in the story of Ea and Atar-ḫasis (*CT*, XV, 49, iii 4 ff. and 37 ff.). See Sidney Smith's restoration of the text in *RA*, 22 (1935), 67 f. A parallel Sumerian story is *HGT* No. 1. See *The Sumerian King List*, p. 39, n. 113.

60. For the myth of Enlil and Ninlil see Barton, *MBI*, No. 4; Chiera, *SEM* 77, and Pinches in *JRAS*, 1919, pp. 190 f. Note that the word ukkin / *puḫrum* is not explicitly used.

61. *Enûma eliš*, Tablet II 16–26.

62. Ibid., Tablet II 123–129. Heidel, *The Babylonian Genesis*, p. 27, translates, following a suggestion by Delitzsch, 1, 127, *ip-šu pi-ia ki-ma ka-tu-nu-ma ši-ma-tam lu-šim-ma*, as "May I through the utterance of my youth determine the destinies, instead of you." Though possible, this interpretation seems unlikely. The gods continue to "determine destinies" long after Marduk has received the powers he here desires. It is therefore improbable that his powers should have voided theirs, and we have accordingly retained the translation "as," "like unto," for *kîma*, the more so since that is the meaning which *kîma* usually has.

63. Ibid., Tablet IV 3–10, 13–16.

64. Ibid., Tablet IV 28–32. We have quoted the passage in Heidel's rendering (*The Babylonian Genesis*, p. 27).

.65. The account which *Enûma eliš* gives of how Marduk became king is of the greatest importance for the light which it throws on the origin and early nature of the Mesopotamian kingship. It shows the king as primarily a leader in war, chosen by the general assembly to provide unified leadership in the emergency. We hope to treat of it in detail in a later article.

66. The word bala means "term of office." As *nomen actionis* of the verb bal, "to turn," its basic meaning would seem to have been "turn." For the semasiological development involved Deimel, *ŠL* 9:1, aptly compared Latin *turnus*. Besides being used of the royal office, it applies to temple offices: guda, bappir ("brewer"), nedu ("janitor"), kisal-luḫ ("court-sweeper"), buršuma ("elder"), etc. Such an office was held in turn by various individuals throughout the year, each holding it for a stated period (bala). The right to hold a specific office for a specific period of the year (bala) was inheritable and could be transferred by sale. Inherited offices were called bala gub-ba, e.g., bala gub-ba N-a(k), "offices to which N. has succeeded (lit. 'stepped into by N.')," as contrasted with kù-ta-sa$_x$ N-a(k), i.e., (offices) which N. bought with money. For the contrast see *PBS*, VII, 2, No. 182. The following may serve as an example of the use of the word: bala é ^{d}Ig-alim-ka itu 6-àm Ur-^{d}lamma dumu Lugal-ušum-gal-ke$_4$ ì-dab. "The term of office in (lit. 'of') the temple of (the god) Igalima lasting six months does Urlamma the son of Lugalushumgal hold" (*RTC* 288:2–3; cf. the bala's of four, two, and twelve months mentioned in the following lines, and see also *ITT* III 6575 and *ITT* II 1010 + V 6848). The holder of a bala was designated as a lú bala, i.e., "man of a bala," translated as *be-el pa-ar-ṣi*, "holder of office," in *HGT* 147:14.

Akkadian borrowed the Sumerian word as *palû* and restricted it to "term of royal office." Since in the older Assyrian royal inscriptions this term is one year, *palû* there means "regnal year." In Babylonia, however, the ruler's term of office was conceived as the total period during which he served; hence *palû* has there the meaning "reign."

67. ^{m}*Šarru-kên*(DU) *šar A-ga-dè*^{ki} *palê* ^{d}*Iš-tar i-lam-ma*, "Sargon, king of Akkad appeared in the *palû* of Ishtar" (L. W. King, *Chronicles concerning Early Babylonian Kings*, II [London, 1907], 113, obv. 1 [cf. p. 3 obv. 1]). A *palû* of Enlil is mentioned in an omen text, *CT*, XXVII Pl. 22 10, *palê* ^{d}*En-líl šanāti* (MU-MEŠ) *šarri kêni*(GI-NA) *ina māti ú-šab-šá tarbāṣu šū irappiš*, "Palû of Enlil. The years of a true king he will

cause to be in the land; that fold will grow large." A *palû* of Nergal, the god of the nether world, finds more frequently mention in omen texts; it is synonymous with tyranny, enemy uprising, and everything bad. See, e.g., *CT*, XX, Pl. 31–33, l. 78; ibid., Pl. 34, iv 18; *CT*, XXVII, Pl. 9 l. 27, pl. 10, l. 22, etc.

68. Chiera, *STVC* 25 obv. 14–rev. 23. The passage reads: ^{14d}En-líl-le dumu-ni ^{d}Sú.en-ra mu-un-[na-ni-íb-gi$_4$-gi$_4$] ^{15}urú líl-lá šà-bi a-nir-ra ír(!?)-[gig î-šeg$_8$-šeg$_8$] ^{16}šà-bi-a a-nir-ra u$_4$ mi-ni-[íb-zal-zal-en] ^{17d}Nanna ⌜sub⌝ ní-za hé-me-b[i....] ^{18}di-til-la inim pu-úḫ-ru-um d[ingir-re-ne-ka] ^{19}du$_{11}$-du$_{11}$-ga An ^{d}En-líl-lá-ka-⌜ta⌝ [....] ^{20}Urí^{ki}-ma nam-l[ugal-bi....ba-an-túm] ^{21}u$_4$-ul kalam ki-gar-ra-ta [....] ^{22}bala nam-lugal-la [šu bala ba-an-ak-ak] ^{23}nam-lugal-bi bala-[bi bala kúr-ra šu bala ba-an-ak]. The third sign in l. 17 appears to be sub (KA + KU. Since it is once glossed su-ub, see Deimel, *ŠL* 33:6, it is presumably to be read as su$_{11}$ + úb). Reduplicated sub, sub-sub, is translated as *šu-kin-nu* "proskynesis" in Akkadian (Deimel, *ŠL* 33:6), and this or a similar meaning may be assumed also for the unreduplicated word. Its use in our phrase recalls the use of *šukênum* in the Old Assyrian texts from Asia Minor as a technical term for submitting to the jurisdiction of a court. It seems probable that Nanna, whose case was adjudged by the assembly of the gods, had first formally submitted to the jurisdiction of that court. Enlil now reminds him that this bound him to accept his verdict, the "Let it be!" which the assembly pronounced. For the term "Let it be" see the passage from the *Lamentation over the Destruction of Ur*, quoted below, p. 168. With our restoration of ll. 22–23 compare the phraseology of *PBS*, X, 2, No. 15, obv. 21: é-zi-da bala-bi bala-kúr-ra šu-bal-ak-a-bi, "the term of the righteous temple, which has been changed for a different term."

69. Kramer, *Lamentation over the Destruction of Ur* (*AS* XII [Chicago, 1940]). For the structure of the poem as well as for its date and historical background see my review in *AJSL*, 58 (1941), 219–224.

70. Kramer, *Lamentation over the Destruction of Ur*, p. 32, 152–164. Except for ll. 152–153, our translation differs from his (ibid., p. 33) on minor points only. In l. 152, since puḫrum does not take the determinative KI, we must read ki sag ki-a ba-da-gál-la. For sag, "people," "(one's) folks," "(the) members of a family," cf. sag = *nišê*, Howardy, *Clavis* 129:34, and ki-sag-gál-la = *ašar emûti* and *ašar kimâti* ibid., 451:75–76.

71. It seems likely that this phrase refers to a promise by which the members of the assembly bound themselves to abide by the decision taken in the assembly.

72. In *Encyclopaedia of the Social Sciences*, IX, 355, and VII, 11. Compare also O. Schrader, *Reallexikon der indogermanischen Altertumskunde* (2d ed.; Leipzig, 1917–1929) article "König" §14:1–3 (I, 620–621) and article "Volksversammlung" (II, 609–611). Closely parallel patterns are found also in ancient Greece, where the institutions of the Homeric age are especially pertinent (see Glotz, *The Greek City and Its Institutions* [New York, 1930], Part I, chap. i, esp. pp. 39–57) and in ancient Israel (see A. Menes, *Die vorexilischen Gesetze Israels* (*Zeitschrift für alttestamentliche Wissenschaft*, Beiheft L. pp. 21–23, and especially the chapter "Der Staat und seine Organe," pp. 88–96). Noteworthy, though less striking, are the parallels found in the organization of the Hittite state (see Hardy, "The Old Hittite Kingdom," *AJSL*, 58 [1941], 214–215).

10. The Reign of Ibbī-Suen

1. References to Enlil's wrath are frequent in Ibbī-Suen's letters, see e.g. the letter to Puzur-Numushda of Kazallu, Falkenstein *ZA*, 49, 60 ff. lines 15 ff. and Kramer in Pritchard *ANET* pp. 480–481.

For the views of following generations see the Lamentation over the Destruction of Ur, Kramer *AS* XII and *ANET* pp. 455–463. Cf. also *AJSL* 58 (1941) 221 f. and Falkenstein *ZA*, 49, 320–324.

2. See Nies, *UDT* 100 dated to Shū-Suen 9 and mentioning *u₄ I-bí-ᵈSú.en* TÙN *šu-ba-an-ti-a* "The day when Shū-Suen assumed the crown(?)." We consider it certain that TÙN here stands for AGA "crown" (thus also Oppenheim, *Eames Coll.* p. 110 to L. 20) because of *PBS* X 4 No. 2 ii 16–17 ᵈ*En-ki en gal Eridu*ᵏⁱ-*ga-ke₄* TÙN-*zi-mah sag-mà ha-ma-ni-in*⌐*gar*⌐, "may Enki, the great lord of Eridu(g) place the exalted true crown upon my head" (cf. also *TRS* 13 iv 53) and since the simple signs are often used for the corresponding *gunû* forms (see Poebel quoted by Hallock, *AS* VII p. 10, note 13, p. 51 to ll. 19–21 and p. 58 to l. 154 f., also apud (Meek, *HSS* X p. x, note 7). The TÙN of Amar-Suena(k) is mentioned in *TÉO* 6046 iv 11, which lists the price of gold inlays for it. See now also the material presented succinctly by E. Sollberger, *JCS* 7 (1953) 48 f. The new text MAH 19352, in conjunction with Nies, *UDT* 100, would appear to suggest that the king was crowned successively in Nippur, Uruk, and Ur. Should this interpretation prove true, we may see in the successive coronations survivals from the time when Uruk and Ur were independent monarchies.

3. So far our only evidence is that of the Sumerian King List. See *AS* XI p. 122. Since Falkenstein has shown (*WO* 2, [1947] 45) that the King List incorrectly makes Shū-Suen the son of Amar-Suena(k), whereas in reality he was the son of Shulgi(r), the authority of the King List in such matters cannot be considered beyond question. To the evidence for Shū-Suen's paternity quoted by Falkenstein (Chiera *SRT* 23 11 8 and 18) should be added *BRM* III 52, the seal used by Shū-Suen when he was as yet only *šagub* of Uruk. In it he mentions Shulgi(r) as his father. A Sumerian rather than a Semitic reading of the name of Amar-Suena(k) is indicated by writings showing that it ended in -*k*; see, e.g., the writings with -*ke₄* in the formula for his second year quoted by Schneider in *ZWU* [and by the writing A-*már-sin-na-ra* in *Nik.* 3803 iii 10; Kramer, *Orientalia* N.S. 22 (1953) plate XL].

4. See Appendix at the end of this article.

5. See *UET* III 1242, a text dated to the sixth (Legrain: eighth) year of Ibbī-Suen which mentions *Ma-ma*[?] *ama lugal* "Mama...the mother of the king."

6. *Gemé-ᵈEn-líl-lá* is mentioned as "queen" (*nin*) in the fifth year of Ibbī-Suen (*UET* III Nos. 376 and 379) and again in his fifteenth (Legrain: twenty-fourth year (*UET* III 1383). Note also the mention of her name in Hackm. *BIN* V No. 6, 27. That she was not married to Ibbī-Suen until after his first year as king may be concluded from *CT* XXXII 43 iii 25, dated to that year, in which she is mentioned as "princess" (*dumu-munus lugal(-ak)*) only, not yet as "queen" (*nin*). On the basis of this passage it has been concluded that she was the daughter (Keiser, *Patesis* p. 34) or the sister (Schneider, *Götternamen*, *An. Or.* XIX p. 202) of Ibbī-Suen.

Since it is not very likely that Ibbī-Suen should have married his own daughter, Schneider's implicit assumption that her title *dumu-munus lugal* in *CT* XXXII 43 iii 25 was carried over unchanged from the preceding reign of Shū-Suen seems preferable. A comparable case is that of the prince *Lugal-á-zi-da*, who occurs with the title *dumu lugal* "son of the king" under Shulgi(r) (Nik. 530, 3) as well as under Amar-Suena(k) (*RA* 10 210; cf. Keiser, *Patesis* p. 33, note 2). Though we have here spoken in terms of a carry-over of titles from one reign to another we are actually inclined to go a step farther and to assume that titles such as *dumu lugal(ak)* and *dumu-munus lugal(ak)* are to be analyzed—like German "Königssohn" and "Königs-tochter"—as "son of *a* king" and "daughter of *a* king," not as "son of *the* king" and "daughter of *the* king." They should therefore be translated simply "prince" and "princess." Compare also the parallel *a-nun-na-ke₄-ne* "descendants (lit. 'seed') of princes" = "nobles." See *JNES* 5 (1946) 135, note 11 [see above, chap. vii].

7. This can of course be only a guess. The possible objection that the formula for Ibbī-Suen's fifth year shows that he had a daughter of marriageable age is not valid since the title *dumu-munus lugala(k)* given to Tukîn-ḫatta-migrisha need not mean that she was the daughter of Ibbī-Suen. See the preceding note.

8. Ir-Nanna(k) is mentioned as *sukkal-maḫ* as late as Ibbī-Suen's second year (e.g., Gen. *Tr. D.* 83; *ITT* 6032). His successor, ᵈ*Nin-líl-ama-mu* (known as simple *sukkal* as early as A.S. 8, see Nies *UDT* no. 126 and cf. *UET* III 165, I.S. 7, where he is styled *rá-gaba*) first occurs with the title *sukkal-maḫ* in I.S. 12 (Legrain 20) *UET* III 45, cf. the more complete copy of the seal in *UET* I 97. He seems in his turn to have been followed by Libur-ᵈSuen, first mentioned in I.S. 21 (Legrain 21) in *UET* III 286 ii. Ir-ᵈNanna(k) came of a virtual dynasty of *sukkal-maḫ*'s. His grandfather *La-ni* held that office under Shulgi(r) (cf. Gen. *TD* 5537 Š.29 and 5538 Š.32 [year count adjusted in accordance with F. R. Kraus, *Orientalia* N.S. 20 (1951), 385–398]). Lani's son (see *SAK* p. 196b′ = AO 4198, see note c) *Ur-ᵈŠul-pa-è* is mentioned in the seal impression of an undated text (Lutz, *UCP* IX p. 118 TN 45) and probably served through the reign of Amar-Suena(k). A *sukkal-maḫ* *Ìr-mu* occurs in A.S. 3 (*BE* III 36) and in Š.S. 1 (*RA* 9 39–64 No. 13.7). Whether he may be identified with Ir-Nanna(k) is doubtful. Ir-ᵈNanna(k) is first mentioned as *sukkal-maḫ* in Š.S.1 (*ITT* 810). His seal stating that he was the son of *Ur-ᵈŠul-pa-è* occurs in *RTC* 429. A mention of him when he was as yet a mere *sukkal* may be found in Gen. *Tr. D.* 85 (dated to S. 47). On this dynasty of *sukkal-maḫ*'s see de Genouillac's discussion in *Tr. D.* p. 10.

The influence of Ir-Nanna(k) on the affairs of the empire may be gauged from his titles listed in his inscription *SAK* p. 148 f. In addition to being *sukkal-maḫ* and governor (*ensi(g)*) of Lagash he is "governor" (*ensi(g)*) or "commandant," i.e., "military governor" (*šagub*) of a series of towns and districts on the border of the empire. This is clearly a means of making available, where it was most needed, authority which could make rapid high-level political and military decisions.

On the reading of Ir-Nanna(k)'s name cf. the Vocabulary Dossin *RA* 21 178 col. iii. 14 *ir*: ARAD:*te-ru-u*[*m*] (read thus with Landsberger *MSL* II p. 149) and ibid., 16 *ur-du*:ARAD:*wa-ar-du-um*. According to this entry ARAD is perhaps preferably to be read *ir* when it means "courtier," "palace servant" (*tīrum*) and *urdu* when it means "slave." The relationship of *ir* to *urdu/arad* and the whole question of the status of the high government officials in the Sumerian state—as their titles show their offices have clearly developed out of those of the house servants of the ruler—is one which badly needs further investigation.

9. See the date formula for the seventh year of Shū-Suen. The place of the year named from the marriage of Tukîn-ḫaṭṭa-migrisha is indicated by *UET* III No. 1554, an account dating to that year, which lists leftover stock from the preceding year as belonging to *mu en-am-gal-an-na* ᵈ*Inanna ba-ḫun*, i.e. to I.S. 4 (See i 1–7 and cf. ii 1–5).

10. See *CT* XXXII 19–22, which lists very substantial taxes in cattle collected from the region at the mouth of the Diyala in the second year of Ibbī-Suen. The tax in question is the *gú ma-da* (Pl. 22 vi 18), there is also a small item for *máš-da-ri-a ezen-maḫ* (Pl. 22 vi 25–26) and a note (ibid., l. 27) that there are no *mu-tù lugal* items.

11. The myth of Emesh and Enten (see Kramer, *Sumerian Mythology*, pp. 49–51; Landsberger, *JNES* 8 248) contains a passage listing the services which Enten "Winter" renders Ibbī-Suen (Barton *MBI* 7 v 5 ff.) and it is a fair assumption that the composition was written in his reign, almost certainly in the most auspicious first years. Another literary document which seems to have been written in his time —more precisely in the second year of Ibbī-Suen—is the so-called History of the Tummal (*HGT* 6 and 7; *PBS* XIII 48 ii). The text, which states that it was written "according to(?) the word of *Lú-*ᵈ*Inanna*, the AŠGAB:GAL of Enlil" (KA *Lú-* ᵈ*Inanna* AŠGAB:GAL ᵈ*En-líl-lá-šè sar-ra*, *HGT* 7 obv. 11–12) ends with the words: "From (the year) 'Amar-Suena(k) became king' (= A.S.1) to (the year) 'Ibbī-Suen, the king, envisaged En-am-gal-an-na the *enu* of Inanna of Uruk on the (omen) kid' (= I.S. 2) I have been leading Ninlil to the Tummal" (*ki* ᵈ*Amar-*ᵈ*Sú.en lugal-ta en-na* ᵈ*I-bí-*ᵈ*Sú.en lugal-[e] En-am-gal-*⌈*an-na*⌉ *en*⌉ ᵈ*Inanna Unug*ᵏⁱ *máš-e in-pà-da* ᵈ*Nin-líl Tum-ma-al*ᵏⁱ*-šè ì-DU-DU* (*HGT* 7, var. *HGT* 6 *ì-DU-DU-en*, *PBS* XIII 48 iii [*ì-DU*]-*DU-dè-en*). A later addition recording Ishbī-Erra's building of the *É-kur-ra-igi-gál-la* of Enlil has in two of the copies (*HGT* 6 and *PBS* XIII iii) been moved up by the copyists to a position before the statement of authorship. *HGT* 7 preserves the earlier arrangement.

12. See *OIP* XLIII p. 170.

13. See Cameron, *History of Early Iran*, p. 57, and ibid., note 40, citing *MDP* X No. 121 and XVIII No. 79.

14. See Reissner, *TU* Nos. 50 and 75.

15. See Keiser, *STD* No. 311.

16. See Myhrman, *BE* III No. 133, Chiera *PBS* VIII No. 157.

17. Animals are provided by "the palace" and "the officiating *ensi(g) (ensi(g) bala(.ak))*" in I.S. 4 (Legrain: 5) Nos. 107, 110, and 113; in I.S. 5 (Legrain: 6) Nos. 122, 128, 136, 137, 138, 188; only in one case, 130, from the *é-REC* 344 or 345, i.e., "the cattle-feeding establishment"(?). The deliveries from the "officiating *ensi(g)*" still occur in No. 158 from I.S. 6 (Legrain: 8) but have been entirely replaced with deliveries from the *é-REC* 344 or 345 in the texts from I.S. 7 (Legrain: 9), cf. Nos. 173, 175, 182, 193, 206, 240. As for curtailments in the offerings note that the normal sequence of offering places: "the gate," ᵈ*Ḫa-ià* (thus according to

unpublished text from Nippur), "the place of the throne," and "the statue of Amar-Suena(k) at the Kar-zagin" is reduced by "the statue of Amar-Suena(k)" in 232 (I.S. 7) and 257 (I.S. 8), and has only *ᵈḪa-ià* in 168 and 185 of I.S. 7. All text references here given are to *UET* III.

18. The crumbling of the empire is referred to in the following omen texts: (1) Rutten, *RA* 35 pl. iv No. 7. *i-nu-mi I-bí-ᵈSú.en ma-zu i-ba-al-ki-tù-šu a-ni-u-um ki-am i-sá(!)-kin*, "When the country of Ibbī-Suen rebelled against him it (lit. 'this') was set down thus." (2) ibid., pl. III No. 6 (cf. von Soden, Orient. NS 15 423 f.) *a-mu-ut sú-ḫu-ra-im ší I-bí-ᵈSú.en ba-* ... (?) *ma-ti-šu i-ba-al-ki-ti-šu*, "Omen of the defection under (lit. 'that of') Ibbī-Suen, of .... of his country—it rebelled against him." We are unable to explain the form of the last verb. (3) Goetze, *YOS* X 36 i 13 f. (see also Goetze, *JCS* 1 261 f.) *šum-ma hašûm ki-ma NÍG.NA₄ hu-ur-ru-ra-at a-mu-ut I-bi-ᵈSú.en ša ma-tum ip-hu-ru-nim*, "If the lung is pitted like a purse (suggested by Landsberger; cf. Howardy, *Clavis* 235.15 and note *YOS* X 14 10 f.) it is the omen of Ibbī-Suen under whom the country assembled (to choose another ruler)." (4) *YOS* X 31 xii 45 ff. (and *JCS* 1 262.) *šumma mar-tum qá-qá-ad ṣe-ri-im ú-ba-nu-um qá-qá-ad er-hi-im ih-ta-ni te-er-tum ši-i ša ša-ah-ma-aš-ti I-bi-ᵈSù.en*, "If the gallbladder is formed like the head of a serpent, the processus pyramidalis like the head of a locust, that message is of the riots under Ibbī-Suen." (5) *YOS* X 26 i 21 (*JCS* 1 262, n. 54). *šumma 2 báb ékallim i-li a-wi-lim ékallamᶦᵃᵐ i-re-di ša-nu-um šu-um-šu a-mu-ut ᶦI-bi-ᵈSú.en ša ša-ah-lu-uq-tim*, "If the 'palace gate' (on the liver) is double: the (personal) god (i.e., 'the will') of a (free-)man will guide the palace, its other name is: omen of Ibbī-Suen concerning destruction." We interpret the meaning of this to be that the will of a member of the commonalty will prevail over that of the crown. This omen (if *šumma 2* is to be emended with Nougayrol, *JAOS* 70 112a to *šumma 3*) may be the same as (6) ibid., 24 10 (cf. 22 11) *šum-ma báb ékallim 3 i-lí ma-tim ékalla-am i-re-du-ú ša-nu šum-šu a-mu-ut I-bi-ᵈSú.en ša ša-ah-lu-uq-tim*, "If the 'palace gate' (on the liver) is triple: the (personal) gods of the (members of the) country will guide the palace. Its other name (is) omen of Ibbī-Suen concerning destruction." (7) ibid., 22 12 *šum-ma báb ékallim 4 a-mu-utᶦI-bi-ᵈSú.en šaša-ah-lu-uq-tim*, "If the 'palace gate' (on the liver) is quadruple it is the omen of Ibbī-Suen concerning destruction." That these omens refer to a state of divided authority seems clear. It is confirmed by ibid., 24 11, which gives the same omen and the interpretation: *ti-bu-ut šar ḫa-am-me-e ša-nu šum-šu ḫi-iš-bu a-na ékallim ú-ul i-ru-ub*, "the rise of a usurper, its other name is: the wealth (of tribute and taxes) will not enter the palace." With this should be compared the failure of the *ensi(g)*'s to send in their contributions to the *eššéšu* offerings for Nanna due under the *bala* turnus in the seventh year of Ibbī-Suen, see note 16 above.

19. *PBS* XIII 9. Duplicates are the unpublished texts Istanbul Ni. 4489 + 4093 + 3045 (= B), a copy of which was kindly placed at my disposal by S. N. Kramer, and 3N–T. 306 (= C) from the recent finds at Nippur. Since *PBS* XIII 9 is the only one of these texts that has so far been published we use it as basis for our treatment. We hope at a later time to give an edition of the series of which this letter formed a part.

20. B: om.

21. B: *-bi-*.

22. Restored from B and C.

23. C: *-a-*, B: om.

24. B and C: *-du$_{11}$*.

25. B: om.

26. B and C: om.

27. Tentatively emended according to B and C which both read *á-šè mu-e-da-ág*. But A may have varied here: *im-tu-[r]e-⌜en⌝*.

28. *1 še-gur-ta-àm* according to B (except for omission of *še*) and C.

29. Thus also B. C: *ba-an-du$_{11}$*.

30. Thus also B and C.

31. B and C: om.

32. C: om.

33. Thus B. C: om.

34. B: om.

35. Thus seemingly B (though the sign inscribed in ŠÁR could be 30 as well as 40).

36. B: + *-ke$_4$*.

37. B and C: *-re-en*.

38. Thus B and C.

39. Thus B. C: *-ni-*.

40. B mistakenly: *-re-en*.

41. Restored from B.

42. C: + *-d[è]*.

43. B and C: om.

44. Thus B. Emend probably to *120(gur)-ta(!)-àm-⌜e⌝*. This emendation has been accepted in the translation.

45. This form of address and the whole correspondence between Ishbī-Erra and Ibbī-Suen show clearly that Ishbī-Erra was in the service of Ibbī-Suen, most likely as a high military officer. Since Ibbī-Suen in the Kazallu correspondence calls him a man from Mari we may assume that Ishbī-Erra was a foreigner(?) who had taken service with the king of Ur and had advanced in the army through his obvious military and administrative talents. As shown by the correspondence Ibbī-Suen himself placed Ishbī-Erra in charge of Isin and Nippur. The assumption sometimes made that he was a ruler of Mari who had conquered Isin is thus to be abandoned. For the general question of the historical validity of the Ur III royal correspondence we refer to Falkenstein, *ZA*, 49, 73 and Güterbock *ZA*, 42, 15. We incline toward Falkenstein's judgment that these are genuine letters stylistically reworked. Even though they should prove to be, in Güterbock's words, "bereits literarische Gestaltungen," the general picture of events and attitudes which they give is probably in its main lines a trustworthy one.

46. We assume *-e-da-* to represent *-'-da-* "with me."

47. Sumerian *ma-da* is translated as MIN (= *ma-a-tum*) "country" in *CT* XII 38 ii 12. Cf. also K 2355 i 24/25 (*CT* XVI 9–11) and *S.Gl.* p. 179. Its use in older sources suggests, however, that it had also a more specific—and probably basic—meaning. Such a meaning is clearly required here where it is plainly distinguished

from *kalam*, i.e., Sumer proper. A clue to what that meaning may have been is offered by Gudea Cyl. A xiv 8–9, where *ma-da gú-sag šár-šár-ra-na Gú-edin-na* ^d*Nin-gír-su-ka-ka*, "in his *mada* abounding in early legumes, in Ningirsu(k)'s Gu-edinna(k)" stands parallel with and in contrast to *uru dù a á-dam-gar-ra-na Gú-giš-bar-ra* ^d*Nanše-ka*, "in his (lands) build (up with) cities and settled (with) populations, in Nanshe's Gu-gishbarra(k)" (ibid., 11–12). From this passage it would appear that *ma-da* means "level land such as may be found on the edge of the desert" (*gú-edin-na*), sparsely inhabited if at all, and contrasting with the well-populated settled areas dotted with towns and villages. Etymologically *ma-da*—clearly a loanword from Akkadian (or Proto-Akkadian?)—could perhaps be connected with the root *m-h-d* from which Arabic has *mahdun* "soil," *muhdun* and *mihādun* "flat terrain." Related to *ma-da* is possibly *ma-a*:MA:MIN (= *ma-mu-u*):*ma-a-tum* listed in the Chicago Syllabary No. 117 (see Hallock *AS* VII p. 19, cf. S^c 98 and VII *S.Gl.* p. 179). It could represent an instance of a loan without final *-a* from *mahd*. Certain early occurrences of loans of the type without *-a* are, however, not easy to find and its range in time is yet to be established. Finally *ma-du-um* "moat" "low ridge"(?), which occurs, e.g., in *OECT* I pl. 7 iii.9 and in the Warad-Sîn inscription VAT 2678 (see Poebel, *AOF* 9, p. 283) should be considered. It may be a late loan from an Akkadian word *mādum* from the same root, though seemingly after some semantic development. The precise relation of these words to Akkadian *mātum*—if such relation exists—is not clear to me. The most satisfactory solution is perhaps to relinquish the suggested connection with Arabic *m-h-d*, and to assume instead an Akkadian *māt-um* as source of the various Sumerian loans. That the unvoiced Sumerian sound, which we conventionally represent by *d* should be used to render Akkadian *t* is normal.

48. See Schneider, *ZWU* pp. 60 f. A. Goetze writes us to this point: "Stephens and I investigated many years ago the dating practices of Ur III. It became quite clear that, during that period, the event mentioned in the date formula is by no means an event of the preceding year. During the earlier part of a year an *ús-sa* formula is always used. As soon as an event takes place which merits furnishing a year's distinctive name, this new name is formulated and announced to the offices of the realm presumably by royal decree. We listed all dated tablets and the point within a year from which on the new date was used came out well. Of course there remained a small overlap. There is never a year which begins right away with the new name (as it does indeed in Old Babylonian times)."

References to events used for date formulas outside the formulas bear this out rather well (Cf. Keiser, *STD* 74 quoted by Schneider and as other examples, e.g., Gen. *Tr. D.* 86 and *TD* 5485). It may accordingly be assumed that the sacking of Šaš(šu)ru(m) referred to in Schneider, *DDU* 83 (A.S. 2) and of Šaš-šu)ru(m) and Šuruṭḫum referred to in Riedel, *RA* 10 208; BM 103, 435 (A.S. 4); Gen., *Tr. D.* 2 (A.S. 4); and in Gen., *TD* 5545 (A.S. 4) constitute military successes previous to and different from the one that is commemorated in the formula for the sixth year of Amar-Suena(k).

49. The prices of oil (*ì-giš*), barley (*še*), and fresh fish (*ku₆-gibil*) in the seventh and eighth years of Ibbī-Suen are given in texts published in *UET* III as follows:

Seventh year (Legrain I.S. 9): No. 1165, 1–3: *2 gur ì-giš 1 gín-a 2½ sìla-ta kù-bi 4 ma-na*, "2 gur oil (at the rate of) for one shekel (silver) each 2½ sila (oil), its silver is 4 mana." Eighth year (Legrain I.S.: 10): No. 1046, 1–3: *5 sìla ì-giš mu 10 (sila) še-šè 4 sìla mu 20* (sila) *ku₆-gibil-šè*, "5 sila oil for 10 sila barley, 4 sila (oil) for 20 (sila) fresh fish." No. 1182: *5 sìla ì-giš Nu-úr-ᵈSu.en 5 sìla Mu-ni-maḫ mu 10 (sila) še-ta 4 sìla Nu-úr-ᵈSu.en 4 sìla Mu-ni-maḫ mu 20 (sila) ku₆-gibil-ta* ... "5 sila oil Nûr-Sîn, 5 sila (oil) Munimaḫ, for 10 (sila) barley each; 4 sila (oil) Nûr-Sîn, 4 sila (oil) Munimaḫ, for 20 (sila) fresh fish each." 1185 1–2 and 3–4: *5 sìla ì-giš mu 10 (sila) še-sè 4 sìla mu 20* (sila) *ku₆-šè*, "5 sila oil for 10 (sila) barley; 4 sila (oil) for 20 (sila) fish." No. 1187 2–3: *2½ sìla ì-ta mu 5 sìla še-ta-šè*, "each 2½ sila oil for each 5 sila barley." No. 1201 i, 1–9: *28 gur 182½ sìla ì-giš ki Ga-ti-e-ta* ..... *ì-bi* ..... *1 gín-a 2½ sìla-ta*, "28 gur 182½ sila oil from Gatie ..... its oil is ..... (at the rate of) for one shekel each 2½ sila oil." Further prices—at approximately the same level—may be found in the undated No. 1207. Tabulated, the quoted prices are:

silver (*kù*)	1 shekel
barley (*še*)	5 sila
oil (*ì-giš*)	2½ sila
fresh fish (*ku₆-gibil*)	12½ sila

With this may be compared the following normal rates from the time of the Third Dynasty of Ur:

Barley (*še*): 1 gin *kù-babbar* = 300 sila (Hussey, *STH* II 24 rev. 1 Š. 44), 1 gin *kù* = ca. 223½ sila (ibid., obv. 10–11. Š. 45), 1 gin *kù* = 300 sila (*TEO* 5680 i 9′–10′, Š.S. 2), = ca. 340 sila (ibid., i 5′–6′, Š.S. 2), 1 gin *kù-babbar* = 450 sila (Pohl, *TuMHC* 99, 1–2, Š.S. 8).

Oil (*ì-giš*): 1 gin *kù* = 13⅓ sila *ì-giš* (*TEO* 6046 iv 13–14. A.S. 4), 1 gin *kù* = 13⅓ sila (*TEO* 6052 iii 8–9. A.S. 5). Fresh fish (*ku₆-gibil*): 1 gin *kù* = ca. 600 sila (*TEO* 6046 ii 2–3, A.S. 4; *TEO* 6052 ii, 3–4. A.S. 5).

50. Compare the not too dissimilar prices cited in the Narām-Sîn text *SRT* 2 (for reconstruction see for the present Güterbock *ZA*,n.F. 8, 24–27 and add *STVC* 94; the recent excavations at Nippur have produced many new duplicate texts) in a description of hard times obv. 6–8. We would read (cf. Güterbock, *ZA*,n.F. 8, 35) *u₄-b[a ì 1 gín]-⌈e⌉ ½ sìla[-ta-àm] še[:gur 1 gín]-⌈e⌉ ½ sìla[-ta-àm] [síg 1 gín]-⌈e⌉ ½ ma-n[a-ta-àm] [ku₆ 1 gín-e giš-ba-an-e sa₁₀(?)-e]*. On prices in times of famine see in general Meissner, *BuA* I p. 362.

51. On the king's responsibility for fertility see Frankfort, *Kingship*, pp. 307–312. If written in the context of a recent famine and of adverse treatment at the hands of the gods, Ibbī-Suen's specific insistence in the later inscription *UET* I 289 that he is "one highly skilled in carrying out correctly any and all rites" (*me níg-nam-ma si-sá-e-da gal-zu-bi* ii 35–36) almost looks like a deliberately defensive statement.

52. See now also Falkenstein, *JAOS* 72 (1952) 42 and Goetze, *JCS* 7 (1953) 32 f.

53. Taha Baqir, *Sumer* 4, 103.

54. Letter for Puzur-Numushda to Ibbī-Suen and the latter's reply. For the reply see Falkenstein's treatment *ZA* 49 (1949) 59–79. A fuller text and Puzur-Numushda's original letter are contained in the unpublished tablet A 7475 in the Oriental Institute's collections.

55. Thus Kramer, *AS* XII pp. 44–45 l. 244.

56. Thus Gelb, *Hurrians and Subarians*, p. 25 and 38–39; Crawford, *JCS* 2, 14; Falkenstein, *ZA*, 49, 75, and 320–321; Kramer in Pritchard, *ANET*, p. 460.

57. Besides the conclusive geographical argument note that *Subir* as an ethnic and political collective is always plainly *Subir*, never *lú Subir*, whereas the *Sua* are typically referred to as *lú Su-a*.

58. *BE* XXXI No. 3; see Falkenstein's treatment in *WO* 1, 377 ff.

59. See the correlation above which shows that Ishbī-Erra's thirteenth year falls immediately before the year for which the list from Ur itself, *UET* I No. 292, inserts a note concerning Ibbī-Suen's defeat.

60. They have now been confirmed by new texts from Nippur, Old Babylonian *lú* series A line 393: *lú-dingir-zà-tag-ga = ša ilum is-ki-pu-šu*; the passage shows that *zà ... tag* means *sakāpum*, "to overthrow." Our attention was kindly drawn to the passage by Landsberger, who is editing the series.

61. See *AJSL* 58 (1941) 221 and V. E. Crawford, *JCS* 2, 13–20.

62. e_{11} "cause to come down (from a stronghold)."

63. *CT* XXXII, 26 iv 15; Nies, *UDT* 95, cf. ibid., 129; Gen., *Tr.D.* 42, 9. On *níg-dab₅*, "materials taken in charge for cultic purposes," see Oppenheim, *Eames Coll.* p. 92 I 9 a.

64. See *CT* XXXII, 31 iii and ibid., 11 iv. Compare in both cases the totals, which distinguish between royal "expenditures," *zi-ga*, and "gifts," *níg-ba*.

65. Note Jac. *CTC* 5, 1–3: *1 sìla A-bí-zi-im-ti mu-tù u₄-ná-a-ka-na ki-ba ba-na-a-gá-ar*, which we would now render "1 lamb for Abī-simtī. It has been substituted for her (customary) incoming deliveries for the *bubbulum* day." This seems to refer to income usually assigned to her rather than coming from her.

66. Nesb. *SRD* xix, Legr. *TRU* 126, Nik. 488.

67. *ki Ur-ᵈIg-alim REC* 344 *nin-ta* "from U., the feeder of cattle(?) of the queen." On *REC* 344 see Thureau-Dangin in *ZA*, 20, 400, note 5, Landsberger *OLZ* 1931 Sp. 133. Thureau-Dangin suggested a meaning "butcher"; we believe "feeder of cattle" to be more accurate and would tentatively see in the sign the older form of later *ušnutillû*.

68. Cf. Langd. *TAD* 55 and duplicate copy (?) No. 64, A.S. 3, 26th of *Diri(g) Ezen-me-ki-gal*; *CT* XXXII, 31 iii, A.S. 6, 26th of *Šeš-da-kù*; Oppenheim, *Eames Coll.* H 13 A.S. 6(!) third month, no day; *Bos. TS* 98, A.S. 6, 26th of *Ezen-ᵈNin-a-zu*; *Legr. TRU* 315, A.S. 6, 25th of *Ezen-an-na*; *CT* XXX 11 iv 26th of *Ezen-me-ki-gál*; ibid., 26 iv A.S. 7, 26th of *Ezen-ᵈNin-a-zu*; *Nies, UDT* 129, A.S. 8, 26th of *Ezen-ᵈSul-gi*; *Jac. CTC* 5, A.S. 8, 27th of *Á-ki-ti*; *Nies, UDT* 95, A.S. 8, 26th of *Ezenmaḫ*; *Gen. Tr.D.* 42, A.S. 9, 26th of *Ezen-ᵈNin-a-zu*. The texts which specifically mention the *bubbulum* day are marked with an asterisk.

69. Note also her appearance as GÌR ibid., 108 l. 119 dated Š.S. 9.

70. SAL +·KU SAL + TÚG.

71. See Landsberger, *JNES* 8, 1949, p. 295.

72. Note SAL + TÚG = *nin, giš, nam-*, and *gál*.

73. Note *ù-mu-un, ág-, me-e, na-ám-, ṭu-mu*, and *zé-ba-àm*. On the use of a few word signs, INIM, IGI, and GÌR, probably to be read with their *Eme-sal* values.

enem, ibi, and *miri,* see Falkenstein, *WO* 2 (1947), 46–47 and the literature there quoted. DINGIR in l. 19 is probably part of the partly obliterated personal name that follows it.

74. Note *ᵈEn-líl-lá, lugal, dingir,* and *kalam.*

75. Thus, rather than *Dab₅-ba-tum* since *dab₅* occurs only as a determined, not as a free, phonetic value in Ur III and Isin-Larsa.

76. Landsberger (*ZA,* 30, 67 f.); cf. Koschaker, *Studien zur Gesetzgebung Hammurapis,* pp. 226 ff.

77. We read ᵈ⌈AMA⌉(?)-X-⌈LUM⌉ ⌈sukkal⌉-mu sà-bi-tum-ma kaš-a-ni zé-ba-àm, "the beer of the tapstress A., my handmaiden, is sweet."

78. On the syntax—apposition to the subject—see Falkenstein, *WO* 2 (1947) 44 f. To the examples there quoted add perhaps the formula for introducing dynasties in the Sumerian King List, see *AS* XI p. 76. 43 f. and passim, and cf. Poebel *OLZ* (1912) 292–293.

79. The pair *giš-gi-na* and *giš-sa₁₁-du* occurs as terms for parts of a loom in Hussey, *STH* II No. 6 i.13–14 passim and (with the variant *giš-níg-gi-na* for *giš-gi-na*) in Ḫ: ḫ. 5, 318 and 305 where they are translated as *mu-ka-nu* and *a-su-u.* The meaning *giš-gi-na,* the "(firmly) fixed," "stationary," wood, would seem to be "cloth beam," since that is the stationary part of the loom, in contrast to the warp beam, which is movable so that the warp may be stretched. This meaning is confirmed by our passage which mentions the *giš-gi-na* in connection with the cloth and contrasts it with the *giš-sa₁₁-du,* mentioned in connection with the warp. The latter term, the Akkadian translation of which also occurs in the sense of crossbeam of a door (Ḫ: ḫ 5 202), seems according to its etymology (*sa₁₁-du* "top [of the head]") to denote specifically, or perhaps only originally, the warp beam (i.e., the upper beam) of the vertical loom. Landsberger, unpublished MS of Ḫ: ḫ in the Chicago Dictionary files, as early as 1935, translated *giš-níg-gi-na* as "festes Gestell," *giš-sa₁₁-du* as "Kopf," "Querbalken." The sign TÚG in ll. 5–6 has the proper form and is distinguished from ŠÈ, which occurs in l. 18. The rather unexpected space after TÚG in l. 6 may be taken as an indication that the copyist found a lacuna in his original at this point. On this use of blank space see *AS* XI pp. 15–17. If we supply ⟨dun-⟩ the passage yields the well-known *túg-dun-dun,* Akkadian *kandu* "warp."

80. We follow Falkenstein in interpreting *a-al-la-ri* as a cry of joy.

81. *na-á[m-ḫi-l]i sù-ga-an,* "make full of attractiveness," is imperative.

82. Translate *ku₅-da* in l. 17 with Landsberger as "dragon" and restore with him *šu ḫé-íb-[m]ú,* "may salute (thee)."

83. We read and translate *ba-sa₆-ge-na-mu ba-zil-zil-i-na-mu,* "My (Shū-Suen) who wert pleased thereat, who wert cheered thereat."

11. The Assumed Conflict Between the Sumerians and Semites in Early Mesopotamian History

1. Breasted, *Ancient Times. A History of the Early World* (2d ed., 1935), chap. v secs. 13–17. Practically all the more recent histories share this view; Eduard Meyer,

Geschichte des Altertums, Vol. I, 2 (3d ed., 1913); King, *A History of Sumer and Akkad* (1916); Hall, *The Ancient History of the Near East* (7th ed., 1927); etc.

2. *SAK* 56 k.

3. Ibid., 152 vi 2; the Sumerian King List (Langdon, *OECT* II, Pl. III) vi 24 f.

4. The fall of Kish is mentioned before that of Uruk and the rise of Sargon in the legendary text edited by Güterbock in *ZA*,n.F. 8 (1934) 25, l. 2. It is also vouched for by the fact that Sargon rebuilt and resettled this city after he had defeated Lugalzagesi. Poebel, *HGT*, No. 34 iii 34′–38′, iv 33′–37′.

5. Shown by his title ensi gal ᵈEn-líl, "grand *ishakku* of Enlil" (*SAK* 154 i 15 f.) and by the statement, ibid., ll. 36–41: u_4 ᵈEn-líl lugal kur-kur-ra-ke$_4$ Lugal-zà-ge-si nam-lugal kalam-ma e-na-sì-ma-a, "When Enlil, king of all lands, had given Lugalzagesi the kingship of the country."

6. The Sumerian King List (Langdon, *OECT* II, Pl. III) vi 31–36: A-ga-dè$^{<ki>}$ Šar-ru-ki-in....-ba-ni nu-giri$_{12}$ qa-šu-du$_8$ Ur-ᵈza-ba$_4$-ba$_4$ lugal A-⟨ga⟩-dèkⁱ lú A-ga-dèkⁱ mu-un-dù-a lugal-àm, "In Agade Sargon (*Sharru(m)kín*) —his....was a date grower—cupbearer of Urzababa, king of Agade, the one who built Agade, became king."

7. Poebel, *HGT*, No. 34 i 12–61, ii 12–61, vii 26′–35′, viii 1′–25′, and see Poebel's discussion, *HT*, pp. 217–222.

8. Shown by his title ensi gal ᵈEn-líl (*HGT*, No. 34 i 10–11) and by the statement, ibid., iii 7′–12′: [Šar-um-ki] ⌜lugal⌝ kalam-ma-ra ᵈEn-líl-le lú-ga[b]-bí-ru nu-na-sì a-[ab-ba] igi-nim-ma-ta a-ab-ba sig-sig-šè ᵈEn-líl-⌜le⌝ [mu-na-sì], "To Sargon, king of the land, Enlil gave no opponent, from the upper sea to the lower sea Enlil gave unto him." See also Poebel, *HT*, p. 219.

9. *SAK*, p. 152, No. VI 2 i 3–5: Lugal-zà-ge-si lugal Unukⁱ-kà lugal kalam-ma. In the inscription *HGT*, No. 34 + 3′–8′, he uses only titles denoting rulership of cities: *bêl qaqqar* Unukⁱ *šar qaqqar* Uríkⁱ, "lord of the territory of Uruk, king of the territory of Ur."

10. Poebel, *HGT*, No. 34 vii 15′–23′: ⌜Šar-ru-ki⌝ *šar* Agadèkⁱ ...... *šar* Kišⁱkⁱ ...... *šar* KALAM-MAkⁱ. As king of Agade only: *HGT*, No. 34 i 33–36, ii 30–32, x 35′–37′, xv 15–17; *PBS* XV, No. 41 viii 14–16. As king of Kish only: *HGT*, No. 34 vi 31′–33′, xi 11′–13′; *PBS* XV, No. 41 vi 1–3, xiii 15–17. As "king of the land" only: *HGT*, No. 34 iii 1–3 and 31′–33′, iv 1–3, 30′–32′, and 50′–51′, viii 26′–28′; *PBS* XV, No. 41 ix 9–11 and 13–15, x 22–24.

11. Since the title "king of the land (kalama)" is used—exclusively—by the Semite Sargon, it is clear that it cannot designate leadership of the Sumerian race as opposed to the Semitic. It is obviously a title with essentially political and geographical connotations. This agrees with what we know of the history of this term, for lugal kalama, "king of the land," meant originally merely "king of the Nippur region." as Poebel has shown, kalama, "the land," is a variant form of Eme- SAL kanaǧa, "the land," and of Eme-KU kinǧi(r), "southern Babylonia, Sumer" (*HT*, p. 152; cf. *GSG*, p. 2, n. 2). The latter form, kinǧir, must go back to older *kinǐǧir (the i is preserved as a in kanaǧa, kalama) and is to be analyzed ki-Niǧir, "territory Niǧir," "the Niǧir region." Inasmuch as the Niǧir which occurs here can develop into a later form Nippur, and inasmuch as we have the direct statement of ancient

commentators that ki-Niğir (written ke-en-gi = ki-N(i)ği(r)), "territory Niğir," *is* Nippur (King, *Seven Tablets of Creation* I 217, No. 32, 574 rev., l. 5), there can be little doubt that Niğir actually represents an older form of that name.

The history of the word Niğir and the terms in which it occurs may be outlined as follows:

(1) In Nippur itself the ancient form of the city name, Niğir, would seem to have developed into *Níbir > *Níbur > Níppur. On ğ > b see Poebel, *GSG* §79. This development is, it should be noted, as yet known only from Eme-SAL. However, it may well have occurred also in the Nippur dialect, which had leanings toward Eme-SAL (see Poebel, *Altorientalische Studien Bruno Meissner zum sechzigsten Geburstag .... gewidmet* .... II 167). Perhaps the occurrence of the Akkadian word *bukannu* (loanword from Sumerian giš-gan, presupposing a pronunciation bu(š)gan in *ana ittišu*, which represents the legal language in Nippur, might be quoted; $i > u$ by assimilation to the preceding labial *b*. The Sumerian *b* was, as so often, heard by the Akkadians as p (cf. bala:*palû*, Buranun:*Purattu*, etc.). It is reduplicated since it follows a short stressed vowel.

(2) Outside Nippur, in regions speaking Eme-SAL, the name Niğir had a slightly different development: *Niğir > *Šiğir > Šimir > Šumir, the latter being the well-known term Shumer by which southern Babylonia was designated by the Akkadians. On Eme-KU n = Eme-SAL š see Poebel, *GSG* §83 and *ZA*,n.F. 4 (1929) 84–87. On Eme-KU ğ = Eme-SAL m see Poebel, *GSG* §76. On $i > u$ by assimilation to following *m* cf. sim:sum, nim:num, etc. The change may well have taken place after the word was borrowed by Akkadian, since there $i > u$ between sibilant and labial as in *šimu > šumu*; cf. Speiser, *Mesopotamian Origins*, pp. 55 f.; the usual derivation of *šumir* from kinğir by palatalization of *k* is rightly criticized by Speiser on the grounds that we have no evidence that palatalization occurred in that language. (His deduction that *šumir* accordingly must be an Elamite word is hardly probable now when it can be shown to be a normal development of *Niğir.)

(3) In Eme-SAL regions, possibly different from those where Niğir became *Šumir*, the term ki Niğir, "the Nippur region," was pronounced ka Nağa(r) (on the preference for the vowel *a* in southern Eme-SAL [dialect from Lagash] see Poebel in *ZA*,n.F. 3 [1927] 259), which developed regularly into kanama > kalama. On ğ > m in Eme-SAL see Poebel, *GSG* §76; on n > 1 before a labial see ibid., §64.

For the understanding of the semasiological development which changed Šumir, Kinğir, and kalam from their original meanings "Nippur" and "Nippur region" into geographical terms for southern Babylonia as a whole the parallel development of the city name Kish into a term meaning "world" or the like (Kiš = *kiššatu*, Deimel, *ŠL*, No. 425. 2. On *kiššatu*, "world," see Delitzsch, *HW*, pp. 360 f. and the equations šár, "horizon," ul-šár-ra, "firmament circle," "horizon" = *kiššatu* there quoted) is very instructive. We have indications that the kings of Kish at a very early date succeeded in gaining supremacy over most of the rival city rulers in Babylonia (according to the text edited by Witzel, *Orientalia* N.S.5 [1936] 331–346 their rule extended to Uruk in southern Babylonia) so their title would naturally become imbued with a meaning beyond what it actually said, king of the city-state Kish, and imply also the supremacy over other city-states which the kings of Kish held. For that reason we find that other kings, as e.g., Mesanepada of Ur, prefer it to their own title (in Mesanepada's case, king of Ur) when they can claim fairly universal dominion, because it already expressed that idea. Through such usage the original title "king of Kish" lived on (in the old orthography of the time of the kingdom of Kish, before determinative for place was used) down to Assyrian times as a title implying worldwide dominion. The same development must be behind the later usage of Šumir, Kiñgir, and kalam. At a very early time the kings of Nippur must have dominated the other cities in southern Babylonia so that their title "king of Nippur" came to imply supremacy of all southern Babylonia. To that period dates naturally also the supremacy of the god of Nippur, Enlil, over other Sumerian gods. Because of these implications of the title lugal kiñgira(k), "king of Nippur," other kings would adopt it—as was the case with the title lugal Kiši(k)—when they had widened their influence to correspond to that of the old Nippur kings; so ki Niĝir > kiñgi(r), used mainly to express this secondary implication, i.e., supremacy over southern Babylonia, became divorced from the city to which it really referred and came to mean southern Babylonia. The same development may be assumed for the dialectal form lugal kalama(k) (or better, umun kalama(k)!). Since this title seems to be closely connected with Uruk (see Poebel, *HT*, p. 153) it represents in all probability the pronunciation of lugal ki Niĝir-ak in the dialect of that city. Used by the Uruk kings to designate authority over southern Babylonia as a whole, kalama took on that shade of meaning: "southern Babylonia," "the (whole) land," and as such it was borrowed back into the main dialect, Eme-ku, where we find it as the term for "the land." The Akkadians, finally, borrowed the third form, Šumir, also originally meaning just Nippur, to designate the same geographical conception, southern Babylonia.

12. Poebel, *HGT*, No. 34 + 3′–32′. See also ll. 33′–34′.

13. [For this reading, i.e., Kù-ᵈBa ba₆, see Thureau-Dangin, *Les homophones sumériens*, p. 40. E. A. S.]

14. The Sumerian King List (Langdon, *OECT* II, Pl. III) v 36–41 and vi 9–14, and cf. vi 31–33.

15. [An analogous situation may be observed in the Hurro-Semitic group of Nuzi. E.A.S.]

16. The complete list of the deities mentioned by Sargon is: An, Enlil, Inanna, ᵈA-MAL, Utu, and Dagān. The last two are of no interest to us here since their mention has no bearing on the Babylonian conflict with which we are concerned. Utu appears exclusively in the curses against those who would destroy the inscriptions, and his occurrence there is naturally dictated by the fact that he was god of justice (the passages are: Utu alone, *HGT*, No. 34 iii 42′ and iv 41′. With Enlil, *HGT*, No. 34 ix 3′–5′; *PBS* XV, No. 41 xi 8′–10′. With Enlil and Inanna, *HGT*, No. 34 xi 21′–24′). Dagān, god of the country on the Middle Euphrates, is mentioned only in connection with Sargon's later campaigns which took him to that region (*PBS* XV, No. 41 v 13′ ff. + *HGT*, No. 34 v 1′–3′; *PBS* XV, No. 41 vi 19′ ff. + *HGT*, No. 34 vi 1′–4′) and has nothing to do with the early wars that made Sargon master of Babylonia. As for the other gods, little need be said about the Sumerian character of An and Enlil. Inanna, written ᵈINNIN, can only be the Sumerian goddess;

for in this period the sign was not used for the Semitic Eshtar, who was consistently written *Eš₄-tár*, as may be seen from proper names. That the last, ᵈA-MAL, was a Sumerian deity is indicated by the more explicit form ᵈA-MAL-gig-du₁₁-ga, "disease-decreeing ᵈA-MAL," which is found in *CT* XXIV, Pl. 13, l. 49 (cf. ibid., Pl. 25, l. 100). The identification with the Akkadian ᵈ*Bennu*, god of epilepsy (?), given there, throws light on ᵈA-MAL's character and gives point to the mention of his battle mace in Sargon's inscription (*HGT*, No. 34 vii 26′–32′).

17. The roles which according to the inscriptions the various gods played are: Enilil "judged" Sargon's "case," i.e., the dispute with Lugalzagesi (ᵈ*Enlíl dín-su i-dì-nu-ma*), *PBS* XV, No. 41 x 2′–5′. The captured Lugalzagesi Sargon "brought in fetters (cf. Landsberger, *ZA*,n.F. 1 (1924) 216² and 'Fauna' p. 87) to the gate of Enlil" (ᵍⁱˢsi-gar-ta kà ᵈEn-líl-lá-šè [e]-túm / *in ší-ga₄-rim₃ a-na báb* ᵈEn-líl *u-ru-uš*), *HGT*, No. 34 i 23–31 and ii 22–29; *PBS* XV, No. 47 viii 4′–13′. Enlil "gave Sargon no opponent" (*Šar-um-ki ....-ra* ᵈEn-líl-le lú-ga[b]-bí-ru [var. lú-gab-ru] nu-na-sì, Akkadian *Šar-ru-kí .... ᵈEn-líl ma-ḫi-ra la i-dì-šum*), i.e., he made him undisputed master of the country (*HGT*, No. 34 iii 1–6, iv 1–6, v 13′–15′, vi 18′–20′, viii 29′–31′; *PBS* XV, No. 41 x 25′–28′). He "gave him (the territory) from the upper sea to the lower sea" (*HGT*, No. 34 iii 7′–12′ ff. and vii 32′–37′ ff.; *PBS* XV, No. 41 iv 1′–3′ and xiii 9′–13′). Sargon puts up statues in front of Enlil (*HGT*, No. 34 ix 22′ and xi 8′) and consecrates booty(?) to him (*PBS* XV, No. 41 x 20′). In unclear context Enlil is mentioned (*PBS* XV, No. 41 xiii 3′; cf. xv 1′). Active help Sargon received also from his personal god, ᵈA-MAL. It was with the battle mace of ᵈA-MAL that he won his decisive victory over Lugalzagesi and the ensi(k)'s following him (*HGT*, No. 34 vii 26′–32′ + *PBS* XV, No. 41 vii 1–6; Lugalzagesi is here referred to only as "the king" but comparison with *HGT*, No. 34 i 12–32 and ii 12–29 shows clearly that the same battle is meant). Sargon has dedicated an inscription to ᵈA-MAL in which he designates him as "his (personal) god" (*HGT*, No. 34 vi 29–30). Sargon's religious titles show that he had special relations with Inanna, An, and Enlil; he was MAŠKIM-GI₄ of Inanna, *pa₄-šiš* of An, and ensi(k)-gal of Enlil (see *HGT*, No. 34 vii 18′–25′). The same titles appeared apparently in the damaged passages *HGT*, No. 34 i 1–11 and ii 1–11. *HGT*, No. 34 ix 30′ ff. leaves out *pa₄-šiš* Anim, perhaps through a copyist's error.

18. The deities involved are, as shown in n. 16, ᵈA-MAL, Inanna, An, and Enlil. Of these ᵈA-MAL was Sargon's personal god; Inanna was the city "god" of Agade, Sargon's own city; An was the city-god of Uruk, the city of Sargon's opponent, Lugalzagesi; and Enlil, who had authority over all of Babylonia, represents that political unit. It is not strange to find the city-god of Uruk in close connection with Sargon, who had defeated his city; for the very fact that Sargon had been able to defeat Lugalzagesi showed that An favored him and preferred Uruk to be ruled by him. That the gods actually appear in Sargon's inscriptions as representatives of political entities is also indicated by the order in which they appear in Sargon's titles: Inanna, An, Enlil; for this is the historical order in which Sargon gained authority over the political entities for which they stand: first Agade, then Uruk by the victory over Lugalzagesi, and lastly all of Babylonia. In the curses, on the other hand, where their political significance is not important, they are listed in the

order of the accepted pantheon: An, Enlil, Inanna (see *HGT*, No. 34 v 22'–30').

19. II. de Genouillac, *TRS*, Nos. 64 and 66; Legrain, *PBS* XIII, Nos. 15, 43, and 47. The text has been well edited in transliteration and translation by Güterbock in *ZA*,n.F. 8 (1934) 25–33. A few points where we differ from his interpretation will be discussed in the following notes.

20. KI-UD-BA. Güterbock (*ZA*,n.F. 8 (1934) 28, n. 7) refers to *TRS*, No. 16: 10*a*, and *OECT* I 8: 27 and points out that in none of these passages can KI-UD-BA have the usual reading kislaḫ-ba, "on its uncultivated ground." He proposes "in diesem Zeitpunkt," which must be approximately what is meant. We have tentatively read ki-u_4-ba, i.e., ki-u_4-b(i)a, "in that place and day" = "then and there" (?).

21. We read ku(g) ^{d}Inanna-ke$_4$ ka-bi IG bí-in-kíd(!), "that gate holy Inanna threw open."

22. *TRS*, No. 66 seems to have the better text: si a-an-sá-e-ne, "they make straight," i.e., "they send straight in," or with Güterbock, "they deliver correctly."

23. É-gal A-ga-dè^{ki}-ka a-gim sag mi-ni-ib-[íl] must mean "in(!) the palace of Agade it rose like waters."

24. These reasons may have been stated in the obscure ll. 55–59. It is difficult, however, to divine the exact meaning of the passage. The two first lines should perhaps be rendered PAD(!)-^{d}INANNA-bi ku(g) ^{d}Inanna-ke$_4$ šu-te-gá nu-zu I-TÚK-gim é ki-gar silim-dam la-la-bi nu-um-gi, "This tribute holy Inanna did not know how to receive, like a . . . . she did not tire of the pleasure of completing (var. dù-ù-dè, "of building") the house which had been founded" (on la-la-bi . .-gi cf. IV R 9: 22). Güterbock translates the first line, "Diese Speiseopfer konnte die heilige Inanna nicht annehmen," and leaves the second untranslated.

25. Thureau-Dangin in *RA* 9 (1912) 112 i 1–14.

26. Since the assumed racial conflict between Sumerians and Semites has long been considered the fundamental issue in older Mesopotamian history, one around which the known historical facts were grouped in presentations of that history, a few words should perhaps be said as to what ought to take its place. As I hope to show elsewhere, the basic factor is purely political, a continual struggle between unifying and disuniting forces in the country itself. The earliest phase of this struggle brought the rise of the city-states, with their thorough concentration of power in the hands of the ensi(k) internally; externally merely short-lived, loosely knit, larger states of feudal character: one city-state dominating, not ruling, the others. A second important phase was introduced with Narâm Sîn, who endeavored to give the larger state endurance by administrative measures, to create a true central administration. These efforts culminated under the Third Dynasty of Ur but failed in their purpose of creating a nation with deep-rooted feeling of unity. The following period of Isin and Larsa constituted politically a relapse to the period of city-states, until Hammurabi's short-lived empire succeeded in laying the foundations of a smaller but more lasting, chiefly north Babylonian, state.

12. An Ancient Mesopotamian Trial for Homicide

1. See in general Landsberger, *Die babylonische Termini für Gesetz und Recht* in *Symbolae ad iura orientis antiqui pertinentes Paulo Koschaker dedicatae* (1939) 219–234,

J. G. Lautner, *Die richterliche Entscheidung und die Streitbeendigung im altbabylonischen Prozessrechte* (Leipzig, 1922), and cf. Frankfort et al., *The Intellectual Adventure of Ancient Man* (Chicago, 1946), pp. 206–207.

2. See especially Lutz, *Sumerian Temple Records of the Late Ur Dynasty* (Berkeley, 1938), Part I, no. 83 iv.

3. On the *mišarum* decrees see Landsberger, *Die babylonische Termini*. On the general question of the character of the "codes" see W. Seagle, *The Quest for Law* (New York, 1941), pp. 102–117.

4. The text was studied jointly by S. N. Kramer and the writer after the finding of 2N-T. 54, and our joint attempt formed the basis for several popular preliminary accounts. Since then we have both continued work on the text. Professor Kramer's latest statement may be found in Kramer, *From the Tablets of Sumer*, Ch. 8 pp. 52–55. The translation here presented—while differing on many points—owes much to our joint work and to the thoroughly stimulating, valuable, and enjoyable experience of cooperating with him.

5. *PBS* XII 114.13.

6. Cf. the Eshnunna Code §48 to which Landsberger drew our attention.

7. Lautner, *Die richterliche Entscheidung*, pp. 74 ff.

8. Haupt, *ASKT* no. 17 and dupl. Langdom, *BL* no. 194.

9. Kramer, *Sumerian Mythology*, pp. 43–47; cf. *JNES* 5 (1946) 132–134 [see above, chap. vii], and *The Intellectual Adventure of Ancient Man* (Chicago, 1946), pp. 152–156.

13. On the Textile Industry of Ur under Ibbī-Sîn

1. Cf. *MJ* V, p. 392.

2. See our review of Legrain's publication in *AJA* 57 (1953) 125–128.

3. All text references are to Legrain's publication in *UET* III when not otherwise specified.

4. The formula for the nineteenth year of Shu-Sîn, which follows the rubric ⌈ká⌉-e gál-[la] in 1505 i, and the formula for the first year of Ibbī-Sîn, which follows the rubric diri mu-tù níg-šɪᴅ in 1504 vii, both apply to items which have reference to the previous year's stocktaking and account balances. The date of 1505 is therefore I.S. 1, that of 1504 I.S. 2.

5. On the basis of the preserved credit totals in 1505 and reading the slightly unclear figure in viii 27 as $3,600 + 3,600 + 600 + 540 + 4 + x = 8,380 + x$ (this reading seems to accord best with the range suggested by a totalling of what remains of the individual credit items) we estimate the total amount of wool handled by the account at a minimum of 19,275 talents (gú), or around 6,435 tons. Of this some 6,155 talents, or around 2,000 tons, seems to have been new wool coming in from the sheepshearings. The very large figures of 1504 vii 19–20 are curious and, if correct, of great interest. A photo kindly made available to us by the Iraq Museum allowed us neither to confirm nor to challenge Legrain's copy.

6. For a tentative suggestion about its identity see below note 32.

7. Compare the similar expression sila-a gál-la, "placed in the street," in 1634 (túg uš-bar) and 1781 (grain).

8. Legrain's copy of the traces is confirmed by the photo mentioned above in note 5. The position of the DINGIR sign excludes a reading ⌜d EN⌝-⌜zu⌝-ta and permits only d⌜šu⌝-⌜d⌝⌜EN⌝-⌜zu⌝-ta. It should be noted that according to the photo a blank space of the length of one-third of a column separates this line from the preceding one.

9. On the reading and meaning of gukkal see Landsberger *MSL* II p. 52, line 255, and note.

10. On the reading of udu EME-gi as udu uli-gi(r) see on the one hand K 43362 (*CT* XIX 21 alam:*nabnítum*) iii.34: EME(ú-li)-gi:...., and on the other cases like sipa udu uli-gi-ra-ke₄-ne (i.e., sipa(d) udu uli-gir-ak-ene) quoted above, in which the final -r is expressed in writing because it forms a syllable with a following vowel.

The term udu uli-gi(r) denotes a species of sheep rated below the "fat-tailed sheep" (udu kungal/gukkal) and above the "black sheep" (udu gi₆). See e.g., *YOS* IV 237 vii 199, 205, 211. It yielded a wool, the name of which is written síg-gi (see e.g., 1504 and 1505 quoted above, also *CT* VII 25, K. 15815 and elsewhere) and which rated below "standard wool" [síg DU] and above "black wool" [síg gi₆]). See e.g., the listings in no. 1535. The writing síg gi represents in all probability a fuller sig gi(r) and contains the same element gi(r) that appears in the name of the sheep from which it comes, udu uli-gi(r). If so, sig gi(r) should possibly be compared with síg-gir₅, listed in Hh XIX 36 (Landsberger MS. ed.) as síg-(gi-ri)gir₅:*gur-nu*, "medium (thickness) wool" (The gloss gi-ri need indicate no more than syllabic final -r as e.g., in gir/giri "foot"). It occurs between síg-sig:*qa-at-na-a-tum* "fine," "thin" wool and síg gur₄-ra:*kab-ra-a-tum*, "coarse," "thick" wool. For occurrences of udu uli-gi(r) see Deimel, *ŠL* 32.11 and 537.55, Howardy, *Clavis* 35.11 and 505.80, Schneider, *Orientalia* 22, 26a, and Legrain's index in *UET* III.

11. On igi-nim, explained as Elam and Iamutbal, see Gelb, *Hurrians and Subarians*, pp. 92 f. and p. 86, and note that these sheep were in the care of the ensi of Eshnunna.

12. Our emendation of 1505 is based on the corresponding entry of 1504, for which the photo shows a fairly clear Áš-nun^ki-na-ta. Both this and the assumed Áš-nun^ki-ka of 1505 conform to standard Ur III writings of the name. See *AS* VI, pp. 2 f.

13. The photo of 1504 confirms Legrain's copy except that the ki appears to be partly broken away. Whether an I- could have occurred between ki and -tu appears doubtful. Probably ⌜ki⌝-⟨I⟩-tu-ra-a etc. On Ituria, ensi(k) of Eshnunna(k), and his floruit see *OIC* XLIII p. 196. He is last mentioned in I.S. 1.

14. On the reading šakan and on the function of this official as a comptroller authorizing expenditure see below note 41.

15. sag-gá appears to represent a *nomen actionis*; note the form igi nu-sag-gá in 1528. We consider it a lexical (thus rather than graphical because of the different g-sounds!) variant of zag-ga. See Hh XIX 29–30 síg igi-zag-ga:*na-as-qa-a-tum*, síg igi-zag-ga:*bi-ri-e-tum*, "selected wool."

16. Slavegirls sent to help in the sheepshearing at various places are frequently mentioned: 1446 (in Lugal-^dSú.en^ki), 1454 (in Bad(i)bira:šà Bàd-bí-ra-ka), and 1441 (in the [grass-]lands of Umma:šà ma-da Umma^ki).

17. For sag-bi see Nies *UDT* 42: 30 gú 8 ma-na síg na₄-mah-ta gú-na 6 ma-na

4 gín-ta sag-bi 3 gú 3 ma-na, "30 talents 8 mana wool according to the large (weighing-) stone. In each talent is 6 mana and 4 shekel (additional weight). Its adjustment (sag) is (thus) 3 talent and 3 mana."

18. The term é-du$_6$-la designates in the Ur III texts a supply point for small quantities of stores such as "wool" (no. 1538), "hides" (no. 1284), "grain" (nos. 916, 919, 920, and 950), "oil" (1131), and others. The é-du$_6$-la could have attached to it "orchards" (1106, 1368) or "fields" (1367, 1369). It was usually named from a person, who presumably administered it, e.g., A-hu-ni dumu lugal 1369, Lugal-SIG-BU dumu Ur-^{d}KAL ensi-ka *HSS* IV 5 vi. Ur-^{d}Ba-ba$_6$ dumu Ur-^{d}KAL ensi Gír-su^{ki} *TU* 126 x, Da-da gala Nibru^{ki} (919 passim, see Legrain's index), Ad-da-mu dub-sar (1538) Da-hi-iš-a-tal rá-gaba Nibru^{ki} (950, 1284), Ur-Gipara(k) *TU* 254.

The two inventories of stores kept in é-du$_6$-la's *HSS* IV no. 5, and *TU* 126 are remarkable for the variety of goods listed; they range from metal utensils, weapons (maces), furniture, cartwheels, balances, boxes, vats, querns, and supplies of linen, wool, and cloth, to various woods, aromatics, oils, and foodstuff such as grains, milk and cheese, honey, dates, wine, etc. In almost all cases only small quantities are kept in stock.

The precise function of the é-du$_6$-la is not yet clear and it is likewise uncertain whether a connection exists between the é-du$_6$-la of the Ur III texts and the word du$_6$-lá:*ridûtum*. For the latter note e.g., erim-huš:*anantu* I (*CT* XVIII 47 Rm 2, 429 iii 12–14 where du$_6$-lá:*ri-du-tú* and é-du$_6$-lá:*e-du-lu-u* occur in a group with la$_4$-lah$_4$:*šá-la-lu*. Note also lú é-du$_6$-lá:*ša ri-du-ti* line 266 in the Old Babylonian lú series (Landsberger's MS. ed.) a passage to which Landsberger called my attention. In favor of assuming a connection and of seeing in the é-du$_6$-la a *bît ridûti*, "succession house," in which the successor of a high official learned administration at firsthand is the relative frequency of princes (dumu lugal) and sons of ensis among the occupants of the Ur III é-du$_6$-la's.

19. An emendation to ^{d}Šu-^{d}Sú.en appears excluded by Legrain's copy and the photo.

20. Thus seemingly 1504 according to photo. 1505 appears to have ⌈síg⌉(!?) túg(!?) nir-ra lá-àm, "wool from cloth wound around the loom beam," Cf. Hh XIX 221 túg nir-lá-lá:*ni-i-ru*, "Webertrumm (das am Webstuhl verbleibende Tuchende)" (Landsberger MS. ed.).

21. The signs *RÉC* 344 and *RÉC* 345 (AB) are very close to each other in form and were, it would seem, not well distinguished in the Ur III period. On *RÉC* 344 see Thureau-Dangin *ZA*, 20, 400, note 5, Deimel *LAK* no. 535, and Landsberger *OLZ* (1931) Sp. 133. From the context in which the sign occurs in the pre-Sargonic period Thureau-Dangin tentatively proposed the meaning "butcher." Calling for the time being the sign *RÉC* 344 or 345 sign x we learn from the texts published by Legrain that the x and the é-x, which he managed, received animals: sheep and cows (e.g., 1225 and 1208) probably for the purpose of fattening them (cf. 1060 rev. ii 6'–8' where the x receives a ram and a lamb for the é-udu-ŠE, the "sheep-fattening house." Cf. also 1232 and 1237). From the é-x are delivered—after the sixth year of I.S.—the animals needed for the king's *eššešu* offerings (130, 173, 175, 182, 206) and the x also provides grain-fed sheep for "the king's table in the Nanna temple"

(gišbanšur lugal šà é-ᵈNanna-ka-šè 153). A translation "fattener of sheep and oxen" is thus perhaps to be preferred to that of "butcher."

If the meaning "fattener of sheep and oxen" for *RÉC* 344 should prove correct it would become tempting to see in that sign the hitherto missing older form of the sign *ušnutillû*, which, in its reading kuš₆, kuruš, and kurušda denotes *mārû* "fattener of cattle" (See ea IV 182–184 = Chicago Syll. 174–176) and á : a IV, 163–168, both in Landsberger's MS. ed. Cf. also Ur-e-a = *nâku MSL* II 284 gu-ru-uš var. gu-ru-DI). The form of *ušnutillû* in the Old Babylonian period is almost exactly that of *RÉC* 344, the only difference is that the upper right hand oblique wedge has its longest extension downward from the wedge head.

22. That gu means "flax fibers" may be seen e.g., from *PBS* II no. 6 = *BE* XXXI no. 4 line 1 ff., a text dealing with the preparation, spinning, and weaving of Inanna's bridal linen.

23. The cryptic term urudu-níg-sun-nu-da occurs perhaps as urudu-níg-sun-d[a] in the important text no. 368, according to which bronze was made from 45 shekel an-na, 6 mana Meluhha copper, and 6 shekel urudu-níg-sun-d[a].

24. Cf. nos. 1637, 1748, and 1758.

25. Cf. Oppenheim, *Eames Coll.* p. 92 I 9a.

26. The reading deₓ-deₓ or di₄-di₄ for TUR-TUR was arrived at independently by Landsberger and us on the basis of the parallelism of de-de-le and de-de-el with gal-ga-al-le, ga-al-ga-le, and ga-al-ga in *SK* 51 obv. 5–7. Landsberger quotes in addition the gloss de-de to TUR-TUR in SCHEIL *RA* 13 137 text XIX.

27. On these two gods see Gelb, *Archiv Orientální* 18 (1950) 189–198.

28. We are in the dark as to the function of this structure and of the old woman inhabiting it.

29. 1504 has a variant text which may perhaps be restored [za-gaba] ᵈNanna za-gaba [ᵈNin-ga]l ù za-gaba [. . . .] . . .-. . .-è-dè(?). We conceive the term za-gaba as representing za-gab(-ak) "(precious) stones of the breast," i.e., breast ornaments. Cf. the stones "suitably placed on the pure royal breast" (gaba kù lugal-a-ke₄ me-te-aš gál-la) in the spells for the royal insignia in IV R 18.3 iv 10-11. As here used the term denotes not only the stones themselves but also the place or vault in which they were kept. In this usage the term occurs also in nos. 341 and 344. The first of these is a record of beads of carnelian (NA₄-ZA-GUL:*sāmtu*) deriving in part from votive gifts, in part from the "tithe" of the seatraders, which were transferred from the storehouse (é-kišib-ba) of the Gá-nun-mah and added to the jewels (za-gaba) of Nanna and of Ningal. The second text, 344, is a receipt by the silversmiths for gold bars, hammered(?) gold, gold beads, etc. which had been stripped from some object or objects, the name of which is imperfectly preserved, and which has been returned (to the silversmiths) from the jewel(-depositorie)s of Nanna and Ningal, probably as working materials.

30. On the reading kín-kín see Oppenheim, *Eames Coll.* p. 146 W 30a.

31. The reading balag(?)-di(?) seems compatible with the photo of 1504. Since Abī-simtī is frequently referred to in texts from Amar-Sîna(k)'s reign in connection with offerings at the *bubbulum* day (u₄ nú-a) i.e., the day the moon is invisible, and since the rites on the *bubbulum* day involved laments accompanied by the balag

drum (cf. the balag u₄-nú-a *STD* 207 iii. 87 and elsewhere) it is not surprising to find a balag singer in her service. The lady in question, Bí-zu-a, was probably her sister, for she is mentioned in Gen. *TD* 5484.7 (A.S.5) as Bí-zu-a nin (SAL + KU) nin (SAL + TÚG). With the problems connected with Abī-simtī we hope to deal in more detail elsewhere.

32. In many respects the Gá-nun-mah would fit the picture well: in terms of size, in terms of its function as a storehouse, and as actually containing chapels for Nanna and Ningal in its midst. The za-gaba of Nanna, shown by our text to have been a part of the Wool Office, is mentioned in connection with the Gá-nun-mah in text no. 341 (see above note 29) and it seems possible to interpret that text as a transfer within the Gá-nun-mah itself, from its é-kišíb-ba to the za-gaba. The latter might well be sought in the é-kù-za-gìn, "house of gold and lapis lazuli," which was located in the Gá-nun-mah (see no. 345). Finally it should be noted that when the wool is fully processed the finished cloth is delivered either to the Gá-nun-mah or to a certain Ur-Shulgira(k), who seems to have had very close connection with it. See below. While full certainty can hardly be reached the Gá-nun-mah would so far, in terms of known structures, appear to have the best claim to being the Wool Office. In its favor is also the fact that the findspot of the bulk of the archive, the Registrar's Office, is not very far from it in space.

33. As further evidence of royal connections should perhaps be mentioned a payment of "wool stipends to the singers of the king in the great 'academy'" (síg-ba nar-lugal-é-umún-gu-la-ke₄-ne) 1504 col. x end. The presence of "singers" makes us tend to see in the term é-umún, which we have translated "academy," the Sumerian prototype of the Akkadian *bît mummi* (On this see Heidel, *JNES* 7 (1948) 102 ff. and the literature there quoted). On umún:*mu-um-mu* see Deimel *SL* 339.9. The final -n seems to have varied with -m (as does e.g., that of ezen, cf. Oppenheim, *Eames Coll.* p. 92 I 9a. For other examples see Poebel *MAOG* 4 (1929) 167 f. and *JAOS* 57 59) for, when followed by a vowel the word often occurs as umú(n)-me (see e.g., ki umú(n)-ma *SEM* 73.13, 18, 19). In the é-umún-gu-la stood, as suggested by no. 1587 rev. col. v, a statue of Enki.

34. See no. 55.

35. See 1515, 1520, 1577. The zabar-dab₅ was an official in charge of the royal tableware: bronze cups, knives etc. His establishment, the é-zabar-dab₅, seems at this period to have served—besides its original function?—as a storing place for wool (1543 cf. 1542) and cloth (1226). According to no. 106 it also possessed an é-*RÉC* 344, a "house of the cattle fattener."

36. For aslag, "fuller," as the reading of LÚ-TÚG, Landsberger refers us to the Princeton Voc., Goetze *JAOS* 65 221 line 39: as-la-ag:LÚ-TÚG:min (= *lu-ú*) *tu-kul-la-ku*:*ás-la-ku* and *OECT* IV pl. XXXIII iv LÚ-TÚG:*aš-la-a-ak-kum*.

37. On the reading of PA + GIŠGAL see Deimel *ŠL* 295.81 and especially Landsberger *ZA*,n.F. 9 76. The materials indicate two variant pronunciations [su-li-]li borrowed as *sulilû* (*HGT* 106 i. 15) and zi-lu-lu, borrowed as *zilulû*. Further Akkadian translations are *sahhirum* and *sahhirtum*. (The unique translation *taš-hi-rum* is perhaps, with Landsberger, to be considered a mistake for *sah-hi-rum*.)

Important for the meaning of the term in the Ur III period is Chiera *STA* 10, which lists wages paid to groups of slave girls under male overseers (ugula). In this text PA + GIŠGAL designates the girl listed first in a group and receiving the highest wage (50 sila). She would appear to be the head girl of the group and to hold a position of authority under the foreman. In the totals she is counted just as are the other workers whereas the foremen are not.

The bridge from a meaning "head worker" to the later use of zilulu and *sahhirum/ sahhirtum* is not easy to find. Perhaps the zilulu/*sahhiru* had as a chief duty the routing out of the workers from their homes to work. If so, a rendering "recruiter," "mobilization officer" might be tentatively considered (note the use of *sahārum* in *TCL* XVIII 91 7–10 and 15–17). Such a rendering would suit fairly well both *CT* XV 50.14 whereas after a military disaster the highest officials have to act as common recruiters to raise a new army quickly in the emergency, and in the Theodicy (Landsberger *ZA*,n.F. 9 66 line 249) where the easy life and the swagger of the elder brother as a small man in authority is resented; in line 247 under the image of a lion, in 249 under that of a recruiter.

38. Note the unusual term tu-ra instead of the expected mu-tù-ra.

39. There is a positive balance of 520 33.5/60 skeins of flax fibers. Restore ŠÁR before the preserved number of skeins in the total for "expenditures and stock on hand" in viii.4. Restore similarly 420 before the figures for "slavegirls in one month" in viii.3, bringing them to 429 20/60 which, added to the sum of individual total in col. vii (2307 35.5/60), gives a total labor figure of 2756 55.5/60. Since the credit in col. ii was 2757 the balance zero given in col. vii.9 is fair enough.

40. Cf. e.g., *TÉO* 6054.

41. Our reading šakan rather than GÌR or ANŠE is based merely on the belief that the term has ultimate connection with the payment for níg-šakan-na to persons serving as maškim's in *PBS* IX 4 iv.

42. The translation of sa-gi₄ as "prepare" is Landsberger's. He refers to Chiera *SLT* 3 i.9 sa ab-gi₄-a:*šu-t*[e]-*er-su-um* and to *CT* XLI pl. 46 BM 23116 rev. 6–7 u₄-da sa ab-gi₄-gi₄:*u₄-ma-am šu-te-er-sú*, sa a-an-gi₄-gi₄:*uš-te-ri-sí*, all forms of an adjectival stem *ersû*.

43. We hope at some later time to discuss the work of the fuller jointly with Landsberger.

44. We see in Kimura(k) a place-name rather than a term for the bleaching pit. The etymological basis on which de Genouillac made his attractive suggestion of the latter meaning (*RA* 7 111 ff.) seems doubtful to us.

14. The Waters of Ur

1. The report on the findings and method of the *Survey of the Central Diyala Region*, ready in manuscript since 1938, is scheduled for the last of the volumes of the Iraq Expedition reports and so has not yet appeared.

The Survey of Central Sumer was proposed by the writer when he was appointed Annual Professor of the Baghdad School in 1953–1954. It was carried out under his direction as a joint project of the Baghdad School and the Iraq Department of Antiquities. Preliminary accounts based on reports from the field are "Mesopotamian

Mound Survey," *Archaeology* 7 (1954) 53–54, Goetze, "Archaeological Survey of Ancient Canals," *Sumer* 11 (1955) 127–128, with map facing page 128, and Jacobsen, "La géographie et les voies de communication du pays de Sumer," *RA* 52 (1958) 127–129. See also Jacobsen, "Early Political Development in Mesopotamia," *ZA* 52 (1957) 96–99 [see above, chap. viii], and the article by V. Crawford in *Iraq* 22 (1960) 197–199.

The Survey of Accad, directed by Robert M. Adams, was undertaken jointly by the Baghdad School and the Oriental Institute of the University of Chicago. A preliminary report on results was given by Robert M. Adams, "Settlements in Ancient Akkad," *Archaeology* 10 (1957) 270–273, map on page 270. A more detailed report is Robert M. Adams, "Survey of Ancient Watercourses and Settlements in Central Iraq," *Sumer* 14 (1958) 101–104, with period maps.

The Diyala Basin Archaeological Project was undertaken jointly by the Oriental Institute and the Directorate General of Antiquities for the Iraq Development Board. It carried out, under the direction of the writer, an archaeological investigation in the Diyala River Basin with the purpose of identifying ancient irrigation and agricultural practices, with special attention to draining facilities and salinization of soils. The program included both a ceramic surface survey in charge of Robert M. Adams, excavations in charge of Mohammed Ali Mustafa and Fuad Safar, palaeobotanical investigations in charge of Hans Helback, and an extensive program of textual study. See Jacobsen, "Salinity and Irrigation Agriculture in Antiquity" (Mimeographed report, iv + 104, maps), Jacobsen, "Summary of Report by the Diyala Basin Archaeological Project...," *Sumer* 14 (1958) 79–89, and Jacobsen and Adams, "Salt and Silt in Ancient Mesopotamian Agriculture," *Science* vol. 128, 1251–1258.

2. Some Tigris supplies were brought into Sumer by Entemena shortly before the Agade period. They grew steadily in volume and importance, so that by Old Babylonian times the feeder and the lower part of the Iturungal were considered a main branch of the Tigris.

3. Note: (1) *Sippar*. Hammurabi built the walls of Sippar, surrounded it with a moat, dredged the Euphrates down to Sippar and let it flow along a protective quay. *LIH* 58 i 10–20 and Akkadian version ibid., 57 i 9–ii 1. (2) *Kish*. Date formula for twenty-fourth year of Samsuiluna mentions the building of the wall of Kish on the bank of the Euphrates. See e.g., *HGT* no. 99. (3) *Nippur*. The Euphrates is shown on the ancient map of Nippur (probably of Cassite date) as touching the north side of the sacred quarter of the city. For a copy of the map see Kramer, *From the Tablets of Sumer* (Indian Hills, Colorado, 1956), p. 274. (4) *Shuruppak*. Location on the Euphrates is mentioned in the Gilgamesh Epic Tablet XI 11–12. (5) *Uruk*. Location on the Euphrates may be inferred from the Gilgamesh Epic Tablet VI 176. (6) *Larsa* and (7) *Ur*. See the letter Ungnad, *VAB* VI, no. 43, 27–28, mentioning "the Euphrates from Larsa to Ur."

4. The location of the upper part of the Irninna canal at Sippar is shown by the letter of Abieshuh, Ungnad, *VAB* VI, no. 78. Its tail end can be shown from the Ur-Nammûk topographical texts, published by Kraus in *ZA* 51 (1956) 45–75, to have joined the Zubi (see ibid., 58 f. §4 and sketch on Taf. V. The broken name of

the district dealt with in 4 we would restore as ÙR + Úki rather than as Akshak) at a point where the latter flows southward, the former first east then northeast to confluence. This point can hardly be other than the point of confluence east of Jemdet Nasr of the Euphrates branch from Sippar, which flows east, with the branch from Abu Ghubar, which here flows south, traced on the ground by Adams and Crawford. The large mounds below the point of confluence should represent ancient Puš.

5. For the route from Babylon up the Araḫtum to Sippar and continuing up the Euphrates see Oppenheim, *Dreambook*, p. 313. For Luhaiat on the Araḫtu see the Date formula of Abieshuh, Ungnad, *Datenlisten*, no. 204.

6. The name occurs as áb-gal and apkal (NUN-ME), Akkadian *Apkallatum, Aplakattu,* Greek Pallacottas. Arrian, *Anabasis* VII.21 describes how Alexander sailed south from Babylon on the Euphrates (i.e., on the old Araḫtum course, which at that period had long been the main Euphrates branch) down to the mouth of the Palla-cottas. On the Apkallatum at Abiak see Kraus, *ZA*, 51, 56.

7. On the Me-ᵈEn-líl-lá from Kish south to Marad see Kraus, *ZA*, 51, 57.

8. The identification of Madinah with Bàd-tibiraki was established by fragments of inscribed cones discovered by Dr. Crawford during our visit to the site (see above, n. 1 on Crawford's report in *Iraq* 22).

9. Identification of this canal with the Iturungal (cf. Diri IV 182 i-su-ru-(en)-gal:íD-UD-NUN:šu, 183 i-dar-en-gal:íD-UD-NUNki:šu, II R. 50 ii.10 íd-erín-ga:i-tu-ru-un-gal, and the variants íd-urú-en-gal and íd-UD-NUNki in the two copies of the Utu-hegal inscription) is suggested by the fact that the latter must have followed an identical course. (1) The writing of the name Iturungal as íd-UD-NUNki seems to identify it as the "Canal of Adab (UD-NUNki)." (2) Proximity to Zabalam seems indicated by *SRT* 3 iv 6–7, which mention Iturungal (íd-UD-NUN)-gá, "in my Iturungal," in close connection with a-šà Zabalam (ZA + SUḪ-UNU)ki-ga, "on my field of Zabalam" (the reason for the writing -ga for expected -gá are not clear to us). (3) It is mentioned as íd-urù. en-gal (written EN-URÙ-GAL) in the Umma text *Nik.* 153. (4) Its touching upon the region of Uruk is indicated by the fact that An-àm of Uruk built a temple of ᵈGa-í-sur-ra, "the mistress of the Iturungal" (Scheil, *RA* 12, 193). (5) In the myths of Nanna's Journey to Nippur and Inannak's Journey to Eridug the Iturungal is mentioned and can refer only to the common course of the canal here discussed and the Euphrates south of Larsa.

For the takeoff of this canal from the Euphrates at Ka-sahar-ra see on the one hand the round trips *Nik.* 116 and Oppenheim, *Eames Coll.* G 20: Umma-Ur-Kasah-harrak-Umma, and on the other *Nik.* 119, where a boat is towed (gíd-da) to Ka-sahar-ra and floated (diri-ga) down to Nippur, then towed in one day from Nippur back up to Ka-sahar.

10. It is possible that this name applied only to the course south of Girsu. For identification see Gudea Cyl. A ii 4–5.

11. *YOS* VIII no. 156: 4. The canal is also mentioned in *BE* XVII/1 no. 3 line 14 and in *OBI* no. 33, both of Cassite period.

12. *SEM* 97 obv. ii.

13. This is suggested by the name of the city-goddess (*SEM* 98 ii 32), which

seems to be Ninlil. For the presence of the ceremonial barge of Nanna of Ur at Shuruppak in the month of Akitu see Legrain, *TRU* no. 349 listing offerings in Shuruppak for má-gibil-lá-Uríki-e-ki-áĝ and cf. the name of the processional barge ĝišmá-ki-áĝ-Uríki in Hh IV 337, *MSL* V, p. 179. See also Landsberger, *Der kultische Kalender der Babylonian und Assyrian*, LSS VI/1–2 (Leipzig, 1915), p. 74.

14. For the myth as a whole see Kramer, *Sumerian Mythology*, pp. 47–49.

15. For this myth see ibid., pp. 64–68.

16. For reading see *MSL* II no. 779. Topographical considerations favor identification with the city Ki-is-sikki mentioned by Sennacherib in the account of his first campaign (Sidney Smith, *The First Campaign of Sennacherib*) in col. i line 48 between Eridug and Nimid-Laguda.

17. *STVC* 29 rev. iii and *STVC* 28 and *SLTN* 100 and *PBS* X/4 no. 6 obv.

18. The identification of Magan with Egypt and Meluhha with Ethiopia rests on clear and firm evidence. See the sane statement by Streck in *VAB* VII/3, pp. 794–795 and the later review of the evidence by Albright in *JEA* 6, 89–98, 295; 7, 80–86. Landsberger, *ZA*,n.F. 1 (1924) 217 and Weidner, *AOF* 16 (1952–1953) 6–11, base their location of Magan on the east and south coast of Arabia on a subjective judgment that the Sumerians could not have traded south of Arabia to the Red Sea. In view of the clear evidence of Mesopotamian influence in Egypt in predynastic times (see e.g., Kantor, *JNES* 11 [1952] 239–250) and the representations of Mesopotamian type ships there, such judgments may legitimately be questioned. Oppenheim's recent postulate of an "eastern" trade with Magan and Meluhha—presumably points in India—and his statement "The toponyms Makkan and Meluhha have then been, as is well known, transferred to two other far-off countries situated in the southern limits of the geographical horizon," *JAOS* 74 (1954) 16, seem to us to have no verifiable basis in any fact.

15. About the Sumerian Verb

1. The field of Sumerian grammar is not one in which one can move with much confidence. The Sumerologist who examines his presuppositions knows only too well how many unknowns enter into his slightest decisions, how unproven, perhaps unprovable, are even his most fundamental assumptions about the writing and about the spoken forms it can and cannot symbolize; and he knows how subtly these endless assumptions differ from one scholar to the next. The suggestions about the Sumerian verb which we present here can thus be no more than subjective guesswork. We have tried, however, to make educated guesses and to guess systematically. We have also sought to collect pregnant examples showing distinctive contrasts or variations in the hope that these examples may continue to be useful even if our guess from them should prove to be wrong. The compass of the article precludes any attempt at detailed correlation with other views; we assume that the reader will be familiar with the large and valuable literature on Sumerian grammar so that he will be able to judge for himself where we follow and where we depart from earlier results. Our debt to Thureau-Dangin and Poebel is manifest on almost

every page, as is our debt to Benno Landsberger, to whom this volume is dedicated. We should have wished to offer to this master of the profound and unerring insight the sure decisive solution, a contribution less fraught with uncertainties, but we thought we could honor him best by honoring a promise made, as it were, under his aegis, the promise in *MSL* IV 2 to attempt a study of the structure of the Sumerian verb.

2. In Sumerian, as in other languages, elements that go to make up a form may be seen to follow one another in the form according to a fixed order of rank. Such an order, embracing as it does the constitutive elements of all occurring forms clearly lays to hand a valuable framework for morphological analysis and classification, one not imposed upon the language from outside but inherent in its own structure.

Observing the extant forms we may distinguish as rank prefix 1 (Pr. 1) all elements found to occur immediately before the root only, as rank Pr. 2 all elements found to occur immediately before the root or before an element of rank Pr. 1 only, as rank Pr. 3 all elements found to occur immediately before the root or before elements of rank Pr. 1 or Pr. 2 only, and so forth, Correspondingly we may distinguish as rank suffix 1 (Su. 1) all elements found to occur immediately after the root only, as rank Su. 2 all elements found to occur immediately after the root or after an element of rank Su. 1 only, and so forth (cf. Gleason, *An Introduction of Descriptive Linguistics* [New York, 1955] pp. 112 ff.).

It follows from the principles on which the rank classes have been distinguished that two elements belonging to the same rank can never occur together in a form; they are potential substitutes, "replacives" of one another, and so mutually exclusive.

It also follows that as the elements in a rank class are potential replacives of one another so will the meanings which they carry likewise be capable of replacing one another; and since a term can meaningfully replace another in a context only if it is relevant—not if it is irrelevant—the meanings of the elements in a rank class can be assumed to have a common relevance. This forms them into a class with the term of their common relevance constituting the class meaning.

The degree of certainty with which an underlying rank order can be recovered will clearly depend in large measure on how representative is the corpus of forms available for comparison. If the corpus is incomplete it may lack forms that would distinguish adjoining rank classes, and these classes may accordingly appear coalesced in the reconstruction. This is not a serious drawback, especially since the presence of two different class meanings in the thus coalesced rank will often furnish a clue that two separate ranks are involved. More serious is the fact that the distinction of two ranks may often rest on a few forms or even a single form which may be open to doubt. In such cases we have on the whole tended to give credence to the evidence if it did not conflict with other known data, preferring to err on the side of over-differentiation rather than on that of oversimplification.

Our reconstruction of the rank classes of the Sumerian verb is presented as a whole in the figure on p. 268.

3. The prefix has been discussed in detail by Falkenstein in *ZA* 48 (1944) 69–118 on the basis of an extensive collection of examples. We base our suggestions about

the meaning of the prefix on the remarkable frequency with which two entities are found in counterpart relation with each other in these examples.

4. The existence of a prefix na- of positive statement was conclusively demonstrated by Falkenstein in *ZA* 47 (1942) 181–223. As for the specific force of this prefix it may be noted that the grammatical texts which may be assumed to refer to it render it by *šu* and *šuāti* (á-A IV₂, *MSL* IV 194, line 163, na-a: NA: *šu-u*; ea IV 105, *MSL* IV 194, né-e: NA: *šu-ú*; AO 17602, *MSL* IV 130–47, lines 9–21, in series u, a, i, e, ul, al, il, ša, ši, na, ba, ab, ta rendered by *šu-ú ri-qu* KI-TA [mistake?] and in lines 22–34 by *šu-a-[ti]* AN-⌜TA MURU[?!]-TA⌝). From these data it seems possible to conclude that na- varied in pronunciation toward ne—possibly in differentiation from vetitive na—and that it has third-person reference to subject (*šu*) or object (*šuāti*). This seems confirmed in some measure by its etymology since it would appear to consist of a third-person pronominal element -n-, "he," "she," "it"(?), and a relater -a, "in," "for." Since na- ranks with the prefixes, i.e., with modal elements expressing the attitude of the speaker (first person) to the occurrence he presents, it would seem that its third-person reference must be seen as contrasting with the inherent first-person reference of the other members of the prefix category and one may assume transfer—by empathy of speaker with subject or object— from first- to third-person attitude to the action.

As actually used (see Falkenstein's careful presentation of materials in *ZA*, 47, 181–223) na-, "within him," seems to present an act not objectively, in itself, "he did," but subjectively, in its psychological matrix of impulse, inner urge, decision to act, in the subject, "he saw fit to do." The following examples may serve to illustrate.

Impulse: en-e níĝ-du₇-e pa na-an-ga-àm-mi-in-è, "the lord saw fit not only (n-ga) to let the proper things appear" (ibid., E.8; on construction of n-ga see n.6 below); É-an-na-túm-me gal na-ga-mu-zu, "Eannatum also saw fit to make it (i.e., the oath sworn by Umma) greatly known" (ibid., E.4). Following this statement we are told how Eannatum sends animals as messengers to the deity by whom Umma swore. Clearest is Stele of the Vultures xix 16–20: [... ᵈNi]n-ĝír-zu-ka-ka šu e-ma-né-ba suhur^ku₆ saĝ-šè ĝin-ĝin-ba É-an-na-túm-me KA a-tar-re, "[Two suhur-fishes in the boundary canal of Ni]ngirsu he set free (saying:) 'Suhur-fish, go ahead! Eannatum is publicizing it.' (At whatsoever's command etc.)."

Inner urge: ama-ni ul-la mí na-mu-un-e, "his (Nanna's) mother, delighted, felt urged to praise him as follows (durative)" (ibid., B.2); ku₆ mudur šu-na na(!)-mu-un-ĝál me..., ku₆^kuš e-sír ĝìr-na na-mu-un-si me..., ku₆ izi ab-šà-ga na-mu-un-zalag me..., "she (the goddess of fishes, Nanshe) sees fit (by inner urge of her piscine nature) to put a fish as scepter in her hand..., sees fit to put fishes as sandals on her feet..., sees fit to light fishes as fires (to light the way) in the midst of the sea..." (ibid., B. 10). The reference in the last line appears to be to phosphorescence.

Various: min-na-ne-ne ki ᵈEn-líl-lá-ta húl-la nam-[ta]-è, "in joy the two of them felt ready to come out from Enlil (having obtained their wish)" (ibid., A.31). At times the volitive element almost fades out as it does, e.g., in English "will" used as a helping verb. In such cases "saw fit to" shades into simple "happened to," as e.g., en-na We-du-um-li-bur ù Nin-ᵈUtu-mu na-an-ga-ti-la-ni igi-ni-šè ì-gub-bu, "as long as Wedum-libur, and also Nin-Utu-mu, will live (i.e., has it in him to live, is up to living) she will serve him" (ibid., F.2).

Of interest is also *MSL* IV 163, lines 12–15, where nam-ga- is translated as MIN (i.e., *tu-šá-ma*), "apparently," *mi-in-di*, "surely," *ap-pu-na*, "moreover," and *pi-qá-at*, "no matter whether. . . ." We do not know of any occurrence of nam-ga- in these meanings in any connected text, but it would seem that they represent a usage in which the presumptive force of na- for empathic projection into the subject's feelings is used hesitantly.

5. In *GSG* §§542–544, Poebel, abandoning his earlier view, suggested that the prefix a- is merely a phonetic variant (Umlaut) of i/e-. Since no phonetic reasons for such a change are apparent in the materials, however, and since the Old Babylonian grammatical texts list separate a- and i- paradigms with separate meanings (cf. e.g., *MSL* IV 82, lines 97–99 and 100–102), the autonomy of the prefix a- is hardly open to doubt. The prefix u- is attested in imperative forms such as ǧen-nu, "come" (*VS* II, No. 31 ii 20; *ASKT* No. 17 obv. 22–23), ga-nu:*al-kam* (*KAR*, No. 111 obv. 3), gur-u:*nashiramma* (*SBH*, No. 82:27–28), ǧar-ù, "set up (a lament)" (unpubl. CBS 8318 i. 5 ff. and dupl. Genouillac, *Kich* II, Pl. 49, D.53), ǧál-lu, "open up" (Kramer, *SLTN*, No. 35 ii 11; Inanna's Descent, line 75, cf. line 76), ⌜ǧá⌝-nu-u[m-z]é-en:*al-ka-a-nim* (*MSL* IV 91, line 96, etc.), and in un-ǧáˢᵘ-ù-bí-tab:*li-iṣ-ṣip ap-pu-na* (Elev. of Inanna; *RA* 11 [1914] 144–145, line 11 and elsewhere).

The ranking of these prefixes after the modal prefixes and before the prefix n-ga- is indicated by forms such as hé-an-du (*UET* III, No. 51; hé-a. . . also to be restored in *MSL* IV 88, 1e and 1f, on the basis of an unpublished duplicate from Ur as Landsberger kindly informs me), hé-ab-sá (*ITT* III, No. 5213), hé-an-ši-díb (*ITT* IV, No. 6900), hé-àm (*passim*) nu-al-til (*passim*), nu-an-na-áǧ-e (*BE* III, No. 10:8), nu-ši-in-ga-ma-ni-ib-túm (i.e., nuš-i-n.ga-ma-ni-b-tum) (*AS* No. 12, p. 28, line 101) and by the occurrence of these elements in imperative forms, which shows that they must belong to a rank different from that of the imperative (profix) and following it. For rank before n-ga-, see for u- the form un-ǧáˢᵘ-ù-bí-tab, for i/e- the form nu-ši-in-ga-ma-ni-íb-túm quoted above, for a- an-ga-kala(g), "is as mighty" (Barton, *MBI*, No. 3 i 24; cf. n. 6 below).

As for the grammatical meanings carried by the prefixes u-, a-, and i/e-, we must obviously look for clues to cases in which Akkadian translation varies consonantly with them. Such a case is the Sumerian preterit form which Akkadian regularly translates with a permansive if it is formed with a- prefix, with a preterit if it is formed with i/e- prefix. Cf. e.g., *MSL* IV 82, lines 97–99, ab-ǧar:*ša-ki-in*, a-ǧar: ⟨*šaknāku*⟩, e-ǧar:⟨*šaknāta*⟩, but lines 100–102 have ì-ǧar:*iš-ku-un*, ì-ǧar:⟨*aškun*⟩, ì-ǧar:⟨*taškun*⟩; ibid., p. 108, lines 105–7, sá an-du₁₁:*ka-ši-id*, sá-a-du:*ka*⟨*-aš-da-ku*⟩, sá e-du:⟨*kašdāta*⟩; ibid., p. 111, line 20, an-gub:*na-zu-uz*, but p. 112, line 26, has ì-gub:*iz-zi-iz* etc. From this difference of translation we may conclude that the prefix a- has a force similar to that of permansive, i.e., that it indicates that the action persists in, and lastingly conditions, the subject. A particularly clear Akkadian example is *alik harrāna* in Gilgamesh Epic, Yale vi 24, which denotes not only that Enkidu has traveled the road but that he remains conditioned by that experience, knows the road, "is traveled." In contrast, the i/e- prefix forms, rendered as simple preterits, imply no such lasting conditioning; this prefix merely indicates that the subject underwent the occurrence denoted by the verb, coming out of it much as he was when he went in.

If the a- prefix with preterit thus indicates persistence in the subject, conditioning of him by a *past* occurrence, it may be assumed that the a- prefix with present/future form indicates similar conditioning of the subject by a *coming* occurrence: inclination toward it, obligation toward it, being destined to it. That this is actually the case may be seen from examples such as an-ta-bal-e-da, "who shall be minded to cross over it (i.e., the boundary canal)" (Entemena Cone A vi 16), ab-ha-lam-me-a:*ša*... *u-sa-za-ku-ni*, "who shall be minded to destroy it" (Rimus b 12; Hirsch in *AOF* 20 [1963] 68, rev. xiv 24 and xiii 20), máš-dà bi-íb-sar-re buru$_5$-a ab-zi-zi:*ṣa-bi-ta ú-ka-aš-ša-ad e-ri-ba i-di-ik-ki*, "he is (obliged) to chase off the gazelles, (obliged) to scare the crows up (off the field)" (*MSL* I, Tf. 4 i 31–34), ^{d}Mar-tu ta-àm an-du$_{12}$-du$_{12}$-un, "why am I (destined) to marry Martu" (*SEM*, No. 58 iv 30), ki-gub-ba-bi àm-zukum-e-dè:*manzassu akabbas*, "I (a captive goddess) was (destined) to tread his premises (i.e., to be taken to the enemy's place to work there as a slave)" (K.41 ii 10′; *PSBA* XVII [1895] Pls. I–II).

The implication of conditioning of the subject by a coming occurrence, of being destined, makes it easy to understand that the a- prefix is the preferred prefix with imperatives since they impose just such compulsion on the subject: e.g., ğen-na (i.e., ğen-a), "Go!" I.e., "you are (obliged, destined) to go!" It also, insofar as conditioning of the subject by the occurrence implies inclination, bent toward realizing it, explains why Akkadian in the translating of clauses with verbs in the a- form shows a marked preference for rendering with participles. For the Akkadian participle typically presents an agent as prone or inclined to an activity (active participle) or as conditioned by an act (passive participle). Examples are gis-kak ur$_5$-šà-ga an-da-ab-lá-ám:*u-ṣu mu-šak-kir lib-bi u ha-še-e*, "the arrow, nailer of liver to lung (i.e., the arrow, which is so conditioned that it nails...)" (Elev. of Inanna; *RA* 12 [1915] 74–75, lines 1–2), za-e ab-ti-la-[bi-me-en]:*at-ta-ma mu-bal-liṭ-[si-na]*, za-e ab-silim-bi-[me-en]:*at-ta-ma mu-šal-lim-[ši-na]*, "you are their reviver, you are their preserver" (IV R 29, No. 1 rev. i 5–8), en-e u$_4$-da al-ti-la:*a-di u$_4$-um bal-ṭu*, "as long as he is living" (IV R 20, No. 2 rev. 7 f.), dingir nam-kù-zu-an-dìm-me-a:*ba-ni ne-me-qí-im*, "(personal) god, creator of know-how (less colloquial term: 'effective knowledge')" (*LIH*, No. 99:16–17).

As for the structure of the prefixes u-, a-, i/e- it may plausibly be suggested that we are dealing with an understood pronominal element followed by casemark (relater) -u of tangentive, a of illative, and e of allative. The referent of the understood pronominal element, since the prefixes indicate a degree of conditioning of the subject, may be assumed to be the subject. On this analysis we may then interpret the prefix a- as denoting "into," i.e., "inwardly affecting, the subject," and i/e- as "externally touching on, but not affecting or lastingly conditioning, the subject." For the casemark (relater) -u we assume a middle value between -e "externally adherent," and -a, "included," namely "internally adherent," "position on inside of border," and call the relation one of "tangentive." See, further, notes 7 and 13 below and cf. Louis Hjelmslev, *La catégorie des cas* ("Acta Jutlandica" VII

1 [1935]) pp. 127–136 (Système sublogique), esp. pp. 128 ff. As member of a prefix rank denoting the degree of conditioning of the subject by the action we assume—as indicated above in the text—that understood pronominal element plus -u denotes restricted, temporary, conditioning (approximately: "instantly, without delay"). It is hardly necessary to stress that the value thus assumed for -u is hypothetical. In its favor is its relevancy in terms of the Sumerian case system and the considerable degree of unity it gives to the use of u throughout the verb.

6. Since Sumerian does not seem to have had initial consonantal clusters, it may be assumed that the sonors n and m of n-ga and m-ga were syllabic in nature and could begin a form. The existence of a syllabic n in Sumerian is suggested by variation between ni/ì and in in the writing of the initial syllable of the city name Isin, presumably pronounced ṇsin, and writings such as -ni-in-i, . . .n-ne-i. . ., and e-en for ne discussed below in n. 12 (end). Syllabic m may be suspected to underlie the writing im, contrasting with i-im- in the paradigm of *alākum* in *MSL* IV.

As for the use of n-ga-, it may be noted that the pronominal element n- can refer, it would seem, to following as well as to preceding verb. The pattern -n.ga-$\sqrt{}_1$. . .-n.ga-$\sqrt{}_2$. . .$\sqrt{}_3$ denotes "not only $\sqrt{}_1$ and $\sqrt{}_2$ but $\sqrt{}_3$." As example may serve lugal-mu za-gin$_x$ a-ba an-ga-kalag a-ba an-ga-a-da-sá a-ba za-gin$_x$ šà-ta ğeš-túg-PI-ga šu-dağal mu-ni-in-du$_{11}$, "O my king, not only who is (as) mighty as you, and who rivals you, but who is from (mother's) womb (as) liberally endowed with intelligence as you?" (Barton, *MBI*, No. 3 (and *TRS* 13) i 22–27 and passim). Other examples of this construction are found at the beginning of the Myth of the Creation of the Pickax (cf. n. 4 above) and in the Kesh Hymn (*OECT* I, Pl. 42, lines 18–20 and passim).

7. For rank after n-ga- see un-ğá^{gu}-ù-bí-tab:*li-iṣ-ṣip ap-pu-na* (*RA* 11 144–145, line 11). The prefix may be analyzed as consisting of an understood pronominal element and casemark (relater) -u of tangentive. The referent of the pronominal element would seem to be the next action stated by the speaker, and the prefix thus indicates that the first action is a constitutive part of the second action, is "internally adherent" to it, or—*mutatis mutandis*—"subjunct" to it.

8. Etymologically the element m may well be related to the m of me-a, "where," and perhaps also to the m of me, "we," "us." On the close relation of the personal pronouns to adverbs of place see nn. 12 and 19. Cf. also as a parallel the use in Italian of the adverb *ci*, "here," for first plural in oblique cases, *ni* (see Otto Jespersen, *The Philosophy of Grammer* [London, 1924] p. 214). The most frequent use of m# is as accollative to denote cursive approach toward the speaker's area, "hither," e.g., nin-zu ^{d}Nin-líl-le i-im-du:*be-lit-ka* MIN (i.e., ^{d}*Nin-líl-le*) il-la-ka, "your mistress, this here Ninlil, is coming" (Myth of Enlil and Ninlil; *JRAS*, 1919, pp. 190–191), but use as decollative for movement away from speaker's area, "hence," is not uncommon. Besides the example quoted above note e.g., lú É-ninnu-ta im-ta-ab-è-è-a, "the man who shall take it (i.e., the statue) hence out of Enninu" (Gudea St. B viii 6–7).

Special mention deserves the use of m in correlation with durative for nearness and cursive movement through time, approximately "were going on (doing)." As examples, may serve the story of Lahar and Ashnan, line 30, i-im-gu$_7$-ù-NE nu-mu-un-dè-si-si-eš, "they (i.e., the Anunnaki) were going on eating and did not become satiated with it," and line 33, i-im-naĝ-naĝ-NE nu-mu-dè-si-eš, "they were going on drinking and did not become satiated with it," where the change in the prefix from noncontact m// to contact mu- correlates with that between durative and punctive suffix. A closely similar example is found ibid., lines 64–67: ĝeštin níĝ-du$_{10}$ i-im-naĝ-naĝ-NE kaš níĝ-du$_{10}$ i-im-du$_{10}$-du$_{10}$-ge-[NE] ĝeštin níĝ-du$_{10}$ ù-mu-un-naĝ-eš-[a-ta] kaš-du$_{10}$ ù-mu-un-du$_{10}$-ge-eš-a-ta, "They were going on drinking the good wine, they were going on regaling themselves with the good beer. When they had drunk the good wine, when they had regaled themselves with the good beer." Further examples are amar-bi gùd-ba-a ì-im-ša$_4$, "its (i.e., Imdugud's) young one went on lying in its nest" (Lugalbanda Epic, line 93), and lú-huĝ-ĝá-a-ni ninda-ni-gu$_7$-e (sandhi for ninda a-ni-gu$_7$-e) túg àm-mu$_4$-mu$_4$:a-gi-ir-[šu] a-ka-lam ú-ša-k[al] ù ṣu-ba-ta ú-lab-ba[-aš], "he is to feed his hired man and go on clothing him" (MSL I 83, lines 18–20).

The combination of cursive, accollative, m with a following regional contact prefix mu-, ma-, or mi- serves to render both motion and arrest. (On the translation of these forms by Akkadian t-forms see MSL IV 25.) An instructive example is CT XV, Pl. 8, rev. 39 ff. The lamenting goddess—presumably envisaged in bovine form—intends to hide from Enlil's "word" so that his neatherd will not find her. In her general statement (rev. 2–6) the form used is consistently na-mu-pà-dè, "may he not find me." In the following lines (7–8), however, she expresses hope that he will seek far away from her hiding place, and this envisaged distance produces a change from na-mu-pà-dè, "may he not find me," to nam-mu-pà-dè, "may he not come over and find me": lú-ù ki-bí-kin-kin e-ne nam-mu-pà-dè e-ne ⟨...⟩ é-ri-a ì-kin-kin e-ne nam-mu-pà-dè e-ne ⟨...⟩, "The neatherd will search the region, may he not come over and find me. ⟨May⟩ he ⟨not come over and find me⟩, in the desert he will seek, may he not come over and find me, ⟨may⟩ he ⟨not come over and find me⟩." Instructive are also the verbal forms in Gilgamesh's advice to Enkidu in Gilgamesh, Enkidu, and the Nether World (Gadd in RA 30 [1933] 128–129, lines 57–71), in which all the verbs denoting a movement and following contact are formed with nam-mu-un- whereas those which imply no such sequence show simple na-an-. The choice of -mu- to indicate contact is probably dictated by the speaker's (Gilgamesh's) sense of emotional closeness with Enkidu (see n. 11 below). When the narrator later relates what happened in Hades (Kramer, From the Tablets of Sumer, Fig. 70) he uses the more objective im-ma-ni-in-.

9. Cf. also ^{ĝiš}ĝišimmar en-na 3-kùš al-sukud-e a ab-bal-e, "he is to water (a-b-bal-e) the palm trees as long as he is growing them toward the height 3 ells (a-l-sukud-e)" (PBS VIII 1, No. 21:13–15).

Ranking of 1// after the u of previousness is indicated by forms such as ù-ul-gíd (Falkenstein, Gerichtsurkunden, No. 215:8) and ù-ul-dím (ibid., line 20). Ranking before the prefixes of regional contact is perhaps indicated by al-bí-in-e$_{11}$-dè:i-tel-li (Langdon, BL, Pl. VIII 8–9), but reading and analysis of the form are not very certain. The line e-ne-ém-ma-ni gaggul-àm-ma-al-šú:a-mat-su kak-kul-lu ka-tim-tu (var. -ti):ki-ma ka-tim-ti kat-mat-ma (var. omits -ma) in SBH, No. 8:64 f., is most likely sandhi for gaggul-àm al-šú, "is covered up as a kakkullu-pot."

10. In diagram form the prefixes used for specific entity indication may be listed as follows:

	1st p. sg. "me"	Near 3rd neuter "it here"	Far 3rd neuter "it there"
Allative, "on"	mu	m-mi	bi
Dative, "for"	ma	ma-ma	ba

11. In briefest compass mu- may be said to denote "closeness" to the speaker if by closeness we understand not only closeness in space and time but also emotional closeness, empathy, involvement. The purely spatial indication of mu- is pinpointed, as it were, by the use of mu- in functional overlap for allative first person "on/at me"; its further implications of speaker empathy are seen most clearly from its preferential correlation with first and second person goal and from variations in its use with 3rd person goal. In trying to illustrate its use we may begin with instances in which mu- seems used without stress on specific correlation with a pronominal goal.

mu-, "here"

The following may be mentioned as particularly instructive examples.

(1) The ditilla texts from Telloh are styled from the place in court of the court reporter. Outside of direct quotations mu- hardly occurs in them except in one special usage: in statements that documents, witnesses, or persons accused were brought into court, i.e., into the immediate presence of the recording scribe. As examples may serve *ITT* II, No. 3532, dub-bi ki-di-ku₅-ne-šè Dingir-sa₆-ga-a mu-túm, "that tablet D. brought here to the place of the judges" (Falkenstein, *Gerichtsurkunden*, No. 45:10–11), and *ITT* III, No. 6545, mu-tu-mu-a, "that he will bring him (a deserter) in." Similar instances are found in *ITT* III, Nos. 3547, 5246, 5286 iii, 6567, in *ITT* V, No. 6754, and in *Bab.* 3 (1910) Pl. VII, No. XIX.

(2) The Code of Lipiteshtar also uses mu- extremely sparingly in the body of the code. Exceptions are statements of entry into the house of the man with whom the paragraph deals; cf. col. xvi 27–29, sağ-rig₇ é-ad-da-na-ta mu-un-tùm-ma, "the dowry she brought from her father's house," and col. xvii 26, é-a nu-mu-un-da-an-tuš, "he will not let her dwell with her (his wife) in the house." In both cases the styling is from the house as if the paragraph was a clause in a contract written there.

(3) Building and votive inscriptions meant to be read *in situ* are styled from the place of the inscription, and mu-("here where I am speaking to you") is accordingly the standard prefix for the central verbal forms recording the building (mu-dù, mu-na-dù) or presenting (a mu-na-ru) recorded. Characteristic change in the use of prefixes, noted by most scholars who have dealt with the subject, is found in Lugalkinishedudu's vase inscription A (*SAK*, p. 156, line 36), where the acts (by Enlil) which led up to the state of affairs surrounding the dedication of the vase are told in e- forms, whereas that state and the dedication itself are told in mu- forms. Similarly, in the vase inscription of Lugalzagesi the events leading up to the present

fortunate state of the country are told in e- forms, while the description of the present state and of the dedication of the vase is in mu- forms. In Entemena Cone A likewise the events leading up to the canal-building operations which the cone commemorates are stated in e- forms, the commemoration in mu- forms. Often the distinction between i- and mu- sets off earlier works from those which the inscription commemorates; cf. e.g., Gudea Brick B 6–10, lú É-ninnu ᵈNin-g̃ír-su-ka in-dù-a é Gír-su-ka-ni mu-na-dù, "(Gudea) the man who built the Eninnu of Ningirsuk built here for him his Girsu house," or the clay nail of Gungunum (*SAK*, p. 206, a) col. ii 7–9, É-hi-li-a-ni in-dù É-gi-na-ab-tùm-kù-ga-ni mu-na-dù, "he built her Ehili and built here her pure store for her."

(4) An interesting stylistic use of forms with and without mu- to indicate near and far occurs in a passage of an Ishme-Dagan hymn (*PBS* X 2, No. 14) and its duplicates: "May the Tigris and Euphrates bring to you (here: hu-mu-ra-ab-tùm) the abundance of the carp flood, and may their canal tails (i.e., the far-reaches of the canals feeding from them) reach far for you (out into the desert: ha-ra-sud-e), may their banks grow grass and herbs for you (here: hu-mu-ra-an-mú), and may joy stretch out for you (to far off: ha-ra-ab-lá), may your orchards (here around the town) range honey side by side with wine (ki hu-mu-ra-ni-íb-ús) and may those good fields (far out beyond town) grow mottled barley for you (ha-ra-ab-mú), may they heap up their grain piles for you (out there: ha-ra-dub-dub), may cattle pens be built for you (out there in the steppe: ha-ra-dù-dù) and sheepfolds broaden out for you (out there: ha-ra-dag̃al-dag̃al)."

mu-, "here with me/you"

Turning from these examples to cases in which the regional reference of mu- is correlated with specific pronominal reference in the form we may conveniently begin with the data furnished by the *alākum* paradigm published by Landsberger in *MSL* IV, OBGT VII. Arranging the forms in parallel vertical columns according to the presence of first person, second person, third person or zero directive-dative pronominal goal of the action, we may set up the instructive paradigm.

Since present and preterit forms with first person singular goal are not given by the paradigm, we have listed instead the relevant imperative forms. To facilitate comparison we similarly list imperatives for present forms with first person plural goal and give the present form in the notes only. We have not included in the paradigm the corresponding forms of plural verb with plural goal (they are 1st p. pl. goal in lines 231, 239, 235, 234; 2nd p. pl. goal in lines 233, 241, 237, 245; 3rd p. pl. goal in lines 298, 310, 301, 313; no goal indicated in lines 141, 169, 147, 175) since they follow the singular forms with plural goal in their use of mu-.

It will be seen from this paradigm that a correlation exists between stated pronominal goal of the action and choice of prefix. Two sets of prefixes contrast mu-/-m-mu- on one side, -m-/-m-ma- on the other. Occurring forms are mu imperative/present/preterit I₁; àm-mu imperative/present I₂; im-mu preterit I₂; àm present I₁; i-im preterit I₁; àm-ma present I₂; im-ma preterit I₂.

Of the two contrasting sets the set -m-/-m-ma- may be considered the basic one since it is the one used when there is no stated pronominal goal in the form that could interfere with the choice of prefix. The basic -m-/-m-ma- is found also with stated first person plural and third person singular and plural pronominal goals, a fact which suggests that these goals do not—or need not—affect the choice of prefix. It is quite otherwise with stated first person singular and second person singular or plural pronominal goals. These goals regularly call for the contrasting set of prefixes mu-/-m-mu-. It will be noted that both mu-/-m-mu- and -m-/-m-ma- indicate closeness to the speaker, "here," and that both sets are identically rendered in Akkadian by ventive. The difference between them must thus be sought in some difference of degree or quality of the "here" denoted, one such degree or quality preferred with first person and second person singular goal, the other not.

mu-, "here" of emotional closeness

In looking for a clue to this difference we must look for instances in which the condition for the variation between the two prefix sets can be even more sharply pinpointed than in the paradigm, occurrences in contexts identical except for one single identifiable variant factor.

Such an instance is furnished, it would seem, by the phrase gù àm-ma-dé-e, "it said to it as follows (durative)," which is part of the standard introduction of quoted speech in the Dispute of the Plow and the Hoe. The phrase has close counterparts in other stories where gù...dé is similarly used in the formal introduction of quoted speech, but there the prefix chosen is mu-; cf. e.g. Enmerkar and the Lord of Aratta, line 68: En-me-er-kár dumu dUtu-ra gù mu-na-dé-e, "She (Inanna) said to Enmerkar son of Utu as follows (durative)." The phrase is a standard one, and many other examples could be quoted. As will be seen, the two phrases differ from the forms of the paradigm given above by having a dative rather than a directional pronominal goal, third person singular, and they differ from each other in that in one case, gù àm-ma-dé-e, this goal is third person neuter, a thing, and in the other, gù mu-na-dé-e, third person personal, a person. Otherwise the contexts are exactly the same. In both cases the storyteller presents one of his characters as close by and spoken to, and one can hardly assume that the closeness with which a storyteller presents his main characters would vary in degree; rather, as suggested by the concomitant variation of neuter and personal, it must be a variation in kind of closeness. The closeness of mu- is not only spatial but also emotional, allowing empathy and identification; that of -m-ma- remains spatial and does not encroach upon the emotions. In other words we may say that mu- renders a subjective personally involved "here," while -m-ma- renders rather an objective merely observed "here."

The reference of mu- to personal pronominal goal was first noted by Falkenstein in his discussion of *TCL* XVI, No. 89 (*OLZ* 36 [1933] 303–304), where the approach of the evil eye to things is consistently described as ba-te, to people as mu-na-te, and where the verbs describing the harm it does to things are formed with -m- (im-), to people with mu-. A further example is Shurpu IX 119–28, where the form bí-in-tag is used of the water touching things (cedar, *hashurru*-tree), mu-un-tag of the water touching persons (An, Ki, En-ki, the man, son of his god).

Attempting to generalize from the examples discussed we would suggest that the speaker can indicate closeness to himself by means of prefixes formed with m.

VENTIVE

	1st p. sg. goal	2nd p. sg. goal	3rd p. sg. goal	No. pron. goal
I₁ Imp./Pres.	[ğá-a- **mu-šè**]* / [alkam ana ṣeriia]	60 **mu**-e-ši-du / illakakkum	49 àm- ši-du / illakaššum	àm- du / illakam
		88 **mu**-e-ši-ğen / illikakkum	77 i-im- ši-ğen / illikaššum	74 i-im- ğen / illikam
I₂ Imp./Pres.	16 ğá- nam-**mu**-še / atlakam ana ṣeriia	58 àm-**mu**-e-ši-du / ittallakakkum	55 àm-ma-ši-du / ittallakaššum	52 àm-ma-du / ittallakam
		86 im-**mu**-e-ši-ğen / ittalkakkum	83 im-ma-ši-ğen / ittalkaššum	80 im-ma-ğen / ittalkam

	1st pl. goal		2nd pl. goal	3rd pl. goal
I_1 Imp./Pres.	191 ǧá-a- alkam niāši	me-a†	208 **mu**-e-ne-du íllakam kunūši	262 [àm- n]e-du íllakam šunūši
	211 i-im- illikam niāši	me-ǧen	213 **mu**-e-ne-ǧen illikam kunūši	274 i-im- ne-ǧen illikam šunūši
I_2 Imp./Pres.	195 ǧá- nam- atlakam niāši	me-a‡	205 àm-**mu**-e-ne-du ittallakam kunūši	265 àm-ma-ne-du ittallakam šunūši
Pret.	215 im-ma- ittalkam niāši	me-ǧen	217 im-**mu**-e-ne-ǧen ittalkam kunūši	277 im-ma-ne-ǧen ittalkam šunūši

* The form is reconstructed on the basis of the parallel ǧá-a-mu-še-en-zé-en : al-ka-a-nim a-na ṣe-ri-ia in line 102.

† The imperative form is given for comparison with the 1st person singular goal form. The corresponding present form occurs in line 199: àm-me-du : i-il-la-kam ni-a-ši.

‡ The imperative form is given for comparison with the 1st person singular goal form. The corresponding present form occurs in line 203: àm-ma-me-du : it-tál-la-kam ni-a-ši.

Within these prefixes he has (if we omit consideration for the moment of mi-, -m-mi-, and ma-) a choice between two sets, -m-/-m-ma- and mu-/-m-mu-. The first set indicates objective closeness, the second subjective closeness implying a degree of empathy and emotional involvement on his part. Per se either of these sets can be used with any one or with no stated pronominal goal of the action, but because of what they connote there is a pronounced tendency toward preference of mu-/-m-mu- with the nearest pole of the pronominal axis, first person singular, goal in the speaker himself, and -m-/-m-ma- for the farther pole of the axis, third person neuter, which, as a thing, normally does not invite empathy. In the middle range of the axis, third person personal, the choice will vary rather more, dependent upon the speaker's attitude toward the person involved.

A number of further examples of correlation of mu- with stated pronominal goal may be cited. They have been chosen for contrast with parallel forms without mu-.

(1) Comitative goal. Cf. gi-dub-ba-zu e-da-ğál:*na-ši-a-ta* (2nd p. sg. goal: "is with you"), mu-da-ğál:*na-ši-a-ku* (1st p. sg. goal: "is with me"), an-da-ğál:*na-ši* (3rd p. sg. goal: "is with him"); nu-e-da-ğál:*ú-ul na-ši-a-ti*, nu-mu-da-ğál:*ú-ul na-ši-a-ku*, nu-an(!)-da-ğál:*ú-ul na-ši* (MSL IV 70, lines 58–64). Closely similar are the comitative infixes denoting ability in the subject: mu-da-:*e-li-i*, e-da-:*te-li-i*, an-da-:*i-li-i* (MSL IV 145, lines 400–402) and mu-da-:*qá-du-ú-a* (MSL IV 143, line 357), e-ta-:*qá-du-uk-ku* (line 361), un-da:*qá-du-uš-šu* (line 364). Further examples are a-ba-a mu-da-an-ná, "who will lie down with me" (PBS I 1, No. 6:42), contrasting with za-ra hé-da-an-ná (ibid., line 43), "with thee may lie down"; nam-mu-da-du, "may not go with me" (Lugalbanda Epic, line 272), but na-e-da-du, "may not go with thee" (ibid., line 274); ur-re-bi me-e ní ba-da-te e-ne nu-mu-da-te:⟨*nak-ri šu-ú*⟩ *ana-ku ap-lah-ma šu-ú ul ip-lah-an-ni*, "I was afraid of that enemy, he was not afraid of me" (K. 41 ii 7; PSBA XVII, Pls. I–II [cf. dupl. Langdon, BL, No. 71:31]).

(2) Allative goal. sağ-túm-ma mu-un-gar:*ma-gi-ir-tam iq-bi-a-am* but sağ-túm-ma i-ni-in-gar:*ma-gi-ir-tam aq-bi-šum* (MSL IV 72, lines 173–76); mu-un-ti-ti:*ú-re-še-an-ni*, nu-mu-un-ti-ti:*ú-la ú-re-[še-an-ni*] but an-ni-ib-ti-ti:*ú-re-ši-[šu*], nu-un-ni-ib-ti-ti:*ú-la ú-re-ši-šu* in MSL IV 74, lines 232–235.

(3) Directional goal, šu te-mu-še-eb:*mu-úh-ra-an-ni*, "receive from me (lit. 'hold near the hand toward me')," but šu-te-en-še-eb:*mu-hu-ur-šu*, "receive from him" (MSL IV 124, lines 2–3); á-mu-šè [h]u-mu-un-ag-eš, "let them make for (i.e., go to) my side," in Gilgamesh and Huwawa (JCS 1 [1947] 12) line 51 but á-ni-šè ba-an-ag-eš, "they made for his side," in line 53.

(4) Dative goal. gur-mu-na-a[b]:[*te-er-*] ⌜*ra-aš*⌝-*šu*, "return it here to him," but gur-ru-na-a[b]:[*t*]*e-er-šu*, "return it to him" (MSL IV 124, lines 6–7).

Interesting differences in treatment of the third person personal goal are exemplified in RTC, No. 19, which records an exchange of gifts between Barnamtarra and the wife of the *ishakku* of Adab and also tells of gratuities given to their respective messengers. The wife of the *ishakku* of Adab gave Barnamtarra's messenger Malgasu a gratuity in Adab (mu-na-sum), and later Barnamtarra gave a gratuity to the Adab messenger in Girsu (e-na-sum). The use of mu-na-sum for the giving to Malgasu, although that action was farther in space and time from the recording scribe than the giving to the Adab messenger, described by e-na-sum, is clearly dictated by the greater emotional closeness of Malgasu as being "from here" and "one of us" to the scribe. Also interesting is the variation in Stele of the Vultures, obv. iv. In telling about Inanna's naming of Eannatum the scribe shares, by using mu-, in Eannatum's gratification (mu-ni-pà). Shortly afterward (col. v 24–25) that same naming is again referred to in connection with a new naming of Eannatum by Ningirsu. Here the scribe shares in the import of the new naming (col. v 29: mu m[u]-ni-sa₄) and records the now less close earlier naming without mu: e-ni-sa₄-a-ni. Later in the same text (rev. i 10) the scribe tells in objective historical narrative that Eannatum gave the Ummean the net of Utu and that the Ummean swore him an oath by it: nam e-na-ta-ku₅. The scribe's attention is on the net. Immediately afterward the oath itself is quoted and the scribe's attention switches to Eannatum and to sharing in his triumph: lú Umma^{ki}-ke₄ É-an-na-túm-ra nam mu-na-ku₅-du zi ^{d}Utu . . . (rev. i. 8–11), "The man of Umma swore here to (our) Eannatum: 'By the life of Utu. . . .'"

Lastly a few examples of mu- with first person singular subject forms may be noted. In *TRS* 69.7–8 Inanna, boasting of her might, says an a-ba-a in-dúb(?) g̃á-e-me-en mu-un-dúb ki a-ba-a in-. . . g̃á-e-me-en mu-un-. . . , "Who was making the heavens tremble? It was I here made them tremble; who was . . .ing Earth? It was I here . . .ed it." The use of mu- serves as does the emphatic form of the independent pronoun to focus attention on the speaker. In the Shulgi hymn *TCL* XV, No. 13 (dupl. Barton, *MBI*, No. 3), Enlil(?) promises to decide a fate for Shulgi and immediately proceeds to do so. The statement begins lugal nam gi₄-rí-íb-ta(r)-ar nam-du₁₀ gú-mu-rí-íb-ta(r)-ar, "King, let me determine a fate for you, let me here determine a good fate for you." The forms reflect transition from a general promise, indeterminate as to time and place, to decisive following-through, determining the fate "here." Finally, the variation of forms in the story of Shukallituda quoted by Kramer in *ArOr* 17/1 (1949) 404 and 402, n. 16, deserves attention. Inanna in stating her determination to find Shukallituda uses the mu- form: lú-g̃íš-du₁₁-ga-mu kur-kur-ra ga-mu-ni-pà im-me, "She said: 'Let me find from out of all the lands the man who cohabited with me." In the following line the storyteller records that she was not finding him nu-um-ma-ni-in-pà-dè, using an -m-ma- form, and earlier the father of Shukallituda in suggesting that she would not find him (p. 402, n. 16) likewise used an -m-ma- form: nu-um-ma-ni-in-pà-dè-en, "she will not find thee therein." The difference affecting the choice of prefix would seem to be that though all three forms look toward an ultimate confrontation of Inanna with Shukallituda this confrontation is in the last two forms seen from outside by speakers not directly involved, in the first form subjectively by the speaker as prospective participant.

12. See *GSG* §§487, 491, and 494; Falkenstein, *GSGL*, §63a–b. The data presented by the texts are, however, rather more varied and complex than the traditional listing given above would lead one to expect. A few points may be mentioned here.

(1) Outside the ergative (zero-case) ranks understood pronominal element—absence of explicit mark of pronominal reference—is common with all singular forms. It seems to be mandatory for all but the first of infixes of the same subseries if they occur together in a form. Since infixes of the form P + a and P + i rank

first in their respective subseries they are less susceptible—perhaps not susceptible at all—of occurring with understood pronominal element.

(2) As for the occurring explicit marks, it may be noted that in the ergative ranks only singular pronominal element seems so far attested. These marks are first person # ranking perhaps directly before the a- series, second person e ranking directly before the e- series (see n. 15), and third person personal n, third person neuter b, both ranking directly before the root. In the first:second person pair #:e the marked form, e, is restricted to denoting second person singular and the unmarked form, #, can denote both first and second person; or we may state this in the form that # denotes the larger class of "participant in the speech situation," e its narrower subclass "addressee." As example may serve the paradigm ğar:*šakānu* in *MSL* IV, OBGT VI. The marked second person singular form occurs in lines 97–99, ab-ğar:*ša-ki-in*, a-ğar:⟨*šaknāku*⟩, e-ğar:⟨*šaknāta*⟩, and in lines 118–120, in-⌈na⌉-an-ğar:*iš-ku-un-šum*, i[n-n]a-ğar:⟨*aškunšum*⟩, [i]n-na-e-ğar:⌈*taškunšum*⌉, but the rule of the paradigm is to use the unmarked form for both first and second person as e.g., in lines 136–138 and passim: mu-na-an-ğar:*iš-ku-un-šum*, mu-na-ğar:⟨*aškunšum*⟩, mu-na-ğar:⟨*taškunšum*⟩.

(3) Outside the ergative, i.e., when the pronominal element (infix component) occurs with accollatively used zero-case or with any other case, the pronominal elements seem more broadly used with considerable overlap of function. The mark e occurs not only as expected with second person singular reference (cf. *GSG* §§487, 491a, 494a) but also with first person, third person, and third neuter singular reference. The mark n seems compatible not only with third person singular reference (cf. *GSG* §§487, 491a, 494–496) but also at times with first and second person singular reference. Examples of such usage are the following.

(a) e with first person singular reference: za-e ⌈ğá⌉-a-ra ki mu-e-a-éğ-a-ta, "ever since you (felt) love for me (mu-e.a-(e)eğ-a-ta)" (Kramer, *From the Tablets of Sumer*, Fig. 76, line 22); É-kur mah-mu dalla mu-e-a-è, "you made my great Ekur stand forth splendidly for me (mu-e.a-(e)è)" (*SRT*, No. 11:41); á-šè mu-e-da-a'i(A-A)-áğ, "you gave me commission (mu-e.da-e-ağ)" (3N-T. 311; unpubl.); ğen-mu-e-da, "come with me" (*RA* 8 [1911] 164, obv. ii 46; cf. photo on plate facing p. 161); mu-e-da-ğál-la-àm:*na-šá-ku-[ma*], "I carry (lit. 'it is with me')" (Angin III 24, 25, 26); ní mu-e-DU:*ú-par-ri-da-an-ni*, "he frightened me" (K.41 ii 5′; *PSBA* XVII, Pls. I–II); mu-e-túm-mu-un-nam, "if it is you bring her unto me (mu-e.e-tum-en or mu-e.#-tum-en)" (Enki and Ninhursag, line 224); a-na-aš nu-mu-un-e-ši-íb-še-ge-en:*am-mi-nim*(!) *la ta-ma-ga-ri-nu*, "why do you not accede to me (nu-mu-n-e.ši-b-šeg-en)" (*SBH*, No. 69 obv. 16–17); ği₆-pár-kù-ğá hu-mu-e-ši-in-ku₄-re (var. + -en), "may you come in to me in my pure Giparu" (Ninmeduga, line 66).

Assimilated to a preceding vowel this first person singular e occurs in mu-ù-da-gub-a-bi, "the one of them who has waited for me (mu-e.da-gub-abi)" (Barton, *MBI*, No. 3 vi. 11; cf. line 13), šu ba-mu-u₈, "release me (ba-mu-e.e)" (*PAPS* 107 [1963] 409, line 9), and šu ba-àm-mu-u₈, "release me (ba-a-m-mu-e.e)" (ibid., p. 509, line 36).

(b) e with third person singular reference: lú ki-sikil ne-en sa₆-ga-ra ne-en mul-

la-ra : *ar-da-tu šá ki-a-am dam-qát ki-a-am ba-na-a-⌈at⌉*, lú g̃ìš na-e-du₁₁ lú ní-su-ub-
[su]-⌈ub⌉-ba:*man-ma-an ai ir-he-e-ši man ma-an ai iš-ši-iq-ši*, "With a girl so nice,
so fair, would not a(ny) man cohabit, would not a(ny) man kiss?" (Myth of Enlil
and Ninlil; *JRAS*, 1919, p. 191, lines 20–21). To the allative in the verb, e, which
stands for e.e, corresponds in the noun the personal dative -ra, which usually
replaces allative -e with nouns denoting persons (cf. *GSG* §496; Falkenstein, *GSGL*,
§123d). For the presumably more original construction of the noun with e cf.
lú-tur-sa₆-ga-e ne nu-mu-un-su-ub-bi, "Shall I not kiss the nice child?" (Myth of
Enki and Ninhursag; *BASOR* "Supplementary Studies" No. 1, p. 14, lines 92 and
112; cf. lines 95 and 115). Instructive for the interpretation of e in g̃ìš na-e-du₁₁
and ne ní-su-ub-[su]-⌈ub⌉ as allative infix third person singular is the parallel ningal ᵈEn-líl ᵈNin-hur-sag̃-ra g̃ìš mu-ni-du₁₁ ne mu-ni-sub_x (EREN + UH; cf. later
munsub), "with Ninhursag the great lord Enlil cohabited, kissed" (Barton, *MBI*,
No. 1 xi 5–8), which shows construction with the allative infix third person singular
ni. A further example of e with third person singular reference is *SEM*, No. 77 ii
10: ᵈEn-líl níg̃ nam-šè mu-e-tar-ra-[šè], "Enlil (in response) to what had been
decided for him (lit. 'on him') as doom (left town)." The later version (*JRAS*,
1919, pp. 190–191) has here mu-un-tar-ra-šè.

(c) e with third person neuter singular reference. Far more frequent than third
person personal singular is third person neuter singular reference of e. The corresponding cases of the noun are -a and, more rarely, -e and -šè. In the inscriptions of
Gudea e is regularly assimilated to preceding a in contact; in later periods this
assimilation does not seem to take place. When e occurs before the root e the writing
shows a vowel a between e and the root, possibly as mark of hiatus.

As examples from the inscriptions of Gudea may be quoted šeg₇ an-na hé-da-a-gi₄
a ki-a hé-da-a-gi₄, "may the rains be held back in Heaven under him, may the
waters be held back in the Earth under him" (St. B ix 19–20); é-a dù-ba mul-kù-ba
gù ma-ra-a-dé, "he spoke to you about the pure star of (i.e., announcing) the
building of the house" (Cyl. A vi 1–2); garza-g̃á mul-an-kù-ba gù ga-mu-ra-a-dé,
"I shall speak to you about the pure heavenly star of my rites" (Cyl. A ix 10); ud
siskur_x-ra mu-na-a-g̃ál, "the dawn found him (lit. 'the day come into being for
him') in prayer" (Cyl. A xiii 28); ud im-zal a mu-a-tu₅, "the day passed, he bathed
in water" (Cyl. A xviii 3); É-ninnu an-ki-ta-til-bi igi-a mu-na-a-g̃ál, "Eninnu,
finished from top to bottom (adv. of manner in -bi), was here for him before (his)
eyes" (Cyl. A xx 10); uru-na ú-šub-ni zà-bi-a mu-da-a-ná-àm, "in the (outlying)
border districts of his city (both) the strong man and his underling could lie down to
sleep (the latter not having to keep watch)" (Cyl. B xviii 10); šu-zi ma-ra-a-g̃ar,
"I have put hand truly unto it for you" (Cyl. B ii 20); iti é-ba ba-a-ku₄, "the new
moon entered into its house" (Cyl. B iii 7); níg̃-ba-g̃á ba-a-gi₄-da, "who will come
back to (i.e., contest) my grants" (St. B viii 19–20). For occasional construction with
-šè rather than with -a cf. ᵍⁱˢgigir-za-gìn-šè mu-na-a-silim, "they (i.e., two kinds of
wood) seemed sound to him for the pure chariot" (Cyl. A vii 19).

As examples from texts of Old Babylonian and later times may serve [šu-íl-l]a-mu
an-né ba-e-ús [me-ri]-ma-al-la-mu ki-e ba-e-ús, "my raised hand I (Inanna) press
against Heaven, my implanted foot I press against the Earth" (*VS* II, No. 28:10);

cf. *ASKT*, No. 21, where the construction with allative (e) of the noun is exemplified. More usual is construction with -a in the noun as e.g., in [aia-mu An] lugal aia dingir-re-e-ne un-e [bar]á-kù-ga ba-e-tuš ama-mu ^{d}Uraš nin-dingir-re-e-ne An-da ki-nú-kù-ga e-ne-sù-gal-ba-e-du$_{11}$, "my father, king An, father of the gods, sits (enthroned) above the people on a pure throne dais, my mother Urash, queen of the gods, grandly disports herself with An on a pure couch" (*SRT*, No. 6:85–88); ur é-tùr-ra hul-ù ná-a-ba lag nam-ba-e-šub-e:*kal-ba šá ina tar-ba-și rab-șu lim-niš kur-ban-na la ta-na-as-suk* (Nergal hymn, line 25; Zimmern in *ZA* 31 [1917/18] 112–117), "do not viciously throw a lump of earth at the dog in the cattle pen when it has lain down (lit. 'in its having lain down'—construed 'the dog which lies in the cattle pen' in the Akkadian translation); sağ-ği$_6$-ga igi-⌈ğá⌉ mu-e-ğál, "the black-headed people are before me" *SEM*, No. 51 ii 9; dupl. *PBS* I 2, No. 104 rev. 9, has mu-un-ğál); dingir di-ğá la-ba-e-gub, "no god sat (as judge, lit. 'stood') in my case (*PBS* X 2, No. 6 rev. i 33); níğ Ki-en-gi-ra ba-a-gu-⟨ul⟩-la kur-ra ga-àm-mi-íb-gu-ul, "what it has destroyed in Sumer let me destroy in the highland" (Barton, *MBI*, No. 3 vi 22–23); tilla-a nam-⌈ba-e⌉-gub-bu-dè-en, "do not stand around in the square" (*SEM*, No. 70:12; dupl. *BE* XXXI, No. 51); mu-ur-ra ud ba-e-zal:*ina gu-šu-ri a-bit*, "I passed the day (Akkadian: 'the night') on the beams (of the ceiling)" (K.41; *PSBA* XVII, Pls. I–II, iii 1–2); é-bi Ni-na-ab^{ki}-a ga-su$_8$-en-[dè-en] ga-ba-e-su$_8$-en-dè-⌈en⌉, "to that house in Ninab let us proceed, thereunto let us proceed" (*SEM*, No. 58:20). As examples of construction with -šè and of alternance with infix -n-ši- may serve ga-an-ši-su$_8$-dè-en Umma^{ki}-a sig$_4$ Kur-šà-ga-šè ga-an-ši-su$_8$-dè-en (var. ga-e-su$_8$-dè-en), "let us proceed toward it, toward brick-built Kurshaga in Umma let us proceed" (Inanna's Descent, line 312); ga-e-su$_8$-en-dè-en Bàd-Tibira^{ki}-a É-muš-kalam-ma-šè ga-an-ši-su$_8$-en-dè-en (ibid., line 322), Text M adding the line Bàd-tibira É-muš-kalam-ma-šè ğìr-ni-šè ba-e-su$_8$-eš, "they proceeded at her heels (lit. 'toward her feet') toward Emushkalamma and Badtibira"; ga-e-su$_8$-dè-en ^{ğiš}hashur-gul-la edin Kul-ab^{ki} ^{ğiš}hashur gul-la edin Kul-ab^{ki} ğìr-ni-šè ba-e- su$_8$-re-eš, "let us proceed, at her heels to the destroyed apple tree in the Kullab desert, (to) the destroyed apple tree in the Kullab desert they proceeded" (ibid., line 331); kur-šè ga-e-su$_8$-en-⌈dè⌉-en, "let us proceed to the highland" (*TuM* n.F. III [1961] No. 5:15). It should be mentioned that a possible variant interpretation of the examples with su$_8$ is to assume a root ere written e-re$_7$ or e-RE$_7$-re.

Instances of e separated from the root e by a written a are ^{d}En-si$_{11}$-ga an-na ba-e-a-è$_{11}$-dè (Lugalbanda Epic, line 253), kur-ra ba-e-a-è$_{11}$ (Inanna's Descent, lines 5 ff.).

(d) n with first person singular reference. Examples in which the pronominal infix component n seems to occur with first person singular reference are umun šà-zu ma-da nu-mu-un-da-ğál-e:*be-lum šá lib-ba-ka* ⌈*la te*⌉-*ep-ta-a*, "Lord who opened not thy heart for me (n.da)" (*SBH*, No. 44:10–11); un-ni-in-rig$_5$, "when he had granted unto me (n.i)" (Hammurabi; *OECT* I, Pl. 18, col. i 11); sağ-e-eš hu-mu-ni-rig$_7$, "as a gift may she grant unto me (n.i)" (Warad-Sin; *UET* I, No. 127:49); a-ba mu-un-da-ab-sá-a . . . a-ba mu-un-da-ab-sì-ge:*man-nu i-šá-an-na-an-ni* [*ia*]-*ti man-nu ú-maš-šá-la-*[*an-ni*] *ia-ti*, "who competes with me (n.da), who compares with me (n.da)" (*SBH*, No. 56:1–3); ní-gal hu-mu-un-da-ri (var. hé-da[?]-

ri):*nam-ri-ir-ri lu ra-ma-ku*, "a great splendor is verily upon me (n.da)" (Angin IV 17); šu-[ni] mu-un-ši-in-ir:[*q*]*a-ti-šu úb-lam-ma*, "he stretched out his hand toward me" (K. 41 ii 5–6; *PSBA* XVII, Pls. I–II [cf. dupl. Langdon, *BL*, No. 71:29–30]; older text *CT* XV, Pl. 25, lines 6 and 7, has mu-ši-in-ir); lú-lul l-me-a mu-un-na-ab-bé-e-[NE]:*šá sar-rat-mi i-qab-bu-ni*, "they tell to me (n.a): 'she is the one who is false'" (*ASKT*, No. 21:53–54).

(e) Examples in which n occurs where second person pronominal infix component e is expected are LIB-BAR in-na-ab-ag-e-NE:*ú-paq-qu-ka*, "(the people) watch you (n.a)" (hymn to Utu; IV R 17, lines 19–20); kur-ra gun- g̃ùr-ru gun hé-en-na-an-g̃ùr-ru:*šá-du-u na-áš bil-ti bil-tú liš-ši-ka*, "may the tribute-bearing highland carry tribute to you (n.a)" (IV R 18, line 5; cf. lines 10–11, 12–13, 14–15, 16–17); za-e sila zi-da šu àm-mi-ni-[ib-mú]-mú:*ka-a-šu su-le-e kit-tum i-kar-rab-ki*, "the righteous street salutes you (n.i)" (*SBH*, No. 53:7–8); ┌ù┐ nu-mu-un-na-ku-ù-NE:*ú-la i-ṣa-al-la-la-ki*, "they cannot sleep because of you (n.a)" (*RA* 24 [1927] 36, obv. 15 and rev. 17); ᵈEn-líl-le igi-zi mu-un-ši-in-bar, "Enlil looked truly toward you (n.ši)" (Iddin-Dagan hymn *TCL* XVI, No. 88:11–13; dupl. *PBS* V, No. 64 [with var. e for un]; *SRT*, No. 52).

To explain this broad use of e and n is not easy, but one might consider the possibility that they are basically elements of spatial indication so that e would denote essentially "the one where you are" and n "the one where he is." While "the one where you are" would normally serve to denote "you," it could as needed be used also for "I (here) where you are" and "he/it where you are." In favor of such an assumption is the obvious relation of e to the demonstrative pronominal suffix -e, which seems to have much the same range as to grammatical person. With clear second person reference it occurs in variation with -zu in izi C 25–26 (VAT 9714; unpubl.), ki-zu-neⁿⁱ-neⁿⁱ:*it-ti-ku-nu*, ki-e-ne-ne:MIN (= *ittikunu*), and in its use in address, e.g. lugal-e ud me-lam-bi nir-g̃ál, "you king here, a storm the glory of which is noble" (see *JNES* 5 [1946] 132 f., n. 9, for further examples [see above, chap. vii]). With third person and third neuter reference it is translated *annû*, "this," in Old Babylonian and *šū*, "the one in question," in Old Akkadian (see *GSG* §§223–226), and the full gamut of personal reference would be covered if—as seems highly probable—we may identify it with the e of the full form of the personal independent pronouns g̃a.e, "I," za.e, "thou," an.e, "he, she."

(4) The second personal plural pronominal infix component occurs in the *alākum* paradigm in *MSL* IV consistently as e-ne. As noted in *MSL* IV 10 and *JNES* 22 (1963) 18 f. [see below, chap. xvii], the infix shows explicit casemark (.a) only in the imperative forms, and it is not clear whether the e-ne which occurs in indicative represents a contracted form of ene-a or a variant ene-# with zero casemark rather than -a. The Neo-Babylonian grammatical texts list e-ne-a:*ku-nu-ti* (*MSL* IV, NBGT I 149) with e-ne-ne-a (ibid., line 150), e-ne-šè:*a-n*[*a*] *ku-nu-ti* AN-TA (ibid., line 156) with un-ne-šè, an-ne-┌šè┐, in-ne-šè, en-ne-šè (ibid., lines 157–160), and similar series with casemarks -da and -ta (ibid., lines 161–170). Also NBGT II gives e-ne:*ku-nu-*[ti] in line 206 and e-ne-a:*ku-nu-*┌*šim*┐(?) in line 207. In context e-ne occurs in Lugal-e X 26 as variant of the form with doubled n: en-ne in ní-me-lám-mu ba-e-en-ne-en-dul (var. ba-e-ne-en-dul):*pu-luh-ti mé-lam-mi-ia ik-tum-*[*ku-*

nu-ti], "my splendor and glory (Akkadian: 'fear of my glory') covered you," and in line 25 in giriš-gin$_x$ šu ha-ba-e-en-zé-en(?)-sìg(?) (var. ha-ba-e-ne-e[n-sìg]):*ki-ma kur-ṣip-ti e-mi-iš-ku-nu-[ti]*, "as a moth I crushed you." Note, further, Lugal-e XIII 10: a-ba šu in-[n]e-ši-in-túm:*man-nu qat-su ub-lak-ku-nu-ši*, "who stretched out a (helping) hand toward you?" The form of the pronominal element, although we have here read it consistently as e-ne, can unfortunately, not be considered altogether certain. The reading e-ne allows explanation of the variants en-ne and in-ne, i.e., prefix i + (e)nne, as due to lengthening of the n only; it also gives a higher degree of unity to the paradigm since the reading of the pronominal infix component third person as ne is certain. Accordingly e-ne, "you," might be interpreted as "thou" (e) + "they" (ne). None of these considerations seems altogether decisive, however, and a reading e-dè with variant en-dè must still remain a possibility.

As competitor to the second person plural pronominal infix component e-ne seems to occur also the element enzen. In the rather badly preserved form found in Lugal-e X 25 (quoted above), šu ha-ba-e-en-zé-en(?)-sìg(?), enzen seems to take the place of e-ne as infix. More frequently, however, it seems to be used as a suffix in forms with second person singular infix changing the singular reference of the infix to plural, much as the addition of the plural suffix -eš to a form with third person singular subject-infix of transitive active preterit changes the singular reference of the subject-infix to plural. Examples of such usage seem to occur in Inanna's Descent, lines 261–262 (cf. the parallel lines 239–240): dingir hé-me-en-zé-en inim ga-mu-ra (var. F: -ri)-an-du₁₁-en-zé-en (var. E omits-en-zé-en) lú-u$_x$ he-me-en-zé-en nam-zu ga-mu-ri-ib-tar-en-zé-en (var. F omits en-zé-en; var. E: dè-eb-. . .-re), "If you be gods let me speak a word with you, if you be men let me decide for (lit. 'on') you thy (*sic*!) fate" (*PAPS* 107, 512). The text is unfortunately in a bad state of preservation, as is also that of Lugal-e XII 30–31, where traces in the various versions seem combinable into similar forms: ha-ra-an-x-SUB-zé(!?)-en and mí zi-[dè-e]š hé-en-du₁₁-en-[z]é(?)-en. Such combination must, however, for the present be considered highly questionable.

(5) The third person plural pronominal infix component occurs as ne in the *alākum* paradigm in *MSL* IV and in the Neo-Babylonian grammatical texts as e-ne, e-ne-ne, un-ne-ne, an-ne-ne, un-ne, an-ne, in-ne, etc. (see *MSL* IV, NBGT I 185–201 and NBGT II 234–255). The reading as ne—probably representing ñ.e with long n tending to form syllable top—can be shown from forms in which it occurs contracted with following a and is written with the unambiguous sign na rather than with NE/DÈ.

As examples of infix ne.a contracted to nä written either ne or na may serve mu-ne-dù, var. mu-na-dù, "he built for them," and KIB mu-na-dù, var. mu-ne-dù (Sollberger, *Corpus*, Ent. 45–73). For other examples see Sollberger, *Le système verbal dans les inscriptions "royales" présargoniques de Lagaš* (Genève, 1952) pp. 74 f. From the Ur III period note e.g. PN₁ ù PN₂-ra ù-ne-a-du₁₁ (*ITT* V, No. 6975) besides PN₁ ù PN₂-ra ù-na-a-du (*YOS* IV, No. 119), and hé-ne-sum-mu (*ITT* IV, No. 8002) besides hé-ne-ab-sum-mu (*ITT* II, No. 2751) and hé-na-ab-sum-mu (*YOS* IV, No. 134), "may you give to them." In texts of the Old Babylonian period

the writings ne and na continue; cf. e.g. íd a–ba mu-ne-ba-NE, "they gave them the
river in its (stage of being full of) water" (Inanna's Descent, line 264; cf. line 265
and see also lines 241–242), besides šu-ne-ne-a in-na-sum, "she gave him to them
into their hands" (ibid., line 342), and ur-saǧ-bi-ne-er gù mu-na-dé-e, "said to its
(i.e., Kullab's) warriors as follows (durative)" (Gilgamesh and Agga, line 52; *AJA*
53,8). Frequently, however, length of the n of ne is indicated by double writing and
occasionally its function as syllable top is shown by the writing nin rather than nn;
cf. mu-un-ne-dè-en-ku₄, "she entered therewith to them" (*SRT*, No. 6 obv. ii 7),
nam-hé-en-ne-íb-tar-re, "may she decide as fate unto them" (*SAK*, p. 220, e ii 13),
saǧ-e-eš mu-ne-in-rig₅-eš, "they granted to them as a gift" (*SRT*, No. 36:41),
inim in-ne-en-du₁₁-ga, "the word he spoke to them" (Lugalbanda Epic, line 238),
and mu-un-ne-ši-in-hal-hal-la:*i-zu-us-su-nu-ti*, "he divided among them" (*CT*
XVI, Pl. 19, lines 62–63) besides sig₄ É-kur-ra-ke₄ sa₆-ga-zu ᵈEn-líl-ᵈNin-líl-ra
hu-mu-ni-in-íb-bé, var. hu-mu-un-ne-íb-bé, "may the brickwork of Ekur speak
favorably of you to Enlil and Ninlil" (*TCL* XVI, No. 88 iv 9–12), where ne is
rendered alternately as ni-in-i... and ...n-ne-i.... Note also ba-an-du₁₁-ni-ib-
ku₄-re-eš-a (var. ba-an-di-ni-ib-ku₄-re-eš-àm and ba-e-en-di-ni-ib-ku₄-re-eš-àm),
"they entered thereinto (ni) away from them (ne-di > n.di), in Lugalbanda Epic,
line 84, where ne.di > n(e).di is written alternately ...n-du, ...n-di, and e-en-di.

13. The system of casemarks (relaters) occurring in the affixes of the verb is
presented in diagram form (the pronominal element involved being symbolized by
"P" or by a square, the part of it affected in the case relation being indicated by
shading).

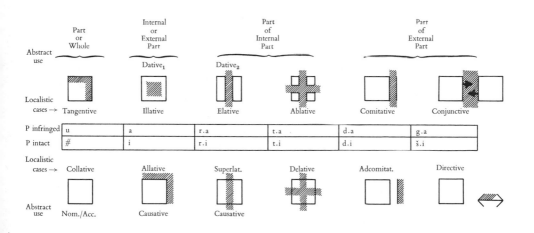

The dimensions within which this system operates are generally those of (1)
"degré d'intimité" or "cohérence-incohérence" and (2) "direction" or "rapproche-

ment-éloignement" as defined by Hjelmslev in his study *La catégorie des cas* ("Acta Jutlandica" VII 1) pp. 128–136 (Système sublogique).

The particular form which the dimension of "cohérence-incohérence" takes in Sumerian is that of "inhérence-adhérence"; it seems statable as one of contrast between interiority and surface relations. The particular form which the dimension of "rapprochement-éloignement" takes seems to be one of degree of closeness in a contrast whole:part (internal:external). Hjelmslev's alternative overall term for this dimension, "direction," is therefore not so suitable; rather, the Sumerian cases appear to show essential neutrality as to direction as such. They focus attention on a relation but do so without specific indication as to whether the relation is coming into being, exists, or has ceased to be; in spatial terms that amounts to saying that "to" and "from" the relevant position are not explicitly distinguished.

The four basic cases are collative (#), illative (a), allative (i/e), and tangentive (u).

The collative, distinguished by zero mark, appears to denote a togetherness of two entities amounting to complete coincidence, immanence of one in the other. The entities are engaged in this relation as wholes. As illustration of the collative relation may serve igi zid mu-ši-bar, "he opened the eye truly toward him" (Gudea Cyl. A i 3; cf. *GSG* §§392–393). The relation here expressed by the zero-case after zid (*adverbialis*) holds between zid and the verb and is that of the togetherness, immanence, of a quality ("truly") and the bearer of the quality (the act of opening). Very similar is the use of zero-case (collative) with the subject of intransitive verb. The togetherness, immanence, here expressed is that of the action and its performer. As we have mentioned, the Sumerian cases can express equally well the existence of a relation of either its coming into being or its having ceased, and we may distinguish these latter uses of the collative as accollative and decollative respectively. As accollative the zero-case appears with the infixes n# and b# of intransitive verbs, e.g., in DU-nu-dumu-mu ki-ta-mu-šè tuš-a-ab:*al-ka ma-ri ti-šab ina ša[p-li-ia]*, "come, my child, sit down below me" (*KAR*, No. 111 obv. 3 and rev. 3). The relation expressed is one of incipient togetherness of the action ("sitting") and a place ("below me") and as means serve with the infix b# the zero-case used as accollative, with the noun the directional case -šè indicating "approach toward." As accollative we may consider also the zero-case in its use to mark the direct object of a transitive active verb. It denotes there the coming into being of the togetherness of the action and the undergoer of the action, and it serves very much the same function when used with subject of a passive verb. As decollative, denoting that a relation of togetherness or immanence has ceased, the zero-case occurs, as far as we can see, only in the ergative infixes which denote subject of transitive active preterit, such as e.g. n# and b#. The action has left the agent, the subject, to lodge in the undergoer of it, the direct object. This use of the zero-case is not found with the noun.

The use of the illative, which has the casemark a, is sufficiently well known to call for little comment. The relation it denotes corresponds closely to that denoted by the Akkadian preposition *ina*, "into," "in," "from within." As an example of the last of these meanings may serve ki-a:*iš-tu er-ṣe-tim*," from within the earth" (Lugal-e VIII 26).

The allative, which has the casemark i/e, denotes a relation to surface or border: "at," "on." It too can denote "to at," "at," and "from at." The last of these meanings seems to underlie its use with the noun to denote the subject of active transitive verb as the departure point of the action.

The tangentive, lastly, has the casemark u and appears to denote an internal relation to surface or border. It is not used with the noun but seems to survive in the possessive pronominal suffixes (see below). In the verb it occurs in several of the prefixes, most clearly perhaps in the prefix mu. As the other cases it is essentially neutral as to direction since it can denote equally well the coming into being, the existence, and the having ceased of the relation. As illustrations may serve šu-ni mu-ši-in-ir, "he stretched out his hand toward me" (*CT* XV, Pl. 25, line 7), where direction is toward the speaker's place (mu-), and túg-mu mu-un-kar, "he took away my clothes" (ibid., line 9), where direction is from the speaker's place (mu-).

Besides the four basic cases, for which simplex markers are characteristic (#, a, i/e, u), a number of cases with more complex markers occur. These complex marks are generally formed with simplex mark a or i/e, so that the simplex mark stands in partitive parataxis with a preceding substantival element which then in its turn is in partitive parataxis with the stem of the word or element that takes the casemark.

There appear to be eight such complex casemarks used in the verb. They establish relations to the interior (ra) or exterior (ri) of a vertical median, to the interior (ta) or exterior (ti) of a horizontal (or vertical) median, to the interior (da) or exterior (di) of a lateral zone, to the interior of a lateral zone of interplay (ga), and to a line of direction (ši/še).

A clear example of ra (elative) in its basic localistic use occurs in mu-na-ra-dé-e, "he pours out (wine) for her" (*SRT*, No. 1 iv 39–40; cf. Falkenstein in *ZA* 45 [1939] 187). Note also its use for "out of" with the noun in such cases as lugal lugal-e-ne-er, "a king out of the kings" (*LIH*, No. 58:37; cf. Poebel in *OLZ* 18 [1915] 134–135). A clear example of ri (superlative) is found in im-mi-ri-bal-bal, "he crossed over it (a mountain range)" (Enmerkar and the Lord of Aratta, line 171), and note its occurrence with nouns, respectively clauses, in mu-5-àm mu-10-àm ba-zal-[la]-ri, "after (lit. 'over and across') that five to ten years had passed." For other examples see *AS* XII, p. 96. The essential neutrality as to direction of these and the other complex-mark cases is suggested by the use of ra also for personal dative, which suggests underlying "down into," "inwardly affecting," as a possible meaning besides "out of," and the similar use of ri for "unto you." For da (comitative), "from with" besides "with" and "to with," see Falkenstein, *GSGL*, §34 a 2, and note the value "amidst" besides "from" for ta (ablative). That še can denote not only "toward" but also "away" is shown by mu-ud-bi-ta-bi e-šè-ğar, "its earlier name he discarded (lit. 'set away from it')" (Urukagina Cone B + C xii 34–35; cf. col. viii 7–9), and perhaps by am-ti-la šu-bi-šè i-im-lá, "a live wild ox hung from its (Imdugud's) talons" (Lugalbanda Epic, line 65). Essential for the relation expressed by ši/še (directive) is thus apparently the fact of direction as such, not whether "to" or "from."

The original meanings of the substantival elements which form part of the complex casemarks seem relatively transparent, and one may perhaps venture the guess that d of da/di is cognate with da, "arm," so that da, "with," is originally "in the arm of," di "at the arm of," and that ši/šè (full form eše) is cognate with eše, "rope," "line," so that eše, "toward," is originally "on the line of." In the case of ta/ti the Akkadian translations of ta by (w)ištum, "(from) in the middle," qereb, "in midst" (ŠL II 140, 13), and ina qabal, "in midst" (ŠL II 139, 19), suggest strongly a meaning "middle" for the element t. Only in the cases of the r of ra/ri and the g of ga is there no clear indication. Whether in all of these cases we are dealing with original consonantal roots or rather with contracted forms on the pattern da-a > dâ > da and da-i/e > dê > de we prefer to leave undecided.

The oppositions of meaning in which the various cases stand within the system are, it will be noted, very frequently—perhaps generally—those of class and sub-class, such as e.g., rectangle and square, not those of class and class, such as e.g., rectangle and circle. (On this feature of grammatical opposition see e.g., Roman Jakobson, "Beitrag zur allgemeinen Kasuslehre," *Travaux du Cercle linguistique de Prague* VI [1936] 246 f., and Hjelmslev, *La catégorie des cas*, pp. 112 f.) As example may serve the opposition between ta, denoting relation to internals of a median (horizontal or vertical) and ra, denoting relation to internals of a vertical median only.

Besides the localistic use to designate relatively concrete spatial relations some of the cases have developed also a more abstract use to serve as so-called "logical" or "grammatical" cases. In our discussion of the collative or zero-case we have already dealt with such abstract use of it as subject case (nominative) and object case (accusative) and have seen this use as based on original localistic use for "togetherness." Similarly, the illative (a) and the elative (ra) develop "abstract" use as datives, probably over their use to indicate the coming into being of relations "into" and "down into" as "inwardly affecting." The first of these (a- dative) can be used in the verb for all persons; the second (ra-dative) seems restricted to use with first and second person singular although one late case of use with third person singular seems attested (see below, Pr. 19). (Outside the verb a is used as dative after possessive pronouns, ra as personal dative with both nouns and pronouns.)

The allative (i/e) and superlative (ri), finally, developed "abstract" use as causatives to mark the person caused to act. Outside the verb the allative in -e develops ergative function as mark of subject of transitive active verb. Of the two causative, ri seems restricted to use in the verb and to use with second person singular.

Comparison of the case system of the verbal affixes thus outlined with the case system found outside the verb in the pronoun and in the noun shows rather close affinity with the case system of the pronoun, less affinity with that of the noun. Since the verbal affixes are generally pronominal in nature this is only natural.

The case system of the independent personal pronoun shows, as does that of the verbal affixes, a collative in # which serves to mark subject of intransitive and transitive verb, both active and passive (nominative), as well as to mark object of transitive active verb (accusative). (For the forms of the personal pronouns see Poebel in *GSG* §§173–205 and *ZA* 39 [1930] 134 ff. and Falkenstein, *GSGL*, §§12–13. That the final e of g̃ae, zae, and ane is part of the stem, not a case element, was shown by Poebel in *GSG* §177.) The case system of the noun differs here significantly in that it restricts the collative in # to use as a kind of *casus patiens* for subject of intransitive and passive verb merely and for object of transitive active verb. For *casus agens*, subject of transitive active verb, the case system of the noun uses not collative in # but rather allative in e.

Both the case system of the pronouns and that of the verbal affixes use the illative case in -a for personal dative (note esp. this use with possessive pronouns in the Ur III ditilla texts; see Falkenstein, *Gerichtsurkunden*, No. 31, n. 12′). The case system of the noun differs from them by preferring allative in -e (Falkenstein in *ZA* 45, 181–183) for such use. All the systems use the elative (ra) for personal dative, but in the verb this use is largely restricted to first and second person singular.

Both the case system of the pronouns and that of the verbal affixes use the case-mark u, which does not occur in the case system of the noun. In the verb, u occurs in relatively clear tangentive function, e.g., in the prefix mu-, where it indicates location on the inside border of the speech area (m). In pronouns it occurs in "abstract" rather than localistic use in the possessive pronominal suffixes g̃u, "my," and zu, "thy." For the understanding of this extension of usage of the tangential, Roman Jakobson's analysis of the genitive (specifically the Russian genitive) as a limiting case (*Travaux du Cercle linguistique de Prague* VI pp. 255 f.) is instructive. Jakobson points out that the genitive "stets die Grenze der Teilnahme des bezeichneten Gegenstandes am Sachverhalte der Aussage ankündigt" and that "Der G. an sich besagt nur, dass der Umfang der Teilnahme des Gegenstandes am Sachverhalte der Aussage geringer als sein gesamter Umfang ist." To express this limiting function of the genitive, respectively of the possessive, the tangential was obviously well suited.

Points on which the case system of the pronouns agrees with that of the noun against the case system of the verbal affixes are primarily the use of the genitive -ak (actually hardly a proper case element since it is not mutually exclusive with the case elements) and the similative -gin$_x$, which do not seem to be used in the verb. Conversely, the conjunctive ga does not seem to appear with pronoun or noun, where the Akkadian loanword u, "and," fulfills its function. That di and ti have so far not been found with pronouns and nouns may be due to accident only; the superlative ri is attested with the noun in the meaning "after" (lit. "over and across"; see above).

It may also be noted that as illative (a) in the verb more and more comes to be used for dative its purely illative function is taken over there in some measure by the allative (i/e); note especially the use of the infix -ni- for both "in" and "on it." In the noun, on the other hand, illative (a) not only tends to maintain itself in its illative function but to take over from allative (e), which is becoming relatively rare. Allative (e) also appears to lose out to dative -ra in the noun with words denoting persons, presumably because a relation of "on" or "at" a person would tend to affect him emotionally or "inwardly," so that dative is preferred. It maintains itself with words denoting nonpersonals.

The causative, which in the verb is expressed by allative (i), has in the noun completely coalesced with dative and is expressed by dative (-ra) with personals, by allative (e) with neuters.

Provisionally the differences of usage of the three case systems may be shown in diagram form as follows:

	Noun	Pronoun	Verb
u	. . . . .	(Tangentive) ⟶	Tangentive
	. . . . .	Possessive	. . . . .
#	Collative (*adverbialis*)⟶	(Collative) ⟶	Collative
	Object case⟶	Object case ⟶	Object case
	Subject case intr. pass.	‖Subject case⟶	Subject case
e/i	Allative ⟶	Allative⟶	Allative
	. . . . .	. . . . .	+ Illative use
	Subject case tr. act.	‖.	. . . . .
	Causative (neut.) ⟶	Causative (pers./?)	Causative (pers./neut.)
	Dative (pers./neut.)	‖.	. . . . .
a	Illative⟶	Illative ⟶	Illative
	+ Allative use	‖.	. . . . .
	. . . . .	‖Dative (pers./?) ⟶	Dative (pers./neut.)
ra	Elative⟶	Elative ⟶	Elative
	Dative (pers.) ⟶	Dative (pers.)⟶	Dative (1/2 pers. sg.)
	Absorbs allative (pers.)	‖.	. . . . .
	Absorbs causative (pers.)	‖.	. . . . .

14. A few further comments on the ranking of the infixes may be in order.

(1) As may be seen from e-bé Íd-nun-ta Gú-edin-na-šè íb-ta-ni-è, "he led its (i.e., the boundary's) ditch out from the Idnun canal to Guedinak" (Entemena Cone A ii 1–3), the order of the infixes is infix ending in a, ta, preceding infix ending in i/e, ni. This order will be found to be generally observed in the Sumerian verb; the infixes in a all rank before those in i/e.

(2) The subdivision into infixes with personal and infixes with neuter pronominal reference, the former preceding the latter in the form, is seen particularly clearly in cases where the same infix occurs twice in a form and differently ranked. This difference in rank, which must reflect a difference in function, can be attributed to the difference of personal and neuter reference. An example is [nam-é]-hul-a-na mu-un-na-ta a-nir-gig-ga-bi im-da-ra-da-ğá-ğá, "the fate of his (i.e., Nanna's) destroyed house she (i.e., Ningal) presented (lit. 'brought close') to him, a bitter lament for it (lit. 'its bitter lament') she was setting up with him (da) anent it (ra; lit. '(arising) out of it') besides it (da)" (*AS* No. 12, p. 26, line 85). Similar is nin-e gù eme-gin$_x$ ne-a im-ma-da-ra-da-[dé-e] (*PBS* X 4, No. 6 obv. 12), "the lady (i.e., Ninmara) cries out because of this (i.e., the defiling of her treasures stated in lines 10–11) to him (da; i.e., Enlil, mentioned in lines 5–7) besides them (da; i.e., the defiled treasures) like a . . .(?)." The -a of ne-a and the infix -ra- which resumes it in the verb both denote "(arising) out of" = "because." A further example is ud ki-šár-ra ma-ra-ta-è-a dingir-zu ᵈNin-ğiš-zi-da ud-gin$_x$ ki-ša-ra ma-ra-da-ra-ta-è, "the daylight which issued out for out from the horizon was your personal god

Ningishzida, he is able (da) as is the daylight to issue out for you (ra) anent it (ra; lit. '(arising) out of it,' i.e., the temple building) from the horizon (a resumed by ta in the verb)" (Gudea Cyl. A v 19–20). The passage states that Gudea's personal god can emerge from the ground—he is a chthonic god—in faraway regions and exert his powers to bring the needed building materials for the temple. Other cases are èš-za sahar-ta ma-ra-ra-an-íl-la, "in your mansion, in what he has raised up for you (ra) from out of the dust (ta resumed by ra in the verb)" (Lugal-e; *SRT*, No. 21 iii 12), and níĝ(!)-bar(!)sur-ra ma-ra-⸢ra⸣-an-e₁₁-NE, "they bring it (i.e., the upholstery of the plow) up for you (ra) out of (ra) the mangle" (Plow and Pickax, line 110 [*BE* XXXI, No. 50:4, restored from unpubl. 3 N-T. 529]). Note also the varying order of a-bi dug-šè ù-mu-e-ni-ši-in-gi₄:*me-e šu-nu-ti ana kar-pa-ti ti-ir-ma*, "when you (e) have made him (ni) return that water to (šè resumed by ši in the verb) the pot (Akkadian simplifies to 'return that water to the pot and ...'),'' in *CT* XVII, Pl. 32, rev. 9–11, where ni with personal reference (causative) precedes ši with neuter reference, and ᵈNin-urta á-zág-e kur-ra ĝìr mu-e-ši-ni-gub-gub:[MIN *A-sak-ku ina šadî-*]*i ú qa-a-ka*, "Ninurta, the Asakku awaits you (e.ši) in the highland (a resumed by ni in the verb)" (Lugal-e IV 4), and ᴁi šà mu-ši-ni-ĝál, "(you are ...-grain rooted in great waters) and thereby (a, contracted with nominalizing a of dù-a in line 12, resumed by ni in the verb) you have made be unto me (ši) life's breath and courage (lit. 'heart')" (Gudea Cyl. A iii 13), where ši with personal reference precedes ni with neuter reference.

(3) The order of the infixes within the gender subseries seems, to judge from the forms ma-ra-da-ra-ta-è (P.ra-P.da-N.ra-N.ta) and im-da-ra-da-ĝá-ĝá (P.da-N.ra-N.da), to be -ra-ta/da, the mutual order of ta and da remaining uncertain. In the formula iti-ta ud-XXII be-ta-ra-zal (Schneider, *AnOr* VII 84, lines 11–12; cf. Falkenstein in *ZA* 45, 193 f.) one may assume gender differentiation and translate "out of the month (ta resumed by ra in the verb) twenty-two days had flown by for (lit. 'from,' ta infix) me" if the passage is not, as suggested by Falkenstein, a conflation of two variant formulas. As the mutual order of ta and da remains uncertain, so also does that of -a and -ra. We assume that a preceded. That in the i/e series i preceded ri seems indicated by *PBS* X 4, No. 14 obv. i 11–12: ᵈEn-ki-ke₄ á-ni ba-ši-in-DU girin sug ⸢ba⸣(!)-ni-gir₈-gir₈-e ᵈEn-ki-ke₄ mud-me-dím-ní-te-a-na šà-bi ⸢ĝiš-túg⸣-PI-ta ù-mu-e-ni-ri-gi, "Enki reached out his arm, pinching off a pinch of clay from the Apsu, when Enki in (a resumed by e in the verb) a tremor (lit. 'his tremor') making the limbs tremble had reflected (gi:*malāku*; *ŠL* II 85, 45) with (ta resumed by ri in the verb) understanding upon (e resumed by ni in the verb) its meaning (he said to his mother Nammu etc.)."

15. In departing from the traditional view which ranks the second person singular subject element e of transitive active preterit immediately before the root and assigning to it instead a rank immediately after the infixes of the a-series and before those of the i/e-series we base ourselves on passages in which this e is seen to occur earlier in the form than such infixes as ni and ši and later than such infixes as da and ta. Examples are su kalam-ma mu-e-du₁₀ níg-si-sá ka-ka mu-e-ni-ĝar, "the muscles of the nation you eased, righteousness you placed in all mouths" (Iddin-Dagan hymn *SRT*, No. 52 ii 9'–11', and dupl. *TCL* XVI, No. 88 iii); níĝ-si-sá Ki-en-

gi-ki-Uri mu-e-ni-g̃ar, "you established righteousness in Sumer and Akkad" (Lipiteshtar hymn *TCL* XVI, No. 87 iv 1–3, and dupl. *UMB* XVII 2 [Dec., 1952] p. 25); ka-zu ka-mà um-me-te šu-um-du-um-mu ka(!)-za ù-ba-e-ni-dab₅, "when you have neared your mouth to my mouth, when you have seized my lip in your mouth" (*SRT*, No. 31:23–25); sag̃-e-eš ù-mu-e-ni-rig₇, "when you have granted it to him as a gift" (*CT* XXXVI, Pls. 31–32, rev. 18); a-gin_x g̃en-mu-šè èn mu-e-ši-tar:*ki-ma a-na a-la-ki-ia taš-ta-lu*, "how you gathered intelligence (lit. 'asked') about my campaign" (Lugal-e XII 15); lú-siskur-ra-ke₄ mu-gub-ba-bi (var. + -ir) igi zi ù-mu-e-ši-bar, "when you have looked truly toward the man of prayer and ..." (*AS* XII, line 431); and (with contraction of i-m-ma-e- to imme) lú-tur-mu ud um-me-ši-nig̃in ud um-me-ši-lá, "my little one, when you have rounded up the storms here for it, when you have hitched the storms here to it (i.e., the chariot of Ishkur)" (*CT* XV, Pl. 15, line 16). For occurrence of e after na, da, and ta note a-gin_x mu-un-né-du₁₁ (var. mu-ne-du₁₁), "how could you say to him (né/ne rendering contracted -na-e-)" (Lugalbanda Epic; *OECT* I, Pl. 7, line 37, and dupl. *SEM*, No. 1 v 35), g̃iš-ši-g̃ar-kù-an-na-ke₄ nam-ta-e-g̃ál:*ši-gar šame-e ellūti*(KÙ-MEŠ) *tap-ti*, "you (Utu) have opened the pure bolts of heaven" (IV R 2, lines 2 f.), ᵈMu-ul-líl-le mu-ganá-ùr im-da-e-[u₅], "Enlil, you rode the harrow thereover" (*KAR*, No. 375 obv. ii 46, and dupl. V R 52, No. 2 obv. 8′ f.).

At variance with these passages—most of them Old Babylonian in data—is, as far as we know, only one text, the late grammatical text *MSL* IV, NBGT II 267 ff. (Bertin's text). Its late and isolated testimony can hardly overweigh the consistent evidence of the earlier data.

Localistic accollative use of e# is probably to be reckoned with, but in most cases the form is difficult to distinguish from allative since contracted e-e and e# will both be written e. For possible examples see the discussion of e as pronominal element above in n. 12; we have in almost all instances considered interpretation as allative, contracted e-e the more probable one.

16. On the use of the i/e- allative form as a causative, i.e., as mark of the agent object in a causative relation, see our remarks in *MSL* IV 28 ff. The paradigm which can be set up for these forms includes both infixes and prefixes used in functional overlap. Starring conjectural or otherwise uncertain forms we may state the paradigm as follows:

CAUSATIVE

	Prefix	Infix		Prefix	Infix
Sg. 1 p.	mu		Pl. 1 p.		me
2 p.		*ri	2 p.		*ene
3 p.		ni/n#	3 p.		*ne/ni
3 n.	bi				

The paradigm may have to be extended to include mi and -m-mi for close neuter causative agent object. The conditions governing choice between ni and n# for third person singular and ne and ni for third person plural are not yet clear.

In the case system of the noun the causative seems to contract syncretism with the dative, so that the corresponding casemarks are there -ra for personal, -e for neuter causative agent object.

A few examples of causatives of the verb gu₇:*akālu*, "to eat," causative "to feed," "support," literally "to make someone eat," may serve as illustrations of the use.

First person singular causative: imp. ğen-na kin-du ù-mu-ag (var. ù-mu-e-ag) ninda gu₇-ù-mu-ub, "go, when you have done work support me (on your earnings; lit. 'make me eat bread')" (*PBS* I 2, No. 103 rev. 7 [dupl. *TCL* XVI, No. 45]).

Third person singular causative: imp. ninda gu₇-ni-ib, "feed him" (*VS* X, No. 204 vi 10); pres. ninda an-ni-íb-gu₇-a, "she will support her" (*BE* VI 2, No. 4:15; cf. the sandhi writing lú-huğ-gá-a-ni ninda-ni-gu₇-e:*a-gi-ir-*[*šu*] *a-ka-lam ú-šá-k*[*al*], "he will support his hired man," in *MSL* I, Tf. 6 iii 18–20); mu-ni-íb-gu₇-ù-NE, "they were feeding him" (Lugalbanda Epic, line 250); pret. a-bi lú-kúr-ra ù-mu-ni-naǧ, "when he has made a stranger (dative ra resumed by causative ni in the verb) drink that water" (Falkenstein, *Haupttypen*, p. 60); ù-mu-ni-gu₇ ù-mu-ni-naǧ⌈-ǧá⌉-ta ì-níg-diri-ga ga-mu-na-ra-ab-šub, "after I have made him eat and made him drink I shall leave in excess of it (ra) a surplus (of) cream for him" (*SRT*, No. 3 iii 12–13). Construction with n# for ni occurs in ᵈEn-ki-ke₄ unu-e Nibruᵏⁱ-àm a-a-ni ᵈEn-líl-ra ninda mu-un-gu₇-e, "Enki at the sanctuary in Nippur was feasting (lit. 'making eat bread') his father Enlil" (*OECT* I, Pl. 4, lines 5–6).

Third person neuter causative: ukù-e ú nir-ğál bí-gu₇-me-en, "I (Urnammu) am the one who fed the people princely food" (*TCL* XV, No. 12:75; cf. Falkenstein in *ZA* 50 [1952]85); á-dam nu-še-ga-ni s[ug-g]e₄ bí-i[b]-gu₇-e, "you make the swamp swallow up the settlements not obedient to him" (*TCL* XV, No. 19:45; cf. Falkenstein, *Götterlieder* I 41).

First person plural causative: ninda-mu hé-ğál ninda-zu ga-gu₇ (var. ga-me-gu₇), "let my bread be, let me eat your bread (var. 'let me feed us,' lit. 'make us eat your bread')" (Gordon, *Sumerian Proverbs*, No. 1:8).

Third person plural causative: lú za-e-ginₓ kin-du ù-mu-ag ama-ne-ne ù ad(!)-da-n[e-ne] ninda an-ni-íb-gu₇-ù-NE, "men like you when they have done (collective) work support (on their earnings; lit. 'make eat bread') their mothers and fathers" (*PBS* I 2, No. 103: 9–10); munus-e lú-IGI-NIĜIN-ne ninda e-ne-gu₇-a, "which the queen fed (lit. 'made them eat') to the retainers" (*DP*, No. 166; cf. [1 ú]-IGI-NIĜIN: *baʾulātu* in *ŠL* II 449, 230).

17. The infixes n and b which rank directly before the root we analyze as n# and b#, i.e., as consisting of a pronominal element followed by casemark zero, which marks the collative case. Structurally they are thus identical with the other collative infixes—the zero infix first person singular ergative ## before the a-series, the e infix second person singular ergative e# before the e- series—as well as with the suffixes of subject and object indication which we likewise analyze as ending in zero-mark. They differ from the corresponding collative prefixes in having a pronominal component denoting an entity rather than an adverbial component denoting area (m, b) or point (l, n).

The pronominal elements n and b are used with third person reference (for exceptions see n. 12 above) and differ from each other in that the indication of b seems to be exclusively anaphoric, that of n not exclusively so. In addition there is a dominant tendency, noted already by Poebel (*GSG* §447), to restrict n to personal, b to neuter and collective reference. As third person elements n# and b# contrast with the second person element e#, ranking before the e- series, and with the first person element ##, tentatively ranked before the a-series. The contrast is fully operative, however, only when these various infixes serve to denote the subject of transitive active preterit, i.e., when the collative is used abstractly as ergative, and even then the zero-infix (##) is frequently used for both first and second person (see n. 12, section 2). In other, localistic, use of these infixes the contrast of person is less sharp, and e# may conceivably appear (see n. 15, end) with third person and third neuter reference interchangeably with n# and b#.

The zero-mark of collative case, which the infixes n# and b# share with the infix e# and the zero-infix ##, was defined above as denoting a relation of togetherness of two entities amounting to coincidence, immanence of one in the other. As all Sumerian cases it can indicate the coming into being of the relation (accollative), the existence of it (collative proper), and the ceasing of it (decollative), but in the verb these uses are so distributed that transient uses (accollative and decollative) are found only in affixes preceding the root, prefixes, and infixes, existential use (collative proper) only in suffixes following the root.

Distinction may be made also between the collative in its basic localistic use and in more abstract use as a "logical" or "grammatical" case.

Examples of its localistic use are fairly common. We may consider, first, instances of localistic use of b# and n# and choose as examples mainly imperatives of intransitive and passive verbs since here the subject is a virtual second person singular and there is no direct object, so that "grammatical" use of b# and n# (for subject or direct object element) does not come into consideration. Such examples are ur-ge₇-re sar-ra-ab-zé-en, "chase the dog (e)" (*PBS* I 1, No. 135:34–35), na₄-šam mè-ta ᵍⁱˢtukul-ta ur-ge₇-re ninda siba-tur-ra sar-ra-ab:*šam-mu i-na ta-ha-zi ki-ma kal-bu ša ka-par-ri ú-kaš-ši-du-šu*, "*shammu*-stone, from the battle with weapons be chased (as) a dog (e) out of the bread (ninda.a) by the shepherd boys (.e assimilated and contracted after tura)" (Lugal-e X 15; Akkadian translation very free: "they chased the *shammu*-stone from the battle like the dog of the shepherd boys [understood: 'is chased away from their food']"), lú-líl(!?)-lá-ke₄ sar-ra-ab-zé-en, "chase away the tempter to vagrant fancies (.e; lit. "the man of the idle wind')" (Kramer in *JAOS* 69 [1949] 202, line 31; for líl:*zaqīqu*, "wind," "spirit," "phantasy," cf. *CAD* XXI, s.v. *zaqīqu*; central meaning "wind" is clear from the synonyms *mehū* and *iltānu* and is extended as in "spirit" related to *spirare*, "to breathe," "to blow"), ᵍⁱˢillulu ús-sa-ab (var. ús-sa-àm), "follow the throw-stick (.e assimilated and contracted after illulu)" (Gordon, *Sumerian Proverbs*, No. 1:145; sense seems to be: "follow through with the attack and make your mother happy by your bravery, or make your personal god happy, i.e., follow your own inclination, and run away"), šen-šen-na ús-sa-ab:*re-de-e qab-lu*, "follow the battle advance (.e, normal with ús, replaced by .a; see n. 13 above" (*RA* 12 [1915] 74–75, line 4), DU-nu dumu-mu ki-ta-mu-šè tuš-a-ab:*al-ka ma-ri ti-šab ina ša[p-li-ia]*, "come, my child, sit down below me (.še)" (*KAR*, No. 111 obv. 3 and rev. 3), á-zi-da-mu-šè g̃en-na-ab:*ina im-ni-ia a-lik*, "walk to my right (.še)" (*CT* XVI, Pl. 7, line 264), am-gal-lú-sár-ra-gaz-za-gin$_x$ ní-ba-hi-šè g̃ar-ra-ab:*ki ri-mi rabî-t ša ma-du tu i-du-ku-šu a-na zi-it-ti na-aš-ki-in*, "as a great wild bull killed by a multitude be set out into portions (.še)" (Lugal-e X 14), tur-tur-bi til-la-ab:*ina şu-uh-hu-ri nag-mir*, "be finished in manner of diminishing (# modal *adverbialis*)" (Lugal-e XI 26), gaz-e-dè til-la-ab:*i-na pu-su-si na-ag-mir*, "be finished in manner of grinding (# modal *adverbialis*)" (Lugal-e X 13).

As will be seen, there is in all of these examples only one case relation in the sentence which the verbal infix b# could resume, that to the single noun which the verb governs. In the noun this relation finds expression not only as in b# by accollative, zero-case, but also by directive (.še) and by allative (.e). Common to all these cases is their ability to indicate approach to impending contact, so that one is led to assume this meaning, accollative, establishing of a relation of togetherness, for the zero-case of b#, which correlates with all of them. For the particularly close relation in meaning between the zero-case in modal-*adverbialis* function and the directive note the well-known variation of igi-zid# ... bar and igi-zi-dè-eš ... bar (*GSG* §§392–393).

Very much the same usage is found with the element n#. Without restricting ourselves as we did with b# we may quote lú-á-zi-ga-bé ^dNanna sá hé-en-e, "may Nanna reach that evildoer (.e)" (*STVC*, No. 52 rev. ii 11 [dupl. *TCL* XVI, No. 50]), ^dEn-líl ì-du ^dNin-⟨líl in⟩-ús:MIN (i.e., Enlil) *il-la-ak* MIN (i.e., Ninlil) *i-re-ed-di*, "Enlil was walking along, Ninlil followed him (n#)" (Myth of Enlil and Ninlil [*JRAS*, 1919, 190–191, col. ii 7] as restored from duplicates *MBI*, No. 4, and *SEM*, No. 77), dù-a-bé an-sù-bé ù-ni-sù..." (Civil in *RA* 54 [1960] 62 f., lines 109–110), "he is to suck on all of it (.e); when he has sucked on it (ni)...," and e₄-bé an-tu$_x$-tu$_x$ e₄ ù-ni-tu$_x$ (ibid., lines 123–124; see also lines 136–137), "he is to bathe in that water (.e); when he has bathed in the water (.e resumed by ni in the verb) ...." Further examples are ù ì-bi-la Du-du-ke₄-ne du₁₁-ga-ne-ne-a ba-ni-ge-né-eš mu dug₄ ì-bí-la-ne-ka ba-an-ge-na-šè..., "and the heirs of Dudu confirmed it by their statement (.a resumed by ni), because it was confirmed by the statement (.a resumed by n#) of the heirs..." (Falkenstein, *Gerichtsurkunden*, No. 99 [*ITT* III, No. 5279] lines 28–30, where the infix ni suggests original construction with e replaced as often by a; see n. 13 above). Similar cases are du₁₁-ga-na ba-an-ge-in (Falkenstein, *Gerichtsurkunden*, No. 125:7), dug₄ Ur-g̃AR-ka ba-an-ge-in (ibid., No. 174:9), dug₄-ba ba-an-ge-in (ibid., No. 186:10′), sig₄ nam-tar-ra ^giš ù-šub-ba ma-an-g̃ál, "the predestined brick was in the brick mold (.a) for me" (Gudea Cyl. A v 7), igi ^dNanna-ka hé-en-sa₆, "may he prosper before Nanna (.a)" (*UET* I, No. 71:38–39), ^giš gu-za-gub-ba-na suhuš-bi na-an-ge-né, "may she (Inanna) not fix securely into the throne he sets up (.a) its legs" (Gudea St. C iv 13–15). Examples with directive in the noun are ^giš ma-gur$_x$-šè da-an-u₅ me-e é-šè da-an-u₅, "let me mount up on the boat (.še), me, let me mount up to the cabin (.še)" (*VS* X, No. 199 iv 13; cf. line 14), g̃iš LA[G]AB-mu kur-šè mu-da-an-šub, "my *pukku* fell from me toward the nether world" (*BE* XXXI, No. 35:5, with Kramer's collations in *JAOS* 60 [1940] 246 f.). In these examples the zero-case of n# seems, as that of b#, to serve as accollative resuming a directive (šè) or allative (e), though the latter is frequently replaced by a. Of interest is the variation of n# and ni shown by the examples of Civil in *RA* 54, 62 f., and Falkenstein, *Gerichtsurkunden*, No. 99. It would seem that ni (contact infix) is the preferred one with precise statement where attention is on the actuality of completion of the action ("they confirmed," "when he has sucked on it"), whereas with more incidental reference or with coming action the less precise noncontact form (n#) is sufficient.

As further examples of b# in localistic use may be mentioned the forms ğar-àm-ma-šè-[íb]:*na-aš-ki-na-aš-šu[m]* and ğar-àm-ma-šè:*na-aš-ki-na-aš-šu* in *MSL* IV, OBGT VI 67 and 70. As will be seen, presence and absence of b# in the Sumerian corresponds to variation of suffix in the Akkadian between -*šum* and -*šu* and therefore indicates that b# must have reference to the goal point of the verbal action since that is the reference of the Akkadian suffixes. Furthermore, since both Sumerian forms imply direction (šè), it must seem probable that the difference between them has reference to eventual contact. With this agrees that as used elsewhere in the paradigm -*šum* seems to look toward contact rather more than -*šu*, it renders Sumerian -na- and -še- while -*šu* renders the noncontact comitative -da-. Interpretation of b# as accollative, direction to impending contact, would thus seem to fit the case.

As for the use of the zero-case in n# and b# abstractly as a "grammatical" case, there is no need to offer examples of these infixes in their use for subject elements third person personal and neuter transitive active preterit. For their factitive use as indicators of explicit or implicit direct object the clearest examples are pairs of imperatives such as zi-ga:*ti-bi*, "rise," contrasting with zi-ba-ab:*šu-ut-[bi]*, "raise," and zi-ga-an:*šu-ut-[bi]*, "raise," in *MSL* IV, OBGT IV i 1, ii 1 (cf. *GSG* § 521). The rule that addition of b# gives the verb factitive force holds in almost all cases, and exceptional "deponent" forms are exceedingly rare.

As far as we can see, interpretation of n# and b# as direct object elements must still rest on these cases pointed to by Poebel. Instances of n# and b# elsewhere, e.g., in transitive active present future where direct object reference can seem plausible, are by no means unusual, but full certainty about the interpretation is usually difficult to obtain. It would be helpful if we could demonstrate that in such forms n# and b# vary consonantly with their respective preference for personal and neuter-collective reference, according to whether the direct object involved is of personal or neuter gender. Such demonstration, however, does not seem possible with any degree of certainty.

Lastly, mention may be made of the use of b# as substitute for causative-allative third person -ni-. Relatively clear instances are furnished by the paradigms *MSL* IV, OBGT VI, VIII, and IX. In these paradigms causative is regularly formed with infix -ni-. When the form contains the infix -ri-, however, this causative -ni- and also the third person transitive active preterit subject element seem to be suppressed, and in their place b# occurs, conceivably as a decollative (#) indicating emanation of the action from both subject and causative agent object (b, "them"). The pattern of occurrence may be seen from the diagram below, which contrasts the noncausative I and I_2 forms with -ra- and -ri- infix with the corresponding III and III_2

forms. The expected causative infix -ni- and ergative (subject third person singular transitive active preterit) which are replaced by b# are shown inclosed in parentheses.

	I			III
216	ma-ra-an-ğar *iš-ku-na-ak-kum*	217		ma-ra-ni-in-ğar *ú-ša-aš-ki-na-ak-kum*
58	kas$_4$ mu-ri-in-du$_{11}$ *il-su-ma-[kum]*	62	kas$_4$	mu-ri-(ni-)íb(-n)-[du$_{11}$] *ú-ša-al-sí-ma-k[um]*
128	sá mu-ri-in-du$_{11}$ *ik-šu-da-ka*	130	sá	mu-ri-(ni-)íb(-n)-du$_{11}$ *ú-ša-ak-ši-da-ka*

	I$_2$			III$_2$
60	⌐kas$_4$ im⌐-ma-ri-i[n-d]u$_{11}$ *il-ta-ás-ma(!)-[kum]*	64	kas$_4$(!)	im-ma-r[i-(ni-)íb(-n)-du$_{11}$] *uš-tál-sí-ma-k[um]*
120	s[á] im-m]a-ri-in-du$_{11}$ *ik-ta-aš-da-kum*	122	sá	im-ma-ri-(ni-)íb(-n)-du$_{11}$ *uš-ta-ak-ši-da-ku*

18. The stem-suffixes differ in an important respect from the other suffixes and from infixes, prefixes, and profixes (except nu-); they alone can occur with nonfinite forms of the verb, infinitive and participle. Their function of indicating the relative places (point and duration) in time of action and subject at the moment contemplated by the speaker may be expressed graphically if we symbolize the subject by "S," the occurrence denoted by the verb (the action) as a line ——, and duration in time by dots. We use our usual symbols $\sqrt{}$ for the root and # for zero in a given rank.

Form	Description	Position in Time of subject and action
$\sqrt{}$-#- # : Post-actional	Punctive:	————S
$\sqrt{}$-ed-# : Pre-actional	Punctive:	S————
$\sqrt{}$-#- e : Intra-actional	Durative:	—..S..—
$\sqrt{}$-ed- e : Pre-actional	Durative:	..S..————

19. The suffixes which make up the rank of subject and object elements may be analyzed as consisting of a pronominal-adverbial deictic core followed by the zero-mark of collative case.

The collative serves here to denote existence of the collative relation only, not also its coming into being (accollative) or having ceased (decollative). Accordingly the subject and object elements denote the subject with intransitive verb, passive verb, and transitive active verb durative (pres./fut.) only. With transitive active punctive (pret.) verb, where the action is no longer "together" with, immanent in, the subject but has lodged in the object they denote the object.

Structurally the deictic core of the subject and object elements may be seen as consisting of a central pronominal-adverbial element denoting an entity in the area of the speaker (sg. #, pl. de) or addressee (sg. e, pl. ze). The reference to speaker's area can be further emphasized by addition of a prepositive en (*hic*), that to addressee's area by addition of a postpositive en (*iste*). The system of contrasts thus created is fairly complex; it seems to move—perhaps under the influence of Akkadian—toward a simplified pattern: singular first person -en, second person [-en, third person -#, plural first person -enden, second person -enzen, third person -de (durative) and -eš.

In diagram form the underlying original contrasts may be shown as follows. We use as approximate renderings for the central elements indicating entity in speaker's area "this one" and "these ones," for those indicating entity in addressee's area "that one" and "those ones"; and we use "here" (*hic*) for prepositive en, "there" (*iste*) for postpositive en.

		hic		*iste*		
Sg. 3rd p.			#		"this one"	= "he"
1st p.		en	#		"this one here"	= "I"
2nd p.			e	en	"that one there"	= "thou"

		hic		*iste*		
Pl. 3rd p.	punctive		eš		"yonder ones"	= "they"
	durative		de		"these ones"	= "they"
1st p.	exclusive	(en)	de		"these one (here)"	= "we"
	inclusive	en	de	en	"these ones here and there"	= "we"
	exclusive		de	en	"these ones there"	= "we"
2nd p.		en	ze		"those ones here"	= "you"
		en	ze	en	"those ones here and there"	= "you"
			ze	en	"those ones there"	= "you"

In detail the following points may be noted.

Singular first person. The basic meaning of -en.#, "this one here," seems to survive in occasional use of -en.# as mark of (near) third person. Note e.g., egi-re šà-ba-a-ni še-ša₄ nu-uš-gul-e-en:*ša ru-ba-tum lib-ba-ša da-ma-ma ul i-kal-la*, "the queen's heart cannot hold back (its) mourning" (*ASKT*, No. 17 rev. 25), and the Old Babylonian examples i-ni-in-ku₄-re-en, "he brought (a statue) into it," and šu in-na-bar-re-en, "he released for him," listed by Falkenstein in *Bagh. Mitt.* II (1963) 8, n. 28.

Singular second person. Analysis of the second person mark as e + en was considered by Thureau-Dangin on the basis of the orthographical distinctions in AO 5403 between second person i[n]-na-te-⌈e-en⌉:[*te-eṭ-h*]*i-šu-u*[*m*] and first person in-na-te-en:*e-eṭ-hi-šum* (obv. 2–3) and the similar first person ba-an-na-te-en:*e-ṭè-hi-šum*, second person ⌈in⌉-na-te-e-en:*te-eṭ-hi-šum* and second person [i]n-da-ǧá-re-e-en:*ta-ša-*⌈*ka*⌉*-áš-*⟨*šu*⟩-*um* (Thureau-Dangin in *RA* 11 [1914] 43; *MSL* IV,

OBGT V). In favor of such analysis is the occurrence of a second person element e in the ergative and in izi C iii 25–26 (VAT 9714 unpubl.): ki-zu-ne^{ni}-ne^{ni}:*it-ti-ku-nu*, ki-e-ne-ne:MIN (i.e., *itti-kunu*) as also the parallel #:de, e:ze in the paradigm.

Plural third person punctive. The mark eš is restricted to use with punctive. The usual assumption that this element is related to the numeral eš, "three," is not supported by the earlier orthography which writes it éš.

Plural third person durative. The mark de is restricted to use with durative. The reading of this element as de rather than as ne, the customary reading, seems to be advocated by syllabaries and variant writings. (1) The lexical series á-A:nāqu VII 110–12 (*MSL* IV 196) indicates reading de of the sign NE/DÈ when it is used to write plural mark: (de-e):DÈ:*ma-du-tum, i-na, a-na, ma-ri-tum* KI-TA, "plural, in, to, durative suffix." (2) de rather than (e-)ne as the form of the third person plural durative mark is indicated by variant writing with de$_4$ (TE) in the form i-sil-e-NE:*idallalu*, "they will publicize," in an Old Babylonian bilingual text (Genouillac) *Kich* II, Pl. 3, C. 1 rev. 19 ff.): erin-e kalam-e i(!?)-si-le-dè:*ṣa-bu ù ma-tum da-li-li-ka i-da-la-lu*, nam-á-gal-zu dingir-gal-gal-e-ne ⟨i-⟩si-le-de$_4$:*li-ú-ut-ka i-lu ra-bu*(!)-*u$_4$-tum i-da-⌐al⌐-la-lu*, "the people and the country will spread (publicize) your praises, the great gods will spread the word about your power." As indicated, we consider the writing dingir-gal-gal-e-ne-si-le-de$_4$ sandhi for dingir-gal-gal-e-ne i-si-le-de$_4$. (3) Writing with da for NE/DÈ of the third person plural durative mark occurs in dingir-gal-gal-e-ne nam ha-ba-ra-tar-ru-da (var. nam-ha-ba-da-an-tar-ru-dè): *ilāni^{meš} rabūti^{meš} li-ru-ru-šú*, "may the great gods curse him" (*CT* XVII, Pl. 34, lines 39–40), and in e-ne ma-an-ma-ma-da:*šú-⌐nu⌐i-šak-ka-nu-ni*, "they were establishing for me" (*SBH*, No. 47:27–28).

Since the vowel e of the verbal suffixes generally tends to develop into a in post-Sumerian times (see *GSG* §476), the writing with da apparently reflects such a phonetic development of the third person plural durative mark from de to da.

Plural first person exclusive -(en)de. Use of simple third person plural durative de, "these ones" = "they," also for first person plural exclusive "these ones" = "we," is well attested. The occurrences suggest an original contrast between exclusive first person plural ("we" = 1st p. + 3rd p.) represented by de and en.de and inclusive first person plural ("we" = 1 st p. + 2nd p. (+ 3rd p.)) represented by de.en and en.de.en. The distinction, which has no counterpart in Akkadian, seems, however, to have been lost by Old Babylonian times.

For de, "we" (excl.), cf. me-dè me-en-zé-en-bi:*ni-nu ù at-tu-nu*, "we and you" (*MSL* IV, OBGT I 467), where the context shows that de, "we," of me-dè (< (i)-me-dè) cannot be meant to include the addressee. Particularly instructive is the parallel set of forms ga-ba-ab-túm-mu-dè, "let us carry (him) off" (1st p. pl. co-hortative), and ga-an-ši-su$_8$-dè-en, "let us proceed toward it" (1st p. pl. cohortative) in Inanna's Descent, lines 296 and 312. The distinction between -dè (excl.) and -dè-en (incl.) is carefully observed also where the forms recur in lines 317 and 322 and in lines 327 and 331 and so must be considered intentional on the part of the scribe. We cite the text as given by N = CBS 13902 (*PBS* V, No. 22; photo published by Kramer in *PAPS* 85 [1942] Pl. 9) for lines 296, 312, 317, and 322 and by 0 = CBS 15162 (*PAPS* 85, Pl. 10) for lines 332 and 327. For line 331 we have only M = YBC

4621 (JCS 4 [1950] 212–213). On the usage in this last text see below. Phonetic or orthographical reasons for the distinction are not apparent since the environments of the two forms seem to be much the same; in both cases the suffix follows a stem in u and is in its turn followed by a new word beginning with a consonant (kù in lines 297, 318, 328, Bad-tibira^{ki}-a in line 322, ^{giš}hašhur in line 331). In terms of meaning, however, it will be noted that the first person plural of ga-ba-ab-túm-mu-dè, "let us carry (him) off," is exclusive, for the carrying is to be done by the speaker and his fellow demons and Inanna, the addressee, is to be left to proceed alone to her city, whereas the first person plural of ga-an-ši-su$_8$-dè-en, "let us proceed toward it," is inclusive, for the proceeding is to be done by both the speaker and his fellow demons and by the addressee, Inanna.

That the suggested distinction tended to be lost in Old Babylonian times is indicated by variants in which it is not observed. Thus in the case of the contrasting forms in Inanna's Descent one version (M = YBC 4621) shows indiscriminate variation: ba-ab-túm-dè-en (line 296), ga-ba-ab-túm-mu-dè (line 317), ga-ba-ab-túm-mu-un-dè-en (line 327) and ga-e-su$_8$-en-dè-en (line 322), ga-e-su$_8$-dè-en (line 331). To this scribe the distinction must have ceased to exist.

For the form -en.dè, "we," likewise exclusive, may be quoted MSL IV, OBGT I 466, me-en-de ù me-en-zé-en:ni-nu ù at-tu-nu, which precedes me-dè me-en-zé-en-bi with same translation in line 467. Other occurrences are PBS X 2, No. 11:26, me-en-dè Ga-ša-an-an-na ^{d}Lamma-sa$_6$-ga-me, "as for us, Inanna is our kindly guardian angel," where the speaker contrasts herself and her group with another addressed one (me-en-zé-en) in line 28. Note also the late text SBH, No. 73:12, me-en-dè šà-ab umun-e na-mu-un-hug̃-e-en-dè:ni-nu lib-bi be-li i nu-ni-ih. As in the case of dè, the function of -en.de within a distinction between exclusive and inclusive seems later to have been lost. Note that PBS X 2, No. 11:21, shows variant me-en-dè-en.

Plural first person inclusive -enden. The basic meaning of -en.dè.en, "these ones here (with me) and there (with you)," seems to survive in occasional use of -enden as mark of (near) third person plural. An example of such use is furnished by the beginning of the Myth of Enlil and Ninlil (*JRAS*, 1919, 190–191, lines 1 ff.): Dur-an-ki uru-na-nam (< uru-anene-àm) àm-dúr-ru-ne-en-de-en:ina MIN (i.e., Duranki) ali-šu-nu šu-nu ú-ši-bu, "In Duranki, their city, they (our city deities) settled." Note also its use in Lahar and Ashnan as third plural direct-object suffix: ^{d}En-ki (var. + ke$_4$) ^{d}En-líl-bi (var. -ra) du$_{11}$-kù-ga-ne-ne ^{d}Lahar ^{d}Ašnan-bi Du$_6$-kù-ta im(var. omits) -ma-da-⌈ra⌉-[ab-è]-dè-en-dè-en (*MBI*, No. 8, with dupl. BE XXXI, No. 15), "Enki and (var. 'for') Enlil with their pure word had Lahar and Ashnan come out of Duku." The form is common in inclusive use as e.g., in Gilgamesh's injunction to Enkidu: g̃á-nam-ma ga-an-ši-su$_8$-re-dè-en-dè-en, "come let us proceed toward him" (Gilgamesh and Huwawa, line 112). Many similar examples may be found in Falkenstein's article on the cohortative in ZA, 45, 169–180.

Plural first person inclusive -de.en. An example of -dè-en in inclusive usage contrasting with exclusive -dè is ga-an-ši-su$_8$-dè-en, "let us proceed toward it" (Inanna's Descent, line 322; discussed above). As with the other first person plural elements discussed, the contrast of inclusive with exclusive seems to have been lost in Old Babylonian times; the difference "here":"not here" may have been slightly more resistant. For use of -dè-en, although the context calls for exclusive first plural, cf. *TCL* XVI, No. 80, where the spokesman for the three men of Adab in explaining to the king what they do for a living uses ı-ag-e-dè-nam, "we (exclusive!) do (not here)"; compare a ga-nag̃-en-dè-en-e-šè, "let us (incl.) drink (here and now) water," later in the same text. Compare also me-dè-en, "we" (excl.), in *LKA*, No. 76 obv. 5–21.

Plural second person -zé.en. The form -zé-en seems regularly to replace -en-zé-ne as second person plural mark in imperatives after b, as e.g., du₁₁-ga-na-ab-zé-en (Inanna's Descent, lines 234 and 243). The reasons for this use are not clear. More suggestive is the use of zé.en in the ventive forms of the *alākum* paradigm in *MSL* IV, *OBGT* VII:

114	g̃en-na-	an-zé-en	: *al-[ka]*
96	⌈g̃á⌉-nu-u[m-	#-z]é-en	: *al-ka-a-nim*
99	⌈g̃á⌉-a-	mu-u[n]-še-en-zé-en	: *al(!)-ka-ni-iš-šu[m]*
102	g̃á-a-	mu-	še-en-zé-en	: *al-ka-a-nim a-na ṣe-ri-ia*
120	g̃en-	ba-	an-zé-en	: *at-la-ka*
105	g̃á-nam-	ma-	#-zé-en	: *at-la-ka-a-nim*
108	g̃á-nam-		an-še-en-zé-en	: *at-la-ka-ni-iš-šum*
111	g̃á-nam-	⌈mu-	še-en-zé-en⌉	: *at-la-ka-nim a-na ⟨ṣe⟩-ri-ia*

As will be seen, -zé-en replaces -en-zé-en in the forms translated as imperative ventive when no specific goal (infix) is present in the form. The simplest explanation would seem to be the assumption that the first en of en.zé.en implies location in the unspecified ventive range, i.e., opposite the speaker. Persons already so located (en.zé-en) will not be ordered to go there; only persons not already so located (#.zé.en) will be so ordered. Conceivably, therefore, -zé.en denotes second person at greater remove from the speaker than -en.zé.en. Consonant with such differentiation would seem also the use in the difficult passage *PBS* V, No. 1 vi 1–2: zi-an-na zi-ki-a i-pà-dè-en-zé-en za-zu-da hé-im-da-lá ᵈEn-líl zi-an-na zi-ki-a i-pà-dè-zé-en za-ne-ne im-da-lá, "You (gods) will swear by the life of Heaven, by the life of Earth, may he be joined with you and yours; Enlil, you (and yours over there) were swearing by the life of Heaven, by the life of Earth, he has been joined to you!"

20. Reasons for positing a nominalizing element zero besides the nominalizing element a are many. We may mention first that Sumerian has not only a verbal noun in a (*nomen actionis*) but also one in zero (*nomen agentis*). Here belong also the two forms of the adjective, one in a and one in zero, since the Sumerian adjective is actually merely the intransitive *nomen agentis*. Nominalizing zero may also be assumed for the enclitic verbal forms -men, "I am," -men, "you are," -àm, "he is," etc. in their appositional use (see Poebel, *AS* III [1932] pp. 3 ff.) as e.g., with Hammurabi ... -men, "I Hammurabi," since their function here is that of a noun, respectively of an independent personal pronoun. Similarly, the late development of enclitic -me-eš, "they are," into simple mark of plural is more easily understood if we can postulate besides, e.g., lugal-me-eš, "they are kings," a nominalized zero

form lugal-me-eš.#, "they who are kings," as intermediary to lugal-me-eš, "the kings."

As examples of clauses in zero besides such in a may serve e.g. lugal ᵈEn-líl-le ki-áĝ-šà-ga-na in-pà, "the king whom Enlil envisaged in his loving heart" (Šū-Sīn Pivotstone A; *SAK*, p. 200, b 5–7; cf. ibid., c 3–5, d 7–9, etc.), and En-an-e-du₇ en ᵈNanna nam-gal-nam-en-na šà-kù-ta nam-šè an-na-tar (see photo), "Enanedu, *entu*-priestess of Nanna, for whom from a pure heart he determined as destiny the great destiny of *entu*-ship" (Gadd in *Iraq* 13 [1951] 27), íd-da ᵈNanna-gú-gal mu-bi, "the canal the name of which is Nanna-gú-gal" (enclitic i-m(e), not expressed in writing, to be analyzed as i-m(e).#, i.e., 'of which canal its name is...,' rather than as i-m(e), 'of the canal its name is...')" (Ur-Nammu clay cone B; *SAK*, p. 188, i col. i 10–11).

16. Ittallak niāti

1. The directional-datival pronominal goals specified in the paradigm are first person "to me," "to us"; second person "to thee," "to you"; third person "to him," "to them." Their distribution varies with the direction of the motion implied in the verbal form. First and second person, typically imagined as close to the speaker and forming suitable goals only for motion directed toward the speaker such as is expressed by ventive, are limited in the paradigm to ventive forms of the verb. Third person, equally well imagined as near to, or far from, the speaker, is listed with both ventive and nonventive forms equally.

2. These meanings are: (1) "locative" e.g., *harrānam alākum* and—with abstract nouns denoting a condition—(2) "ingressive," "entering upon a condition," e.g., *labirûtam alākum*.

3. The presence of a meaning "from" has mainly been noted with one of a double accusative. Description has therefore tended to be in terms of use of double accusative and of the construction of specific verbs rather than in terms of a general variant meaning of the accusative. We base our preference for the latter mode of description on the principle that simplicity and convenience of description is furthered if purely rational meanings are, as far as possible, assigned to particles and morphological elements rather than described as constitutive parts of variant lexical meanings of verbs or nouns. Thus we would analyze *imhuršu* as *imhur* "he received" + *šu* "from (acc.) him" exactly as we would analyze the parallel *imhuršum* as *imhur* "he received" + *šum* "for (dative) him." The alternative analysis, seeking the ablative relation in a variant lexical meaning of the verb: "to receive from" besides "to receive," would lead to *imhur* "he received from" + *šu* "him" (direct-object acc.) and by implication to *imhur* "he received for" + *šum* "him" (direct-object acc.). Thus the two forms distinguished from each other in the expression, -*šu* and -*šum*, would be thrown together by the analysis as mere allomorphs of the direct-object accusative of the third masculine singular pronominal suffix, and the lexicon would be burdened with two variant "meanings" for *mahārum*: "to receive from" and "to receive for," besides "to receive." In the case of otherwise intransitive verbs such variant meanings would be active transitive. Though theoretically possible such analysis seems less simple and convenient.

One point should perhaps be mentioned. In many languages it is not uncommon to find that an entity which with active turn would have been expressed as an indirect object, or construed with a preposition, is with passive turn made the subject of the passive verb. Note e.g., English constructions such as "I was told" for "me was told" or "I was offered" for "me was offered." Similarly in Danish "jeg er budt fem Kroner" for "mig er budt fem Kroner." Correspondingly Akkadian can construe *ekmêk*, "I am robbed," where with active turn *ittiia* or *-anni* would have been used.

4. B. Landsberger, "Der 'Ventiv' des Akkadischen," *ZA* 35 (1924) 113–123.

5. Ibid., 118.

6. Ibid.

7. I.e., preterite, present, and imperative. The latter must be counted as a prefix-form with prefix 0 or possibly 00.

8. We hesitate to use the term since no phonemic analysis of Akkadian has yet been undertaken.

9. We have not been able to undertake a systematic study of all instances of suffixed accusative pronominal suffix first person singular. In view of the contrast *i:ni*, singular:plural, we should be inclined, however, to analyze a possible form *ikšud-ni* "he caught me" as *ikšud* + *n̄* (rank 3'su.) + *i* (first singular accusative) rather than as *ikšud* + *ni* (first singular accusative).

10. *ZA*, 35, 118.

11. See Gelb, *MAD* II, pp. 171 f.

12. The occurrence of prefix forms of the verb ending in *a* in Old Akkadian has been demonstrated by Gelb, *Old Akkadian Inscriptions in Chicago Natural History Museum* (1955), p. 190. The forms with *a* occur as "subjunctives," i.e., restricted to use in clauses only, and it is to be noted that they occur as variants of, not as replacement for, the normal "subjunctive" in *u*. Examples are šu-NIGÍN 10 LAL 2 AB + ÁŠ-*bu-ut Mu-tu-tu* É *a-na* DINGIR-*a-zu iš-du-da* (no. 1:9–12), AB + ÁŠ 1 (PI) ŠE *Gi-nu-nu a-na Dar-e-tum i-ti-na* (no. 3:7–10), *in* É *ši uš-da-a-bí-la* (no. 10:8), *šu a-na Šu-ni-tum a-ti-na* (no. 21: 5 ff.), and ŠE-HAR-AN É-*ni-um su Na-bí-um in i-te-su ik-su₄-ra* (no. 14:30). The form appears to survive into Old Babylonian where it is the one characteristically used before following ventive, or visitive and departive, elements. Cases without such following elements are difficult to spot with certainty since the possibility of interpretation as a ventive with elided *m* is not always easily excluded. We shall restrict ourselves, therefore, to one example only, the form *ik-šu-da-ka* translating sá mu-ri-in-du₁₁ in the paradigm *OBGT* IX line 128, *MSL* IV, p. 109, which the paradigm clearly distinguishes from the ventive *ik-šu-da-ak-ka* translating sá ma-ra-an-du₁₁ in line 91. The form occurs in context in *Lugal-e* XI.41 in the address to the *šadānu* stone du₅-na šu-mu sá nu-mu-ri-ib-du₁₁:šal-ṭi-iš qa-a-ti la ik-šu-da-ka, and though our copy of the translation is late there can be little doubt that it goes back to an Old Babylonian original.

As to the meaning of the form in *a*, an assumption that it serves merely to mark the "subjunctive" is hardly possible in view of the fact that in conjunction with the ventive element it is found equally in clause and in main sentence. A clue to its meaning may be offered by the parallel use of forms in *u* and in *a* in the attestation of witnessed transactions in the documents published by Gelb, for if—as its use else-where indicates—the form in *u* is used to attest binding action, established fact, the form in *a* may possibly denote the only other thing likely to occur in a document as attested by witnesses, statement of agreement, of willingness to undertake obliga-tion. On such an assumption the passages quoted above might be translated "total of eight witnesses (to the fact) that Mututu agreed to measure the house for Ilum-asû" (no. 1:9–12), "witnesses (to the fact) that Ginunu agreed to give 1 PI of barley to Dar'etum" (no. 3:7–10) "in the house for which I have agreed to have renumera-tion made (?) (let me weigh out for you the rest of the price)" (no. 10:8), "that which I agreed to give to Šunîtum" (no. 21:5 ff.). For 36:6–9 we venture no trans-lation. The meaning proposed would fit particularly well in the quotation from Lugal-e "my hand was not agreeable to seize thee amain" (i.e., "I could hardly bring myself to seize thee by force"). In fact, since the *šadānu* stone is present among Ninurta's captive foes, but clearly does not deserve to be there because it is highly thought of by Ninurta, a note of reluctance in connection with the statement of its capture is definitely demanded by the context. In favor of a meaning indicating agreeableness, approachableness, in the subject is also the fact that such a meaning would form a bridge to the volitive West-Semitic *iaqtula* form with which it is clearly formally related. On the latter see W. Moran, *Or.* NS 29 (1960) 1–19.

The existence of a form in *i* in Old-Babylonian was noted independently by Landsberger and von Soden. Examples of its occurrence are given by von Soden in *GAG* §82 e. To these may be added the important letter Fish, *Letters of the First Babylonian Dynasty* 4 = 888, to which Landsberger drew my attention, and *CT* IV 22a (Schorr *VAB* V no. 61). The last of these passages states that certain debts amounting to 9 shekel silver *A-hu-ši-na a-na A-wi-il-ilim* DUMU-NI *i-zu-uz-zi*, "Ahushina had to assign as share to Awīlilim his son." The suggested force of the *i* modus, "action under compulsion," is guessed from the context. It fits, however, quite well also in *CT* VI 40a (Schorr, *VAB* V no. 61, 153) ll. 11–12, where the hire of a slave is stated with the addition *it-ti ra-ma-ni-šu-ma il-ta-ba-aš-ši*, "he has to keep himself in clothes." It also suits the context in its various occurrences in Fish, *Letters*, no. 4. The writer of the letter, a woman, tells in l. 15 that when the addressee visited her she was too happy to bother him with her affairs: *ah-du-ú-ma ṭe₄-mi mah-ri-ka ul aš-ku-un-ni* "I rejoiced, so that I had to not lay my (various) matter(s) before you," and in l. 24 she complains that she was so upset that *a-ka-la-am ù me-e ú-ul e-li-im-mi*, "I had to not taste food and drink," i.e., that "I could not eat or drink." She is greatly worred about the hard times: *i-na ki-mi-na-an-na ma-am-ma-an-ni a-na ma-am-ma ú-ul i-ha-ba-at-ti ga-du-um bi-ti-ia la a-ma-at-ti … bi-ti lu-ba-li-iṭ-ṭi … la a-ma-at-ti*, "at present anybody has to not lend to anybody. I, together with my household, must not die, … I have to keep my household alive … I must not die." In *TCL* XVII. 81.5, finally, a passage quoted by von Soden, the writer, after reporting various calamities, goes on to say: "Your mother cannot help being ill (marṣatti)." Tentatively we may therefore see in the mode in *i* a mode of compelled action. For possible remnants of an *i* modus in Arabic see Wright, *A Grammar of the Arabic Language*, 3rd edition, Vol. II §247.

13. The traditional statement that the modal element (e.g., subjunctive -*u*) occurs

only with forms which in the indicative end in a consonant is clearly paralogical; it answers a question about morphology (form expressive of meaning) in terms of a different universe of discourse, phonetics (form viewed apart from meaning).

14. For the sake of clarity and easier orientation we have not considered the dual in our diagram of the person-gender-number system. Its inclusion would serve only to widen the gap between the system of marks and that of meanings to be expressed.

15. At a still earlier stage *šarrum i* and *atti ta* were undoubtedly subjects consisting respectively of a noun and pronoun in apposition and pronoun and pronoun in apposition.

16. Albrecht, *Zeitschrift für alttestamentiliche Wissenschaft*, 1896, 120, quoted in Brockelmann, *Grundriss*, I, 424.

17. The Akkadian Ablative Accusative

1. The range of occurrence is formulated as if Akkadian had only direct-object accusatives and prepositional accusatives, which is by no means certain. As other groups of accusatives become established the formulation must be adjusted accordingly.

2. The word "never alone" should probably be dropped in view of the likely existence of occasional elliptic constructions such as the example from *TCL* VII No. 68 quoted below under *nadānum*.

3. The form mu-da-an-šub may be analyzed as consisting of the prefix mu-, a first person singular ablative infix -' -da-, "from me" (cf. Falkenstein, *GSGL* §70 a.l), and an infix -n- denoting "into," "in," which resumes the directional postposition -šè of kur-šè, "toward the nether world."

The existence of a Sumerian infix -n- identical, or almost identical, in meaning with the locative -ni- may be seen from cases such as *ITT* III 5279 iii. 3–5 ù ì-bí-la-Du-du-ke₄-ne du₁₁-ga-ne-ne-a ba-ni-ge-né-eš mu dug₄-ì-bí-la-ne-ka ba-an-ge-na-šè..., "and the heirs of Dudu confirmed it by their statement (*lit.* made it firm in their word). Because it was confirmed by the statement (*lit.* was made firm in the word) of the heirs...," where the locative relation expressed by the postposition -a (du₁₁-ga-ne-ne-a and dug₄-ì-bí-la-ne-ka) is resumed by -ni- in the active transitive statement, by -n- in the passive statement of the same event. Further examples offers Civil *RA* 54 (1960) 62 f. ll. 109–110, dù-a-bé an-sù-bé ù-ni-sù..., "he is to suck on all of it. When he has sucked on it...," and 123–124, a-bé-an-tuₓ-tuₓ a ù-ni-tuₓ..., "he is to bathe in that water. When he has bathed in the water..." (see also ll. 136–137), where the locative relations expressed by -e (dù-a-bé, a-bé) and by -a (a representing a-a) are resumed by -ni- in the futurum exactum statements, by -n- in the pres/fut. statements of the same events.

Examples in which this -n- is used to resume a preceding postposition -a are e.g., the passives du₁₁-ga-na ba-an-ge-in, MLC 109.7, Falkenstein, *Gerichtsurkunden*, No. 125 dug₄-Ur-GAR-ka ba-an-ge-in, *ITT* II 4159 9, Falkenstein, *Gerichtsurkunden*, No. 174, dug₄-ba ba-an-ge-in, *ITT* III 6569 10′ Falkenstein, *Gerichtsurkunden*, No. 186, the intransitives sig₄ nam-tar-ra ᵍⁱˢù-šub-ba ma-an-ĝál, "the predestined brick was in the brickmold for me," Gudea Cyl. A v. 7, igi ^{d}Nanna-ka hé-en-sa$_6$, "may he prosper before Nanna," *UET* I 71.38–39, and the transitive active ^{giš}gu-za-gub-ba-na suhuš-bi na-an-ge-né, "may she (Inannak) not fix securely into the throne he sets up its legs," Gudea St. C. iv. 13–15.

Whether we are here dealing merely with a special function of the still highly problematical all-person -n- or with a separate element we are not yet able to say.

4. Cf. Von Soden, *Or* 30 (1961) 158, n. 2.

5. Louis Hjelmslev, "La Catégorie des Cas" (Aarhus [1935]), p. 96.

6. If "accusative" is taken as a term for form only, not for meaning or form and meaning, and if "of relation" is understood as "of unspecified relation," the term "accusative of relation" would indicate that accusative form in Akkadian sometimes does not have its usual function of limiting meaning to accusative meaning but indicates instead that any case meaning is applicable. To maintain that such an all-case form exists it would be necessary to show clear instances of accusative form where the contexts demand nominative function and genitive function and dative function. We do not believe such instances exist.

7. A definition of accusative meaning for Akkadian has not yet been worked out and it seems best for the time being to state it in terms of the aggregate of specific relations compatible with accusative form and not with any other case form. Ultimately it will perhaps be possible to show that the accusative, both direct-object accusative and prepositional accusative corresponding to prepositions such as *itti* and *eli*, renders essentially surface relation and contrasts with the nominative, both subject nominative and prepositional nominative corresponding to prepositions such as *ina*, which renders essentially interiority relation.

Bibliography

Books

1. *Philological Notes on Eshnunna and Its Inscriptions*, *AS* VI (Chicago, 1934).
2. *The Sumerian King List*, *AS* XI (Chicago, 1939).
3. *Cuneiform Texts in the National Museum, Copenhagen, Chiefly of Economic Contents* (Leiden, 1939).

Books written conjointly with others

4. *Tell Asmar and Khafaje. The First Season's Work in Eshnunna, 1930/31*. By Henri Frankfort, Thorkild Jacobsen, and Conrad Preusser. *OIC* XIII (Chicago, 1932).
5. *Sennacherib's Aqueduct at Jerwan*. By Thorkild Jacobsen and Seton Lloyd, with a preface by Henri Frankfort. *OIP* XXIV (Chicago, 1935).
6. *The Gimilsin Temple and the Palace of the Rulers at Tell Asmar*. By Henri Frankfort, Seton Lloyd, and Thorkild Jacobsen, with a chapter by Günther Martiny. *OIP* XLIII (Chicago, 1940).
7. *The Intellectual Adventure of Ancient Man. An Essay on Speculative Thought in the Ancient Near East*. By H. and H. A. Frankfort, John A. Wilson, Thorkild Jacobsen, William A. Irwin (Chicago, 1946). Reprinted as *Before Philosophy* (Pelican Books, 1949). Partly reprinted in *The World of History*. Edited by Courtland Canby and Nancy C. Gross (New York, 1954).
8. *Most Ancient Verse*. By Thorkild Jacobsen and John A. Wilson, with an introduction by David Grene (Chicago, 1963).

Contributions to books by others

9. *Sumerian Lexical Texts from the Temple School of Nippur*. By Edward Chiera. *OIP* XI (Chicago, 1929). Therein: "List of Parallel Texts," pp. 8–13.
10. *Clavis cuneorum, sive signorum Assyriorum linguis Latina Britannica, Germanica . . . composita*. By Gert Howardy (London, Leipzig, and Copenhagen 1904–1935). Therein: autograph of cuneiform signs.
11. *Oriental Institute Discoveries in Iraq, 1933/34. Fourth Preliminary Report of the Iraq Expedition*. By Henri Frankfort. *OIC* XIX (Chicago, 1935). Therein: "A Hittite Hieroglyphic Inscription from Hines," pp. 101–103.

NOTE: Starred entries are included in this book.

12. *Glydendals Verdenhistorie* I–III (Copenhagen, 1936). Edited by W. Norvin and A. Olsen, Therein: "Mesopotamien," I, pp. 40–80.
13. *Khorsabad I. Excavations in the Palace and at a City Gate.* By Gordon Loud, with chapters by Henri Frankfort and Thorkild Jacobsen. *OIP* XXXVIII (Chicago, 1936). Therein: "Inscriptions," pp. 129–133.
14. *Khorsabad II. The Citadel and the Town.* By Gordon Loud and Charles B. Altman. *OIP* XL (Chicago, 1938). Therein: copies, transliterations, and annotated translations, pp. 103–104.
15. *The Temple Oval at Khafajah.* By Pinhas Delougaz, with a chapter by Thorkild Jacobsen. *OIP* LIII (Chicago, 1940). Therein: "The Inscriptions," pp. 146–150.
16. *Pre-Sargonid Temples in the Diyala Region.* By Pinhas Delougaz and Seton Lloyd, with chapters by Henri Frankfort and Thorkild Jacobsen. *OIP* LVIII (Chicago, 1942). Therein: "The Inscriptions," pp. 289–298.
17. *Stratified Cylinder Seals from the Diyala Region.* By Henri Frankfort, with a chapter by Thorkild Jacobsen. *OIP* LXXII (Chicago, 1955). Therein: "The Inscriptions," pp. 48–52.
18. *MSL* IV. By B. Landsberger, R. Hallock, Th. Jacobsen, A Falkenstein (Rome, 1956). Therein: "Introduction," pp. 1*–50*, and with contributions to "Part I: Emesal-Vocabulary," pp. 1–44.
19. *The Interpretation of Dreams in the Ancient Near East.* By A. Leo Oppenheim. Transactions of the American Philosophical Society 46/3 (Philadelphia, 1956). Therein: translation of Gudea Cyl. A iv 7–vi 14, pp. 245–246.
20. *Sumerian Proverbs: Glimpses of Everyday Life in Ancient Mesopotamia.* By Edmund I. Gordon (Philadelphia, 1959). Therein: "Notes on Selected Sayings," pp. 447–480; "Additional Notes," pp. 547–550.
21. Introduction to *Cradle of Civilization* by Samuel Noah Kramer. *Great Ages of Man, A History of the World's Cultures* (New York, 1967), pp. 6–7.

Articles

22. "Nyere Assyriologisk Litteratur," *Historisk Tidskrift niende rekke* 5/3 (Copenhagen, 1927) 486–496.
23. "On the Chronology of the Agade Dynasty," *Acta Orientalia* 5 (1927) 302–309.
24. "An Unrecognized Text of Ilu-mutabil," *AJSL* 44 (1928) 261–263.
25. "Further Additions to 'Le syllabaire accadien'," *ZA* 39 (1929) 223–225. With F. Geers.
26. "How Did Gilgamesh Oppress Uruk?" *Acta Orientalia* 8 (1930) 62–74.
*27. "The Investiture and Anointing of Adapa in Heaven," *AJSL* 46 (1930) 201–203.
28. "The Chief God of Eshnunna," *Actes du Congrès International des Orientalistes* (Leiden, 1932) 55–56. Republished in *OIC* XIII.
29. "The Ancient Name of Khafaje," *Atti del XIX Congresso Internazionale degli Orientalisti* (Rome, 1938) 91–96.
30. "The Inscription of Takil-ili-su of Malgium," *AOF* 12 (1937–1939) 363–366.
*31. "The Assumed Conflict Between the Sumerians and Semites in Early Mesopotamian History," *JAOS* 59 (1939) 485–495.
32. "Parerga Sumerologica," *JNES* 2 (1943) 117–121.

*33. "Primitive Democracy in Ancient Mesopotamia," *JNES* 2 (1943) 159–172.

34. "Temples, Mesopotamian," in *An Encyclopedia of Religion* (New York, 1945). Edited by Vergilius Ferm, 770–772.

35. "Religions, Mesopotamian," *An Encyclopedia of Religion*, 483 485.

36. "The Oriental Institute: Thirty Years and the Present," *JNES* 8 (1949) 236–247. With John A. Wilson.

37. Comments to S. N. Kramer, "Gilgamesh and Agga," *AJA* 53 (1949) 17–18.

38. "Some Opinions about an Unidentified Statue," *Sumer* 7 (1951) 75–76.

39. "An Agricultural Document from Nippur," *Sumer* 7 (1951) 77–78.

40. "Nippur, Nov. 25, 1953," *Archaeological Newsletter* No. 6 of *ASOR*, 1–4 (with map).

*41. "The Myth of Inanna and Bilulu," *JNES* 12 (1953) 160–187. With cuneiform copy (Plates LXVI–LXVIII) and an appendix (187–188) of S. N. Kramer.

*42. "On the Textile Industry at Ur under Ibbī-Sîn," in *Studia Orientalia Ioanni Pedersen . . . dedicata* (Copenhagen, 1953) 172–187.

*43. "The Reign of Ibbī-Suen," *JCS* 7 (1953) 36–47.

44. "Mesopotamian Mound Survey," *Archaeology* 7 (1954) 53–54.

45. "Enmerkar and Ensukkuššdanna," *Orientalia* NS 23 (1954) 232–234. With S. N. Kramer.

46. "Texts and Fragments," *JCS* 8 (1954) 82–86.

47. Cuneiform copy *apud* A. Feigin and B. Landsberger, "The Date-list of the Babylonian King Samsu-ditana," *JNES* 14 (1955) 138.

48. "Appendix: Copies," *apud* R. Harris, "The Archive of the Sin Temple in Khafajah (Tutub)," *JCS* 9 (1955) 106–120.

49. "An Old Babylonian Charm Against *merḫu*," *JNES* 14 (1955) 14–21. With B. Landsberger.

50. "Henri Frankfort (24.II.1897–16.VII.1954)," *JNES* 14 (1955) 1–3. With P. Delougaz.

*51. "Early Political Development in Mesopotamia," *ZA* 52 (1957) 91–140.

52. "Salt and Silt in Ancient Mesopotamian Agriculture," *Science*, Nov. 21, 1958, Vol. 128, No. 3334, pp. 1251–1258. Reprinted in *The Bobbs-Merrill Reprint Series in Geography*, G-105. With Robert M. Adams.

53. "Summary of Report by the Diyala Basin Archaeological Project June 1, 1957, to June 1, 1958," *Sumer* 14 (1958) 79–89.

54. "La géographie et les voies de communication du pays de Sumer," *RA* 52 (1958) 127–129.

*55. "An Ancient Mesopotamian Trial for Homicide," *Studia Biblica et Orientalia* III, *Analecta Biblica et Orientalia* XII (Rome, 1959) 130–150.

*56. "*Ittallak niāti*," *JNES* 19 (1960) 101–116.

*57. "The Waters of Ur," *Iraq* 22 (1960) 174–185, with Plate XXVIII.

*58. "Toward the Image of Tammuz," *History of Religions* 1 (1961) 189–213.

*59. "Formative Tendencies in Sumerian Religion," in *The Bible and the Ancient Near East: Essays in Honor of William Foxwell Albright* (New York, 1961). Edited by G. Ernest Wright, 267–278.

60. "Babylon," *IDB* I 334–338.

61. "Euphrates," *IDB* II 180–181.
62. "Tigris," *IDB* IV 642, 1 fig.
63. "Ur (city)," *IDB* IV 735–738, 7 figs.
64. "Enmerkar and the Lord of Aratta," *Trudy Dvadcat' piatogo Meždunarodnogo Kongressa Vostokovedov*, (Moscow, 1962–1963) I, pp. 173–174 (summary in Russian).
*65. "Religion" (in this book titled "Mesopotamian Gods and Pantheons"), in "Babylonia and Assyria," *Encyclopaedia Britannica* (1963), II, 972–978.
*66. "The Akkadian Ablative Accusative," *JNES* 22 (1963) 18–29.
*67. "Ancient Mesopotamian Religion: The Central Concerns," *PAPS* 107/6 (1963) 473–484.
68. "Note sur le rôle de l'opinion publique dans l'ancienne Mésopotamie," *RA* 58 (1964) 157–158.
*69. "About the Sumerian Verb," in *Studies in Honor of Benno Landsberger on his Seventy-fifth Birthday, April 21, 1965, AS* XVI (Chicago, 1965). Edited by H. Güterbock and T. Jacobsen, 71–102.
70. "The Battle Between Marduk and Tiamat," *JAOS* 88 (1968) 104–108.
71. "Some Sumerian City-names," *JCS* 21 (1967, issued 1969) 101–103.

Reviews

72. "New Royal Inscriptions," review of *PBS* XV, in *AJSL* 46 (1929) 67–71.
73. "Gilgamish in English Verse," review of C. Campbell Thompson, *The Epic of Gilgamesh*, in *AJSL* 46 (1930) 208–209.
74. Review of O. E. Ravn, *Babylonske og assyriske Kongers historiske Indskrifter (ca. 2800–500 f. Kr.)*, in *AOF* 12 (1937) 70–71.
75. "New Texts of the Third Ur Period," review of *TuM* NF I/2 in *AJSL* 55 (1938) 419–421.
76. Short notice of C. Frank, *Kultlieder aus dem Ischtar-Tamūz-Kreis*, in *AJSL* 56 (1939) 309.
77. Review of S. N. Kramer, *Lamentation over the Destruction of Ur*, in *AJSL* 58 (1941) 219–224.
78. Review of James Philip Hyatt, *The Treatment of Final Vowels in Early Neo-Babylonian*, in *Classical Weekly*, Vol. 36, No. 9, *December 14, 1942*, 100–101.
79. Review of O. Neugebauer and A. Sachs, *Mathematical Cuneiform Texts*, in *BASOR* 102 (1946) 17–19.
80. Review of S. N. Kramer, *Sumerian Literary Texts from Nippur in the Museum of the Ancient Orient at Istanbul*, in *BASOR* 102 (1946) 12–17.
*81. "Sumerian Mythology: A Review Article," review of S. N. Kramer, *Sumerian Mythology: A Study of Spiritual and Literary Achievement in the Third Millennium B.C.*, in *JNES* 5 (1946) 128–152.
82. Review of N. Schneider, *Die Götternamen von Ur III, AnOr* XIX, in *Orientalia* NS 16 (1947) 391–398.
83. Review of L. Legrain, *Ur Excavation Texts* III, in *AJA* 57 (1953) 125–128.

Lexical Index to Jacobsen's Writings

NOTE: Entries are listed according to number in bibliography. An * before an entry number indicates that the discussion is republished in this volume. The correspondences are as follows: 31 = chap. 11; 33 = chap. 9; 41 = chap. 5; 42 = chap. 13; 43 = chap. 10; 51 = chap. 8; 55 = chap. 12; 56 = chap. 16; 57 = chap. 14; 58 = chap. 6; 65 = chap. 2; 66 = chap. 17; 67 = chap. 3; 69 = chap. 15; 81 = chap. 7. Discussions are separated by commas, articles by semicolons. Page numbers given are to the original article.

SUMERIAN

#- *69:73, 75
-#- *69:84, note 12, 87, note 13, 88–91, note 18
-# *69:note 20, 101
-#.#- *69:91–92
-#.# *69:99, note 19
-#.di- *69:94
-#.e- *69:93, note 16
-#.ra- *69:92
-#.ši- *69:94

a- 18:3*, 12* ff., 20* ff.; *81:note 7
-a- *69:note 5, 76, 78–79, 87, note 13, 88–91, 92
-a 18:28*; *69:101, note 20
A 15:149
a-abba(k) *81:139 ff., note 21, note 28
abba *33:note 44
abba uru *33:note 44
áb-gal *57:note 6
abzu *81:139, note 21
(gišmá) addir(= A.PA.BI+GIŠ. PAD.DIRI) 20:462

ad-e-éš—gi₄ *41:note 77
a-da-al(-lam) 77:224
á gada mu-tù-ra-bi *42:182
a-gar 3:9–10
á—gar 20:455
á-giš-gar-ra ki engar-gu-ke₄-ne-ta *42:177
á-giš-gar-ra-aš *42:181
a-huš-gi₄-a *67:note 20
a-ka NN ba-a-gar 3:11,note 3
al- 20:470
alala 49:note 25
gišal-tag 5:note 41
-àm 20:451; *55:147–148
ama 16:292
ama-ab-zu-da 16:292
amar-maš-du₃ 45:234
amaš 32:note 6
a/i-m-mi 18:29*
a-na-àm 20:453
AN AN AN 6:156
an-edin 40:4
an-ta—gál *67:note 24

AKKADIAN

PROPER NAMES

Index